Introduction to

Learning & Teaching

Infants through Elementary Age Children

Early Childhood Education
providing lessons for life

www.EarlyChildEd.delmar.com

Introduction to

Learning & Teaching

Infants through Elementary Age Children

Barbara A. Nilsen, Ed.D.
Gini Albertalli, M.S. Ed.

DELMAR

THOMSON LEARNING ™   Australia   Canada   Mexico   Singapore   Spain   United Kingdom   United States

DELMAR

THOMSON LEARNING

Introduction to Learning & Teaching: Infants through Elementary Age Children
by Barbara A. Nilsen, Gini Albertalli

Business Unit Director:
Susan L. Simpfenderfer

Executive Editor:
Marlene McHugh Pratt

Acquisitions Editor:
Erin O'Connor Traylor

Developmental Editor:
Melissa Riveglia

Editorial Assistant:
Alexis Ferraro

Executive Production Manager:
Wendy A. Troeger

Project Editor:
Amy E. Tucker

Production Editor:
J.P. Henkel

Technology Project Manager:
James Considine

Executive Marketing Manager:
Donna J. Lewis

Channel Manager:
Nigar Hale

Cover Design:
Tom Cicero

For permission to use material from this text or product, contact us by
Tel   (800) 730-2214
Fax   (800) 730-2215
www.thomsonrights.com

Library of Congress Cataloging-in-Publication Data
Nilsen, Barbara.
  Introduction to learning and teaching : infants through elementary age children/Barbara A. Nilsen, Virginia Albertalli.
    p. cm.
  Includes bibliographical references and index.
  ISBN 0-7668-1539-0
  1. Early childhood education--United States--Handbooks, manuals, etc. 2. Education, Elementary--United States--Handbooks, manuals, etc. 3. Child development--United States--Handbooks, manuals, etc. 4. Active learning--United States--Handbooks, manuals, etc. I. Albertalli, Virginia. II. Title.

LB1139.25 .N55 2001
372.973--dc21   2001017190

NOTICE TO THE READER

Contents

Preface

Careers in education can take many pathways and result in a wide variety of job possibilities. This book is written on the premise that all educational careers begin with a foundation knowledge of the child and family. In any building, the foundation is one of the most important aspects, but is rather mundane in appearance. It is in the upper part of the building that the structure takes on its distinctive appearance. We are attempting to build a foundation that is strong, yet individualized to the myriad options for careers in teaching. In this book, we are presenting a wide view into the reality of being a teacher. In Chapter 1, you will find some Reality Check passages that present facts, figures, and concepts to help you make career decisions. Throughout the text, you will find some of the knowledge you will need (you are at the beginning of this journey) and some hints at the types of encounters you will have with children of varying ages. This book is meant to be an exploration of a career in teaching, as well as related careers. As with any building project, changes can be made in the blueprint and construction along the way. You should anticipate that this could happen, so we invite you to use this book to begin to explore, reexamining your own plans along the way.

You may be wondering about the title *Introduction to Learning and Teaching: Infants through Elementary Age Children.* Those words were carefully chosen to communicate and emphasize the simple fact that learning comes before teaching (and while teaching, as well). There is a great deal of preparation ahead of you and we want to introduce the idea that your educational preparation for teaching is more than memorizing theorists' names and their contributions, or knowing how to construct a lesson plan. True learning is life–changing; it is the kind of learning we hope you will experience as you work with this book.

Features in this book will guide your thinking and learning. Learning objectives are listed at the beginning of each chapter so you will know what you should be learning in that chapter. You can assess your learning against these intended outcomes.

✳ CHAPTER EMPHASES

Each chapter introduces you to a subject area, orienting you to the importance of that area to learning and teaching and then leading you into three areas: child development, curriculum, and assessment.

Understanding the Developmental Area and Its Issues

The discussion of the topic or developmental area examines some of the background, issues, and importance of that area. This section is designed to inform you of some of the latest research and thinking, as well as some of the controversies that may exist. As a developing professional, you need to know that many experts on education have widely disparate opinions. Because education deals with humans, it is not as predictable and replicable as science, so teaching professionals need to rely on theories, past practices, and proven methods while using their own philosophies and wisdom. This preliminary section in each chapter will help you form your own position.

Understanding Child Development

The main focus of each chapter is on **development**: the teacher's development and the child's development, including the teacher's relationship with the child's family, who are the child's first teachers. While this is not a child development textbook, we believe that teachers must be grounded in knowledge about children and families, as well as subject content and techniques of teaching. *Whom* we teach is intertwined with *why* we teach, *what* we teach, and *how* we teach.

This book is based on the concept that once you know about children in a general way, you will be better prepared to know each child you teach in a specific and personal way. More importantly, you will then be prepared to help each child learn in a way that is meaningful to her or him.* It is a continuous cycle of learning and teaching, and learning and teaching, with learning always coming first.

You may have a career goal in mind, such as becoming a sixth-grade teacher, kindergarten teacher, or infant teacher, but you may not be aware of the broad range of roles and options revolving around each career choice. This book examines a broad range of children's ages for a variety of reasons. Because you are at the beginning of your career preparation, you may be focused only on one particular grade or age group. Perhaps you are at the opposite point—just knowing you want to be a teacher but undecided on an age group you would like to teach. From what we know about children, the developmental features of one age or stage overlap with others; even if you eventually decide to teach sixth grade, knowing about children's development in the early years will help you understand those sixth graders better. If you are thinking of teaching younger children in preschool settings, it will be helpful for you to be aware of the development and teaching challenges of upper grades in order to see the importance of the foundation you are providing. Development occurs in a continuous motion, spiraling and building on previous learning and experiences.

Figure P–1 provides some of the many options open to you as a teacher. They vary in the type of setting or program and in requirements for preparation. This book is designed as an exploration of many of these to help you make a more informed career choice.

When you look at child development, you always must begin with what is genetically inherited, that raw material from which a unique individual will emerge. **Nature** is that which is inborn, genetically coded, and universal to all humans. It is the hereditary component of development. In this context, **nurture** is the word used to describe all of those experiences that build on those innate possibilities. Development

*For ease of reading, we alternate gender-specific pronouns throughout the book by using "her," "hers," "she," etc. in the odd-numbered chapters and "him," "his," "he," etc. in the even-numbered chapters.

development—Progressive physical, psychological, and social changes in human beings.
nature—The inborn, genetically-coded capacities and limitations of an individual.
nurture—The environmental, experiential influences on development that derive from social interactions.

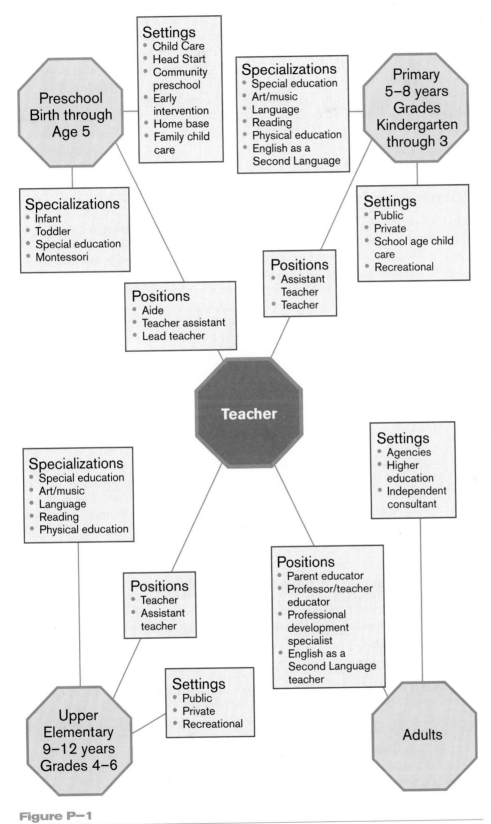

Figure P–1

Options within teaching careers.

depends on the nurturing of that which is inherited, learning that takes place from the moment of birth, enabling children to talk, act, think, and interact with the world into which they were born. People's worlds are neither isolated nor stable. Often, beliefs evolve, and misunderstandings take place, because people assume that everyone's views and beliefs are similar to their own. We will attempt to broaden your understanding of how people are alike and how they are different and some reasons why that is so. We will consider children's diverse learning styles and capacities. Teachers must adapt to children's uniqueness and developmental ranges. We will also consider diverse ethnic, cultural, and life circumstances and explore strategies to help you make every child feel accepted and valued.

Curriculum for the Developmental Domains

While this book is not designed as a "how-to-teach" book on **pedagogy**, it presents the notion that how and what we teach is based on what we know, not only of the actual subject matter, but also of the child and ourselves. Suggestions for **curriculum** are included to present ways that you can think about and plan for your classroom environment, learning, and create and facilitate opportunities for each child to develop within that particular domain. These are suggestions to add to your pedagogical repertoire, as well as to provide a vision of a teacher's work. Again, we emphasize the learning and teaching cycle throughout the book; the topic of curriculum is included for you to begin thinking about your developing educational philosophy and pedagogy.

Assessing Learning and Development

Friedrich Froebel

(1782–1852) German educator and nature lover who emphasized self-activity as the foundation for learning. He started his own school for children under six, calling it *children's garden,* or "kindergarten" in German, where children used balls, blocks, and cubes for playful learning activities. His principles of gardening and play were widely used throughout Europe and the Western world.

How does a teacher know when the lesson is learned? Assessing learning and development involves observing and evaluating behavior and projects, and formal testing to ascertain if the teaching objective has been met. Each chapter includes a section with suggestions for the kinds of assessment methods you can use to measure each child's progress. Different domains of development and curricular content call for different kinds of assessment. This is another area of knowledge you will need to build. And, while this book is intended only as an introduction and foundation, it should help you build awareness that learning, teaching, and assessing are integrally linked.

✳ CHAPTER FEATURES

Each chapter will draw your attention to theorists, definitions, and quotes and end with review activities for additional learning opportunities.

Theorists

When you first meet someone new, you usually learn very little about that person in your first encounter. You may or may not remember the person's name, a unique characteristic, or the relationship that person has with someone else. That is the beginning of knowing a person. This book will introduce you to theorists such as **Friedrich Froebel**, one of the many philosophers, historians,

---

✳ **pedagogy**—The art or practice of teaching according to a particular philosophy or method.
curriculum—The planned activities for learning a skill or concept.

and other important contributors to the field of education. The handshake icons will remind you that you are just beginning your relationship with these people. Throughout your career, you will be learning more about how their personal lives influenced their ideas, about their major work and accomplishments, and how their ideas influence what teachers do every day.

Definitions

Important words within the text are printed in color and repeated along with definitions at the bottom of the page. This will make it convenient for you to check your understanding of the word or concept. Previously in this section you saw definitions for **development**, **nature**, and **nurture**. These terms are also included in a comprehensive glossary at the end of the book.

Scenarios

SCENARIO	Nita teaches toddlers in a child care center located on a college campus. Besides the four toddlers in her *family,* there are four more who are the *family* of her co-teacher, Jack. This arrangement helps each adult know the four children very well, with the children having a consistent adult to depend on for attention and fulfillment of needs. Nita and Jack quietly talk over their plans for the next day while the children are resting or napping in the afternoon. Each takes responsibility for bringing in objects or supplies so the plans can be carried out. Jack is very creative and thinks of some very unusual items for the children to explore. Nita's strength is her love of books, so she is constantly bringing in new books for which Jack can usually find props, or physical objects that connect to the story, since toddlers need that sensory stimulation to help them remain interested and remember the story.

Throughout the text we have included scenarios like this one as glimpses into the lives of hypothetical classroom and teacher experiences. We hope these will illustrate the concepts and provide examples of how teachers can address the developing child while implementing the curriculum.

Words of Wisdom

We also want to introduce you to people who are working with children today: in family child care homes, child care centers, private and public schools, and children's literature and product development. Sometimes we will hear from families, the child's first teachers, as they speak of their ideas about school, teachers, and their hopes for their children.

We have gathered the voices of these people so you can "hear" a sample of viewpoints about learning and teaching. An owl icon will alert you to the Words of Wisdom box within the text. We hope you will listen to and reflect on these words and consider these tidbits of advice from other people.

WORDS OF WISDOM

Olav Ostvold, a teacher in Norway, wrote these words when we asked him to give beginning teachers some advice:

"There are so many 'prophets' who have uttered the ultimate wisdom that it's easy to get lost! Still, I can give you one very good example of wisdom: An older teacher, author, and priest once told me 'You can examine a rose with an open hand, but not with a clenched fist.' At the time it seemed like some nonsense from an old man—today it makes perfect sense. You can reach the inner mind and gain the trust of a difficult child if you are open-minded, willing to admit your own mistakes, etc. If you are stubborn, or too harsh, and the student's well-being is less important to you than your own progress, the whole thing is a lost cause. This old man also told me that humor is the best tool a teacher has at hand. In other words, a teacher with no sense of humor will not remain a teacher very long."

REVIEW ACTIVITIES

One of this book's primary principles is that learning requires active participation. You will practice that principle not by just reading the text and memorizing definitions, but by constructing your own learning through several different kinds of Review Activities at the end of each chapter. Exercises to Strengthen Learning, Internet Quest, Reflective Journal, and Related Careers are included to stimulate your thinking about learning and teaching.

Exercises to Strengthen Learning

Just as doing exercises strengthens your body, the exercises in this book will help strengthen your understanding of the concepts presented in each chapter. The activities are usually age-specific, so you can select the age group you are most interested in, or sample different ages as you go through the book, to explore career choices. The exercises often include case studies or observation assignments to illustrate chapter principles.

Internet Quest

Another way you can learn about learning and teaching is to search out your own paths. With that task in mind, and to give you practice in using the resources available on the World Wide Web, we will send you on some Internet quests in each chapter. Each of you has different interests. Each quest will take you to an individual knowledge destination. We will be sending you off on a technological journey, introducing you to the wealth of information found on the Internet, and trusting you will learn to be selective and analyze its worth.

Reflective Journal

The information, concepts, or principles you find yourself thinking about beyond assignments or outside the classroom are the topics that help you better understand yourself, a specific child, or a subject, and that is the knowledge that will change your life. We encourage you to reflect and write about topics that are personally important to you. The end of each chapter contains reflective journal assignments. As you continue this journal throughout the book, you will be forming your own educational philosophy, which will not only be an assignment in the last chapter of the book, but which will continue as you pursue your educational and career goals. This is the introduction, so this will be your *beginning* educational philosophy, written down so that 5, 10, or 25 years from now you can look back at it and see what still pertains and what has changed. The world will change, you will change, schools will change, and so will your philosophy, but this will be the beginning.

RELATED CAREERS

Not only is this book intended to help you make a more informed career choice, it also may lead you to consider NOT becoming a teacher. The diagram entitled Related Careers (Figure P–2) will introduce you to other career possibilities. You saw in

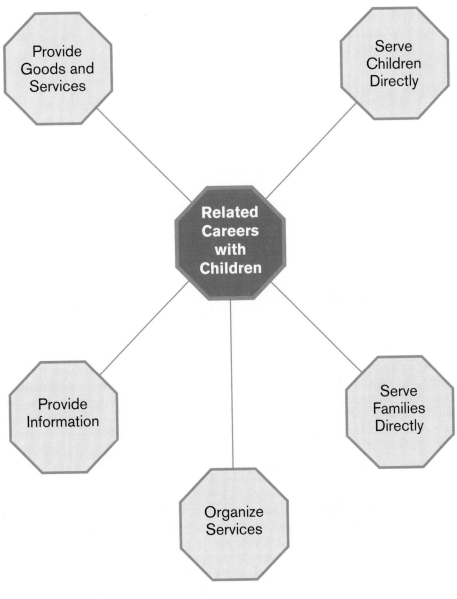

Figure P–2

Careers related to teaching.

Figure P–1 that there are a number of settings, programs, and age ranges from which to choose. These Related Career diagrams at the end of each chapter present the idea that although you may want to work with children, you can do so in other ways than being a teacher. These careers are divided into five categories.

* Serve Children Directly—Working with children in a variety of roles that may not be in a traditional classroom teaching setting
* Serve Families Directly—Working with individual families in some helping profession
* Organize Services—Making referrals or helping make services availabe, rather than actually performing the service directly
* Provide Information—Writing, researching, or communicating information useful for children or families
* Provide Goods and Services—Designing, manufacturing, selling, or providing goods or services needed by children and families, or by the people who work with them

＊ USES FOR THIS BOOK

We, the authors, envision many purposes for this book. It can be used as the basis of coursework for the six goals with thirteen competency areas of the Child Development Associate: a safe, healthy learning environment; physical and emotional competence; social and emotional development and positive guidance; a positive productive relationship with families; program management; and professionalism. It is a text that can be used for an introductory course in teacher preparation at the associate or bachelor degree level. The accompanying Instructor's Manual suggests learning and teaching strategies toward each of those purposes. Other accompanying materials will help the instructor augment the textbook.

＊ SUPPLEMENTS

Instructor's Manual

An Instructor's Manual is available that provides chapter overviews, key terms, suggestions for lectures, and interactive exercises to use in class to emphasize important chapter concepts and augment reading in the textbook. Each chapter guide also addresses the various uses for the book: preparation for working with infants, toddlers, preschoolers, primary, or elementary age children. If you are using the textbook for one of those purposes, you will find teaching strategies aimed at that specific audience.

Computerized Test Bank

An extensive test bank is available for those who use them. We take the stand throughout the book that tests are not the ultimate measure of outcomes, and we believe this is true for adults as well as children. However, we know you do not rely solely on test scores, but also on students applying their knowledge through assigned projects. The exercises at the end of each chapter can be adapted into graded assignments to measure outcomes, as well as content measured by testing. The computerized test bank includes convergent content questions for vocabulary and concept checks, as well as essay questions for critical thinking and communication of ideas. Specific questions may be selected for use with students preparing to teach infants, toddlers, preschoolers, primary, and elementary age children.

Online Resources™

The Online Resources™ to accompany *Introduction to Learning and Teaching: Infants through Elementary Age Children* is your link to early childhood education on the Internet. The Online Resources™ contains many features to help focus your understanding of the learning and teaching process.

* Sample Chapter and Preface.
* Critical Thinking Forum—Students are asked to consider a scenario from the text and respond to questions that require critical thinking skills.
* Web Activities—These activities direct you to (a) Web site(s) and allow you to conduct further research and apply content related to learning and teaching of infants through elementary age children.
* Web Link—For each chapter, a summarized list of Web links is provided for your reference.
* Sample Quizzes—Questions are provided on-line to test your knowledge of the material presented.
* On-line Early Education Survey—This survey gives you the opportunity to let us know what features you like and what features you want to see improved on the Online Resources ™.

The On-line Resources ™ icon appears at the end of each chapter to prompt you to go on-line and take advantage of the many features provided.
You can find the Online Resources™ at <www.EarlyChildEd. delmar.com>.
usermane: n3yt9h4   password: delmar44

The authors and Delmar make every effort to ensure that all Internet resources are accurate at the time of printing. However, due to the fluid, time-sensitive nature of the Internet, Delmar cannot guarantee that all URLs and Web site addresses will remain current for the duration of this edition.

Students, remember: you are at the beginning of the journey and the adventure is in the exploration. We wish you a smooth journey with a scenic view that reaches the destination of a satisfying career working with children and families.

❋ ACKNOWLEDGMENTS

The authors are indebted first of all to our families, who provided support, encouragement, fast food, and laundry and other household assistance. This book is a team effort that extended far beyond the two authors. We acknowledge and thank our colleagues from the National Community College Early Childhood Teaching and Leadership Institute for their guidance and support of our conviction that all children have a right to a quality education, which begins with the teacher. We thank Vassar College for their photos of children. We also want to thank the Delmar team, Erin O'Connor

Traylor for her support and Melissa Riveglia for her nudges, Publisher's Studio for their attention to detail, and the many reviewers who improved this text with their insightful and helpful suggestions.

Nancy Baptiste, Ed.D.
New Mexico State University
Las Cruces, New Mexico

Wendy Sue Bertoli, M.Ed.
Lancaster County Career and
Technology Center
Willow Street, Pennsylvania

Mary Lou Brotherson, Ed.D.
Nova Southeastern University
Fort Lauderdale, Florida

Jane Catalani
San Antonio College
San Antonio, Texas

Martha Dever
Utah State University
Logan, Utah

Claude Enfield
Northland Pioneer College
Holbrook, Arizona

Linda Estes, Ed.D.
St. Charles County Community
College
St. Peters, Missouri

Teresa Hopkins, Ph.D.
Germanna Community College
Locust Grove, Virginia

Susan Kent, Ph.D.
Ohio State University
Newark, Ohio

Judith Lindman, M.Ed.
Rochester Community and Technical
College
Rochester, Minnesota

Frank Miller, Ed.D.
Pittsburg State University
Pittsburg, Kansas

Ruth Sasso
Naugatuck Valley Community-
Technical College
Waterbury, Connecticut

Barbara Payne Shelton, Ed.D.
Villa Julie College
Stevenson, Maryland

Wenju Shen, Ed.D.
Valdosta State University
Valdosta, Georgia

Rosemary Wolfe, Ph.D.
Anne Arundel Community College
Arnold, Maryland

The Learning Teacher

Objectives

After reading this chapter and completing the review activities, the learning teacher should be able to:

1. State why teaching is a professional career.
2. Critically identify personal motivators for considering a career in teaching.
3. Explore the knowledge, skills, and attitudes necessary for effective teachers.
4. Begin to develop an education plan.

✳ WHAT IS A TEACHER?

"A teacher is one who makes himself progressively unnecessary."

–Thomas Carruthers

"Who dares to teach must never cease to learn."

–John Cotton Dana

"When teaching, light a fire, don't fill a bucket."

–Dan Snow

"In teaching others we teach ourselves."

–Proverb

"Teaching is the greatest act of optimism."

–Colleen Wilcox

"Every day, through my students, I touch the future."

–Sharon Christa McAuliffe

The Family as First Teachers

In its broadest definition, a teacher is a person who guides another to a higher level of knowledge or skill. The parents and family are the child's primary teachers. Within the family the child is taught social norms, learning the *rules of the tribe*. Children learn the functional skills of self-care such as eating, dressing, and personal hygiene, and the names of objects, people, and places in their world. They learn to use languages to first make their needs known and later to communicate ideas, describe events and negotiate the system of the family and beyond. As they grow older, they use the system of the family along with information and experience from a wide world to shape and refine their own values and beliefs. They learn what is acceptable and what is nonacceptable behavior within specific environments. Children learn that the rules of behavior vary among situations such as eating at home versus eating in a restaurant or speaking a native language with the family versus speaking the country's mainstream language at school. They learn to do everyday tasks to help the family function that may be distinctive from other families' tasks (Figure 1–1).

Community Teachers

The child is also taught by community members such as scout leaders, music and dance teachers, sports coaches, and cultural and religious leaders. These people may have extensive training and education within their specific field. Children have a way of cutting through barriers of societal status; they recognize the role of that person in teaching them and reward them with the name "Teacher." Unpaid volunteers in these teaching categories deserve the respect and the right to bear the worthy name of teacher, but the teacher we will be exploring in this book will be the formally prepared, college-degreed person in the occupation of teaching.

Professional Teachers

You are reading this book at the beginning of your teacher preparation program. You have a long road ahead and this book is a road map to help you investigate and explore a realistic view of what teaching involves. Most roads on a map are not straight and there are many from which to choose. Some are streamlined, some are picturesque, and some have difficult terrain to navigate. Many times as you follow the roads, the turns take you to destinations you did not expect at the beginning of your journey.

Figure 1–1

Children learn a million
things from caring adults.

This book is a beginning point on that journey toward teacher preparation. Some of you may stop at convenient points along the way. You may be using this book in a course to prepare you to work as a teacher's aide in a classroom to assist a state-certified, degreed teacher. You may be using this book to earn a credential that verifies basic competencies in some aspect of a career with children. You may be using this book in a program that leads to an associate's degree and prepares you to work with some independence in some settings. You may be using this book in a foundations of education course, preparing you for your state's requirements for teacher licensure. All 50 states have college requirements of at least a bachelor's degree, most have teaching examinations, and some require a master's degree within a specified period of time. Your professional preparation depends on the work setting, the age of the children you want to teach, and the state in which you will work. Introductory course work in any of these pathways will lead to future studies of greater depth and breadth of knowledge in teaching.

All teachers study a balance of course work covering a general knowledge called general education or the liberal arts (Figure 1–2 on page 4). Such courses include mathematics, science, behavioral science, history, and languages, and are part of teacher preparation. Teachers generally study all courses at their introductory level during the first two years of college. They return to those areas of study during their third and fourth years of college to gain depth and breadth of knowledge. As a teacher moves into study at the Master's level, the teacher has usually identified an area of teaching to explore and research in greater depth.

Banner and Cannon (1997) have said, "Above all, teaching requires learning itself; and, if possible under demanding conditions that face so many teachers, it requires mastery of a subject." In their book *The Elements of Teaching* (1997), they reinforce the idea that the three essential components of good teaching are the act of

| CDA | ASSOCIATE DEGREE | | | Bachelor of Science | Bachelor of Arts |
Child Development Associate	**AAS** Associate in Applied Science	**AS** Associate in Science	**AA** Associate in Arts		
Theory & Pedagogy– 120 hours of college-level coursework in competencies = approx. 9 credits Practice–480 work hours Advisor observation/portfolio = approx. 3 credits *Discretion of higher education institution	Theory & Pedagogy & Practice 2/3 = approx. 40 credits	Theory & Pedagogy & Practice 1/2 = approx. 30 credits	Electives May be Theory & Pedagogy. Practice usually does not transfer 1/4 = approx. 15 credits	Education 1/2 = approx. 60 credits in Professional Education	Arts and Sciences 3/4 = approx. 90 credits
Comparison of early childhood preparation using the American Association of Community Colleges suggested model for AAS, AS, and AA degrees		General Education 1/2 = approx. 30 credits	General Education 3/4 = approx. 45 credits		
Terms: Theory: coursework in child development, diversity & exceptionality curriculum & implementation, family & community, and assessment Practice: Supervised field experiences, student teaching, practicum General Education: Humanities, mathematics and technology, social sciences, biological and physical sciences, the arts, personal health and fitness	General Education 1/3 = approx. 20 credits Total 60–64	Total 60–64	Total 60–64	1/2 = Arts and Sciences (General Education)	1/4 = approx. 30 credits Other
NOTE: This is a general model with approximate distributions.				Total 120	Total 120

Figure 1–2

Careers in teaching require education at various levels of preparation.

gaining knowledge, the knowledge gained by that act, and the process of learning how to teach. They present some very strong reasons why teachers should be thinkers and that teaching is:

* knowing and mastering a subject enough to understand its significance in relation to other fields and to contribute to further knowledge in those fields.

* embodied in the act of learning; the teacher keeps on learning more and has a quest for a deeper understanding, a lifelong pursuit.

* conveying the spirit of love of learning to others, with the teacher so enthralled with the subject that the enthusiasm is contagious.

* learning from others, including the students, focusing on what students know rather than what they do not.

* justifying learning for its meaning other than just passing a test.

Teaching is learning, reflecting, collaborating with others, and continuing to learn. It is an active process that needs opportunities for trying and testing ideas. That is why field experiences, moving from observation to student teaching, are included in teacher preparation programs. The model for learning becomes: introducing the knowledge base, watching experts, trying it out, reflecting on what worked and what did not, and perfecting the techniques.

✳ WHY DO YOU WANT TO BE A TEACHER?

"I want to be a teacher because I just love kids."

"I want to be a teacher because it's a respected profession."

"I want to be a teacher because I want to make a difference in people's lives. There is one particular teacher who really turned my life around and I want to be just like him."

"I want to be a teacher because it pays well and you have summers off."

"I want to be a teacher because that's all I've ever thought about doing from the time I was little."

I Just Love Kids

The young of any species are genetically and biologically designed to be attractive, at least to their mothers, and usually to the species as a whole (Figure 1–3). "Psychologists and evolutionary biologists agree that it is natural, and also necessary—that is,

Figure 1–3

The young of any species hold an attraction.

adaptive—for mothers and their infants to be attached or bonded. . . .There is nothing sweeter than a picture of some sort of animal mother with her infants—even hyenas and bats look cute in a mother–infant tableau" (Small, 1998). Most people experience a pleasant fascination with a kitten, puppy, newly born zoo or farm animal, or a human infant. The young are fascinating to watch in their struggle to attain skills that are taken for granted by adults. The struggle to stand, to move about and find food, and finally to become an independent member of the group is an engaging process. Often emotions are stirred at the helplessness of the young, with their crude attempts and victorious accomplishments. These same feelings lead some people to think, "I want to be instrumental in helping a child in that process of growth." Children can be cute and endearing, giving love and affection, and some people assume that being a teacher will be a pleasant experience of being surrounded by adorable beings all day.

REALITY CHECK

While some children are adorable and endearing all of the time, most children are adorable only some of the time. The rest of the time they are functioning emotionally and behaviorally at a developmental level that may be self-centered or without self-control. They have not developed the ability to understand that events occur independent of them and they are unable to express emotions and ideas in a way that is understandable or socially acceptable. In other words, their behavior may be difficult to like. There may be children who are in your class who have personalities and characteristics that clash with yours, who have values that are different, or behaviors that you cannot tolerate.

Another reality in "liking kids" is the notion of what kids (children) are like. This knowledge is gained from experience within our own cultural context. Today the teacher must be prepared to teach children of many different cultures, beliefs, languages, socioeconomic groups, and life circumstances. One may have a student who is being raised by a grandparent with four generations in the home. Another child may have a parent in jail. A student of yours may have spent a part of his or her young life in a refugee camp separated from all that is familiar. There may be more than one child whose holidays, customs, and foods are totally different from yours. You may have a student whose parents are millionaires, who fly all over the world, and are in constant contact through telephone, fax, and computer. You may have children in your class whose parents seem distant, controlling, overprotective, or maybe even abusive. Will you be able to "like" all those children and their families equally?

While liking children may be the first step in your choice to become a teacher, the reasons will have to go beyond that for a sustaining, effective career. The overall purpose of this book and the introductory course you are taking is to help you explore all your reasons for becoming a teacher.

It's a Respected Profession

You certainly would not begin to prepare for a career for which you personally had little respect. Probably your family respects education and is supportive of your educational pursuits. You may have relatives who are teachers. You see that teachers rank highly in career status lists and you think that teaching is a profession that will bring you that same status in the community (Figure 1–4).

OCCUPATION	PRESTIGE SCORE*	MEDIAN WEEKLY EARNINGS, 1997**
Physician	86	N/A
College/university professor	74	N/A
Registered Nurse	66	710
Secondary school teacher	66	NA
Elementary school teacher	64	662
Police officer	60	697
Librarian	54	638
Firefighter	53	707
Bookkeeper	47	420
Mail carrier	47	677
Secretary	46	410
Carpenter	39	482
Childcare worker	36	202
Truck driver	30	506
Janitor	22	313

Figure 1–4

*Adapted from National Opinion Research Center. (1994). *General social surveys 1972–1994: Cumulative codebook* (pp. 881–889). Chicago: Author.
**Adapted from U.S. Department of Labor. (1998). *Employment and earning, January* (pp. 209–214). Washington, DC: U.S. Government Printing Office.

REALITY CHECK   The respect and status afforded to the teacher depends on many variables. Of course, just being in a job may not bring respect if one's attitude and behavior do not warrant it. Respect is earned through interactions that demonstrate the possession of certain characteristics valued by the other party. These may be very different from situation to situation. In some situations, a person who uses technical terms, complex sentences, and references to big names in art, history, philosophy, and psychology is respected for advanced learning. That same demeanor in other circumstances may be interpreted as acting superior and failing to relate to others. Perceptions of the teacher as a professional vary according to the setting, information being taught, the student's family attitude, and age of the students. The teacher who assumes that respect comes with the profession may find otherwise. Entrants to the field should be aware that to gain the respect and status of a community takes work and time. It does not come automatically with the title.

More recently, schools and teachers have come under criticism for American children failing to score as high on achievement tests as expected, especially when compared with other modern countries. Bernard Spodek, noted researcher and spokesperson on teacher preparation, said in an interview, "In the last two decades society's expectations of teachers have increased. We hear about schools failing. The reason the public sees schools failing is because this same public is expecting so much more from teachers than it ever did before . . . so expectations go up while resources to meet those expectations go down" (Allison, 1999a).

Teachers today are getting much of the blame for falling test scores and the educational system (teacher preparation in particular) has been the focus of calls for restructuring and reconceptualizing. You may be caught in the middle of a changing system. School reform and restructuring are important issues. The role of the teacher has changed drastically in the last 50 years and so the focus of this book is on the teacher as a learner who is ready to adapt to a changing world. It is hoped you will have a more realistic idea of what a teacher's responsibilities are.

I Want to Make a Difference in Children's Lives

Perhaps you have selected teaching as a career because you had one or more influential teachers who made a profound impact on your life. There may be teachers who stand out in your memory of school or those who made a difference in your school or community. There are numerous heartwarming stories about teachers who believed in a student who then went on to perform great things, attributing them to that teacher. In the following words from a master teacher, see the contrast between DeQuan's first teacher and his second.

WORDS OF WISDOM
Listen to what Kim Hughes, Teacher of the Year for South Carolina, 1999, says about her motivation for teaching:

"I remember DeQuan, a second year kindergartner who was labeled by his former teacher as a troubling distraction, an ultimate failure before the age of six. In my classroom I struggled to find something of value in DeQuan that we could build upon, something he cared about or longed for. I found it in his ability to comprehend and extend the story's context. Naturally, he became a favorite facilitator of our literature circles, thus enabling his peers a chance to pay closer attention to the meaning of the text. DeQuan left our kindergarten with a sense of empowerment, competence, trust and optimism in the power of his choices. Together we worked and reworked his developing sense of self so that he could experience 'what could be,' rather than 'what was inevitable.'"

Making a difference is a worthy motivation and we hope you will be one of those influential teachers. Research says that adult-child (we could extend that to teacher-child) relationships are some of the most frequently reported protection factors against school-age risk of low academic achievement (Garmezy, 1994). A long career in teaching brings you in contact with hundreds and thousands of children: each unique, each from a different family situation and at a different point in their development. Some say there is a critical window between kindergarten and third grade to intervene in and short-circuit those learning and behavior difficulties that lead to school failure and dropping out. The risk of academic failure can be predicted at school entry with about a 75 percent accuracy rate (Pianta, 1999). You will want to be one of those who address the risk factors before it is too late.

The Abecedarian Project, a 20-plus-year longitudinal study of the effects of a quality early childhood program, has indicated that while academic benefits are present in the early school years, it is social benefits that are most promising (Figure 1–5). The children who were in the program graduated from four-year colleges at twice the rate of their peers, and held onto jobs at higher rates than similar age-mates (Ramey & Ramey, 2000).

Teachers can make a difference. Research studies such as one conducted in Texas (Rivkin, Hanushek, & Kain, 1998) demonstrated that it was the influence of teachers more than any other variable that influenced student achievement. Supportive results have been obtained by other researchers (Jordan, Mendro, & Weerasinghe, 1997).

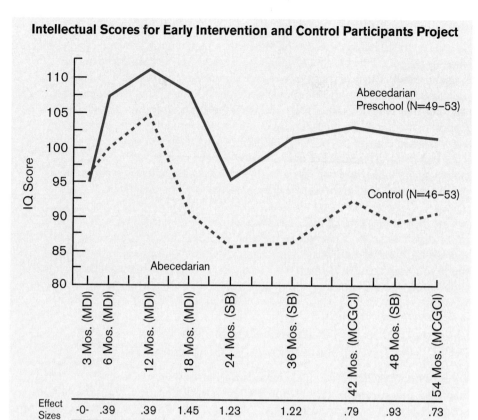

Figure 1–5

Abecedarian Project brought results. (Used with permission of Craig Ramey, Civitan International Research Center, Birmingham, AL <http://www.circ.uab.edu>)

If as a teacher you can catch that teachable moment and interest a child in science, or score a breakthrough in reading or math comprehension, you will gain great satisfaction and realize it is a life-changing moment. This can happen with a great many of the children you will teach. The goal of teaching is to reach every child, helping each one advance in knowledge and development. That goal is within the reach of all dedicated, well-prepared teachers.

REALITY CHECK There will be those children in your classroom whom you cannot reach. Some children, because of their life situation or other factors, will be impossible for you to teach and it may not be the child's fault. It may be that you are the barrier because of a personality conflict with the child. It may be you have a different value system or your own prejudices get in the way. It may be your own teaching style that just cannot be comprehended by the child. Not all teachers are good for all children. This is where close self-reflection is needed. Teachers should look inward

continued

before deciding that the child is unteachable. Professions that require high energy and high caring, like teaching, often are marked by burnout. Fifty percent of young teachers leave the field after five years (Henke, Geis, & Giambattista, 1996). Many of those give reasons other than burnout—for example, starting a family, moving, going to higher-paying jobs—but anecdotal evidence points to some suspicion about underlying factors. They may be disillusioned with what the job is all about; they may feel isolated and without support or resources from colleagues or administration, or have encountered children who exasperated or frustrated them to the point of self-doubt. Sometimes reality sets in and the person genuinely feels she has made a mistake. For them, moving on may be the wise choice. For others who feel tension and stress, remedies and help are available through peer mentoring and professional development opportunities that help them feel more prepared to face the difficult challenges.

There will be children whose lives are so difficult that academic learning is much less important than survival, either physically or psychologically. There will be children who pass through your class who are not memorable. There will be those who will shine and others you will remember with a sigh of relief, for despite your best efforts you were not able to reach them and you were glad to see them pass on to the next teacher. The hope is that, somewhere along the way, someone else can reach them.

I Want to Be a Teacher Because it Pays Well and You Have Summers Off

Public school teachers have made inroads for better wages and benefits, often attributable to unionization. The National Center for Education Statistics (NCES) reported that the average annual teacher salary in 1997–98 was $39,385 (1998). Most public schools have summer vacations of at least two months, allowing an alternative wage-earning opportunity. This increases the yearly earning potential of a teacher who can work at some other job for two months. Tenure, which protects a qualified teacher from being dismissed except on severe grounds, is usually achieved after a probationary period of three years of successful teaching (Mukamel, 1996). Teachers who are parents are attracted to a 10-month schedule with workdays and vacations coinciding with their children's, thus reducing child care costs and increasing the amount of time parents can spend with their children. For many, teaching is a career that is very compatible with family life and brings a comfortable lifestyle.

Teachers may work in private schools that have specialties, connections with religious affiliations, or a philosophy of teaching that makes the work environment an added enhancement to the wages. These positions may offer a comparable (but usually lower) wage, benefits, and calendar year similar to the public school setting. For teachers who are parents, an added benefit may be reduction in their children's tuition.

REALITY CHECK Public school teachers' wages vary greatly from state to state and even from district to district within a city. Even though the national average salary for public elementary and secondary school teachers is around $40,000, the cost of living also varies among locales. Just looking at the dollar figures may not tell the whole economic story. State certification requirements demand at least a bachelor's degree and, in many states, a master's degree. Other professions with the same amount of education often start out at higher wages. A study of 1992–93 degree recipients done five years after graduation showed careers in education generating lower average annual salaries (Figure 1–6 on page 12).

continued

Teachers usually have requirements for additional professional development that may not be provided by the school; thus, it becomes the teacher's expense. In many school districts, the stipends for supplies in the classroom are extremely meager. Teachers often purchase supplies and classroom materials themselves without reimbursement. Teacher tenure is not in effect in every school district or system, making job security tenuous depending on school district enrollment. A teacher might enjoy and be very effective teaching a particular grade, but even with tenure, if there is no need for the teacher in that grade and another grade position is open, the teacher must accept and adapt to that position or face a loss of employment. Teacher tenure across the country is under scrutiny; it may be a disappearing teacher benefit in the future.

For the teacher who is also a parent, planning for holidays and vacations to synchronize with one's children only works if you live and work in the same district. School calendars vary widely. The teacher's school day and calendar may vary from district to district in the same area. Teachers have obligations for additional training, meeting days, and after-school events that may take place when their children are out of school, so child care is a consideration. These are the practical aspects in selecting a career.

Because of the lack of a public subsidy, teachers in private schools may not earn wages or benefits comparable to teachers in public schools. Public school elementary and secondary teachers received 25–119 percent more than private school teachers (NCES, 1998). Private and parochial schools do not receive public tax funding as public schools do, and depend on tuition, fund-raising, and organizational support. This fiscal base is less dependable, varies from year to year, and is a burden on families. Teachers in private schools usually do not have tenure. If there is no tuition reduction for teachers' children and it becomes necessary to enroll them in public school, the teacher's own children may have a different school calendar.

Unfortunately, those who teach young children in child care settings, Head Start, or preschools make very low wages. A national study found average wages were between $13,125 and $18,988, with only 20 percent receiving health benefits.

Teachers in centers accredited by the National Association for the Education of Young Children (NAEYC) typically received higher wages (Whitebook, Howes, & Phillips, 1989). Parental payments coupled with state subsidies are the major income source for these programs; thus, the resources are just not there for higher wages. This has spurred a national call for increased public funds to raise child care teachers' wages in all early childhood programs, but the picture is bleak. Because of the low wages in child care programs, teachers change jobs frequently. High turnover is an adjustment both for the worker and the child. Teachers often must develop political advocacy skills to attempt to change working conditions for themselves that will ultimately benefit children and families. Higher salaries will attract and retain better qualified and satisfied teachers, resulting in better programming and quality outcomes for children.

I've Always Wanted to Be a Teacher

You've been (for approximately 11,000 hours) watching teachers for years (Figure 1–7 on page 13). It looks easy and you think you could do at least as well as they have. You just assign the students some work, stay ahead of them in the book, give tests and correct papers, and talk to a parent now and then. It can't be so hard, especially if you are teaching preschool, where they just play, or primary grades, where they are just learning beginning levels of reading, math, and science.

Average Annual Salary of 1992–93 Degree Recipients in April 1997	
Engineering	$44,524
Health professions	$39,421
Mathematics and other sciences	$38,148
Business and management	$37,454
Social science	$35,536
Public affairs/social services	$30,563
Humanities	$30,179
Biological sciences	$29,331
Psychology	$28,197
History	$28,147
Education	$26,513

SOURCE: McCormick et al, 1999.

Figure 1—6

Teachers' salaries in comparison to other professionals. (From McCormick, A. C., Nunez, A. M., Shah, V., & Choy, S. P. (1999). *Life after college: A descriptive summary of 1992–93 bachelor's degree recipients in 1997.* Washington, DC: U.S. Department of Education, National Center for Education Statistics.)

REALITY CHECK   Whether they are on a tennis court, on a piano keyboard, in a hair salon, or at a computer terminal, when you watch experts do anything, it always looks easy. It is a challenge to interact with a number of children all day, helping each one to progress in development and subject areas, and working toward goals that may not always be important or attainable. Many schools are pressuring teachers to better prepare students for competencies needed for standardized testing. The group of children that a teacher works with will be diverse in cognitive abilities, cultural background, developmental level, family values, health, life experiences, and even language. The teacher must be able to address the different strengths and needs of individual students. The teacher uses her own cognitive abilities for perception, memory, judgment, and values, necessitating an adjustment to each child's way of acquiring knowledge and skills. The Occupational Outlook Handbook (1998–99 edition) published by the U.S. Department of Labor (1998) says the teaching profession "requires a wide variety of skills and aptitudes, including a talent for working with children; organizational, administrative, and record-keeping abilities; research and communication skills; the power to influence, motivate, and train others; patience and creativity" (p. 179). Because of the increasing complexity of our society, with rapidly expanding knowledge and changes in the type of educational outcomes, from work skills to thinker skills, the teacher assumes many roles in the course of a day. Allison (1999b) ponders this question, "Can the majority of teachers switch effectively among their many roles, and still obtain excellence in every domain? Children and families always will have a bottomless well of needs. When is 'enough' enough?" (p. 259).

Teachers themselves must know their subject areas deeply, understand how individual children think and learn, and create a variety of experiences that actually work to produce learning and help children reach competence. For each grade level, there is usually a defined curriculum with expected outcomes for knowledge and skills. Children must attain a certain level before moving to the next level.

Figure 1—7

"I want to be a teacher just like you."

"They just play." Throughout this book you will notice an emphasis on play. It is not just for the preschool child; hundreds and even thousands of research studies have found that both children and adults learn best through play (Duckworth, 1987; Fromberg & Bergen, 1998; Garvey, 1999; Jones & Reynolds, 1992). While the early childhood years look like "just play" to the observer, children learn through their play. Primary and elementary age children also learn through play, but the rigors and expectations of the school may not accept that "active learning" model.

Informed decision-making is considering many factors, advantages and disadvantages, and coming to a logical conclusion based on the facts. The purpose of this section was to help you explore the many reasons why you want to be a teacher, not to discourage you, but to help you consider the realities. Teachers have a lot to learn. The next section provides you with some of the areas of knowledge that a teacher needs.

✳ WHAT DOES A TEACHER NEED TO KNOW?

In the early days of American education, all a teacher needed to know was more than the students. There was no such thing as teacher training or certification. We have come a long way from that casual system to a very complex and multibillion dollar industry. There is much you need to know to be a teacher. Here are a few things to start thinking about.

It may seem obvious that before you can teach, you must learn. You already have the notion that the learning to which we refer is not just reading, writing, mathematics, and science but has a much broader meaning. Learning involves a change in behavior. An old adage is, "The lesson is never learned until the behavior changes." It is more than getting a passing grade on a test, or being able to match definitions with vocabulary words, or recognizing all the categories of poisonous plants. The lesson is not learned until those vocabulary words become a part of our language and behavior and we avoid those poisonous plants. The teacher is, first and foremost, a learner. Before we look at the *what* of teaching, it is most important to look at the *who*: first, ourselves; then, the children and families we will meet along the way, in addition to our colleagues. This chapter will start you on that road to discovery.

Learning about Yourself

SCENARIO You are strapped in the airplane seat and the airline attendant is reviewing the safety procedures. You are instructed that in case of loss of cabin pressure, the oxygen mask will drop down. If you have a child with you, you are to place the mask on yourself before placing one on the child.

The reason is that if you did this in reverse order, you may be affected while placing the mask on the child and not be able to extend further care to the child. This is a metaphor for teaching. You must examine yourself, your nature and your own learning, before thinking about teaching the child.

The following sections will help you look at yourself, what you bring to your teaching, and what you might need to add or take away.

Ecology of Human Development.

Who are you? What are you like? How are you different from, and yet the same as, other people? Zoom your lens out to the moon; then focus the lens on yourself right at this moment (Figure 1–8). Here you are, one little person, at this point in time on the earth. It makes one feel insignificant, yet each of us is a unique individual, like no other at any time since time began or will be again. Urie Bronfenbrenner of Cornell University, a great thinker of our time, set forth a more scientific model for considering a person's place in the universe in his book *The Ecology of Human Development: Experiments by Nature and Design* (1979). **Ecology** is a term from biology, but Bronfenbrenner uses it to relate to human development. Thinking of human development this way helps us discover who we are, how we have come to be like this, and what forces have an impact on us, as well as those we have an impact upon. Figure 1–9 offers a visual picture of the explanation that follows.

Urie Bronfenbrenner

(1917–) Russian born, professor emeritus at Cornell University. One of the world's leading scholars in developmental psychology and child-rearing and one of the founders of Head Start.

Nature. Human development begins with the biological characteristics you inherit from your parents. The genetic code that is distinctly you, DNA (deoxyribonucleic acid), is a combination from all the ancestors on your mother's and father's sides. Trillions of possibilities exist, but as luck or design would have it, this is what you have to work with: no more, no less. You have physically inherited the determinants of your sex, your skin, your hair and eye color; the shape of your head, teeth, and hands; and possibly a particular weakness in an organ. You have a voice that may sound just like another family member's; you may have a laugh or a personality characteristic that there was no way for you to learn but was genetically programmed. You have a brain capacity and a certain way of processing information over which you have no control. You have talents or lack thereof just like a forefather or foremother. These and thousands of other characteristics are the basis of who you are; they are the influences of who you will become. This is the core of your ecology.

---

ecology—Biological term referring to the mutual relations between organisms and their environment.

Figure 1—8

Viewing ourselves from an outside perspective. (Courtesy of NASA)

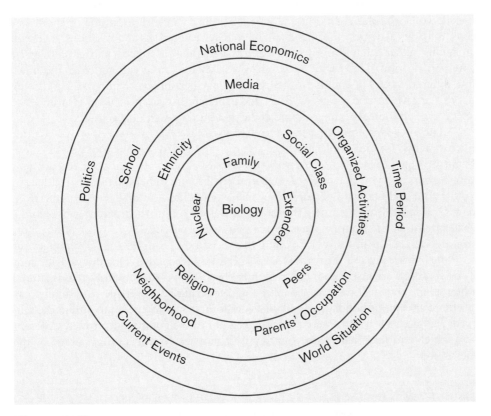

Figure 1—9

The sociological ecology. (Adapted from Bronfenbrenner, U., 1979). *The ecology of human development: Experiments by nature and design.* Cambridge, MA: Harvard University Press)

Nurture. The remaining influences on you are the nurture forces: those that affect your life by direct teaching, modeling and examples, or subtle messages and far-flung events over which you have no control, but that have an effect on you. The categories of those influences are: microsystems, mesosystems, exosystems, and macrosystems.

Microsystems are very close, personal, and primary influences. You might guess that family is the most significant influence. Being born into a family not only brings you inherited characteristics, but also conveys beliefs, values, attitudes, and mannerisms that range from how you cut your food to what you call your genitals. Your immediate family, such as parents and older siblings, and then extended family, such as grandparents, aunts, uncles, cousins, and close family friends, are the primary socializing agents who profoundly influence you. As you interact with them, you are watching and listening, taking in information and forming patterns of behavior, either as you are instructed or in opposition to what you are taught.

A feature of this microsystem is that it is dynamic and constantly evolving. Your parents have their own ecology that is constantly changing, and this affects your life. For example, suppose you were born into a family as the second child. Your parents already have a relationship and routines established with their first child, your older sibling. Then you come along and your presence changes all that. The family routine changes. Your needs further divide the communal pot. *You change everything.* In turn, your family, of course, affects you. This is what is known as the reciprocal nature of systems. You are affected by and in turn affect your environment; it works both ways. Other systems within your microsystem will be different for each person. These systems are those activities, roles, and experiences that are a part of your life. They may include your school, neighborhood, Scouts or other youth clubs, music or sports lessons, religious activities, a job, and family holiday celebrations and vacations. These all are highly influential in forming your identity, and you also make an impact on them by your participation. These systems change as you change, or as you get older and move into different stages of your life. Some systems may become more important and some nonexistent when other activities, roles, and experiences take their place. However, the effects are still there, helping to build and contribute to each new venture.

The **mesosystems** are the interrelations or overlap of two or more of your microsystems. One example is when your parents go to your school's Curriculum Night or Open House to speak with the teacher about you, and your teacher tells your parents that you are a whiz at puzzles. Perhaps your father did not realize that, so he goes out and buys you puzzles. Your mesosystem has now affected your microsystem. Or a friend from your neighborhood joins your Scout troop and now rises to the challenge of all the honor badges, while you had been content to plod along. Now you are caught up in the competition to attain more badges, thus changing your scouting experience and the whole troop's performance record. Or suppose your family celebrations are associated with religious observances. Your microsystem is altered when family and religious participation come together and overlap. Your family may celebrate a religious holiday for its social significance, but you begin to attend the religious services to learn the sacred meanings, and now celebrate it in a totally different way, which you may share with your family. The microsystem is thus affected by the mesosystem.

---

microsystems—Interpersonal relationships experienced in face-to-face settings, including family, school, youth groups, and religious organizations.

mesosystem—A combination of microsystems that influences the individual as the individual affects the microsystems, producing a change in both systems.

The **exosystems** are the realms with which you have no direct contact or over which you have no control but which have an effect on you. It could be your parents' employment or their circle of friends, the local town board or school board, the media, or innovations in technology. The local school board decides that all children must wear uniforms to school. Because they disagree with the philosophy of that requirement, your parents decide to move to a different part of town where there is no such requirement. Your life is changed forever because of a school board decision. Or just think of the changes that have taken place in the last five years alone with the use of the Internet. How people talk with each other, the ways and rate at which they exchange information, how they shop, all have changed because advanced computer and communications technology made this possible. Who knows what is next!

The **macrosystems** are the broader contexts in which all other systems operate. They include political systems and economic systems; the basic beliefs and values of the culture and religions; and the historical time in which you live. As mentioned earlier, our lives have been changed because of the Internet. The Internet is a component of the macrosystem that grew tremendously in the late 1990s and was not a part of the lives of most people in the 1980s. It is a part of many children's lives today; it is part of their microsystem, with toddler computer learning programs that the parent may be unsure of how to even load into the computer. When today's children are adults and look back on childhood, the historical context will be much different from that of their parents.

Because of the dynamics of these interrelated systems, you can chart your own ecology at only one given point in time. It will probably be different a year from now and it may be different only a day from now, depending on events in your own family, town, nation, or world. It is helpful, however, to gain insight into yourself today as that pinpoint on the globe, and to begin reflecting on the factors that have made you the way you are. The next section is a closer examination of some other factors about you.

Learning about Your Own Learning. Along with your biological inheritance comes a certain way of processing information. Much progress has been made in the field of cognitive learning theory based on new ways to actually see the brain work and understand it better. Your brain has already taken in and stored billions of bits of information, much of it trivial, extraneous stimuli from your environment such as the sound of a clock ticking, the sight of a fleck of dust floating through the air, or the feel of the waffle ridges in an ice cream cone. Most likely, you do not think of those things until they are called to your attention, such as in the preceding sentence. Then you are able to consciously retrieve them. By the next paragraph, they will have faded back into their little spaces and, not brought up again, they will stay there, perhaps for a long period of time. But they are there for you. New stimuli will search your past memory to find a match. Aha! There it is. If the stimulus is a new one, there is no match. It will take conscious effort to put that into storage and another similar sensation to bring it out again. That is a very simple explanation of learning. Teaching is providing those experiences that either make connections or matches with prior sensations, or presenting new experiences and then making connections with them again before they are lost.

---

exosystems—Those spheres of influence that indirectly affect the individual and over which the individual has little or no control.

macrosystems—Systems based on values, traditions, and beliefs that exercise power over vast resources or numbers of people and over which individuals have no control.

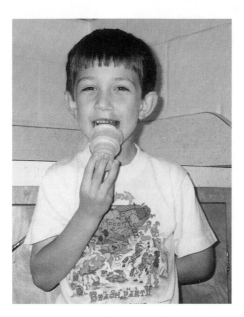

Figure 1–10

Can you feel the cone? Taste and smell the ice cream?

What makes us remember things? We remember information when we chunk it, or group ideas together in organized ways, linking it to other similar pieces of information. Learning is especially effective when enhanced by multiple sensory experiences. When you read about the waffle ridges on an ice-cream cone, your memory connected it with the image of the patterns of ridges and depressions, and the shadows, colors, and shape of the cone. This perceptual imagery is connected to memories of other objects of a similar triangular shape, and hopefully the sweet taste of the cone and the ice cream it held. Can you picture it? Now imagine, if you can, never having had that sensory experience. Suppose you have only seen a picture of an ice cream cone, and have never experienced the reality of one in the physical world (Figure 1–10). How vivid and extensive would your recall be? Not very. It is likely your perception and imagery of that object would be two-dimensional, flat, and dull, limited to sight without memories of the texture, the smell, or the taste. So what does that mean for a teacher? When teachers present a concept, hopefully the child has had a similar experience or can make some kind of a mental match or connection to that concept; it is even better if that match or connection is paired with multiple related matches. If the child has no cognitive associations to make with that concept, how can a teacher present new information in a way that makes it meaningful and lasting? The teacher can use the precepts of cognitive learning theory: link the new information to many sensory experiences, along with repetition, and it will be remembered. Teaching and effective learning depend on firsthand, tangible, sensory experiences to stimulate the brain to learn and remember.

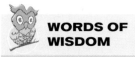

WORDS OF WISDOM   Mary Jamsek is a Master Teacher at the Child and Family Laboratory at the University of Texas at Austin. She reflects about thinking and learning, and of continuing to learn:

"It seems that the longer I work with children the more I see that there is still more to learn. Children may be children, essentially unchanging, and principles of working with children (curriculum, guidance,

continued

child development) may remain the same, but each child makes the equation yield a slightly different answer."

"After 12 years I feel that I am proficient in certain aspects of teaching, still needing to grow and learn in other areas, and I know that there are ideas I don't even know about yet. I never miss an opportunity to seek out experts–the children in my class, their parents, my co-teachers and colleagues, workshop and conference presenters, and books and journals. I never feel like an opportunity to learn is a waste of time. Even if it's a subject I'm well versed in, there's always a new perspective or a chance to retrieve information from some new dusty corner of my overcrowded brain."

"I find that my passions change, both personally and professionally. I might discover a new topic or revisit an old one with new eyes provided by added years of experience. The excitement of the new, the challenge of the unknown, and the desire to figure out the where, what, when, how, and why keeps me fresh in my classroom and in my life–a positive for me and the children with whom I spend my days."

In your reflection regarding memory, recall, and learning (as in the past few paragraphs of this section), you have been performing **metacognition**, *thinking about thinking,* just as Mary did in the passage she wrote. The teacher as a learner must perform metacognition as a reflective technique to self-analyze personal prior experiences in order to relate them to the task of teaching. Then the teacher attempts to imagine the prior experiences of the students, how the concepts will make connections with their prior experiences and learning, and how to stimulate connections, chunk information, and surround it with multisensory experiences to help them learn. Not everyone learns in the same way, so it is helpful if the teacher knows his own learning style and that of his students.

From the fields of psychology and biology come two related theories seeking to explain differences in how people learn. Learning style theory is based on the work of Carl Jung (1927); it is looking at the different ways humans perceive experiences, make decisions, and interact with others. It categorizes those differences into sensation versus intuition, logical thinking versus imaginative feelings, and extroversion versus introversion. The Myers-Briggs type indication (McClanaghan, 2000) applied Jung's work and created tools and tests (or instruments) for self-analysis of these styles, and many have worked to interpret and apply the personality-type theory to the fields of business and education. By examining her own personality type and those of the children in the class, the teacher can recognize the processes of learning and modify teaching techniques to address the learning styles of the children in the group. The Internet Quest section at the end of this chapter contains the addresses of Web sites that can help you to assess your own personality type. In the Reflection section, you may consider how that affects your learning and thus your teaching. How will you teach children who learn differently than you do?

Howard Gardner's many publications, beginning with *Frames of Mind: The Theory of Multiple Intelligences* (1983) and in later ones (1993, 1999a, 1999b) describe seven human intelligences: linguistic, logical-mathematical, spatial, musical, bodily-kinesthetic,

---

metacognition–The ability to reflect on one's own thinking process–thinking about thinking.

interpersonal, and intrapersonal. An eighth has been added: naturalist intelligence (Campbell, Campbell, & Dickinson, 1996). Gardner attributes contributions from both a person's biology and culture when explaining different aptitude levels in various content and competence areas (Silver, Strong, & Perini, 1997). As a self-learner, the teacher can recognize in a student which abilities are strongest and which are less developed. Recognizing the likelihood that children in the group may have opposite strengths, an appropriate selection of teaching strategies and especially assessment tools needs to be taken into consideration (Figure 1–11).

Culture is another factor in learning style. It is estimated that by 2026, 70 percent of American students will be nonwhite or of Hispanic origin (Garcia, 1995). Griggs and Dunn (1995) have done an extensive study of Hispanic-American students and their learning styles. They found most of these students experienced late-morning peak energy levels, and preferred a cool environment, conformity, peer-oriented learning, kinesthetic instructional resources, a high degree of structure, and variety, as opposed to routines and a field-dependent cognitive style. Latham (1997) points out that even as this demographic change is taking place, individual schools' teaching methods have remained relatively unchanged, traditional, and homogenous. He describes the KEEP (Kamchameha Early Education Program) project in Hawaii (Tharp, 1982, 1989), where students had improved performance on standardized tests when teachers adapted their classroom approach to be congruent with Hawaiian social culture. The Hawaiian approach did not work with Navajo school children, who have a different social culture. This indicates that a culturally responsive pedagogy is important in helping diverse populations attain success. Knowing one's own learning style, and that of the students and their cultures, is an important starting point for the teacher.

Figure 1–11

You will be teaching all kinds of children.

Learning About Your Biases. For teachers in a society that consists of many different groups of people from all over the world, the classroom community is an excitingly diverse place and challenging as well. It is a diverse culture in which people are speaking many different languages, thinking in many different ways, and valuing different things. You want to be a fair and unprejudiced teacher, as well as one who is teaching knowledge and skills that will prepare your students for life in society. You have explored your own place in that society because of the family into which you were born, the community and world situation around you, and your own personality and learning style. Now you will take a microscope and closely examine your inner feelings that could contribute to or prevent your respecting all children and treating them fairly.

As a product of the society you explored previously, you can use that framework when you look at other people. Because of your own background, certain **prejudices**, **stereotypes**, or **biases** may exist that will be roadblocks to equality in our classrooms. Schneidewind and Davidson (1997) called this the *Filter of Oppression*. Through socialization we have developed biases through which we view others and these biases lead to oppressive attitudes and behaviors (Figure 1–22 on page 22). We need to heighten our awareness of these biases within ourselves, reflect on their origins, and examine the negativity they exact upon us personally. We then can examine the damage our partisan notions and attitudes do to people when we react to them not as unique individuals, but as members of this preconceived grouping. The lesson is learned when we realize the unfairness of this and seek to interact with each person without these prejudices.

These biases may influence the teacher's perception of the child, her expectation for the child's potential, and ultimately the attention the teacher gives that child. We encourage you to perform a self-examination of your own attitudes, prejudices, and biases, and work to eliminate them from your life.

Learning about Children and Families

If you were preparing to be a nurse, you would need to learn about medications, treatments, and medical procedures; the nurse needs to know all this as it applies to the patient. If you were preparing to be an architect, you would need to learn about strengths of various building materials, types of building design, and the kinds of foundations needed to support the building's weight. The architect needs to know all this as it applies to the building's purposes, and how it will serve the people who inhabit it. So it is with teaching: there is much to learn about yourself, the body of knowledge or content you will teach, and how to teach that knowledge. You need to know all this to teach the students in your classroom. Think of yourself as a researcher, seeking to find answers to questions about each child's life situation and how best to impart the mandated curriculum in a meaningful way. Knowing about the child, and

---

prejudice—An attitude of prejudging, usually in a negative way; a rigid and irrational generalization about an entire category of people.

stereotype—An assumption about what people are like based on previous associations with them or with people who have similar characteristics, or based on information received from others, including the media, whether true or false.

bias—Discriminating against a person or group based on prejudice.

The areas of oppression include:

 * Racism—The belief that human beings have distinctive characteristics that confer superiority of one race over another, giving that race the right to more power and resources. This is oppression based on skin color, which is a biologically inherited trait.

 * Sexism—The belief that one sex is superior to the other, usually a perception of male superiority over the female; in our society, males have the dominant power in private as well as public life.

 * Classism—The belief that certain people deserve differential treatment because of their power, wealth, or family influence.

 * Agism—An attitude that subordinates a person or group because of age.

 * Heterosexism—Classifying people based on the dominant sexual orientation.

 * Linguicism—Discrimination based on the language a person speaks as their first language.

 * Anti-Semitism and other religious oppression—Discrimination against non-Christian religious groups or Christian groups not of the majority culture.

 * Ableism—An attitude towards a person with a physical or emotional disorder that limits the perception of their ability in other areas.

 * Competitive individualism—An attitude supporting competition that evaluates an individual's success or failure measured against another person.

Figure 1—12

Filters of oppression. (From Schneidewind, N., & Davidson, E. *Open minds to equality: A sourcebook of learning activities to affirm diversity and promote equality* (2nd ed.). © 1997 by Allyn & Bacon. Reprinted/adapted by permission)

how he or she grows, develops, and learns is the theme throughout a teacher's learning and the foundation of this book.

Principles of Child Development. As described in the Introduction, development is affected by nature—inherited traits, characteristics, and abilities—as well as by nurture—those interactions with people and the environment that effect changes. Some constants regarding development are universal for all children.

 * Development moves in an orderly progression from simple to complex, building on those abilities that have already been acquired. Cross-cultural research indicates that physical, intellectual, language, and social-emotional development occurs all over the world in the same progression (Konner, 1991). Children learn to roll over, sit up, crawl, stand, and then walk, in that order. Other developmental features have an equally predictable progression, with identifiable milestones or accomplishments. At the beginning of their social development, infants are not concerned with the activities of others when they experience bodily needs. They are self-centered, considering only

their own needs by reflex. As children age, they begin to adapt their demands to the accessibility and willingness of others to provide for them. Young children have little control over their expression of emotions. They cry out, laugh without restraint, show violent anger, and have little desire or ability to control those responses. As they grow older, they learn what is socially acceptable and may develop an increasing range of strategies to express those emotions.

* While development moves in a predictable progression, the rate of that progress varies for individual children. Some children walk at nine months and some not until fifteen months, although those children and their unique and individual patterns may be perfectly normal. Each child has her own timetable for the accomplishment of milestones. That rate is determined by a multitude of factors, beginning with genetics, environment, prior experiences, encouragement, and even culture. While some children develop independence in self-care at a very early age, in other cultures children are dependent much longer.

* Social, physical, language, intellectual, creative, and emotional developments are not isolated from each other; experiences in one area may influence or delay development in another. Physical development of the small muscles is necessary for writing ability. Attention span, sometimes affected by emotional development, is necessary for learning to read (Figure 1–13). Traumatic events such as a severe illness or hospitalization may delay language development even though the illness may not affect any of the components of the brain or body areas needed for speaking.

Figure 1—13

Development occurs in a predictable progression.

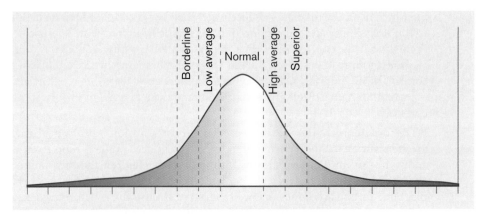

Figure 1–14

Development can be described by a bell-shaped curve, with most milestones reached within the range of average age.

* Development is profoundly affected by social and cultural contexts. Going back to Bronfenbrenner's ecological model (Figure 1–9) on page 15, all those concentric circles of influence or systems in the diagram have an impact on how and when the child changes. To be effective, learning experiences in the classroom must be culturally congruent with children's lives outside the classroom, building on what children already know without devaluing important objects and relationships (Hyun, 1996).

Child development is both generalized and specific. It embodies universal principles and milestones, yet each child is a unique individual who is influenced by genetics, temperament, environment, experiences, and child-rearing practices, language, gender, and religion. The teacher as a learner should be well-grounded in child development principles, stages, and characteristics and should recognize the differences that may affect that development.

We have included a Developmental Checklist in Appendix A for children from birth through age nine from Allen and Marotz (1999) and for children through age twelve from Estes (1998). As you read this book and its various sections, refer to this checklist to identify the various developmental areas and milestones that occur throughout early childhood.

Exceptions in Child Development. If we think of the traditional **bell curve** (Figure 1–14), all development occurs within that curve, with most of it within the range of normal, or the middle portion of the curve. There are variations and exceptions that occur at both ends. Those differences will be found within your classroom, so it will be important for you to learn about these possibilities. This section will introduce some of them, but you will learn more about them throughout your career preparation. New diagnoses and strategies are being discovered, making it necessary for

bell curve—A common type of graph, more or less in the shape of a bell, that displays the normal distribution of statistical frequencies of items, features, or attributes, with the average, and usually majority, feature being examined falling most frequently in the median, and with lesser values/frequencies displayed on either side of normal.

you to update your knowledge base throughout your career. It may be that you will be the one to discover the difference: whether it is an area where a child is gifted or talented, has a developmental delay that interferes with the progress of moving forward in a particular area, or if the child has a different ability or disability in learning. In later chapters, you will learn more about identifying and adapting teaching strategies to accommodate these differences, which can occur in any area of development.

WORDS OF WISDOM   "All children are gifted. They just open their presents at different times and in different ways." Anonymous

Developmental Exceptionalities.   The Individuals with Disabilities Education Act (1975), reauthorized in 1990, PL 94–142, requires mandatory "free, appropriate public education for every child between the ages of three and twenty one years" regardless of how, or how seriously, she may be handicapped. The Americans with Disabilities Act of 1990, PL 101–476 amended the act to include and serve those children from birth through age 5. The Rehabilitation Act of 1973, PL 93–112, prohibits discrimination against the handicapped. These laws stipulate that all children with handicapping conditions be served in the **least restrictive environment**, meaning that the child should have every opportunity to function in settings offered to all other children their age, and should be afforded any additional assistance to make that happen. That least restrictive environment may consist of an increasing amount of intervention in the form of:

* a regular classroom setting with fully integrated curriculum.
* a regular classroom with occasional consultation help.
* an itinerant teacher providing regular but partial-day instructional sessions.
* a special teacher who provides partial-day instruction, and most or all instruction for several days with a prescriptive plan.
* homebound or segregated instruction.
* a self-contained totally segregated classroom.
* a special day school.
* a residential school.

There is a diagnostic and institutional need to assign a label to groups of people who share certain characteristics. While it is important to understand that need, you should remember as a teacher to see each child as an individual and to try not to allow the label or its expectations interfere with seeing the child's abilities and strengths. While one area of a child's development may be impaired, other areas are not necessarily affected and are ready for the same kind of experiences provided to all children. As you read the list of identified disabling conditions, think of the areas of strength that you could work with as a teacher, not just the areas of need.

least restrictive environment—The instructional setting most like that of nonaffected peers that also meets the needs of the student with the disability.

The federal legislation guaranteeing appropriate education for individuals with a range of special needs or disabilities has been amended many times, as more becomes known about differing abilities and the effectiveness of intervention and remediation tactics. Below is a list headed "child with a disability" from IDEA (Individuals with Disabilities Education Act of 1990 PL 101–476, section 602[3]), with explanations adapted from Allen and Schwartz (1999) and Bowe (2000):

* Mental retardation—Not the preferred designation used by people who work with children. The American Association on Mental Retardation (AAMR, 1992) defines mental retardation as "substantial limitations in present functioning. It is characterized by significantly sub-average intellectual functioning, existing concurrently with related limitations in two or more of the following applicable adaptive skill areas: communication, self-care, home living, social skills, community use, self direction, health and safety, functional academics, leisure and work."

* Hearing disabilities—Including deafness or hearing loss so severe that the individuals cannot process language

* Speech or language disabilities—Diminished ability to communicate due to physical or cognitive functioning

* Visual disabilities, including blindness—Visual loss severe enough that it is not possible to read print, or requiring large print or print under special conditions

* Emotional disturbance—Behavior disorders or problems such as infantile autism or childhood schizophrenia

* Orthopedic disabilities—Difficulties caused by the absence or nonfunctioning of arms, legs, or digits

* Autism—A disorder that includes emotional unresponsiveness and social-cognitive deficiencies

* Traumatic brain injury—Injury to the head that causes neurological damage to the brain resulting in spatial confusion, distractibility, memory problems, impulsivity, or aggressiveness

* Other health disabilities—Health disorders such as heart problems, leukemia, asthma, sickle-cell anemia, hemophilia, diabetes, or cystic fibrosis that may limit strength, vitality, and alertness

* Specific learning disabilities—Normal IQ but difficulties with reading or processing information

* Multiply disabled—Having more than one disability; one may or may not be associated with another (Adapted from Allen & Schwartz, 1999; Bowe, 2000)

The classroom teacher is part of the team that determines the proper placement for the child. Each child labeled as "disabled" must have an *individualized education program* (IEP), a written statement agreed upon by the parents, the local special education planning team, and the child (if appropriate). It includes:

* a statement of current levels of educational performance.

* a statement of annual goals, including short-term instructional objectives.

* a statement of the specific educational services to be provided, and the extent to which the child will be able to participate in regular educational programs.

* the projected date of initiation and anticipated duration of such services, and appropriate objective criteria and evaluation procedures and schedules for determining, on at least an annual basis, whether instructional objectives are being achieved (PL 94–142, Education for All Handicapped Children Act of 1975).

Once the child is identified as disabled, the school is also mandated to provide free and appropriate education for that child. That education may include in-classroom enrichment, a consultant teacher, a resource room where the child goes for one-on-one or small group work with a specialist for portions of the day, or special class or school. The practice of **inclusion** of children with disabling conditions within the regular classroom places a responsibility on the teacher to adapt to and meet the needs of a wide range of children. The teacher is part of the team for that child, planning the IEP to meet the child's exceptional needs. Thus, the teacher must know about the physical and cognitive features of children with disabilities and how to meet the individual needs of each of those children. While this can be interesting and rewarding, it is also challenging. In any typical group, there will be children with a wide range of abilities in different developmental areas. Project Star (Finn & Achilles, 1990) indicated inclusion was only successful when class size was reduced to a group 13 to 17 students. Most public school classrooms have many more than 17 students. Proponents of inclusion point out that children with special needs benefit from friendships and contact with classmates who don't have special needs. A program for children who require special education teachers or aides calls for increased collaboration skills on the part of the adults, who must coordinate special services with the plans of the classroom teacher. Full-inclusion classrooms that meet the needs of every student may oblige the teacher to change standard classroom practices.

As you continue your education as a teacher, you will study the areas of cognitive differences; you may even decide to specialize in teaching children with developmental disabilities, or the gifted and talented.

Social/Cultural Influences on Child Development. Children are different because they come from different families and backgrounds. Every family socializes or teaches their children how to get along in the world in a different way (Figure 1–15 on page 28). Some socialization factors can be categorized, though we should be very cautious about forming stereotypical ideas about whole groups of people.

Economic—One in five children in America lives in poverty, according to the United States Census data, and one in every four children under six is designated as poor. Unfortunately, the rate of poverty in America is, at the time of this writing, increasing (Figure 1–16 on page 28).

Several studies show that children of poverty have more instances of delayed physical development and score lower on test scores of cognitive ability than children from medium-income families. Additionally, poverty among preschool children is likely to adversely affect school completion years later. While the teacher cannot attack the poverty, the teacher must work with the effects.

Cultural—Each culture defines its normal behavior. Behavior that is perfectly normal in one culture may be perceived and labeled as abnormal in another. We learn cultural behaviors from our family, peers, and neighbors and they affect our social behavior. When cultures confront each other, there is an unsettling feeling and unconscious measuring of one against another. In the United States, the European influence is so strong that **Eurocentrism** (the belief that this culture is superior) is institutionalized, finding its way into all values, customs, and behavior. This can be a profound disadvantage for children from another culture seeking some familiar object, language, or even a face that looks like theirs.

---

inclusion–Students with disabilities are educated with nondisabled peers with supports and services provided as needed.

Eurocentrism–Focus on beliefs and concerns relevant to Western societies.

Figure 1—15

Preservation of culture is accomplished in many ways.

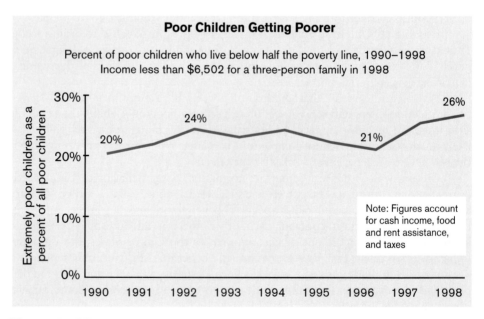

Figure 1—16

Poverty in America, especially among its youngest, is increasing, not decreasing (Used with permission from Children's Defense Fund.) Children's Defense Fund. 2000. *The State of America's Children Yearbook, 2000*, p. 8. Boston: Beacon Press.

The nation's schools are changing and becoming more ethnically, racially, and linguistically diverse (Figure 1–17 on page 30). The proportion of children under the age of 18 who are of white European descent is projected to decline steadily and rapidly, from 69 percent in 1990 to 50 percent in 2030. The number of children who are Hispanic, or African-American or of another non-Caucasian race is expected to climb from 30 percent to 50 percent (Hernandez, 1995).

The teacher needs to be aware of the multicultural nature of the world, the global community in which most children live and move. The teacher must use that sensitivity not just in a culturally mixed classroom for the well-being of those children, but also in the homogeneous classroom to serve as a guide for those children's developing perceptions and sensibilities. The first step for the teacher is to learn about the cultures represented in the group setting. De Melendez and Ostertag (1997) have developed a simple Class Profile to begin gathering this information in categories such as social class structure, ethnicity, religious affiliation, language other than English, family configuration, and exceptionality. This is included in the Review Activities: Exercises to Strengthen Learning at the end of the chapter.

The next step is to search for more information on any of these designations that are not familiar to the teacher. This will develop what Lynch and Hanson (1992) call **cultural competence**. The teacher takes action based on that knowledge, and decides what to incorporate into the environment and curriculum that will represent each child's culture. It may take the form of culturally related materials such as:

* Visuals—Including posters, pictures, and photographs
* Manipulatives—Including puzzles, cooking tools, personal ornaments, or items such as blocks, buttons, or shells for sorting and classifying
* Art supplies—Those familiar to the culture, colors representative of diverse skin tones, and culturally traditional crafts
* Music/movement—Instruments, recorded music, songs, and dances from the culture
* Holiday celebrations—Culturally traditional foods and customs
* Literature—Books with all kinds of ethnicities and differences represented and stories of everyday-life commonalities

Learning about Families. Every family is unique. Our own family experience gives us a bit of firsthand knowledge about families, but there is much to learn. Social, economic, cultural, and political forces are constantly influencing families and in turn affecting their children. Many families with working adults depend on child care during the working hours for care of their preschoolers, and before and after school (and during school breaks) for school-age children. As the child matures, self-care becomes an issue for families and the community. Determining when a child is responsible enough to care for herself is an individual family decision based on the child's maturity level and the neighborhood in which they live. Schools are taking a greater role in providing programs for older children for academic and recreational enrichment. Working families report that when a child is too ill to go to school, the family is in a predicament. The child either goes to school sick, or the parent stays home and loses income, or some alternative arrangement is hastily made. The teacher

---

cultural competence—A working knowledge of the values, beliefs, customs, food, and language of various cultures.

Population by Race and Hispanic Origin: 1990 to 2050 (in thousands. As of July 1, resident population)

Year	Total	Race					Not of Hispanic Origin			
		White	Black	American Indian[1]	Asian[2]	Hispanic origin[3]	White	Black	American Indian	Asian
ESTIMATE										
1990	249,402	209,180	30,599	2,073	7,550	22,549	188,601	29,374	1,802	7,076
PROJECTIONS										
Middle Series										
1995	262,820	218,078	33,144	2,241	9,357	26,936	193,566	31,598	1,931	8,788
2000	274,634	225,532	35,454	2,402	11,245	31,366	197,061	33,568	2,054	10,584
2005	285,981	232,463	37,734	2,572	13,212	36,057	199,802	35,485	2,183	12,454
2010	297,716	239,588	40,109	2,754	15,265	41,139	202,390	37,466	2,320	14,402
2020	322,742	254,887	45,075	3,129	19,651	52,652	207,393	41,538	2,601	18,557
2030	346,899	269,046	50,001	3,515	24,337	65,570	209,998	45,448	2,891	22,993
2040	369,980	281,720	55,094	3,932	29,235	80,164	209,621	49,379	3,203	27,614
2050	393,931	294,615	60,592	4,371	34,352	96,508	207,901	53,555	3,534	32,432
Lowest Series										
2050	282,524	213,782	44,477	3,383	20,882	62,230	157,701	40,118	2,793	19,683
Highest Series										
2050	518,903	381,505	81,815	5,384	50,199	133,106	262,140	71,863	4,295	47,498

[1] American Indian represents American Indian, Eskimo, and Aleut.
[2] Asian represents Asian and Pacific Islander.
[3] Persons of Hispanic origin may be of any race. The information on the total and Hispanic population shown in this report was collected in the 50 states and the District of Columbia, and, therefore, does not include residents of Puerto Rico.

Figure 1–17

The racial and ethnic makeup of the United States is changing. (Source: U.S. Department of Commerce, Bureau of the Census. (1996, February). *Population projection of the United States by age, sex, race and hispanic origin: 1995–2050* (Current Population Reports. Series P–25–1130). Washington, DC: Author.

who learns about each child's family situation better understands all the child's needs, not just those related to intellectual development (Figure 1–18).

When a child moves from one teacher to another, whether it is a grade change or a move to another district, communication between the two teachers can yield a great deal of information about the child's development, behavior, idiosyncrasies, needs, and best approaches. The new teacher listens carefully to the teacher who has had experience with the child and who can offer suggestions regarding the approach that has worked best with that child. Is this not the same procedure that any teacher should use when communicating with the child's family? They are the child's first and primary teachers. They have observed and assessed that child's development for years. They have firsthand knowledge of the child's behavior and individuality, and the methods that work best to tap into the child's cooperation and manageability. Along with biological factors, the biggest influence on the child is the family; it makes sense to listen to those experts. The teacher who sees the family as a source of information about the child and as a partner in the learning process will be the most effective teacher. Chapter 2 will explore this principle in depth, giving the rationale and methods for family involvement in the child's education.

Learning about Learning and Teaching

There are many different theories about how people learn, develop, and change. You will be studying theories that are contradictory and theories that are similar. Learning about learning is a dual process. You will be learning about your own learning processes, and the processes by which others learn. You saw earlier in the discussion on learning styles that everyone does not learn in the same way, so learning about learning will help you become a better teacher. The many theories, philosophies, and methods of teaching will also be part of your preparation. This section will introduce you to learning and teaching theories.

Figure 1–18

The teacher can better understand the child in the context of the family.

John B. Watson

(1878–1958) American psychologist, called the Father of Behaviorism. He worked at the University of Chicago and at Johns Hopkins University, performing elaborate experiments with laboratory rats to explain learning through classical conditioning.

John Locke

(1632–1704) English philosopher; believed that children are born with temperaments and propensities but that adults channel children's impulses and create differences among people.

B. F. Skinner

(1904–1990) American psychologist; systematically studied learning, which he called operant conditioning. Wrote *Verbal Behavior* (1957) and *Schedules of Reinforcement* (1957).

Learning about Learning. How do you learn?

"I learn best by repeating and repeating the information and getting a reward for learning it."

"I know I will learn it when I'm ready."

"I learn best if I have someone to explain it and show me examples and actually show me how to do it."

These three attitudes about learning relate to three major **theories** about how development and learning take place. Learning is defined as a relatively permanent change that occurs as a result of experiences in the environment. Our beliefs and knowledge about how people change affect how we teach. Those beliefs and knowledge are the basis for our educational theory or philosophy. As you progress through your preparation, and throughout your career, you will be continually modifying your own educational philosophy. Your teaching, or pedagogy, will be based on that philosophy. The following are three of the major theories of development and learning, explaining the theoretical background of the answers to the question, "How do you learn?"

Behaviorism. "I learn best by repeating and repeating the information and getting a reward for learning it."

With the Industrial Revolution and assembly line production came the idea that learning could take place in the same way. It entailed a body of knowledge presented in an orderly fashion, under controlled circumstances, step-by-step, with rewards for lessons learned and punishments for failures. Consequently, schools were structured on the factory model. This kind of learning was supported by the ideas of **John B. Watson**, who believed that he could mold any infant, regardless of that infant's inborn capabilities, into a doctor, lawyer, or artist, or even beggar man or thief, through repeated linked experiences that aroused emotions. His best-known experiment involved an eleven-month-old child named Albert. Watson and colleague Rosalie Raynor showed Albert a rat and at the same time made a large noise behind Albert. After several repetitions, they ceased the loud noise and found Albert was still afraid of the rat. Albert had learned to fear the rat because the sight of the rat was associated with a startling sound. Thus, they confirmed that the negative or positive emotions associated with an experience could eventually be brought about without the actual stimulus. This work in classical conditioning brought rise to the philosophy of **behaviorism**, the theory that learning is solely responsible for behavior. It was based on the earlier concept of *tabula rasa* proposed in the eighteenth century by English philosopher **John Locke**. That theory asserts that a newborn's mind is a blank surface that is influenced by environment and experience. Locke's theory rejected or ignored biological factors as having the potential to influence learning or differences in learning strategies.

Watson's work was expanded by the American psychologist **B. F. Skinner**. He observed that a stronger response is elicited by a pleasurable reinforcement, which increases the probability that the response will be emitted again. He believed that positive reinforcement worked better than punishment.

theory—A framework of ideas or principles that guides the interpretation of facts and acts as a basis for action.

behaviorism—The theory that views learning as the most important aspect of development and proposes that behavior can be objectively measured through stimulus-response relationships.

Teachers may have students repeat an action over and over, such as writing a spelling word 100 times; the student is rewarded with a star, a smiley face, or a good grade. From then on, the student supposedly spells the word correctly, without the star, smiley face, or good grade. The teacher is thus using a behaviorist approach. In the classroom, positive reinforcements such as smiles, nods, praises, or high grades are often used to shape behaviors, or to encourage a repetition of the behavior. These positive reinforcements are rewards for desired behaviors. Negative reinforcement is the removal of an aversive stimulus to increase the probability of a response. An example would be a student who gets a bad grade, but then finds that if he studies, he gets a good grade; the student has learned that studying increases the probability that he will not get the aversive stimulus (a bad grade). The form of learning in which behavior can be changed by its consequences is known as *oparent conditioning*.

The traditional academic or teacher-dominated classroom is not totally behaviorist in practice but does use the industrial model of repetition and reward and skills-outcome-based orientation. Many modern educational theorists support the bases of traditional education.

Maturationism. "I know I will learn it when I'm ready."

The **maturationist** point of view contends that development will occur in a natural progression and will evolve with minimal interference from adults. A famous maturationist was Jean-Jacques Rousseau, a French philosopher (1712–1778) who held that adults should allow the child to *unfold,* passing through stages of development that are predetermined and individual for the child. Later maturationists include Erik Erikson, Jean Piaget, and Arnold Gesell. We will learn more about Erikson and Piaget in later chapters. In a program that strictly adheres to maturationist philosophy, the motivation for learning and subject matter come from the child. One such program is Summerhill (Neill, 1960), where the adults support the children's interests. Some private and alternative schools use this method, as do many home schooling situations.

A distinguishing feature of the maturationist theory is the notion that there are critical or sensitive periods where a certain kind of learning or development should take place. The theory asserts that if specified development does not take place during a critical period, the developmental opportunity is likely lost. It may, however, be acquired later, although with difficulty. Humans appear to have a propensity for *sensitive periods* rather than critical periods. For example, learning a second language is much easier in the first four years of life than it is at fourteen years of age, when it can be done, but not as easily, and perhaps never with the full sound range and accent.

Humanism. "I learn best if I have someone I trust explain it and show me examples and actually show me how to do it."

This statement reflects the theory of **humanism** as related to learning and self-motivation, in which the child has no need for external stimuli or rewards. Abraham Maslow (1908–1970) and Carl Rogers (1902–1987) were the leading proponents of the humanistic view. We will learn more about Maslow in later chapters. The humanistic view of learning maintains that before learning can commence, the individual's physical needs must be satisfied, as well as those for love, support, and acceptance.

Which is right? All these theories have some features supported by research and many of them may make sense to you. You might examine your own abilities to trace the origins of your learning. You might sing like the grandparent who died before you were born. You never forget to brush your teeth at night because as a child you

---

maturationist—Espousing the theory that the child will learn and develop according to a genetically determined pattern from conception through adulthood, with the adult's role being to support and follow the child's lead.

humanism—Theory that emphasizes the uniqueness of the individual and the search for self-actualization.

received a coin for your bank every night after you brushed. You remember hoarding possessions but now freely share them, or you may stay away from dogs because of a bite you received as a child. These ways in which you learned might exemplify features of one or more of the theories. Most teaching professionals do not ascribe wholly to all the tenets of any one theory but instead apply certain aspects of each to certain circumstances. Refer to the theory comparison chart in Figure 1–19 to begin to see the parallels and the contrasting viewpoints.

Learning about Teaching. It is not enough just to know the subject matter; you must know your pedagogy, or how to teach that body of knowledge. You will have courses in teaching methods based on certain philosophies of teaching, with emphasis on the model that the professor or the school of education has deemed the best. The model guides the classroom arrangement, the time schedule, the equipment and materials, and the teacher's role. The methods of a model are based on one of the fundamental philosophies of development mentioned earlier. They are also based on the instructional setting, and the age and developmental stage of the children within that setting.

Early Childhood. Many models exist for teaching during a child's early years (infancy through age eight), though studies have shown that early childhood teachers primarily use an eclectic approach incorporating individual aspects of the many models. The following brief overview highlights some of the teaching models you may observe. You will develop your own philosophy of education, perhaps wholly immersing yourself in one of these models or selecting components that feel comfortable to you and fit the developmental levels of the children with whom you will work.

* High/Scope, also called the Perry Preschool Project, is used in many Head Start programs as a cognitively oriented program emphasizing key experiences through Planning, Recall, and Small Group times. The teacher observes and plans individually with the child, who explores through the senses and works with materials to sort and classify objects, make comparisons, discover relationships, and put things in sequence.

* The Bank Street Approach was developed at the Bank Street College of Education, emphasizing children's total development through a play-based setting as children interact with each other and the materials. The teacher's role is to provide the environment, observe, enhance the play, and note the development that unfolds.

* Montessori programs follow the teachings of Maria Montessori, the first woman physician in Italy. She worked primarily with children who had mental disabilities. She discounted the developmental stage theories and believed that, by providing the right environment and learning materials that have structured uses and correct ways to use them, learning would occur. In repeating activities with these materials, the teacher's role is to provide the vocabulary, pointing out the attributes or concepts that the materials demonstrate. The materials themselves provide the positive feedback, since they are self-correcting, only having one way they can fit, such as a puzzle, or pegs of graduated sizes that fit in holes that will only accept the right-size peg.

* Reggio Emilia is a city in northern Italy known for its preschool programs based on the philosophy of Loris Magaluzzi. The image of the child is one of strength and ability, while the role of the teacher is to provide the environment, materials, and experiences based on the children's interest (Figure 1–20 on page 36). Further, it is the teacher's obligation to document the children's work to show them progress and involve families. Many people have been enthralled

Age	Freud's Psychosexual Stages	Erikson's Psychosocial Stages	Piaget's Cognitive Stages	Kohlberg's Moral Reasoning Stages	Gardner's Creative Stages
Birth–1 year	ORAL–Ego directs babies' sucking activities. If oral needs are not met, may develop thumb sucking, fingernail biting, smoking, overeating.	BASIC TRUST VS. MISTRUST From warm responsive care, infants gain confidence that needs will be met. If they have to wait long for comfort, mistrust develops.	SENSORIMOTOR Acts on world through senses building schema—basic structures of information.		
1–2 years	ANAL–Exercises power over holding urine, feces. If toilet training is too demanding, may result in extreme orderliness or messiness.	AUTONOMY VS. SHAME Wants to choose and decide for herself. Autonomy fostered when permitted reasonable free choice without shame.		Stage 0 Preconventional Stage Egocentric—"I should get my way."	
2–3 years			PREOPERATIONAL Use symbols to represent sensorimotor discoveries. Develops language, make-believe. Egocentric. Judgments based on intuition rather than logic of conservation.		Instinctively creative in art, music, drama, language.
3–4 years	PHALLIC–Id impulses transfer to genitals. Oedipus conflict for boys and Electra conflict for girls—unconscious sexual desire for opposite-sex parent. Complexes resolved when child later identifies with same-sex parent and develops strong superego taboo.	INITIATIVE VS. GUILT Make-believe play and ambition and responsibility. Too much parental control and too many demands lead to guilt.			
4–5 years					
5–6 years				Stage 1 Unquestioning Obedience	
6–7 years	LATENCY–Sexual instincts die down, superego further develops. Acquires social values outside family and from peers.	INDUSTRY VS. INFERIORITY Capacity to work and cooperate. Negative experience leads to feelings of incompetency.		Stage 2 Instrumental Purpose Self-Interest–"You do this for me, I'll do this for you."	
7–8 years			CONCRETE OPERATIONS Logical reasoning, conservation, still concrete thinker.		Concentration on rules and practical ideas.
9–10 years				Stage 3 Conventional Conforms to social rules for acceptance, approval of family and peers.	Search for literal messages rather than metaphors. Copy and collect.
10–11 years			FORMAL OPERATIONS Can deal with abstract symbols.	Stage 4 Social-order Maintaining Duty to uphold laws for good of society.	
Adolescence	GENITAL–Puberty causes sexual impulses of phallic stage to reappear. Resolution leads to mature sexuality.	IDENTITY VS. IDENTITY CONFUSION Tries to seek place in society and with others. Negative outcome is confusion about adult roles.			Convergence of creativity to plan, implement, and evaluate a project. Takes risks. Attempts new projects, preserves individuality.
Young Adulthood		INTIMACY VS. ISOLATION Quest for relationships.		Stage 5 Social Contract Protection of majority	
Middle Adulthood		GENERATIVITY VS. STAGNATION Giving to next generation, accomplishment.		Stage 6 Universal Ethical Abstract moral guide for all humanity	
Old Age		EGO INTEGRITY VS. DESPAIR Life evaluation.			

Stages are not fixed and often overlap with residual attitudes and behaviors from preceding stages prematurely. Some never reach the upper stages of psychosocial, cognitive, or moral development.

Figure 1–19

Comparison of theories of child development.

Figure 1—20

The schools of Reggio Emilia, Italy, are known throughout the world for their children's visual representations.

with the children's paintings and sculpture, which have traveled worldwide. These works are the children's representations of what they see, using "a hundred languages" and various media and styles to express their perceptions to others. This is *emergent curriculum* coming from the children's ideas rather than the teacher's premade plans. This is also called the *project approach,* where the theme or subject to pursue is based on the children's interests.

✳ Constructivist programs are based on the principles of Jean Piaget, focusing on the student's interaction with the materials, and integrating all the learning areas around a theme or concept that involves the whole child's development. The teacher plans through a *curriculum web* of related activities around a main theme such as Water: with art, music, large muscle activity, manipulatives, math and science activities, and a story all about Water. The teacher's role is in setting the environment, knowing and planning for the interests of the child, and helping the child make connections between various learning activities. This curriculum model is called the *developmentally appropriate* model. The constructivist model is one that is espoused by teachers and learners of all ages, based on the premise of the learner's active participation, constructing her own learning through experiences.

Elementary Grades. Grade schools have tried numerous models for curriculum instruction. Most schools are organized by grades signified by age, meeting in one classroom with one teacher. The method the teacher uses to teach the lessons is determined by specific training and also by the administrative policies of the school. The lessons may be organized into separate subjects, providing skill instruction in reading, spelling, grammar, literature, mathematics, science, social studies, health, and physical education. Other instructional strategies combine subjects into a more integrated approach, such as writing and social studies, literature and history, or mathematics and health. The teacher may use different teaching methods for different subjects. The teacher may use lecture, films, workbooks, or demonstrations to transfer facts and ideas. Students may be engaged in experiments, projects, or reports for active learning and as a way of demonstrating learning. Questioning is an age-old teaching strategy, with the teacher using both open-ended questions for divergent thinking (such as "How many ways can you warm your hands?") and closed questions for convergent thinking (such as "What is the difference between gloves and mittens?").

Some models you will learn more about in the future include:

✳ Direct instruction—The teacher presents the information or demonstrates the concepts the students practice independently, and then the teacher evaluates the student's response (Figure 1–21). In this method, the teacher controls the environment and the information conveyed, as well as the feedback or evaluation of the student's progress. The efficiency of this model is balanced against the inability to individualize for the students' varying levels of ability.

✳ Objectives—The intent of the lesson is clearly stated as an objective to reach a specific goal or group of goals. Lesson plans designate (1) the task required of the learner, such as to "identify, compare, solve," or "state"; (2) the conditions or limitations of the task, such as "after reading the chapter, after studying the slide under the microscope"; and (3) the expected level of performance, such as "with at least 85 percent accuracy" or "identify the misspelled words."

✳ Experiential learning or inquiry method—The intent of this teaching strategy is for the student to be actively involved in an experience that will not only be enjoyable but will give her the opportunity to discover the concept, test it out, and make connections with prior knowledge. This is also called the

Figure 1–21

Direct instruction by the teacher of groups of children is one teaching method.

constructivist method, that is, the student is constructing knowledge from the experience. This helps the student develop critical thinking skills to analyze the problem, collect the data, and come to a conclusion. Science and mathematics lessons use this method effectively. Students may sort objects by color or other attributes. They may place and count them in groups of 10. They may weigh those groups to see if certain classes of 10 objects weigh more or less than others and theorize why that is the case.

* Role playing and games—Another strategy of teaching is to use dramatic play, placing the student in the role of another person and to think in the first person about an event or situation. Because it takes higher-level thinking, beyond egocentricism (Piaget's term for the ability to only see things from one's own point of view), role playing works best after age eight or nine. By this age, children can imagine what the person must be feeling or thinking and use that perspective to attack dilemmas, such as "What if you were one of the Pilgrims on the Mayflower? What would you be most concerned about after you survived the trip? Act out your actions and talk about your thoughts," or "What if you were one of the Native Americans watching the Pilgrims emerge from the Mayflower? What effect would their coming have on your way of life? Whose country is it?"

    Games can effectively be used to practice skills such as matching (card games such as UNO®), counting (Monopoly®), and logic (checkers and chess). While enjoyable and relatively stress-free, games also develop social skills such as taking turns and cooperating.

You will develop many methods of pedagogy that during your preparation and practice years. Another aspect of the teacher's knowledge base is how to determine if the students have learned anything while in your class as a result of your lessons and learning activities. There are many ways of assessing learning. A further discussion of this topic is in Chapter 6 on Cognitive Development. In the interim, consider the following few methods.

Learning about Assessing Learning. You are very familiar with a number of evaluation tools, since you have experienced them yourself. Perhaps the most obvious is one of your least favorite methods of evaluation.

Tests. There are many kinds of tests.

* Teacher-generated tests—You have taught a lesson and you want to measure if the students can give with the answers you expect. These can be objective tests such as true or false, fill in the blank, list, or provide reasons. Essay examinations that ask the student to discuss or compare and contrast are subjective and depend on the teacher to make a judgment about the level of understanding derived from the explanation. This method is used primarily with grade-school and older children, and not in early childhood (Figure 1–22)

* Criterion-referenced tests—These tests are given to determine the developmental level at which a student knows the material or can perform a skill. This can be used as a screening tool for placing a student at the appropriate level for further instruction. Criterion-referenced tests can be geared for any age group and are useful in determining developmental levels and giving indicators of serious developmental lags.

* Standardized tests—These tests, produced by specialists to measure a specific knowledge area or skill, are first submitted to a select population (standardized); it is then assumed that the results from that group will be comparable to the results from other, similar groups taking that test. These, too, are

Figure 1—22

Individual tests are a method of assessing learning.

developed for children of all age ranges, and for a variety of purposes. One of the obvious shortcomings of such a test might be the differences between the standardized group and the child to whom the test is administered. Many have been shown to be biased against certain factors such as gender, race, culture, socioeconomic level, or social experience.

Performance-Based Evaluations. The teacher observes the student to see the results of the lessons demonstrated by that student.

* Checklists and rating scales—A predetermined list of criteria is used against which the performance of the student is observed and measured. Developmental checklists are useful in the early childhood years to measure progress in various areas. Other checklists can be constructed for older grades to measure specific knowledge and skills in select subject areas. Rating scales are similar to checklists but allow for recording a range or various levels of meeting academic or developmental criteria, using such terms as Never, Sometimes, and Always, or Beginning, Practicing, and Mastery.

* Anecdotal recordings—The teacher observes and writes a detailed account of a child's academic or developmental performance (Figure 1–23 on page 40). This is a standard early childhood assessment method that gives a snapshot of an incident or segment of behavior in a natural setting without undue pressure on the child. It is done unobtrusively so the child's behavior is not changed by her knowledge that she is being watched.

* Portfolio—The teacher and the child select samples of work that demonstrate the student's proficiency. This method is gaining acknowledgment as an authentic assessment method. It can be used from the age of one year on, as soon as the child is producing any kind of work, with children as young as

Figure 1−23

Observation and recording is another way to assess learning.

three and four helping in the selection process. Watching a child's writing progress from scribbling to cursive is a wonder to behold.

The role of assessment and evaluation is an important strand in a teacher's preparation. Everyone wants to know, "How am I doing?" The child needs to know, families want to know, and the teacher and administration want to know of the child's progress. Effective evaluation goes hand in hand with instruction. In every chapter that presents an area of children's learning and development, there is a section on assessment to give you an idea of how the teacher knows if learning has occurred.

SUMMARY

Professional teaching requires college preparation. Within the profession, there are levels of education that correspond to the responsibilities an individual may assume as a teacher. In the United States, individual states set the requirements for preparation of teachers in various settings. Teacher preparation includes coverage of a common body of knowledge that includes work by major theorists, a common language, and common practices based on child development. Individuals are motivated to become teachers for a variety of reasons. By exploring personal values and feelings, the rewards and drawbacks of teaching, and awareness of career options you can determine the best position in the field of education for your career. There is much to learn.

KEY TERMS

ecology	stereotype	Eurocentrism
microsystems	bias	cultural competence
mesosystems	bell curve	theory
exosystems	least restrictive	behaviorism
macrosystems	environment	maturationist
metacognition	inclusion	humanism
prejudice		

REVIEW ACTIVITIES

Exercises to Strengthen Learning

1. Think back to the teacher who made the biggest difference in your life. What was the difference that teacher made? List 10 specific characteristics of that teacher that you admire. Describe an incident involving this teacher that is an example of a good teaching practice.

2. Think about a teacher you had that you consider a poor teacher. List ten characteristics about that teacher that led you to believe the teacher was poor. Describe an example of this teacher's poor teaching practice and tell how you would handle the situation differently.

3. Visit a classroom of your choice and use the Class Profile (Figure 1–24 on page 42). Observe, and then speak with the teacher for further assistance in completing the profile.

4. Look at the catalogs from three colleges that offer preparation for state certification as a public school teacher. Compare and contrast the general education, content, and field experience courses and requirements at these colleges. Look for performance standards, course descriptions, and the number of credit hours required in each category for graduation. Which program do you think offers the best preparation for your career goal and why?

Internet Quest

1. Begin your Internet quest by using the key word phrases "teacher preparation" and "teacher qualifications." Visit at least three Web sites for each search. List the sites you traveled to and write a brief description of each. What did you learn that was new to you?

2. Find the qualification requirements for a child care teacher or certified teacher in your state.

3. Find a Web site about the Myers-Briggs personality type inventory. Discover your own type and consider how this will affect your teaching, especially when you are teaching children who have a different personality type from yours.

4. Search for sites regarding exceptionalities and the law regarding the school's responsibility to meet the needs of students with an exceptionality, such as autism, Tourette's syndrome, giftedness.

Planning for Cultural Diversity:
Developing a Class Profile

Responsive and developmentally appropriate planning and teaching require a
good knowledge of the children you teach. Teachers can prepare a class profile
based on the elements of diversity. The form below can be used to create your
class profile.

CLASS PROFILE

Grade Level: _____   Date: _____

Ages: _____   Class size: _____

Area: Urban ___ Suburban ___ Rural ___   How many Girls? ___ Boys? ___

Social class structure	Ethnicities present	Main religious affiliations	Languages other than English

Family configurations present	Exceptionalities present	Comments, points to remember

Summary/highlights:

Figure 1—24

Class profile. (From de Melendez, & Ostertag, 1997)

Reflective Journal

What I learned about myself and my values in regard to teaching will affect what I do
as a teacher in the following way . . .

REFERENCES

Allen, K. E., & Marotz, L. R. (1999). *Developmental profiles: Pre-birth through eight* (3rd ed.).
Albany, NY: Delmar.

Allen, K. E., & Schwartz, E. S. (1999). *The exceptional child: Inclusion in early childhood education* (4th ed.). Albany, NY: Delmar.

Allison, J. (1999a). A tribute to a great scholar and colleague: A conversation with Bernard "Bud" Spodek. *Childhood Education, 75*(5), 262.

Allison, J. (1999b). On the expanded role of the teacher. *Childhood Education, 75*(5), 259.

American Association on Mental Retardation (AAMR). (1992). *Mental retardation: Definition, classification, and systems of support.* Washington, DC: Author.

Americans with Disabilities Act. (1990). PL 101–336.

Banner, M. J., & Cannon, H. C. (1997). *The elements of teaching.* New Haven, CT: Yale University Press.

Bowe, F. G. (2000). *Birth to five: Early childhood special education* (2nd ed.). Albany, NY: Delmar.

Bronfenbrenner, U. (1979). *The ecology of human development: Experiments by nature and design.* Cambridge, MA: Harvard University Press.

Campbell, B., Campbell, L., & Dickinson, D. (1996). *Teaching and learning through multiple intelligences.* New York: Allyn and Bacon.

Children's Defense Fund. (2000). *The State of America's Children Yearbook, 2000,* p. 8. Boston: Beacon Press.

de Melendez, W. R., & Ostertag, V. (1997). *Teaching young children in multicultural classrooms.* Albany, NY: Delmar.

Duckworth, E. (1987). *The having of wonderful ideas and other essays on teaching and learning.* New York: Teachers College Press.

Education for All Handicapped Children Act. (1975). PL 94–142.

Finn, J. D., & Achilles, C. M. (1990). Answers and questions about class size: A statewide experiment. *American Educational Research Association, 27,* 557–577.

Fromberg, D. P., & Bergen, D. (1998). *Play from birth to twelve and beyond: Contexts, perspectives and meanings.* New York: Garland.

Garcia, E. E. (1995). The impact of linguistic and cultural diversity on America's schools: A need for new policy. In M. C. Wang and M. C. Reynolds (Eds.), *Making a difference for students at risk: Trends and alternatives.* Thousand Oaks, CA: Corwin Press.

Gardner, H. (1983). *Frames of mind: The theory of multiple intelligences.* New York: Basic Books.

Gardner, H. (1993). *Multiple intelligences: The theory in practice.* New York: Basic Books.

Gardner, H. (1999a). *Intelligences reframed: Multiple intelligences for the 21st century.* New York: Basic Books.

Gardner, H. (1999b). *The disciplined mind: What all students should understand.* New York: Simon & Schuster.

Garmezy, N. (1994). Reflections and commentary on risk, resilience and development. In R. J. Haggerty, L. Sherrod, N. Garmezy, & M. Rutter (Eds.), *Stress, risk and resilience in children and adolescents: Processes, mechanisms and interventions* (pp. 1–19). Cambridge, UK: Cambridge University Press.

Garvey, C. (1999). *Play* (rev. ed.). Cambridge, MA: Harvard University Press.

Griggs, S., & Dunn, R. (1995). Hispanic-American students and learning style. *Emergency Librarian, 95*(23), issue 2, 11.

Henke, R. R., Geis, S., & Giambattista, J. (1996). *Out of the lecture hall and into the classroom: 1992–93 college graduates and elementary/secondary school teaching.* Washington, DC: National Center for Education Statistics, U.S. Department of Education.

Hernandez, D. J. (1995). Changing demographics: Past and future demands for early childhood programs. *The Future of Children, 5*(3): Retrieved February 28, 2001, from the World Wide Web: <http://www.futureofchildren.org/lto/08_lto.htm>.

Hyun, E. (1996). New directions in early childhood teacher preparation: Developmentally and culturally appropriate practice (DCAP). *Journal of Early Childhood Teacher Education, 17*(3), 7–19.

Individuals with Disabilities Education Act. (1990). PL 101–476.

Jones, E., & Reynolds, E. (1992). *The play's the thing: Teachers' roles in children's play.* New York: Teachers College Press.

Jordan, H. R., Mendro, R., & Weerasinghe, D. (1997). *Teacher effects on longitudinal student achievement.* Paper presented at the Center for Research on Educational Accountability and Teacher Education, Indianapolis, IN.

Jung, C. (1927). *The theory of psychological type.* Princeton, NJ: Princeton University Press.

Konner, M. (1991). *Childhood: A multicultural view.* Boston: Little, Brown.

Latham, A. S. (1997). Responding to cultural learning styles. *Educational Leadership, 57*(7), 88–89.

Lynch, E. W., & Hanson, M. J. (1992). *Developing cross cultural competence: A guide for working with young children and their families.* Baltimore, MD: Paul H. Brookes.

McClanaghan, M. E. (2000). A strategy for helping students how to learn. *Education 120*(3), 479.

McCormick, A. C., Nunez, A. M., Shah, V., & Choy, S. P. (1999). *Life after college: A descriptive summary of 1992–93 bachelor's degree recipients in 1997.* Washington, DC: United States Department of Education, National Center for Education Statistics.

Mukamel. E. (1996). *Trapezoid forum on teacher tenure.* Retrieved February 28, 2001, from the World Wide Web: <http://www.roccplex.com/bhs/trapezoid/tenure/forum.html>.

National Center for Education Statistics (NCES). (1997). *Characteristics of stayers, movers, and leavers: Results from the teacher followup survey: 1994–95.* Washington, DC: Author, U.S. Department of Education.

National Center for Education Statistics (NCES). (1998). *Estimated average annual salary of teachers in public elementary and secondary schools, by state: 1969–70 to 1997–98.* Table 79. Retrieved October 25, 1999, from the World Wide Web: <http://www.nces.ed.gov/pubs99/digest98/d98–079.html>.

National Opinion Research Center. (1994). *General social surveys 1972–1994: Cumulative codebook* (pp. 881–889). Chicago: Author.

Neill, A. S. (1960). *Summerhill: A radical approach to child rearing.* New York: Hart Publishing Co.

Pianta, R. C. (1999). *Enhancing relationships between children and teachers.* Washington, DC: American Psychological Association.

Ramey, C., & Ramey, S. (2000). *Persistent effects of early childhood education on high-risk children and their mothers.* Retrieved November 9, 1999, from the World Wide Web: <http://www.circ.uab.edu/craigramey/abceffect.htm>.

Rehabilitation Act of 1973. (1973). PL 93–112.

Rivkin, S. G., Hanushek, E. A., & Kain, J. F. (1998). *Teachers, schools and academic achievement.* Working Paper Number 6691. Washington, DC: National Bureau of Economic Research.

Schneidewind, N., Davidson, E. (1997). *Open minds to equality: A sourcebook of learning activities to affirm diversity and promote equality* (2nd ed.). New York: Allyn and Bacon.

Silver, H. F., Strong, R. W., & Perini, M. J. (1997). Integrating learning styles and multiple intelligences. *Educational Leadership, 55*(1), 22–27.

Skinner, B. F. (1957). *Schedules of reinforcement.* New York: Appleton-Century Crofts, Inc.

Skinner, B. F. (1957). *Verbal behavior.* New York: Appleton-Century Crofts, Inc.

Small, M. F. (1998). *Our babies, ourselves: How biology and culture shape the way we parent.* New York: Teachers College Press.

Tharp, R. G. (1982). The effective instruction of comprehension: Results and descriptions of the Kamchameha early education program. *Reading Research Quarterly, 17*(4), 5503–5527.

Tharp, R. G. (1989). Psychological variables and constants: Effects on teaching and learning in school. *American Psychologist, 44*(2), 349–359.

United States Department of Labor, Bureau of Labor Statistics. (1998). Occupational Outlook Handbook. Washington, DC: United States Government Printing Office.

United States Department of Labor. (1998). *Employment and earning, January* (pp 209–214). Washington, DC: United States Government Printing Office.

United States Department of Commerce, Bureau of the Census. (1996, February). *Population projection of the United States by age, sex, race and hispanic origin: 1995–2050* (Current Population Reports Series P–25–1130). Washington, DC: Author.

Whitebook, M., Howes, C., & Phillips, D. (1989). *Who cares? Child care teachers and the quality of care in America.* Final report of the National Child Care Staffing Study. Oakland, CA: Child Care Employee Project.

For additional learning and teaching resources, visit our Web site at www.EarlyChildEd.delmar.com.

RELATED CAREERS

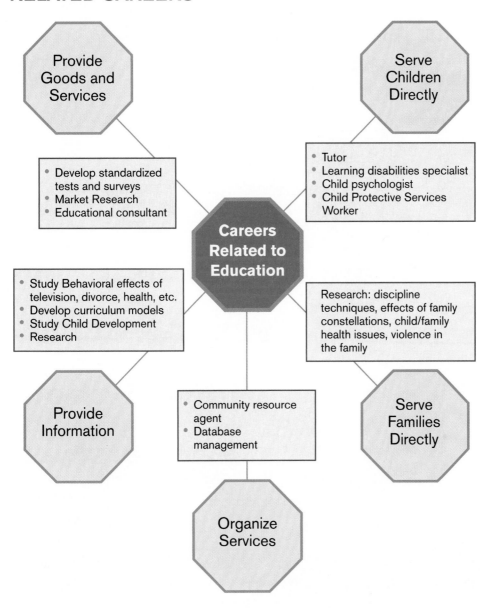

Provide Goods and Services

- Develop standardized tests and surveys
- Market Research
- Educational consultant

Serve Children Directly

- Tutor
- Learning disabilities specialist
- Child psychologist
- Child Protective Services Worker

Careers Related to Education

- Study Behavioral effects of television, divorce, health, etc.
- Develop curriculum models
- Study Child Development
- Research

Research: discipline techniques, effects of family constellations, child/family health issues, violence in the family

Provide Information

- Community resource agent
- Database management

Serve Families Directly

Organize Services

Figure 1—25

Careers related to education.

Learning and Teaching with Families— Home/School Partnerships

Objectives

After reading this chapter and completing the review activities, the learning teacher should be able to:

1. Explain the role of the family in a child's education.
2. Enhance the partnership between school and family.
3. Build relationships with families regardless of culture, language, socioeconomic status, or developmental abilities of the child.

✳ UNDERSTANDING THE PARTNERSHIP WITH THE FAMILY

SCENARIO Briana, a kindergarten teacher, sent a letter to the homes of all her new students before school began. In it, she introduced herself and told of her hopes and plans for the students. She listed the days she'd be in the classroom getting it ready for the school year and invited families and children to drop by. She included a response postcard for the parents to fill out and send back specifying some of their hopes and dreams for their child. She also included a sheet of paper for the child to draw on and bring to school on the first day to begin decorating the bulletin board. Briana carefully read the school enrollment forms to acquaint herself with each child's background; she did research on any allergies, medical conditions, or special needs, and on their diverse cultural or religious backgrounds, so she is prepared for each child. She made a card file with important information to remember and noted questions to ask when she meets the family. She believes strongly that these preparations will make for a good school experience for the children and their families.

In any **partnership**, the partners enter with strengths to contribute and bring with them an acceptance and appreciation for the strengths and limitations of the other partners. The partnership evolves as each partner develops an understanding and appreciation of the others. All of the partners define and reconcile the ultimate objective and individual responsibilities.

The dynamics of the home/school partnership are similar. Initially, the relationship can be seen as a triangle, with the child and family very close together and the teacher at a distance (Figure 2–1 on page 48). As the partnership matures, the teacher draws nearer to both the child and family for the time they are together. They work as a team, each with distinctive strengths and contributions to the partnership, and each having responsibilities to the others.

The notion of the parent as educator was championed in Europe by many theorists of the Enlightenment period. **Johann Pestalozzi**, Swiss educator and theorist said, "For children, the teachings of their parents will always be the core, and as for the schoolmaster, we can give thanks to God if He is able to put a decent shell around the core" (Pestalozzi, 1951, p. 26).

In early America, European immigrants perceived the duties of parents as educators of their children and were strongly influenced by their religious beliefs and cultural heritage. European immigrants to the New World had strong patriarchal family structures and an interdependence on homesteads and small businesses that were necessary for survival. Slaves were frequently separated from their kinfolk, with only some of those families reuniting after

Johann Pestalozzi

(1746–1827). Swiss educator and theorist, called the Father of Parent Education. He emphasized the importance of the home as the child's first educator in *How Gertrude Teaches Her Children.*

✳ **partnership**—Two or more individuals or organizations working together toward mutually beneficial goals.

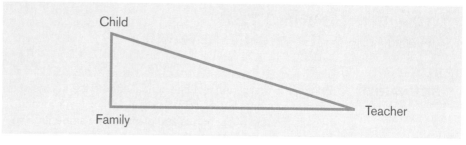

Figure 2–1

The teacher becomes a part of the child/family relationship for a short while.

the Civil War ended in 1865. Native American family structures also were disrupted by the arrival of the Europeans to the North American continent, and by the efforts to educate in the white man's ways by separating children from their families and placing them in boarding schools.

The early 20th century saw a rise in the importance of education, bringing with it recognition of the role of the family in cultural assimilation and child development. Many movements, such as those that brought about settlement houses and early kindergartens, were formed to counteract the negative forces of poverty, and to promote a new attitude embracing humanism and belief in the child's innate goodness (Weber, 1969). Parenting was affected by new philosophies recommending strong discipline, such as that found in behaviorist John B. Watson's advice, "Never hug and kiss them, never let them sit in your lap. If you must, kiss them once on the forehead when they say goodnight. Shake hands with them in the morning" (Vincent, 1951, p. 206). Conversely, at the same time in the early decades of the1900s, the Child Study Association of America was emphasizing "love, support and intelligent permissiveness" (Brim, 1965, pp. 169–170). Out of this newfound interest in and focus on parenting, parent cooperatives emerged in various university communities in Massachusetts, New York, and California. The Parent Teacher Association (PTA), founded in 1897, saw its membership grow from 60,000 in 1915 to 1.5 million in 1930 (Schlossman, 1976).

The Depression years, 1930–1940, brought new concerns for families, with the White House Conference on Child Health and Protection in 1930 recommending parent education as part of the system of public education (Pennsylvania Department of Public Instruction, 1935, pp. 9–10). The most renowned parent educator of this time was Dr. Benjamin Spock, who published *Baby and Child Care* in 1946. He stressed a more child-centered approach to child-rearing that was interpreted as permissiveness. Popular magazines in the 1950s stressed the importance of the child/parent relationship and parental involvement in school.

The whole nation got involved in family life and education with the Civil Rights Act of 1964, which guaranteed equal opportunity of education, and in research studies such as the Coleman Report on Equality of Educational Opportunity (Coleman et al., 1966), which pointed out the importance of effective home support of education. The War on Poverty and the establishment of Head Start in 1965 set parent involvement in education as a new national priority. Longitudinal studies such as Lazar's (1983) pointed out that "closer contact between home and school and greater involvement of parents in the education of their children are probably more important" than generally realized by administrators (p. 464).

By the 1980s and 1990s, as more and more families consisted of two working parents, or of single working mothers or fathers, the time available for parental and

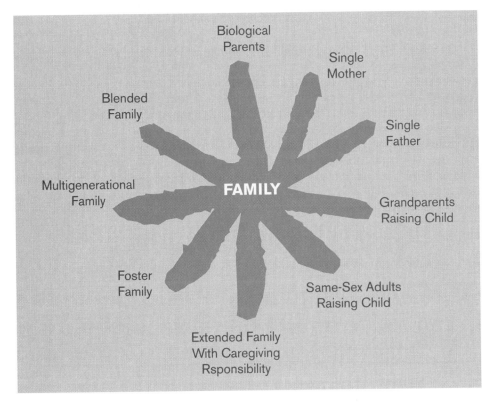

Figure 2—2

There are all kinds of families.

home involvement with the child's education had been reduced. Congress passed the Family Medical Leave Act (PL 103–3) in 1993, allowing for unpaid time away from work for the birth or adoption of a child, or the serious illness of a child, spouse, or dependent. Corporations and businesses have begun to recognize the effect of family responsibilities on their employees and have voluntarily instituted "family-friendly" policies including tax-free set-asides, flexible working hours, child and dependent care subsidies, on-site child care, and parent education programs during working hours. Many concerns such as poverty, domestic violence, homelessness, and drug and alcohol abuse still affect the family, the child, and ultimately the teacher.

Who Is the Family?

To understand the partnership between schools and families, you must first understand the meaning of "family." The traditional definition of mother, father, and related siblings who live together is only true for a portion of today's families. Nationwide, the percentage of families headed by a single parent increased from 22 percent in 1985 to 26 percent in 1995. In this chapter, we define family as the **primary caregivers** with whom the child lives and who has legal custody of the child. Even this definition can be strained by such arrangements as nonresidential joint custody, foster parenting, grandparent caregivers, or any number of different family constellations (Figure 2–2).

primary caregiver—Individual who provides the majority of physical, social, emotional, and economic support to a child.

The Teaching Family. Contemporary families are diverse in their makeup and life situation. It is not unusual for the mother of a preschooler to be a high school or college student herself. In many families, the work schedules of parents prevent the family from gathering as a complete unit on a daily (or in some families even a weekly) basis. Families in which parents are living in separate households or living with other adults not biologically related to the child are becoming common. Each of these different family situations carries different social, economic, and educational implications.

The family is the child's primary and first teacher. How do family arrangements affect the way in which a teacher communicates or interacts with individual families? How does the family affect learning? The role of the teacher is to see the child in the context of the family and to find the best methods to reach and involve the family in the child's school life. To do that, the teacher gathers information to identify who those primary caregivers are.

* Who does the child live with?
* Who takes responsibility outside of school for making sure the child is prepared for the school day?
* Who feeds the child?
* Who helps the child with homework?
* Who brings the child to school?
* Who nurtures the child?
* Who has legal custody of the child?
* Who has a biological connection to the child?
* Who initiates contact with the school?
* Who does the child define as family?

The teacher must know who has legal rights concerning the child, and of those people who do, who will interact with the school or program. A nonjudgmental attitude is extremely important to developing good working relationships on behalf of the child. The teacher gathers information from many sources to ascertain the most significant individuals in a child's life. Information forms filed at the time of enrollment in the school or program provide information about who is in the child's family and who is legally responsible for the child. The policy of the school or program dictates to whom the teacher may release information, and that individual is normally the responsible adult making legitimate decisions concerning the child. This is the formal, legal part of the partnership.

Secondly, the parents or legal guardians will also identify who else needs to be involved in the child's education. Many parents attend school open houses and conferences, or they may volunteer for classroom events and activities, but they may also delegate some or all of these interactions to grandparents, extended family members, or other caregivers. The most important thing is that someone in the family take an interest in the child's school life. These grandparents, aunts, uncles, siblings, or cousins are also a part of the partnership.

Special attention and effort needs to be given to significant adults who appear to have no interest in the child's education or who express feelings of anger or distrust regarding the education of the child. Family members may influence the child's attitude toward education in both positive and negative ways, and building a partnership with those disengaged individuals is challenging, but very important for the child's success in school.

The U.S. Department of Education (1994) stresses the importance of family involvement in the child's education in three main roles.

* Families have control over student absenteeism and reading material and television watching in the home, all indicators and modifiers of the child's achievement.
* Literacy particularly depends on learning activities in the home, especially the activity of reading aloud to children.
* Family activities can enrich the child's experiences and are important to the child's school success.

Contributions and Benefits of the Partners

Each partner brings strengths and contributions to the partnership and each benefits in a different way. The child, the teacher, and the family influence each other as they work together.

The Child. When home and school form a partnership, the child benefits most from continuity. When family and school work together and support each other, the child feels the security of a unified caring network. In this network, the primary attachment of the child to the family is not terminated; it is enhanced by a working partnership between home and school. When family members are involved with the school, the child is witness to the mutual respect of teacher for family, and family for teacher and school. This secure base and cooperative spirit enhances academic performance and cognitive skills (Powell, 1989).

Children who have very different economic or **cultural** backgrounds from that of the teacher or of the majority of their classmates experience discontinuity. A child whose family does not speak English in the home has more barriers to confront than simply language. There is usually an accompanying cultural atmosphere as well; there may be foods, customs, holidays, and ways of relating to one another that may be very different from others in the classroom. Even the way the child is treated at home and how they are treated at school can be so different as to be stressful and confusing. In many cultures, children are not expected to be independent and self-reliant, and experiencing those values and expectations at school may make them uncomfortable. The teacher's role is to gain knowledge of the culture and adapt the classroom atmosphere to include as many sights, sounds, and behaviors of that culture as possible. Children from economically deprived situations may find the classroom too stimulating, too full of abundance. Understanding teachers help these children learn to accept and trust the classroom environment, and be responsible for the classroom materials. These steps, which the teacher can take to bridge home and school, will benefit the child.

The teacher's knowledge and skills provide for an educational climate that meets the specific needs of the children and enables the teacher to see each child as a unique individual with capability and potential (Figure 2–3 on page 52). The knowledgeable teacher will design lessons and learning activities that address the child's developmental level, but also challenge the child to learn and develop further. Partnerships formed with the family have a positive effect on achievement. Because such an alliance is a model for a positive attitude toward school, it encourages the motivation to learn. When the teacher and family know each other, and respect and work together, the child can have a sense of familial belonging and acceptance at school.

---

culture–Patterns, beliefs, thoughts, manners, and tastes that are common to a group of people and passed on from generation to generation.

Figure 2–3

The teacher is the bridge between home and school.

WORDS OF WISDOM Kim Hughes, the teacher who spoke about DeQuan in Chapter 1, also talked about the teacher's impact on families:

"I feel the impact of my teaching when children I taught some 16 years ago and their families continue to be a part of my life. Recently, Kelly contacted me to share the excitement of becoming a freshman majoring in education. The abused and neglected Kelly I met as a four-year-old had little chance of a productive life. Her short lifetime had been filled with monsters many of us pretend do not, cannot, exist in our world today. I was determined to make a difference in this young life, to develop a nonjudgmental relationship with both Kelly and her mom, to listen with my eyes and ears, to celebrate their strengths and accept their vulnerabilities unconditionally."

"Continuous efforts to understand, support and guide her family led to success in breaking a family cycle of poverty, ignorance, undereducation and low self-esteem. Today, Kelly's mom enjoys her work as a data technician for a large medical practice and Kelly delights in the never-ending possibilities she will enjoy as a college graduate. I know that I have made a significant difference in the life of this family."

The Family. A discussion with parents yielded the following responses:

"I want a teacher for my child who . . .

. . . is helpful, strict, friendly, and sensitive."

. . . is very understanding."

. . . reads more books in a year than my child does."

. . . is attentive to my child's individual needs."

. . . doesn't try to replace me as the parent."

The qualities described are important to parents and may be difficult to fulfill all of the time. If teachers could, their relationships with families would be much more cooperative and helpful for the child. The family knows the child best; their initial and primary contribution to the partnership is that knowledge of the child's physical, medical, social, and intellectual history. The family knows what makes the child happy or sad, what the child's strengths and interests are, and what hopes they have for the child. They present the child in a social context that helps the teacher better understand the child. When a family tells the teacher they have moved five times in the last year, that gives the teacher valuable information about the child's possible emotional and educational experiences. When the family informs the teacher that they live on a farm where each child has many morning chores before school, the teacher gains an understanding of the child's world. When the teacher learns that the family has only been in this country one month after a yearlong wait in an immigration resettlement program, the teacher will benefit from that knowledge.

Close home/school partnerships offer respect to the family, fostering their acceptance and empowerment. The partnership looks to the family as a contributor, and not a liability, nor a need to be filled or fixed. This model of solidarity is one that yields many benefits. The Cornell empowerment project that helped parents see themselves as worthwhile participants with the school yielded impressive results for the families, schools, and communities involved (Cochran & Dean, 1991).

The family can make many valuable contributions of their talents, time, and culture to enrich the classroom (Figure 2–4). Family members may be musical; or they may be able to demonstrate a craft or special talent; or provide resources that can enhance learning, such as zoological specimens or family pets, or paper trimmings from a print shop; or they may share unusual vocations or hobbies. Families provide outreach into the community. The whole class benefits from their special contribution, but especially the child of that family, seeing their life affirmed and accepted.

Often what begins as a school involvement activity can lead to social, educational, or employment opportunities. Head Start successfully used parent involvement activities not only to provide extra adults in the classroom but also as on-the-job training for those adults. Many Head Start personnel began as involved parents, who then advanced to assistant teacher positions, thus gaining access to training and education to become a Child Development Associate (CDA), with many eventually

Figure 2—4

When families are involved in school, children's performance increases.

attaining college degrees and pursuing a career in education. Parent teacher associations also provide a social and service outlet for parents, as well as training in leadership, motivating many to enter politics or education-related careers.

When people feel they have a valuable, appreciated contribution, they may become advocates for the school, another valuable asset for all parties. Due to the increasingly consumer-oriented climate in education, involved family members learn more about school systems and how they work. They can make more informed choices for their own child and hold schools accountable for their objectives. When families are involved in schools, whole communities benefit.

The Teacher. The teacher brings to the partnership a knowledge base that includes child development principles along with some background in psychology and philosophy, resulting in an objective perspective from which to view the child. The teacher brings extensive educational experiences as well, knowing what concepts to teach and the ways to teach them. The teacher sees the child in relation to developmental milestones and appropriate behavior, or in their interaction with peers in a school setting (which may be different from the way the child acts at home). The teacher also assesses the child's development and behavior in part by comparing him to children from prior teaching experiences (Figure 2–5).

This knowledge base can be a resource to families through which they may better understand their child and the learning process. Of course, it is tricky to be a resource, yet not appear as a know-it-all or a direction-giver. In building partnerships with parents, teachers must remain professional; that is, motivated by a desire to serve, but taking an objective, emotionally separate stance from the family. While the teacher as a professional has an accumulation of specialized knowledge, this learned proficiency may feel threatening to some parents. By practicing the communication skills of active

Figure 2–5

The teacher's knowledge of child development can assist the child and the family.

listening and reflection, the teacher can help the parent feel comfortable. "Listening is a combination of hearing what another person says and involvement with who is talking. The good listener responds reflectively to what the speaker is saying. She restates, in her own words, the feeling and/or content that is being expressed—and doing so, communicates understanding and acceptance" (Bolton, 1979). The teacher brings a specialized knowledge to help family members know (not to dictate to them) what is best for their child; it works best for the child when there is a partnership.

As teachers work with family members, they may meet individuals whom they admire and enjoy spending time with. Some of these relationships may begin to cross the line from professional to personal. Because the teacher is working with a child in a professional capacity, it is important to also keep the teacher-family relationship on a professional basis. Through self-reflection, a teacher becomes aware of personal values and perceptions concerning parents and family. Thus, the teacher's own family experiences and socialization may affect their work and interactions with other families. Is there a class or income difference between the teacher and the children's families? Is there a racial or cultural difference making one or the other uncomfortable because of unconscious prejudice or bias? "Ethical practice dictates that helpers [teachers] seriously consider the impact of their values on individuals they work with and the conflicts that might arise if values are sharply different. Simply because you do not embrace an individual's values does not mean that you cannot effectively work with that person. The key is that you be objective and respect that individual's right to autonomy" (Corey & Corey, 1998). People feel most comfortable in assuming the values they hold are held by all or that they *should be* held by all, but a conscientious teacher attempts not to make value judgments of others, offers acceptance, and works toward mutual understanding. However, teachers must also determine when a family practice is truly harmful to the child, and then follow professional guidelines for intervention.

Partnerships with Families of the Child with Special Needs

SCENARIO

Alicia was registered for preschool at the age of three. Her grandmother brought her to school while her mom was at work. The medical history indicated no problems. Grandma would often say to the teachers, "She is so stubborn. She just won't listen and just gets what she wants without talking. She does just what she wants to do." The teachers worked with Alicia, got acquainted, and helped her to learn the routines, but they also noted her behaviors and lack of language skills. They documented Alicia's behaviors—not just the problematic ones—and found inconsistencies. After a few weeks, the teachers asked Alicia's mother to meet with them after school. Alicia's mother broke down and cried, "Finally, someone will listen. I think something is wrong, but my mother just keeps saying she's stubborn." After a full professional evaluation, Alicia was found to have a profound hearing loss. With corrective devices, Alicia could hear enough to feel part of things; she made progress in language development, and her behavior underwent a dramatic change.

Sharing Concerns. When a child enters a group setting such as school or child care, it often is the first time that people outside the family have an opportunity to closely observe the child. When those outside observers are knowledgeable about child development, they apply their learned frame of reference to each child, and sometimes detect something out of the ordinary. This can be a difficult time for the family, and for the teacher who may be the one to raise a concern about the child's development. Suggesting that something may not be developing normally in the child is a very sensitive communication. Ideally, the teacher and family share their observations and concerns and develop a plan for the child to be fully evaluated by a specialist. The teacher must be careful not to suggest or diagnose a dysfunction, but rather to provide information that can help with further assessment.

WORDS OF WISDOM A parent who asked to remain anonymous wrote this agonizing account of her struggle with the school regarding her child's learning disability.

"My daughter was in preschool the first time a teacher pointed out that she had very weak writing and drawing skills. At the time, the teacher thought it was developmental, so she capitalized on the areas she was strong in. By the time she was in fifth grade, her teacher asked if she had ever been tested for a learning disability. She was distractible and distracting to other children. At that time, I felt the teacher should learn to manage the children."

"By junior high school, things fell apart. Changing classes, different teachers, and assignments from many different directions became overwhelming. I asked that she be tested and the results were that she had a learning disability. The school and teachers developed a plan and worked as a team to implement the plan at school and at home. We communicated weekly and she started to do much better. I felt so guilty for not having her tested sooner. I worried about whether or not she could attend college. My daughter is a senior in high school now. Over the years, she has continued to build on her learning strengths that were identified in preschool."

Emotional Response to Diagnosis. Once the evaluation is completed, a diagnosis is made and further steps are outlined. At the time of diagnosis, however, the family will often go through stages that are not unlike the stages of grieving (Chinn, Winn, & Walters, 1978; Chinn, 1984).

* Denial—A refusal to accept the diagnosis, clinging to those areas that are developing as proof the child is developing normally
* Projection of blame—"If only . . ." looking back at pregnancy, heredity, trying to find a reason
* Fear—Worry about the future or extreme ranges of the disability
* Guilt—Thinking they should have done something differently or thinking it is retribution for misdeeds
* Grief—Disappointment that the child may not reach expected potential
* Withdrawal—Embarrassment, inability to explain the child's differences to others
* Rejection—Turning away from the child or failing to follow through in intervention
* Acceptance—Recognition and setting realistic expectations for the child

The role of the teacher is to support the family by understanding these emotional responses, providing sensitive but accurate information, and furnishing both informational and supportive resources.

The Teacher and Family Involvement. The law provides for family involvement in every step of the intervention process. The Education for All Handicapped Children Act of 1975 (PL 94–142) and later Amendments of 1986 (PL 99–457) and 1997 (PL 105–17) stipulate familial involvement and focus on families as members of the intervention team. This team writes the **individualized education program** (IEP), which delineates the rights of parents to be notified concerning evaluations or changes in diagnoses, review records, obtain independent evaluations, consent to placement, and challenge and appeal decisions.

The teacher's role is to treat families who have a child with special needs as individuals, and to afford them respect and dignity. Gestwicki (2000) suggests these roles.

* Clarify information—Interpret or reinforce communication from other sources regarding terminology, diagnosis, and treatment
* Be hopefully realistic—Rejoice in small successes without raising false expectations
* Help parents let go—To not be overprotective
* Increase parent involvement in the classroom—Invite participation but allow the classroom time to be a respite
* Know available community resources—Supply information for both himself and the family and in certain cases for other parents
* Help reestablish self-confidence—Provide for social linkages with other parents for emotional support

Opportunities for Family Involvement

Kelley-Laine (1998) suggests two patterns for family involvement: collective and individual.

Collective. Many families feel more comfortable with group activities, where the agenda is less personal and less focused on any one individual or family (Figure 2–6 on page 58).

* Orientation sessions—Often there are many details that families need to know at the beginning of a school year or upon entering a new school or center. Inviting all the families to come at one time is efficient and begins the socialization/interaction process for families. All the information presented should also be in writing to reinforce the presentations and discussions, and to refer to later, as well as for those who could not attend.
* Parent meetings—There may be special issues of concern to families of a particular class or of a whole school. By bringing families together to present the

individualized education program (IEP)–The IEP is an education program developed by a committee comprising parents, school administrators, and sometimes the affected student, that describes the special education and services designed to meet the needs of a student with a disability.

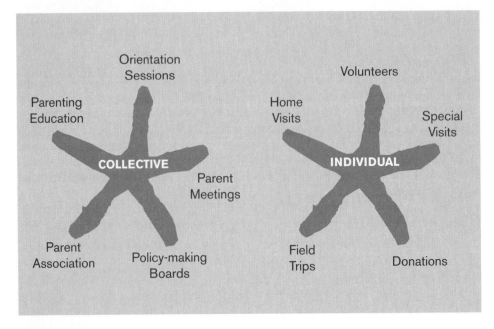

Figure 2–6

Various modes of family involvement. (Adapted from Kelley-Laine, K. (1998). Parents as partners in schooling: The current state of affairs. *Childhood Education, 76*(6), 342)

issue and discuss it, the school is demonstrating openness and a willingness to inform as well as listen.

* Policy-making or advisory boards—Parent advisory boards, elected school boards, and policy councils can be used to achieve a representative and democratic voice for families in the school's or program's policies. All families are invited and encouraged to participate, either by serving or by voting. Such organizations promote the flow of information and serve to keep their representatives abreast of significant developments. The structure of elections and representation allows for participation and two-way communication. Head Start is a prime example of empowering families through its Policy Council, in which families are involved in making decisions that affect or enhance the program.

* Parent associations and class councils—The PTA is the most widely recognized example of this type of family involvement (Figure 2–7). This organization has had varying successes throughout the years, depending on the leadership involved. An accepting, inclusive administration attempts to reach as many families as possible and provide for their specific needs.

* Parenting education—The school can be a resource for assisting parents and families to be more effective in guiding their child's development and direction. These efforts to offer knowledge and support to parents may take many forms, and entail different purposes, with varying results. One popular model is Parent Effectiveness Training (PET), based on the work of Thomas Gordon (1975); another is the later Systematic Training for Effective Parenting (STEP) by Dinkmeyer and McKay (1983). Adaptations for preschoolers and teens have also been developed. These models have been found to be effective with middle-class parents but less so with low-income groups (Gestwicki,

Figure 2—7

Involving families in decision making is an empowering strategy for home/school interaction.

2000). Specific targets such as teen parents, non-English-speaking individuals, or hard-to-reach parents require various strategies and often a less structured and peer-led group. Seefeldt and Barbour (1994) describe the effectiveness of programs that allowed participants to choose and plan their own topics, emphasizing again the empowerment model.

Individual. The teacher and families have opportunities for individual involvement that are limited only by time and creativity.

* Volunteers—There is always a need for extra hands in a classroom, from assisting with daily routines to participating in special projects. Enlisting the assistance of available family members brings benefits to all; the teacher is freed up to do other tasks, the family member feels useful, and the child has two important people close at hand. Families can be substantial and vital resources to the school.

* Special visits—A family member may have a special talent or skill to demonstrate or share with the class. When these skills reflect a part of the child's culture, such as making pasta, learning a festival dance, or hearing a tribal story, the whole class is enriched; the child has a sense of enhanced continuity between home and school and the family feels acceptance and respect.

* Donations—Many are generous with time, talents, and needed items. A grandparent with a backhoe can dig a hole for a sand pit, while another may have a business that can provide the sand (Figure 2–8 on page 60). Business surpluses such as paper, filing cabinets, or used computers are always useful treasures. Painting walls in the school, planting shrubs or flowers, or designing a school Web page are all possible contributions from families who may not be able to help in other ways.

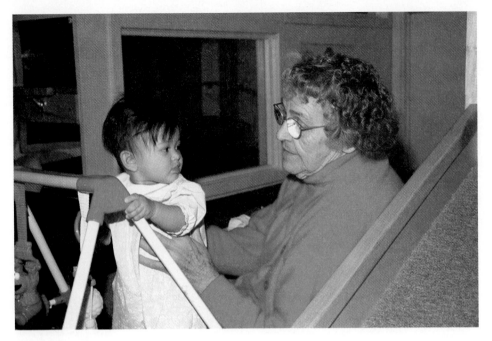

Figure 2—8

Special visits by family members bring a sense of pride to the child and enrich the curriculum.

* Field trips—Outside the regular classroom, volunteers are needed to chaperone field trips. Extra supervision outside the classroom gives everyone peace of mind and benefits the parent and child because of the shared experience, which they can talk about at home.

* Home visits—One of the best ways to get to know a child in his family context is to make a home visit. The intent of the initial visit is not to judge or inspect but to better understand and develop a relationship with the family. Bringing an activity that involves the child or the parent and discussing the parent's goals for his child gives focus to the short, friendly visit. In certain instances, where most of the formal education program is taking place in the home because of home schooling or illness, such home-based parent-teacher communication and interaction are crucial. In these cases, the home visit revolves around addressing the needs of the children and the continuity of their education.

Families will likely represent diverse cultural/racial groups. A conscientious teacher will avoid stereotyping based on the type of home in which a child lives. Home visitors should include individuals who are representative of cultures and races of the families they are visiting.

Communication. Face-to-face communication is always the best way to assess not only verbal interaction, but also accompanying body language. It is indispensable for immediate processing of responses and direct verbal negotiation, and for making the messages comprehensible and clear to all participants. However, because of the structure of the educational or family setting, daily or even frequent conversations are not always possible; other methods may be used to keep the lines of communication open (Figure 2–9).

 * Telephone—The next best thing to a face-to-face conversation may be a telephone call. Whether it is purely social to keep in touch or for a specific purpose, the discussion should be handled diplomatically, with the teacher realizing that a call from school may carry some anxiety. Serious concerns or difficulties are best handled face-to-face if that can be arranged. Telephone answering machines with prerecorded notices and updates on the latest curriculum topics have been used effectively by some teachers and also as a way for the family to leave a message for the teacher.

 * Newsletters—These regular one-way communications can inform, demonstrate learning with samples of children's work, or suggest learning activities and invite participation. Readability and a tone of friendliness and collaboration make newsletters an effective communication tool. The newsletter as a tool can be enhanced by offering some manner of response or by involving families in the actual writing and production. With more and more families having access to e-mail, an electronic newsletter is becoming a viable option; as a complement and extension, the school may host a school Web site on the Internet, with pages for each classroom.

 * Personal notes—Sending a note home may be the only way a teacher can communicate with the family. Whenever writing such a note, the teacher should be aware of the impression it will give, beyond the intended message: a teacher's note with spelling errors, a sarcastic tone, or commands for the

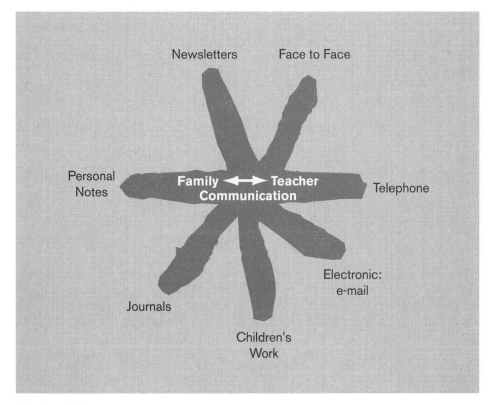

Figure 2–9

Family–teacher communication can take many forms.

family to follow destroys the approach and purpose of the communication (Figure 2–10). Personal notes, too, may be sent electronically.

* Journals—Many teachers use journals sent back and forth between home and school for each partner to write thoughts, ideas, and questions. Some teachers of young children focus the journal on the escapades of a teddy bear or other stuffed animal that goes home with one child and then with another, back and forth between the classroom and the home. This is a creative experience for the family and provides a shared experience. It also invites comparison and contrast among the families, so they can learn more about each other.

* Pamphlets and articles—Teachers can duplicate and send home pertinent information produced by others regarding a topic of mutual interest.

* Children's work—This is often a neglected area of communication between home and school. When a child tells a story about a school event, the family shares in the child's perception of the experience. The teacher's comments can amplify work by explaining, for example, "This is Charles's first attempt at cursive writing."

* Parent conferences—Children's progress and related concerns are often discussed at scheduled, formal parent-teacher conferences. These consultations require thoughtful and comprehensive teacher preparation to assemble work samples and an agenda of what information is to be discussed. Nilsen (2001) suggests communication be descriptive, positive, and personal (Figure 2–11).

Giving the family specific details about the child's progress in all developmental areas from the achievement, rather than the deficit, point of view enables the parent to see the child's developmental level without unduly emphasizing the deficits. Communicating what strategies the teacher is using to help the child progress in certain areas shows the family the teacher is making a genuine and skillful effort toward positive outcomes. These conferences are personal and so are held in a place where the discussion is private and the teacher and family can feel free to speak candidly in the discussion.

To the parents of Jose Perez:

Jose's drawing of our school was selected for the community art show at the high school. The art show is on Saturday from 11 A.M. to 4 P.M. We are very proud of Jose.

Sincerely,
Mrs. Stone

Para la familia de Jose Perez:

El dibujo que Jose hizo de nuestra escuela ha sido seleccionado para la exposicion de arte de la comunidad a llevarse a cabo en la escuela superior. La exposicion se llevara a cabo el sabado de 11 A.M. a 4 P.M. Estamos muy orgullosos de Jose.

Sinceramente,
Mrs. Stone

Figure 2–10

Communication may need to be modified to meet all families' needs.

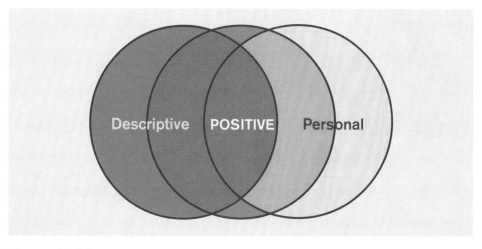

Figure 2–11

The teacher's communication should be descriptive, positive, and personal.
(From Nilsen, B., 2001)

Teachers need to handle all information gathered about the family in an ethical manner. Much of what a teacher gathers is used only within the parent/teacher partnership to plan or enhance the child's education. In most cases, there is no benefit to sharing that information with other teachers, counselors, or administrators. If there is an educational need to meet with others regarding that information, the family has a right to know with whom the information will be shared, and frequently the family has a legal right to have that information shared only if they grant permission in writing. It is very important to define the educational partnership for the parents if it is to include school personnel other than the classroom teacher. No family or personal information is ever to be shared outside the school (to professionals or noncustodial family members) without the written permission of the legal guardian. The National Education Association Code of Ethics of the Education Profession states that the teacher "shall not disclose information about students obtained in the course of professional services unless disclosure serves a compelling professional purpose or is required by law" (NEA, 1998). This principle is also included in the NAEYC Code of Ethics (1997). Schools have written policies and processes related to sharing personal, student, or family information when such sharing is shown to be an educational necessity.

Overcoming Barriers to Home/School Partnerships

Partnerships of any kind have barriers to overcome, and the home/school partnership is no exception (Figure 2–12 on page 64). Differences among people and their expectations, or changing circumstances and misunderstandings, are impediments to mutual understanding; they can undermine the partnership's effectiveness. A few such barriers (some of which you may have thought of already) and their possible solutions include time, attitudes, language, and illiteracy.

Time. The teacher and the family are busy; there are many demands on their time, in relation to the roles and responsibilities they assume within, as well as apart from,

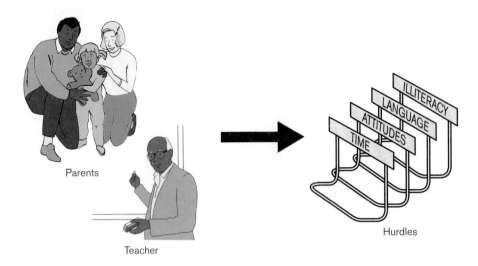

Figure 2–12

There are many hurdles to effective home/school relationships.

the partnership. The teacher who sets a high priority on interaction with families will strive to manage time and organize work, and to keep families informed and feeling a part of school life. The teacher can make it easier for families to allocate time for involvement by minimizing the demands on them and by investigating solutions to other considerations such as transportation, child care, or parking. Effective partnerships devise alternatives that accommodate the family and their needs—whatever it takes to make involvement happen.

Attitudes. It is hoped that the teacher and family realize the benefits of a dedicated partnership. However, it is a partnership of human individuals, and sometimes differing attitudes are present or conflicts arise. There may be a bias about "people like that" on either side; teachers or families may have previous experiences that preclude a willingness to fully participate, or they may have a misunderstanding about roles. Open communication may help to overcome these barriers, but does not ensure that all families will participate in a meaningful way. Each family should be respected for its individual level of participation, from those who are earnestly involved to those who are not at all involved. Teachers should make efforts to maintain an alliance with families to their fullest capacity without sacrificing their role of classroom teaching.

Language. Many families do not speak English fluently or, in some cases, at all. Often, the children are more adept at speaking English. To communicate with those families that do not speak English, the teacher should find translators or some means to communicate important words and phrases to the family in their native language. Some teachers keep a translation book handy or develop a list of common phrases to send home in notes, such as "James did well in math today!" or "Teacher conferences are on Tuesday. What time can you come?"

Illiteracy. Many parents cannot themselves read or write. It is up to the teacher to find a comfortable way to communicate to these parents without embarrassing them. Often an illiterate parent has been inspired to learn to read after building a trusting relationship with a child's teacher. Oral messages are essential; many illiterate individuals have a support person to read written messages to them, but a phone call or personal conversation will ensure that information was received.

✳ DEVELOPMENT AND CURRICULUM FOR FAMILY PARTNERSHIPS

Child development influences family involvement with child care providers and schools. The partnership is different for a family with an infant in child care than it is for the family of a sixth grader. The teacher plans parent involvement in the curriculum (intentional activities with an objective) that takes into account family dynamics. Family involvement is intentional and a strategic component of the curriculum.

As children develop toward independence, the parent/child relationship changes, which in turn changes the teacher/parent relationship (Figure 2–13). For example, as an infant enters child care, the bond between the child and family is strongest. The child care teacher does everything possible to support that bond. As the child grows older and enters school, daily contact between teacher and family is reduced. The attachment relationship becomes less of an issue and the peer group becomes a greater influence on the child. These changes result from normal development and need to be recognized and accommodated in the partnership. Depending on the type of school and the age of the child, family members have different opportunities for educational involvement. The following presents the most common patterns of family involvement in different settings and at different developmental stages.

Infant Development

The infant forms an attachment to significant adults, usually the parents, immediately after birth. It is in this relationship that the infant must find security and comfort; this attachment is believed to be the foundation for all later psychological and emotional development (Erikson, 1963; Ainsworth, 1973; Bowlby, 1969; Sroufe, 1996). It is from this secure base of attachment that the infant becomes capable of developing relationships with others. The relationship is formed with the family through continued mutual interactions. As the infant comes to develop confidence that physical and emotional needs will be met, he then generalizes that conviction and extends that

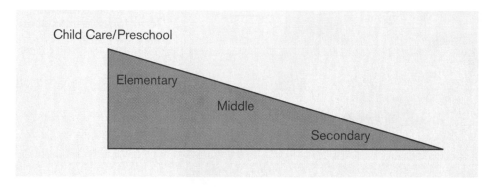

Traditional Home/School Involvement

Figure 2–13

Family involvement in the school usually decreases as the child gets older for a variety of reasons.

trust to all who care for him. When that infant is cared for by a child care professional, the child's world of trust extends to that person as well. The caregiver does not replace the parents or family members; rather, the caregiver expands the network of those on whom the child can depend.

Curriculum for Infant/Family Relationships. When an infant enters child care (whether center-based or family child care), an attachment to the caregiver/teacher is added to the child's social and emotional relationships. Working together, the family and teachers learn about each other's routines and develop a partnership in caring for the infant. The infant's physical status may at times undergo abrupt changes, so it is important for teachers and family to communicate daily regarding eating and sleeping patterns and other physical conditions.

In the first year, there are many developmental milestones and the teacher is a resource to the family in helping them anticipate and understand the changes their child is going through, and in anticipating those changes. For example, a developmental milestone occurs at about seven months when the infant experiences separation anxiety accompanied by a response of fearfulness or shyness, possibly even with the familiar teacher. The family can be alerted to this milestone's approach and the parent and child comforted through this potentially difficult period. Here again, mutual trust between all partners—family, child, and teacher—is needed. Because the first year has a sequence of developmental landmarks, including the first smile, first roll over, first sit up, first pull up, and maybe even first step, the child care teacher, and not the parent, may be the first to see these milestones occur. Teachers need to use sensitivity about those "firsts," knowing how important it is for the family to have been the discoverers. A thoughtful teacher may say, "Watch in the next day or so, he's just about to take his first step."

How do busy families and teachers find time to develop this relationship and interact together with the child? Some teachers and parents develop transition rituals that are repeated each day (Figure 2–14). The daily presentation of a favorite blanket to the teacher by the parent is an example of a transition ritual. The child has learned to trust the parent to be careful of his blanket and by observing the parent turn this special item over to the teacher, the child (by example) learns trust for the new person

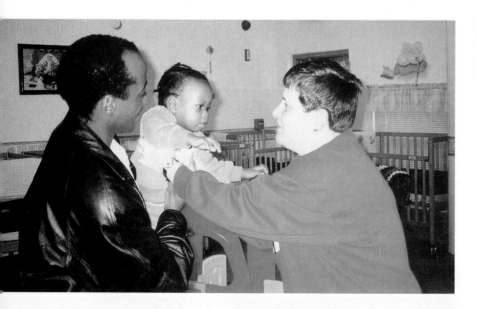

Figure 2—14

The family must feel comfortable in trusting the caregiver.

who has entered his life. Of course, the teacher appreciates the importance of making sure the blanket is safe and available to the child. Daily consistency of transitions from home to school to a familiar caregiver in a familiar setting allows the infant to build that important trust.

In the child care setting, the family is usually the consumer, paying for the services of the center or family child care home. This reciprocal relationship of paying for and providing services places the family and teacher in a more formal partnership, often by way of an express contract. This may give the family a sense of proprietorship and control over the program. On the other hand, because the services are vital to the family's efficacy, some families find themselves unwilling to influence change because they need the services so badly. This is where communication within the partnership plays a significant role.

Toddler Development

The toddler is in the developmental stage of exercising autonomy, the independence won from mastering walking or at least some form of locomotion, and now is more demanding of the caregivers' attention. This puts strain on all the partners: the adults in the family, the teachers in the child care center, and the child himself. Daily communication between home and school at drop-off and pickup times helps to keep everyone up to date on what consistent limits are to be set, and how to allow independence for the toddler, but without complete concession.

Curriculum for Toddler/Family Relationships. The teacher is an important resource for families during the toddler years. For example, a parent may be very frustrated while trying to shop with a toddler. The parent describes the toddler as running away at every chance and loudly yelling "No!" when brought back to the parent. The teacher can help parents understand that this is an indicator of healthy development of the child's independence and when the child masters a sense of self-control the persistence of this behavior will decline. The teacher can help parents strategize how to manage this temporary difficulty in a way that allows the child to work toward independence without frustrating parents or creating dangerous situations. They may suggest taking another responsible individual on shopping trips to keep track of the child and allow him to travel more freely while the other adult shops. They may recommend that the parent avoid shopping with the child until this developmental struggle passes. The teacher may also, in response, provide more opportunities for the child to feel independent in the classroom. Because the teacher is an expert on child development, he can help parents learn to anticipate and handle both struggles and accomplishments during these years.

Some parents worry that the child will not feel secure with a new teacher, but also fear the child becoming too attached to the teacher and less attached to them. How can the teachers of infants and toddlers work with parents to alleviate these fears and enhance the child's development? The teacher should regularly reassure parents that they are the most important individuals in the child's life.

Preschool Development

A preschool child of three through five years continues to be highly influenced by his family. The child arrives at the preschool setting with the influences that include his family's structure, his position in the family, the family's discipline and parenting styles, sibling relationships, and family events. Communication between teacher and family tends to include the child's viewpoint as the child becomes more verbal. The child now may say, "My teacher says I don't have to eat all my peas," which may be in conflict with family policies. Many teachers have heard announcements of family developments not ready for public notice by an excited and eager preschooler; a child may announce that they are "getting a new baby" before the family is ready to make a public announcement (of a "fact" that may or may not be accurate). A child may misinterpret a conversation he overheard; he may misinterpret events at home, and then tell the teacher misinformation. The child also relays information about school to the family that, once again, may not be accurate. Gini relates the following story:

WORDS OF WISDOM

"When my son was a four-year-old, he was very anxious about a picture at school that he told me showed a bird eating her baby. I asked the teacher about it and it took a few minutes to realize that he had misinterpreted a picture of a large bird feeding a baby bird. The teacher and I had seen the picture as an image of nurturing, but my son saw it as a nightmare!"

Curriculum for Preschool/Family Relationships. In many Head Start and pre-K settings, children are bused to school, so daily contact between the child's family and the school is not face to face; thus other methods are necessary to establish a partnership. At this age, family involvement in the classroom for assistance and enrichment offers that opportunity, for those families whose schedules allow it. The family member who is able to contribute time and talent has the opportunity to see classroom activities, his child interacting with other children, and the teacher's skills in managing the whole group. This brings a new perspective to the parent. The teacher also gets a new perspective on the child by observing the interaction between parent and child. The child sees continuity between home and school, mutual respect and acceptance that raises self-esteem. "I am in the midst of people who care for and accept me."

WORDS OF WISDOM

Heather Bridge Fraser conducted action research in a preschool in Birmingham, England. She writes "that preschool children's thinking and learning occurs within the context of their home culture, rather than through preschool learning activities that are unrelated to them. This research suggests that it is parents and the home culture that are at the centre of children's lives and learning. Therefore, it is parents who are in a powerful and important position to influence much of the content and context of the preschool curriculum. Parental involvement is most beneficial when it creates and facilitates links between children's home lives and their related play and learning in preschools. Staff can use "living play" as the launch pad for developing rich realms of children's learning. Such living play is based on children's real lives. It is interesting and relevant to children *now*."

Heather's words emphasize the importance of knowing what the home context is and adapting curriculum to it rather than from some book of ideas or predetermined theme in which the children may not be interested. Until the teacher knows the children and the families from which they come, curriculum should not be tightly planned.

In parent cooperative programs, parent involvement takes on a more intensive form, with parents taking turns acting as teachers and assistants in the classroom. They usually are more involved in the decision-making processes of the school as part of their responsibility.

There are additional opportunities to engage the family in their preschooler's education. At this age, children love to bring things into school to show the teacher or the class. They may want to introduce a favorite toy, a picture from a trip, or even a new sibling. The teacher makes time for these important displays and helps the child to manage his excitement and apprehension regarding sharing important objects with the class.

Primary Age Development

Although many children have been in school settings as preschoolers, the first day of school looms as a significant milestone for both families and children. The child is now entering a mandatory system. Families themselves have experienced school with varying degrees of success, and they bring with them experience, prior knowledge, and perhaps an emotional response when they walk into the school building.

Perhaps this will be the child's first ride on the school bus, perhaps it is the first time the child and parent refer to the teacher by a surname rather than a first name, or perhaps the cafeteria holds a new experience. Previous to this, families could select from a wide range of settings where their child would be cared for and educated. Public policy dictates standards for curriculum, setting, and teacher qualifications once a child reaches the age of five or six. How does this change the way a family relates to their child's educational setting? Does the family have less control over the education of their child than they had in previous years? Schools have traditionally been considered the venue of children and teachers, leaving the family on the outside. Research and changes in philosophy now work to counteract that notion.

The developmental shift of the allegiance and influence of family to include the teacher and peer group occurs during these years (Figure 2–15). The child will often say to his family, "My teacher says . . .," denoting a higher authority than the parents. This often places the family in a comparable position to that of an outsider, leaving the

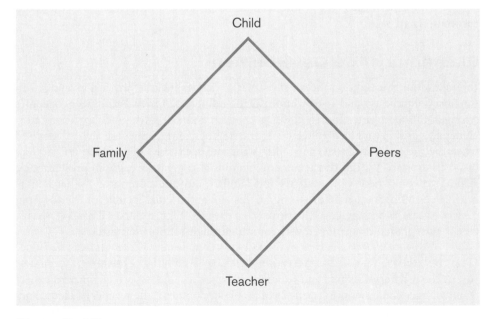

Figure 2—15

Once a child is in school, peers enter the relationship.

family feeling alienated and usurped. The teacher can prepare families for these situations before they occur, informing them of their child's natural developmental character, and offering assurances that the school and the teacher do not have motives of undermining the family. The emphasis again is on partnerships.

During the primary years, friendships separate from family friendships develop, while at the same time family values remain most important to children of this age. As the child's world expands, it includes the teacher and new friends in the more formal school environment: "Billy told me to. . . ." As the child develops toward independence, the family begins to feel the separation and minimization of the familial influence. This can also create a barrier to involvement in their child's education.

Curriculum for Primary Age Family Relationships. The wise teacher devises strategies to overcome these challenges. The teacher prepares families for the child's burgeoning independence and wider circle of influences. The teacher assures the family that the values they have instilled form the foundation for all future social relationships and that they are still the primary influence on the child. The teacher initiates communication with parents to furnish opportunities for involvement in education. Most school settings hold an open house or curriculum night soon after school begins in the fall. The teacher emphasizes that education is a partnership between the family and the school, and that communication from the family is welcome and desirable. The teacher may outline some activities to expect during the year that will involve and encourage family interaction, such as reading books, or bringing specific items or pictures to school, or creating or completing a project at home to later bring back to school.

The teacher should pay special attention to devising strategies for family involvement with families who do not attend open houses or school conferences. Likely, it is not a lack of interest in their child's education and development that prevents family members from attending these events. Other issues may prevail, such as conflicting work schedules, illness, separation or divorce, or fear of school due to their own negative experiences in educational institutions. The teacher must devise ways to circumvent or overcome these barriers and make all families feel comfortable, welcome, and accommodated.

Elementary Age Development

In grades four through six, the most dramatic changes include physical growth (with the onset of puberty) and socialization, as the influence of friends and peers becomes stronger. Students enter fourth grade as children and exit sixth grade as adolescents. Generally, girls mature into puberty earlier than boys, and families are always surprised when they attend a spring event in fifth grade and see these "young women" in their boys' classrooms. Within this generality, there is also great diversity in growth rates, leading to comparisons by students and families and questioning of "What is normal?" Peer influence becomes strong at this age and a child's circle of friends from previous years may change, to the surprise of parents (Figure 2–16). This is especially true if sixth graders are grouped with middle- or high-school youngsters.

Curriculum for Elementary Age Family Relationships. Just as the teacher of infants and toddlers is a resource and expert on what to expect from younger children during periods of rapid development, the teacher of elementary age children can again assist families with the many issues that arise during the surge toward adolescence. Teachers can help define the wide range of "normal" for children of this age, easing concerns for both children and their families. With the approach of ado-

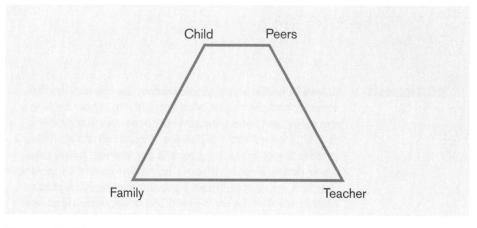

Figure 2—16

Peers become a very strong influence, sometimes stronger than teacher and family.

lescence, children's strong peer allegiance may cause them to want their families to stay away from school. In this stage of peer comparisons, and as the family enters into the arena, children may be critical of family members' appearances, the car they drive, or the way they talk. They also may not want the dialog between teacher and parent to get specific, thus keeping their school behavior private so parents will not pressure them to do better or behave differently. The teacher can recognize these normal feelings and schedule family involvement at school separate from classroom activities, unless by mutual consent of all partners so that involvement can take place in a more inclusive environment.

Another issue that arises in the classroom at this age is the development of romantic and sexual attraction among children. Children in today's world are exposed to a great deal of information and misinformation regarding dating, sexual attraction, and sexual relationships through television, movies, and songs. This exposure is reflected in classroom behavior as children, in their struggle to grow up, ineffectually imitate adult behaviors. A teacher in a fifth or sixth grade classroom has specific training and education regarding this developmental stage and will work with families to define age-appropriate behavior for their children.

We live in a mobile society. The class is rarely composed of the same children all year long. The teacher is a resource for helping families and students make transitions in and out of this particular classroom or from middle school to high school. Some may be making transitions from private to public school, from home school to public or private school, or a self-contained classroom to a setting in which different teachers teach each subject. Not only is this transition a change of environmental and educational setting, but it also symbolizes the official recognition of adolescence. How can teachers help parents and students through this transition? Many schools have parent/student orientations at the new setting to address issues including "what to expect": from changing classes to how to open a combination locker.

Building family partnerships becomes crucial when the teacher or the parent has a concern about the child's behavior or education. If a foundation of trust and openness has been built, both the teacher and parent can discuss their concerns openly. Families and teachers can problem-solve and devise a plan of action to which both parties can commit, and which is workable for the teacher, the family, and the child.

✳ ASSESSMENT OF HOME/ SCHOOL RELATIONSHIPS

SCENARIO James Robert is a sixth grade teacher; he has noticed that excuses and permission slips brought into school by Amber are in her own handwriting. He is concerned that Amber is doing things without her parents' knowledge. When Amber's mother comes in for the teacher's conference, James asks about Amber's recent illness. The mother confirms that Amber was sick with a sore throat. As James is showing Amber's mother some of the child's work, his observations lead him to believe that the mother cannot read. When he asks her to sign the attendance sheet, she drops it, and then sets it on the table without signing it. From now on, James calls Amber's mother on the phone to confirm important events and issues, rather than sending home written notices. He also invites her to volunteer in the classroom for activities that do not involve reading or writing so that she will be comfortable being involved with Amber's schooling.

What kind of a partner is James? Can you think of other strategies that James can use to strengthen the home/school relationship?

Assessing the home/school relationship begins with the attitude and behavior of the teacher. Figure 2–17 is a self-assessment to begin thinking about your own attitudes.

The goal of assessing the home/school relationship is to determine how the teacher can best communicate with and engage the family. The teacher will ask direct questions, make observations, and draw conclusions based on these observations.

Sometimes in the course of working with children and families, the teacher learns information that is unpleasant, potentially embarrassing, or personal. With few exceptions, the teacher is legally and morally bound to maintain confidentiality regarding family information. One exception to this is reporting child abuse and neglect. As the teacher gathers and assesses family information for the purpose of forming the learning partnership, the teacher may become aware of events and situations that cause him to suspect abuse or neglect. That is as far as the teacher's assessment need go. At this point, the teacher is required by law to report his suspicions to the proper authorities.

It may seem like a contradiction after such a strong emphasis on the family partnership to address the issue of child abuse reporting here. However, if we look at the teacher's role in the act of reporting as a partner's way of getting help for the family, especially the child, it makes sense, and thus is vital to this chapter's discussion. Teachers and child care workers are mandated reporters by law in every state. A mandated reporter must report any "reasonable cause to suspect" a child has been maltreated. Not reporting suspected neglect or abuse could result in legal action.

The teacher has frequent opportunities to observe children's physical condition and behavior, both of which give indicators of abuse and neglect. These indicators

As a Teacher, I Believe That I Should . . .	Always	Sometimes	Never	Essential	Not Important
1. Listen to what parents are saying.	❏	❏	❏	❏	❏
2. Encourage parents to drop in.	❏	❏	❏	❏	❏
3. Give parents an opportunity to contribute to my class.	❏	❏	❏	❏	❏
4. Have written handouts that enable parents to participate in the classroom.	❏	❏	❏	❏	❏
5. Send newsletters home to parents.	❏	❏	❏	❏	❏
6. Contact parents before school begins in the fall.	❏	❏	❏	❏	❏
7. Listen to parents half of the time during conferences.	❏	❏	❏	❏	❏
8. Contact parents when a child does well.	❏	❏	❏	❏	❏
9. Allow for differences among parents.	❏	❏	❏	❏	❏
10. Learn what objectives parents have for their children.	❏	❏	❏	❏	❏
11. Learn about interests and special abilities of students.	❏	❏	❏	❏	❏
12. Visit students in their home.	❏	❏	❏	❏	❏
13. Show parents examples of the student's work.	❏	❏	❏	❏	❏

Figure 2–17

Parents as partners in education. (From *Parents as partners in education,* 5/E by Berger, Eugenia Hapworth, © 2000. Reprinted by permission of Prentice-Hall, Inc. Upper Saddle River, NJ)

may include injuries that do not seem accidental, unkempt appearance, poor hygiene, developmental delays, or the child's actual disclosure or account of an incident of abuse. The teacher's role is to observe, ask nonleading questions, record precisely what is observed, write down quotes, and immediately follow the school's policies. Those policies should include a way to report "reasonable cause to suspect" to authorities. The teacher need not prove that abuse or neglect is occurring, but he must accurately report the exact details of his observations to authorities. Every state has child maltreatment laws and a reporting phone number. Remember that this is to protect the child and get help for the family if the suspicions are substantiated.

SUMMARY

The family is the child's first and most important educator. Because of this, it is important for the teacher to build a partnership with the family so the child experiences consistency. The teacher enhances the partnership between school and family by building trust and communicating clearly in a manner and in language comfortable for the child and family. The teacher monitors his personal biases and appreciates cultural, language, socioeconomic, and developmental differences among those families served. As children mature, the relationships within the partnership change. The teacher anticipates this and helps the family prepare for these changes.

KEY TERMS

partnership

primary caregiver

culture

individualized education program

REVIEW ACTIVITIES

Exercises to Strengthen Learning

1. Draw a picture of the family in which you grew up. When your picture is done, write the answers to the following questions in a personal journal.
   a. Who did you look up to or admire in your family?
   b. Who made decisions in the family about how money should be spent?
   c. What are three rules your family had?
   d. Who had most responsibility for discipline?
   e. Who selected child care or babysitters?
   f. Who was most responsible for communication with the school?
   g. Do you remember any occasions when your parent(s) went to school? What was it like?

   After you have answered these questions, list three personal values you have acquired from your family. Are these values universal to all families? How can you develop acceptance of families who do not hold these values?

2. Interview parents of an infant/toddler, a preschooler, a primary age child, and an elementary age child.

   Suggested questions.
   a. Where and in what setting is your child educated?
   b. What are the strengths of your child's teachers?
   c. How do you get information about what is happening at school?
   d. When was the last time you went to your child's school? For what purpose? What was it like?

   When you have completed your interviews, summarize the similarities and differences in responses you received from parents. Did parents give the impression that they were part of a partnership with the teacher who educates their child? What ideas do you have that could strengthen the partnership?

3. Case Example

   Toni and Celeste are identical twins in your infant/toddler room. Their mother, Jane, is a single parent who works full time from 7 A.M. until 3 P.M. as a practical nurse at a hospital. Your center does not open until 8 A.M. so the twins' grandmother brings them to the center. Jane also has a first grade son who comes home from school at 3:30 P.M.

    a.   Who do you want to include in the parent/teacher partnership?

    b.   What type of information is it important for you to know each day about the twins?

    c.   What type of information is it important for you to relay to the family each day about the twins?

    d.   What special considerations might identical twins need?

    e. Describe three strategies you could use to enhance communication with the family and to strengthen the teacher/parent partnership.

4. Case Example

You work in a rural Head Start center where children are bused to the program Monday through Thursday. Many of the families are part of a migrant workforce that lives in this area for three months out of the year. On Friday morning, the families are invited to come along with their children for parent education classes.

    a.   Attendance has never been great but has been dwindling. What might be the reasons?

    b.   What are some of the barriers you see to increasing attendance?

    c.   Can you think of ways to get more families involved?

5. Case Example

You teach third grade in an inner-city school. Most of the students in your class live in high-rise apartments. You have tried to make home visits but cannot gain access to their buildings. You have sent home journals for family responses but seldom get them back. You try to phone but most of the families do not have listed phone numbers. Some do not even have phone service. You are really getting discouraged at this family involvement effort.

    a.   What can you do? To whom can you talk for support? Ideas?

Internet Quest

1. Search the Internet for sites for parents. Compare and assess three sites.

2. Find sites about parent education programs: one for new parents, one for preschoolers, and one for school age children. Compare the sites' information about parental involvement in the child's learning or school.

3. Find sites that provide information for teachers on family involvement. Find five good pieces of advice to share with your classmates.

4. There are many Web sites that are culture-specific. Explore at least three of these and look for information regarding family involvement with school.

Reflective Journal

What I learned about partnering with families will affect what I do as a teacher in the following ways . . .

REFERENCES

Ainsworth, M. (1973). The development of infant-mother attachment. In B. Caldwell (Ed.), *Review of child development research* (Vol III). Chicago: University of Chicago Press.

Bolton, R. (1979). *People skills: How to assert yourself, listen to others, and resolve conflicts.* New York: Simon & Schuster.

Bowlby, J. (1969). *Attachment and loss* (Vol. I, Attachment). New York: Basic Books.

Brim, O. (1965). *Education for child rearing.* New York: Free Press.

Chinn, P. C. (Ed.). (1984). *Education of culturally and lingusitically exceptional children.* Reston, VA: Council for Exceptional Children.

Chinn, P. C., Winn, J., & Walters, R. H. (1978). *Two-way talking with parents of special children: A process of positive communication.* St. Louis, MO: C.V. Mosby.

Cochran, M., & Dean, C. (1991). Home-school relations and the empowerment process. *Elementary School Journal, 91*(3), 261–269.

Coleman, J., Campbell, E. Q., Hobson, C. J., McPartland, J., Mood, A. M., Weinfield, F. D., & York, R. L. (1966). *Equality of educational opportunity.* Washington, DC: U.S. Government Printing Office.

Corey, M., & Corey, G. (1998). *Becoming a helper.* Pacific Grove, CA: Brooks/Cole Publishing.

Dinkmeyer, D., & McKay, G. D. (1983). *Systematic training for effective parenting.* Circle Pines, MN: American Guidance Service.

Education for All Handicapped Children Act. (1975). PL 94–142.

Education for All Handicapped Children Act, Amendments (1986). PL 99–457.

Erikson, E. H. (1963). *Childhood and society* (2nd ed.). New York: W. W. Norton.

Family Medical Leave Act. (1993). PL 103–3.

Gestwicki, C. (2000). *Home, school and community relations: A guide to working with parents* (4th ed.). Albany, NY: Delmar.

Gordon, T. (1975). *Parent effectiveness training.* New York: Peter H. Wyden.

Individuals with Disabilities Education Act Amendments. (1997). PL 105–17.

Kelley-Laine, K. (1998). Parents as partners in schooling: The current state of affairs. *Childhood Education, 76*(6), 342.

Lazar, I. (1983). Discussion and implications of the findings. In Consortium of Longitudinal Studies, *As the twig is bent.* Hillsdale, NJ: Lawrence Erlbaum Associates.

National Association for the Education of Young Children. (1997). *NAEYC position paper: Code of ethical conduct.* Washington, DC: Author.

National Education Association (NEA). (1998). *Code of ethics of the education profession.* Retrieved February 28, 2001 from the World Wide Web: <http://www.nea.org>.

Nilsen, B. (2001). *Week by week: Plans for observing and recording young children,* (2nd ed.). Albany, NY: Delmar.

Pennsylvania Department of Public Instruction. (1935). *Parent education.* (Bulletin 86). Harrisburg, PA: Author.

Pestalozzi, J. F. (1951 [1969]). *The education of man.* New York: Philosophical Library, 26.

Powell, D. R. (1989). *Families and early childhood programs.* Washington, DC: National Association for the Education of Young Children.

Schlossman, S. L. (1976). Before Home Start: Notes toward a history of parent education in America 1897–1929. *Harvard Educational Review, 46*(3), 436–467.

Seefeldt, C., & Barbour, N. (1994). *Early childhood education: An introduction* (3rd ed.). Englewood Cliffs, NJ: Merrill/Prentice Hall.

Spock, B. (1946). *Baby and child care.* New York: Duell, Sloan & Pearce.

Sroufe, L. A. (1996). *Emotional development: The organization of emotional life in the early years.* New York: Cambridge University Press.

U.S. Department of Education. (1994). *Strong families, strong schools: Building community partnerships for learning.* Washington, DC: Author.

Vincent, C. E. (1951). Trends in infant care ideas. *Child Development, 22*(3), 199–209.

Weber, E. (1969). *The kindergarten.* New York: Teachers College Press.

 For additional learning and teaching resources, visit our Web site at www.EarlyChildEd.delmar.com.

RELATED CAREERS

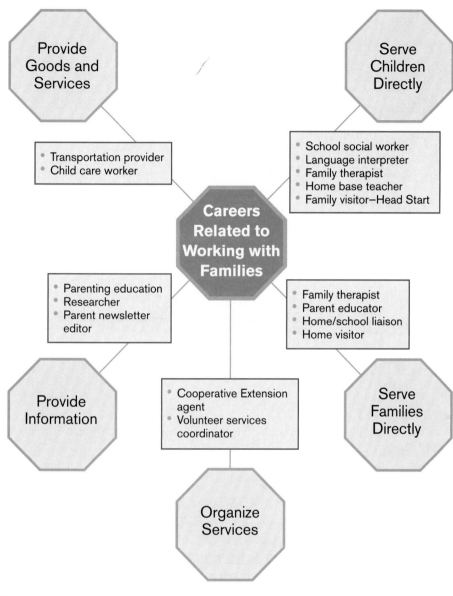

Figure 2–18

Careers related to working with families.

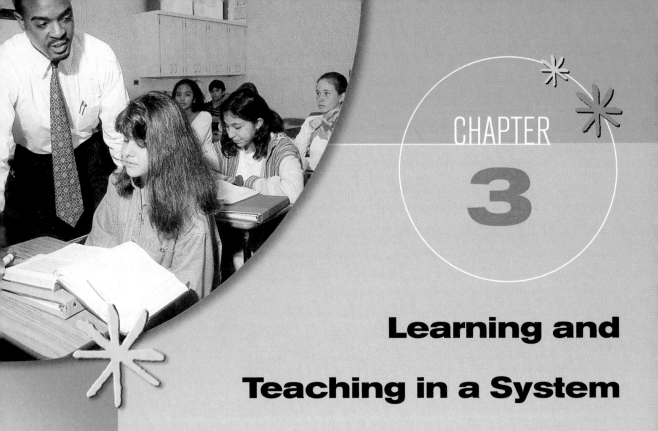

Learning and
Teaching in a System

Objectives

After reading this chapter and completing the review activities, the learning teacher should be able to:

1. Describe what a system is and explain how forces outside and components within the system influence the total system.

2. Describe at least three current education systems in the United States.

3. Explain the influence of the developing education systems in the United States on cultural groups in the United States.

4. Explain the influence of cultural groups in the United States on the development of the education systems in the United States.

SCENARIO Peter is a teacher in a suburb of a small city. Unemployment is high, and the community where his school is located has had many families move into it with young children. Many of these families do not speak English as their primary language. Peter works in a public school supported by local property taxes and subsidies from the state and federal governments. The school budget increase was voted down by local taxpayers and there is no anticipated expansion of state or federal aid. Although Peter has four additional children in his classroom this year, he has no additional help, nor does he have more supplies than last year. The textbooks that Peter uses are quite old. They include few examples of leaders from any cultural group other than European American.

Donna works as a teacher in a school that serves a large population of Native American children. Many of the children's parents and grandparents attended boarding schools where they were prohibited from speaking their native language, practicing native customs, or seeing their families. This school encourages the involvement of family, supports the study and practice of Native American customs and the use of their native language, and enjoys strong community support.

Brian teaches at a Head Start program in southern Mississippi. His program receives funding directly from the federal government; the purpose is to prepare children of poverty for kindergarten. This program has traditionally been a half-day program emphasizing family involvement. In the last three years, family involvement and registrations have declined because most adults in the community have jobs and need to place their children in full-day programs. Head Start federal funding for the half-day program is adequate, but it is not sufficient to fund full-day programs.

Sharra works in a private primary school. The board of directors of the school is made up of parents of the children who attend the school. The parents would like to change the school's policy, which does not require teachers to be state certified. They are aware of research that concludes that teacher training increases the quality of education children receive. As the board begins to research this proposal, they find it will increase tuition because they will have to offer higher salaries to certified teachers. Many parents cannot afford higher tuition and, if it is increased, they will have to pull their children out of the school.

Each of these four teachers works within the education system in the United States. Their resources, curriculum, and guidelines for education are influenced by groups in power and policy makers. These influences are at the federal level and the state level and in the community of families that they serve. Educating the younger generation has been a priority of all peoples. Over the years, the perception of who should be educated, the manner in which they should be educated, and the content of that education has changed.

Imagine yourself as a teacher entering one of these four classes. Who are the students? What do they look like? What are their cultural heritages? What languages do they speak at home? What skills and knowledge do they possess? To what degree is the classroom or school meeting their educational needs? What are the influences that affect the capacity of these classrooms to meet the needs of the children? How do we improve education for all children? What will the classroom look like as you gaze out over it? The class you see may look completely different from the one this teacher sees today (Figure 3–1).

In her book *Other People's Children: Cultural Conflict in the Classroom* (1995), Lisa Delpit states, "To improve education . . . we must recognize and address the power differentials that exist in our society between schools and communities, between teachers and parents, between poor and well-to-do, between whites and people of color. Further, we must understand that our view of the world is but one of many, that others see things in different ways."

Figure 3–1

The world is changing and so is the classroom.

✳ THE POWER CONNECTION

Public education in the United States is a function of government: federal, state, and local. The national government oversees the military academies and the Bureau of Indian Affairs, which operates 187 schools in 23 states, and appropriates funds that it then distributes to the states. The U.S. Department of Education, whose secretary is part of the president's cabinet, promotes education through grants and the collection and dissemination of information. Various presidential initiatives have profoundly affected education, such as Reagan's and George Bush's policies for parental choice and Clinton's Goals 2000 plan to upgrade and reform education. George W. Bush placed the emphasis on literacy and school accountability.

State governments are given responsibility for education by the Tenth Amendment to the Constitution. State boards of education have responsibility for private and public elementary, secondary, and vocational education, including setting curriculum, school facility standards, and quality and standards for professional personnel; recommending state education laws, and administering federal programs.

Local governments make decisions regarding school governance and finance. They implement federal, state, and local regulations and policies, tax to raise funds for education, oversee the facilities and personnel, and act as liaisons between the school and the community. The superintendent is the board of education's appointee who administers the program, carrying out policies and curriculum as directed by the board of education and overseeing principals, school-based management teams, and community advisory committees.

Power is money and therein lies the tension between these three governing levels. Federal and state mandates fund a large portion of local school budgets, thereby wielding power over decisions and policies. Local boards of education, believing they know what their local school district needs, either accept or reject outside influence and funding. Often, poorer districts cannot raise sufficient funding through property taxes for quality education. In some communities, citizens resent having to pay for the education of children whose parents are not property taxpayers. These are some of the power issues that the public education system faces.

A Look at Systems

In any system, there are individuals or groups who have more influence than others on the system's policies and practices. These leaders may use their influence to shape a system that works equitably for all, or they may use their influence to shape a system that favors some individuals or groups over others. In the history of education in the United States, the distribution of benefits has not been equitable, usually reflecting the policies and practices of mainstream society.

A **system** is an organization of individual units that function as a whole. A change in one unit of the system affects the whole system. The electrical system in a car is one example. When the system is in perfect working order, you are not aware of the individual components working together to keep the car running smoothly. The battery, fuses, wires, spark plugs, and generator function very differently, but all depend on each other for the total system to work well. What happens when the generator fails to work? The battery does not become fully charged when the car is running, and soon the battery will not have enough energy to start the engine.

✳ **system**—An organization of individual units that function as a whole.

The car also has a system of subsystems. For example, there is a fuel system, a steering system, a cooling system, and a braking system. Each system depends on all the other systems to make the car run smoothly. A fault in one individual component of a subsystem (such as the electrical system) may cause the total system to fail. Like a car with its various subsystems, the educational system also has subsystems.

Educational Systems

An educational system is the organization of systems and subsystems that allow cross-generational learning to take place in our society. Civilization cannot take place unless **cross-generational learning** is present. This learning of skills by children from their parents and other adults is the basis of education (Newman, 1998).

There are as many models of education systems as there are models of cars. Both educational and automotive manufacturing systems are influenced by culture and scientific study. Just as cars have become safer and more efficient through research, educational systems have changed as research uncovers optimum teaching practices. Preference or function determines some educational practices and organizations, just as an automobile may take the shape of a utility vehicle or a fancy sports car. Both systems depend on fuel. The educational system needs money to operate, while a car needs gasoline. Both the educational system and the automobile system are steered and controlled, with the driver controlling the car, and those who invest money in it controlling the educational system.

Educational systems in the United States are similar to automobile systems in that preference and function are determined by who has control over the system. When cars were first developed, they were very expensive and available only to a privileged few. The same is true for education in the United States. As cars became mass produced, they were marketed to a wider population, but still were not available to all. As the education system in the United States developed, it reflected European cultural values and did not accommodate the cultural values of all.

Institutional Bias

Early automobile marketing and advertising were directed to white males. A female could drive a car, but cars were designed to accommodate the larger male body. An individual of color might have the resources to own a car, but cars were the symbol of white males' success and power, and both subtle and blatant advertising messages made this clear. Policies and practices in institutions such as schools, hospitals, the police, and the workplace reflect the values and sometimes the prejudice and discrimination of the people in power. This **institutional bias** can be subtle or blatant. Often the bias is so ingrained and accepted that individuals do not see the policy or practice as bias.

An example of blatant educational bias would be the history of denying access to public education to African Americans. Although this practice is no longer legal in the United States, subtle institutional bias continues. More subtle institutional bias would be not including African American folk tales in a folklore curriculum, or not including stories by African American authors in a high school literature book.

---

cross-generational learning–Knowledge transferred from an older generation to a younger generation.

institutional bias–Unequal access to the benefits produced by a system that is supported and integrated throughout the system.

This institutional bias becomes even subtler as we look at who becomes involved in organizations that support schools. All parents are welcomed and encouraged to join the parent-school organization, but if meeting announcements are not sent out in the home language of families, how can they feel truly invited to join? If the after-school community service club meets in the home of an individual from an affluent neighborhood, will all children and families feel welcome and comfortable? Figure 3–2 is an example of institutional bias related to English as the mainstream language, the language of power and control.

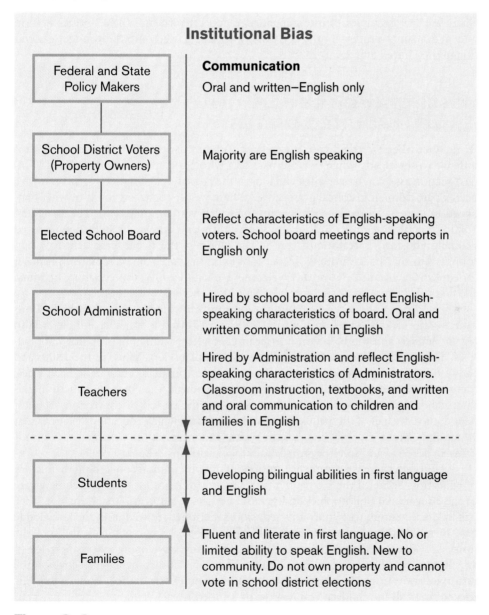

Institutional Bias

	Communication
Federal and State Policy Makers	Oral and written—English only
School District Voters (Property Owners)	Majority are English speaking
Elected School Board	Reflect characteristics of English-speaking voters. School board meetings and reports in English only
School Administration	Hired by school board and reflect English-speaking characteristics of board. Oral and written communication in English
Teachers	Hired by Administration and reflect English-speaking characteristics of Administrators. Classroom instruction, textbooks, and written and oral communication to children and families in English
Students	Developing bilingual abilities in first language and English
Families	Fluent and literate in first language. No or limited ability to speak English. New to community. Do not own property and cannot vote in school district elections

Figure 3–2

In this example of institutional bias, families with limited ability to speak English have both limited access to the benefits of the educational system and a limited ability to change the system. They may not be aware of school policies, programs, or information that would help their child succeed in school.

The body of knowledge passed from one generation to the next in public education is determined by those in power. Different cultural groups have divergent ideas and values about what that body of knowledge should include and in what manner it should be conveyed. Traditionally in the United States, the individuals with the power to make such decisions have been of European American descent. Much of the theory and resultant teaching practices have their roots in European American values.

These educational values emphasize and exemplify the perceived-as-desirable attributes of independence and self-determination. The historical examples and role models of Daniel Boone and the story of the Boston Tea Party reinforce this value. There are few examples of interdependence and reliance on others—values held in esteem in many cultures—in the body of knowledge passed onto the younger generation in the United States.

✳ HISTORY OF EDUCATION IN THE UNITED STATES

Remember when we asked you to step back and look at yourself from the moon? It is difficult to see clearly when you are part of a whole, or up close and involved. This next section asks you to step back and look at the educational system of which you have been a part from an historical perspective. Where we are today is a result of what happened in history, and affects the system for which you are preparing. The struggles; political, social, economic, and religious forces at work; and issues still to be resolved will help you form a realistic picture of the world of the twenty-first century classroom. With that backward and deeper look, you may see some alternative purposes for education, examine if it is truly welcoming all children with an equal opportunity, and commit to improving the system's inequities wherever you find them.

The history of United States education can be divided into three periods. Education in the United States during the 1600s and 1700s was available and directed to few individuals and was based on European-centered teaching philosophies and practices. This period was one of exclusion. As the population expanded in the 1800s and early 1900s, due in part to the immigration of people from many cultures and countries, there was a perceived societal need to convert individuals to a common American cultural standard through public education. This was the period of conversion. The last period, the later half of the 1900s, is that of inclusion, in which education "assumes that ethnic and cultural diversity enriches the nation and increases the ways in which its citizens can perceive and solve personal and public problems" (Banks, 1999).

Although there is an immense amount of documentation concerning the history of education, some of the history remains unwritten. As more people become aware of the educational philosophies and practices of those cultures outside Europe, they will be documented, with innovative educators identified; in so doing, the knowledge base of successful teaching practices will expand. Perhaps you will contribute to the history of education by taking part in a research study, developing a new approach to an education problem, becoming a policy maker, or writing a new perspective on the history of education. Most importantly, what will you use from the lessons of past history to reach all the children you work with tomorrow?

The Beginning of Cross-Generational Learning in North America

The first people immigrated to the North American continent thousands of years ago. Many historians believe they arrived by crossing the Bering Strait. As they populated the continent toward the south, they settled in isolated groups, each developing a distinct culture and language (Hodgkinson, 1992). Each individual Native American group developed a process for cross-generational learning to take place. The North Cheyenne culture valued education for the positive effect it had on the community. Cross-generational learning taught the young to become fully aware of and learn from visions, dreams, and closeness to the world around them. The North Cheyenne looked at the broad picture and used **inductive reasoning** to discover lessons. The North Cheyenne scholar was an observer of and listener to life's forces, and showed great respect to knowledgeable individuals (Rowland, 1996). This cultural and intellectual training was purposeful and planned, but did not conform to the values of European-influenced education, which tended to transmit and value learning through **deductive reasoning**.

Deductive reasoning is attained in Piaget's stage of formal operations, usually by people who have progressed through high school and college thereby causing some people to make the assumption that less technological societies and cultures do not have advanced reasoning power. This was used as the rationale for excluding Native American and African American people from education. In cultures where formal schooling is limited, however, logical thought and conclusions have been demonstrated using both deductive and inductive reasoning (Retschitzki, 1989).

A Period of Exclusion

As more and more people arrived on the North American continent, the groups from Western Europe gained control over other societies. The Europeans brought their concept of education to this country and, because they had the most influence, the education system in the United States reflected the values, beliefs, and practices of Europeans. Figure 3–3 (on page 86) illustrates the stages in educational history of exclusion, conversion, and inclusion.

The European Immigration. In 1492, when Columbus arrived on this continent, there were three million people living here (Hodgkinson, 1992). The first English settlement on the American mainland was established in 1607 in Jamestown, Virginia. From this time on, European immigrants continued to settle on American soil. Once survival was assured, education of children became a priority. By 1642, Massachusetts required settlers to educate their children. Puritan parents believed that children should be taught to read so they could read the Bible. In 1647, the Old Duluder Satan Act required all towns consisting of 50 or more families to teach all children to read and write. Although this law required all children to become literate, it allowed domestic education to be substituted for that of formal learning institutions. Most girls received domestic education, while boys received formal schooling (Brinker, 1999), with most schools educating the male children of European settlers.

As the population of European settlers increased, formal systems of education expanded. At the same time, reforms in Europe began to influence formal education there, which in turn influenced American education. Two European men who advocated

---

inductive reasoning—Coming to a conclusion based on the examination of individual facts. For example: The cake tastes good, the candy tastes good, and the pie tastes good. All have sugar; therefore, sugar must be the common ingredient that makes them taste good.

deductive reasoning—Coming to a conclusion by applying a general principle to a specific fact. For example: Sugar tastes good. Cake has a lot of sugar in it. Cake will taste good.

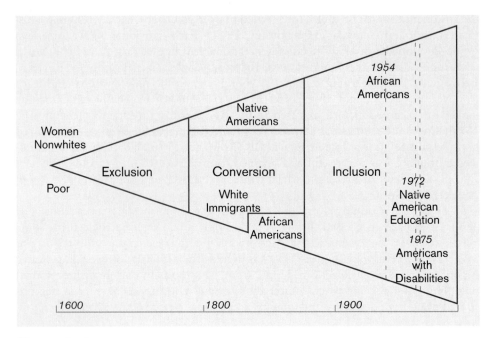

Figure 3–3

The educational system has gone through periods of exclusion, conversion, and inclusion.

for a literate population were John Calvin and Martin Luther. Both valued education for the purpose of encouraging the reading of the Bible. Cross-generational learning in the European tradition took the form of formal education, with a concentration of transmitting knowledge and cultural values through reading.

"In 1728, at the age of six, Samuel Adams began formal schooling at the Boston Latin School. Like the two dozen boys who presented themselves for admission, Samuel read a few verses from the King James Bible. The curriculum was fixed and had not changed in decades with the teacher drilling most of the students in their lessons" (Fowler, 1997).

Education in the 1700s. During the 1700s, the United States began to struggle with the task of educating its inhabitants. Benjamin Franklin and Thomas Jefferson both believed the population should be educated. Franklin thought schools would prepare individuals for the world of business, while Jefferson conceived of an educational system that would provide leaders who could keep the country free.

Africans who came to this country as slaves during this time were not considered in these education efforts. In Africa, traditional education was considered a concern of the entire society. "In the traditional context, education gave the child a sense of security, belonging, identity, and accomplishment. It was not only a process of preparation, but also a process of participation in the life and work of his or her group or community" (Bah-Diallo, 1997). Not only were Africans discouraged or prohibited from participating in the system of education developing in the United States, but also the basic foundation of family and community in which traditional African education took place was torn apart by slavery.

By the mid-1700s, boarding schools or seminaries for women were being opened. Although some schools recognized that women had the potential to perform academically as well as men, there continued to be strong objection to educating females in academic subjects. The belief persisted that the education of females should concern itself with domestic skills (Brinker, 1999).

The Revolutionary War (1775–1783) united the settlers as they fought for independence from England. By the end of the war, the citizens of 13 colonies had established a government ruled by laws, founded on a guarantee of the basic rights of individuals to life, liberty, and the pursuit of happiness. These rights of citizenship were not applied to all inhabitants of the United States, but did lay the groundwork for these basic rights being protected for all citizens in the future. The struggle to protect these basic rights in the United States continues today.

A Period of Conversion

After the American Revolution, a common American identity began to develop. For most of the next two centuries, one significant purpose of education in the United States was to support a common set of beliefs, customs, knowledge, and skills in the population. During this period, more and more of the population were included in publicly funded education efforts. The goal of educating each individual with a common pedagogy toward common national goals was not always successful or productive.

Education in the 1800s. The reform movement in the early 1800s was a result of unrest in the country. Crime and poverty were high. "Of all the ideas advanced by reformers, none was more original than the principle that all American children should be educated to their fullest capacity at public expense. . . . Reformers viewed education as the key to individual opportunity and the creation of an enlightened and responsible citizenry. They also believed that public schooling could be an effective fight against juvenile delinquency and an essential ingredient in the education and assimilation of immigrants" (Martin et al., 1995). One of the most vocal education-for-all reformers was **Horace Mann**, who was Secretary of the Massachusetts Board of Education. He is credited with the public school movement, which included better school buildings, intellectual progress of students, employment of women as teachers, and the establishment of teacher training institutions. He advocated public school for all young people—rich and poor—to develop their full abilities as the hope for the future.

Horace Mann

(1796–1859) He began an educational awakening movement (1820–1860) of basic elementary education for all children. He was Secretary of the Massachusetts Board of Education.

In many American cities, African Americans continued to be excluded from public school efforts, and the education of women still tended to deal with domestic issues. There were some opportunities for women to attend private academic schools and some institutions of higher education began admitting African Americans and women.

Before the Civil War, missionary schools were opened to educate Native Americans. These attempts failed for the most part because the teachings were intended to encourage Native Americans to give up their beliefs and convert to Christianity. The effort was abandoned (Styron, 1997). The availability of education for primary and secondary age white children grew during the first half of the nineteenth century through the "common school" movement. Society began to value education as a means of increasing the nation's productivity and equalizing opportunity for its citizens. As the number of common schools increased, the body of identified educational knowledge grew, as did the need for trained teachers.

In 1839, the first state normal school for teacher education opened in Lexington, Massachusetts, under the administration of Horace Mann, offering a two-year teacher training program that included content subjects, as well as instruction on the art of teaching. The normal school movement led the way in gathering and disseminating reliable information upon which effective educational judgments could be based (Borrowman, 1965). Many of today's teacher education colleges in the United States began as normal schools. Listen to the words of nineteenth century teacher Mary Swift, as she describes the first time she is asked to "teach."

WORDS OF WISDOM

"This morn, Mr. Pierce wished to try the experiment of having one of the scholars hear the recitation in Philosophy. Accordingly he gave me the charge of recitation. The feeling caused by asking the first question tended rather to excite . . . but feeling the necessity of sobriety—I was enabled to play the teacher for a short time" (Borrowman, 1965).

Post-Civil War. After the Civil War, efforts to expand education to all populations persevered. The motivation to expand educational opportunity was often guided by the interests of the European American population. One goal of education was to convert individuals to European values. The Indian Boarding Schools were organized under the Bureau of Indian Affairs (BIA) to Americanize Native American children. Captain Richard Pratt began a trend with the 1879 opening of his Carlisle

Booker T. Washington

(1856–1915) Founded Tuskegee Institute for African American vocational education.

Indian Industrial School in Pennsylvania. Pratt felt that the "natives" must have their inherited culture stripped away in order for them to become productive members of society. He summarized his beliefs in his statement: "Kill the Indian, save the Man." (Styron, 1997). Indian boarding schools did not allow Native American children to live with their families, nor to speak their native language, dress in the manner to which they were accustomed, or practice religious rituals. The curriculum taught English and trained children as laborers. Due to this effort in education, many Native American children lost touch with their language, culture, and spiritual foundations. In an effort to show the impact of the experience at the Hampton Institute in Virginia, upon arrival Native American boys were asked to pose for a photograph in their traditional clothing (Figure 3-4). They were then forced to wear uniforms while enrolled in the school and photographed again to document the changes that occurred as a result of the Institute's program (Styron).

W. E. B. du Bois

(1868–1963) The first African American to graduate from Harvard; part of the rising Black middle class. Founded the Niagara Movement, later to become the National Association for the Advancement of Colored People (NAACP).

The Freedman's Bureau within the War Department established schools for African Americans to address their plight during and after the Civil War. The literacy rate among African Americans, estimated then at 5 percent, rose to 40 percent by 1890 and 70 percent by 1910. "One of the most lasting benefits of the Freedman's Bureau was the schools it established. . . . During and after the war, African Americans of all ages flocked to these schools. The freed person shrewdly recognized the ways to the planters' power—land, literacy, and the vote" (Martin et al., 1995). Two champions of education for African Americans were **Booker T. Washington** and **W. E. B. du Bois**.

Washington recognized the need for vocational skills and founded Tuskegee Institute in Alabama for that purpose. He knew African American children needed an education to compete in a free society. Du Bois was the first African American to graduate from Harvard and promoted the education of the *talented tenth* in university settings to join the business, professional, and intellectual elite. Unlike Washington, he emphasized traditional education and political action to advance the cause of equality for African Americans.

Figure 3–4

Boys arrive at Indian boarding school, 1872. (Courtesy of Duke University, Rare Book, Manuscript, and Special Collections Library.)

Education in the 1900s. As the United States entered the twentieth century, education was universally available through a system of urban and rural schools. Many rural children attended one-room schools in a multi-age grouping of children (Figure 3–5 on page 90). Teachers were adept at instructing and maintaining control of children with a variety of learning levels and abilities. Education was available to both boys and girls; it was seen as a means of unifying immigrants who hailed from a variety of European countries and of preparing a workforce for the country. For these children, public schooling was not just education in literacy and arithmetic, but in the American way of life. Here is part of Gini's grandmother's story.

WORDS OF WISDOM Pierra arrived with her mother, father, and grandmother to this country in 1908 from Italy when she was two years old. "I must have been about seven years old. A family friend's daughter who lived across the street took me to school. I spoke no English, and was put in kindergarten at St. Michael's Catholic School. A few years later, we moved to a nicer home and I transferred to Public School Number 3. When I was fourteen, I had finished grammar school and got a job in a dress factory for $22 a week" (Albertalli, 1990).

Figure 3–5

Many one-room school houses existed all across America (such as this one, which has been well preserved by people with an interest in history).

John Dewey

(1859–1952) The leading reformer of the Progressive Era, who emphasized student-centered learning.

The leading reformer of this period was **John Dewey**, who emphasized that education should concentrate on the students' interests rather than the subject matter. He said, "Education therefore is a process of living and not a preparation for future living" (Archembault, 1964). The Progressive movement Dewey started emphasized how to think, rather than what to think, with curriculum using the scientific method of observing, experimenting, and thinking divergently. This replaced the rote memorization process of learning.

Public school education continued to be available to all children, but it was not an equitable education. In many areas of the United States, African American children had to attend schools separate from those of white children. Often, the schools for African Americans lacked resources and equipment. The positive side was that African American teachers became visible role models of educated adults to children who attended those schools. Because African Americans were often denied the opportunity for education and professional employment, their children did not have the opportunity to see very many highly educated individuals of their race.

A Period of Inclusion

Starting in the mid-twentieth century, educational opportunity began to broaden to people of color, women, the poor, the disabled, and many other disenfranchised groups. A period of legal and social action changed the system.

The 1954 *Brown vs. Board of Education of Topeka* decision made racial segregation unconstitutional. This ruling alone did not stop all racial segregation in public schools in the United States, but over the course of the next decade, the ruling was enforced. Enforcement meant using federal troops or the National Guard to assure the safety of black students in all public schools.

The 1964 Civil Rights Act prohibited discrimination in employment and education on the basis of race, color, religion, and national origin. This act extended the rights of individuals to attend and work in publicly funded schools. With the threat of losing tax support if discrimination continued, organizations were sharply motivated to comply with this ruling.

In 1972 and in 1975, respectively, the Indian Education Act and the Indian Self-Determination and Education Assistance Act were passed. Since the adoption of these measures, many Native American communities have organized their own schools in which children are immersed in Native American cultural values, language, and practices.

The Chief Leschi School, a tribal school operated by the Puyallup Tribe, opened in 1996 and serves students from 92 different tribes. Every day, all children participate in "Circle," a cultural activity in which the children sing native songs and play drums. In addition to cultural activities, the Leschi School sets goals for the children to become proficient as writers and life-long learners. By interweaving both culture and academics, the school helps the children develop pride and improved self-esteem. Parents are engaged in the learning process through their involvement in cultural activities (Leschi, 2000).

The U.S. Department of Labor Title IX Education Amendments of 1972 prohibit sex discrimination against employees and against students in educational programs receiving federal funds. Title IX states that

> "No person in the United States shall, on the basis of sex, be excluded from participation in, or denied the benefits of, or be subjected to discrimination under any educational program or activity receiving federal funds."

This law has made an impact on the education of women. "In 1994, women received 38 percent of medical degrees, compared with 9 percent in 1972, women earned 43 percent of law degrees, compared with 7 percent in 1972, 44 percent of all doctoral degrees to U.S. citizens went to women, up from 35 percent in 1977" (Bailiwick, 2000).

The 1975 Education for All Handicapped Children Act guarantees that all children with disabilities from ages three to twenty-one have a right to free and appropriate public education. (Later amendments extended this to apply to children from birth.) This education must take place in the *least restrictive environment* in which the child's needs can be served. Previous to this act, many children had to live in institutions away from their families or received no educational services at all because their local school districts did not have educational services that met their needs. For example, school districts often could not provide for the education of deaf children because teachers who knew sign language, or speech and hearing specialists, were not available. With the employment of individuals in these areas of expertise, hard-of-hearing and deaf children could be educated in the local school district. The act also redirected the burden of educational costs for children with handicaps to the school district in which the child's family resides. This removed the financial burden from many families and made available services they could not previously access because of cost.

When guidelines were established to make cars crashworthy, more fuel efficient, and safer, automobile designers were obligated to reconsider what the car should look like. They thought about the changes necessitated by law and how they could be implemented. The changes benefited society by making cars pollute less and making car travel safer, but it was not always easy for car manufacturers to adjust.

As with automobile design evolution, a similar process of change is true for school systems. The legislation mentioned previously had an impact upon the educational systems in the United States, but not without struggles, failures, and revisions. Providing that least restrictive environment is still an individual struggle between school district and family. As students with handicapping conditions were given the

Figure 3–6

Students with differing abilities thrive in settings in which accommodations have been made.

right to attend schools supported by federal funding, those schools had to decide how to offer appropriate services and support, and in what manner they would address required accommodations and adapt existing classrooms and school grounds to serve all students. Teachers who never had a child with disabilities in their classroom needed to learn to teach children with exceptionalities (Figure 3–6).

Providing equal educational opportunity has not yet been achieved because school budgets based on tax rolls are insufficient in some areas, while more than sufficient in others. This leaves some of the most at-risk children in districts with the least resources. Providing gender equity is nonnegotiable, but in some areas it is very controversial. In the area of sports and athletics, where funding and resources were in much greater proportions for males, school systems needed to create opportunities for female athletes. Many thought there would not be enough interest, but quite the contrary; female athletics have become very popular due to equal access.

✳ EDUCATIONAL SYSTEMS IN THE UNITED STATES

Families send their children to school to receive an education. Because there is such variety among people in the United States with regard to values, culture, and economic resources, and the body of knowledge families want passed to their children, the education system is very complex. Public education is available to all children from the age of six to eighteen free of charge, but it does not always meet the educational goals and expectations of every family. Those who have the financial resources or time may choose to educate their children outside the public school system.

Public Schools

Public schools are supported by taxes; regulated by various local, state, and federal agencies regarding policy and curriculum; and are free to every child. The organizational structure of a public school system pictured in Figure 3–7 shows that there is a hierarchy in the decision-making power within the system. The state education department usually sets curriculum guidelines for public schools. The school board comprises elected individuals who live within the school district and sets administrative policy for the school district and both hires and dismisses teachers and administrators. The school board hires an administrator (the school superintendent) to oversee the administrative policies in the district. Each school building has a principal who administers that school. Classroom teachers report to the principal.

How is this a system? It is a hierarchical organization in that a change in policy by the school board (for instance, a change in minimum class size) will affect all levels of the organization below it (see Figure 3–7). What other entities are present in this system and how do they affect the total system?

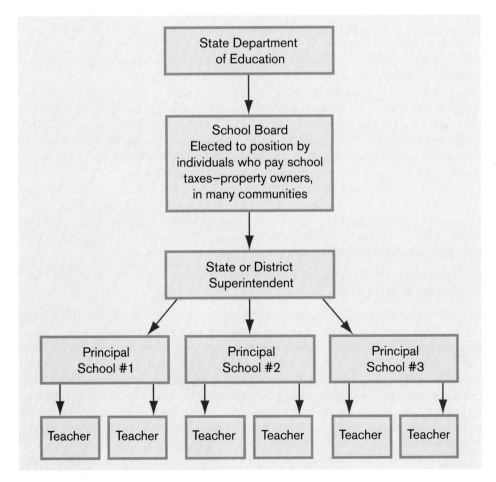

Figure 3–7

Public school model.

In many communities, the public schools are supported by taxes levied on privately owned property, and only those individuals and businesses who own property may vote on school issues. Basing school taxes on property values affects the system in many ways. If property values in the school district are high, then the district is usually able to collect enough funds to keep buildings in good repair, keep class sizes low, and compensate teachers generously. Where property values are low, it is difficult for school districts to maintain safe buildings, competent staff, and smaller class sizes. A second issue related to property taxes supporting education is that, in some communities, the individuals who decide district issues through their vote do not have children, have grown children, or are not involved in education. The budget items they approve may be very different from the budget items parents of children would approve.

How do children affect the education system in a community? Gini's son was born in a population bulge. The year he was born there was a very high birth rate compared to the years prior to and after his birth. Each year, his elementary school had to add a teacher to his grade because classes were over the maximum allowable size by about one or two students. Classes were shuffled around each year, and he ultimately benefited by being in small classes. The district also had two other schools experiencing the same bulge. Rather than hiring three teachers to take care of the bulge at three different schools, the district decided to shuffle children around in all three schools so that only one extra teacher had to be hired. This was a cost-effective decision on the part of the taxpayers, but the children who were shuffled to a new school, as well as their parents, were not very pleased.

One innovative approach to public schools is the charter school. "Charter schools are independent public schools, designed and operated by educators, parents, community leaders, educational entrepreneurs and others. They are sponsored by designated local or state educational organizations who monitor their quality and integrity, but allow them to operate freed from the traditional bureaucratic and regulatory red tape that hog-ties public schools" (Center for Education Reform, 2000). Families choose to send their children to charter schools for a variety of reasons, the most significant of which is that the family may have more impact on the operation of the school than they would in a traditional district public school.

Many public schools are reluctant to have a charter school open in their district. The funding allocated to individual children follows them to the charter school, leaving less for the district school. Proponents of charter schools respond by saying that because charter schools are efficient and of high quality, the district system is strengthened and that individual schools in the district system are held more accountable.

Private Schools

Private schools are usually supported by tuition charged for each pupil who attends the school. There may also be other nonpublic funds that support the school, such as those from religious organizations, endowments, grants, and charitable donations (Cromwell, 1997). Since parents directly support the school, they have more direct influence on the policies and practices in a private school. Private schools must comply not only with public policy regarding compulsory education, but also the guidelines for curriculum content established in each state. The board of directors of a private school is usually made up of those who support the school financially, such as parents, or the sponsoring organization, such as a church (Figure 3–8).

A private school usually has a specific philosophy, and families with similar philosophies tend to use such schools; for example, Montessori schools or schools with multi-age classrooms. Some private schools charge very high tuition that only financially well-off families can afford. A private school may be associated with a specific religion that is prac-

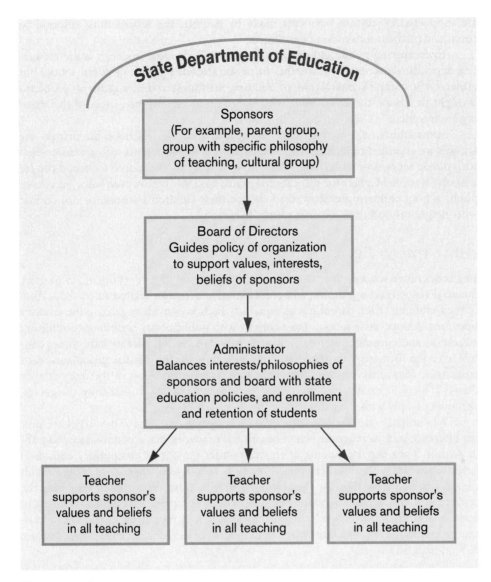

Figure 3—8

Private school model.

ticed by the families and children who attend the school. Some private schools immerse children in a specific language or culture . Other private schools follow specific child management practices, focus on a single academic or artistic area, or follow the teaching of a particular educational theory or practice. Some private schools provide educational services not available in public school, such as early childhood education for children whose families meet certain income guidelines or for children below a specific age.

As a system, a private school is somewhat isolated from the community as a whole, so a public education policy change may not affect it. An example would be a change in what is required to be served for public school lunches. If the private school does not participate in the public school lunch program or accept public funds to provide lunches, then it would not be affected by this change. Private schools tend to be more tightly aligned to parental demands than public schools. Because private schools are supported by tuition payments made by parents, the school must respond to parental demands or risk losing enrollment.

In comparing public and private schools, "an individual student's academic success depends not so much on whether he or she attends a private or public school but rather on a complex interaction of abilities, attitudes, and strengths or problems brought to school; the skills and knowledge of teachers; and the quality of the learning environment" (Cromwell, 1997).

Some additional differences between public and private schools are that private schools are attended by choice. They are an alternative for parents who are dissatisfied with public schools or have other reasons for wanting their children to attend private schools (National Center for Educational Statistics, 1997). However, some parents of public school children are allowed to choose their children's school, or can choose what neighborhood they live in as a way of choosing.

Alternative Schools

In a cooperative school, parents *are* the school. A group of parents organizes to share financial costs, teaching duties, and administrative decisions related to the education of their children. Each parent has an equal say in choices made regarding the school's operation. Cooperative schools must comply with public policy regarding compulsory education and curriculum content. In a cooperative school, parents have direct control over the management of the school as a group. As long as the group can reach consensus, all will feel they influence their children's education in the manner they desire. If an individual parent holds a differing view on a policy issue from the group, she must comply with the majority's wishes.

Why might a group of parents opt for a cooperative school? They may have similar interests, such as religious beliefs or cultural practices, not accommodated in public school. They may be parents of children under the age of compulsory education (usually age six) with no other options available for a school experience for their children. They may have thought about home schooling, but do not think they have the resources to educate their children by themselves. The parent group is motivated to consolidate time, knowledge, materials, locations, and money to provide their children an education in which they have a high level of decision-making power (Figure 3–9 on page 98).

Parents who homeschool their children must register with their local school district and comply with public policy regarding compulsory education and curriculum. A home school network is a group of families who educate their individual children in their individual homes. Groups of homeschool families network to provide social activities for their children, share teaching strategies, and support each other. Many school districts have several families who are homeschooling their children, and these families may have a newsletter or Internet chat room to communicate with one another. Some homeschool networks have regular meetings. Parents in such arrangements have a high degree of control over the content of the curriculum and the strategies used to teach their children. They have control over both the environment and when teaching occurs.

Preschool Education

Many children in the United States are in some kind of program outside the home in the years prior to public schooling. These programs take many forms, but all serve some kind of educational objective (Figure 3–10 on page 99).

SCENARIO   Ever since she had been a young girl, Marilyn wanted to be a teacher of young children. Marilyn works in a prekindergarten classroom operated within the public school system. She is a certified teacher with a master's degree in education and an undergraduate specialization in early childhood studies. Marilyn's salary is $32,000 and she receives medical and retirement benefits. She is a member of a teacher's union. She is required to work 185 days per year from 8 A.M. until 4 P.M. She is supervised by her building principal, and district policy is set by the school board elected by the property owners within her district. Marilyn has been with the district for many years and plans to retire from this job in several more years.

Ever since he had been a young boy, Gaylord wanted to be a teacher of young children. Gaylord is a head teacher in a child care center supported by parent fees. He has a high school diploma and has completed two college courses. Gaylord earns $12,000 per year and has no benefits. He works 240 days per year from 7:30 A.M. until 3:30 P.M. The center's owner supervises him. He takes courses at the local college and from the Internet and hopes to earn a bachelor's degree in the next five or six years. He has been at the center for two and one-half years and is the most senior member of the staff other than the owner. He plans to leave as soon as he receives his bachelor's degree to work in the public school system. The other teachers in the center also have high school diplomas.

While parents are at work or school, someone must care for their children. Most of the cost of care is the responsibility of the family. Parents pay directly for 60 percent of the child care costs in this country (Stoney & Greenberg, 1996; Mitchell, Stoney, & Dichter, 1997), spending an average of 8 percent of family income (Casper, 1995). With child care costs an average of $100 a week for a preschooler and more than that for an infant, a parent making little above the minimum wage may have to spend 25 percent of her income or more on child care. Parents may try to make arrangements by working different shifts, enlisting the help of other family members or neighbors, or arranging for unregulated care in the neighborhood. These types of makeshift arrangements may keep the child safe and supervised, but neglect the child's education. The average tuition for a four-year-old's child care is greater than the annual tuition and fees at a public college, in some cases twice as much (Schulman & Adams, 1998). All the latest studies point to the importance of language and literacy experiences in the early years, with learning beginning long before the child is enrolled in school. The preschool education system in this country is less advanced than in other industrialized nations and deemed to be average or mediocre because of the lack of a stable funding (Cost, Quality, and Child Outcomes [CQCO] Study Team, 1995). This is because of the lack of national commitment to quality preschool education and care.

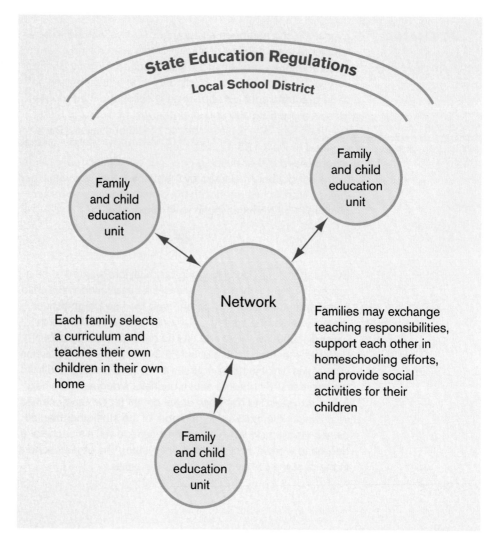

Figure 3—9

Home school model.

The education and care of this country's youngest children are less regulated, less organized, and less consistently supported by public funds than is education for children in kindergarten through college. Because of this and the great need for families to look to the community for child care and education, a mosaic of systems has developed. There are great discrepancies among the systems due to lack of consistent standards or similar funding streams.

Child Care. No national license or standard exists for people who care for and teach children six weeks to five years old. The education of the caregiver/teacher has a direct impact on the developmental gains the child will make during her early years, yet because of the lack of public funding, people who hold these positions generally make low wages. "The fundamental dilemmas of early childhood services are delivery, fragmentation, lack of equitable access, and quality. . . . For decades, well-intentioned individuals, mostly women with limited employment options, subsidized the early care and

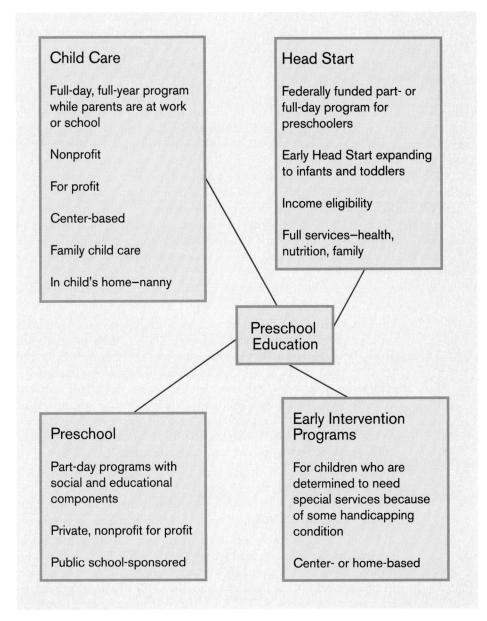

Figure 3—10

Preschool education systems.

education system because they were not offered adequate compensation and benefits. Such subsidization coupled with a marketplace economy has kept wages low and deterred many from entering the field in private and public sectors" (Copple, 1991).

Each state chooses how or whether to regulate staff qualifications, staff-to-child ratios, and the attributes of the environment children function in each day. In general, these regulations are far below those that guide education from kindergarten forward. Each state or community can also choose whether to subsidize the cost of early childhood education. Once again, the cost of early childhood education usually falls upon the shoulders of the child's family. Nationally, there is a lower proportion of subsidy going toward the cost of early childhood education than for any other level of education through college. Therefore, families pay a higher portion of the cost for early childhood education. Since there is a limit to how much a family can pay, the funds available for early childhood education are constrained. Compensation and education requirements for teachers are low.

This is described as the **trilemma** in preschool education; the balancing of teacher-to-child ratios, staff salaries, and total cost of services. Without sufficient funds from either parents or subsidy, salaries must remain low and the quality of education for young children suffers. If ratios are lowered to provide more individual care, costs increase and parents cannot afford the care. Several initiatives have been started throughout the country to address these issues and to bring more money into the early childhood education system to enhance the quality of care for young children.

It is crucial to increase the quality of care for young children in this country. "While the first three years of life is critical to brain development, quality infant and toddler care is almost always hard to find. Recent research on the brain development of children has shown that how children grow and develop depends on the interplay between nature (the child's genetic development) and nurture (which includes their nutrition, surroundings, care and stimulation)" (Children's Defense Fund, 1999). Options for early care and education are:

* Child care centers—Child care centers consist of both profit and non-profit organizations that care for several children, usually in classrooms grouped by age range. The classes usually have a teacher and at least one teaching assistant. In a high-quality center, there are low teacher-to-child ratios, there is low staff turnover, and teachers are highly educated in both general education and early childhood. The organizational structure of a child care center may include a board of directors, a director, teaching staff, teaching assistants, and support staff, or it may only consist of a center owner and teaching staff.

* Family child care—Child care that takes place within the teacher's home is family child care (Figure 3–11). That individual may be licensed or may be an unlicensed informal provider. Once again, regulations vary greatly by states in regard to training and environment.

* In-home child care providers—For those who can afford individual service, children may be cared for in their own home by a person who may be referred to as a mother's helper, nanny, governess, or au pair. In these situations, the family sets the criteria for education and experience and is responsible for designing the types of activities in which the child will be involved while with the caregiver. This is the least regulated type of child care, depending fully on the family to use judgment in selecting and supervising the caregiver. It is important to remember that this is part of the educational system, for anything you do with a young child is part of learning and cannot be ignored as unimportant just because it is not in a school setting. Informal care, whether in the child's home or the caregiver's home, requires employer/employee relationships, including income tax and Social Security withholding.

trilemma—Multifaceted dilemma in the child care system, balancing ratios, salaries, and the cost of service.

Figure 3—11

Many children are cared for in the homes of relatives or nonrelatives. There are state regulations for family child care homes.

This adds to a community's economic base by enabling parents with young children to remain in the workforce.

Here are the stories of two typical child care providers.

SCENARIO   Joanna lives in a small house and has children in her care from 5 A.M. until midnight. Sometimes she keeps children overnight if their parents are called in to work. Because children come and go throughout the day, she is never sure from one day to the next how many she will have, nor can she effectively plan daily activities. She tries to attend some local training programs, but often she cannot because an unexpected child is at her house. Joanna has a fenced-in yard where the children can play, and a television room for quieter times. Her home is clean and she provides nutritious food for the children. Her income fluctuates from week to week because the number of hours she can charge for child care varies.

Esperanza also has a family child care business. She is registered with the local resource and referral agency for child care and accepts most of her work from that office. The agency matches parent needs with child care services. Esperanza has

continued

an associate's degree in early childhood education and continues to take courses toward her bachelor's degree. She accepts children in her home between the hours of 3:30 P.M. until 8 A.M. She is able to offer after-school services to families, as well as services to parents working the night shift. With guidance from the resource and referral agency, she has a written policy she gives to parents and she requires a signed contract for services. Her population of children is consistent and a comfortable routine has been established with them so she can include developmentally appropriate enrichment activities. She is a leader in the local professional organization and works with a state-level committee to raise standards for early childhood education.

Head Start. Head Start is an educational program available for infants and toddlers (Early Head Start) and preschool children of poverty. The goal of the program is to socially and academically prepare children for kindergarten. The program is fully subsidized by the federal government and not only offers education services for a child, but also works with the child's family to help them receive health and social services. Early Head Start and Head Start have led the way in setting standards for infant, toddler, and preschool education by identifying and establishing comprehensive program standards and measures to which each program is accountable. These standards and measures are based on national research findings concerning the best educational and developmental practices and are uniformly enforced throughout the United States.

Preschool. Many part-day programs are available from a variety of sources. Churches, community centers, and individuals may offer preschool programs for socialization, specific academic curricula, or as a service to parents who need a few free hours. The programs range from cooperative play groups where parents take turns supervising the activities to very structured learning situations where such things as computer skills, gymnastics, foreign language, or early reading are encouraged. The regulation for such programs varies from state to state, along with teacher qualifications and the way the programs are administered. For the most part, these programs are totally funded by the participants and are not part of the public sector.

Early Intervention Services. This is a collaboration among systems. For children under school age who require special services because of developmental delays, services can be provided in various ways. The child can be placed in a group of typical children in a child care, preschool, or Head Start setting, receiving special services in that setting. For more intense intervention, the child may attend a program specifically for children with special needs, where specially trained personnel in physical, occupational, speech, and language therapy are available throughout the day to administer treatments and intervention strategies to assist in development. Or, the child may receive the necessary therapies at home with itinerant therapists visiting on a regular basis. Most of the cost of services for a child with special needs is covered by private insurance or by early intervention funding through the public school.

As you can see, the system of services for preschool is so fragmented that many people do not consider it a system of all. Although high-quality care and education are available, they are not affordable or accessible to all preschool children in the United

States. It is not until children reach the age of six that a free education is guaranteed. That education, although not always as high in quality as it has the potential to be, has a monitoring system of rules and regulations in place to meet minimum standards. Those minimum standards for public education are usually much higher than the minimum standards required of preschool programs.

☀ THE FUTURE OF THE EDUCATIONAL SYSTEM

Education reforms of the late 1900s have changed the system's curriculum, pedagogy, organization, and technology. In the 1960s and 1970s, in reaction to the Russians launching Sputnik into space, greater emphasis was placed on science, with new curriculum developed and education begun at an earlier age. Experimentation with open education, multi-age grouping, and student-centered education meant a resurgence for the philosophies of Dewey. During the 1980s, education was criticized for not being competitive in the global economy. The pendulum swing calls for a return to basic education. In the late 1980s and 1990s, state and local control of schools proposed deregulation and school choice. President Clinton's Goals 2000 in the Educate America Act of 1994 included greater emphasis on math and science; adult literacy; lifelong learning; safe, drug-free schools; teacher preparation; and parent participation. In the early 2000s, a shift to looking at workplace needs brings business and industry into the education arena. Three themes dominate and will influence education in the early years of the twenty-first century.

National Goals and Standards

In movements to improve education, there is much thought and debate about clearly defining what a student should know and be able to do and how that will be measured. Many professional organizations are developing standards that will be discussed in later chapters of this book. The measurement of how individual students meet those standards is part of a monumental assessment explosion. Tests and portfolios are proliferating the education market and are used not just for individual measures of achievement, but to measure the effectiveness of the teacher, the curriculum, the school, the district, and even the state.

Accountability

Using standards and assessments, schools administrators and individual teachers are subject to accountability measures. Positive and negative sanctions are being used, such as teacher bonuses for higher test scores or threats of school closures or takeovers for low scores.

How do you assess whether or not a system is doing the job it was designed to do? One way is to define specifically what you want the system to accomplish. For example, when you purchase a car you expect the outcome to be that you will be able to transport yourself safely, conveniently, and when you want to the destinations you choose. Your performance goal can be stated, "As a result of purchasing this car, I will have safe, convenient transportation to the destinations I choose for the next three years." If, after two years, the car does not start or a wheel falls off while driving, you can measure the success of our goal. You could say you achieved 66 percent of your goal by having two out of three years of trouble-free driving. Is this outcome good enough? How will it impact your purchase decision for your next car? What improvements do you want to see in performance the next time that you measure the outcome? What changes do you need to make?

Outcome-based assessment looks at the impact of the educational experience on children. How are children different as a result of being involved with a particular system or organization? The results must be measurable and a comparison must be made to a previously established standard. The standard may be a minimum performance level for competency in a specific area or a comparison to performance levels obtained previously.

The staff at Memorial Elementary School in Valparaiso, Indiana, uses a systems approach to design curriculum and meet staff–determined performance outcomes. In a plan to improve language arts instruction, they set a goal to "evolve into a premier school for communication arts instruction." Their measure of success was in tracking third-grade standardized test scores. The systemic approach included strategies for staff training, remedial curriculum, and several efforts to motivate children to read, such as providing one free book to each student and bringing published authors to the school. As a result of their efforts, their third-grade students scored two standard deviations above the mean score.

WORDS OF WISDOM

Gregory D. Wilson, Ph.D., Principal of Memorial Elementary School in Valparaiso, Indiana, explains the systems approach this way:

"We have spent the previous three years developing our instructional strategies in the area of language arts. We have made strong progress and are pleased with our students' performance in the classroom, as well as on national achievement tests. We knew it was time to focus our attention on improving mathematics instruction. Our stated mission is 'to improve our mathematics instruction so that students will be more successful in reading, writing, and problem-solving mathematics.' For two years, the teachers and I met with a consultant as a whole staff, in small groups, or as grade-level teams in our quest for instructional improvement."

"True reform and change will occur only when strong collegial analyses are a part of the process. An administrator must provide leadership and strong commitment and be involved in all aspects of the process. Evaluation and follow-up of each step must occur so that the necessary adjustment can be made for the whole process to be successful."

Basic Skills

In a conservative backlash to the perceived failure of the child-centered philosophy of education and with declining test scores, many schools are pursuing more rigorous literacy, mathematics, and science foundations, sometimes at the expense of music, art, and physical education. Magnet or charter schools are being formed as a choice for parents who want a special curriculum, special interest for their child, or as an alternative to poorly performing schools. The "excellence in education" movement is refocusing on the primary mission of the schools to prepare productive citizens.

SUMMARY

The education system in the United States has come a long way in educating all of its inhabitants, but there are still areas for further growth and research. Universal education is provided for children, usually from the age of six to age eighteen. Should universal education be expanded to include younger children and college students? Do undocumented aliens have a right to free public education? What are the indicators of an education system that treats both males and females equally? How much money is enough to educate the population of the United States? How will we change teaching practices as we learn more about learning and about the brain through technological advances? How will computer technology and virtual classrooms affect school systems?

What is the future of education? We will have to continue to test the practices and theories developed with European-centered approaches with respect to diverse populations. We will have to look at the teaching practices of other cultures and use those that prove most effective in our systems in the United States. We must identify leaders of education from other cultures and work with them to lead education reform in the United States. We must integrate education innovations and approaches from other cultures into American education and assure that each student is educated in a manner that respects and capitalizes on cultural strengths.

Systems are an organization of individual units that function as a whole. Change in one unit of the system impacts all of the system. The education system in the United States is made up of subsystems, some of which include the public school system, the private school system, and the system of early childhood education. The education system should meet the needs of all cultural, socioeconomic, racial, gender, sexual orientation, and language groups to transmit knowledge from the previous generation to the succeeding generation. As the population in the United States changes the education system must change with it. Organizational change must be comprehensive; whether it is in creating a school system that is more inclusive of children with disabilities, individuals who speak other languages in their homes, or whether the change is designed to meet higher standards of academic learning.

KEY TERMS

system	inductive reasoning
cross-generational learning	deductive reasoning
institutional bias	trilemma

REVIEW ACTIVITIES

Exercises to Strengthen Learning

1. Attend a school board meeting.
   a. Do school board members represent the racial, cultural, socioeconomic, and language characteristics of the students and families served by the district?
   b. What issues were discussed?
   c. How were decisions made?
   d. Who will be affected by the decision?
2. Visit a private school. Interview the principal, a teacher, and a parent.
   a. What is the educational philosophy of the school?
   b. Why do parents choose to send their children to this school?
   c. What are the racial, cultural, socioeconomic, and language characteristics of the students and families served by the school?
3. If you were to organize a cooperative school for fourth through sixth graders, what would you and the parents need to consider?
   a. How would decisions be made?
   b. What resources would you need?

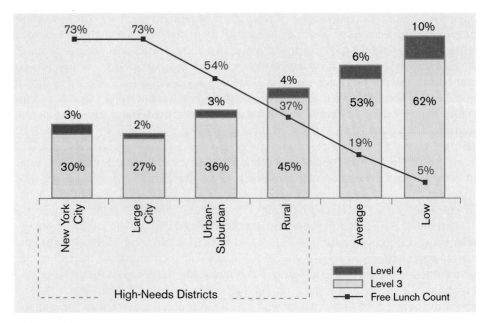

Figure 3-12

Student poverty and achievement on the grade four language arts exam.
(From New York State Department of Education, 2000)

    c. What rules would you have?

    d. In the event of a crisis, who would be responsible?

4. Interview three elderly people of different racial or cultural groups.

    a. Ask them to describe their school experience.

    b. Did they ever experience any limits to their education as a result of their race or culture?

    c. How do they think education in the United States today is different from when they attended school?

5. Examine Figure 3-12.

    a. How is student achievement in the grade four language arts exam correlated to student poverty?

    b. What systems affect student achievement?

Internet Quest

1. Find and compare three sites that have the keyword multicultural education.

2. Search for sites that link the words poverty and education. Locate two reports and analyze the impact that poverty has on a child's education.

3. Tour the ERIC database maintained by the U.S. Department of Education. Make a list of the topical areas that you can access in that database.

Reflective Journal

This is what I learned about the history of education systems in the United States . . . It will affect what I do as a teacher in the following way . . .

REFERENCES

Albertalli, P. (1990). *Nanna's story*. Unpublished manuscript.

Archembault, R. D. (Ed.). (1964). *John Dewey on education—selected writings* (p. 430). New York: Random House.

Bah-Diallo, A. (1997). *Basic education in Africa*. United Nations Educational, Scientific and Cultural Organization. Retrieved February 28, 2001, from the World Wide Web: <http://www.jica.go.jp/e-info/e-subsahara/mbp001.html>.

Bailiwick. (2000). *Overview of title IX*. Retrieved January 2000, from the World Wide Web: <http://www.bailiwick.lib.uiowa.edu>.

Banks, J. (1999). *An introduction to multicultural education*. Boston: Allyn and Bacon.

Borrowman, M. L. (1965). *Teacher education in America: A documentary history*. New York: Teachers College Press.

Brinker, K. (1999). *Genius shall not pine unrewarded*. Retrieved October 19, 1999, from the World Wide Web: <http://www.georgetown.edu/centers/cepacs/education.html>.

Casper, L. M. (1995). What does it cost to mind our preschoolers? *Current Population Reports* (U.S. Bureau of the Census Publication No. 70–52). Washington, DC: U.S. Government Printing Office.

Center for Educational Reform. (2000). *Making schools work better for all children*. Washington, DC: Author.

Children's Defense Fund. (1999). *The state of America's children yearbook*. Washington, DC: Author.

Copple, C. (1991). *Quality matters: Improving the professional development of the early childhood workforce*. Washington, DC: National Association for the Education of Young Children.

Cost, Quality, and Child Outcomes (CQCO) Study Team. (1995). *Cost, quality and child outcomes in child care centers, technical report*. Denver, CO: University of Colorado.

Cromwell, S. (1997). *A recent U.S. Department of Education report looks at differences and similarities of public and private schools*. Retrieved February 28, 2001, from the World Wide Web: <http://www.education-world.com/a-admin/admin035.shtml>.

Delpit, L. (1995). *Other people's children: Cultural conflict in the classroom*. New York: The New Press.

Educate America Act, Goals 2000. (1994). PL 103–227.

Education for All Handicapped Children Act. (1975). PL 94–142.

Fowler, W. M. (1997). *Samuel Adams, radical puritan*. New York: Addison Wesley Longman.

Hodgkinson, H. (1992). *The current condition of Native Americans*. Charleston, WV: ERIC Clearing on Rural Education and Small Schools. Retrieved February 28, 2001, from the World Wide Web: <http://www.ael.org/eric/nextbib.htm>.

Leschi. (2000). *Chief Leschi school*. Retrieved February 28, 2001, from the World Wide Web: <http://www.leschi.bia.edu>.

Martin, J., Roberts, R., Mintz, S., McMurry, L., Jones, J., & Haynes, S. (1995). *America and its peoples: Volume one to 1877*. New York: HarperCollins College Publishers.

Mitchell, A., Stoney, L., & Dichter, H. (1997). *Financing child care in the United States: An illustrative catalog of current strategies*. Kansas City, MO: Ewing Marion Kauffman Foundation.

National Center for Educational Statistics. (1997). *Public and private schools: How do they differ?* Retrieved February 28, 2001, from the World Wide Web: <http://www.nces.ed.gov/pubsearch/search.asp>.

New York State Department of Education. (2000). *2000–2001 budget priorities*. Albany, NY: Author.

Newman, R. M. (1998). *A history of formal education*. Retrieved February 28, 2001, from the World Wide Web: <http://www.shianet.org/~reneenew/HUM501.html>.

Retschitzki, J. (1989). Evidence of formal thinking in Baoule airele players. In D. M. Keats, D. Munro, & L. Mann (Eds.), *Heterogeneity in cross-cultural psychology*. Amsterdam, Netherlands: Swets & Zeitlinger.

Rowland, F. C. (1996). *Identifying scholars on the tribal community*. Paper presented to Native Research and Scholarship Project, Orcas Island, WA.

Schulman, K., & Adams, G. (1998). *Issue brief: The high cost of child care puts quality care out of reach for many families*. Washington, DC: Children's Defense Fund.

Stoney, L., & Greenberg, M. (1996). The financing of child care: Current and emerging trends. (Special issue on financing child care.) *The Future of Children*, 6(2), 83–102.

Styron, E. H. (1997). *Native American education; Documents from the 19th century.* Special Collections Library, Duke University. Retrieved January 10, 2001, from the World Wide Web: <http://www.duke.edu/~ehs1/education>.

For additional learning and teaching resources, visit our Web site at www.EarlyChildEd.delmar.com.

RELATED CAREERS

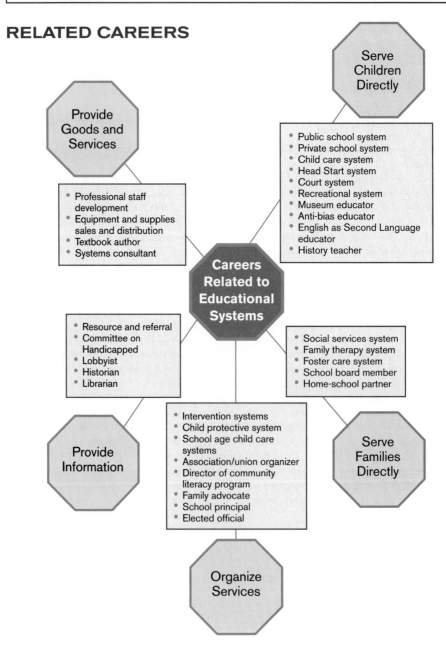

Figure 3–13

Careers related to educational systems.

The Learning Teacher and the Classroom Environment

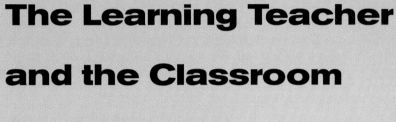

Objectives

After reading this chapter and completing the review activities, the learning teacher should be able to:

1. Explain the environment's impact on learning.
2. Identify potential safety hazards in the building, classroom, and outdoor environment.
3. Modify environments to provide a safe learning environment.

SCENARIO Tobias has just been hired and the administrator takes him to his assigned classroom. Tobias looks at it and says, "Is this all there is?" The administrator says, "Well, we do have a general supply room with other pieces of furniture and things, but it's rather sparse, because the other teachers have already made their choices. We operate on a small budget. You can ask for more, but I can't promise anything." Tobias begins to think of how he can furnish his classroom like he did his apartment. He made furniture, scouted secondhand stores, and made use of donations. He begins his quest.

You can furnish and decorate a classroom the same way you would furnish and decorate your bedroom or a whole house. Your first consideration is the space that defines the room in terms of fixed dimensions of width, length, and height. Then, there are those physical attributes like doors and windows that must be accounted for when thinking of furniture arrangements or bulletin boards. Lastly, lighting and temperature controls provide comfort and ambiance for the activities occurring in the room. The entryway gives the first impression of what is inside. Identifying who this place belongs to is done with name plates or signs. Classrooms with signs, posters, and symbols of the people who are learning and growing within make a good first impression (Figure 4–1.)

Then, there are categories of *things* that go into the room. Furniture is defined as those large standard pieces that perform a function and may or may not be movable; they are the constant around which other smaller pieces and accessories are arranged. Smaller pieces can be moved around to perform various functions and give variety to the room arrangement. Supplies are used up and must be replaced periodically. Scattered around the room are the memorabilia and objects selected by its inhabitants that give evidence of their interests, hobbies, culture, and values. Soft places invite resting, relaxing, reflecting, and dreaming. Storage places hold treasures and additional items to be used later, or cast-off things that indicate a change in inter-

Figure 4–1

An inviting entryway gives promise of more good things inside.

ests. The room's arrangement and its contents change over time depending on the needs and the changing life stages of the people using the room. "An environment is a living, changing system. More than the physical space, it includes the way time is structured and the roles we are expected to play. It conditions how we feel, think and behave; and it dramatically affects the quality of our lives" (Greenman, 1988, p. 5).

No matter what the room or classroom, these basic principles of arrangement and content are the same. "Knowledge of the relationships between physical surroundings and actions is a practical tool the teacher can use for many purposes" (Loughlin & Suina, 1982, p. 5). The environment is called the **third teacher**, with the family being the first teacher and the classroom teacher the second. The classroom environment acts as a teacher that redirects behavior by way of furniture placement, and by having interesting spaces that beckon and attract. The environment manages materials by arranging them attractively, organizing them with convenient storage, and incorporating a variety of colors, shapes, textures, and purposes. The environments we inhabit are "contributors to our experience," adding to pleasant memories or contributing to unpleasant ones. This chapter will explore the classroom environment, with its furniture, materials, and supplies, and show how environment differs by program type. Teaching philosophy and, inevitably, budgets, will also be addressed, as well as the influence on those factors by the teacher and the children.

✳ UNDERSTANDING THE CLASSROOM ENVIRONMENT AND ITS EFFECT ON LEARNING

SCENARIO

You walk into a restaurant and the smiling greeter says, "Welcome to Guiseppe's. How many in your party? Smoking or nonsmoking? Would you like a window table or one on the patio? Right this way, please." You are led through a room with subdued lighting and soft music, full of people in quiet conversation, to a table covered with a crisp tablecloth, glowing candle, and fresh flowers. The greeter says, "I hope you enjoy your dinner. May I bring you something to drink?"

What message has that environment conveyed to you about Guiseppe's? Do you think you will enjoy your time there? How can that same atmosphere be translated into a classroom?

SCENARIO

You are greeted at the door by Mr. Blackhawk. He smiles as he calls you by name and says, "Good morning. I can't wait for you to see what we have to do today. You'll want to go over to the Learning Station right away and see what is there. Your friends have already started and have a place for you to join them." You cross the classroom, which smells of balsam boughs the teacher has placed in a large jar. You pass by the

continued

continued

✳ **third teacher**—The environment as a primary influence on behavior and learning.

work you did yesterday, which is mounted on colored paper along with all the other students' work. Each is inscribed with their names—Jeremiah, Rasheem, Caroline, Kyle—and they are captioned, "Works of Distinction." As you drop off your coat in your labeled spot, you find a pebble placed on a piece of paper that says, "Take me to the Learning Station." You navigate across the room around tables and desks arranged in various configurations. You find your classmates with their pebbles, examining each one and matching them to a chart with the names of various types of rocks. "Oh, we needed that one. We turned off the lights so we could see the sparkly ones. Yours fits right here. Mr. Blackhawk says that as soon as our research is done, we can turn this into a project for the science fair."

Components of the Environment

Mr. Blackhawk's classroom environment is welcoming physically, socially, emotionally, cognitively, aesthetically, and culturally. Let's examine some of the factors that made it so (Figure 4–2).

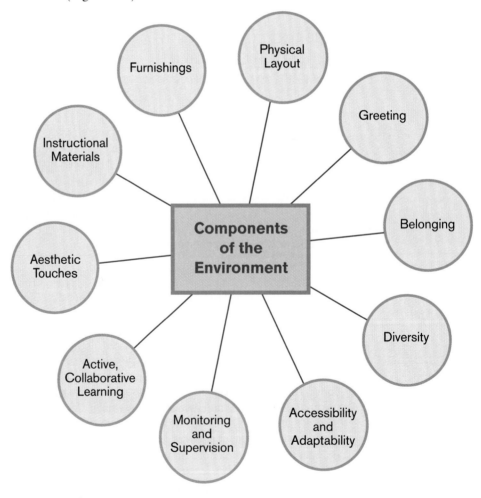

Figure 4–2

Components of the environment.

Greeting. The environment, no matter how meager or grand the budget, is not as important as the welcoming atmosphere of acceptance and friendliness. It is the teacher who sets that mood overtly in greetings and interactions, and subtly through body language and enthusiasm. The first sights and sounds as a child arrives set a tone. The teacher plans the entry to the classroom in a way that is pleasing to the eye, with a feeling of safety and belonging. When the students have places for their belongings, a greeting ritual, and an arrival routine that helps them make the transition as they arrive, the climate is conducive to learning.

WORDS OF WISDOM Jim Sullivan writes, "I remember my first director job in Miami. I put up a sign on my office door that said, 'WELCOME, BIENVENIDOS,'' and a woman who had been working in the center for over 12 years came up to me, almost in tears, and told me how much it meant to her to see her language (Spanish) in the school. (This was the first time ever!) It is important for people (parents, children, and teachers) to see themselves and their lives reflected in the classrooms. Photos of families work wonders!"

Belonging. Everyone wants to feel a part of the group and the teacher can help make that happen by reducing competition and promoting cooperation and collaboration (see Figure 4–2). By displaying all children's work and giving it respect in the way it is presented, the teacher says that each one is valued. The teacher plans for each child to make a contribution to a joint project, requiring participation.

Diversity. The sense of belonging extends to *each* individual, as a member not only of the class, but also of the global community. The teacher assures that the environment is culturally diverse, whether or not the students are. There are artifacts of various cultures and pictures on the wall that depict people of every race, as well as abilities, not dressed in "native" costumes or being helped, but performing everyday tasks common to all people. Thus, each child who enters the classroom will find a familiar face, sound, or sight, and in this way each child will come to accept those who are different from him. The teacher leads in this acceptance through the environment, as well as in his words and actions.

Physical Layout. The arrangement of the furniture in the room demonstrates the teacher's philosophy of education by collaboration. Straight rows of desks may indicate a philosophy of structure and looking to the teacher as the source of knowledge, whereas tables and circles symbolize a community of learners, with the teacher as a facilitator or guide. Learning centers throughout the classroom confirm the teacher's belief in the active, individual, and small-group learning approaches.

Furnishings. The room includes desks for students and teacher, or tables and chairs that comfortably fit the user. When seated, feet should touch the floor, with legs bent at right angles. Areas related to instruction are also part of the furnishings, such as cabinets, bookcases, and storage units. Items not in use should be stored away both for preservation and to keep the appearance of the room neat and not visually overstimulating.

Instructional Materials. These are materials or objects necessary for instruction, such as chalkboards, televisions, overhead projectors, computers, books, paper, and writing implements. These teacher aids should be in good repair and used for variety in lesson presentation and demonstrations. With more and more classrooms equipped with computers, many with Internet linkage, the resources and opportunities for learning are limitless. Books, such as textbooks, reference books, and books for leisure reading, including periodicals, should be current, plentiful, and accessible as needed. By providing many kinds of paper and a variety of writing tools, the teacher stimulates writing and drawing. Community sources for donation of these materials can be explored, such as printing businesses for cut scraps or promotional materials no longer needed.

Aesthetic Touches. The teacher plans not just the physical environment, but the sensual one as well. By heightening every sense, even that of smell, the teacher is using the whole brain approach. The sight, touch, and smell of balsam branches or other natural materials link learning with pleasant memories. A room that is alive with color, and has interest-catching displays, objects, and activity areas, indicate that the people who use it are afforded a multitude of possibilities. "Aesthetics is a worthy but often unconsidered goal when designing a visual environment. . . . Children are more likely to grow up with an eye for beauty if the adults around them demonstrate that they value aesthetics" (Gonzalez-Mena & Eyer, 1997, p. 94).

Active, Collaborative Learning. The teacher has provided materials and a structure for discovery. One-dimensional learning from the printed page about the attributes of various types of rock formations can in no way compare to the hands–on experience of actually manipulating the rocks, analyzing them, comparing them to each other, classifying them into categories, and explaining their attributes to others. That use of the scientific method engages learners in lifelong lessons, not just about these rocks, but about how to investigate and find answers to questions not yet asked. Collaborating with others affirms knowledge and shares and magnifies the lessons learned, both cognitive and social (Figure 4–3). The teacher has taught a lesson more important

Figure 4–3

Active involvement in project work make children excited about learning.

than transferring data; he has transferred a thirst for learning. Kolbe, Shepherd, and Eaton (1994, p. 11) call this making "ordinary things look extraordinary."

Monitoring and Supervision. Active, child-centered learning does not mean that the teacher is merely a spectator. The teacher has provided both support, so the learning results in positive outcomes, and supervision to assure the children's safety. The teacher will intervene if children start hurling pebbles across the room or tasting the pebbles in the course of their investigation. The teacher's most fundamental responsibility is the children's physical safety. If insults are hurled rather than pebbles, the teacher will also intervene with strategies, not to suppress and stifle, but to mediate and assist in peaceful problem-solving that not only addresses this situation, but can be generalized to other, similar situations. The mentoring and supervision extends beyond simple behavior control to observing, reflecting on, and discussing how the children are interacting with one another and the concepts of the desired learning outcomes.

Accessibility and Adaptability. By law and by conscience, the classroom must be accessible to persons with handicapping conditions that may include physical, visual, aural, or learning impairments. The teacher assesses the classroom's suitability for the children's abilities and makes any necessary adaptations to the environment so each child can find maximum success as independently as possible. This is part of the *least restrictive environment*.

Environment and Learning

Much attention has been given to early childhood environments but less to primary and elementary classrooms. Some studies on the effects of environment on learning have resulted in the following guidelines that can help teachers plan the classroom environment.

- ✳ Student performance is not hindered by noise coming from group work in the classroom (Arends, 1994).
- ✳ Snacking assists learning. Reading speed and accuracy increase when students are allowed to have water and snacks (MacMurren, 1985).
- ✳ The teacher's desk does not need to be the focus of the room. Teachers who have less need for control and give children more autonomy place their desks away from the front of the room (Arends, 1994).
- ✳ Colors affect mood, emotional states, psychomotor performance, muscular activity, breathing and pulse rates, and blood pressure (Hathaway, 1993).
- ✳ Blue and green foster relaxation, while red and orange in instructional areas induce anxiety (Weinstein, 1981).
- ✳ Calm, relaxed environments promote learning. Psychologically or emotionally negative environments inhibit learning (Midjaas, 1984).
- ✳ Attractive additions to school décor, such as posters, plants, and flowers, and showcases where students' work was displayed were common elements in successful schools (Rutter, Maughan, Mortimore, & Ouston, 1979).

In a two-year study (1995–97) that included classroom observations, as well as interviews with and surveys of hundreds of teachers, students, and parents, Foster-Harrison and Adams-Bullock (1998) conducted research on classroom environments for grades four though twelve. The results yielded what these groups believed to be most important in the classroom.

* Teachers—Computers, television, class libraries, use of color on walls, and flat-top student desks. They also listed individual climate control, phones, and names on the door, which add to the professional environment.

* Students—Comfortable reading furniture and student desks, cleanliness, color, carpeting, and decorative additions. Students also wanted teachers to have access to phones and their names on the doors.

* Parents—Computers, learning centers, student work on walls, television, comfortable reading furniture, use of color on the walls, and decorative plants and accessories. Parents believed the environment affected academic performance and behavior.

Comfort, cleanliness, and aesthetics are all important to the learning environment. While teachers may not have control over the size of the room, its care, furnishings, and arrangement can enhance or diminish student performance (Figure 4–4). The environment can also be the cause or the remedy for problem behavior in the classroom. Dodge and Colker (1995) present the process of identifying the problem behavior, its possible environmental causes and making some changes to the environment rather than trying to rely on children's self-control. They suggest, for example, if running in the classroom is a problem then the cause may be too much open space and a remedy to the environment might be to rearrange the furniture to divide the space so wide-open space and long aisles in the classroom are eliminated. It is much easier to rearrange furniture than to constantly be monitoring and trying to control undesirable and perhaps unsafe actions.

Figure 4—4

A pleasant décor is a common element in successful schools.

The Aesthetic Environment

One of the pioneer proponents of the importance of aesthetics in the environment was **Maria Montessori**. She emphasized those materials and environments needed for children to perform the work of learning; teachers who espouse this philosophy give great attention to the environment. Montessori proponents ensure that classroom furnishings are child-sized and that all activities in which the children take part can be done without adult assistance. The classroom is organized into centers, with individual work space for each child defined by rugs or mats. Children's interaction with materials are called *work tasks* (Montessori, 1965).

The classroom is influenced by the Montessori ideology of beauty, one she developed when working with poor children in the slums of Rome. Materials are made of wood and other natural materials attractive to the eye and to the touch, emphasizing the importance of sensory integration with learning (Lillard, 1996; Standing, 1962). Each piece of equipment is designed to teach a specific concept in a sequenced order of challenge. The materials are self-correcting, needing no adult consultation about the right or wrong choices the materials may invite. The teacher's primary roles (Roopnarine & Johnson, 1993) are to prepare the classroom environment so the children can work with the materials, and to assist, but not lead, all the while respecting each child's individuality. Montessori's emphasis on individual work tasks and structured lessons have been adopted by a few early childhood programs, but the de-emphasis on social interaction has placed her philosophy in conflict with other philosophies. However, the principle of an environment with well-organized sensory materials is one that all learning settings could adopt.

Maria Montessori

(1870–1952) Italian physician whose interests included children institutionalized for mental retardation. She opened Casa di Bambini (Children's House) in 1907 in the slums of Rome, where she cared for children during the day, emphasizing health, cleanliness, and sensory training in an environment of beauty and order.

Reggio Emilia Schools and the Environment. Environment means the external conditions and influences affecting the living organism. The word *habitat* comes to mind. One of the most celebrated systems of preschools in the world today is found in Reggio Emilia, Italy. The environments, the children's work, and the teachers' philosophy have been praised around the world. The founder of the Reggio Emilia preschools, Loris Malaguzzi (1984) said, "We also think that the space has to be a sort of aquarium that mirrors the ideas, values, attitudes and cultures of the people who live within it". That philosophy is apparent to any visitor to these neighborhood schools. Barbara recalls her visit there.

WORDS OF WISDOM
"On my visit in 1996, I was enthralled with the inviting entryway of each of the schools we visited. The entryways resembled foyers of comfortable homes, with soft furniture in small groupings, art and decorations on the walls, and a large antique armoire or ornate desk as a focal point. Many of the schools had formerly been neighborhood homes that had been renovated with lifted ceilings, opened walls between rooms to large arches, glass partitions that created a feeling of vast space, and light flooding in everywhere at changing angles throughout the day. There were interesting, real things—not toy replicas—to handle and work with in each room. It might be a real bass drum, a telescope aimed at the sky, or a real balance scale to weigh various kinds of grains, pasta, and beans. Mirrors reflected and amplified the light and objects, as well as the movements of the inhabitants, creating a moving mural. The furnishings were made of natural materials softened by a patina of use and care. Even the sleeping places for toddlers were intriguing: large baskets with openings

continued

through which they could come and go at will. Many rooms had a little space into which one, two, or three children could retreat and observe the action, think, read, or even nap. Each *atelier* (art studio) was supplied with real art supplies not ordinarily seen in young children's classrooms, like oil paints and canvases, overhead projectors and shadow screens, real clay and a kiln, photography equipment, and more. The contents of the atelier reflected the *atelierista's* (studio teacher's) area of expertise, such as water wheels, clay, masks, or photography, as well as the projects the children were working on. The outside spaces were also beautifully planned, with large overhanging shade trees, grassy areas interspersed with brick-paved areas, flowers, shrubs, fountains and small water pools, natural paths, and trees to climb. The aquarium or habitat that Reggio models reflects the philosophy of the child being capable and respected" (see Figure 4–5).

Environments for ALL Children

What does it feel like to be in one room for a whole day, day after day? When planning an environment for such a space, it is important to consider the people who will be there, their basic, as well as changing, needs, and the functions that will be performed there. In schools, the environment is supposed to be planned with children in mind. The building, the hallways, and the rooms are arranged to provide spaces for children. The furniture and equipment are proportioned for both the children and the adults in the room, and grouped to fill the needs of the activities going on there. Playing and working, eating and eliminating, moving and being still, being together and being alone are all issues to address in the planned environment.

Figure 4–5

In the schools of Reggio Emilia, Italy, the classroom and the outside yard are considered the child's *habitat*.

Two educational philosophers have emphasized the importance of the teacher's role in planning the environment. John Dewey (1966) wrote, "We never educate directly but indirectly by means of the environment. Whether we permit chance environments to do the work, or whether we design environments for the purpose makes a great deal of difference. And any environment is a chance environment so far as its educative influence is concerned unless it has been deliberately regulated with reference to its educative effect" (p. 19). John Goodlad, author of *A Place Called School,* said in an interview, "The role of the teacher today? No different than it has always been—to provide for every child the richest kind of environment where the youngster can develop as a responsible human being. All the teacher can do is to create an environment" (Stone, 1999, p. 265). Environment is the total experience: physical, emotional, cognitive, and social. The teacher is responsible for planning all domains of the child's school experience.

All children should be considered when environment planning. The Americans with Disabilities Act passed in 1990 mandates that all public buildings be accessible to people with physical disabilities (Figure 4–6). This means that every school should accommodate a child in a wheelchair or with a walker. The school administration and teachers are responsible for any modifications to the building and to the room to be sure the child can function in as many activities as any other child; again, this is known as the least restrictive environment. Materials and supplies should be on accessible shelves. There need to be a variety of work space heights and attention must be paid to aural and visual stimuli. Does the classroom have extraneous noise that makes it difficult for a child who has hearing impairments or is easily distractible? Is the classroom too visually stimulating with colors, shapes, and moving objects? Perhaps sound-absorbing materials need to be added, or some spaces that restrict or reduce visual stimuli.

Many factors go into the decision of whether an aide may assist a child with special needs. The teacher's role is to protect the child's safety, just as with all the other children, and at the same time to not overcompensate by not allowing the child to try

Figure 4–6

All children's needs must be considered in planning the classroom environment.

the activities the other children are doing. Expectations of the child in those areas not affected by a disability should not be lower; instead, materials and activities should be open-ended for a range of abilities, interests and levels, to increase the likelihood that every child can find success.

Children's home lives should be represented respectfully in the classroom in materials and activities that are relevant and sensitive to their differences. However, the teacher should take care that, while he is ensuring an environment that portrays diversity, he does not unnecessarily single out or highlight any one theme. Varied and inclusive representation can take the form of:

* pictures of people from all races, nationalities, and abilities represented as they are today.
* literacy materials and music that reflect children's cultures and accommodate handicapping conditions.
* activities and books that are screened for underlying bias and incorrect portrayals of all people.
* recognition that family constellations often vary from the "typical" mother/father/child type.

Teachers must be attentive to meeting the needs of children with learning disabilities by making accommodations for their different ways of learning. Some directions may need to be tape-recorded in addition to being written. Some children may need more time for activities and testing, or a clear indication of coming transitions. Some provisions may need to be made in the room arrangement to reduce distractions such as outside noise or activities or visually stimulating room accessories. There should be a space where children who prefer to work alone can do so without being ostracized. This is not a time-out area, but rather a private space to which a child can choose to go to work quietly, observe the rest of the class, or just relax.

Planning for the environment involves much more than arranging a room. It reflects the teacher's objectives, but should also be influenced by the children who learn there. As with every other teacher role, this planning is complex and interwoven with intangible factors other than counting desks and chairs.

✳ SAFE ENVIRONMENTS

The teacher's primary task is to keep children safe while they are in the school environment. Local, state, and national standards, along with inspections by the fire department and the department of health, regulate the physical safety features of child care centers and classrooms in public and private school buildings; however, day-to-day individual classroom safety is the teacher's responsibility. There are three main risk factors in childhood injuries (Robertson, 1998, p. 166).

* Environments—Including objects, hazardous materials, unsafe equipment, lack of safety devices
* Behavior—Child: developmental level, lack of knowledge, high stress, lack of self control; adult: inattention, lack of knowledge, high stress, lack of self control
* Conditions—Location hazards such as water, electricity, heights, obstacles, machinery

Planning for the environment, then, is not only a way to create effective and inviting learning and interaction, it is also to ensure the children's and teacher's safety. All classroom furnishings, equipment, materials, and supplies should be selected with care. Marotz, Cross, and Rush (2001) have outlined a few important guidelines.

1. Carefully consider children's ages, interests, and developmental abilities; check manufacturer's label for recommendations.

2. Choose fabric items that are washable and labeled flame-retardant or nonflammable.

3. Look for quality construction; check for durability, good design, stability, absence of sharp corners or wires.

4. Select toys and equipment made from nontoxic, lead-free materials.

5. For children under age three, avoid toys and play materials that have small pieces.

6. Select toys and equipment appropriate for the amount of available play and storage space.

7. For younger children, avoid toys with electrical parts, as well as toys propelled through the air with force.

8. Choose play materials that children can use with minimal adult supervision.

9. Supervise children at all times, being cognizant of potentially dangerous materials, equipment, or activities.

Children must be physically safe before they can concentrate on learning and developing. Children's safety is perhaps something the learning teacher has not considered as the role of teacher. Accidents *do* happen, despite the most meticulous precautions. Knowledge of and certification in basic first aid and cardiac pulmonary resuscitation (CPR) may be teacher requirements (check with your state and school's or program's regulations). When an accident occurs, first aid should be administered and a judgment made regarding further treatment or assistance from a health professional (Figure 4–7 on page 122).

Child care programs and schools should have written policies concerning accidental exposure to potentially infectious body secretions and provide training in **universal precautions** to safeguard against such an accident. This includes wearing disposable latex gloves whenever there is a possibility of contacting blood, vomit, urine, feces, nasal secretions, or saliva. Infectious materials, such as contaminated clothing and diapers, must be isolated in labeled plastic bags and handled with care. The increasing incidence of blood-borne pathogens such as hepatitis and HIV make this critically important for teachers and caregivers. Every child care program and school should have an accident report form (see sample in Figure 4–8 on page 123) and a standard policy for its use.

Hazard Awareness and Emergency Procedures

WORDS OF WISDOM
Barbara relates: "I was at the zoo watching a mother orangutan supervise her very tiny baby as it climbed higher and higher on the wire fencing. The mother held out her hand just under the baby, without touching it, letting it wobble higher and higher, eventually out of her reach. That visual image has remained with me for years as an example of allowing, yet minimizing, risk. The teacher's first responsibility is the safety of the children, whether it is protecting crawling infants, climbing toddlers, swinging preschoolers, racing elementary children, or experimenting

continued on page 124

universal precautions–Special measures taken when handling bodily fluids, including careful hand washing, wearing latex gloves, disinfecting surfaces, and properly disposing of contaminated objects.

Emergency breathing techniques for the infant and child.

If vomitus or foreign objects are visible, use the tongue-jaw lift to open the mouth. Then use a finger to quickly check for the object. Remove if visible.

Position child on his back. Gently tilt the head up and back by placing one hand on the child's forehead and the fingers of the other hand under the jawbone. Lift upwards (head tilt/chin lift). **Look** for the chest to rise/fall. **Listen** for breathing. **Feel** for breath on your cheek.

For an infant, place your mouth over the infant's nose and mouth creating a tight seal. Slowly and gently, give two small puffs of air (one to one and one-half seconds), pausing between breaths. Check (look/listen) for breathing at the rate of one breath every three seconds. If air does not go in, reposition and try to breathe again.

For a child one to eight years, place your mouth over the child's mouth forming a tight seal. Gently pinch the child's nostrils closed. Quickly give two small breaths of air (one to one and one-half seconds per breath). Continue breathing for the child at a rate of one breath every three seconds. If air does not go in, reposition and try to breathe again.

Lift your head and turn it to the side after each breath. This allows time for air to escape from the child's lungs and also gives you time to take a breath and observe if the child is breathing.

Figure 4—7

First aid must be administered when an accident occurs. (From Marotz, Cross, & Rush, 2001)

INCIDENT REPORT FORM

Fill in all blanks and boxes that apply.

Name of Program:_____ Telephone No.: _____

Address of Facility:_____

Child's Name:_____ Sex: M F   Birthdate: __/__/__   Incident Date: __/__/__

Time of Incident: ___:___AM/PM   Witnesses: _____

Parent(s) Notified By: _____ Time Notified: ___:___AM/PM

Location where incident occurred: ☐ playground ☐ classroom ☐ bathroom ☐ hall
  ☐ kitchen   ☐ doorway   ☐ large muscle room or gym   ☐ office ☐ dining room
  ☐ stairway   ☐ unknown   ☐ other (specify): _____

Equipment/product involved: ☐ climber   ☐ slide   ☐ swing   ☐ playground surface
  ☐ sandbox   ☐ trike/bike   hand toy (specify): _____
  ☐ other equipment (specify): _____

Cause of injury (describe): _____
  ☐ fall to surface; estimated height of fall _____ feet; type of surface: _____
  _____
  ☐ fall from running or tripping   ☐ bitten by child   ☐ motor vehicle   ☐ hit or pushed by child
  ☐ injured by object   ☐ eating or choking   ☐ insect sting/bite   ☐ animal bite
  ☐ injury from exposure to cold   ☐ other (specify): _____
  _____

Parts of body injured: ☐ eye   ☐ ear   ☐ nose   ☐ mouth   ☐ tooth   ☐ other part of face
  ☐ other part of head   ☐ neck   ☐ arm/wrist/hand   ☐ leg/ankle/foot   ☐ trunk
  ☐ other (specify): _____

Type of injury: ☐ cut   ☐ bruise or swelling   ☐ puncture   ☐ scrape   ☐ broken bone
  or dislocation   ☐ sprain   ☐ crushing injury   ☐ burn   ☐ loss of consciousness
  ☐ unknown   ☐ other (specify): _____

First aid given at the facility: (e.g., pressure, evaluation, cold pack, washing, bandage): _____
  _____

Treatment provided by: _____
  ☐ no doctor's or dentist's treatment required
  ☐ treatment as an outpatient (e.g., office or emergency room)
  ☐ hospitalized (overnight) no. of days: _____

Number of days of limited activity from this incident: _____ Follow-up plan for care of the
child: _____

Corrective action needed to prevent recurrence: _____

Name of official/agency notified: _____ Date: _____

Signature of staff member: _____ Date: _____

Signature of parent: _____ Date: _____

(Courtesy of Pennsylvania Chapter, American Academy of Pediatrics)

Figure 4–8

Sample accident form. (Courtesy of Pennsylvania Chapter, American Academy of Pediatrics)

early adolescents. When a child is learning and exploring, anticipating potential hazards and the possibility of injury is weighed against perceiving the child's developmental stage and the relative need for that exploration."

Unintentional injuries, primarily from motor vehicle accidents, are the leading cause of death among children aged one through fourteen (Figure 4–9). This indicates the vulnerability of children in cars, so families and schools need to take precautions to always use seat restraints for all children. Burns, drowning, and suffocation follow for ages one to nine, with firearms coming third after traffic accidents and drowning for the ten to fourteen age group. The next highest incidence categories can be prevented by adult supervision. There should be barriers to hazardous places, and restriction of access to dangerous substances that could burn, suffocate, or result in a fatality. The classroom and school can be perilous places if the teacher is not exercising awareness, caution, and prevention.

A profile of risk for accidental injuries shows that the following characteristics or factors make a child a higher risk: boys; children in single-parent or low-income families; children who live in crowded neighborhoods; and children who are aggressive, highly active, or antisocial (Bussing, Menvielle, & Zima, 1996; Christoffel, Donovan, Schofer, Wills, & Lavigne, 1996; Starfield, 1991). A sobering statistic for this age group is that African American boys have the highest death rates, primarily because of higher rates of accidents and homicide (Singh & Yu, 1996).

Building Safety

The younger the child, the more potential dangers there are, and thus the greater the vigilance required of the adult. Adults who set limits and define rules of conduct also contribute to a safe environment.

SCENARIO Catherine is a prekindergarten teacher assistant. She heard the teacher discuss with the children what to do if a loud bell rang. It would be a "fire drill" and the children were to line up and exit the building through certain doors as quickly as they could. The third week of school, the alarm went off. As they hurried the children into the hall, one of the children began to cry, and then another, and the crying spread among all the prekindergarten and kindergarten children, who were screaming and crying, "We don't want the school to burn down." What went wrong, Catherine wonders?

Planning a safe environment begins with the building itself. Schools, child care centers, and regulated family child care businesses are subject to local health, safety, and fire codes, as well as specialized regulations. Inspections are conducted at regular intervals, but a safe environment is a moment-by-moment task. The location of the building contributes to its relative safety or jeopardy. Consideration should be given to traffic, air pollution, and excessive noise to minimize dangers from those factors. Building materials that are free of hazardous contaminants, low windows, doors installed with safety glass, and good lighting are all essential elements of a safe building.

10 Leading Causes of Death, United States 1998, All Races, Both Sexes

Age Groups

Rank	<1	1-4	5-9	10-14	15-24	25-34	35-44	45-54	55-64	65+	Total
1	Congenital Anomalies 6,212	Unintentional Injury and Adv. Effects 1,935	Unintentional Injury and Adv. Effects 1,544	Unintentional Injury and Adv. Effects 1,710	Unintentional Injury and Adv. Effects 13,349	Unintentional Injury and Adv. Effects 12,045	Malignant Neoplasms 17,022	Malignant Neoplasms 45,747	Malignant Neoplasms 87,024	Heart Disease 605,673	Heart Disease 724,859
2	Short Gestation 4,101	Congenital Anomalies 564	Malignant Neoplasms 487	Malignant Neoplasms 526	Homicide & Legal Int. 5,506	Suicide 5,365	Unintentional Injury and Adv. Effects 15,127	Heart Disease 35,056	Heart Disease 65,068	Malignant Neoplasms 384,186	Malignant Neoplasms 541,532
3	SIDS 2,822	Homicide & Legal Int. 399	Congenital Anomalies 198	Suicide 317	Suicide 4,135	Homicide & Legal Int. 4,565	Heart Disease 13,593	Unintentional Injury and Adv. Effects 10,946	Bronchitis Emphysema Asthma 10,162	Cerebro-vascular 139,144	Cerebro-vascular 158,448
4	Maternal Complications 1,343	Malignant Neoplasms 365	Homicide & Legal Int. 170	Homicide & Legal Int. 290	Malignant Neoplasms 1,699	Malignant Neoplasms 4,385	Suicide 6,837	Liver Disease 5,744	Cerebro-vascular 9,653	Bronchitis Emphysema Asthma 97,896	Bronchitis Emphysema Asthma 112,584
5	Respiratory Distress Syndrome 1,295	Heart Disease 214	Heart Disease 156	Congenital Anomalies 173	Heart Disease 1,057	Heart Disease 3,207	HIV 5,746	Cerebro-vascular 5,709	Diabetes 8,705	Pneumonia & Influenza 82,989	Unintentional Injury and Adv. Effects 97,835
6	Placenta Cord Membranes 961	Pneumonia & Influenza 146	Pneumonia & Influenza 70	Heart Disease 170	Congenital Anomalies 450	HIV 2,912	Homicide & Legal Int. 3,567	Suicide 5,131	Unintentional Injury and Adv. Effects 7,340	Diabetes 48,974	Pneumonia & Influenza 91,871
7	Perinatal Infections 815	Septicemia 89	Bronchitis Emphysema Asthma 54	Bronchitis Emphysema Asthma 98	Bronchitis Emphysema Asthma 239	Cerebro-vascular 670	Liver Disease 3,370	Diabetes 4,386	Liver Disease 5,279	Unintentional Injury and Adv. Effects 32,975	Diabetes 64,751
8	Unintentional Injury and Adv. Effects 754	Perinatal Period 75	Benign Neoplasms 52	Pneumonia & Influenza 51	Pneumonia & Influenza 215	Diabetes 636	Cerebro-vascular 2,650	HIV 3,120	Pneumonia & Influenza 3,856	Nephritis 22,640	Suicide 30,575
9	Intrauterine Hypoxia 461	Cerebro-vascular 57	Cerebro-vascular 35	Cerebro-vascular 47	HIV 194	Pneumonia & Influenza 531	Diabetes 1,885	Bronchitis Emphysema Asthma 2,828	Suicide 2,963	Alzheimer's Disease 22,416	Nephritis 26,182
10	Pneumonia & Influenza 441	Benign Neoplasms 53	HIV 29	Benign Neoplasms 32	Cerebro-vascular 178	Liver Disease 506	Pneumonia & Influenza 1,400	Pneumonia & Influenza 2,167	Septicemia 2,093	Septicemia 19,012	Liver Disease 25,192

Data Source: National Vital Statistics System, NCHS, CDC

Figure 4–9

Leading causes of death by age. (Source: National Vital Statistics System, National Center for Injury Prevention and Control/Centers for Disease Control)

Fire exits should be checked regularly to ensure they are not blocked and regular building evacuations must be practiced. The word "drills" has a totally different meaning for children, so some other term like "practice evacuations" is suggested. How could Catherine and the rest of the staff have better prepared the children for this practice evacuation?

The teacher should receive training in evacuation procedures that include proper exit routes (Figure 4–10). Attention should be given to classroom routines, including room arrangement, so there are no impediments to rapid exit and no chance a child will be left behind. All staff should be informed as to what they should take with them from the room, such as daily attendance sheets, lists of emergency numbers, and protection from weather. School policy should specify a site away from the building for a long-term evacuation. Families should be informed of the off-site location should a long-term evacuation become necessary. Smoke and carbon monoxide detectors should be installed in every occupied space and in maintenance areas, as well as available and working fire extinguishers. A secure entry system is a necessity, with all doors locked, yet open from the inside.

Keeping Children Safe from Abuse

Protecting children from potentially dangerous people is also the responsibility of the teacher. The teacher protects the children by being meticulous about releasing the child only to authorized adults, and by being vigilant both inside and outside the building and on field trips. Within the classroom, the teacher also protects children from physical and psychological harm caused by other children. By preventing or intervening in cruel teasing, ridicule, and physical assault, and by applying classroom management techniques that deter and stop such actions, the teacher provides a psychologically safe environment.

The teacher provides a mentally healthy environment by recognizing the uniqueness, strengths, and needs of the whole child. And it should go without saying that the teacher refrains from using ridicule, which could put the child under psychological stress.

Unfortunately, child abuse affects as many as 500,000 children anually in the United States. School personnel and child care workers are **mandated reporters** by law in every state. People working with children are under penalty of civil action if they fail to report suspicions of abuse. This is the arm of protection that professionals extend around the child and his family. It is sometimes the only way the abuser can get help for the stress factors that contribute to such actions against a child and assistance in preventing further abuse.

Child abuse can take on several forms, each with specific symptoms.

* Physical abuse—Unexplained bruises, welts, burns, lacerations, abrasions, or fractures, human bite marks, child exhibiting behavioral extremes

* Neglect—Frequently hungry, inappropriately dressed for the weather, poor hygiene, left alone or inadequately supervised for long periods of time, needs medical or dental care, exposed to unsafe living conditions, truancy

* Sexual abuse—Difficulty walking or sitting; torn, stained, bloody undercloth-ing; pains or itching in the genital area; venereal disease; weight gain/loss; prob-lems with hygiene; sexually knowledgeable beyond expectations for his age

* Emotional neglect—Failure to thrive, neurotic traits, developmental lags, self-destructive behaviors

When child abuse is suspected, the teacher should take immediate action, fol-lowing the established procedures of the center or school. The reporter does not need to prove the abuse or determine who the abuser is. All that is needed is *reason to sus-pect*. It is important to get help for the child by documenting the event, if witnessed, or eliciting trustworthy disclosures from the child; it is then the teacher's obligation to transfer the responsibility of proof to trained professionals for observation and assessment. This is essential to protect the child. Every state has a child abuse hotline or law enforcement agency designated to receive the report.

The Indoor Environment

There are some general guidelines for creating indoor environments that help learn-ing occur. Recommended group size varies with the age of children: infants (8), tod-dlers (12), three-year-olds (14), four- to five-year-olds (20), six- to eight-year-olds (24) and nine- to twelve-year-olds (28) (National Association for the Education of Young Children, 1998, p. 47). There needs to be sufficient space: the minimum space requirements per accreditation standards (NAEYC) is 35 square feet of usable indoor floor space and 75 square feet outdoors. The space should be inviting to children, with furnishings proportioned to their bodies, so that when they sit in the chairs, their feet rest on the floor. The classroom space is divided into areas definable by function, with spaces for individual work, small groups, and large groups. There should be suf-ficient storage for those supplies and materials that are not in use, and open, labeled shelves readily accessible by the children for supplies in current use.

The room should be aesthetically pleasing, with a variety of colors and textures, both natural and artificial lighting, and materials that absorb sound to minimize excessive noise (Figure 4–11). The room should be cleaned regularly, with furnishings kept in good repair, and have a water supply nearby for drinking and for hand washing. Electrical outlets should be covered or have childproof safety caps, and cooking should be confined to a separate area with a fire barrier. The room should be arranged to promote visibility among areas in a way that allows for free movement that will not cut across, but rather around, learning domains like block-building, dramatic play, or book-reading areas. The classroom should reflect the children's cultural identities, as well as those of the global community, by accurately portraying families and the daily activities of real people. The classroom should provide separate storage space for each child's belongings that is labeled and readily accessible to the child. Abundant books and other literacy materials should be made readily available to the children, and there should be a sufficient supply of other materials to support learning objectives.

Bathrooms must have a toilet and sink for every 15 children. A bathroom in close proximity to the classroom is a practical consideration, with fixtures sized and outfitted for the children's developmental level. The bathroom should be cleaned and maintained often, and presented to the children as an extension of the classroom, with wall pictures and health and safety reminders, such as hand-washing posters.

The Outdoor Environment

While the teacher does not normally decide on the location of the child care center or school, hopefully the setting is inviting from the moment it comes into view. Many school buildings are intimidating institutional structures that portray a less-than-welcoming image. Their appearance may "act as barriers to the development of warm, trusting relationships, a sense of community, and feelings of ownership and belonging" (Shepherd & Eaton, 1997, p. 45). Signs, ground plantings, and window décor

Figure 4–11

This indoor environment has sufficient space, furnishings, and materials for learning to occur.

Figure 4–12

Children also enjoy a natural habitat.

can add a welcoming touch to even the most formidable building and teachers can have impact on making this happen.

Outdoor time is an important part of any school child's day and should be considered another part of the curriculum. The site and equipping of outdoor space is also usually beyond the teacher's control, but some modifications can be made to the area to make it more conducive to children's enjoyment of the outdoors. Moore (1998) calls this the *microclimate,* those places that protect children from climate extremes, providing sunny and shady spots, breezy and protected areas, and warmer and cooler spaces. They are places where the children can be protected from precipitation or move away from standing water, with surfaces that protect, yet provide a variety of textures and cushioning. Trees and plantings should provide shade and wind block; they contribute to the study of nature's seasonal changes (in climates where they occur), and furnish a habitat for birds, animals, and insects for the children's contemplation (Figure 4–12).

Play yards should be designed with as much attention as is given to interior spaces, to meet a full range of educational goals: not just for physical and recreational activities but also for social gathering, investigation of the natural environment, and fantasy. They should be adjacent to the indoor area for ease of transition and access to bathrooms and equipment and supplies. If the play yard is just outside the window of the classroom, it can be an extension of the indoor learning environment for studying plants, animals, and changes in weather conditions. Equipment should be arranged so that small groups of children can cluster in a social grouping area with the equipment as the shared experience, under adult supervision. Younger and older children should each have their own separate outdoor places: infants separated from toddlers, toddlers from preschoolers, preschoolers from primary age children, and primary age from elementary age children. Each of these age groupings has specific physical, social, intellectual, and supervisory needs.

✳ ENVIRONMENTS PLANNED FOR SAFETY AND LEARNING

Providing an environment conducive to learning is the teacher's responsibility. The environment must be safe and healthful, planned with the child in mind, and offer an invitation to learn.

Safe Learning Environments for Infants

SCENARIO Andy read in the morning paper that a piece of infant equipment was being recalled by the manufacturer. He copied down the information and took it into work that morning. When he checked, he found the piece that was in his classroom was not one of those listed, but he posted the notice on the family bulletin board just in case any of them had the item being recalled.

Infants seem to need many pieces of equipment these days for their routine care. This is especially so as more is learned and revised about the necessity, design, and safety of various pieces of equipment, as well as good practices in infant care. The infants' teacher must keep abreast of the latest safety alerts to protect the infants from harm and to use the environment in a way that stimulates their development in all domains.

Indoor Environments for Infants. Because of their inability to remove themselves from danger and their complete dependence on adults, infants must be isolated from all physical dangers. One of the most important safety precautions is the Back to Sleep campaign, which urges placing infants on their back to prevent SIDS (Sudden Infant Death Syndrome). Studies have shown that babies placed on their stomach to sleep are at higher risk for SIDS. In 1995, 3,279 babies in the United States died of SIDS. Other accompanying risk factors for SIDS are: male gender, low birth weight, African American, mothers who smoke, and young mothers. The SIDS rate among Northwest American Indian and Alaskan Natives was dramatically reduced between 1993 and 1996, attributable to a number of factors that centered on parent education about sleeping position and secondhand smoke (U.S. Centers for Disease Control, 1999). Another safety precaution for infants focuses on eliminating walkers on rollers and jump-ups that clamp on doorways. These are not safe and have been found to cause injury to legs and hip joints.

Infant classrooms include spaces designated for sleeping, since infants require several sleeping periods during a day. There needs to be a raised surface for diaper changing that is safe for the child and comfortable for the adult. Infants need time to be down on the floor, looking at each other and using equipment that will stimulate them to move closer or try to touch or move objects. This, of course, should be carpeted and comfortable. Eating times for bottle-fed infants are in the arms of adults who gaze into their eyes and talk to them, so the adult needs to be in a comfortable rocker that cannot pinch crawlers' fingers. For infants at the self-feeding stage, safe highchairs or small tray tables and chairs provide the social atmosphere that meals should bring. (See the layout from Lee [1997] in Figure 4–13 for all of these attributes.)

For the environment to meet the learning needs of infants, it must first provide space to move. Olds (1983) stated, "Sensorial and motoric experiences are the bedrock upon which all intellectual functions are built." There need to be areas for calm, quiet activities such as large-piece puzzles, shape sorters, and books to look at, handle, and chew. These activities involve manipulating objects, using all senses, and taking in information for later reference. Exploration is the main learning objective at this stage. Of course, since the mouth is a primary sensory receptor at this age, objects that have been mouthed by one child should be cleaned and disinfected before they go back into circulation for all. This necessitates having many objects, and many

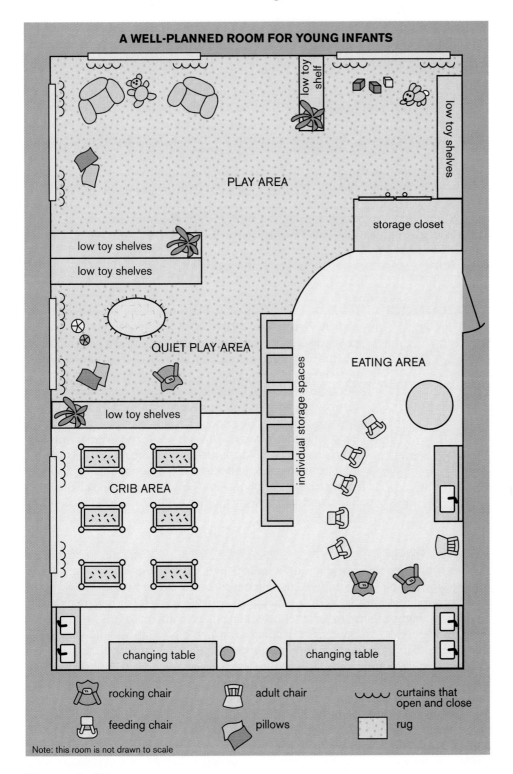

A WELL-PLANNED ROOM FOR YOUNG INFANTS

low toy shelf

low toy shelves

PLAY AREA

storage closet

low toy shelves

low toy shelves

QUIET PLAY AREA

EATING AREA

low toy shelves

individual storage spaces

CRIB AREA

changing table ◯ ◯ changing table

🐻 rocking chair   🪑 adult chair   〰〰 curtains that open and close

🪑 feeding chair   ▱ pillows   ▦ rug

Note: this room is not drawn to scale

Figure 4—13

Room layout. (Used with permission from Lee, J. M. (1997). In E. S. Szanton (Ed.), *Creating child-centered programs for infants and toddlers.* New York: Children's Resources International.)

duplicates of each. See Figure 4–14 for a list of common infant/toddler manipulatives. These are toys that can be handled and "manipulated" to learn lessons of sound, shape, and matching. These toys help infants build cognitive structures of color, quantity, and textures. A high-quality infant toddler program has a wide variety of such pieces of equipment. They are the tools of learning.

As the child progresses in large muscle development, his area of exploration widens and demands preparation. Boundaries can be set by prudent furniture arrangement, preventing the child from going places that are dangerous or inappropriate. Learning to move is fostered by equipment and activities that are challenging but not impossible or dangerous. Crawlers need warm, smooth surfaces on which to crawl, with interesting objects at eye level. An infant bulletin board can be made with pictures beneath clear acrylic sheets on which to crawl. If the pictures are of the babies and families in the group, it is even better. Separate but observable areas for sleeping, eating, and playing, as well as parent reception areas, are needed.

Outdoor Environments for Infants.

SCENARIO   Maxine sees that two of the three infants are awake and rolling and crawling around on the rug. It is a beautiful day, so she gently places sleeping Evan in a carrier and lifts Lori and Jared into the buggy and straps them all in. She wheels the buggy out onto the playground and sets Evan under a shade tree. After she checks the grass for any twigs or other things that may have appeared since yesterday, she places Lori and Jared on the grass. She says, "Oh, feel how cool and smooth the pretty green grass is." She sits down on the grass, rocking Evan's carrier gently as he sleeps and helping Lori roll over from tummy to back, and then back to tummy again. "Good rolling today, Lori. Show Jared how. He'll be doing it soon. See, Jared, you can see the sky and the tree when you learn to roll over."

The outdoor exploration begins with a smooth path on which to wheel a stroller or cart past interesting things to look at. The outdoors should be explored close up in areas prepared for crawling, such as grassy areas or artificial turf. For beginning walkers, there should be things to pull themselves up on and hang on to, and gentle slopes or ramps to traverse. An assortment of equipment should be available, including movable objects that can be pushed and pulled and balls to roll and throw. Natural objects to explore, such as trees and bushes, stimulate the sense of touch and texture. The sense of hearing is stimulated with sounds such as birds chirping at a bird feeder, wind chimes in a tree or hung under the eaves, or water flowing through a low play trough. As in any environment, safety is a primary concern, with pre-use checks done for possible hazards. Infants put everything into their mouth, so pebbles and other small objects should be eliminated from the area. Swing seats should be constructed of resilient, lightweight material and have a strap-in seat to prevent children from falling out (Frost, 1992).

A separate play yard for infants and toddlers should include: roofs or canopies for shade, fabric and flapping things like flags and banners, decks or platforms on which to climb and sit, slides, play houses or tunnels in which to crawl and hide, logs

Types of Equipment and Materials

SOFT	HARD
Cloth puppets	Blocks
Cloth and soft plastic dolls	Hard plastic dolls
Dress-up clothes	Cars, trucks
Fur	Plastic curtains
Pillows	Sand
Mats	Paper
Rugs	Cardboard
Cloth curtains	Books
Water	Posters
Clay	Plastic, wood mobile
Paint	Wood
Cloth wall hangings	Linoleum
Glue	Baseball
Ribbon	Plastic bottles
Cushions	Catalogs
Cloth mobile	Magazines
Rubber balls	Buttons
Sponge balls	Metal cans
Cloth scraps	Sandpaper
Foam scraps	
Yarn	

OPEN	CLOSED
Puppet	Puzzle
Doll	Zipper
Water	Button/buttonhole
Sand	Snaps
Clay	Stacking rings
Blocks	Windup doll
	Windup mobile

SIMPLE	COMPLEX
One-piece puzzle	Four-piece puzzle
Doll	Doll clothes
Clay	Clothes fasteners

INTRUSION	SECLUSION
Bike	Large box to hide in

HIGH MOBILITY	LOW MOBILITY
Bike	Sit and spin
Toy cars, trucks	Slide
Stroller, buggy	Books
Balls	Blocks
	Clay
	Painting
	Puzzles
	Water
	Sand

Figure 4–14

Common infant/toddler manipulatives. (From Watson, Watson, & Wilson, 1999)

or benches, and storage for small equipment. Greenman and Stonehouse (1996) have designed such a play yard (Figure 4–15).

Environmental Curriculum for Infants. The environment influences the development and learning of infants by providing stimulation of and practice for swiftly developing physical abilities, beginning language, and cognitive and social skills. Infant locomotion skills need space to develop. Equipment can enhance this, but is not required. What is required is an adult who anticipates safety hazards and removes them, and removes unforeseen hazards as they present themselves.

The environment supports the curriculum of infant development by providing for active exploration in the following areas.

* Physical—Places for infants to lie, roll, crawl, creep, and pull up safely; objects to grasp, manipulate, carry, fill, and dump

* Intellectual—Sensory experiences provided throughout the day through interaction with an adult, with materials to touch, smell, hear, and sometimes taste

* Language—Responsive adults who listen to the infant's developing sounds and first overtures at verbalizations, talk to the infants about things in the environment and the routines taking place, spaces where adults and individual infants are in close, face-to-face positions for communication

* Creative—Materials in the environment that the infant can act upon to change

* Social—Infants placed in proximity to each other to see each other and begin to communicate, but where they are protected from unintentionally harming each other

* Emotional—Secure environments that can be relied upon for basic stability, yet changing in small ways to remain interesting

The routines of the day, and the pieces of equipment that support those routines, such as high chairs, infant seats, cribs, and changing tables, represent opportunities for learning that adults can be trusted to meet needs, the most valuable lesson the infant is learning.

Safe Learning Environments for Toddlers

Because toddlers are mobile and inquisitive, their environment must be both safe and conducive to exploration. Toddlers pull themselves up and climb; thus, equipment must be stabilized so it does not topple over or lead the toddler to higher dangers that he cannot handle. Floor surfaces should be carpeted to protect little bodies from the falls that will inevitably occur. All the sanitary and environmental precautions for the infant room carry over into the toddler room. Duplicates of toys are a must because it is in a toddler's nature to want what the other child has and take it forcibly because of immature social skills. All toys, equipment, and materials should be free of sharp edges, nontoxic, and large enough not to present a choking hazard. Electric outlets should be protected with inserts and toilet facilities should be close by, with accommodations for small bodies such as safety seats, low sinks, or stable steps. See Figure 4–16 (on page 136) for hazards common to young children and the areas that should receive careful scrutiny to protect little ones from harm.

Indoor Environments for Toddlers. Toddlers have a need for variety and choice of play areas within the classroom. They need large muscle activities to motivate them to walk, run, climb, push, and pull. For the youngest children, the

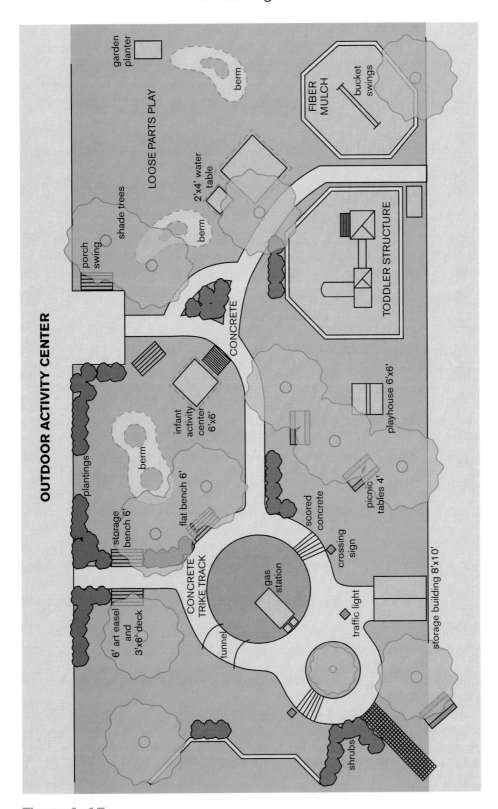

Figure 4–15

Outdoor play yard. (Reproduced by permission, *Prime Times* © 1996.
Redleaf Press: St. Paul, Minnesota)

Ingestion	Choking, poisoning, internal burns from small objects, pins, medications, toxic substances, plastic bags, balloons, large food pieces, allergic reactions to food
Falls	Changing tables, stairs, climbing on furniture or play apparatus not properly anchored or cushioned
Falling objects	Unsteady furniture, heavy items on upper shelves with parts hanging
Cuts, eye injuries	Sharp corners and edges on doors, cabinets, furniture, sharp objects, protrusions that poke such as handles and knobs
Pinches	Doors, cabinet doors, car doors and windows, rocking chairs and glider chairs, adult exercise equipment
Burns and electrocution	Electrical outlets, exposed wires, hot liquids, hot foods (especially uneven heating in microwaves)

Figure 4—16

Major safety hazards for the toddler.

environment and the people in it *are* the curriculum. The learning environment is designed to:

* empower each child to become a confident, lifelong learner and a secure, caring person.
* promote all aspects of development: large and small motor, cognitive, perceptual, social, emotional, language, creative, and expressive.
* nurture a positive self concept that includes acceptance of cultural and family background.
* be free of racial or sex role bias or stereotype and encourage all children to accept diversity.
* provide a wonderful place for childhood (Greenman & Stonehouse, 1996, p. 193).

Outdoor Environments for Toddlers. The outdoor environment should also be prepared for the curious toddler who puts everything into his mouth. Plants, flowers, pebbles, equipment, and space must all be considered hazards to be controlled and monitored. Toddlers are gaining autonomy (a sense of personal self-identity and independence); opportunities must be provided for them to safely exercise this newfound skill. They need places to climb, crawl, dump and fill, run, and slide, and to be protected as much as possible from potential danger. Supervision is the key to safety, with a ratio of three to four children per adult and a group size of no more than 12.

Toddlers need an outdoor play space separate from older children because the equipment and surfaces are different. Well-tended grass (that has not been recently chemically treated) or even bare ground is the best surface for crawling and walking. At least six inches of cushioning material are needed beneath equipment for each twelve inches of apparatus height. Sand and water, both inside and outside, provide a basis for learning the properties of liquids and granular solids as they are poured from one size and shaped container to another. The weight differences between full and empty containers and the float/sink concept of water play are all abstractions gained from the play environment. Water play in shallow containers is always done under supervision; and sand play as well, to prevent children from swallowing it or getting it in their eyes. The adult does more than just provide the equipment and materials at this stage to maximize learning. The adult describes the materials: "Oh, this pail is full of water," or makes an observation of the child's actions: "You poured water from the little cup into the big blue pail," and suggests other ways to use materials: "Do you want to try this funnel? It's a way to pour into the little hole in the bottle." The acquired concepts of full, little/big, blue, and the funnel and its function are all outcomes of the adult's interaction with the child and the environment.

Environmental Curriculum for Toddlers. Lowman and Ruhmann (1998) suggest a toddler environment of:

* simplicity (large motor zone, dramatic play zone, messy zone).
* seclusion (a place to be alone).
* softness (homey and noise absorbing).
* sensuality (visual, tactile, auditory, olfactory).
* stimulation (challenging with next step, open–ended materials).
* stability (favorites for repetition and practice).
* safety (big enough to climb on and manipulate, not so small as to be swallowed) and sanitation (daily cleaning routine with one tablespoon bleach to one quart of water).

The toddler is working towards autonomy; thus the environment allows freedom of movement and manipulation, but with the adult providing safe materials, supervision, and extension of the activities the child chooses. Whether the child is rolling something around on the floor, throwing nonbreakable objects, looking out the window, or climbing up on a piece of equipment, the teacher's role is to both provide safety and describe the activities in words. The teacher should administer encouragement and praise, rather than prohibitions and constant exhortations to "Be careful." The "no-nos" should be restricted and the "Yes! Look what you did!" increased. In that way, exploration of the environment embodies the curriculum. "It is understood that the *spirit* of learning, not the content, is the prime concern" (Greenman & Stonehouse, 1996).

Safe Learning Environments for Preschoolers

SCENARIO Elias is a new teacher in a classroom with no large muscle equipment. Children began climbing on a shelf to the top of a wooden refrigerator and jumping off. They did it safely and without injury, but it would have been better to provide both the equipment and supervision for their need to climb and jump. Preschoolers have ingenious ways of providing themselves with an interesting and challenging environment. The teacher's role is to provide for their need to move and try out and strengthen their muscles and imagination in a safe environment.

Preschoolers have a sense of the dangerous hazards to avoid and have enough muscle control to maneuver through the environment. By this age, children are less likely to put foreign objects and substances in their mouth. They have coordinated the large muscles with the small, and can move about in a reasonably safe manner. They are beginning to use words to communicate, instead of physical force, and to explain what they need to augment their play. They can now independently toilet, eat, dress themselves, and negotiate with other children for what they need, using imagination and ingenuity. All this competency does not mean they are not at risk for accidents. In any given year, about a quarter of all children under five have at least one accident that requires some kind of medical attention (U.S. Bureau of the Census, 1996). Close supervision is necessary, with the classroom adult/child ratio for this age being six to eight children to one adult in the group of no more than 18.

Indoor Environments for Preschoolers. The preschool environment includes a welcoming place with a cubby or shelf area for personal belongings. The furniture is sized to fit preschooler's bodies and is in good repair. The displays in the room are of children's work, and diverse populations of people with all kinds of family constellations represented. The room is well organized, so that materials are easily accessible and easily replaced using picture labels, as well as simple word labels. There are separate areas of the room with comfortable furnishings for quiet activities. Areas of active play have barriers to contain the play to that area. The art area has protected surfaces so spills are not a worry and a source of water for cleanup is nearby, as well as a place to dry or store finished work. Cover-ups are provided to protect clothing from messy play. Equipment, materials, and activities are not gender specific in order to extend all experiences to both boys and girls in the classroom.

A typical preschool classroom includes areas for block building, dramatic play, sand and water play, a quiet area for reading and listening, an art area, and a table area for activities such as puzzles and small manipulatives, as well as snack and games (Figure 4–17).

Outdoor Environments for Preschoolers. The outdoor environment for preschoolers requires a variety of equipment to meet their developmental levels and interests. Just as they do indoors, some children choose quiet, passive activities, while others select more active ones. Sand and water play areas have the same requirements and equipment needs as indoors, but the children can be freer, without concern for spills. Manipulative areas can be provided for in a number of ways by confining small muscle equipment to a table area. Large muscle activities require surfaces that allow for wheeled vehicles like bikes, scooters, and rollers skates to roll easily, as well as climbing and swinging areas with sufficient padding underneath to protect from falls. Outside, children can pay attention to another tactile dimension: the sand is warm on top and cool underneath. They can master pedaling a tricycle. The teacher's role is one of safety supervision, but he is also there to amplify children's discoveries, model a deference for all life, from worms to ants, and inspire closer observation of nature by calling attention to a bird's warble or a cloud pattern.

Environmental Curriculum for Preschoolers. The classroom environment contains equipment, materials, and supplies that are integrally connected with the program's goals. The curriculum is offered with long periods of free-choice time, supervised for safety and needs assessment, and extended by the teacher's probing questions and suggestions, rather than dictates. Learning in all areas of development can be assessed by observing children while they participate in these learning

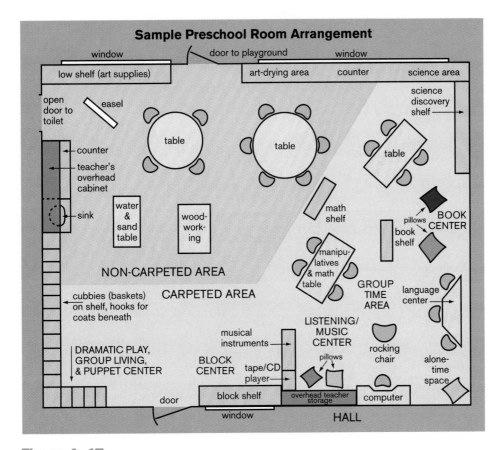

Figure 4–17

Preschool room arrangement. (From Jackman, H. L., 2001)

area activities. A preschool classroom arranged for play/learning is well equipped and arranged in learning centers (Figure 4–18, on page 140).

* The sand and water area is large enough to accommodate several children, with nonslip surfaces, close to a sink, along with a wide assortment of containers, tubes, scoops, and cleanup tools. In this area, children experiment with the Piagetian conservation concept that content volume does not change even with various shaped containers. The role of the teacher is to observe, describe the actions, and point out the cause and effect of those actions.

* The block area is on a flat, carpeted surface with low shelves stocked with unit blocks (those that are in proportion to each other, one unit, a double, a quadruple, halves, quarters, and cylinders) and ramps and accessories such as vehicles, play people, fabrics, and writing materials. Block play with unit blocks is the foundation of mathematics and geometry. The role of the teacher in this area is to observe, describing to the children using words like balance, enclosure, and cylinder, and to provide suggestions of other materials that could supplement the building.

* The dramatic play area stimulates role-play and is often equipped with pretend household appliances and accessories, or theme-based equipment to portray a grocery store, shoe store, pet store, fire station, doctor's office, or bank. This area stimulates social studies concepts about the many contribu-

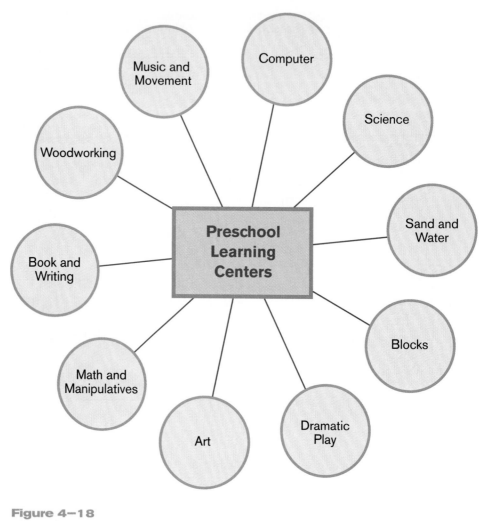

Figure 4–18

Preschool learning centers.

tors to community life. Additional pieces, such as dolls, clothing, props, and literacy materials, add to the realism and richness of the interactions. The teacher's role is to supply the materials, especially those that reflect the children's family lives.

* The art area provides a place to explore all kinds of media for drawing, painting, sculpting, cutting, rolling, gluing, and producing. The area contains a free space for working, such as a low table, and has nearby shelves stocked with a variety of supplies for the children to choose from. Ideally, the area should be near water for ease of cleanup and have a space for drying paintings and safe storage of finished products. The teacher's role is to provide the materials and encourage their independent use by guiding the child not so much to imitate the teacher's ideas, but rather to follow his own ideas. The teacher allows the child to create, destroy, and try again.

* The math and manipulative area contains equipment for small muscle development such as puzzles, small blocks, games, and items for sorting and classifying. The materials are displayed on low shelves for self-selection, an arrangement High Scope Curriculum calls the *find, use, return cycle* (High/Scope Press, 1995). The role of the teacher is to rotate these materials, keeping some consistent for repetition and mastery and some variable for challenge. These materials help children form math concepts by grouping, sequencing, patterning, and counting (Figure 4–19).

* The reading and writing area contains a wide variety of books that children can select from to read through or have read to them. There are writing materials of all kinds: pens, pencils, markers, and crayons, and all kinds of paper: lined, unlined, construction paper, card stock, envelopes, and stickers. The teacher's role is to select appropriate books, rotate the collection, making it relative to the children's interests, and select at least one book a day featured in a book time to instill a joy of reading in the children. The teacher is a role model for writing by keeping anecdotal notes on observations in the classroom and writing dictated stories, captions for artwork, charts, and class notes.

* The woodworking area provides real tools, wood, and other materials to construct permanent objects, helping the child see the concept of the part and the whole. The teacher's role, besides providing materials, is to supervise for safety and to reinforce the importance of construction for both boys and girls.

* The music and movement area is equipped with space for children to move to a variety of types of music. Prerecorded music tapes or CDs and musical instruments from various cultures enrich the area, as do props such as scarves, hats, batons, and costumes. The teacher's role is to provide culturally relevant materials and guidance for the children in using the equipment.

* A computer area is equipped with one or more computers with programs appropriate for the children's age and several chairs for shared computer use.

Figure 4–19

Well-equipped learning centers allow preschoolers to select and get involved in activities.

The computer is a tool for developing small muscle coordination, language, and literacy. The teacher's role is to support its use by providing materials for the area, observing, describing the children's actions, and connecting the computer activities with others in the class, such as art, blocks, science, math, and reading. Computers linked to the Internet serve as resources for both children and teachers to search for information when working on projects.

❋ The science area contains live animals and fish to give children firsthand experiences in observing the attributes of living things, such as habitat, food, physical characteristics, and the life cycle. Plants and physical objects such as earth and rock samples provide opportunities for investigations and comparisons. The tools of science, such as microscopes, magnifying glasses, specimen containers, and trays for collecting and sorting are in this area as well as reference books.

One of the ways children can begin to learn about the environment is to take an active part in its care. They are ready for what educational reformer John Dewey called "learning by doing" (Dewey in Paciorek & Munro, 1999). He described the University of Chicago school that experimented with various models of curriculum. One was the work model, where children accomplished meaningful work by using tools, cooking, sewing, and weaving. Young children can learn to be quite adept at peeling potatoes, sweeping floors, scrubbing tables, and shoveling snow. It is not work to them, but fun; and in the meantime they are learning physical skills, and even more importantly, a work ethic: it is satisfying to work and see the positive results. This is not to suggest making children into laborers, but simply that the care of the classroom environment can extend beyond watering the plants and feeding the fish. Sanding down a wooden shelf, smoothing the sharp edges, and applying a finish coat (outside, of course) is a learning activity of real value. This is care of the environment that brings with it many lessons.

Safe Learning Environments for Primary Age Children

SCENARIO You walk down the hall and look in each classroom. You cannot see into some because the windows are covered with paper. Another has the door wide open, with paper flowers on the door and music softly playing. The next room is totally silent, although it is full of children sitting at desks. The next room has soft fabric draped across the windows, partially shading plants in various stages of growth on the windowsill. As you walk by the next room you smell the aroma of gingerbread baking and see the teacher and children seated on the rug and on soft pillows while they take turns reading the story *The Gingerbread Man.*

What does each of these environments tell you about the teacher or the curriculum? In which room would you feel most comfortable?

Much less attention is given in research literature to the learning environment for school age children, yet the same principles apply to its importance in the whole scheme of learning and teaching. Primary age children, especially kindergartners or first graders, may be entering a large, institutional building for the first time. They may be walking to school or riding a school bus, venturing farther from home and family than ever before. These youngest school children should have recommendations regarding their safety and protection, both from their families and from the school. Safe routes, bus practices, early dismissal procedures, stranger warnings, and early arrivals are all issues to be addressed by the school, the teacher, and the family. Older, more experienced children may be subject to the same risks as younger ones, although they think they can handle them. Sometimes it is this confidence that places them at the most risk. Continual safety lessons and reminders are part of the teacher's role in keeping children out of harm's way.

Indoor Environments for Primary Age Children.

SCENARIO Priscilla is a first grader attending a new school on the first day of the school year. She has come to school on the bus and descends the bus steps with less enthusiasm than her fellow riders. She follows the crowd through the double doors into the big hallway. A woman there says, "Good morning. If you are in first grade, follow the yellow tape on the floor." Priscilla looks down and there it is. She follows it down a hall, down a flight of stairs, around the corner, and down another hall. She sees a big #1 on a door and steps closer. Out comes a woman who smiles and says, "Are you one of my first graders? What's your name? There are some children waiting to meet you inside. Andrew Carmine will take a picture of you for our bulletin board. We're glad you are here!"

The classroom environment in elementary schools is dependent on the room's organization. In self-contained classrooms, students are with one teacher for the entire day. The teacher is responsible for planning, implementing, and assessing the curriculum, as well as for managing the class. The classroom has the equipment needed for reading, writing, mathematics, social studies, science, and sometimes even music and art. The philosophy of teaching, and the style and personality of the teacher, are reflected in the room arrangement and displays.

The elements of the primary classroom environment can be categorized in the following ways (Figure 4–20, on page 144):

* Furniture in the classroom includes desks and tables suitable for sitting or standing, chairs that fit the children, and shelves that hold frequently used items for student accessibility. The furniture is arranged for various pedagogical approaches, such as whole-group teacher-directed activities, where all the children pay attention to the teacher; small-group activities, where children are clustered at tables working together; or individual activities, with each child at a separate desk or work station.

* Raw materials are the supplies used to make products. Literacy materials such as paper and writing tools are available to record information and transmit messages. A variety of other materials are available for use in art, science, math, and social studies.

* Tools transform the materials and are used to conduct experiments and explore ideas. They are useful for measuring, weighing, joining, and viewing. They can be scissors, staplers, glue and tape, measuring and weighing instruments, or different kinds of microscopes and magnifying glasses.

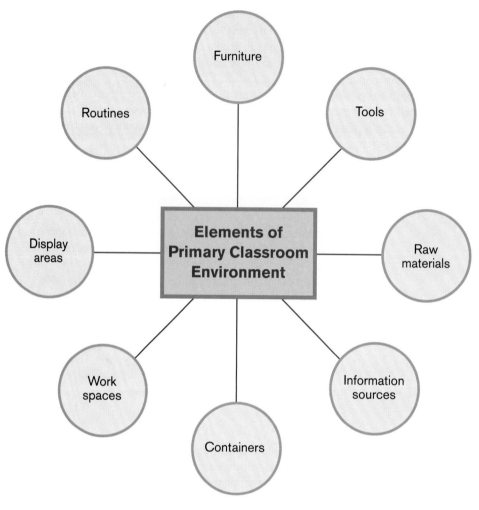

Figure 4–20

Elements of primary classroom environments.

* Information sources are in abundance, such as books, posters and charts, maps, printed matter, labeled specimens, computers, and other technology, such as overhead and slide projectors.

* Containers available for transporting materials and display include some that are watertight, racks, envelopes, bags, baskets, and boxes of all kinds and sizes.

* Work spaces are flexible to allow for work on various kinds of projects, and can include a water source, adjustable height and size for individual or group work, and chalkboards, bulletin boards, and easels.

* Display areas used to document work include bulletin boards, hanging areas, racks, and shelves. Flat surfaces are used to display three-dimensional work.

* Routines are conveyed visually through written directions, labels, news boards, lists, and sign-up sheets. These serve as reminders and reference points and meet the needs of different kinds of learners.

The classroom arrangement is dictated by the pedagogical style of the teacher. When you think of a classroom you probably open the memory box of rooms with rows of desks facing the teacher and the teacher's desk at the front of the room. The traditional, directive style of teaching called for paying attention to the teacher as the one who imparts knowledge, with the students the receptors of that knowledge. The teacher who uses a nonauthoritarian approach where learning is divergent and inventive, with students active in the learning process, will probably have a less traditional classroom setting. The student's desks may be in small groupings, or large tables may replace some or all of the desks. Just as a home's environment reflects its inhabitants, so the classroom reflects the teacher's philosophy. As you develop your own educational philosophy and pedagogical style, you will begin to form ideas for the classroom's physical environment that will be in concert with your ideas.

Outdoor Environments for Primary Age Children. Outdoor play is a favorite time for primary age children, who may be under stress to sit and concentrate for longer than their bodies and minds can tolerate. When they come outside, it is like they are exploding from a bottle.

SCENARIO	Sophie has led her second-grade class to the playground when her colleague Alex comes out with his class. The children run like the wind, laughing at and delighting in the butterflies that have pervaded the playground. Alex comes over and begins to engage Sophie in a conversation about the new administrator. Sophie says, "Oh, I know. She has to get real!" or Sophie says, "I'd love to talk with you, but I want to go over and see what kind of bug Abigail and Shawana have just captured. Talk to you later."

Many teachers see outside play or recess as a time for socializing with each other or tuning out. There is a definite role for the teacher outside as well. The teacher, of course, supervises all areas to be sure that no unsafe actions are occurring, intervening as necessary before they reach a serious level. Besides supervision, the teacher observes and can use the time to evaluate the children's progress in physical, social, and emotional development by watching their active play. The teacher can support and expand play episodes with suggestions, open-ended questions, and redirection of play that appears headed for a dispute. Planning for outdoor play can enrich children's options for more organized activities where they can learn teamwork, cooperation, and the rules of sports conduct. The teacher uses outdoor time to extend learning with such activities as measuring shadows, observing natural phenomena, or taking mini-field trips.

Outdoor areas should have an outer barrier to traffic, animals, and unauthorized persons. Studies have shown that children feel freer when there is a fence boundary than when there is none. The outdoor area should have a variety of surfaces, such as soil, grass, sand, flat hard sections for wheeled vehicles, and cushioned surfaces under climbing equipment. While outdoor time is often freer of planned activities, it still should be viewed as a learning opportunity. This is not chatting and socializing time for teachers, but instead a time to focus on the children's activities, both for safety supervision and enhancement of both physical and cognitive learning. Outdoor areas used before and after school and during recess provide a physical outlet, an opportunity to learn and practice physical skills, and a social atmosphere different from indoors, and they can provide a time of learning math, science, social studies, and literacy skills as well. It all depends on the teacher's role in supporting and planning for the outdoor learning. There should be free play times without adult planning, but outdoor areas are also conducive to planned lessons. An outdoor environment revives attention and provides real learning opportunities in nature, in terms of weather, astronomy, geology, and biology.

Outdoor areas are most often playgrounds, with climbing, balancing, and swinging equipment, and playing fields for baseball, soccer, and basketball (Figure 4–21). Nearby sports equipment storage is a must. The learning that takes place during sports activities depends on the supervision and the supervisor. Physical skills honed in this learning environment can bring the child self-esteem and lifelong physical fitness. Provision should be made for children who desire independent activities or less strenuous ones. This is an age of small, same-sex groups, so picnic tables, benches, and conversation pits provide a space for this activity.

The world range of this age child has expanded into the nearby neighborhood. Lessons on pollution, solid waste accumulation, and neighborhood deterioration can provide meaningful learning experiences that incorporate the neighborhood around the school. Middle school students in Minnesota discovered deformed frogs on a pond exploration field trip. Their quest for answers took them all the way to the U.S. Environmental Protection Agency, which was also stumped for a cause even after many scientists and the students gathered more deformed frogs in Minnesota. No definitive theory has been substantiated to date (Hayes, 1998). Learning outside school may include trash pick-up, a newspaper/bottle drive, or measurements of various kinds, incorporating many areas of the curriculum, such as science, math, literacy, and social studies. This has the long-term goal of good citizenship and an awareness of the balance between nature and man's survival.

Environmental Curriculum for Primary Age Children. Just as a home reveals the values, personality, and interests of its residents, the classroom often reveals those same characteristics of the teacher. An artistic teacher will have a room rich in art affirmation, with prints of master painters, mobiles hanging from the ceiling, and activities for integrating the standards of the mandated curriculum with art.

Figure 4–21

Free play times are for releasing energy, practicing skills, and social interaction.

The same is true of the teacher with an interest in music, technology, history, or anything else. The depth of the teacher's knowledge and commitment to learning will spill over into the environment, making it a place for children to explore with the teacher.

The environment should support all areas of the curriculum. The choices of equipment, books, materials, and objects to explore and manipulate should all be relevant to the area of study.

* Reading—Biographies of and collections of books by an author being studied
* Mathematics—Tools to weigh, measure, and manipulate
* Science—Equipment to view objects close up or far away, living and nonliving things to observe and compare
* Social studies—Maps, artifacts, and cultural items
* History—Time lines, reference books, objects from the past, and machines

Most children say recess is the best part of school. It is a time of exuberant play, of developing autonomy and self-expression, of choosing playmates, and carrying out their own agendas and playing without the direction or interference of adults.

Safe Learning Environments for Elementary Age Children

More schools are realizing that children need to be able to take pride in and feel a part of their school. They need an environment that reflects their interests, culture, and issues. Hallway and cafeteria murals, courtyard plantings, and art displays—all generated by the students—help them contribute to the environment of the school building.

While physical safety is always the primary concern, this age group needs the teacher's special attention for psychological safety. Their intensifying social interactions and tenuous self-esteem can be easily harmed by cruelty and exclusion. An emotional environment of tolerance, acceptance, and recognition is one for which the teacher is the role model.

When we view Figure 4–9 and see homicide as one of the top four causes of death among five- to fourteen-year-old children, the statistic is staggering. Recent school shootings have made us reconsider if school is a safe place after all. Joycelyn Elders, former Surgeon General of the United States, reported that in 1989 an estimated 430,000 students took a weapon to school to protect themselves from attack at least once during a given six-month period (Elders, 1994, p. 260). She said, "We need to focus on *prevention* of violence. To do this we need to focus our efforts on children and teach them carefully at school and at home" (p. 262). Safety is not just prevention of harm or bodily injury while children are in school; it is also helping them learn methods for solving problems in nonviolent ways. This will be discussed further in Chapter 12.

Indoor Environments for Elementary Age Children.
Departmentalized classroom organization is common in upper elementary grades, where various teachers and classrooms specialize in the instruction of one academic area. The classroom is equipped with specialized materials and equipment for teaching a subject field. Hands-on materials can be readily available for student use, and student work examples can be displayed. The classroom arrangement, furnishings, equipment, materials, and supplies correlate with the subject matter at hand, such as science, math, social studies, or literacy, with books and classroom displays focusing on that subject. The arrangement of the classroom reflects the teaching philosophy and pedagogical style of the teacher. A teacher who believes his role is to impart knowledge in a structured format will arrange desks in rows, with assigned seats to control behavior,

all facing where he stands or sits in the front of the room. The teacher who has a collaborative learning philosophy will arrange desks in small clusters facing each other or arrange tables so students are facing each other. You will decide what style of teacher you will be and that will govern how you design the classroom space.

Risky behavior puts elementary age children in the greatest danger from accidents and peer acceptance-related behaviors such as smoking, drinking, and drug use. Only 25 percent of children reported always using their bicycle helmets (Sacks, Kresnow, Houston, & Russell, 1994). Children of this age need places to congregate for conversation. They are social beings and, as such, practice the art of talking and listening, as well as defining their gender roles. The teacher's role is to provide a place with limited privacy for these conversations, but with the added safety factor of visibility (Figure 4–22).

Outdoor Environments for Elementary Age Children.
Outdoors, this age group benefits from the same kind of environment as the primary age group. Organized sports, often in the form of physical education classes, replace the free play of younger years. The teacher's role may change during this time, depending on school structure. This may be the teacher's planning time or lunch period. If the teacher is expected to stay with the class, then his role may be to plan, assist in, or cheerlead the activities taking place.

Environmental Curriculum for Elementary Age Children.
The world range and environment of older children extends beyond the neighborhood; their environment is the world. Some schools have nature trails and observation points in their outdoor environments that support the curriculum. This not only gives opportunities to observe nature, but also instills a lifelong appreciation for ecology and wildlife preservation. Accessing Internet sites to obtain information about rain forest depletion, global warming, ozone measurements, or population demo-

Figure 4–22

Elementary age children need both privacy and supervision.

graphics can be used in the curriculum, with the added benefit of learning about computers and the Web. Learning activities could center on researching the effects of various colors on people's psychological health or the measurable effects of drugs and alcohol on reflexes and reasoning ability, or measuring the decibel levels in the school cafeteria for a project on making the school a healthier place. These activities also include many other curriculum areas and are relevant the child's life.

In preschool, primary, and upper elementary programs, the outdoor environment may include field trips near and far. Preplanning is necessary to protect the children and maximize the learning experience. Making transportation arrangements, gathering emergency contact phone numbers, and bringing first aid and bee sting kits are the teacher's responsibility.

✳ ASSESSING ENVIRONMENTS

The physical environment is extremely important to the safety, health, and learning of the children with whom you work. Constant vigilance for safety, consideration of the effects of the environment on behavior, and expansion of the environment as children learn and grow are part of the teacher's role. This calls for assessing the environment, gathering data by observation and more formal instruments like safety checklists, and making adjustments based on the data. The environment is an important source of support to the learning and development of every-age child, but it can also be a source of danger. It can also be a possible remedy for problem behaviors. Dodge and Colker (1995) made suggestions of how to assess behavior problems that may be related to the environment, and how making changes in the environment may reduce or eliminate them.

Many checklists exist that can help in assessing both indoor and outdoor environments. An excellent tool for assessing not only the objects in the environment, but also child's interaction with it, can be found in *Prime Times* by Greenman and Stonehouse (1996, p. 220), which is included in Appendix B.

Frost and Wortham (in Frost, 1992) have developed a good checklist for assessing the outdoor environment for ages three through eight that is included in Appendix C.

Harms, Cryer, and Clifford present one of the best known environmental evaluation tools, which includes not only the physical environment, but also how the teacher expands the environment into learning, in their *Infant Toddler Environmental Rating Scale* (1998) and the revised edition of the *Early Childhood Environment Rating Scale* (Harms, Clifford, & Cryer, 1998). See Appendix D for excerpts from these assessment tools.

SUMMARY

The place where you will spend your days with children can contribute to your effectiveness as a teacher, as well as your personal well-being. It is one of the first considerations and should not be overlooked. This chapter presented you with a rationale for the influence of the environment on the program and considerations for you to make in forming your philosophy about how you will set up your classroom's physical environment. The outdoor environment may be out of your control, but you can act as a change agent to make the outdoors a safer, more appropriate place, as well as enhance what already exists. Use this "third teacher" as a partner in developing your learning and teaching philosophy.

KEY TERMS

third teacher

universal precautions

mandated reporters

REVIEW ACTIVITIES

Exercises to Strengthen Learning

1. Infants—Use Appendix B to observe the environment of an infant or toddler classroom.

2. Toddlers—Use Appendix D to observe the environment of an infant or toddler classroom.

3. Preschoolers—Use Appendix D to observe the environment of a preschool age classroom.

4. Primary—Use Appendix C to observe a playground used by primary age children.

5. Design a classroom in which you would like to work.

6. Elementary—Visit an elementary school classroom and observe its environmental elements and what they convey about the teacher's interests, emphasis, teaching philosophy, and curriculum goals, as well as the culture of the students and the teacher, school standards, and safety concerns and precautions.

Internet Quest

1. Find the Web site of the National Safety Board and investigate safety hazards the teacher can help prevent.

2. Use the Internet to investigate the types of cushioning material and depth required under climbing apparatus.

3. Search for a list of common household or classroom plants that are poisonous.

4. Search for Web sites of school safety programs and select three exemplary ones.

Reflective Journal

Because I learned in this chapter that _____, when I am a teacher I think I will _____.

REFERENCES

Americans with Disabilities Act. (1990). PL 101–336.

Arends, R. I. (1994). *Learning to teach* (3rd ed.). New York: McGraw-Hill.

Bussing, R., Menvielle, E., & Zima, B. (1996). Relationship between behavioral problems and unintentional injuries in U.S. children. *Archives of Pediatric and Adolescent Medicine, 150*(1), 50–56.

Centers for Disease Control. (2000). Ten leading causes of death, United States 1998, All Races, All Sexes. Retrieved May 4, 2001, from the World Wide Web: <http://www.cdc.gov/ncipc>.

Christoffel, K. K., Donovan, M., Schofer, J., Wills, K., & Lavigne, J. V. (1996). Psychosocial factors in childhood pedestrian injury: A matched case-control study. *Pediatrics, 97*(1), 33–42.

Dewey, J. (1966). *Democracy in education: An introduction to the philosophy of education.* New York: The Free Press.

Dewey, J. (1999). Three years of the university elementary school. In K. M. Paciorek, & J. H. Munro (Eds.), *Notable selections in early childhood education* (2nd ed.). Guilford, CT: Dushkin/McGraw-Hill.

Dodge, D. T., & Colker, L. J. (1995). *The creative curriculum for early childhood.* Washington, DC: Teaching Strategies, Inc.

Elders, J. (1994). Violence as a public health issue for children. *Childhood Education, 70*(5), 260–262.

Foster-Harrison, E. S., & Adams-Bullock, A. (1998). *Creating an inviting classroom environment.* Bloomington, IN: Phi Delta Kappa Educational Foundation.

Frost, J. (1992). *Play and playscapes.* Albany, NY: Delmar.

Gonzalez-Mena, J., & Eyer, D. W. (1997). *Infants, toddlers and caregivers* (4th ed.). Mountain View, CA: Mayfield Publishing.

Greenman, J. (1988). *Caring spaces, learning places: Children's environments that work.* Redmond, WA: Exchange Press.

Greenman, J., & Stonehouse, A. (1996). *Prime times: A handbook for excellence in infant and toddler care.* St. Paul, MN: Redleaf Press.

Harms, C., Clifford R. M., Cryer, D. (1998) *Early childhood environment rating scale* (Rev. ed.). New York: Teachers College Press.

Harms, C., Cryer, D., & Clifford, D. (1998). *Infant/toddler environmental rating scale.* New York: Teachers College Press.

Hathaway, W. E. (1993). Non-visual effects of classroom lighting on children. *Education 33*(4), 34–41.

Hayes, S. (1998, April 13). The celebrated deformed frogs of LeSuerer County. *Scholastic Update (Teachers' Edition), 130*(13), 6–8.

High/Scope Press. (1995). *Educating young learners: Active learning practices for preschool and child care programs.* Ypsilanti, MI: Author.

Hohmann, M., & Weikart, D. P. (1995). *Educating young children.* Ypsilanti, MI: High/Scope Press.

Jackman, H. L. (2001). *Early education curriculum* (2nd ed.). Albany, NY: Delmar.

Johnson, J. E. (1998). Play development from age four to eight. In D. P. Fromberg & D. Bergen (Eds.), *Play from birth to twelve and beyond: Contexts, perspectives and meanings.* New York: Garland.

Kolbe, U., Shepherd, W., & Eaton, J. (1994). *Mia–Mia child and family study centre handbook.* Sydney, Australia: Macquarie University.

Lee, J. M. (1997). Physical space: Designing responsive environments for infants and toddlers. In E. S. Szanton (Ed.), *Creating child–centered programs for infants and toddlers.* New York: Children's Resources International.

Lillard, P. (1996). *Montessori today: A comprehensive approach to education from birth to adulthood.* New York: Schocken Books.

Loughlin, C. E., & Suina, J. H. (1982). *The learning environment: An instructional strategy.* New York: Teachers College Press.

Lowman, L. H., & Ruhmann, L. R. (1998). Simply sensational spaces: The multi-"s" approach to toddler environments. *Young Children, 53*(3), 11–17.

MacMurren, H. (1985). A comparative study of the effects of matching and mismatching sixth-grade students with their learning style preferences for the physical element of intake and their subsequent reading speed and accuracy scores and attitudes. (Doctoral dissertation, St. John's University, 1996). *Dissertation Abstracts International, 45,* 2791A.

Malaguzzi, L. (1984). *L'occhio se salta il muro. Catalog of the exhibit, "L'occhio se salta il muro,"* published by the Comune di Reggio Emilia, Assesserato Istruzione, Regione di Emilia Romagna.

Marotz, L. R., Cross, M. Z., & Rush, J. M. (2001). *Health, safety, and nutrition for the young child* (4th ed.). Albany, NY: Delmar.

Midjaas. C. L. (1984). Use of space. In J. W. Keefe & J. M. Jenkins, *Instructional leadership handbook*. Reston, VA: National Association of Secondary School Principals.

Montessori, M. (1965). *Dr. Montessori's own handbook*. New York: Schocken Books.

Moore, G. T. (1998). Site planning and layout. *Child Care Information Exchange, 119,* 24–27.

National Association for the Education of Young Children (NAEYC). (1998). *Accreditation criteria & procedures.* Washington, DC: Author.

Olds, A. R. (1983). Planning a developmentally optimal day care center. *Day Care Journal, 1*(1),16–24.

Robertson, C. (1998). *Safety, nutrition, and health in early childhood education.* Albany, NY: Delmar.

Roopnarine, J., & Johnson, J. (1993). *Approaches to early childhood education* (2nd ed.). Upper Saddle River, NJ: Merrill/Prentice Hall.

Rutter, M., Maughan, B., Mortimore, P., & Ouston, J. (1979). *Fifteen thousand hours.* Cambridge, MA: Harvard University Press.

Sacks, J. J., Kresnow, M. J., Houston, P., Russell, P. (1994). Bicycle helmet use among American children. *Injury Prevention, 2,* 258–262.

Shepherd, W., & Eaton, J. (1997). Creating environments that intrigue and delight children and adults. *Child Care Information Exchange, 117,* 42–47.

Singh, G. K., & Yu, S. M. (1996). U.S. childhood mortality, 1950 through 1993: Trends and socioeconomic differentials. *American Journal of Public Health, 86,* 505–512.

Standing, E. (1962). *Maria Montessori: Her life and work.* Fresno, CA: Academy Guild Press.

Starfield, B. (1991). Childhood morbidity: Comparisons, clusters, and trends. *Pediatrics, 88,* 519–526.

Stone, S. J. (1999). A conversation with John Goodlad. *Childhood Education, 75*(5), 265.

U.S. Bureau of the Census. (1996). *Statistical abstract of the United States: 1966* (116th ed.). Washington, DC: U.S. Government Printing Office.

U.S. Centers for Disease Control. (1999). *CDC Media Relations: Infant mortality declines dramatically among northwest American Indians and Alaskan natives.*

Watson, L. D., Watson, M. A., & Wilson, L. C. (1999). *Infants & toddlers: Curriculum and teaching* (4th ed.). Albany, NY: Delmar.

Weinstein, C. (1981, August). Classroom design as an external condition for learning. *Educational Technology,* 12–18.

For additional learning and teaching resources, visit our Web site at www.EarlyChildEd.delmar.com.

RELATED CAREERS

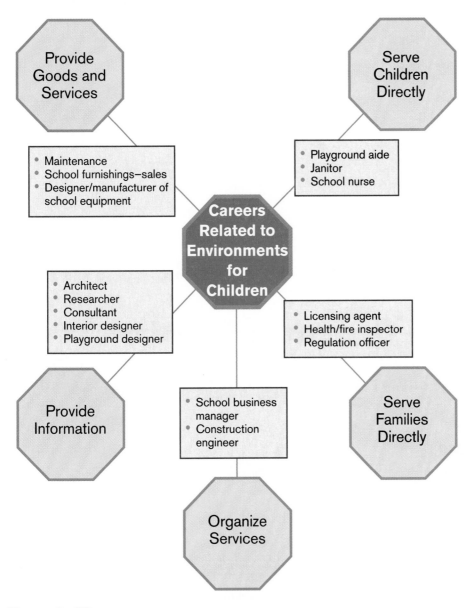

Figure 4–23

Careers related to environments for children.

5

Learning about Teaching the Growing Child— Physical Development and Health

Objectives

After reading this chapter and completing the review activities, the learning teacher should be able to:

1. Explain the principles of physical growth and development.

2. Identify genetic and environmental factors that influence physical growth and development.

3. Apply principles of physical growth and development to learning about and teaching children from birth through sixth grade.

Every morning when you get out of bed, walk across the floor, and take care of body needs like hygiene, dressing, and eating, you are using your body automatically, without thinking about it or appreciating the ability to do so. You did not get to this point in physical development easily: for many people some of these tasks are difficult or impossible. If you think about it, you realize that if children are hungry or sick, or have a physical disorder, learning and other areas of development may be compromised. Let's look at some children and see how it works.

✳ UNDERSTANDING PHYSICAL DEVELOPMENT'S RELATIONSHIP TO LEARNING

SCENARIO   Nine-month-old Lucinda crawls across the floor, grabs a magazine lying on the floor, and tears the pages.

Nine-year-old James, who has muscular dystrophy, crawls across the floor, grabs a magazine lying on the floor, and reads the cover story to his class.

Nine-year-old Corrinda walks across the room, picks up the magazine, thumbs through the pages, but cannot read or speak. Corrinda has autism.

You might have the impression that thinking is a function of the brain, whereas movement is a function of the body, but in truth both functions result from the correlation and interdependence of the brain and body systems. The brain is the center of all body movements. A fit body with a malfunctioning brain certainly is a sad thing to see; the reverse is also true. The mind and body are so integrated that the teacher cannot think just about the brain, but must consider the whole body and the whole child (Figure 5–1 on page 156). This chapter will help you explore what that means.

The Nature of Physical Development

When we examine any component of the individual, we must begin with biology, the genetic and prebirth factors that will influence later **growth** and **development**. These words are often used together (i.e., "growth and development") and they are often used separately with assumed exchangeable meanings; however, they do have their own separate definitions.

Growth refers to those changes measured quantitatively (in numbers), such as height, weight, girth (inches around), teeth, and even vocabulary. Growth occurs throughout the life span, rapidly at the beginning and then slowing into adulthood; at the same time, the body is continuously replacing cells. Inches, pounds, and number of teeth and vocabulary words increase as we age, with each change or growth measured by a number. Of course, any given growth element may have limitations or fluctuations due to many factors.

growth—Physical changes throughout the life span that can be measured quantitatively.

development—Qualitative changes in physical, cognitive, social, emotional, creative, and language domains that proceed from simple to complex according to a universal systematic progression.

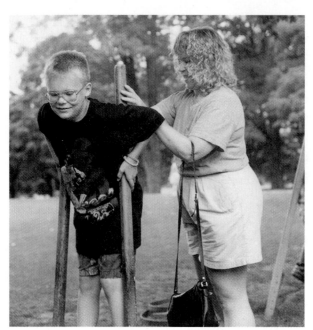

Figure 5–1

Children grow and develop at different rates, but in predictable patterns.

Development refers to the changes that are measured qualitatively (from simple to complex) in several domains: physical, cognitive, social, emotional, creative, and language. Development occurs in an orderly progression, in a universal sequence of milestones, but at variable rates from child to child.

Every cell in the body contains genetic instructions known as chromosomes, which are located in the nucleus of the cell. Cells are composed of genes, the segments of deoxyribonucleic acid (DNA) that transmit hereditary information. A single chromosome may have as many as 20,000 genes. These determine all of our inherited physical characteristics, such as being male or female, colors of everything (brown skin, green eyes, red hair), and body parts' size and shape (ears like our mother, long legs like our father). Some believe the size of our brain, our temperament, and even our taste in music are in part determined by genetics. These can work together for good or bad, purely by chance.

In the embryonic period, between conception and eight weeks, many crucial developmental changes take place. By the end of the third week after conception, the central nervous system has started to form and the beginnings of the eyes can be seen. By the fourth week, the heart and digestive system are appearing; by the fifth week, buds of arms and legs are forming, and by the eighth week, fingers and toes emerge and bones begin to harden. The embryonic period is the most vulnerable to developmental errors. In the fetal period, from the ninth week to birth, most of the major body parts are formed and those parts are growing rapidly (Figure 5–2). Also in those months, refinements of body parts like finger pads, eyebrows, eyelashes, and sexual organs appear and the fetus adds weight. The fetus is now very active and responsive to touch within the womb, but not externally.

Genetic disorders that involve chromosomal abnormalities usually (but not always) result in spontaneous abortions. Some genetic disorders cause no developmental problems, but many can and do. The most common genetic disorder is Down syndrome; roughly one in every 800 to 1,000 infants is born with this abnormality (Rogers, Roizen, & Capone, 1996). These children have distinctively broad, flat facial

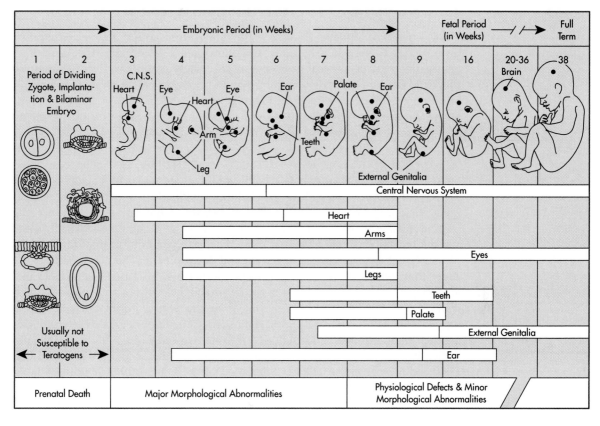

		Embryonic Period (in Weeks)							Fetal Period (in Weeks)		Full Term

Figure 5–2

During the embryonic stage, many changes take place. (From
Charlesworth, R., 2000)

features and often have other physical and cognitive limitations that vary in severity.
Sex chromosome abnormalities are among the most common genetic disorders,
occurring once in every 500 births (Thompson, McInnes, & Huntington, 1990);
they may result in infertility, educational problems (such as Klinefelter and Turner
syndromes), and in some cases a reduced IQ.

Cystic fibrosis is another genetic disorder occurring in about one out of 2,000
births, producing excess mucus in the lungs and thereby reducing the child's ability to
participate fully in physical activities. Spina bifida, a deformity in which the base of the
spine does not close, is linked to inadequate amounts of folic acid in the expectant
mother's diet during fetal development. This may cause reduced cognitive functioning and some lower-body paralysis. Cerebral palsy results from brain damage during
the prenatal or perinatal period and may include paralysis or other muscle dysfunc-
tions. It may also affect vision, hearing, and cognitive functioning.

Today, more and more is being discovered about genetics and there are even
attempts at engineering or manipulating genetic information. Genetic testing prior to
pregnancy can identify potential disorders; amniocentesis, ultrasound, and other tests
may diagnose difficulties prior to birth. Physical growth and development are to some
extent determined by inheritance, but are affected to an even greater degree by environmental factors before, during, and after birth.

The Nurture of Physical Development

Growth and development are affected by biological (nature) and sociological (nurture) factors. General health, safety, and nutrition are three factors that can positively or negatively affect physical development both before and after birth (Figure 5–3). Preventive and medicinal health care, provision of a safe environment, and adequate nutrition are issues for all people, but are particularly difficult for those with limited financial resources. Schools and communities can play a role in increasing the availability of these necessities for healthy physical development.

Prenatal Nurture of Physical Development. The fetus or developing person needs nurture before birth or difficulties may arise. Factors before birth such as the mother's diet, drugs (including prescribed or over-the-counter medications, illicit drugs, nicotine, and alcohol), exposure to diseases, or the presence of preexisting diseases may influence growth and development, during both the fetal period and the remainder of life following birth. The health and nutrition of the mother are obviously important to prenatal growth and development. The developing fetus gets all its nourishment from its mother. If the mother's diet is nutritionally deficient, the fetus depletes the mother's body of the available nutrients at a rate consistent with its own proper development, at a detriment to the mother, until available necessary nutrients fall below detectable levels. Only then is the fetus negatively affected, elevating the risk of stillbirth or death during the first year of life. In 1995, 7.3 percent of all babies born in the United States weighed below 5 lb. 8 oz., compared to 7.7 percent in 1960 and 6.7 percent in 1984 (Children's Defense Fund, 1998). This below-average birth weight places infants at risk both at birth and afterwards. The addition of multivitamins, especially those containing folic acid, to the diet of a pregnant woman significantly reduces the risk of neurological disorders in the developing fetus.

Any artificial substances introduced into the fetus through the mother may be harmful. Pregnancy requires the safe use of prescribed and over-the-counter drugs. Another significant determinant for low birth weight is smoking during pregnancy. The effects on the fetus may extend into lifelong metabolic immunological problems,

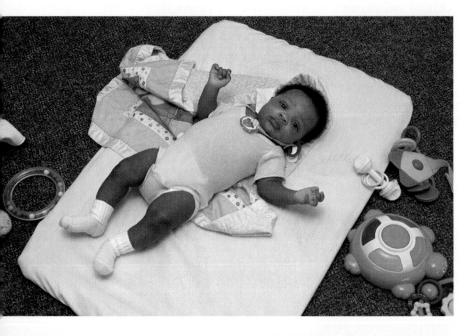

Figure 5–3

Physical growth and development depend on genetics and a healthy environment.

and possible interference with cognitive development and functioning. Drugs such as cocaine and heroin may harm the developing embryo and fetus; documented effects include abnormal body part formation, and brain and neurological disorders, but research is still inconclusive about the long-term effects. Newborns can be born addicted to cocaine and heroin. Fetal alcohol syndrome, which is caused by the mother abusing alcohol during pregnancy, can result in abnormal facial characteristics, stunted physical growth, and neurological problems. These syndromes may or may not be diagnosed at birth and the long-term effects are still being researched. Tests of the effects on the fetus of the father's substance abuse habits have yielded inconclusive results.

Some diseases that the mother has can be passed to the fetus in the womb or during childbirth, including measles, syphilis, diphtheria, influenza, serum hepatitis, chicken pox, diabetes, genital herpes, and human immunodeficiency virus (HIV), which causes AIDS. Other diseases may be passed on later in breast milk. Any of these may cause physical or intellectual impairments of varying severity. Rubella may cause deafness, heart defects, or cognitive disorders, but it is rare and preventable because of the availability of immunization. HIV, however, is a newer and less controllable threat to the infant, especially if the mother has developed full symptoms. Young maternal age, lack of prenatal care, poor nutrition, and the Rh factor also influence the development of the fetus and later development of the child.

Healthy Physical Development. Except for the most severe and irreversible effects on the fetus and infant mentioned previously, **maturation**, the environment, and interactions with others can greatly reduce the overt effects of prenatal risks, resulting in more normal growth and development.

From the very beginning and throughout life, physical health and indeed life itself depends on adequate provision for the body's needs. **Abraham Maslow** was a psychologist who became interested in human behavior and its motivations. He established an orderly progression of needs that must be met from basic physical needs and affective or emotional needs to self-fulfillment. While it does not provide the whole answer to human behavior, his theory does give us some indicators and practical advice for our actions (as teachers and parents) and for interpreting those of others. We can often attribute a person's behavior to the neglect of one of these important areas of need. Maslow's *Hierarchy of Needs* (Figure 5–4 on page 160) begins with the life essentials of food, drink, air, safety, and security.

This hierarchy of needs details the basics of physical nurturing that must be satisfied before learning can commence in the classroom. You know that if you are hungry or thirsty, or smelling fumes, you cannot pay attention to a lesson. Fear of ridicule or violence within the school will also interfere with the ability to learn. While the child is in its care, the school (and the teacher) is responsible for the physical needs of her body, as well as the physical and psychological safety of security.

You probably will be sick more often than usual in your first year of teaching because of greater exposure to more sources of contagion. One of the most important ways to stay healthy is to wash your hands to prevent the spread of disease. Proper hand washing by both children and teacher decreases the cross-contamination of germs. Most people do not wash their hands properly; rinsing,

Abraham Maslow

(1908–1970) Born in Brooklyn of Russian parents; psychologist, rejected behaviorism for humanistic approach, believed in inner strength of the child. Principle: that basic needs of body and mind must be met before learning and self-actualization can be achieved. Major work: *Motivation and Personality.*

---

maturation—Genetically determined patterns of changes in development that occur over time.

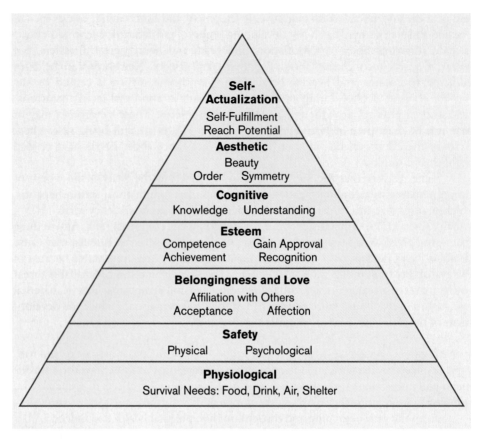

Figure 5–4

Maslow's hierarchy of needs. (Adapted from Maslow, A. H. (1970). *Motivation and personality* (2nd ed.). New York: Harper & Row)

washing, and rinsing again is the correct procedure to keep from contaminating clean hands. See Figure 5–5, for the correct procedure.

These classroom guidelines are suggested for all ages. Teachers and children should wash hands:

⁕ on arrival.

⁕ before handling food.

⁕ after changing diapers or assisting a child in the bathroom.

⁕ after handling items contaminated with mucus, urine, feces, vomitus, or blood.

⁕ after using the toilet.

⁕ at the end of the day or immediately upon arrival at home.

Teachers should keep informed of the children's health through contact with the families and school health professionals. Teachers also must keep written records regarding any health-related incidents or concerns for follow-up discussions with families. Conditions such as diabetes, epilepsy, attention deficit disorder, and physical impairments to hearing, eyesight, or mobility require knowledgeable teachers and possible environmental modifications so the affected child can function as normally as possible. Each child's health record confidentiality must be maintained. Necessary medications are distributed according to school policy.

Procedure:

1. Check location of soap, paper towels, and waste receptacle.
2. Completely wet hands and wrists under running water, with fingertips pointed downward.
3. Apply liquid soap and lather fronts, backs, between fingers, and under fingernail areas for 15 seconds. (Sing the Happy Birthday song twice to time yourself.)
4. Rinse well under running water holding hands downward and leaving water running until you have dried your hands.
5. Dry thoroughly with paper towel.
6. Turn off faucet by using a paper towel to touch the faucet.
7. Discard towel in waste container without touching the container.

Figure 5–5

Proper hand washing is not as simple as it may seem.

WORDS OF WISDOM Sally Skelding of Portland, Oregon, who describes herself as a brontosaurus dinosaur—meaning she has had long experience with teaching children—reminds us of the accommodations that should be made to the environment to welcome ALL children with these questions:

"Are there doll wheelchairs? Are there real items that people with disabilities might use, such as small wheelchairs, walkers, and grabbers? How accessible is the room to get into? How about access to the building? Are there lips on the door entrances where a wheelchair could tip? How about playground accessibility? Are there areas where a child with physical limitations can use the playground, or do they watch from the deck or room? Is there a diversity in meal offerings that reflects the school population or community? What image does the director's office present? How about the outside of the building and the entrance? The rooms need to make a child and parent feel welcome, and by this I mean that a child of any color, ability, or gender feels *safe* when they stand in the doorway and look into the room."

A growing problem in children today is **asthma**, a narrowing of the airways into the lungs triggered by allergies, weather, exercise, infections, smoke, or strong emotions. Difficulty breathing is the most apparent symptom and can lead to blackouts from oxygen starvation. Asthma, whether allergy- or exercise-induced, is a serious but treatable disease that affects an average of 6.9 percent of children between the ages of one and 18 (Centers for Disease Control, 1996), but it is more common among children living in crowded conditions or poverty, where rates are as high as 14 percent (Crain et al., 1994). Childhood asthma is one of the main reasons for children's hospitalization, with one out of 10 children in America diagnosed with it and another one in 10 undiagnosed (Mayo Clinic Health Oasis, 1998). The incidence of asthma has nearly doubled in the last 20 years, with no satisfactory explanation. With treatment, asthma can be controlled by avoidance of triggers, and with allergy injections and medications to open airways.

Another health concern for teachers today is HIV/AIDS. It is estimated that at some point in every teacher's career she will have a child who is HIV-positive in the classroom (Jessee, Nagy, & Poteet-Johnson, 1993). While more and more information is available about the virus, controversy and fear remain. Universal sanitary precautions are the rule. All bodily fluids must be treated as contaminated and handled only with latex gloves, with surfaces and hands disinfected immediately. If a child who is HIV-positive is in the group or classroom, the child and family have the right to keep that information confidential. The child may not need any special considerations. Since it cannot be known if anyone has a specific contagious disease at any given time, universal precautions are always carried out for all, without undue attention to any individual.

Since children may become ill during the day, the teacher must be aware of symptoms such as listlessness, glassy eyes, change in coloring, rapid breathing, coughing, nose discharge, diarrhea, vomiting, or head itching. Any of these symptoms may require the child to be removed from the group until the child is diagnosed and treated to prevent the spread of disease or, as in the case of head lice, parasites. School policies will guide the readmission of the child into the group.

Nutrition for Physical Development and Health. Research shows connections between hunger and poor school performance (Pollitt, 1995; Kruesi & Rapoport, 1986). Breakfasts that consist of high-protein and high-energy foods have been shown to have positive effects on children's cognitive functions, physical endurance, and creativity (Wyon, Abrahamsson, Jartelius, & Fletcher, 1997). In 1997, 73 percent of public schools offered breakfast and lunch programs, and a large percentage of those schools also offered summer lunch programs in low-income areas (Children's Defense Fund, 1998). Unfortunately, according to a report in NEA Today (2000) from the Food Research and Action Center (FRAC) and the U.S. Department of Agriculture (1993), millions of children across the United States begin the school day hungry. Children who are malnourished are more vulnerable to disease, infections, and anemia, and to environmental toxins such as lead poisoning. They are also at greater risk for growth abnormalities and mental retardation.

Along with malnutrition another problem is childhood obesity. Excess weight normally results from an imbalance between calories taken in and energy expended. A child who weighs more than 10 percent above normal weight for her age is consid-

asthma—Condition that causes breathing difficulty because of obstructions in the airways of the lungs. The U.S. Department of Education recognizes asthma as a disability when it affects a child's education.

ered overweight and if she is more than 20 percent above normal weight, she is considered obese. Childhood obesity results from a combination of family and cultural practices, nutritional habits, physical factors such as lack of exercise, and psychological factors. Obesity can cause hypertension and diabetes mellitus, and produce stress on weight-bearing joints. Mental and emotional stress on children who are obese comes from peer pressure, and social acceptance and self-esteem factors. Teachers can help these children by teaching them about genetic inheritance factors and influences and good nutrition and exercise habits, and by encouraging social interactions that are not based on physical appearance.

An important component of any child care or school program is the meal and snack portion of the day. Head Start's nutrition program provides these for approximately 800,000 children nationwide during the school day. The famous milk-and-graham-cracker snack was immortalized by comedian Bill Cosby and later by Robert Fulghum in his book *All I Really Need to Know I Learned in Kindergarten* (1989). School and teacher involvement in children's nutrition is important not only for the provision of basic nutritional needs, but also for children's learning good nutrition habits that will promote lifelong wellness. The U.S. Departments of Agriculture and Health and Human Services have established dietary guidelines for maintaining and improving health that recommend everyone:

* eat a variety of foods.

* maintain a healthy weight.

* choose a diet low in fat, saturated fat, and cholesterol.

* choose a diet with plenty of vegetables, fruits, and grain products.

* use sugars only in moderation.

* use salt and sodium only in moderation.

(U.S. Departments of Health and Human Services, 1990)

The variety of foods consists of 6–11 servings of bread, cereal, rice, and pasta; 3–5 servings of vegetables; 2–4 servings of fruit; 2–3 servings of meat, poultry, fish, beans, eggs, and nuts; and 2–3 servings of dairy products, with fats, oils, and sweets used sparingly (Figure 5–6 on page 164). Serving sizes, which vary with age, will be noted later in the chapter.

A related health and nutrition issue is dental caries, or cavities. Low-income populations are more prone to dental problems because of poor nutrition, with diets high in refined carbohydrates and sweets that contribute to the breakdown of calcium on the teeth. Feeding practices such as putting babies to sleep with a bottle of milk or juice causes the sugar to pool on the teeth, attacking the tooth enamel. Learning proper tooth-brushing techniques and instilling regular tooth-brushing habits can help prevent dental caries.

The daily schedule or routine should provide for an exercise period, preferably outdoors, when the weather allows, where both free-choice and planned activities are offered. The school environment is conducive to all kinds of physical movement. Providing space and equipment can enhance development of strength, endurance, and coordination (as well as skill levels). The curriculum should include learning activities that present concepts of keeping healthy and safe, both physically and psychologically, and the adults in the school should model those health and safety practices themselves. Children of various age groups have different health and safety needs as they grow and develop. Knowing the stages and milestones of development is the foundation for providing the appropriate environment and curriculum to attain these developmental goals.

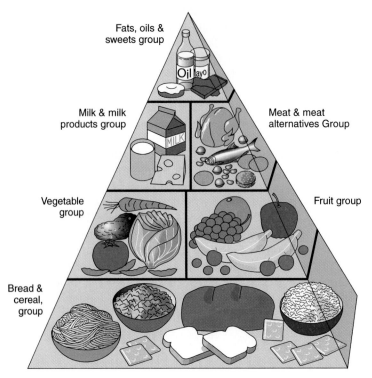

Figure 5—6

The food guide pyramid. (Courtesy of the U.S. Department of Agriculture)

❋ DEVELOPMENT AND CURRICULUM FOR THE GROWING CHILD

Anytime you look at ages and stages of development, it must be through the widest lens possible. While these stages occur in an orderly progression in normally developing children, they are also individual in timing, so some may occur later or sooner and still fall within the realm of normal. Maturation, the orderly progression of changes over time, is universal to all human species, and is programmed genetically. These physical developments, also called motor development, are further divided into gross motor development (body movement from one place to another) and fine motor development (manipulative skills, such as using the hands and fingers to accomplish tasks). But since we are talking about muscles, and not motors, we prefer to use the terms "large muscle" and "small muscle" development.

Physical development occurs in a predictable pattern from the head to the feet (**cephalocaudal**) and from the center of the body to the hands and fingers (**proximodistal**). One way to remember this is how the fetus develops: head first, then the trunk and legs, followed by the arms and little nubs that eventually become fingers. The control of these muscles occurs in this same pattern, such as holding up the head

❋ **cephalocaudal**—The progression of the control of muscles from the head to the feet.

proximodistal—The progression of the control of muscles from the center of the body out to the fingers.

before being able to kick at will; or rolling over by twisting the torso before being able to hold a pencil. Eventually, all these muscles will work together in a complex behavior called *hierarchic integration* (Werner, 1948).

The role of the teacher is to provide curriculum that addresses the developmental stage of the student, regardless of their age, even as an infant. Curriculum begins with preparing the environment with furnishings, materials, and supplies that are age appropriate, functional, and safe. Augmenting the furnishings are the activities the teacher plans to engage the child in active learning by interacting with the environment. An important factor here is the teacher, who is not just a stagehand and an observer, but who is also an encourager, supporter, monitor, enhancer, and appreciator of each child's efforts.

Infant Physical Development and Curriculum

Infants are changing at such a rapid rate that monitoring their physical condition is a critical tool for measuring their well-being. Since the infant cannot say when she is hungry, cold, or hurting, the adult must interpret her behavior for clues to her inner state. A normally active infant who becomes lethargic may not cry, and may thus be exhibiting a serious health symptom. Regular weight gain and progressive physical skill attainment are the usual indicators that the infant is healthy.

Infant Physical Development.

* Growth—During the first year, the baby grows significantly in height, weight, and head circumference. See Figure 5–7 on page 166 for average growth charts.

* Muscle Development—During the first year, the infant's movements include reflexive actions such as:

 Babinski—Spreading toes when sole of foot is stroked

 Grasping—Squeezing any object placed in palm

 Stepping—Moving feet as if walking when held upright with feet against a flat surface

 Rooting—Turning head to the side where cheek is stroked

These are not due to the infant's control over those muscles; they are genetically programmed neurological reflexes. Those reflexes disappear within the first few months of life. The Babinski reflex, for example, disappears by the end of the first year. At the same time, controlled muscle action is developing, such as raising and turning the head, reaching out and batting at objects, and eventually swinging leg and arm together while twisting the trunk to roll over. This coordination of head, trunk, arms, and legs is needed to get to the milestone that marks the end of the infancy stage: walking. Infants who have other disorders such as blindness, hearing impairments, or significant cognitive delays may also experience physical delays.

In the first year following birth, the infant triples in weight and grows approximately 10 inches in length. Bones become harder and muscles increase in mass, and the infant gains strength and control of those muscles. Body proportions change, but the head is still large compared to the rest of the body. One of the earliest sets of muscles an infant learns to control are the eye muscles. Even a newborn has some control of these muscles, moving her eyes and searching for novel things to see. By two months of age, deliberate head movements to look at new objects accompany the eye movements. This visual tracking will continue to develop throughout infancy.

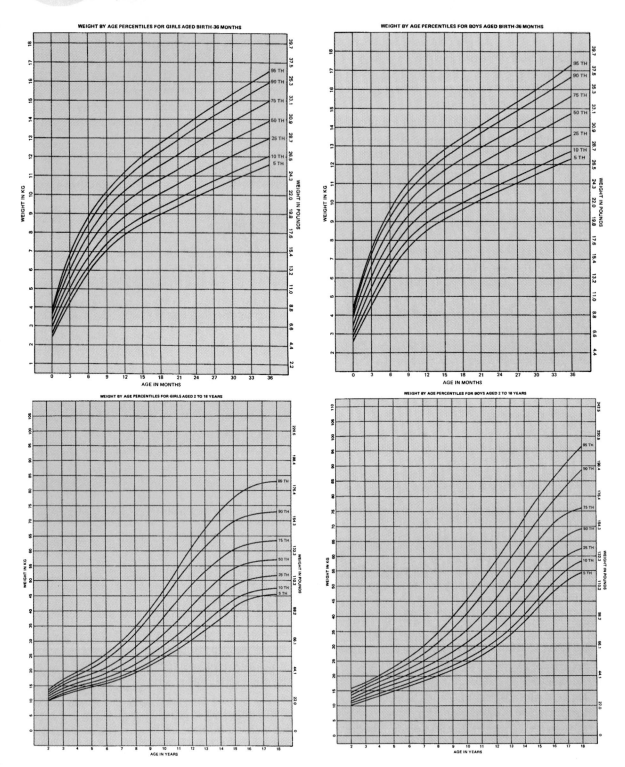

Figure 5-7

Growth statistics. (Courtesy of the National Center for Health Statistics, U.S. Department of Health and Human Services)

SCENARIO
* Two-week-old Caroline holds on to big sister's finger and won't let go.

* At three months, Caroline reaches out and grabs big sister's hair.

* At five months, Caroline grasps the toy placed by big sister on her high chair tray.

* At one year, Caroline drops a small toy over the side of the bathtub and reaches over for it.

Reaching and grasping begin as reflexes that are replaced by deliberate, increasingly controlled movements. Moving in a proximodistal direction, the two-month-old infant moves arms to bat at a mobile or grab at mother's face. At four months, the infant has a palm grasp, using the whole hand without using the thumb. By six months, the thumb is closing around the object as well, and by eight months, the thumb works in opposition to the fingers to grasp small objects. Letting go is harder and develops later than grasping. This small muscle development and control continues to be refined and to work more efficiently over time.

SCENARIO

* At two months, Mario lifts his head and looks in the direction of his dog, Ruff.

* At four months, Mario pushes and pushes and flops over onto his back in Ruff's direction.

* At six months, Mario is up on his hands and knees and rocks back and forth in Ruff's direction.

* By seven months, Mario uses his elbows and hips to scoot over nearer to Ruff.

* By seven months, when Mario reaches Ruff he grabs hold, pulls himself up, and stands up holding on to Ruff.

* At one year, Mario takes a step toward Ruff.

Moving in a cephalocaudal direction (head to foot), the infant gradually gains control of her whole body, working toward the goal of walking. By two months, the infant holds up her head and looks around. Between two and four months, she holds up her shoulders and uses her arms to lift her torso. Between two and five months, she coordinates her legs, one at a time, first to flip, and then to smoothly roll over. She rolls from her stomach to her back first, and then later rolls from her back to her stomach. Between five and eight months, she sits up without support. By six to eight months, she goes from rocking on her hands and knees, to propelling forward with legs dragging, to creeping using hands and knees to move from place to place (Figure 5–8 on page 168). By ten months, she pulls herself up and stands supported. Between seven and thirteen months, she walks around by holding onto things and between eleven and fourteen months, she stands and then walks without support. That walking signals the end of the infancy stage. The pattern of these milestones in development is universal, but the ages at which they occur are individual to each child based on genetic factors, experiences, and the infant's own temperament. Cultural influences may accelerate or inhibit the milestone of walking. In the South African tribe of

Figure 5-8

Infants creep and crawl before they walk, which they do at varying ages.

the San, mothers constantly carry their infants in a sling on their hips, allowing the infant freedom to move arms and legs and to feed at will. Sitting and standing skills are practiced as the mothers support and repeat those actions, so these babies sit and stand earlier than their European peers (Small, 1998).

During infancy, there is a close relationship among nutrition, growth, development, and the ability to resist disease. The child's diet during this time may consist primarily of breast milk or a substitute, with the eventual introduction of soft solids such as cereals and pureed fruits, vegetables, and meat. Children who do not gain weight during this period experience **failure to thrive**, which may be caused by either malnutrition or deprivation dwarfism (Patton & Gardner, 1963), where the growth hormone is suppressed because of emotional abuse or neglect. Poverty contributes to failure to thrive, because of both the lack of adequate or appropriate nutrition and environmental stress factors such as abuse (physical or emotional) and substance-abusing parents.

Dennis (1960, 1973) researched orphanages where children were provided sustenance, but little opportunity for physical movement. Not surprisingly, their physical development was extremely delayed.

Infant Health and Nutrition. The infant's health depends on an environment that is sanitary and as free from contaminants and irritants as possible. Toys, equipment, and linens should be washed frequently. Air should be circulated and filtered so that germs are not reintroduced into the environment. Because of their immature immune systems and limited in-group exposure, which would help build greater immunity, infants and young children are very susceptible to communicable diseases. Pathogens, or germs, are present in respiratory discharges, blood, urine, and feces. Adults and infants can both transmit diseases. Frequent hand washing for all, sanitary procedures when feeding, and thorough cleaning of toys, equipment, and surfaces can reduce this transmission.

---

failure to thrive—Undernutrition that seriously affects physical growth and development, as well as emotional and cognitive development.

Keeping babies healthy begins with the recommended immunizations (Figure 5–9 on page 170).

Because infants have immature physiological systems and so many things in the environment are new to them, their physical state can change very rapidly and quickly deteriorate. The adult must watch for very subtle changes in the infant to gather cues that may be vital to the baby's health and well-being. A crying infant gets attention, but what about the one who all of a sudden is not crying, or is not as active and alert as usual? These can be signs that something is wrong.

Sudden Infant Death Syndrome (SIDS) is the leading cause of death among children under one year, claiming approximately 3,000 two- to twelve-month-olds annually. No single cause has been identified, but some suspected causes include: physiological or neurological abnormalities, a bacterium occasionally found in raw honey, a brain stem defect that impairs the infant's arousal response, the mother's cigarette smoking during pregnancy, or an immature respiratory system (Kinney et al., 1995; Schwartz, Stramba-Badiale, & Segantini, 1998). Many infants appear to be in good health prior to their death, making it especially traumatic for both the families and the caregiver if the death occurs in a child care facility. A major discovery in Europe in the late 1980s prompted the American Academy of Pediatrics to launch a "Back to Sleep" campaign recommending that all babies be laid to sleep on their backs or sides and not on their stomachs. This simple precautionary practice has lowered SIDS deaths by approximately 50 percent (Carroll & Siska, 1996). Parents and caregivers should follow this important advice.

Infants need more than food, diaper changes, and a place to sleep. They need adults who look them in the eye with a smile and acceptance. They need adults who touch them tenderly, speak to them often and cheerfully, describe the routines of the day, and respond promptly to their physical and emotional needs. This means that one adult should be responsible for no more than three or four infants, and the whole group size with two adults should be no more than eight. These arrangements provide for enough adults to meet infants' urgent and emotional needs, as well as act as play partners for cognitive stimulation.

The infant's head is so large proportionate to the rest of her body that she is especially vulnerable to *shaken baby syndrome*. Sometimes a colicky baby (or an exasperating toddler) leads the adult to lose patience and shake the child out of frustration or anger. This quick motion to the body and its resultant whiplash effect on the head and neck can cause serious damage to the brain and spinal cord. This must not occur! It is dangerous to the child and may even be fatal. Nationally, 3,000 to 5,000 children each year are found to have shaken baby syndrome. This problem was brought to national attention with the 1997 death of Matthew Eappen, in which au pair Louise Woodward was charged with involuntary manslaughter.

As recommended by the American Academy of Pediatrics, for the first six to twelve months of an infant's life, breast milk is best suited to the infant's digestive system, as well as providing initial immunologic protection (Wagner & Anderson, 1996). Breast milk is both less likely to trigger allergies and more easily digested than cow's milk. The mother's diet, supplemented with vitamins C and D, helps to provide the nutrition necessary for forming strong bones in the fetus and nursing infant and maintaining bones in the mother. As a breast milk substitute, formula must be mixed with safe water and in accordance with the directions of the manufacturer and infant's pediatrician. The infant should be fed while being held, and not by propping the bottle with a blanket or pillow. Cereal and pureed foods are introduced on the pediatrician's advice, usually one at a time to observe possible allergic or digestive reactions.

Because the infant is rapidly developing control of the body from head to toe, the adult should provide encouragement for each newly acquired skill. Placing a toy in front of a baby just starting to scoot will give her something interesting to strive for.

Recommended Childhood Immunization Schedule

Vaccines are listed under routinely recommended ages. Bars indicate range of recommended ages for immunization. Any dose not given at the recommended age should be given as a "catch-up" immunization at any subsequent visit, when indicated and feasible. Ovals indicate vaccines to be given if previously recommended doses were missed or given earlier than the recommended minimum age.

	Birth	1 month	2 months	4 months	6 months	12 months	15 months	18 months	4-6 years	11-12 years	14-16 years
Hepatitis B		Hep B	Hep B			Hep B				Hep B	
Diphtheria, Tetanus, Pertussis			DTaP	DTaP	DTaP			DTaP	DTaP	Td	
H. Influenzae type b			Hib	Hib	Hib	Hib					
Polio			IPV	IPV		Polio			Polio		
Rotavirus			Rv	Rv	Rv						
Measles, Mumps, Rubella						MMR			MMR	MMR	
Varicella						Var	Var			Var	

Approved by the Advisory Committee on Immunization Practices (ACIP), the American Academy of Pediatrics (AAP), and the American Academy of Family Physicians (AAFP).

Figure 5–9

Recommended immunizations. (From the Centers for Disease Control and Prevention)

Placing a toy to the side of a baby getting ready to roll over, the baby will reach for the toy as a stimulating reward for rolling over. When the baby begins to rise up on her knees and pull up, the adult should provide stable pieces of furniture and equipment that will hold the child's weight for standing and *cruising* (holding on to furniture to get where she wants to go) around.

Infant Curriculum for Physical Development and Health.

Infancy has the most specialized equipment for routine care in the form of cribs, carriers, high chairs, changing tables, and strollers or carriages. Strict criteria for this equipment are established and enforced by the U.S. Consumer Product Safety Commission, but this does not absolve the adult from examining the equipment carefully and using it properly. Besides the customary furnishings, the classroom should be outfitted with equipment to challenge and reinforce rapidly developing large and small muscles. Padded or soft surfaces on which to crawl, stable furniture on which to pull up and support early stages of standing and walking, and chewable, cleanable, small manipulative toys are all useful in helping to develop muscle control. Equipment that can stimulate large muscle development includes balls, push/pull toys, and stable infant play seats (walkers or jump-ups are not recommended).

The activities the teacher plans or does spontaneously should be directly connected with the child's developmental level. Greenman and Stonehouse (1996) call these *prime times* in their book by the same name. The developmental variability from child to child in the first year of life suggests that activities should be one-on-one, delaying group activities until the second year. Spontaneous activities include adult responses to the child's task at hand, such as rolling over, sitting up, crawling, standing or walking, and grasping and letting go. Planned activities should also include acquired skills and those still developing by providing for repeating and practicing mastered skills. Challenging activities introduce and stimulate the next level of development with the adult as a guide, encourager, and enabler. As the child repeatedly performs the activity with the adult's help, the skill is developed. Eventually the child is able to carry out the activity independently, perhaps not perfectly or without some frustration, but the accumulated experience leads to mastery. The following are some suggested activities to promote physical development in the infant (Watson, Watson & Wilson, 1999).

 * Birth to four months—Move the infant's body position from back to stomach in different safe locations to allow her different views and actions in the room. Massage the infant's body, gently bending and stretching arms and legs in a bicycling motion. Fasten balls or small bells securely to baby's booties to stimulate kicking for visual and auditory response. Place objects for grasping within the infant's reach.

 * Four to eight months—Fasten a cradle gym above the baby to stimulate reaching and batting to make noise or movement. Provide uncluttered space where the child can roll around and sit up for short periods of time. Hold the baby and move to music. Provide soft toys that are easy to grasp, and toys that make noise when moved.

 * Eight to twelve months—Provide obstacle-free space for crawling, and low, sturdy furniture to hold onto and climb on. Provide objects small enough to pinch and lift but not swallow, and objects to bang. Push/pull toys can be crawling incentives.

The outdoors also offer a stimulating place for muscle development (Figure 5–10 on page 172). Safe places from which to view the world around them, shaded from sun and protected from wind, are great for infants. Crawlers and early walkers

Figure 5-10

Infants thrive on outdoor play.

can be placed on a blanket, pebble-free grass, or other soft surface, under adult supervision. Washable toys for grasping, moving, and making noise can be brought outside for play. These opportunities can be enhanced by having other children nearby to watch and interact with. The adult, of course, is the primary muscle stimulator by way of massage, physical manipulation of arms and legs, standing the infant up with support, and stimulating walking.

Toddler Physical Development and Curriculum

In the second year of life, the child finds freedom in mobility, discovers words to express wants and needs, and develops a strong will to use both. No longer an infant, and becoming an independent person, the toddler moves through the second year at full speed, which may bring many a bump and bruise.

Toddler Physical Development. Toddlers are those infants who have accomplished upright locomotion. They still may be cruising (holding on for support but walking), or they may have been liberated from the need for physical supports and now rush from one area to another. The toddler's birth weight has quadrupled and height has more than doubled. Bones are hardening (ossification) and the fontanels (skull spaces) are closing. By the end of the second year, the cephalocaudal progress of muscle control is reaching the sphincter muscles needed to control urination and defecation. Also by the end of the second year, 18 to 20 baby teeth (primary teeth) have appeared. As the toddler nears three years, she is sleeping 13 hours a day, including one daytime nap.

Young toddlers walk with feet spread apart, hence the term "toddler," but they move with deliberate action and can run, but not always stop, usually just dropping to the floor or colliding with an object or person. They can crawl up stairs and come down by crawling backwards or bumping down on their bottom. If they are able to reach the handrail, they will climb the stairs one step at a time. As they begin to descend the stairs in an upright position, the observer's heart may skip a beat because toddlers often show no fear and may step right off the edge. Toddlers between their second and third birthdays have much better walking and running skills, stand more erect, and have a more proportionate body to head ratio. This physical attribute allows for a better body weight-balance ratio. The older toddler walks up and down stairs (still usually one step at a time), pedals a tricycle, and throws a ball.

Young toddlers grasp crayons and markers using the whole hand and scribble on and beyond the paper with the whole arm and little fine muscle control (Figure 5–11). They are beginning to feed themselves and drink from a cup. Their grasp-and-release small muscles are exercised by the desire to fill and dump small items, including sand and water, into and out of a container. Piling up and knocking over blocks hold great fascination for them and they will repeat this over and over. They experiment with every item they find, often still using their sense of taste and oral manipulation; therefore, small items need to be eliminated from the young toddler's environment. They can turn the pages of cardboard and cloth books, and they enjoy looking at the pictures of animals and babies. Older toddlers are gaining more control of their hand muscles, holding the pen or marker in a finger and thumb grasp; however, their grasp is usually high up on the tool, which hampers control. They can build towers with blocks, pound clay, and turn the individual pages of a book.

Toddler Health and Nutrition. In this period of rapid growth and development, serious illnesses may slow growth, but adequate health care can ensure that normal growth expectations are attained. There are disparities in the health status of America's children, with children of low-income families more likely to be exposed to lead paint that can affect their nervous system and less likely to receive prompt or routine health care for disease prevention.

Toddlers have built up some immunity to diseases, but a sanitary environment, coupled with frequent hand washing and universal precautions when diapering and cleaning up bodily fluids, are essential to reducing the spread of diseases. Toddlers are acquiring teeth, but have not yet developed sophisticated social or language skills, so biting as a form of primitive communication is a potential danger to other toddlers

Figure 5–11

Young writers use their whole fist to grasp the pencil or marker.

Figure 5-12

Biting happens.

and adults. It will happen! The adult responds by washing the bite and giving sympathy to the bitten child, telling the biter that it hurts when she bites (Figure 5–12). Some children who bite can be deterred with alternative objects to bite, while others just need time to pass through the phase. The best defense is to alert adults, who can prevent, redirect, and be patient.

Keeping toddlers safe is an expanding task because, as their mobility and hand coordination increases, the potential for accidents also increases. All electrical outlets must have protectors to prevent curious toddlers from inserting small objects into them. Stairwells and windows and doors that open should have safety gates or some form of protection against toddlers opening them and falling through. Small objects should be kept away from toddlers because they present a choking hazard. Ropes, cords, belts, and strings, including hood or hat strings, pose the danger of strangulation. Properly secured car seats must be used at all times in the back seat of the car. The child should never be left unattended in a car, a room, or outside. All furniture within reach of the toddler should be heavy enough to not move when the toddler pulls up on it and anchored so she cannot pull it over on her. Chests of drawers and bookcases are hazards because drawers and shelves can become levers for the child to pull the whole piece of furniture over on herself. It's not easy keeping a toddler safe!

The older infant who ate enthusiastically has now turned into a toddler who may be finicky and fussy, and only want to eat one type of food for days on end. The toddler's developing autonomy is demonstrated in eating behavior. Because this decrease in appetite and tendency to prefer a limited number of foods develop at the same time as the drive to be independent, food struggles between the toddler and adult often emerge. Providing a variety of good food choices and avoiding a power struggle over what and how much the toddler eats will help her retain power by selecting foods and amounts. Of course, snacking on nonnutritious foods and drinks should be avoided. Toddlers are beginning to feed themselves, often getting more on their clothing than in their mouths. About 20 teeth have emerged now, including the molars. Toddlers can now brush their teeth after meals: this is an opportunity to establish good dental hygiene. The toddler's food should be cut into small pieces that can be easily pierced with a child-sized fork, scooped up with a spoon, or picked up with the fingers. Premeal handwashing is an important habit to instill. Toddlers need close supervision during meals to prevent them from choking, since they do not chew well and they tend to put many pieces of food in their mouth at a time. A variety of small servings consisting of two teaspoonsful of each foods should be served at each meal, with small servings of nutritious snacks in between (Figure 5–13). Toddlers learn table manners by eating with adults and they also enjoy the social experience of eating with other

---

Child and Adult Care Food Program

Infants

Birth to three months
Breakfast, Lunch, and Snack
4–6 oz. formula

Four to seven months
Breakfast, Lunch, and Snack
4–6 oz. formula
0–3 tbsp. iron-fortified infant cereal (not snack)
0–3 tbsp. vegetables or fruits (not snack)

Eight to eleven months
Breakfast and Lunch
6–8 oz. formula
2–4 tbsp. iron-fortified infant cereal (not snack)
1–4 tbsp. fruit or vegetables

Lunch
1–4 tbsp. meat, fish, poultry, egg yolk, or dried beans *or*
1–4 oz. cottage cheese, cheese spread, or cheese food *or*
½–2 oz. cheese

Snack
2–4 oz. formula or milk or full-strength fruit juice
2 crackers or ½ slice bread

Children

One to two years
Breakfast
½ cup milk
¼ cup fruit juice, fruit, or vegetable
Bread or cereal (¼ cup cereal, ½ slice bread)

Lunch
½ cup milk
Meat or meat alternative (1 oz. meat or cheese, 1 egg, 2 tbsp. peanut butter, or ¼ cup cooked dry beans or peas)
¼ cup (total) vegetables or fruits (more than one choice)
½ slice bread

Snack (select two)
½ cup milk
½ oz. meat or meat alternative *or*
2 oz. plain yogurt or ¼ cup flavored yogurt (*do not serve yogurt and milk at same snack*)

Three to five years
Breakfast
¾ cup milk
½ cup fruit juice, fruit, or vegetable
½ slice bread *or*
⅓ cup cold cereal *or*
¼ cup hot cereal

Lunch
¾ cup milk
Meat or meat alternative (1½ oz. meat, poultry, cheese, or 1 egg, or ⅜ cup cooked dry beans or peas *or* 3 tbsp. peanut butter *or* ¾ oz. nuts or seeds)
½ cup (total) vegetables or fruits (more than one choice)
½ slice bread

Snack (select two)
½ cup milk
½ oz. meat or meat alternative *or*
2 oz. plain yogurt or ¼ cup flavored yogurt
½ cup fruit juice or fruit or vegetable
Bread or cereal (½ slice bread, ⅓ cup cold cereal, ¼ cup hot cereal)

Figure 5–13

Food serving guidelines. (From Robertson, C. 1998)

children. The child's chair should have a footrest or allow her feet to touch the floor and eating utensils should be child-sized and nonbreakable.

Toddler Curriculum for Physical Development and Health. Materials that can be used to promote physical development include:

* plastic soft drink bottles filled with material or objects that make noise or change as the bottle is tipped or rolled, such as macaroni, water with food coloring and oil, pennies, or glitter. (Make sure bottles are sealed with extra-strength glue.)
* bean-filled beanbags to toss (these can be handmade and filled with birdseed or rice as an alternative to beans).
* pinch-type clothespins to latch onto the edges of things and slip-on type clothespins to insert into plastic milk jugs.
* pegboards, stacking and nesting toys, a pounding bench, and plastic jars with matching lids.
* simple dress-up props such as hats, purses, and lunch boxes, and seasonal clothing like mittens and scarves, or swim goggles and sun visors.
* play items inside a plastic swimming pool without water, which holds great appeal for toddlers, who like getting in and out alone, as well as the feeling of coziness inside.

Toddlers love to go outdoors and now they can walk on uneven ground; they can push and pull movable objects around, and experience outdoor features such as snow, sticks, sand, leaves, and grass. While the outdoor environment offers wonderful sensory learning opportunities, it also may contain potential hazards, such as toxic plants and other things toddlers put in their mouths. The adult caregiver must be vigilant. Playgrounds should be specially designed for the needs of toddlers, with resilient surfacing and level areas for wheeled toys, as well as low climbing apparatus and objects to move. Moving, arranging, piling up, and knocking down objects enhance children's physical, cognitive, and emotional development. Hills to climb, run up, or roll down bring special pleasure. Shade trees also provide the sensory experiences of touch and smell. Outdoors water and sand play can eliminate the concern of spills indoors and can be a full-body experience, with children actually getting into the sandbox (which should be covered when it is not in use to prevent animal contamination) or the water in warm weather (Figure 5–14). Adult supervision is a must for these types of activities. Even water in a bucket can pose a drowning hazard to a small child.

Preschooler Physical Development and Curriculum

Three- to five-year-olds can manage many self-care routines and often insist on doing so. They are continuing to smooth out movements and gain control of small muscles. Usually, this is a calmer time than the toddler years, with children exhibiting a longer attention span and newly acquired skills. The preschooler spends more time at chosen tasks such as riding a tricycle, swinging, doing a puzzle, or drawing.

Preschooler Physical Development. The preschooler adds about four to five pounds a year, up to an average body weight of 45 pounds by the age of five, and grows two to two and one-half inches a year, with girls only slightly shorter and lighter than boys. The body has smoothed out, losing its baby fat. The *toddling* has turned into smooth walking, running, and skipping. By the end of the preschool stage,

Figure 5–14

Toddlers enjoy filling, dumping, and controlling substances.

children walk up and down stairs using alternating feet. They can climb and swing with ease and use better judgment about their abilities and the risks that they take.

Preschoolers have much better small muscle coordination than toddlers. They can throw and catch a large soft ball and are using a pencil and scissors somewhat skillfully. They are beginning to print their names and draw pictures that are recognizable, though more symbolic than realistic. By this time, 90 percent of children have firmly established a preference for using their right or left hand.

Preschooler Health and Nutrition. This is usually a time of good health and steady growth and development, and the preschooler is less likely than the toddler to engage in actions that risk life and limb. Illnesses during this span tend to be of a respiratory nature or allergy related. By the end of the preschool years, the typical child sleeps about 10 hours a night, with no nap. Preschoolers have fewer accidents than toddlers, who lack self-awareness, or than primary and elementary age children, who are subject to peer pressure and tend to be risk takers to prove their bravery. Childhood injuries are the leading cause of death among children ages one to fourteen. Most accidental deaths occurring among children ages one to four are linked to motor vehicle accidents (National Center for Heath Statistics, 1998). Preschool children graduate from infant seats to booster seats. They may begin to resist the constraint, but fortunately they are also better able to understand the importance of safety. With some added incentives like tape players with earphones, favorite books, or drawing pads, preschoolers can learn to cooperate with car safety rules.

Influenced by other children's food choices in the classroom, the preschooler is more adventurous in trying new foods than the toddler. The social aspect of eating is important to preschoolers; they enjoy participating in social conversations at the table, although these may interfere with the actual task of eating. Eating skills have improved with the continued development of small muscle coordination; the preschooler can use all utensils fairly well for buttering bread, cutting meat, and drinking without spilling (most of the time). The preschooler is acquiring an understanding of safe choices and is less likely to ingest nonfood items. They understand the importance of brushing teeth and eating healthful foods, although the term "good food" can be confusing, since to the preschooler potato chips are good and candy bars are very good. The preschooler understands bedtime and car safety routines; the basics of using a phone to call for help, and, at least vaguely, the idea that she is vulnerable to disease.

Television is a significant, mostly negative, influence on the preschooler's choice of foods (Gans et al., 1993; Kotz & Story, 1994). Children of this age average about 25 hours per week of television viewing, with the youngest children viewing the most hours per week. Inactivity while watching television, coupled with the influence of high fat, sugary food commercials, have led to increasing preschooler obesity. (See the comparison of advertised foods to recommended foods in Figure 5–15.) Compounding this, more and more meals are eaten outside of the home and many restaurants provide foods high in calories and fat content for their children's meals, setting the course for hypertension, obesity, and vitamin deficiency.

Recommended food serving sizes are smaller than adults might think appropriate. The recommended 1,500–1,700 calories a day for four-year-olds should consist of no more than 30 percent from fat and 10–12 percent from protein, accompanied by low levels of refined sugar. Disagreements over appropriate food choices sometimes lead to a food struggle between adult and child that can have lifelong negative implications on relationships and health and nutrition. Head Start parent education efforts have shown that parents can help children learn to like new foods and eat sufficient quantities from a variety of food groups. For example, when children help prepare their own food (chopping vegetables, stirring ingredients), they are more likely to try the finished product (Fuhr & Barclay, 1998).

Preschooler Curriculum for Physical Development and Health.

Physical activity is important for children's muscle development, stress release, and confidence building. Classroom equipment for large muscle development should be available during free play every day. Many programs schedule gym time a few days a week but this does not allow children to choose activity when they *need* it. Space considerations may require inventiveness, but less space is needed than one might think. A personal-size trampoline with a railing affords a good aerobic workout to a stressed child. Wiffle balls hung on strings from ceiling grids provide good hand-eye coordination practice and an outlet for excess energy.

Small muscle control is still developing. There are all kinds of small manipulatives (equipment that involve the use of small muscles and eye-hand coordination) in school supply catalogs, but some of the best ones can be found in the home. Clothing provides good small muscle practice with zipping and buttoning. Kitchen tools such as hand mixers, potato peelers, cheese graters, orange juicers, pancake turners, chop sticks, and taco presses give practice in different types of hand movements, while allowing the child to connect with her culture. These should all be used under adult supervision.

Every planned and free-play activity that occurs in the preschool classroom provides practice for developing large and small muscle skills.

⁎ Dramatic play—Putting on clothing, pretending to do housekeeping tasks, taking care of dolls, and using toy maintenance tools, such as plastic screwdrivers, hammers, pipes, and fittings

⁎ Art area—Developing small muscles while drawing, writing, cutting, molding, and painting

⁎ Blocks—Developing large muscles when moving hollow blocks and ramps and small muscles with unit blocks and accessories

⁎ Sensory table—Filling, dumping, sifting, and pouring use refined small muscles

❋ Book area—Using small muscles when turning pages or piling books

❋ Science/math area—Using small muscles to examine, explore, and manipulate objects for classification and quantification

❋ Snack and meal time—Using small muscles when manipulating tableware and preparing food by spooning, spreading, or cutting

Outdoors, the preschooler needs and takes opportunities to climb and jump; environments should ensure the area is as safe as possible with height limits for jumping

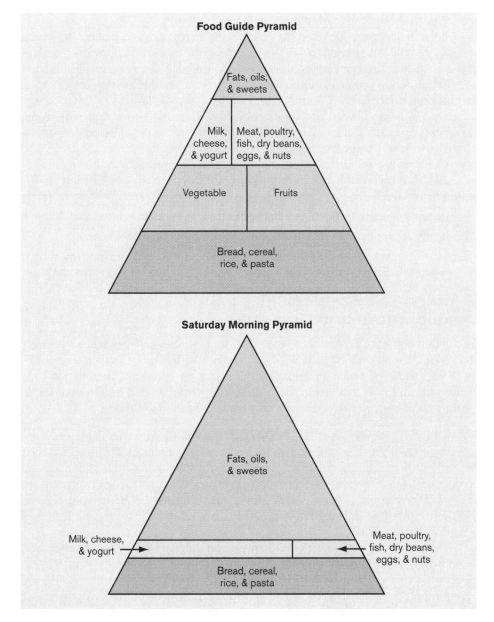

Figure 5−15

Food guide pyramid compared to Saturday morning pyramid. (From Kotz, K., & Story, M. [1994]. *Journal of the American Dietetic Association, 94*(11) 1296–1300)

and cushioned surfaces. Supervised long walks in safe areas and running enhance endurance. Children at this age are beginning to be interested in games, but they have a limited attention span and understanding of rules. Traditional games such as Ring Around the Rosie; Duck, Duck, Goose; and Red Light, Green Light are appropriate for this age. Preschoolers also enjoy foot races that do not emphasize the competitive aspect. They are beginning to use sports equipment for batting, and for kicking, throwing, and catching balls, but protective equipment and adult supervision are still needed to maintain safety. Children of this age love the sensation of speed, whether it is on bicycles, swings, or merry-go-rounds; opportunities should be provided for these activities within safety limitations. Trips to parks with safe, but challenging, activities expand the children's physical abilities.

Preschoolers can understand basic concepts of staying safe and healthy. Books and activities designed to promote good choices can be incorporated into the daily curriculum. The teacher, family members, and peers (as role models) are all-powerful influences on behavior. Adults should pay careful attention to the types of habits they are modeling for observant preschoolers. Children of this age love to cook, an activity that promotes an interest in healthful food and hand-washing practices and boosts their self-esteem. Cooking is especially conducive to cognitive development as preschoolers watch food substances being changed by temperature, measure ingredients, set the table, and grasp the sequence and pattern concepts as they follow simple recipes.

Health programs for preschoolers (Parcel, Tiernan, Nadar, & Gottlob, 1979) should help children:

1. identify feelings of wellness and illness and be able to express them to adults.
2. identify appropriate sources of assistance for health-related problems.
3. initiate independently the use of sources of assistance for health problems, such as applying Bandaids, dialing 911, and recognizing healthy and unhealthy choices.

Primary Age Physical Development and Curriculum

As children enter the early school years, they are physically independent and usually able to care for all their hygiene needs, sometimes with some assistance, and sometimes with some insistence, from their family. They are becoming interested in their own bodies and how they work, so this is an opportune time to instill good health, nutrition, and exercise habits that will help ensure a healthy adulthood.

Primary Age Physical Development. Children develop more complex physical skills such as skating, swimming, or playing a musical instrument in their early school years. During this stage, participating in team sports helps to develop and coordinate large and small muscle actions in conjunction with cognitive functions and social interactions (Figure 5–16). Primary age children can better control small muscles, resulting in drawing and writing that is a more accurate representation of what they know and see.

During the primary grades, children gain an average of five pounds a year and grow two and one-half inches a year. Skeletal and muscular growth is increasing, along with strength and lung capacity. Body dimensions are slimming down and becoming proportionately more adultlike. Body size and shape are becoming more important in defining who children are as they begin to measure themselves against their peers. There is a great deal of variation in height and weight that has little bearing on full growth attainment. Still, concerns are rampant, especially for girls who tower over boys, and for boys who are shorter than the rest. Body differences may also be influenced by diet and activity levels.

Figure 5—16

Girls and boys are aware of differences in their sizes and abilities.

Primary Age Health and Nutrition. This is a stage of physical activity and "industry," as Erikson (1963) calls it; it is a time of gaining adult-level large and small muscle skills. Children of this age are generally healthy, except for short-term infections. Other more serious diseases may occur; symptoms such as decreased appetite or activity level or irritability may be early indicators. Children of this age are very interested in the workings of their body, making this an opportune time for teaching the facts of bodily functions, as well as healthy lifestyle choices to maintain lifelong health.

There is a strong relationship between the physical and psychological domains at this age. During the early school years, children's self-comparisons, along with rigid self-criticism and criticism by others, compounds their sensitivity regarding their physical attributes, affecting their self-esteem. This self-consciousness can extend into reluctance to participate for fear of ridicule, or extreme risk-taking to gain the perceived admiration of others. Thompson, McInnes, and Huntington (1990) found that teasing during this period leaves long-lasting effects on self-esteem and social competence. Cultural norms for masculinity and femininity are also rigid at this age, with children imitating the behaviors of older role models to *try on* their gender roles.

With all the physical activity and steady growth of this period, along with academic pressures, good nutrition is vital. Unfortunately, an estimated 40 percent of children ages five to eight show at least one heart disease risk factor such as high blood pressure, elevated cholesterol, or obesity (Williams, 1990). Children prone to obesity should be under a physician's supervision and care should be taken in the classroom to preserve the child's acceptance, self-esteem, and sense of self-worth. The American

Heart Association (1999) recommends reducing dietary fat, becoming more active, and adult modeling of healthful eating and activity habits for all children. Childhood obesity is often carried over into adulthood, bringing with it serious health risks. One study of children indicated a 54 percent increase in the prevalence of obesity among six- to eleven-year-olds from the 1960s to the 1990s (Troiano, Flegel, Kuczmarski, Campbell, & Johns, 1995; Gortmaker, Dietz, Sobol, & Wehler, 1987). Studies involving twins have verified a genetic factor in the predisposition to obesity (Stunkard, Harris, Pedersen, & McClearn, 1990). The risk factor for obesity is greater with two obese parents, which may indicate a genetic component as well as the parents being poor role models for eating and exercise habits (Deitz & Gortmaker, 1985; Bouchard, Lykken, McGue, Sega, & Tellegen, 1990).

The increase in obesity over the last several decades is attributable to an American diet that is high in refined sugar, fats, and an accompanying sedentary lifestyle that includes little physical exercise. The origins of both these factors can be traced back to the public schools. The average school lunch is notoriously high in fat, with about 37 percent of its total calories accounted for by fat. Schools also disregard U.S. Department of Agriculture guidelines on content and serving sizes (Pannell, 1995). Many schools have eliminated or cut back on their physical education programs, which may have contributed to American children's declining state of physical fitness (Office for Disease Prevention and Health Promotion, Public Health Service, 1984). Ross and Pate (1987) found that only about one-third of elementary school children have daily physical education and fewer than one-fifth have extracurricular activity programs at school.

WORDS OF WISDOM

Bernard Spodek was quoted in an interview:

"Recently *The New York Times* published a front-page article about how schools are eliminating recess. Administrators believed that eliminating recess would provide more instructional time. We wouldn't eliminate adults' coffee breaks in the hopes of increased productivity. Workers perform better with adequate breaks. Likewise research shows that children function better after recess compared to if they just stayed in classrooms doing assignments" (Allison, 1999, p. 262).

Young people watch television an average of almost 20 hours per week (Strasburger & Donnerstein, 1999). Contributing to the decline in physical fitness in addition to two to three hours a day of inactivity are television commercials, which bombard the viewer with advertisements for high-fat, high-sugar foods (Tufts University Diet and Nutrition Newsletter, 1995). Additionally, those foods are usually shown as part of a fun activity (Ogletree, Williams, Raffeld, Mason, & Fricke, 1990). And, while children are watching television or videos, what they are *not* doing contributes to obesity. They are not moving, walking, running, or playing. In fact, Klesges (1993) found that while children are "glued to the tube" they are in a deeply relaxed state that lowers their metabolism, using even less calories than doing *nothing*. Prolonged computer usage by children in place of vigorous physical activity compounds the childhood obesity problem.

This is the age of large muscle coordination for movements such as running, jumping, climbing, throwing, and other sports-related skills, as well as small muscle eye-hand coordination for drawing, writing, modeling, and fine craft work. Equipment includes all kinds of sports apparatus for individual and team sports, and for movement sports such as bicycles, swimming, and skateboarding, as well as arts and crafts materials. Computers are also included, with children using both keyboard and mouse to write, draw, and manipulate graphics.

Primary Age Curriculum for Physical Development and Health.

Schools have become a hub of preventive efforts to intervene in the unhealthy behaviors or social/environmental conditions that are the leading causes of premature death. Risk behaviors established early in life persist into adulthood. For the past 20 years, *Growing Healthy* (National Center for Health Education, 1996), a comprehensive school health curriculum, has been proven to promote knowledge, attitudes, and behaviors consistent with growing into healthy adults. In the primary grades, the curriculum has the following themes and content:

* Kindergarten: Happiness is a Healthy Me—An overview of the five senses that examines features that make children unique from other people and helps them learn good dental practices

* Grade 1: Super Me—Focusing on the body as a machine and expanding knowledge of the five senses, and helping them learn assertiveness skills

* Grade 2: Sights and Sounds—Examining the body's ability to see and hear, and focusing on feelings and how to express them

* Grade 3: Movement and the Human Body—Focusing on the muscular and skeletal systems, and helping children learn about safe self-care

Free-time activities for primary age children include competitive sports, both team and individual (Figure 5–17). Planned activities can enhance muscle development by helping with coordination and stamina, including isolated skills such as foul shots in basketball, throwing and catching baseballs, swimming strokes, gymnastic moves, and hiking over rough terrain. Practicing handwriting, arts and craft activities with various media, carpentry, puzzles, and card and game playing all refine small muscle skills.

The teacher provides opportunities for this age group to experience a wide variety of sports and recreation options and arts and crafts. Exercise habits established in childhood are more likely to continue into adulthood, resulting in a reduced chance of cardiovascular disease (Blair & Meredith, 1994). Children of this age like collecting

Figure 5—17

Most primary age children enjoy active sports.

things and planning their collections' categorization and display. Whether baseball cards, insects, rocks, or the latest toy craze, manipulating and categorizing objects help children use their muscles, as well as their intellect.

Elementary Age Physical Development and Curriculum

Eight- to twelve-year-olds are growing at uneven rates, but are confident movers and doers. They have issues about physical development that are more psychological and emotional than in previous stages, now measuring themselves against each other, their heroes, and their role models. They are exuberant and interested, as long as you keep them moving.

Elementary Age Physical Development.
Most elementary age children have well-developed and controlled muscles for all the basic sports skills, including running, throwing, catching, and batting, along with increased strength and endurance. Their small muscle skills are almost at a mature level, giving them mastery over drawing, writing, and craft making, with girls usually having better small muscle skills than boys of this age.

Toward the end of the elementary school years, some other striking physical changes are taking place. Children may add three to six inches in height per year. Muscles and bones become thicker and denser; strength and endurance are thus increased. This is also a time of awkwardness, not only as a result of the changes taking place in the body, but also because of the changes taking place in the mind.

Hormones trigger dramatic changes at the onset of puberty.

* Primary sex characteristics—Testes and penis in the male; ovaries, uterus, and vagina in the female.
* Secondary sex characteristics—Changing voice, beard growth, ejaculation in boys; breast development and menstruation in girls; body hair in both sexes.

The early maturation of some eleven- and twelve-year-olds dramatically emphasizes the different rates at which children develop. There may be as many as six to ten inches difference in height among children of the same age. Girls are often taller than boys. These drastic differences chip away at the self-confidence of later maturing girls and boys. Shorter and smaller youngsters can be embarrassed by these physical discrepancies. Children's psychological health should be a concern of parents and teachers at this age, which is a critical turning point for a healthy adolescence of good self-image, comfort with their own bodies, and self-assuredness in their social group. An emphasis on physical appearance may result in preoccupation with weight, risk-taking to prove one's worth, and early sexual behavior.

Hormone-induced physical changes also have dramatic effects on behavior, with mood changes in girls as they approach menstruation and increased sex drive in boys as levels of androgen shoot up. Hormonal changes and growth spurts can increase appetite during this stage, and girls especially need more iron to prevent anemia. Social, emotional, and cultural factors enter into food selections, with high–fat fast food the predominant choice. At the same time, undue attention paid to physical appearance can manifest itself in a preoccupation with dieting and reducing body fat. In a study of 500 girls aged nine through eleven in California (presented in testimony before the U.S. Congress in 1999), researchers found that close to 50 percent were dieting, even though only 17 percent were overweight (Zigler & Stevenson, 1993). A study surveyed first, second, and third grade children and found there was already a relationship between television viewing and fat stereotyping in both boys and girls.

This caused the researcher to conclude there is a negative predictor for eating disorders linked to television viewing (Harrison, 2000).

Elementary Age Health and Nutrition. At the threshold of adolescence, concerns about sexuality are on the minds of both young people and adults who care about them. Because the average age of first intercourse has decreased to seventeen for girls and sixteen for boys—with approximately one-fourth of youth reporting first intercourse by fifteen and some younger (Allan Guttmacher Institute, 1994)—these concerns need to be addressed in the elementary years. One pivotal influence for elementary age children is television. The causal relationship between sexually explicit messages on television and unprotected sexual activity is not documented, but of the average 14,000 sexual references a year on television, only 150 refer to sexual responsibility, abstinence, or contraception (Strasburger, 1993).

By this age, young adolescents have definite preferences for particular sports. These choices are influenced heavily by their peers, and fall into two groups: those who choose sports and those who do not. It is not just a matter of physical fitness: numerous studies have indicated that children who play sports or a musical instrument, or participate in community service, get better grades, get along better with peers, and have a higher resistance to drug use (Mahoney 2000; Jenkins 1996). Many fourth through sixth graders choose passive activities such as television and video watching, listening to music, or mall loitering, none of which enhance physical development.

Elementary Age Curriculum for Physical Development and Health. The teacher can help influence and build on positive, existing interests through planned activities linking those interests to some physical activity. Dancing to favorite music, or trips to a nearby natural location, may catch children's interest and initiate some physical activity. Children of this age are less involved with large groups, preferring smaller, more intimate social interactions. The effective teacher takes advantage of this knowledge to help plan appropriate activities.

The Cooper Institute for Aerobics Research (1987) established fitness standards for eight- to twelve-year-olds, called the FITNESSGRAM (Figure 5–18). Looney and Plowman (1990) administered the test to representative groups of children from eight to eighteen years old and found less than half of the children could perform at expected levels of overall fitness. Levels of fitness appeared to decline after elementary

	8-year-old boys		8-year-old girls		12-year-old boys		12-year-old girls	
	Standards	%	Standards	%	Standards	%	Standards	%
Mile run/walk	13 min.	85%	14 min.	83%	10 min.	85%	12 min.	83%
Pull up, palms facing away from body	0		0		1X	72%	1X	32%
Sit-ups, bent leg	25X	55%	25X	50%	35X	71%	30X	69%

Figure 5–18

Aerobic fitness of children. (Adapted from the Cooper Institute for Aerobics Research, 1987, and Looney & Plowman, 1990).

school, with less than one-third of girls between fourteen and eighteen able to do one push-up. This emphasizes the importance of incorporating physical activities in the regular school day to establish the wellness habit.

Even though you may be teaching fourth to sixth graders, drug abuse prevention and sex education begin very early in life through family and society influences. At this age, however, this information is vital to their health, since they are actually making decisions based on the values and ideas they have formed throughout the preceding years. The most successful pre-adolescent prevention programs include self-esteem building, abstinence promotion, school completion strategies, and career exploration. There are many predictors of early sexual activity, including early onset of puberty, history of being abused, poverty, lack of attentive and nurturing parents, cultural and family patterns of early sexual experience, poor academic achievement, ignorance or misinformation about reproduction, parents' own early pregnancy or substance abuse problems, peer activities, and attitudes and beliefs (Bempechat et al., 1989; Allan Guttmacher Institute, 1994).

Some of the same predictors for early sexual activity are also indicated in early adolescent drug and alcohol use. Family risk factors include parental use of alcohol and other legal or illegal drugs, parental absence, inconsistent discipline, and possible genetic tendencies. Difficulties in school can be both the indicator and the initiator of use and abuse of drugs. Peer drug use is perhaps one of the strongest predictor, along with parental influences and alienation from dominant social norms and values (Hawkins, Catalano, & Miller, 1992). Young people involved in prosocial activities such as attending church seemed protected against alcohol and drug use and truancy.

Teachers can take a proactive role in deterring antisocial behavior by motivating, learning, teaching, and raising a child's interest level in some academic or recreational area, as well as providing a stable, caring relationship with the youngster.

The themes and content of *Growing Healthy*'s (National Center for Health Education, 1996) curriculum for the upper elementary grades are:

* Grade 4: Our Digestion, Our Nutrition, Our Health—Learning about the body's need for proper nutrition and the interrelation of nutrition and the ecosystem

* Grade 5: Our Lungs and Our Health—Examining the respiratory system, effects of pollution, and dangers of smoking, alcohol, and other drugs. Students learn first aid and mouth-to-mouth resuscitation for emergencies

* Grade 6: Our Heart and Our Health—Assessing present health and setting health goals for age 18. Learning about the heart and circulatory system and exploring the nature and causes of stress

✳ ASSESSING PHYSICAL DEVELOPMENT AND HEALTH

A child's failure to grow and develop in a progressive pattern is cause for concern. Standardized height and weight charts provide a gauge for physical growth patterns, but those models need to be adjusted for such factors as race and the family's genetic history. Development that is atypical, deviating from the norm or with inconsistent growth patterns, should be evaluated by health professionals. Such development may or may not be indicative of a serious lifelong disability; early intervention may assist in diagnosing, correcting, or arresting any problems. Developmental delays are significant deviations from the expected norms and may be indicators of serious illness or physiological system difficulties. Environments must be modified to allow the child to be included in regular activities. In this way, the child's unaffected areas of development can reach their maximum potential. Early diagnosis of developmental delays is important; both families and teachers should heed warning signals.

Appendix A contains milestones that may be used to assess physical development.

SUMMARY

Physical health, safety, and nutrition are essential to survival, quality of life, and learning. The teacher must prepare an environment conducive to students' physical needs, plan appropriate activities and lessons, and record the progress of each student. In addition, teachers must recognize that there are individual differences in development, but remain keenly aware of warning signals. As a role model, the teacher should practice safe procedures, eat healthful foods, and participate in physical fitness activities.

KEY TERMS

growth	asthma	proximodistal
development	cephalocaudal	failure to thrive
maturation		

REVIEW ACTIVITIES

Exercises to Strengthen Learning

1. Infants—Observe four infants (one month old, six months old, nine months old, and twelve months old) and note the differences in their physical abilities. Note especially how they move and how they grasp objects.
2. Toddlers—Observe three toddlers in a child care setting during mealtime. Make note of their ages, what they ate, how much they ate, and how they ate. Analyze each child's eating patterns in relation to physical development and dietary requirements.
3. Preschoolers—Using the Frost-Wortham Physical Development Checklist (Frost, 1992) in Appendix E, rate the physical development of three children, all of whom are three, four, or five years old, noting the range of variability among children the same age.
4. Primary Age—Watch three hours of children's programming on a Saturday morning. Keep a log of the food products advertised during that time. Analyze the products for nutritional content and the proportion of foods in each section of the food pyramid of recommended food groups for daily intake.
5. Elementary Grades—Using the FITNESSGRAM (see Figure 5–18) or the standards from the President's Council on Physical Fitness <www.indiana.edu/~preschal/testilems.html>, measure the fitness of a group of at least five children ages eight to twelve.

Internet Quest

1. Find the latest dietary and nutritional guidelines for children from birth through age twelve.
2. Keep a food diary for three days and find a Web site that analyzes your dietary intake for calories, vitamins, and minerals.

3. Explore Web sites that present information about partnerships in drug prevention and report on three of the ones you think would be most effective.

4. Find up-to-date information on three children's health issues on the American Academy of Pediatrics Web site.

Reflective Journal

What I learned from this chapter about physical development, health, safety, and nutrition that was most important to me is . . .

Because of what I learned, this is what I will do when I'm a teacher . . .

REFERENCES

Allan Guttmacher Institute. (1994). *Sex and America's teenagers.* New York: Author.

Allison, J. (1999). A tribute to a scholar and great colleague: A conversation with Bernard "Bud" Spodek. *Childhood Education, 75*(5), 262.

American Academy of Pediatrics (1997, December). Breastfeeding and the use of human milk (RE9729). *Pediatrics, 100*(6), 1035–1039. Retrieved February 28, 2001, from the World Wide Web: <http://www.aap.org/policy/re9729.html>.

American Heart Association. (1999). Obesity and overweight in children. Retrieved February 28, 2001, from the World Wide Web: <http://www.americanheart.org/Heart_and_Stroke_A_Z_Guide/obesityk.html>.

Bempechat, J., et al. (1989). Teenage pregnancy and drug abuse: Sources of problem behaviors. *ERIC/CUE Digest No. 58,* ED316615.

Blair, S. N., & Meredith, M. D. (1994). The exercise-health relationship; Does it apply to children and youth? In R. R. Pate & P. C. Hohn (Eds.), *Health and fitness through physical education* (pp. 11–19). Champaign, IL: Human Kinetics.

Bouchard, T. J., Jr., Lykken, D. T., McGue, M., Sega, N. L., & Tellegen, A. (1990). Sources of human psychological differences: The Minnesota study of twins reared apart. *Science, 250,* 223–228.

Carroll, J. L., & Siska, E. S. (1996). SIDS: Counseling parents to reduce the risk. *American Family Physician, 57*(7), 1566.

Centers for Disease Control. (1996). Asthma mortality and hospitalization among children and young adults—United States, 1980–1993. *Morbidity and Mortality Weekly Report, 45*(17), 1–41.

Centers for Disease Control. *Immunization Schedule.* Retrieved June 28, 1999, from the World Wide Web: <http://www.pathfinder.com/ParentTime/Health/imshed_table.html>.

Charlesworth, R. (2000). *Understanding child development* (5th ed.). Albany, NY: Delmar.

Children's Defense Fund. (1998). *The state of America's children* (p. 104). Washington, DC: Author.

Cooper Institute for Aerobics Research. (1987). *FITNESSGRAM user's manual.* Dallas, TX: Author.

Crain, E. F., Weiss, K. B., Bijur, P. E., Hersh, M., Westbrook, L., & Stein, R. E. K. (1994). An estimate of the prevalence of asthma and wheezing among inner city children. *Pediatrics, 94,* 356–362.

Deitz, W. H., & Gortmaker, S. L. (1985). Do we fatten our children at the television set? Obesity & television viewing in children and adolescents. *Pediatrics, 75,* 807–812.

Dennis W. (1960). Causes of retardation among institutional children: Iran. *Journal of Genetic Psychology, 96,* 47–59.

Dennis, W. (1973). *Children of the creche.* New York: Appleton-Century-Crofts.

Erikson, E. (1963). *Children and society* (2nd ed.). New York: Norton.

Frost, J. L. (1992). *Play and playscapes.* Albany, NY: Delmar.

Fulghum, R. (1989). *All I really need to know I learned in kindergarten*. New York: Villard Books.

Fuhr, J. E., & Barclay, K. H. (1998). The importance of appropriate nutrition and nutrition education for young children. *Young Children, 53*(1), 74–80.

Gans, K., Sundaram, S., McPhillips, J., Hixson, M., Linnan, L., & Carleton, R. (1993). Rate your plate: An eating pattern assessment and educational tool used at cholesterol screening and education program. *Journal of Nutrition Education, 25*(1), 19–35.

Gortmaker, S. L., Dietz, W. H., Sobol, A. M., & Wehler, C. A. (1987). Increasing pediatric obesity in the United States. *American Journal of Diseases of Children, 141*, 535–540.

Greenman, J., & Stonehouse, A. (1996). *Prime times: A handbook for excellence in infant and toddler care*. St. Paul, MN: Redleaf Press.

Harrison, K. (2000, October). Television viewing, fat stereotyping, body shape standards and eating disorder symptomatology in grade school children. *Communications Research, 27*(5), 617–.

Hawkins, J. D., Catalano, R. E., & Miller, J. Y. (1992). Risk and protective factors for alcohol and other drug problems in adolescence and early adulthood: Implications for substance abuse prevention. *Psychological Bulletin, 112*, 64–105.

Jenkins, J. E. (1996, Summer). The influence of peer affiliation and student activities on adolescent drug involvement. *Adolescence, 31*(122), 297.

Jessee, P., Nagy, M., & Poteet-Johnson, D. (1993). Children with AIDS. *Childhood Education, 70*(1), 10–14.

Kantrowitz, B. (1991, Summer). The breath of life [Special edition]. *Newsweek*, 52–53.

Kinney, H. C., Filiano, J. J., Sleepter, L. A., Mandell, F., Valdes-Dapena, M., & White, W. F. (1995). Decreased muscarinic receptor binding in the arcuate nucleus in sudden infant death syndrome. *Science, 269*, 1446–1450.

Klesges, R. (1993). Effects of television on metabolic rate: Potential implications for childhood obesity. *Pediatrics, 91*, 281–286.

Kotz, K., & Story, M. (1994). Food advertisements during children's Saturday morning television programming: Are they consistent with dietary recommendations? *Journal of the American Dietetic Association, 94*(11), 1296–1300.

Kruesi, M. J., & Rapoport, J. L. (1986). Diet and human behavior: How much do they affect each other? *Annual Reviews of Nutrition, 6*, 113–130.

Looney, M. A., & Plowman, S. A. (1990). Passing rates of American children and young adults on the FITNESSGRAM criterion-referenced physical fitness standards. *Research Quarterly for Exercise and Sport, 61*, 215–223.

Mahoney, J. J. (2000, March/April). School extracurricular activity participation as a moderator in the development of antisocial patterns. *Child Development, 72*(2), 502–.

Maslow, A. H. (1970). *Motivation and personality* (2nd ed.). New York: Harper & Row.

Mayo Clinic Health Oasis. (1998). *Controlling asthma in children*. Retrieved June 28, 1999, from the World Wide Web: <http://www.mayohealth.org/mayo/9804/htm/ch_asthma.htm>.

Mellin, L. M., Irwin, C. E., & Scully, S. (1992). Prevalence of disordered eating in girls: A survey of middle-class children. *Journal of the American Dietetic Association, 92*, 851–853.

National Center for Health Education. (1996). *Growing healthy*. Waco, TX: Health Edco, a division of WRS Group.

National Center for Health Statistics. (1998). *10 Leading Causes of Death*. Washington, DC: Author.

NEA. (2000, May). When kids show up hungry. *NEA Today, 18*(8), 39.

Office for Disease Prevention and Health Promotion, Public Health Service. (1984). *National Children and Youth Fitness Study*. Washington, DC: Author.

Ogletree, S. M., Williams, S. W., Raffeld, P., Mason, B., & Fricke, K. (1990). Female attractiveness and eating disorders: Do children's television commercials play a role? *Sex Roles, 22*, 791–797.

Pannell, D. V. (1995). Why school meals are high in fat and some suggested solutions. *American Journal of Clinical Nutrition, 61*, 245S–246S.

Parcel, G. S., Tiernan, K., Nadar, P. R., & Gottlob, D. (1979). Health education and kindergarten children. *Journal of School Health, 49*, 129–131.

Patton, R. G., & Gardner, L. I. (1963). *Growth failure in maternal deprivation.* Springfield, IL: Charles C. Thomas.

Pollitt, E. (1995). Does breakfast make a difference in school? *Journal of American Dietary Association, 95,* 1134–1139.

President's Council on Physical Fitness. Retrieved July 26, 2000, from the World Wide Web: <http://www.indiana.edu/~preschal/testilems.html>.

Robertson, C. (1998). *Safety, nutrition, and health in early childhood education.* Albany, NY: Delmar.

Rogers, P. T., Roizen, N. J., & Capone, G. T. (1996). Down syndrome. In A. J. Capute & P. J. Accardo (Eds.), *Developmental disabilities in infancy and childhood: Vol. II. The spectrum of developmental disabilities.* (2nd ed., pp. 221–243). Baltimore, MD: Paul H. Brookes.

Ross, J. G., & Pate, R. R. (1987). The national children and youth fitness study II: A summary of findings. *Journal of Physical Education, Recreation and Dance, 58*(9), 51–56.

Schwartz, P. J., Stramba-Badiale, M., Segantini, A. (1998). Prolongation of the QT interval and the sudden infant death syndrome. *New England Journal of Medicine, 338,* 1709–1714.

Small, M. F. (1998). *Our babies, ourselves: How biology and culture shape the way we parent.* New York: Anchor Books.

Strasburger, V. C. (1993). Children, adolescents and the media: Five crucial issues. *Adolescent Medicine: State of the Art Review, 4,* 479–493.

Strasburger, V. C., Donnerstein, E. (1999, January). Children, adolescents and the media: Issues and solutions. *Pediatrics, 103*(1), 120–.

Stunkard, A. J., Harris, J. R., Pedersen, N. L., & McClearn, G. E. (1990). The body-mass index of twins who have been reared apart. *New England Journal of Medicine, 322,* 1483–1487.

Thompson, M. W., McInnes, R. R., & Huntington, F. W. (1990). *Genetics in Medicine* (5th ed.). Philadelphia, PA: Saunders.

Troiano, R. P., Flegel, K. M., Kuczmarski, R. J., Campbell, S. M., & Johns, C. L. (1995). Overweight prevalence and trends for children and adolescents: The national health & nutrition examination surveys, 1963–1991. *Archives of Pediatrics & Adolescent Medicine, 149,* 1085–1091.

Tufts University. (1995, January). TV food ads feed kids the wrong message. *Tufts University Diet 7 Nutrition Newsletter, 12*(11), 7.

U.S. Department of Agriculture (USDA). (1993, October). *Food program facts* (Fact sheet). San Francisco, CA: Food and Nutrition Service, USDA.

U.S. Department of Health and Human Services. (1990). *Healthy people year 2000: National health promotion and disease prevention objectives* (PHS Publication No. 91–50213). Washington, DC: U.S. Government Printing Office.

Wagner, C. L., & Anderson, D. M. (1996). Special properties of human milk. *Clinical Pediatrics, 35*(6), 283.

Watson, L. D., Watson, M. A., & Wilson, L. C. (1999). *Infants & toddlers* (4th ed.). Albany, NY: Delmar.

Werner, H. (1948). *Comparative psychology of mental development.* New York: International Universities Press.

Williams, L. (1990, March 22). Growing up flabby in America. *The New York Times,* p. C1.

Wyon, D. P., Abrahamsson, L., Jartelius, M., & Fletcher, R. F. (1997). An experimental study of the energy intake at breakfast on the test performance of 10 year old children in school. *International Journal of Food Science and Nutrition, 48,* 5–12.

Zigler, E. F., & Stevenson, M. F. (1993). *Children in a changing world: Development and social issues* (2nd ed.). Baltimore, MD: Brookes/Cole.

For additional learning and teaching resources, visit our Web site at www.EarlyChildEd.delmar.com.

RELATED CAREERS

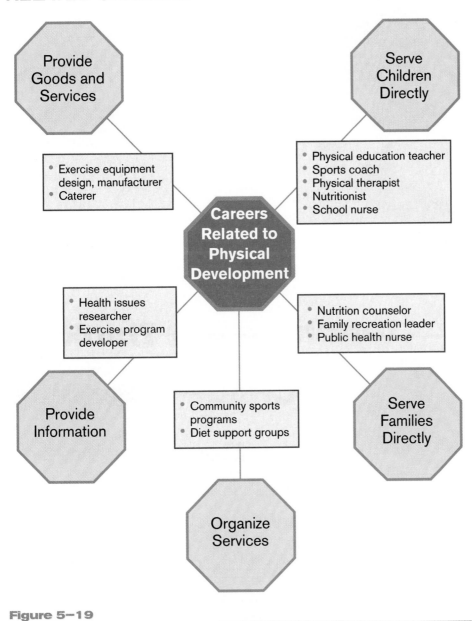

Figure 5–19

Careers related to physical development.

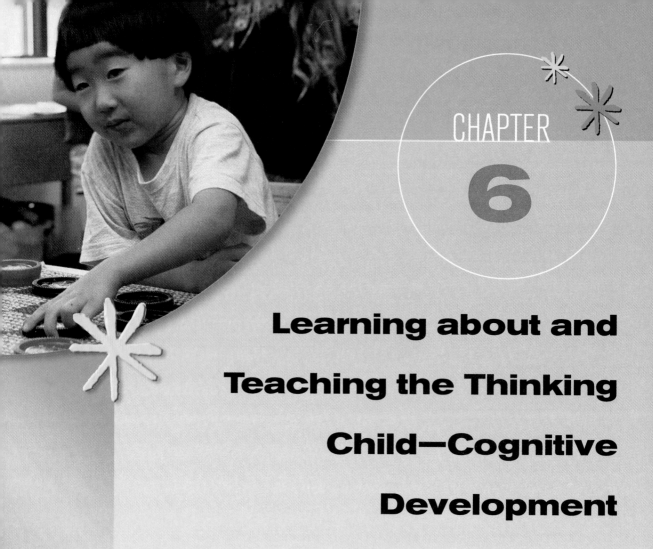

Learning about and Teaching the Thinking Child—Cognitive Development

Objectives

After reading this chapter and completing the review activities, the learning teacher should be able to:

1. Describe the processes that take place as the brain develops.

2. Identify the stages of cognitive development.

3. Explain the teacher's role in supporting cognitive development at various age levels.

❋ UNDERSTANDING COGNITIVE DEVELOPMENT IN LEARNING AND TEACHING

SCENARIO Azim crawls on the floor; he finds a ball, picks it up, shakes it, chews on it, bangs it against the floor, and then throws it. The teacher gets the ball and says, "Let's roll the ball." She rolls the ball to him. It hits his leg and he picks it up and throws it, laughing. The teacher says, "Good throw. Let's roll the ball," and she rolls it to him. He watches the ball, reaches out, and pushes it back to her. She says, smiling, "Yeah, you rolled the ball."

Eighteen-month-old Bruce pushes open the door; he looks up at the top of the door, watching as the automatic door closer pulls it shut. He pushes it open again, looks up, and watches it close again. He repeats this over and over and over.

Carolyn, three years old, and her big sister, six years old, are looking through a book. The big sister points to objects in the book, naming them: "Swimming pool, basketball, wheelbarrow, flower."

Anthony, who is just starting first grade, painstakingly sounds out the words as he writes a thank-you letter to the person who stopped and cared for his dog, who was hit by a car: "TANKS FOR TAKING CAR OF MY DOG SCOTTY WEN HE WS HIT. HE HAS A BROKIN LEG BUT WIL GIT BATER SOON."

Katrina bakes cookies for her fifth-grade bake sale. Her goal is to earn $10 for her class trip and she knows her cookies will sell for 25 cents each and that her recipe makes four dozen. She is thinking about how many batches of cookies she will have to make.

Each of these children is learning. They are learning through watching the effects of their actions on objects, changing patterns, the relationship between sounds and symbols, and how to solve problems using mathematical calculations. Who is their teacher? Can learning occur without a teacher? Can learning occur in spite of a teacher? Can teaching occur without learning?

The most common definition of a teacher is one who imparts knowledge or transfers skills to someone else. In reality, no one teaches unless the another person learns. Learning is more than recitation of a fact or repetition of an action. "It is the ability to perform various types of thinking such as reasoning, problem solving, organizing, and remembering ideas and images" (McCullough, 1992). All areas of development are interdependent; they do not progress in isolation. As we introduce you to cognitive development, keep in mind that it is a complex system that follows principles of orderly progression, with stages and milestones. The expected progression of stages varies for individual rates of development. Cognitive development is affected by genetics, environment, and experiences, and can be hindered by trauma or lack of stimulation.

We live in exciting times: it is only recently that sophisticated technology and techniques have been available to study the brain. Every day, new discoveries are made about the way the brain develops and processes information and how learning occurs. In the last 10 years, revolutionary discoveries of noninvasive techniques such as magnetic resonance imaging (MRI) and positron emission tomography (PET) enable neuroscientists to see how the brain works, and to record and measure activity levels and functions of various parts of the brain. These innovations have brought new attention to the importance of stimulation in the early years. "Neuroscientists stress the fact that interaction with the environment is not simply an interesting feature of brain development; it is an absolute requirement . . . beginning with days of conception" (Shore, 1997). Brain synapses, the connections that carry information between brain cells, multiply rapidly and reach maximum levels by the age of three, gradually declining by half by adolescence. What a staggering thought!

Learning is about making connections between the brain's bits of shared information. Preadolescent children are biologically primed and ready for a teacher who maximizes that potential. During your formal education, you will have opportunities to improve your teaching techniques based on information that will become increasingly available about cognitive development. During your career as a teacher, your continuing education about cognitive development should be a lifelong commitment.

The Nature of Cognitive Development

At birth, the brain is ready to receive, process, store, retrieve, and manipulate sensations and experiences. Cognitive development builds on this early foundation.

Early Brain Development. To know how to teach, you need to know how learning takes place. Brains, like noses, are different in everyone (Figure 6–1).

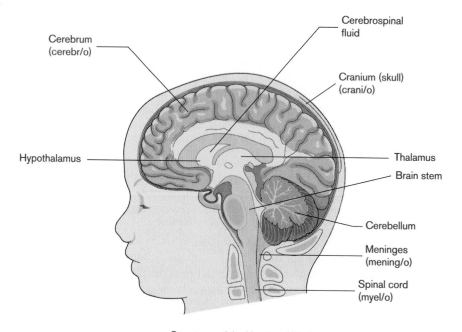

Structures of the Head and Neck

Figure 6–1

Diagram of child's brain.

Like noses, they all have the same function and anatomical similarities, and may even have a family resemblance, but each one is unique. Here are some interesting facts about the brain from Jensen's *Teaching with the Brain in Mind* (1998).

Did you know that:

* ✳ the brain accounts for only about two percent of the body's adult weight, but consumes approximately 20 percent of the body's energy?

* ✳ two-year-olds have the same number of neurons as found in the brain of a healthy adult?

* ✳ you lose 10,000 to 100,000 brain cells a day, but you have more than you will ever need; in fact, you only use one percent of one percent of your brain's processing capacity?

* ✳ almost 10 percent of children under five have photographic memory, as do one percent of adults?

* ✳ the brain prunes away unneeded cells? That is why, if you have not heard the sounds of other languages in your first few months of life, it will be almost impossible for you to make those sounds if you study those languages as an adult.

* ✳ infants who are rocked gain weight faster and develop vision and hearing earlier?

* ✳ the best foods for brain development are leafy green vegetables, salmon, nuts, lean meats, and fresh fruits?

* ✳ the brain's attention cycles last about 90 to 110 minutes; mental breaks of five to 10 minutes are needed every hour and a half?

Think of millions of buttons sprinkled on a huge piece of fabric. You take a needle and thread, sew a button on, and go on to the next button, linking the two together with your stitching. You work from button to button, but between some you take several stitches and go back and forth. At some point when you pick up the fabric, the buttons that are not attached fall off (representing the pruned brain cells). That is a visual image of the connections that experiences make among brain cells.

It is almost impossible to separate the nature and nurture aspects of brain development. The brain is wired and ready (nature) and all sensory experiences (nurture) form synapses between the brain cells. The richer the environment of sensory experiences, the more synapses are formed, and the more brain cells are connected.

During the first 10 years of a child's life, every stimulus and experience, every sight and sound, and every interaction with other people shapes the child's brain. How does this happen? A newborn infant has roughly 100 billion brain cells. Sensory information is received by the **neuron**, a nerve cell that transmits messages in the form of electrical impulses. These impulses pass over a small gap between neurons, the **synapse**, to a motor neuron that initiates a chemical, or neurotransmitter, release across the gap, which may stimulate an electrical discharge in an adjacent neural structure, thus perpetuating the impulse. In the case of a motor neuron, this impulse initiates muscle activity. This is a reflex action that does not involve conscious thought or intentional action. As myelination occurs, insulating the neurons and speeding transmission of nerve impulses, the rest of the cerebral cortex and the brain stem are connected to other nervous system structures, and the infant's abilities expand. "Each

neuron—A nerve cell.
synapse—A small gap between interconnecting neurons.

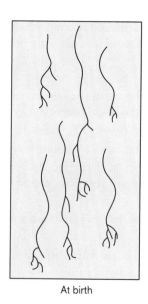

At birth

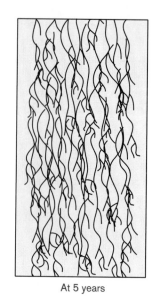

At 5 years

Figure 6–2

Synapses present from birth are expanded and connected through stimulation, reaching their peak by five years of age.

Arnold Gesell

(1880–1961) Developmental theorist who popularized the concept of *readiness,* the physical and cognitive maturity the child develops naturally to a point of readiness for formal school learning. Founded the Gesell Institute of Human Development, where he developed a series of norms detailing children's physical language and personal-social behavior according to chronological age, distinguished from *developmental* age.

neuron is made up of a cell body which is surrounded by **dendrites**, elongated tissues which receive messages. A very long thread of tissue, the **axon**, extends out from the cell body toward other nerve cells. The purpose of the axon is to send messages" (Trawick-Smith, 1997). The connection between the dendrite and the axon is the wiring, or threads, of the brain. When no connection is made, it is called pruning.

In his early years, a child's brain forms twice as many synapses as will eventually be needed. If these synapses are used repeatedly in a child's day-to-day life, they are reinforced and become part of the brain's permanent circuitry. If they are not used repeatedly, or often enough, they are eliminated. In this way, experience plays a crucial role in 'wiring' a young child's brain" (Shore, 1997). See Figure 6–2, which is a sketch of the synapses present at birth and those at five years, when a child has had five years of stimulation by all of the senses forming those important linkages.

Maturationist theorists such as **Arnold Gesell** (1940) attribute the infants' interaction with the environment to the maturing brain. Gesell pointed to embryonic development as the model or pattern for later development, dictated by genetics and modified by the environment. Maturationists believe that, as a secondary role in shaping the individual, genetically determined patterns of change occur as individuals age within their environment. Gesell's scales of infant motor development were widely used in the 1930s and 1940s. The maturationist position was further strengthened by the research of Margaret and Wayne Dennis (1940). They studied traditional Hopi infants who were kept tightly wrapped on cradle boards for the first year of life,

dendrites—The short fibers emanating from the neuron, the receptor sites for axons.

axon—The long fibers of a neuron that transmit impulses away from the cell body to other neurons. Usually one axon per neuron; can subdivide to connect with many dendrites.

restricting their movements, but who began walking at a comparable age to other nonwrapped Hopi babies and Gesell's timetable for walking. But does the maturationist viewpoint apply to cognitive development? Those who are proponents of an unchanging IQ (intelligent quotient) believe so.

Multiple Intelligences. People think in different ways. Not all smart people are smart in the same way. Some people have incredible abilities to remember all kinds of things, or calculate numbers in their head, or know just what to say or do to put others at ease. In 1983, Howard Gardner wrote *Frames of the Mind: The Theory of Multiple Intelligences,* in which he describes intelligence not as a single, localized entity but as originating from many areas in the brain. Gardner identifies types of intelligence and finds that different individuals possess different intellectual strengths and are more receptive to different types of learning experiences than others (Figure 6–3).

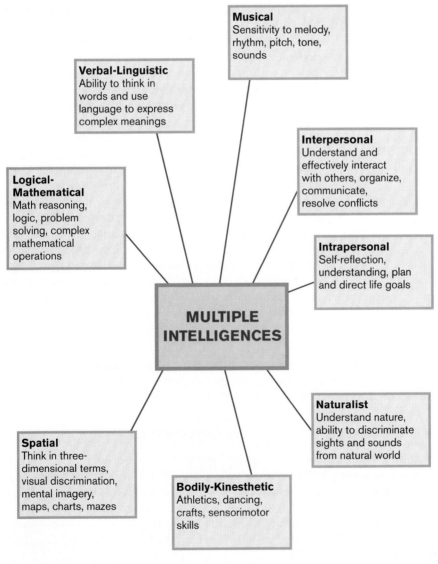

Figure 6–3

Multiple intelligences. (Adapted from Gardner, 1983; Campbell, Campbell, & Dickinson, 1994; and Nicholson-Nelson, 1998)

In *Developing Students Multiple Intelligences,* Nicholson-Nelson (1998) describes each area of intelligence, how the individual learns best, and who is strong in this area of intelligence. It is not surprising that Maya Angelou and Abraham Lincoln are identified as verbally linguistic; Einstein as mathematical-logical; Pablo Picasso, Frank Lloyd Wright, and Bobby Fischer as spatial; Mahatma Gandhi and Mother Theresa as interpersonal; and John Muir, Charles Darwin, and Luther Burbank as naturalist. The teacher's task is to develop learning activities and opportunities that address each area of intelligence. As the teacher plans the classroom environment, develops curriculum, or assesses children, he should make a conscious effort to ensure that each child can approach learning in the manner most useful to them. The teacher should provide many avenues for children to reach their learning goals or competency levels.

SCENARIO   Jack Elm is a third-grade teacher. By the end of third grade, his students are expected to have memorized the multiplication tables up to 10×10 and to be able to use multiplication to calculate accurate answers to simple word problems. Jack understands that this task may come easily to some children, but the majority of children in his room will have to work hard to reach this level of competency by the end of the year. Jack is familiar with Gardner's work on multiple intelligences and provides his children with a variety of approaches to reach their learning goals. He has set up a math area that offers small-group opportunities for interaction to discuss calculations and to practice multiplication tables verbally. He has similar activities available for children to work on quietly by themselves and provides opportunities for them to build models of multiplication problems. He encourages children to draw pictures of math problems and to use color if they prefer as they write out calculations. Jack and the children create a multiplication fact tag game to play outside and two of the children share a song of multiplication facts they have written. Jack makes a conscious effort to address each area of intelligence as he develops his class plan to meet the math skills and competencies goals for third grade.

There is little doubt that individuals have unique capacities to think, learn, and reason. This begins with biological inheritance, but is profoundly influenced either negatively or positively by the environment.

The Nurture of Cognitive Development

As young children interact with their environment, messages are sent between neurons. Six-month-old DeShay reaches out and grabs the spoon and puts it in her mouth (Figure 6–4). She smiles in delight and her father says, "Good girl!" Her eyes and brain work together to allow her to focus on the spoon, physically grasp it, and remember the concept of putting the spoon in her mouth. She receives emotional reinforcement from her father. Through all of this, she has been "connecting the buttons on the fabric of her brain."

The Role of Play in Cognitive Development. "Play includes the idea of pleasure, self-imposed ideas and spontaneous activities, and activity not restricted

Figure 6–4

Many areas of development are working together here.

by reality or instruction" (Gestwicki, 1999). Children play alone, alongside another child, or with other children (Figure 6–5). Children manipulate objects, verbalize, interact with others, imagine, solve problems, experiment, and practice and test their skills during play. Children may build something new with objects, pretend to be another person, or engage in an interactive activity with agreed-upon rules.

Figure 6–5

Young children develop brain synapses during routine interaction with the environment.

Figure 6–6

When children partici-
pate in group games,
they begin to learn to
communicate clearly,
settle disputes, com-
promise, present argu-
ments, and reason
with others.

"For young children, play is the lifeblood of learning, so it is vital that teachers provide extensive opportunities for children to learn through play every time they come to school" (Hendrick, 1998). Play serves an important function in children's cognitive development. Dramatic play is a significant factor in encouraging a child's ability to extend and expand on ideas and to solve problems. "Through play, children pursue their interests . . . discover how the world works . . . communicate with others . . . see how it feels to act like other people . . . practice familiar skills and learn new ones . . . cooperate and solve problems—they learn by doing!" (Phillips, 1991). In dramatic play, children learn the difference between real and pretend, make plans, and use their imaginations. They experiment and draw conclusions and use language to convey ideas to others.

With older children, play often revolves around group games. When children participate in group games, they learn to communicate clearly, settle disputes and compromise, present arguments and reason with others, and creatively solve problems by inventing new rules or games that meet the needs of the group (Figure 6–6). This is different from games played as part of an organized sport team. Children do learn some of the same skills in adult-led sport teams, but the cognitive challenges are much greater when they have to decide how to play a game so that everyone can participate.

SCENARIO

Andrea is a sixth-grade teacher. Her class looks forward to their kickball game every day. Andrea acts as an observer and intervenes only when safety is a concern. The class knows that the rules of the playground prohibit physical violence or inappropriate language. During the school year, Andrea watched the class invent an equitable way to select team

continued

members without hurting feelings, figuring out how to include weaker members of the team in the game, and develop a complex scoring system. Some days, as rules were modified, there was more discussion than game playing. Andrea has no doubt that playing informal ball games has enhanced the cognitive development, as well as the physical, social, and emotional development, of her students.

In addition to cognitive development being influenced by the relationships a child forms with other people and through play, it is also affected by environmental factors such as levels of family violence, availability of medical and dental care, quality of child care and school environments, safety of the environment, and the availability of nutritious food.

Exceptions in Cognitive Development

Alfred Binet, a French psychologist, and Theophile Simon, a physician, developed a psychological examination to diagnose mental subnormality (Binet & Simon, 1912). They constructed a series of problems of increasing difficulty by which they could determine basic intelligence, which they called the *mental age,* when comparing children to other children of the same age. This tool was not meant for measuring academic or achieved intelligence, but rather innate ability. A German developmental psychologist, William Stern (1912), developed the mathematical ratio $IQ = MA/CA \times 100$, or the mental age divided by chronological age multiplied by 100 (100 representing the average IQ), resulting in the child's IQ (intelligence quotient.)

Intelligence, or the ability to learn, is determined by both nature and nurture. Some scholars believe that genetics is the most important factor in intelligence, while others think intelligence is primarily influenced by environment, with most maintaining that intelligence results from the interplay of both. Intelligence tests like the Benet and Weschler scales measure problem-solving skills, from which the intelligence quotient, or IQ, is calculated. From these tests, you can draw inferences regarding school and career success. Differences in cognitive development range along a continuum. On the one end are the gifted and talented, on the other end are those who are developmentally disabled, and in the middle are children with a host of learning disabilities.

Gifted. Children who are exceptional or **gifted** may fall into the categories of geniuses, precocious, or talented with the potential for high:

 * ability (including intelligence).
 * creativity (the ability to formulate new ideas and apply them to the solution of problems).
 * task commitment (a high level of motivation and the ability to see a project through to its conclusion).

Children who are gifted may be divergent (creative) or convergent (linear) thinkers. They may have an insatiable curiosity and an ability to understand abstract

---

gifted—Child who has demonstrated or has the potential for high capabilities of intellect, creative or productive thinking, leadership, visual or performing arts.

concepts far beyond their age, as well as leadership skills and a sophisticated sense of humor. These exceptional cognitive abilities may or may not apply to academic endeavors, however, giving some children the labels of "underachiever" or "unmotivated." Identifying and individual planning for the gifted child depend on the school district, the resources, and the skill of the teacher to plan, assess, and arrange for alternative learning activities.

Learning Disability. The Individuals with Disabilities Education Act (1990) defines a **learning disability** as a "disorder in one or more of the basic psychological

Disability	Description	Accommodations
Attention deficit/ hyperactivity disorder	Easily distracted by unimportant stimulation and may exhibit inattention, hyperactivity, and impulsivity. May appear to daydream and it may be difficult to gain their attention.	Provide quiet, nondistracting area for study. Give simple, brief instructions. Provide written or pictorial "to do" lists. Behavior modification plan. Stimulant medication.
Auditory processing disorder	Problems understanding language, despite normal hearing.	Provide written or pictorial notes of classroom instructions. Earphones. Tactile experiences that support general curriculum.
Dyscalculia	Problems with math and arithmetic. May be due to difficulty with understanding abstract concepts or with writing and recognizing numbers.	Calculators. Sorting/counting objects (beads, abacus, rods). Graphs.
Dysgraphia	Problems with writing that may result from difficulty with hand movement or memory.	Computer with word processing/spell check functions. Speech recognition software. Oral assessment. Scribe.
Dyslexia	Problems with reading that result from inability to distinguish among individual sounds in spoken language.	Books on tape. Break down words to individual sounds. Oral assessment.
Visual processing disability	Problems with understanding written language despite normal vision.	Books on tape. Oral assessment. Verbal instructions.

Figure 6–7

Learning disabilities.

processes involved in understanding or using spoken or written language, which may manifest itself in an imperfect ability to listen, speak, read, spell or to do mathematical calculations. Learning disabilities may be a result of brain injury and include such conditions as perceptual disabilities, minimal brain dysfunction, dyslexia, and developmental aphasia. The difficulty is not caused by problems such as poor vision, poor hearing, or low intelligence. Suspected causes are neurological in origin and may be a result of many things, including lead exposure, fetal exposure to alcohol, or atypical brain development. Indicators of a learning disability include low academic achievement for age and ability level, or a severe discrepancy between areas of intellectual ability, such as oral expression, listening comprehension, written expression, basic reading skills, reading comprehension, mathematics calculation, and mathematics reasoning. There are many types of learning disabilities (Figure 6–7).

One example of a learning disability is dyslexia. Children with near-normal or above intelligence who have severe difficulty in learning to read, particularly in decoding words, probably have a form of dyslexia. Another example of a learning disability is attention deficit disorder (ADD). Children with ADD have a neurological impairment that makes it hard for them to focus their attention. ADD may also be accompanied by hyperactivity, which expresses itself as difficulty in delaying gratification and controlling impulsive behavior. Those affected are usually of normal or high intelligence, but the disorder prevents them from reaching their full academic potential (National Information Center on Children and Youth with Disabilities, 1996).

SCENARIO   David, a third grader, is the first to come up with answers to verbal problems in math. However, he does not perform well on written math tests because the numbers on his math problems are not lined up so that place values correspond, so he miscalculates the answers. He hands in incomplete written math assignments.

Gwen, in fourth grade, loves to read and often has a book hidden on her lap to read during other classes. She keeps a journal on her computer at home and shares some of her entries with her teacher. Her teacher judges her journal writing to be about three grade levels above the class average. When Gwen writes an essay in class, her spelling is poor and her thoughts are disorganized. If Gwen is called on in class, she often is confused and cannot answer the question. Even if the teacher works with her individually, Gwen has difficulty verbalizing responses to questions.

Robert, a sixth grader, sits at a desk, the lid of which he can hardly close because the desk is so full! Today the class is

continued

---

learning disability—"Disorder in one or more of the basic psychological processes involved in understanding or using spoken or written language, which may manifest itself in an imperfect ability to listen, speak, read, write, spell or to do mathematical calculations."

cleaning their desks before winter break. His teacher notices that many of the assignments that Robert said he lost or never got back are in his desk. Also in his desk are two peanut butter and jelly sandwiches (perhaps from the days he told his teacher he lost his lunch), a permission slip for a field trip he had to miss because he did not know where his note was, a pair of old socks, two hats, and three miniature cars. David is not doing well in school this year. He misses many assignments, does not hand in homework, and lost his portion of a large group project. His school record shows that he is of above-average intelligence and scored very high on some sections of the standardized achievement tests last year.

Diagnosing learning disabilities may be difficult. The teacher may recognize a discrepancy between academic areas and behavior indicators and begin to document observations (Figure 6–8). The teacher and the school then pull together a team to define and diagnose the problem, and support the child in learning. As the first member of the team, the child's family should request a screening by the child's physician to rule out vision, hearing, or other health problems. A learning specialist trained in assessing learning difficulties is also part of the team. Based on input from the family, physician, and learning specialist diagnosis, the intervention team can prescribe specific actions. If all the assessment information indicates a learning disability, an Individualized Education Program (IEP) is created for the child that may include special

Figure 6–8

Class participation behaviors vary widely among individual children.

instructional accommodations, counseling, or medication (Figure 6–9). The teacher must stay involved during this time, because it may take several attempts to find the appropriate combination of interventions for the IEP to succeed. All members of the team must remain in close communication with each other. With positive, appropriate intervention, many children with learning disabilities are successful in school.

What kinds of things are included in the IEP for a child with a learning disability?

David now uses graph paper to write his math assignments. He can take his math test over an extended period of time with a break in the middle, use a calculator to check his homework, and explain his work orally to a resource room teacher.

Gwen's IEP states that she should not be called on in class unless she volunteers to respond to an inquiry. She is provided with a computer for all written work and is encouraged to use its spelling and grammar checking functions. If she handwrites assignments or tests, she is not graded on her spelling.

An IEP (Individualized Education Program) is a legal document required for each child with special needs as defined by federal education law. The purpose of an IEP is to ensure that strategies are in place so the child can maximize his learning potential. An IEP should include:

* Information about the child and family
* Date of planning meeting and date invitation to attend was sent to family and planning team
* List of individuals on planning team including:
  —School administrator
  —Special educations teacher
  —General curriculum teacher
  —Family representative
* Evaluation method and results of initial evaluation
* List of the child's strengths
* Child's present level of performance in:
  —Special education setting
  —General curriculum
* Annual education goals and clear, measurable outcomes
* Details on meeting needs that result from the disability through general curriculum, accommodations and modifications
* Strategies that include:
  —Placement in least restrictive environment in which goals may be achieved (may be in special education or general curriculum setting)
  —Related services needed (for example, speech or physical therapy)
  —Supplementary aids needed (for example, audio textbooks)
* Transition plans (for example, from elementary school to middle school)

Figure 6–9

An individualized education program.

Robert receives his assignments in writing, with a copy mailed to his parents because he often misplaces his papers. He has a duplicate set of textbooks at home. The teacher mails weekly reports to his family to let them know of any missed assignments so he can catch up. A learning specialist and the family physician diagnosed Robert with attention deficit disorder. He is taking prescription medication and his teacher, family physician, and family monitor his reactions and progress.

Students, teachers, and families must work together to decide on strategies that minimize the negative effects of learning disabilities. Some approaches include adjusting the learning environment to limit distractions, providing oral or visual directions, and extending the time available to complete tasks. Helping all students recognize each other's strengths and assist each other strengthens the cooperative community of the classroom, enhancing all class members' emotional health.

Achievement levels for children with learning disabilities can be significantly different from their overall intelligence. All of the child in the scenarios are now performing better in their disability areas, but, more importantly, they are not being held back from success in their strong areas. David tutors some of the other children in his class when they have trouble with a new math concept, Gwen has begun to write a chapter book, and Robert hands most of his assignments in on time and is better prepared for tests—and his desk shuts now, too!

Mental Retardation. Mental retardation is the term used for limited intellectual functioning with people who are mentally retarded having IQs of 70 or less. This dysfunction is marked by limited adaptive behavior, and can include an inability to effectively communicate or be personally independent or socially responsible. Mental retardation occurs before the age of eighteen. It may result from conditions of poverty, such as poor nutrition and inadequate health care, child abuse, or neglect; genetic defects, or maternal prenatal use of alcohol, drugs, or cigarettes.

SCENARIO   Tommy is six years old. He does not speak in full sentences and points to objects he wants. His intellectual functioning is on the level of a two-year-old. Tommy is diagnosed with mental retardation.

A common cause of mental retardation is Down syndrome, a genetic anomaly resulting from the presence of an extra chromosome (Figure 6–10). Children with Down syndrome may be mildly, moderately, or severely retarded. They may exhibit physical symptoms such as hearing and visual problems, or seizures and cardiac conditions that may result in premature death. The teacher of children with Down syndrome will work with a team that includes the family, and may include the family doctor, physical therapist, speech therapist, resource room teacher, and special education teacher to develop an education plan that takes into account the unique qualities and strengths of each child.

Autism is a physical disorder of the brain that causes a developmental disability ranging from mild to severe. It is apparent in communication disorders, social withdrawal, severe emotional rigidity, or a combination of the three. It may be caused by Fragile X Syndrome, "the leading cause of impairment in males" (Bowe, 2000). This disorder is caused by damage to the X chromosome; the impact on males is greater than that on females because males have only one X chromosome, while females have two. In males, the symptoms of Fragile X Syndrome may include, "mild to severe hyperactivity, mild to severe retardation, moderate LD (learning disability), autism, or no symptoms at all" (Bowe, 2000).

Figure 6–10

Opportunities for growth and recognition are necessary for all children.

At some point, all teachers will likely have students in their classrooms with a developmental disability. Teachers must be able to recognize signs of cognitive dysfunction, know how to make referrals for assessment, be able to communicate clearly with the child's family and other educators regarding the disability, and be able to carry out their specific assignments from the child's IEP. As you continue your education as a teacher, you will study the areas of cognitive exceptionalities and you may even decide to specialize in teaching children who are gifted and talented or those with developmental disabilities.

✳ THEORISTS IN COGNITIVE DEVELOPMENT

Many theorists have contributed to the knowledge base on cognitive development. Most of these theorists have been males and come from European and European–American backgrounds. As such, the body of knowledge reflects the cultures and gender of the theorists. Today, as researchers from other cultures and women study cognitive development, the body of knowledge is becoming broader.

Two main cognitive development theorists are Jean Piaget and Lev Vygotsky. Their work serves as the basis for understanding the process of learning as an interaction of the developing human brain and the environment.

Jean Piaget

Jean Piaget was a trained biologist who studied environmental changes, first in birds and later in mollusks. He based much of his work in child development on his naturalist observation of his own three children, along with a limited number of other subjects. Some psychologists question his data because of the limited number of children he studied. The cognitive development sequence

Jean Piaget

(1896–1980) Swiss biologist who became interested in the child's construction of knowledge by processes of cognitive development influenced by maturation and interaction with the environment. He developed theories on the stages of cognitive development based on the child's *operations,* the ability to understand and manipulate information.

described by Piaget has been found to be valid in children around the world, although the ages may vary with the culture (Lafrancois, 1980).

Piaget's theory begins with the need of an individual to maintain a state of balance, or **equilibrium**, within his world. The individual needs to find order, structure, and predictability. With each new piece of information taken in through the senses, the brain attempts to make a match, to gain understanding based on prior knowledge or mental patterns. Piaget called these mental patterns **schemes**. As the child is exposed to new information and experiences, the schemes are adjusted to maintain equilibrium. This is called **association**, a match with what is already known or has been experienced. When the information is similar, the schemes are expanded (like adding more related facts to your knowledge of World War II as you study). This process is called **assimilation**. Sometimes new information or experience causes the creation of a new scheme or modifies an existing scheme. This process is called **accommodation** (Piaget, 1952, 1959). Nilsen's diagrams (2001) may help visual learners remember these similar terms (Figure 6–11).

SCENARIO Four-year-old Gina visited her white-haired grandmother, who announced that the neighbor next door had just become a grandmother. When they visited the neighbor, Gina looked puzzled when she saw her and asked, "Where's your white hair?" Gina's existing scheme envisioned all grandmothers having white hair. She tried to make the association between "grandmother" and "white hair" but was in disequilibrium when the schemes did not match. As her grandmother explained what made one a grandmother, Gina accommodated her scheme of "grandmother" through assimilation to include both white- and brown-haired women.

Two-year-old David sees a large boat on the river. This is the first time he has seen a boat. He points and says his approximation for his favorite thing, "Truck." His teacher says, "That's a boat, David. Boats float on water. Trucks drive on the road." As David and his teacher look at other types of boats, he accommodates and develops a new scheme of boat. As he takes a bath that evening, he pushes the soap around on top of the bath water and says, "Boat!" (Figure 6–12 on page 210).

Piaget described four stages of cognitive development in children. The stages describe development that is continuous and progressive, moving through one stage before beginning the next. The stages are related to age ranges, but there is variety

---

equilibrium—The process of new information finding order and structure with prior information. When new information is not linked to prior information, the individual is in a state of disequilibrium.

schemes (schema)—Piaget's term for a mental structure that provides a model for action in similar circumstances. Organized patterns of individual knowledge of objects and their relationships.

association—Matching of new information with what is already present.

assimilation—Absorption of new information, forming expanded schema.

accommodation—Modification of prior information, forming changed schema.

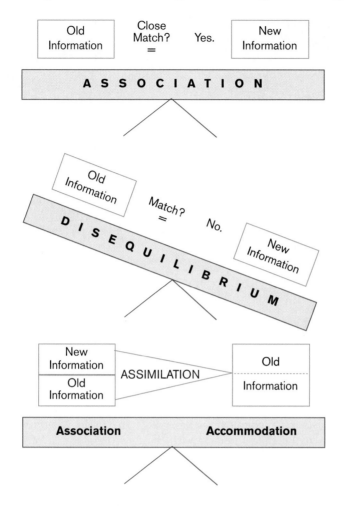

Figure 6–11

Association, disequilibrium, and assimilation. (From Nilsen, B., 2001)

within these ranges among children. He emphasized that "construction is superior to instruction" (Thomas, 1992), which led to the term **constructivism** (Piaget, 1973), which refers to the belief that knowledge is constructed by experience, not just by coming of age and passing through stages. His theory supports the idea that learning takes place through experiences (such as play) and that there is a pattern and age when certain learning usually takes place.

Piaget's cognitive stages (1952) are followed by ages that are approximate. In some cultures, the cognitive characteristics may appear earlier or later, but they all follow the same sequence.

✱ **Sensorimotor stage (birth to two years old):** The child is coordinating sensory perceptions and simple muscle or motor behaviors (Figure 6–12 on page 210). In substages of this period, intentional movement increasingly

constructivism—The interplay between biological development and experiences in which the individual constructs knowledge unique to that individual.

Figure 6–12

Sensory experiences build cognitive structure.

replaces the reflexes present at birth. These are coordinated and regulated by the developing cognitive structures of the brain. Cognitive development occurs as the child interacts with the environment and other people in his world (Figure 6–13).

Figure 6–13

Children hypothesize, experiment, and draw conclusions as they explore their environment.

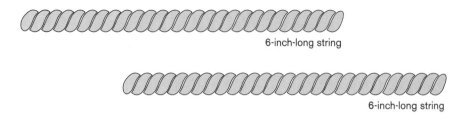

6-inch-long string

6-inch-long string

Figure 6–14

The preoperational child will judge one string to be longer than the other because the ends of the strings are not lined up.

* **Preoperational stage (two to seven years old):** This *intuitive* period is distinguished by the absence of the more sophisticated mental operations or actions that will appear in the next stage. The child makes judgments about quantity and volume based on appearances, rather than the logic that dictates that a change in configuration does not change quantity. The classic experiments of comparing the same lengths of string placed parallel but not even (Figure 6–14), coins spread out on a table and coins in a row, or clay in a large ball and the same amount of clay then broken into smaller balls are used to demonstrate the child's use of appearances or intuition rather than knowledge of quantity or volume. The child in this stage is also characterized by **egocentrism**. The child cannot comprehend that what the child sees is not what another person may see. For example, if the child is looking at a book and sees the pages with words and pictures, the person facing him sees the cover of the book. This demonstrates the child's inability to think about another's point of view. Thus, the statement, "How would you like it if he did that to you?" is incomprehensible to the preoperational child.

* **Concrete operations (seven to eleven years old):** During this stage, the child is developing the ability to perform mental operations, or internalized actions, based on reason and logic. He can mentally combine, separate, order, and transform objects and actions while physically in the same place as the objects. The child is able to manipulate numbers and dimensional concepts such as volume, and take more than one attribute into consideration, unlike the preoperational child in the previous examples. Balls of clay in a single lump or an equal amount in small balls, equal lengths of string parallel but not placed equally left to right, or equal amounts of water in tall glasses or short dishes will not confound the child whose thinking has progressed into this stage. He can explain that the form does not make a difference and, later, in the stage, mentally construct what will happen to the water level in the two differently shaped containers.

* **Formal operations (eleven to adulthood):** In adolescence, the ability to think logically in the abstract develops, continuing into adulthood with the increasing ability to think about one's own thinking.

egocentrism—Interpretation from one's own point of view. The inability to mentally place oneself in another's physical or emotional position.

Lev Vygotsky

(1896–1934) Russian psychologist who observed children's play to form theories about children's thinking. He emphasized the importance of social context, culture, parents, and teachers on the child's development. He saw that children's thinking progressed in dramatic play, as they took on social roles and solved problems through self-talk. His theory includes the concept of *zone of proximal development* and his belief in the importance of language as a factor in cognitive development.

While these stages are attributed to ages, the stages do not change on the birthday in question. Instead, they evolve as part of a dynamic process that is influenced by experiences that vary from one person to another.

Lev Vygotsky

Another developmental theorist to whom educators look to for guidance when planning learning experiences for their students was **Lev Vygotsky**. He emphasized that the child's knowledge comes from his culture, family members, the media, and school. Vygotsky saw two lines of development: the natural line of biological maturation of mind and body and the cultural line through interactions with people. He held that children learned what was important in a society through play. The term used to describe his philosophy is *sociocultural,* with a strong emphasis on language as the cultural trnasmitter.

One of Vygotsky's concepts is the **zone of proximal development**. This concept describes what the child can accomplish during independent problem solving and what he can accomplish with the help of an adult or more competent member of the culture (Berk & Winsler, 1995). What this means is that before a child masters a specific developmental milestone, approximations or attempts have been made, with the assistance of an adult, in which the child *almost* performs the task alone. The teacher uses Vygotsky's theory to assess each child's readiness to learn and master new skills or knowledge. Based on the assessment, the teacher sets up learning experiences that build on what the child has mastered and already knows. This is called **scaffolding**. "Scaffolding is a process by which adults provide supportive structures to help children learn and play (Figure 6–15). Scaffolding occurs at a time when children are faced with a challenge that they can solve independently with a simple hint, question, or a prompt from an adult" (Trawick-Smith, 1997).

SCENARIO

Zane is six years old. Based on his teacher's assessment, he is ready to master reading unfamiliar printed words. One piece of the puzzle is that Zane has a desire to learn to read about his favorite subject, undersea creatures. Other pieces of the puzzle include such things as his knowledge of the fact that printed words can be decoded, and the facts that his vision is clear with corrective lenses and his eyes can physically scan from left to right. He recognizes the letters of the alphabet, can distinguish and identify individual letter sounds in spoken words, and can relate those letters to their spoken sound. With all these pieces in place, the puzzle can come together easily with just a few cues and support from his teacher by providing a book about jellyfish that has words he will have to

continued

✳ **zone of proximal development**–The period of time in which a child is almost able to achieve a developmental milestone.

scaffolding–The adult provides direction and support for accomplishing what would normally be beyond the child's abilities.

Figure 6–15

Before a child can read, many other cognitive milestones must be achieved. The teacher builds on these milestones to help children learn to read.

sound out. Zane is in the zone of proximal development for learning to read. If there were pieces missing, such as not having much experience with reading or printed materials, or if he could not distinguish individual letter sounds, the task of learning to read would be difficult, if not impossible. Zane's teacher knows through observation that the next learning step for Zane is to decode unfamiliar printed words. All the pieces are in place for that learning event to occur. The teacher will provide support and a few cues to Zane, and the wonderful ability to decode the printed word will be his.

As a student of education, you will study Piaget, Vygotsky, and other developmental theorists in depth. You will learn to use their theories and to develop activities and create environments that take advantage of a child's developmental ability to learn. You may even study further, and conduct research and develop theories of your own upon which other educators base their practice.

✳ DEVELOPMENT AND CURRICULUM FOR THINKING AND LEARNING

Cognitive development unfolds in an orderly and timely sequence for most children. Teachers should be aware of the expected developments for the age range of children in their classes. Based on knowledge, the teacher makes decisions about when it is time to introduce the next learning challenge to a child and recognizes when development is not occurring as expected. The teacher is a resource to families regarding the development of their children and shares accomplishments and concerns with them.

"Because of what we know, this is what we do" is a mantra that guides the teacher's professional practice. Now that you know how children of a certain age think, that should guide you in what you teach and the way you teach. Curriculum planning, which will be a major part of your teacher preparation, is based on knowing the developmental stage of the children in your group, the expected outcomes of the grade or program, and a wide array of activities to achieve the outcomes. Planning for cognitive development will involve all the other curriculum areas (to be covered in later chapters in this book, such as reading/writing, math, science, social studies, music, and visual arts. These subjects may be taught separately from each other or integrated into a thematic curriculum. Emergent curricula base learning activities planned to achieve learning goals on the children's interests and ideas. The design of the learning curriculum is part of the teacher's decision-making process. Later chapters will also address emotional development and guiding children's behavior, since the teacher must work with the whole child.

Infants' Thinking and Learning

What is going on in that cute little head, you wonder? Is it just a buzz of incoming sensory stimulation? Is there any processing going on? The answers to these questions are complex and still subjects of research using the latest brain-imaging technology. What we are learning is that the cognitive abilities of infants in their most rudimentary stage are much more sophisticated than we ever realized. Gopnik, Meltzoff, and Kuhl (1999) call infants and young children "scientists in the crib" because "they formulate theories, make and test predictions, seek explanations, do experiments, and revise what they know in the light of new evidence" (p. 161).

Cognitive Development of Infants. Infants are in Piaget's sensori-motor stage. The term itself gives a clue about how children learn at this point: they use their senses and motor (or movement) ability. There is much to learn and explore in the world and infants are stimulated by sensory experiences and motivated to develop motor skills. As the infant begins to control movements, such as grasping and releasing a hand, or masters the muscle control for rolling over, getting up on hands and knees, pulling himself up to stand, and walking, his world expands considerably (Figure 6–16).

In this stage of development, children use their motor abilities and senses to develop schemes. Their behaviors are goal directed, such as an infant rubbing against

Figure 6–16

During the sensori-motor stage of development, children use their motor abilities and senses to develop schemes.

his mother's shirt to cue the mother that it is time to nurse. In the early part of this stage, children deal with the here and now and are only aware of an object when the object is present and stimulating their senses. The game of peek-a-boo is very exciting for a child under one year because it is a surprise that the person behind the blanket is still there! After this, children develop the ability to represent objects in memory. **Object permanence** is the ability of a child to remember an object even after it is out of sight. Children at this stage do not think as adults do. They repeat motions over and over to build knowledge about the properties of objects, such as soft, hard, tasty, smooth, and bumpy. They try and fail and try again, not knowing that their actions may be the cause of the failure.

Infants learn through routines within a secure, nurturing, consistent environment. An infant appears capable of very little, but if you closely observe a newborn you may be surprised at how capable they really are. Most newborns can hear and are capable of recognizing and showing preference for their mother's voice. When a newborn hears the voice of a parent or caregiver, he will often move to the rhythm of the voice's speech patterns. The newborn's eyes can follow a moving object; he likes sweet liquids, and does not like specific smells. These are inborn instincts designed to capture and hold the attention of parents and caregivers and to help the infant make sense of his environment. Throughout the first year, these basic instincts are expanded into more purposeful movements and actions. Primarily, the infant uses these abilities to survive: to develop an attachment with caring adults, trusting that his needs will be met. By the end of the first year, he will use these skills to make some independent decisions for action based on his own goals.

Infants instinctively recognize their mother's voice. Within months, infants develop a strategy to call their mothers or other significant caregivers for comfort, nourishment, or companionship. By the time infants reach their first birthday, they have developed the cognitive ability to anticipate routine events and express displeasure when the routine changes. They have mental representations or symbolic thoughts. They begin simple pretending by mimicking the act of eating, sleeping, or crying, and they begin to use objects in a pretend way.

SCENARIO   Darlene has a favorite bib that her father puts around her neck before each meal. Darlene lifts her head to accept the bib when she sees her father pick it up. Today the favorite bib is in the wash, so her father chooses another one. Darlene recognizes that the object is a bib, but not the one she likes, and before her father can put the bib on, Darlene turns her head away. Darlene has the cognitive ability to anticipate a routine event, recognize a familiar object, and communicate displeasure when the anticipated event does not follow the familiar routine or pattern (Figure 6–17 on page 216).

During the first year, and throughout their childhood, infants gain self-control and mastery. As their physical abilities develop and allow them to reach for and move toward desired goals, their cognitive abilities develop and expand as well, so they can take advantage of their new physical abilities. On the other hand, as cognitive abilities

object permanence—The ability to understand that objects have substance, are external to oneself, and continue to exist when out of sight.

Figure 6—17

By their first birthday, children develop the cognitive ability to anticipate routine events and express pleasure and displeasure.

develop, the child recognizes a favorite toy and practices reaching and holding until he is physically able to do so. When you think of the seemingly helpless newborn, it is amazing to think of the brain development that must occur for the 11-month-old to be capable of selecting and holding onto a favorite toy.

Curriculum for Infants' Cognitive Development. Since so many changes occur in the first year of life, we will divide infancy into sections.

Young Infants: Birth to Six Months. Necessary for cognitive development in the first months of life are the actions by adults who provide such physical needs as food, clean diapers, and a healthy environment, but also respond emotionally to the child, gazing into his eyes, touching him gently, and talking lovingly to him. These actions do not spoil the baby, but rather set the stage for later learning, giving the child the security that will be the basis for later exploration.

"Babies need space and opportunity to move at their current capabilities. They need a place rich with objects to explore through the senses. They need key adults to respond to them promptly, consistently, and warmly, and to interact with them giving them language, face to face so they can begin to understand the process of human communication. They need a place that is safe for them to be in, but one that does not restrict free movement and active curiosity" (Gestwicki, 1999).

In the early months, infants need to have objects to focus on and follow. They need to see familiar objects disappear and reappear. Some of these objects may be the faces of family. As infants mature, a giant step in cognitive development is their realization that they can cause objects to move. The infant watches his sister shake his rattle and delights in the noise. As his sister places the rattle in his hand, he grasps it and shakes it. At first, he is unaware that he is causing the rattle to make noise. As he manipulates the rattle, he becomes aware that it is the motion he makes that causes the rattle to make noise, so he repeats the action, and repeats it, and repeats it!

Mobile Infants: Six Months to Twelve Months. Children at this age need to be able to explore and experience objects that are safe to touch, put in their mouths without being swallowed or causing choking, stand or climb on without falling, and crawl over or walk on without getting injured. They need to hear language relevant to what they are doing and simply verbalized observations. They need to be gently challenged to notice new characteristics about objects or to try using objects in new ways.

SCENARIO Eric's mother holds out the flower and says, "See the pretty flower? It's a purple flower. You can smell it (sniff). It's so sweet. Just like Eric."

Equipment for this age is anything that is safe to lift, throw, chew on, crawl over, or bang on a table. The infant now has the mobility, one way or another, to get to any interesting object, so the first role of the adult is to keep the infant from danger. Manipulation and locomotion are the two tasks and curriculum guides for environment and activities. Providing children at this stage with interesting, safe objects, along with adults who describe the children's actions and marvel at their innovations, enhances cognitive development. Remember, the child is making connections, so the more repetition, similarities, go-together toys, and activities, the more schemes the child will have to draw on later.

Toddlers' Thinking and Learning

SCENARIO Tommy is 15 months old. His mother hides his pacifier in her purse. Tommy remembers this and reaches into her purse when she is not looking to get his pacifier back. In order to do this, Tommy must have the cognitive ability to remember where his pacifier is, even though it has been hidden from his sight. He has obtained the level of object permanence and formed the scheme, or cognitive structure, for the pacifier and where it was hidden.

Eighteen-month-old Sierra piles blocks on a pillow. She has piled blocks before successfully but each time she gets more than two on the stack, it tips and falls. She tries and tries. She moves the building process to the carpet and it works. She has not yet reached the concept of cause and effect. "If I do this (build on a shaky base) the blocks will fall, but if I build on a flat surface, they will stack." This will come in the next few months and the observer who sees Sierra try different surfaces as the base of her constructions will know she has reached that higher level of cognitive development.

Cognitive Development of Toddlers. In the second year of life (still in Piaget's sensorimotor stage), children begin to understand the relationship between cause and effect. Between twelve and eighteen months, they use trial-and-error experimentation to find new ways to play; they can then mentally represent the problem and change their actions as they near twenty-four months old. They can find objects that are

Figure 6—18

In the second year of life children can classify objects by one characteristic, name familiar pictures in a book, and put similar things together and take them apart.

out of sight, classify objects based on one characteristic such as color, put simple things together and take them apart, and name familiar pictures in a book (Figure 6–18).

In the area of language, they understand much more than they are able to say and begin progressing from one- to three- and four-word phrases and sentences. In this stage, children begin to classify similar objects. Initially "they make a number of mistakes because of their concepts; thus all men are 'Daddy,' all women are 'Mommy,' and all toys are 'Mine'" (Hergenhahn & Olson, 1997). This is called *overgeneralization*. It is often humorous, but adults can understand what is happening when they understand the beginning stage of the child's thinking. Of course, the word "No!" is a favorite with two-year-olds as they begin to exercise independence and autonomy. This is a developmental milestone, not a mark of stubbornness or obstinacy.

Young children learn within the context of a relationship with a trusted person. Their language abilities are built through conversations about daily events and their cognitive abilities can be stretched by new experiences that feel safe. The primary caregivers include parents, siblings, and teachers. To provide consistency in the learning environment, it is crucial that this group functions as a team, with the care and development of the child as their central focus.

During the infant and toddler years, children make tremendous strides in their cognitive development. Their cognitive ability and neural connections have grown, based on their experiences. Because of this significant brain growth, it is crucial for future cognitive development that infants and toddlers be given every opportunity to experience the environment and test their new skills. "By the age of three a child's brain has 1,000 trillion synapses—about twice the number as her pediatrician's. This number holds steady throughout the first decade of life. In this way a child's brain becomes super-dense" (Shore, 1997).

WORDS OF WISDOM   Sharon, a teacher of toddlers in the Boston area, relates this observation:

"It was after lunch today and most of the children were down for naps, so it was very quiet. One child, an 18-month-old I'll call Amy, had the play area to herself. There was still one lunch chair left out that we

continued

had not yet put away. (We use a wooden sort with a buckle and detachable tray, like a basic high chair but low to the ground.) Amy picked up one of the dolls and sat it in the chair and buckled it in. As I was going about my duties, I thought to myself, "Hmmm, I wonder what will happen when she looks around for a tray. I wonder if she will even think of a tray." They were still dirty and out of Amy's reach. Hardly before my thoughts were done, Amy went across the room, picked up a Boppy pillow (those semi-round pillows nursing mothers use to help raise the baby), brought it over to the chair, and proceeded to put it around the doll in the chair in the exact manner of a tray!"

"I was amazed not only at her solution, but also at the apparent quickness with which she thought of this. As I said, the thought had hardly finished running through my mind of wondering what she would do when she was off to get the pillow. . . . This served to remind me just what wonderful, smart, creative, problem solvers even the youngest children can be. Sometimes people don't think of infants or young toddlers like this."

Amy made the cognitive connections between the shape of the tray and the shape of the pillow? This is the beginning of that physical knowledge of shapes in the environment. Amy constructed her own lesson in geometry that day!

Differences in cognitive development between children become apparent by the end of the third year. Not all children develop at the same rate. By the age of three, a child should point to and name familiar objects, use two- or three-word sentences, sort objects to a single characteristic, and like being read to. If not, then the child should be checked by a health care provider or early childhood specialist (Allen & Marotz, 1999).

Curriculum for Toddlers' Cognitive Development.

SCENARIO Kelly is 20 months old. She takes all the small, decorative pillows from the living room furniture and carries them one at a time to her bed. Her grandmother asks what she is doing and she answers, "My piwwows" (Figure 6–19 on page 220).

Toddlers need opportunities to manipulate objects that have parts or come in sets so they can sort things according to one-dimensional categories. Kelly has categorized pillows as objects that belong on a bed and has been given the opportunity to arrange the environment the way she understands it. Toddlers also need opportunities to experiment with cause and effect. Many toddlers discover the delight in turning the television on and off to hear the click or flipping a wall switch up and down to watch the overhead light go on and off. A safer device for toddlers is an easily operated flashlight. Other situations in which they may observe cause and effect include rolling a ball or toy car down an incline, pushing keys on a computer keyboard to make changes on the screen, and banging a spoon on a pot to create a noise. Children at this age delight in the tiresome activity of dropping their toys from the high chairs or cribs to watch adults patiently pick them up!

Toddlers should also have the opportunity to put things together and take them apart. Simple puzzles consisting of just a few pieces, a pull train with two or three easily connected cars, or even the experience of trying to put on some of their own clothes (or taking them off!) all provide opportunities for toddlers to strengthen cognitive development.

The objects that toddlers are given to manipulate do not need to be expensive or even toys. Common household objects work just as well, such as pots and pans, plastic

Figure 6—19

Toddlers need opportunities to manipulate objects.

containers, laundry baskets, and empty cereal boxes. Toddlers just need the opportunity and freedom to explore many objects in the manner they imagine. Toys such as puzzles should not be so complex as to frustrate the toddler. For example, a puzzle with five pieces may be too complex for a young toddler, but a puzzle with two pieces may lead to much successful experimentation with "putting together and taking apart."

Preschoolers' Thinking and Learning

As children enter the preschool years, they continue their tremendous growth in cognitive abilities.

SCENARIO   Tamar, age two, points to a big spotted thing out in the country: "Doggie! Doggie!" Big four-year-old sister Tabatha says, "No, silly, that's a cow!" Tabatha has a sophisticated schema of familiar animals. She has classified these four-legged animals into finer categories, such as farm, zoo, jungle, and woodland animals. She looks at the animal and her sensory information sorts out the various attributes of the animal and responds with the correct name, indicating that she has more advanced cognitive ability than little Tamar.

Cognitive Development of Preschoolers. Preschoolers are in Piaget's preoperational stage (two to seven years old). In this stage, children are getting ready to put it all together (Figure 6–20).

During this stage, children solve problems by using their intuition or inference, rather than logical thought. This is illustrated by the child's inability to understand that the amount of or number of objects does not change even though the shape or order is changed.

Figure 6–20

Tremendous cognitive growth occurs during the preoperational years.

SCENARIO

Tabatha says, "There's a big bunch of cows and a little bunch of cows." Eight-year-old Timothy says, "No, silly, it's a herd of cows and they're the same, just this herd is standing closer together. I counted them and there are eight in each herd."

Timothy has developed the concept of conservation, while Tabatha has not. Here, that term does not mean an appreciation for ecology, but rather the understanding that quantity or amount does not change by spreading things out, breaking it up into several smaller pieces, or pouring it into different sized containers. For example, a child in this stage will think there are more jelly beans in a row of five that is spread out and fewer in a row of five that are close together. The child judges "more" by the length of the line the jelly beans make, and not by the number of beans, even though the child may be able to count five beans in each row (Figure 6–21).

Figure 6–21

Children learn to count by sorting and manipulating objects.

SCENARIO Shelly was admonished not to throw food on the floor. She closed her eyes and dropped crusts of bread under her chair. Because Shelly could not see the crusts drop, she did not think anyone else could either. This is a very important concept in understanding this stage of thinking because it helps explain motives and set expectations for children's behavior. The classic, "How would you like it if he did that to you?" line is incomprehensible to the three-, four- or even five-year-old. Mentally, the child cannot put himself on the receiving end of the punch, pinch, grab, or kick. This involves a mental transfer of himself into the body of another that a child of this age cannot accomplish.

An example of preschoolers' cognitive limitations is egocentrism, the inability to perceive what others see.

SCENARIO Paul, age three, and Katrina, age four, are using their problem-solving abilities. They attend a nursery school three mornings a week. Their teacher, Edward, has arranged his classroom with housekeeping/dramatic play, quiet reading, counting/math, art, and large motor areas. Although Edward has set up areas, the boundaries between the areas are not always fixed. Yesterday, Paul went grocery shopping with his grandfather. Today, he is at preschool. Paul joins Katrina in the dramatic play corner of the classroom, which is equipped with a miniature kitchen that has plastic food items and dishes. Paul uses a doll carriage as a grocery cart and says to Katrina, "I'm going shopping." Katrina says, "I'm the money taker and you're the shopper." Katrina crosses the classroom to the art area and cuts up some green paper and says, "Here's your money." Paul gets blocks from the block area and fills his carriage with them. He places the blocks on the kitchen table and Katrina states a price for each item. "Ten for eggs, 47 for all those vegetables, 200 for the cereal. That will be 2,090 for those groceries." Paul gives her a handful of paper. Edward, the teacher, who has been watching, observes: "Wow, Paul, that's a lot of money you paid Katrina!" Paul replies, "I bought a lot of food!" Katrina places money on the table and counts, "One teen, two teen, three teen, *six teen.*" The teacher says, "Yes, your groceries cost 11, 12, 13, 14, 15, *16* dollars!" (Figure 6–22).

What has Edward, the teacher, done to encourage cognitive development in his classroom? What experiences in this scenario contributed to Paul's and Katrina's cognitive development? What is Katrina's zone of proximal development?

Curriculum for Preschoolers' Cognitive Development.
Everything that occurs in the preschool classroom contributes to cognitive development. The organization of the environment contributes to cognition. The cubbies where children hang their coats are labeled with their names and stickers or photographs so they can *read* their proper location. The shelves are labeled with words and

Figure 6—22

As children play, they reinforce and build upon what they have learned to move on to new learning.

pictures of the materials and supplies stored there (Figure 6–23). The schedule provides long periods of uninterrupted time for exploration, as well as predictable routines in which children learn the sequence of expected behavior for group times, meal

Figure 6—23

Labeled classrooms help young children understand that the printed word has meaning and also helps them organize their thinking.

times, and getting ready to go home. These are all part of the school day's structure, but each in their own way contributes to a schema for cognitive development.

The preschool classroom is an environment where children have opportunities to interact with people and objects in creative ways. Many preschool programs ascribe to the play-centered philosophy, with enrichment activities in learning centers. For example, Edward, the four-year-olds' teacher, arranged activity areas in his classroom. He allowed Paul and Katrina to use materials from different areas for creative play. Edward observed the play and described it to the players, while he assessed their social, emotional, physical, cognitive, and language areas of development. He will use their interest to involve them and others in planning a grocery store in the dramatic area, with special emphasis on matching, counting, and prereading activities.

Preschool children need variety in their learning environment. They require equipment that is safe and made for their size. To encourage cognitive development, they need opportunities for dramatic play, such as an office or cooking area, exposure to books, written words to label familiar items, and available writing implements. They need to have opportunities to sort, count, and compare a variety of objects. They need other children and adults to talk to about their activities and ideas. Lastly, they need an adult who observes and assesses when they have mastered concepts and then arranges the environment to gently challenge them to grow further.

Literacy development holds a central place in the preschool classroom. Books and literacy materials such as interesting charts and posters should be available. Good children's literature should be spotlighted every day in an individual, small-group, or large-group reading session that is filled with excitement and positive experiences. Children should see their words in print by dictating stories or bylines for their art work. Symbols should be everywhere in the form of picture labels. Opportunity for mathematical and scientific exploration is provided with equipment and materials to explore and manipulate. A variety of abundant blocks can encourage mathematical concepts of wholes, parts, and combinations. Observing natural objects such as rocks, soil, plants, and animals in the classroom adds to the children's knowledge of the world. Problem solving is used in the social realm to determine who will get to paint at the easel first. Problem solving in the physical realm may involve trying to determine why the block towers keep falling down. Both are opportunities for the teacher to help children construct their own theories, test them out, come up with possible solutions, and observe the results. Children learn every minute, so the learning teacher should assess what is contributing to or hindering that learning and modify the environment, activities, and interactions to contribute to cognitive development.

Primary Age Children's Thinking and Learning

The five- to seven-year-old is making a cognitive shift in his way of thinking, from intuition to logic. He is developing a sense of symbols as representations for other things, so alphabet letters and their accompanying sounds, and numbers and their accompanying quantity now have more meaning.

Cognitive Development of Primary Age Children.
Primary age children are making the transition from the preoperational stage (two to seven years old) to the concrete operations stage (seven to eleven years old). In the primary grades, egocentrism has diminished and the child is able to conserve and represent. This brings a new level of thinking that equips the child for reading and writing, manipulating numbers (both in writing and mentally), and thinking more abstractly about things that cannot be experienced directly through the senses. This stage is one of orderliness: taking in vast amounts of information and coming to conclusions that

are logical and based more on concrete reasoning and less on intuition. Children in the primary grades are developing more logical thinking to solve problems and predict outcomes. They learn to read, write, add and subtract, and are beginning to understand multiplication and division. Eight-year-olds use complex systems to organize collections and belongings. They understand that individuals may have different thoughts and feelings than their own. They can carry out multiple-step directions (Allen & Marotz, 1999). A primary age child has a mental image of a sequence of events involving past, present, and future and can describe them, while the preoperational child needs to act them out to retell them in sequence.

SCENARIO	Ms. Marti is a second-grade teacher. Her class has been learning about different types of seeds. Over the last week, the children have brought a variety of seeds to school in labeled plastic bags. The children have been divided into groups of three and each group has been given a piece of stiff cardboard. Ms. Marti asks that each group decide on a design to make with their seeds, gives them glue with instructions for its use, and asks that they put their finished designs on the back table to dry, and then clean their worktable and wash their hands.

The group that includes Brian, Peter, and James looks at their seed packets and Brian says, "Lets put all the white seeds here, the brown seeds here, and the black seeds here." James says, "Put the big, white pumpkin seeds over here and the big, brown acorns here because they look different from those other seeds." Peter says, "That seed looks like a really big fish eye." Brian arranges the pumpkin seeds in five piles of ten and says, "I found those seeds when I was carving pumpkins." James says, "You have fifty seeds. If we make a fish design, we can use the cucumber seeds for the scales and then use some of the pumpkin seeds for fins."

Peter begins to glue the design together, but gets too much glue on the cardboard. James says, "You squeezed the bottle too hard; wipe it off and don't squeeze so hard." Peter has printed "F" and "I" and asks Ms. Marti what comes next. She reminds him that the final sound is SH. Peter finishes writing "FISH" on the cardboard. Brian carries the project to the drying shelf, Peter wipes off the table, and the three boys wash their hands.

What cognitive abilities are evident in these children from this project? What subject areas are the children exploring? What was the teacher's role in the above scenario? The teacher acted as facilitator of the activity by supplying materials, arranging the group, setting the boundaries of the project, and arranging to have seeds brought to school in labeled packages. She helped the children differentiate among and identify different seeds and interacted with the groups when they needed clarification or guidance. This primary school teacher encouraged an active learning process. The primary teacher realizes that children are beginning to develop individual strengths and strategies for acquiring knowledge and provides learning opportunities for children that accommodate and take advantage of their developing learning styles.

Curriculum for Cognitive Development of Primary Age Children.

Primary school children are usually enthusiastic about learning and attending school. The teacher should work to retain this level of enthusiasm and have it extend beyond the primary grades. In many schools, the teacher is expected to follow a prescribed curriculum to achieve learning outcomes. The teacher can reach these outcomes by interweaving learning activities that motivate and are interesting to individual children, leading them to achieve the identified learning outcomes.

The primary classroom is a resource for learning, activities, and materials for individual, small-group and whole-class use. There are times when individual seat work may be assigned to encourage the child to work out problems or learning activities using his own initiative and resources. Since collaboration is a skill needed in society, small-group assignments are often used. In these, students contribute their own strengths, negotiating with each other when differences of opinion arise, and learn that cooperation and teamwork can bring both results and satisfaction. The teacher should be keenly aware of each child's educational needs and monitor groups to ensure that the learning goals on each child's level are met. Making connections with prior knowledge is always an important principle in cognitive development, so the teacher plans learning activities relevant to the children's knowledge and culture.

The seed activity combined the subject areas of science, art, math, and writing into one activity planned on a thematic web (Figure 6–24). Other activities that took place during this thematic unit were planting seeds, measuring and recording growth, and writing and making a short book about the growth of a seed. Some of the children read *Jack and the Bean Stalk,* made a large paper bean stalk the length of the hallway, and measured it. The class walked to a neighbor's garden to identify what was growing and brought back a bag of potatoes, three tomatoes, and a zucchini. They counted, measured, weighed, and recorded the statistics on the vegetables before making soup out of them. Ms. Marti wrote the soup recipe on big poster paper as they described each step. Ms. Marti told the children that, many years ago, children attended one-room schoolhouses and made soup every day in the winter for lunch. She made a mental note to find a story about one-room schools. Some of the children copied the recipe to take home. Using a thematic approach, Ms. Marti taught reading, writing, math, social studies, and art. If the children are interested in the story of the one-room schoolhouse, she may design a theme unit about that period of history and the one-room school experience. By taking cues from the children, she retains their enthusiasm for learning. She also provides a variety of learning activities that use the children's different strengths in math, writing, art, and speaking.

Elementary Age Children's Thinking and Learning

Elementary age children are making the transition from the concrete operations stage (seven to eleven years old) to the formal operations stage (eleven to adult).

Cognitive Development of Elementary Age Children.

By the upper elementary grades, children have developed the concept of conservation. They can think logically about concrete objects, or objects that they can see and feel. Children in this stage develop the ability to order objects in a series according to increasing or decreasing length, weight, or volume and to classify or group objects based on certain characteristics. "Although concrete operational thinkers have made

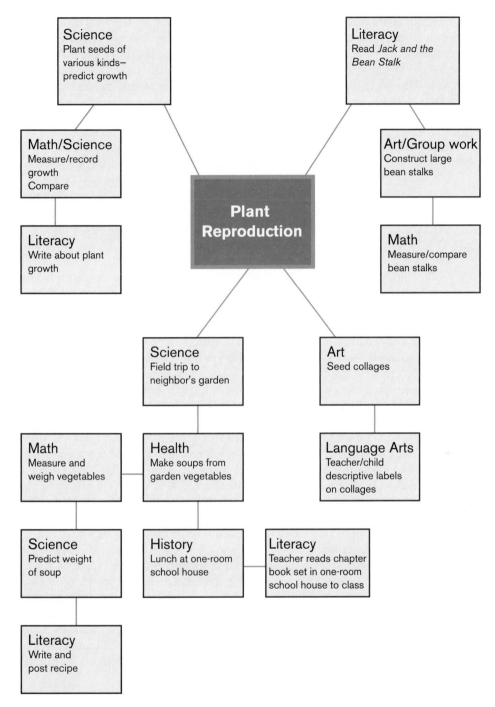

Figure 6–24

Thematic webs provide for cognitive connections among fields of study, making lessons relevant and memorable. Notice which multiple intelligences are incorporated in this thematic web.

important developmental strides, their thinking is still tied to available experiences; they need to solve problems with concrete objects. In working with concrete operational learners, the challenge for teachers is to structure learning activities that provide a concrete foundation for their thinking" (Eggen & Kauchak, 1999). The concrete operations stage is where the child has the capacity to think logically about concrete things, those things the child experiences in everyday life. He can see the ball of clay remolded into a log shape and mentally reform it into a ball, knowing it will be the same size. This reversibility is a characteristic of the mental manipulation possible because the child has attained this level of cognitive development.

SCENARIO Mr. Stewart's fifth-grade class is learning about simple machines. When they study levers, he takes the class to the playground to experiment with weight and leverage on the teeter-totter. He connects this concrete experience with the formulas he is presenting in class because he knows children at this age need to actually weigh and measure for themselves, instead of just reading about it.

In the upper elementary grades, children are entering into the period of formal operations, which means to gain the ability to think logically about hypothetical things. They can mentally reverse not only concrete objects like balls of clay and glasses of liquid but also intangible ideas like truth and justice. They have a better grasp of both sides of an issue, seeing moral and ethical dilemmas in situations like the poor man who steals food for his starving children, or the question of who deserves the limited supply of a cure for a deadly disease. Kohlberg (1969) studied moral development in relation to cognitive development, exploring how children came to judgments about good and bad based on their thinking level.

After the age of 10, the number of synapses produced within the brain is less than the number eliminated through pruning. "As pruning accelerates in the second decade of life, those synapses that have been reinforced by virtue of repeated experience tend to become permanent: the synapses that were not used often enough in the early years tend to be eliminated" (Shore, 1997). Teachers today are exploring the significance of this and using this knowledge to change some teaching practices. For example, children who learn a second language when they are very young do not speak either their first or second language with an accent. Their early experience modifies their cognitive structures for two languages. It is more difficult for children to become fluent in a second language when their instruction begins in high school because that sensitive period for learning languages has passed. It can be done; it is just more difficult. "For most children, middle childhood is a time for settling down, for developing more fully those patterns that have already been set. It is a period for learning new skills and refining old ones. Children focus on testing themselves, on meeting their own challenges as well as those imposed by the environment. The child who is successful in these tasks will probably become more capable and self-assured" (Craig & Kermis, 1994).

SCENARIO Kim is in the sixth grade and, as part of a unit on South America, has chosen to make a South American meal for his family. He will cook for his mother, two sisters, grandparents, and two friends. The recipe he chose serves four so he doubles all the ingredients on the list. As he starts to gather the ingredients, he discovers that there is no onion salt in the cupboard. He thinks about what else might be good in the recipe and

continued

decides to use garlic powder. From a previous experience, he knows garlic powder has a strong taste, so he adds just a little. Because garlic powder contains no salt, he adds a little bit of salt to even out the flavors. At dinner, everyone compliments him on his delicious meal. Kim designs a poster that includes pictures of the food, the cooking process, the dining experience, and an explanation of the origin and cultural significance of the recipe (Figure 6–25).

Kim had to modify a recipe to make enough for his family (Figure 6–25). What did Kim have to think critically about? How was he a problem solver? What subject areas were involved in this project? How did his being able to choose his project help him build upon strengths he already possesses? What did Kim learn from this activity?

Curriculum for Cognitive Development of Elementary Age Children. To develop critical thinking skills, children need to be presented with problems, form hypotheses, and test and evaluate their hypotheses. Memorizing unrelated factual information does not facilitate critical thinking, but simply increases recall which may be limited in duration. For meaningful learning to take place, the teacher must use many strategies to meet the curriculum's learning outcomes while making the learning relevant and connected so it lasts beyond the testing period. The teacher should provide many opportunities for children at this age to work independently on special interests, and to work with others in small groups toward a common goal, avoiding competition among children.

Children at this age begin to gather information from books, the Internet, or interviews to meet a learning goal. Children become aware of their strengths as learners and the teacher provides materials, opportunities, and projects so the child can use those strengths. For example, Kim found it more rewarding to explain his project in the form of a picture essay on a poster, rather than to give an oral or written report.

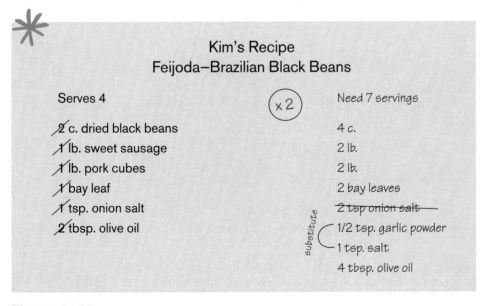

Kim's Recipe
Feijoda–Brazilian Black Beans

Serves 4   (x 2)   Need 7 servings

2 c. dried black beans   4 c.
1 lb. sweet sausage   2 lb.
1 lb. pork cubes   2 lb.
1 bay leaf   2 bay leaves
1 tsp. onion salt   2 tsp onion salt
2 tbsp. olive oil   1/2 tsp. garlic powder
                                              1 tsp. salt
                                   substitute
                                              4 tbsp. olive oil

Figure 6–25

Elementary age children begin to have the cognitive abilities to solve more advanced problems.

Additionally, the room should be arranged so that children can work quietly and independently as they consider and begin to analyze information. They may need a quiet space to think through the steps in a complex division problem or to choose words for a poem. At the same time, the room must be easily rearranged to facilitate partner and group learning. Children will tap into the group members' cognitive strengths to complete complex learning tasks. There should be resources in the room to help them explore, analyze, problem solve, calculate, and draw conclusions. These resources might include dictionaries, atlases, a collection of fiction and nonfiction books at a variety of reading levels, calculators, measuring devices, basic art supplies, a tape recorder, a computer, and a magnifying glass; writing paper and pencils should be readily available to all children in the classroom. Additionally, students need access to a library with current resources, the Internet for research, video equipment, a media or art room, a music room, and building supplies such as hammers, saws, and screwdrivers. A variety of adults with diverse strengths, talents, and areas of expertise should be available to the children for support, information, and guidance (Figure 6–26).

✳ ASSESSING COGNITIVE DEVELOPMENT

Assessment should determine what the student knows and can do in order to identify his needs and plan a curriculum for further learning. The two major teachers' unions have agreed upon standards for teacher competence in assessing students. These standards center on the teacher's skill in selecting, administering, scoring, and interpreting appropriate methods for making instructional decisions about individual students, planning their teaching, developing curriculum, and improving schools (American Federation of Teachers, National Council on Measurement in Education, & National Education Association, 1990).

Figure 6–26

Computers allow the older child with higher level cognitive abilities to manipulate information quickly.

Assessing Infant and Toddler Cognitive Development

Each age group you have been exploring demands a different kind of assessment, both in content and in method. Infants, toddlers, and preschoolers are not test takers; therefore, assessing their cognitive development is done by observing them and recording your observations based on both your knowledge of child development and the individual child's previous progress. Individual curriculum plans based on the assessment can then be made to help the child progress, not only in areas that may be lagging, but also in areas that are at a normal or advanced level. The teacher's role is to help every child progress in every domain.

Assessing Primary and Elementary Age Children's Cognitive Development

In the primary and elementary grades, assessment becomes more formalized and is often dictated by the school district or the state. There are several types of assessments.

* Pencil and paper tests—These may be objective tests with one correct answer for each question in fill-in-the-blank, matching, or multiple-choice format. Open-ended tests ask questions that require essay-type answers formed into sentences with explanations.

* Oral tests—The teacher asks questions of the students as a group or individually to ascertain their levels of knowledge and understanding.

* Performance tests—The teacher observes the student to evaluate his skill level in such things as mathematical computations or science experiments.

All of these methods may be used to assess the student's mastery of the concepts presented, demonstrating learning outcomes. Most schools use standardized tests, produced by testing experts to obtain objective measurements of a student's progress. Some of the controversies surrounding the use of standardized tests are presented in the next section.

Standardized Testing

A **standardized test** compares the test taker with a large group of similar pupils and is administered and scored in the same way for standardization and comparison purposes. For example, a child in sixth grade may take a test that compares his reading comprehension with a large group of other sixth graders. The child's score results from a comparison to the large group score. Millions of standardized educational tests are administered to schoolchildren in the United States each year (McCullough, 1992). Each individual score is compared to the scores of other children who took the test. Most are multiple-choice tests that can be easily graded. Legislators, parents, taxpayers, and schools look to see if an adequate number of the local school district's test scores fall in at least the average range. If so, the school district is seen as having done its job.

Another use for standardized tests is to measure a child's ability to learn in order to determine what and how the child should be taught. For example, testing might indicate that a child in the third grade is not able to calculate math problems at the same

standardized test—Test designed to be taken by a large number of students that are administered, scored, and interpreted in the same way no matter where it is administered.

level as most of her classmates, but instead calculates at the level of most first graders. The teacher will use this information to investigate further. Was the test score accurate? Is the child experiencing a physical problem? What is the child's next learning step in math? Is further testing warranted to provide additional helpful information?

Commercial achievement tests are researched, written, and distributed by private testing companies. Some of the most widely used are (Airasian, 2001):

* California Achievement Tests.
* Comprehensive Tests of Basic Skills.
* Terra Nova.
* Iowa Tests of Basic Skills.
* Metropolitan Achievement Tests.
* Sequential Tests of Educational Progress.
* SRA Achievement Series.
* Stanford Achievement Tests.

What are the problems with standardized testing? In many school districts, the test scores are compared to a national standard. A successful school is seen as one that meets or exceeds the national standard. In recent years, school districts have been asked to be more accountable for what they do, and the measure for many schools is their test scores. With this pressure, schools have begun to "teach to the test." An example of teaching to the test can be found in New York State, where the state administers a standard examination at the end of high school classes for all academic subjects. The curriculum to prepare students for the exam begins in the early years of education. In one elementary school, children missed the solar eclipse because the class did not have time to see or learn about it. It was not on that year's curriculum and the teacher was pressured to prepare the children for the upcoming test. By high school, children are spending weeks studying old tests in academic topic areas to prepare for the final exams. Teachers announce their average test scores from previous years at parents' nights, impressing upon them the importance of good performance, adding family pressure to the high-stakes tests.

On the other hand, the test has encouraged teachers, parents, and students to focus on those areas considered standards for a specific topic. All children who take the test prepare by studying the standard curriculum. The number of children who graduate from high school and cannot read or write well enough to get a job or to go to college is a major concern. Does requiring a minimum score on a standardized reading and writing exam as a criterion for high school graduation mean that students will be better prepared for college and future careers?

Other criticisms of standardized tests are that most are multiple choice and may not measure the full scope of learning. In authentic assessment, the student is asked to apply his knowledge to a specific task. For example, a science student may be asked to perform an actual experiment. Students may also build a portfolio of their work samples to demonstrate their knowledge. English students may collect their best writing samples to submit for evaluation. Another controversy surrounding standardized testing has been that the defined standard or method of testing is not culturally inclusive. For example, cultural beliefs in some Native American tribes bar competitive behaviors in an academic setting. Also, many Native Americans' first language is unwritten, and Native Americans on economically deprived reservations lack the experiences that would enable them to understand the examples that teachers use in classroom instruction. Some standardized tests are also not valid when used with children with special needs. A visually impaired child will not perform well on test questions that require the student to compare two objects on a page or to complete word exercises involving visual cues. Students with motor control problems may have difficulty filling in an answer sheet that requires coloring in small circles. Accommodations are often difficult to arrange.

What do we do with information from standardized tests? Are individual children identified who have acquired less knowledge than is expected for the time period for which they are tested? Are individual children identified who have surpassed the expected level of knowledge for the time period tested? What should be done once an individual child is so identified?

The teacher must understand the defined normal developmental range for the children in his class. The teacher must also be skilled at observation in order to supplement the information supplied by the test with information about how the child functions in the real world. The teacher must understand the child's cultural context and potential barriers to the child's performing well on the standardized test. The teacher must know of available experts to add to the educational team to further assess or intervene in areas of development that are of concern. Most importantly, the teacher must be able to communicate clearly with the family to gather and give information and be able to address their fears and misperceptions in a way that will make the family feel a part of the educational team.

SUMMARY

Cognitive development both follows an expected order and is individual. From the earliest moments, the infant's experience within his environment strongly influences brain development. Piaget and Vygotsky both noted a common pattern and order in children's cognitive development. Gardner identified areas of intelligence in which individuals exhibit certain strengths. The teacher's role is to understand the stages of cognitive development, appreciate different learning styles among individual students, and recognize delays in cognitive development and locate resources and intervention for those children. The teacher then creates an environment in which individual children can operate in their zone of proximal development and master new learning goals. The teacher is a guide, facilitator, and resource for students and families as cognitive development occurs.

KEY TERMS

neuron	equilibrium	egocentrism
synapse	schemes	zone of proximal
dendrites	association	development
axon	assimilation	scaffolding
gifted	accommodation	object permanence
learning disability	constructivism	standardized test

REVIEW ACTIVITIES

Exercises to Strengthen Learning

1. Infants—Let's look at two different experiences for infants. As you read these scenarios, try to identify the events that are stimulating and encourage brain development.

Gary wakes up and is aware of being uncomfortable. His diaper is wet and it is beginning to make him feel cold and starting to irritate his skin. He whimpers as he awakens. A voice says softly, "Hi, sleepy head. Are you ready to wake up?" He is lifted from his bed and pressed against a warm body. "Oh, you're all wet. Let's get you changed," the soft voice says. The wet diaper is taken off and a warm cloth cleans his irritated skin. All the while, the soft voice continues to talk and a familiar face looks intently at him. He waves his hands in time to the rhythms of the voice and smiles at the face. The face smiles back and says, "What a big smile. Are you a happy baby?"

Compare Gary's experience to Tonya's.

Tonya wakes up and is aware of being uncomfortable. Her diaper is wet and beginning to make her feel cold and it burns the sores on her skin. She whimpers as she awakens. As she awakens more, she cries harder. She is very uncomfortable and screams. A pair of arms suddenly picks her up. A voice says, "Yuck, you're soaked." The arms hold her away from the caregiver's body. The wet diaper is removed, a cold cloth wipes her, and a dry diaper is put on. The face she sees above her is unfamiliar and looking at something over her head. The caregiver places Tonya back in her crib without speaking to her and leaves the room.

What did Gary experience and learn during the routine of diapering? What did Tonya experience and learn during the routine of diapering? Educators of infants use daily routines to stimulate cognitive development. The educators are a team of consistent adults that include the parents, other close family members, and child care provider. To optimize learning through routine, they communicate regularly so that the child experiences consistency and builds trust so that learning can take place.

2. Toddlers—Let's look at an experience with a toddler. Try to identify what occurs that encourages cognitive development.

Janine's mother picks her up and says, "It's dark; do you want to come outside and see the night?" Janine's mother holds her close as they walk outside. The air is chilly on Janine's cheeks, but her mother's arms are warm. Her mother says, "Look up, it's the moon. See how bright and round it is?" Janine points and says, "moon." Her mother turns and points again. "See all the little lights? Those are the stars. There are millions of stars. Aren't they pretty?" Janine points and says, "Pretty." Her mother says "Brrr, it's cold outside; we better go inside." Her mother takes Janine back into the house and says, "Oh, it's nice and warm in here!"

What was Janine exposed to during this experience? What may she have learned? What new words may she have heard and how did this experience help her understand the meaning of the words? Why was she not frightened by the dark but relaxed enough to absorb the experience of the dark?

3. Preschoolers and Primary Age Children—Review Piaget's ideas about the preoperational and concrete operational child's intuitive thinking. Try this demonstration on two children, one four or five years old and another seven or eight years old, and compare the difference in their answers.

One of Piaget's experiments that you can duplicate is his demonstration of the abilities of children to use logical thought to understand that as the appearance of an item or substance changes, the amount does not change.

Supplies: Two clear plastic glasses, water, food coloring (or you may use juice), aluminum pie plate, tall clear flower vase.

Process: Have the child fill each glass with an equal amount of liquid. Ask the child if the glasses hold the same amount. Have the child pour the liquid from one glass into the pie pan and from the other glass into the vase. Ask the child if the pan or the vase has more, less, or the same amount of liquid.

Predict the child's answers from what you know of Piaget's theories.

As a final test, ask the child to choose which glass of juice he would like to drink.

How did the children you worked with judge the volume of juice? Which glass of juice did they choose for their snack? What did this activity imply about the cognitive abilities of children?

4. Elementary Age Children—Interview a sixth-grade child. Ask what the child is learning in math class. When you have determined a math concept the child is working to understand, ask him what he already knows to help him learn the new concept. Is this child operating in the zone of proximal development for the math concept he is currently trying to learn? Why do you think this is, and what is your evidence?

Internet Quest

1. Search the Internet for children's toys. Identify two toys that are developmentally appropriate for infants/toddlers, preschoolers, primary school, and elementary school children. Describe each of the eight toys you have chosen and explain why each is developmentally appropriate for the age range of child it was designed for. Describe two ways you could use this toy with children. Explain how a child with a specific disability could use the toy.

2. Select one of the exceptionalities of cognitive development and find Web sites that give more information, as well as a support group for families dealing with that exceptionality.

Reflective Journal

In this chapter I learned the following about _____ (age of child) cognitive development.

When I am a teacher, I will . . .

REFERENCES

Airasian, P. W. (2001). *Classroom assessment: Concepts & applications* (4th ed.). Boston: McGraw Hill.

Allen, K. E., & Marotz, L. R. (1999). *Developmental profiles: Pre-birth through eight* (3rd ed.). Albany, NY: Delmar.

American Federation of Teachers, National Council on Measurement in Education, & National Education Association. (1990). *Standards for teacher competence in educational assessment of students.* Washington, DC: Author.

Berk, L. E., & Winsler, A. (1995). *Scaffolding children's learning: Vygotsky and early childhood education* (p.3). Washington, DC: National Association for the Education of Young Children.

Binet, A., & Simon, T. (1912). *The development of intelligence in children.* North Stratford, NH: Ayer Company Publishers.

Bowe, F. G. (2000). *Birth to five: Early childhood special education* (2nd ed.). Albany, NY: Delmar.

Campbell, L., Campbell, B., & Dickinson, D. (1994). *Teaching and learning through multiple intelligences.* Needham Heights, MA: Allyn and Bacon.

Craig, G. J., & Kermis, M. D. (1995). *Children today*. Englewood Cliffs, NJ: Prentice Hall.

Dennis, W., & Dennis, M. (1940). The effect of cradling practices upon the onset of walking in Hopi children. *Journal of Genetic Psychology, 56, 77–86.*

Eggen, P., & Kauchak, P. (1999). *Educational psychology: Windows on classrooms.* Upper Saddle River, NJ: Merrill.

Gardner, H. (1983). *Frames of the mind: The theory of multiple intelligences.* New York: Harper-Collins.

Gesell, A. (1940). *The first five years of life* (9th ed.). New York: Harper & Row.

Gestwicki, C. (1999). *Developmentally appropriate practice: Curriculum and development in early education* (2nd ed.). Albany, NY: Delmar.

Gopnik, A., Meltzoff, A. N., & Kuhl, P. K. (1999). *The scientist in the crib.* New York: William Morrow.

Hendrick, J. (1998). *Total learning: Developmental curriculum for the young child.* Upper Saddle River, NJ: Merrill.

Hergenhahn, B. R., & Olson, M. (1997). *An introduction to theories of learning.* Englewood Cliffs, NJ: Prentice Hall.

Individuals with Disabilities Education Act. (1990). PL 101–476.

Jensen, E. (1998). *Teaching with the brain in mind.* Alexandria, VA: Association for Supervision and Curriculum Development.

Kohlberg, L. (1969). Stage and sequence: The cognitive–developmental approach to socialization. *Handbook of socialization: Theory in research.* Boston: Houghton-Mifflin.

Lafrancois, G. R. (1980). *Of children: An introduction to child development* (3rd ed.). Belmont, CA: Wadsworth.

McCullough, V. E. (1992). *Testing & your child: What you should know about 150 of the most common medical, educational, and psychological tests.* New York: Plume.

National Information Center on Children and Youth with Disabilities. (1996). *Learning disabilities: Fact sheet #7* <http://www.Idonline.org/ld_indepth/general_info/gen-2html>.

Nicholson-Nelson, K. (1998). *Developing students' multiple intelligences.* New York: Scholastic.

Nilsen, B. (2001). *Week by week: Plans for observing and recording young children* (2nd ed.). Albany, NY: Delmar.

Phillips, C. B. (1991). *Essentials for child development associates working with young children.* Washington, DC: Council for Early Childhood Professional Recognition.

Piaget, J. (1952). *The origins of intelligence in children.* New York: International Universities Press.

Piaget, J. (1959). *Language and thought of the child.* New York: Humanities Press.

Piaget. J. (1973). *To understand is to invent: The future of education.* New York: Grossman.

Shore, R. (1997). *Rethinking the brain: New insights into early development.* New York: Families and Work Institute.

Stern, W. (1912). *Psychologische methoden der intelligenz-prufung.* Leipsig: Barth.

Thomas, R. M. (1992). *Comparing theories of child development* (3rd ed.). Belmont, CA: Wadsworth.

Trawick-Smith, J. (1997). *Early childhood development: A multicultural perspective.* Englewood Cliffs, NJ: Prentice Hall.

 For additional learning and teaching resources, visit our Web site at www.EarlyChildEd.delmar.com.

RELATED CAREERS

Figure 6-27

Careers related to cognitive development.

Learning about and Teaching the Speaking Child—Language Development

Objectives

After reading this chapter and completing the review activities, the learning teacher should be able to:

1. Support the language of the child and the family.
2. Describe the developmental process of acquiring language skills.
3. Discuss strategies a teacher can use to support and facilitate language development.
4. Discuss the roles of culture and cognitive development as they relate to children's multilingual abilities.

❋ UNDERSTANDING LANGUAGE IN LEARNING AND TEACHING

What is language? What was the last conversation you had? How many words did you speak? How did you know what each word meant? How did you know which form of a word to use? How did you learn the language you speak? How did you grow from an infant who could only communicate with a cry to an adult who can intelligibly relate ideas and concepts to others?

Humans communicate with each other through the use of language. With language, they follow a set of rules and use symbols to exchange ideas and information with each other. Although there are a limited set of symbols in any given language, humans are able to arrange a seemingly unlimited array of those symbols to create many different words and sentences and to communicate in many situations (Figure 7–1).

Language is more than just the words that are spoken. Speech is merely the ability to articulate words; language is the ability to communicate with others. Language consists of the spoken words themselves, but also integrates facial expression, gesture, and vocal inflection. Cultural values influence interpretation of the words, expressions, gestures, and intonations used in communicating an idea.

Words are symbols, or sounds to which there is an attached meaning. That all humans have language is universal, but the meanings associated with the sounds of speech are not so. From a sociological perspective, language allows human experience to be cumulative. One generation passes experience on to the next, building on experiences that need not be reinvented by each succeeding generation. A shared recounting of memories depends on a shared language. Each person has individual experiences, but through language, her memories and past experiences are accessible and transmittable to others. Social understandings, viewpoints, opinions, and understandings are intangibles that can only be communicated through language.

Figure 7–1

Although there are a limited set of symbols in any given language, people are able to arrange a seemingly unlimited array of those symbols to create many different sentences and communicate in many situations.

Language is productive; that is, an individual who wishes to communicate to another "understands and produces utterances they have never heard before and they can also create new utterances by recombining elements they already know" (Piper, 1993). For example, David uses the word *play* but has never used the word *playing* before. He has heard several words in conversation that end in *-ing*. He tells his father, "I am *playing* with my kitten." Although no one specifically explained the word *playing* to him, he combined the word *play* with the concept that *-ing* adds to a word to correctly tell his father what he is doing. In other words, David applied the *-ing* sound to an action word in a way that was new for him to accurately communicate an idea.

Language allows people to communicate or think about events or environments that are not necessarily in the here and now. Humans can converse with each other about something that happened yesterday or a century ago; they can also communicate and think about something that will happen in the future. This ability to communicate about events not in the immediate moment is known as displacement; it is this capacity that sets humans apart from all other species that communicate. Other species communicate only about events that occur in the present. A dog barks a warning as a car comes onto the property, but the dog cannot communicate the thought that if a car approaches tomorrow, he will bark.

SCENARIO	Gini asked her son to take the dog outside. She said, "Remember, yesterday he ran away, so be sure to put him on his leash."

How did Gini know to use the word "ran" instead of "run"? How did her son know to buckle the end of the leash *on* the dog's collar and not have the dog stand *on* the leash? When we listen to and record conversations and think about the complexities of language, it is amazing that we speak our native language so easily and that our listeners understand what we mean.

As individuals learn a new language, they hear and understand the meaning of words before they can use the words to communicate ideas. **Receptive vocabulary** refers to those words used by others that an individual understands, and to which she is able to respond. For example, Fiona, age ten months, is asked by her mother to give her a ball they are playing with. Fiona hands the ball to her mother because she can comprehend what her mother says. The words and meaning are part of her receptive vocabulary.

However, at the age of ten months, Fiona does not have the ability to say to her mother, "Give me the ball." The words she is capable of using correctly to convey an idea to another are, for the time being, one-word expressions. The words an individual is capable of using to accurately convey an idea to another are part of their **expressive vocabulary**. Expressive vocabulary development follows the development of receptive vocabulary. Fiona's expressive vocabulary is not yet developed enough to tell her mother to give her the ball, but her level of receptive vocabulary is such that she understands when her mother asks her for the ball.

---

receptive vocabulary—The words an individual understands and can act upon.

expressive vocabulary—The words an individual is able to use to accurately convey meaning to another.

The Rules of Language

The first rule of language has to do with its system of sound. Each individual sound in a language is a separate **phoneme** and each language has rules about the order in which phonemes may be used. There are also principles regarding which phonemes can be used in combination with other phonemes. Phonemes do not necessarily correspond to the written symbols of a language on a one-to-one basis: for example, the letters "s" in "school" and "c" in "center" symbolize the same English phoneme.

SCENARIO	The use of interchangeable symbols for an identical sound often proves to be a big problem for people who are learning to spell. Kim, age six, asks her mother how to spell a word that sounds like "kom." Her mother says "c-a-l-m." Kim replies, "I don't hear an 'L' in the word." Her mother tells her the L is silent in the word calm, which means peaceful and quiet. Kim says, "NO, Mom, I mean in the word dot com." Kim has heard Web site addresses and is trying to understand how the frequently heard term "dot com" fits into her language.

The second rule of language determines how the smallest units of sound that communicate meaning may be combined or strung together. Some **morphemes** are complete words such as the word *run*, while others are sounds that are not complete words, such as *-ing* or *-ed*. In English, the morpheme *-ing* communicates that the action of the root word is in progress (cooking) and *-ed* communicates that the action of the root word occurred in the past (cooked). The rules of morphology also guide the order in which units of sound should be placed.

SCENARIO	A three-year-old boy once gave his mother quite a start when he apparently understood a morpheme as a complete word. He and his mother were walking one day when he asked her, "Mom, what is sex?" His mother was not ready for this talk, but thought she should clarify how much he knew and wanted to know about the topic before launching into a long answer. She said, "You mean like boys and girls?" He looked confused and said, "NO, like bugs, spiders, you know—insects!"

Young children often overgeneralize the rules of morphology. For example, Tomi, age three, is telling his teacher what he did yesterday. Tomi says, " I goed with my Dad to buy rice for supper." Tomi knows that the suffix *-ed* conveys to the listener that an event has occurred in the past, but he has not yet learned that there are exceptions to the rule (Figure 7–2 on page 242).

The rules that govern the order in which we place words in a language, affecting the meanings that are meant to be conveyed to the listener are the rules of **syntax**. For

phoneme—Each separate sound in a language.

morpheme—Unit of meaning in language: root words, prefixes, and suffixes.

syntax—The rules that govern the order in which we place words in a language, which affect the meanings conveyed to the listener.

Figure 7–2

Children learn the rules of language as they converse with others.

example, when the mother asked the boy to put the dog outside, she did not say, "Ran he yesterday away." Even though the words in the sentence are the same, they do not follow the accepted order in the way a speaker strings words together. Again, before children learn the rules of syntax, they often make interesting statements.

SCENARIO

Three-year-old Susan's grandfather gives her a plastic bat and ball for a gift. Susan has seen other children at day care play ball. She asks her grandfather to help her make the "ball hit the bat." Susan is limited in two ways in how she can communicate what she wants to occur. She is still confused about cause and effect, and she has not yet grasped the rules of syntax. These rules tell her the order in which the noun, verb, and direct object appear in a sentence to communicate to her grandfather that she wants to "hit the ball with the bat."

Another aspect of language is the meaning of words and sentences. This is called **semantics**. As children make additions to their vocabulary list, they sometimes use words without knowing what they mean. Sometimes, they invent words to fill a need for something they want to communicate and use the rules of semantics as best they can.

semantics—The meaning of words and sentences.

WORDS OF WISDOM Gini recalls, "My family enjoyed taking rides in the country to look at the beautiful views from the tops of rolling hills that make up the countryside where we lived. My three-year-old brother almost had the idea when he pointed across an overlook to a hill in the distance and said, "Look at the *showence*." He invented his own word to convey the lovely sight (show) that he wanted to call our attention to. Of course, since his invented word conveyed the idea of calling attention to or showing a beautiful view with others, this invented word has remained in our family's vocabulary for 40 years."

The social use of a language is **pragmatics**. What is involved in the process of using words to convey a message to another person? How does the communicator know to ask a question; to use a tense that speaks of the past, present, or future; and what expression to use to get her ideas across to someone else? How does a child ask to join a group at play, or persuade the teacher to let them stay outside a while longer?

SCENARIO Suzanne is working on a computer puzzle in math class. Her teacher sees both that Suzanne is at a critical point in the game and the choice of action Suzanne is about to make. The teacher says, "Are you really going to do *that*?" Her facial expression, voice inflection, and word emphasis all affect the meaning of the question. If the teacher asks the question with a smile and enthusiasm in her voice, she sends the message to Suzanne that she should proceed. If she asks the question with a frown and a questioning tone to her voice, Suzanne will get the message that she is making a bad move in the game.

Communication

Communication is the exchange of ideas or information between two or more people. Case in point: one person has a message to convey to a second person. The way the first person sends that message is affected by her culture, values, past experiences, and language. The first person chooses gestures, facial expressions, word order, words themselves, and voice inflection to deliver an idea to the other person. The person who receives the message is also affected by her culture, values, past experiences, and language, and interprets the gestures, facial expressions, word order, words themselves, and voice inflection to interpret the message's meaning. To communicate successfully, both the conveyer and the receiver of the message must understand the subtle meanings of each other's communication styles and traits (Figure 7–3 on page 244).

Conveying the meaning of words is sometimes difficult even when the individuals who are interacting share the same language and culture; it becomes even more complicated when culture or language differs. The meaning of words can change by way of very subtle voice inflections, facial expressions, and gestures. Janet Gonzalez-Mena (1997) suggests that to successfully communicate across cultures, individuals must educate themselves in five areas of nonverbal communication where miscommunication often occurs.

---

pragmatics—The social use of language.

Figure 7–3

Conveying the meaning of words is complicated when culture or language differ. The meaning of words can change by way of very subtle voice inflections, facial expressions, and gestures.

1. Personal space—The circle of space a person is comfortable maintaining around herself when communicating with others is called *personal space*. The size of this space varies among cultures. In the European-American culture, people usually maintain an arm's length between each other. It is important to observe and respect the personal space of various cultures.

2. Smiling—Smiling is another communications skill specific to each culture. Vietnamese students smile even while being reprimanded; smiling at all times is a common characteristic of the Vietnamese. This is sometimes misinterpreted by people of other cultures.

3. Eye contact—When people from different cultures have the same pattern of eye contact, they feel comfortable with each other. In some cultures, direct eye contact conveys respect for the importance of what is being communicated. In other cultures, direct eye contact is seen as a sign of disrespect.

4. Touch—Each culture communicates through touch in different ways. Touching the head is appropriate in Canadian and American cultures if the person doing the touching is superior in some way to the person being touched. Breaking cultural rules about touching can send a misleading message.

5. Time concepts—Cultures differ in the way they perceive time. A meeting scheduled at noon may mean that the meeting begins right at noon to one culture and that it is important to arrive 10 minutes early to be ready to start at noon. To someone from another culture, it may mean arriving at noon and then getting organized to meet. To others still, it may mean meeting sometime *around* noon.

It is nearly impossible for adults to remember a time when they did not understand and follow most of the rules of their native or first language. It is amazing to think that children sort out most of these complex rules by the time they enter kindergarten.

The Nature of Language Development

Is acquiring language an innate ability? Language theorists have researched and argued over whether or not a child is born with the ability to master language, or if language mastery results primarily from environmental influences. Those who argue that language acquisition is an inborn faculty cite that it occurs naturally in children unless there is a severe cognitive or organic disability present.

Noam Chomsky is a linguist and theorist who believes children have an innate ability to learn language. He observed how rapidly children learn the rules of language. They practice new sounds or word combinations, and experiment with the rules of language. He theorized that there is an area in the brain separate from other sites of cognitive abilities. The language acquisition device (LAD) refers to the specific ability or mechanism a child has to learn the rules of language. Chomsky's theory was supported by cross-cultural studies showing that children from different cultures learn certain universal rules of language in the same sequence. Supporters of Chomsky's theory also describe the critical period for language acquisition: research indicates that children must learn language within a specific time period or risk not being proficient in it. This supposition is demonstrated in children who are bilingual from birth, or who learn a second language very early and subsequently speak both languages without an accent. People who learn language after this critical period in early childhood usually speak second languages with an accent.

Noam Chomsky

(1927–) Debates B. F. Skinner's theory that children are conditioned to talk by hearing parents and other adults. Chomsky argues that all languages share structural characteristics and calls this innate brain capacity for language the language acquisition device (LAD).

The Nurture of Language Development

Many theorists believe that, although children have an ability to learn language and are primed to learn language from birth, they learn language foremost through their interaction with their environment and other people. Jean Piaget postulates that language development follows cognitive development. For example, a child is not able to ask for *more* dessert than her brother unless she has the cognitive ability to understand what *more* means. Piaget theorized that a child learns a concept (such as *more*) and then fits the word symbol to the concept. As vocabulary is accumulated, children communicate more effectively; they develop and refine concepts and continue to label those abstractions. Accompanying the acquisition of words are the processes of assimilation (the symbol for plants is the word flower) and accommodation (not all plants are flowers, only certain colorful ones). Piaget theorizes that, as a child progresses through the stages of cognitive development, her accumulation of language skills progresses based on cognitive growth.

Lev Vygotsky, a learning and development theorist, theorized that children use language to think. With language, they are able to symbolize events that occurred in the past, project future events, and communicate their ideas. Language allows children to label their thoughts.

SCENARIO

Carolyn, age six, is working on a puzzle in the classroom with two of her friends. The teacher provided this puzzle, the first one the children have worked on that does not come in a frame. Putting pieces together by trial and error, the children have completed about half of the puzzle when suddenly Carolyn realizes that all the pieces on the border have one smooth side. Carolyn considers this, predicts, and says, "The pieces with the smooth edge go on the outside." One of her friends begins to look for all the smooth–sided pieces and puts them in a separate pile. The friend says, "Now we can put all the edges together." They call the teacher to the table and Carolyn says, "Look, if we find all the smooth-edged pieces, we can put the outside of the puzzle together." The teacher praises them for figuring this out and asks them what their next step will be.

By carefully observing the girls, their teacher determined that they were in the zone of proximal development for working on a frameless puzzle. By providing the challenging activity, the teacher encouraged the girls to move to a higher level of thinking. Carolyn came to an understanding as a result of her trial-and-error experience with the puzzle; she labeled her understanding with words, and communicated those words to her friend, who then used this input to move the puzzle assembly ahead. "A teacher's ability to plan activities that provide varied linguistic experiences and that result naturally in meaningful communicative interactions is critical" (Kratcoski & Katz, 1998). "Teachers who structure their classroom to allow open discussions find that children talk about what they know and they talk to discover what they do not know" (Moore, 1998) (Figure 7–4).

Language is complex, and the way children master their first language relatively rapidly is still somewhat of a mystery. " If anyone could tell us with any certainty how children do accomplish what they do in language learning, we would not need . . . theory, for we would have entered into the realm of fact" (Piper, 1998). Although the acquisition of language may be a natural phenomenon, language development is nurtured by opportunities to expand vocabulary, express increasingly complex thoughts and concepts, strengthen cognitive abilities, and increase social skills.

Language and Literacy

Teachers use the term *language* to mean several things. Many schools have a language arts curriculum that includes oral communication, reading, and writing. In this chapter on language, we will discuss spoken communication, and in the next chapter we will discuss writing and reading. We will also discuss multilingual children and their families, and how language develops in children who speak more than one language. The development of literacy in children cannot be separated from the development of

Figure 7–4

Language allows children to label their thoughts.

	Language	Literacy
Young Infant	• Cries • Babbles • Responds to caretaker's voice	• Eye coordination • Beings to differentiate verbal sounds
Older Infant	• Receptive language • Limited productive language • Body language for receiving and sending communication	• Begins to differentiate among words • Can point to familiar objects in a book
Toddler	• Receptive language increases • Productive language increases • Puts words together in sentences • Can convey ideas with languages • Likes repetition and patterns in language	• Can handle and turn pages in sturdy books • Is aware that pictures and books contain stories • Begins to recognize landmarks, logos, and street signs • Begins to experiment with making marks on objects • Develops awareness that printed words convey language
Preschooler	• Learns rules and language • Can make up or tell stories • Can carry on conversations	• Aware of printed symbols representing words • Recognizes some letters • Knows that reading and writing follow a pattern established by her culture • May recognize name • Memorizes and repeats familiar stories • Experiments with writing and can write some recognizable letters
Primary	• Increases vocabulary • Masters rules of languages	• Learns to decode printed words • Learns to write sentences • Learns to write short paragraphs
Elementary	• Can participate in persuasive conversation and express complex thoughts verbally	• Begins to read chapter books • Begins to read for information • Writes stories and poems

Figure 7–5

The development of language and literacy is related.

language. Language development is the basis for literacy; they are continuous and intertwined. As a child's language skills develop, so do her early literacy skills. In the older child, vocabulary expands through both participation in conversations with others and reading. The following chart shows the connection between language and literacy development (Figure 7–5).

Multilingual Families and Children

Some characteristics of a language are unique to that particular language and the culture from which it stems. Children learn the rules of the language or languages they are exposed to and use with their family and primary caregivers. "Each language draws attention to alternative ways of encoding events, enhancing similarities of some relationships and contrasting others" (De Villiers & De Villiers, 1979). A child who learns the French language will learn to categorize objects as male or female by using *la* or *le*. Suzi sees a book on the table, points to it, and says to her mother, *"la livre."* Her mother says, *"le livre,"* to confirm Suzi's knowledge of the object but correct her categorizing the book as female. An English-speaking child does not categorize objects this way.

This not only speaks to the uniqueness of language patterns, but also is an example of the way language reflects and is part of culture. Seeing objects as being male or female offers a different perspective for a person who does not attribute such characteristics to objects. From her earliest exposure to speech, the child's culture is being transmitted to her by language. Language symbolizes the child's experiences, thoughts, and concepts. The principles for using those symbols in a particular language give the child a system for classifying experiences and knowledge.

Think of a child who speaks French as placing every object in a box with a picture of a girl on it or a box with a picture of a boy on it. As the child discovers new objects, she must place it in one of the boxes. People who are experienced at putting such objects in correct boxes are nearby to correct, model, and help, so that eventually all of the objects end up in the correct box. Each time the child uses an object, she must retrieve it from one of the two boxes. A child who is learning English places all her objects in one plain box. Each time that child needs an object, she reaches in the box and retrieves it. This simplistic example shows how different languages follow different rules, with the French-speaking child and the English-speaking child retrieving the symbols for objects in very different ways. Think of all the subtle rules and properties of your own language. How does your language shape the way you see, and interact with, the world?

SCENARIO

Sara, an eight-year-old, moved to this country from Mexico six months ago and her first language is Spanish. She speaks Spanish to her grandfather, who lives with her family. Sara's mother speaks both Spanish and English, and as a nurse uses both languages at work. Sara's father is a chef who works with others who speak Spanish. He is taking English lessons and the family works together to practice their English. English is the primary language spoken in Sara's school. Sara's teacher speaks both English and Spanish. Sara speaks English to most of her peers in school but has two friends whose first language is Spanish and she enjoys speaking in Spanish to them.

Sara understands much of what she is required to read in school, and understands much of what the teacher says in English. Her teacher is aware of Sara's level of English comprehension and clarifies new concepts for Sara in Spanish, or she pairs Sara with another Spanish–speaking student to

continued

practice and master new concepts. The teacher encourages and supports Sara as she perseveres in reading, writing, and speaking English.

There is great variety in the policies among states and school districts regarding the issue of bilingual education (Figure 7–6). The mainstream language of the United States is English and there is an accompanying expectation that all citizens will be proficient in English. Since this is a country of immigrants, individuals whose primary language is not English have always been present in significant numbers. School systems in the United States have struggled over the years to develop strategies, both positive and negative, to educate children whose primary language is other than English.

SCENARIO Maria is a sixth grader from France. She has lived in the United States for the last three years and is bilingual, speaking both English and French. Maria says that, "Even though I speak, read, and write well in English, my brain still thinks in French. If I have to think about something that is hard to understand, I find myself translating English to French in my mind before thinking about it." Eva, an adult who has lived in the United States for 30 years, and whose primary language is Swedish, remembers suddenly realizing one day that she was thinking in English. Up until that time, she, like Maria, could speak, read, and write fluently in English, but thought in her primary language.

Figure 7–6

Teachers and the classroom environment they create should support all languages spoken by children and their families.

For many years in the United States, the strategy of teaching English to non-English-speaking individuals has been to replace their native language with English. Native Americans who were sent to boarding schools for education during the late nineteenth and first half of the twentieth century were only allowed to speak English and were punished if they spoke their native tongue. Many immigrant children were enrolled in schools where no one in their classroom could speak their native language. The thinking was that the sooner these children learned English and ceased using their native language, the better off they would be.

WORDS OF WISDOM   Francia Espinosa related her experiences in learning English at age eight:

"To me it's like sounds of words that have no meaning to them. I felt stupid because I was not able to understand what people were saying even though I wanted to communicate. I couldn't understand that it was the language. The teachers thought that by raising their voices I would understand more, which didn't make a difference, of course. It was funny. I didn't realize when it happened that I could understand. I would imitate what people were saying. There was no magic moment when I realized that I knew English."

"For my children, English is their first language because of child care, school, and the fact that my husband is English-speaking. They do speak some Spanish and when they are around people who don't know English, they do use Spanish. This summer they were in the Dominican Republic and were able to communicate with other children. When they heard words they didn't know, they would come to me and sound out the word. It's like the process when we learned our first language. We imitated the sounds and then learned that those sounds had meaning."

Children can best learn a second language in settings in which they are immersed in the new language (Figure 7–7). The goal is to add a language to the child's communication skills, rather than replacing the child's native language. Other strategies include using both the native language and the new language in the classroom. The objective is to support the child's efforts to learn the new language by expanding efforts to communicate and clarifying concepts in the native language as needed. Teachers also need to think about other aspects of children's lives that language depends upon. Family values and culture are captured within language. To preserve a child's ties to her culture, the child must receive support in her first language while learning another language (Figure 7–8).

✳ DEVELOPMENT AND CURRICULUM FOR LANGUAGE DEVELOPMENT

As we look at the ages and stages of language development and learn how infants begin to sort out the sounds of language, we must ask what the infant has been exposed to before birth. Has the fetus sensed her mother's speech patterns as well as those of other people close by? Is she born having already developed synchronization of her fetal movements with her mother's speech patterns?

Prenatal Language Development

During the seventh month of pregnancy, fetus's brain and ears are developed to the point that she can sense sounds. The fetus, like a newborn, becomes habituated to

	Monolingual	Bilingual
Infant	• Crying • Babbles reflect native language	• Crying • Babbles may be more varied and complex than monolingual child
Toddler	• First words • Two-word phrases—begins to learn rules of language, such as word order	• Uses words for both languages as if a single language • Can speak the same total number or words as a monolingual child • Combines rules of word order from both languages
Preschoolers	• Learns semantics and syntax • Able to speak and comprehend one language. • Carries accent in subsequent languages learned after preschool years	• Sorts out semantics and syntax rules of languages and matches each to particular language • Able to speak and comprehend both languages • Speaks both languages without accent

Figure 7–7

Comparison of monolingual and bilingual children from birth.

Figure 7–8

Children can learn an additional language in an environment that supports the primary language and offers exposure to and practice of the second language.

repeated sounds. "Habituation is the repeated presentation of a stimulus, which causes reduced attention to the stimulus" (Santrock, 2000). This means that the fetus or newborn will pay attention to a new sound, but as they become familiar with it, will heed it less. For example, a fetus is surrounded by the sounds of her mother's heartbeat, digestion, and breathing. As the fetus becomes habituated to these sounds, she pays less attention to them. When the fetus senses a new sound, she takes notice and the mother senses this by the fetus moving. As the fetus becomes familiar or habituated to sounds, the response is somewhat less than that of the initial reaction. Researchers study language development by observing this habituation.

Infant Language Development

An infant's receptive language, or her understanding of spoken language, develops before she can actually speak. Initially, between birth and six months of age, the infant's expressive language is characterized by crying (Figure 7–9). She becomes quite adept at communicating need, pain, and displeasure. You may think that all infants cry in the same way for the same reasons. However, across various cultures there is a great deal of difference in how long and in what manner infants cry. This means that infants' cries are intentional and varied to communicate to the caregiver that something is needed, such as food or physical comfort.

The amount of crying is "influenced by an infant's immediate environment" (Small, 1998). Small explains that cross–cultural research indicates that infants in nonwestern cultures cry much less than infants in the United States and Europe. This is due to the cultural goal of independence in the United States and Europe. Parents in western cultures do not respond to an infant's cries immediately but believe that infants sometimes cry for no reason at all. In nonwestern cultures, babies are attended to as soon as they begin to whimper, so they do not cry as long.

Researchers working with infants study their receptive language by observing how they habituate to sounds. Infants between two and five days old can discriminate between two types of sounds, researchers have found. In experimental settings, infants are exposed to syllables such as *bi* until they habituate to that sound. When a new syllable is presented, infants are able to distinguish that it is a new sound and

Figure 7–9

First communication efforts take the form of cries.

react to it by paying closer attention (Laboratoire de Sciences Cognitives et Psycholinguistique, 1999). What do we know from observing an infant's accomplishments in her first year? During the first months, she learns to express need, displeasure, and pain through crying; make eye contact and smile when she is pleased and satisfied, and experiment with sounds. These are the early stages of communication. Many infants carry on long babbling conversations with themselves as they practice the rhythms and patterns of speech.

By the second six months, infants usually understand the names of objects and people with whom they are connected. An infant's first words will likely reflect her environment. An infant raised on a farm may learn words such as cow, tractor, or pig as part of her first expressive language. A child living in the city may use the words bus, light, boat, or pigeon as part of her first expressive language. Infants also use gestures as an early form of communication. An infant will lift her arms in the air to communicate that she wants to be picked up. She will point to an object she wants. Gestures also reflect culture; an infant in Japan, for example, will try to bow (Trawick-Smith, 1997). Researchers have studied how children learn to hear the boundaries between words, and how they learn which word goes with which object, action, or concept, without each word being explained by an adult or older child. Some research indicates that children may follow the gaze of the speaker to learn how to attach words to objects (Saffran, 1999; Infant Language Project, 1999).

Infant Language Curriculum. By nature, infants try to communicate with other people. The people who surround the infant have an obligation to respond to those attempts. Infants' attempts at language are made in response to their routines. The infant feels hungry and cries; someone responds quickly to that message and feeds her. The infant makes eye contact and smiles as feelings of comfort wash over her body. The caregiver smiles back and says, "There, do you feel better?"

The infant's teacher should take advantage of opportunities to respond verbally and with facial expressions to the sounds an infant uses in trying to communicate. The teacher should arrange the room so infants can make eye contact with other children and adults. Changing tables, cribs, and activity areas should be oriented so the infant can see others talking, and can be seen and heard as she tries to join in the conversation. Interesting objects should be present for the infant to gaze at, think about, and comment on. A mirror is fascinating for the infant to study and finally understand that the other infant is just a reflection. The infant can also study her lip and tongue movement and expressions in the mirror.

For the infant whose family speaks a language other than the principle language of the classroom, the teacher should work with the family to learn key words the infant will hear at home and respond to the infant with those words. The teacher should learn how the family pronounces the child's name and how they use that name when calling or speaking to the child. The noise level in the room should be kept under control so the infants can hear conversation and sort out individual sounds. The most important action for an infant's teacher to take is to be responsive to an infant's cries, grins, gurgles, babbling, gestures, and grunts.

Toddler Language Development

During the toddler years, a child builds an expressive vocabulary that starts with approximately 20 words and grows to approximately 1,000, although her receptive vocabulary may be much larger. The toddler begins to combine words into sentences until they are able to tell a story or say what happened to them. This ability to put words together increases the toddler's ability to communicate ideas and concepts.

As toddlers begin to put words together, they experiment and work with the rules of their native language. In English, they eventually realize that a noun and verb express a complete thought. What a sense of power it must give a toddler to say, "Daddy, run!" and have Daddy do just what the toddler had in mind! How wonderful it must be to tell a teacher about something that happened at home, such as "Doggy bark," and have the teacher respond with, "What did your doggy bark at?" The child responds "Kitty" and a conversation has taken place about something that happened in the past.

"The first expansion of the noun phrase usually occurs with the addition of an adjective (*bad doggie*) or a qualifier (*more juice*). After these come, more or less in order, the ordinals (*other spoon*), cardinals (*two bears*), the demonstratives (*this cookie*), possessives (*my hat*) and finally the articles *a, an,* and *the*" (Piper, 1993). With these capabilities, the toddler can begin to communicate more productively and in progressively sophisticated ways (Figure 7–10).

As the toddler approaches three years old, she adds direct objects and pronouns to sentences, and learns to follow the rules of syntax. She begins to use words that end in -*ing* and -*ed*. The toddler also improves on her pronunciation and is thus more easily understood.

Toddler Language Curriculum. The toddler's teacher should create a curriculum that facilitates the rapid expansion of children's language abilities during these years. The teacher should make the classroom something that the children want to know and talk about. The teacher must be approachable—the kind of adult with whom talking and sharing are rewarding experiences.

By responding positively and engagingly when a child speaks, the teacher helps her learn correct pronunciation and build vocabulary by repeating what she says and expanding on her expression. Jerry approaches his teacher with his sneaker in his hand. He says to the teacher, "Foot off," and the teacher says, "Your shoe came off

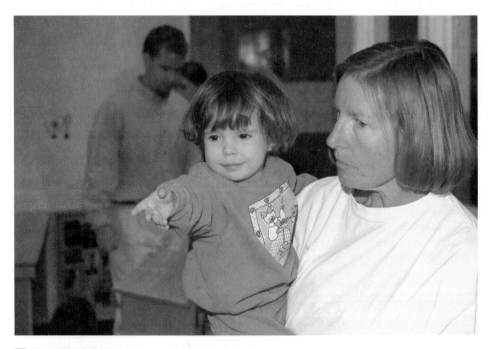

Figure 7–10

Toddlers begin to put words together and work with the rules of their native language.

your foot." Jerry smiles and nods. In this exchange, Jerry successfully communicated to the teacher that his shoe came off his foot. The teacher modeled for Jerry a better way to convey his message so it is clear that his foot is not what came off!

By creating events that are worth talking about, the teacher gives the toddler a reason to communicate. The teacher may put a hat on a stuffed animal to begin a conversation with a child or tie a red ribbon on her wrist to see who notices and says something. Interesting pictures should be located at eye level where children can see them, and then discuss with each other or the teacher what is in them. Photographs of the children involved in activities should be placed at a toddler's eye view to give them another reason to communicate. A mirror is another tool that inspires toddlers to talk.

The teacher should encourage the toddlers' use of adjectives by challenging them to describe things in the room. Questions such as "What did the truck look like?" will lead a child to say such things as "Big truck."

Very simple rhyming songs and nursery rhymes help children become aware of phonemes and morphemes. They begin to enjoy the rhythm of language with phrases such as "Little boy blue, come blow your horn, the sheep's in the meadow, the cow's in the corn." A toddler's first recitation of this poem may simply be "boy blue" and "cow corn," but by hearing it over and over she will, as time goes by, fill in the missing words.

At this age, children need to talk to other people to develop language. If there is a television in the classroom, it should only be on for very short periods of time, with a teacher present. The television is used as one more tool to create events worth talking about. Watching five minutes of *Teletubbies* with an adult should be followed by a discussion of at least five minutes. The teacher may say, "What did Tinkie Winkie do?" to which the toddler may respond, "Jump." The teacher might follow this with, "Can you jump like Tinkie Winkie?"

Computers in the toddler classroom can also be used as part of the language curriculum if they are used as a tool to generate conversations with other people. Toddlers' time spent on computers should be limited to very short periods and the teacher should be present to engage them in conversation about what is happening on the computer. The bright patterns on some computer programs can be very engaging for toddlers and may strengthen some areas of development, but toddlerhood is the age where language development is very rapid and lays the groundwork for later success in reading, cognitive abilities, and social skills. Toddlers learn language by talking to other people.

Toddlers from multilingual families or who use a language other than what the teacher or their classmates speak need opportunities to hear and practice their native language. Ideally, there should be an adult in the classroom who speaks the native language of the child, but many times this is not possible. Teachers can work with parents to learn a child's favorite rhyme or song in her native language and learn to pronounce correctly a list of several common phrases, directions, and names of foods and special items.

Preschool Language Development

During the preschool years, children expand their vocabulary and add about two new words per day (Figure 7–11 on page 256). If development is within normal ranges, they speak clearly and pronounce phonemes accurately. They also work on mastering complex tenses in their language or languages, although they still make mistakes as they experiment with more and more complex communication. Karta tells her child care provider that " I *swimmed* in the lake yesterday with Tommy." She has communicated about something that happened yesterday and has applied the *-ed* rule to the word "swim." Karta's child care provider says, "When you swam in the lake yesterday with Tommy, did

CHILD'S AGE		CHILD'S AGE	
2–2½ years	Joins words in sentences of two or more words.		Uses adverbs, adjectives, and prepositions.
	Knows name and age.		Names some colors and is interested in counting.
	Has vocabulary of over three words.		Looks at books while alone and enjoys reading time.
	Understands long spoken sentences and simple commands.		Talks about relationships.
	Begins using plurals and past tense.		Memorizes a short song, poem, fingerplay, or story.
	Changes pitch or loudness for specific meaning.		Repeats three digits and two to three nonsense syllables if asked.
	Begins using forms of verb "to be."		Uses adjectives and pronouns correctly.
	Uses a few prepositions.		Can copy a recognizable circle or square well if shown a model.
	Uses "I," "me," and "you."		Can imitate a clapping rhythm.
	Uses about 25 phonemes.		Starts to talk about the function of objects.
	Articulates about 10 to 12 vowel types and about 12 to 15 consonants.		Can find an object that's different in a group.
	Points to and names objects in pictures.		Can find missing parts of wholes.
	Names five to eight body parts.		Can classify using clear, simple distinctions.
	Enjoys rhythm in words, nursery rhymes, finger plays, and simple stories.		Knows names of common shapes.
	Understands and responds to almost all adult speech.	4–5 years	Has vocabulary of over 1,500 words.
	Generalizes by calling round objects "ball," and so on.		Uses sentences of five to six (or more) words.
			May use impact, shock, and forbidden words.
2½–3 years	Negatives, imperatives, and commands occur.		May use words of violence.
	Shows variety in question types.		Argues, convinces, and questions correctness.
	Adds as many as two to three words to vocabulary daily.		Shares books with friends.
	Names items in signs and books.		Acts out story themes or re-creates life happenings in play.
	Uses three- or four-word sentences.		Has favorite books.
	Enjoys fun with words.		Likes to dictate words.
	Follows simple directions.		Notices signs and print in environment.
	Points to body parts when asked.		Uses etiquette words, such as please, thank you, and so on.
	Names many common objects.		Enjoys different writing tools.
	Uses an increasing number of nouns, verbs, and pronouns.		Knows many nursery rhymes and stories.
	Draws lines and circular forms in artwork.		May add alphabet letters to art work.
	Knows words or lines from books, songs, and stories.		Creates and tells long stories.
			Can verbally express the highlights of the day.
			Knows many colors.
3–4 years	Asks why, what, where, how, and when questions.		Can repeat a sentence with six or more words.
	Loves word play.		May pretend to read books or may actually read other's name tags.
	Makes closed figures in art.		Holds writing tools in position that allows fine control.
	Begins using auxiliary verbs.		Traces objects with precision.
	Tells sex and age.		Classifies according to function.
	Utters compound sentences with connecting "and . . er . . but," and so on.		Asks what words mean.
	Engages in imaginary play with dialogue and monologue.		Is familiar with many literary classics for children.
	Says full name.		Knows address and phone number.
	Follows two- and three-part requests.		Can retell main facts or happenings in stories.
	Relates ideas and experiences.		Uses adultlike speech.

Figure 7–11

Growth of vocabulary. (From Machado, 1999)

you get cold?" Karta's child care provider used the correct form so Karta could hear it. Karta may then say, "No, we did not get cold when we swam." Karta has learned that the word *swim* does not follow the rules of past tense with which she is familiar.

Preschoolers usually go through a period when they want nothing more than to have a conversation with the people they are close to. They have unlocked the door to communication and, just as a baby who has learned to crawl does not want to stop crawling, they do not want to stop talking! It takes patience to attend to all the child is saying, but it won't be long before the child screens her thoughts before speaking. In the meantime, a teacher must support, respond to, and encourage the child, no matter how fatiguing it may be (Figure 7–12).

Older preschoolers learn and practice the complexities of social conversation in such ways as:

* gaining another's attention by making eye contact, touching, or using words or catch phrases like "Know what?"
* pausing and listening.
* correcting herself.
* keeping listener's attention by not pausing, so another speaker can't jump in.
* taking turns in conversation by developing patience and trying to listen while still holding in mind what she wants to say (Machado, 1999).

Controversy exists over whether or not a child should begin learning a second language at this age, or if the child should master her primary language first. "It may be, then, that when young children are asked to learn a second language for use at school before their first language has sufficiently matured to serve as a source of transferable skills, the learning task is very burdensome and requires more time than older children need—children whose first language skills are available for transfer" (Collier, 1987). Unfortunately, for many children there is no choice because education in their first language may not be available. The positive side of teaching a second language to children at this age is that they will be able to speak the new language without an accent.

Preschool Language Curriculum. The preschool teacher should arrange the room so it has plenty of interesting items and events for children to talk

Figure 7–12

Preschoolers have unlocked the door to communication and want nothing more than to converse with the people they are close to.

about among themselves. The room should be arranged in "areas," with the dramatic play area one of the most important for language development. The dramatic play area should contain items that are commonplace to all the children, but also some items they are unsure about in terms of their identity or use. The dramatic play area should also include items that tie in with the curriculum and the activities of the larger classroom. For example, if the class has recently visited the grocery store, the dramatic play area should include a toy cash register, play money, pretend food, empty food boxes, paper bags, a child's grocery cart, "checkbooks," shopper discount cards, aprons, smocks, name tags, a calculator, scales, paper for grocery lists, and pocketbooks. Foods representative of the children's cultural makeup should be included. The different languages spoken by the children should be evident on cereal boxes and labels and in recipes and magazines. In the dramatic play area, the children will chatter as they pretend to be people they are not and as they try to solve problems and experiment with using items in new ways.

The preschool room should be arranged to encourage group work, so children have many opportunities to converse with each other. There should be two or three chairs around each computer so children can work together and discuss the problems or games they see on the screen. They can also use the computer to have an adult type up their made-up group stories.

During the preschool years, children begin to enjoy dramatic storytelling. The teacher can begin by telling a few action–packed and exciting stories to the class. In time, the teacher can begin a story and prompt the children to add parts to complete it. Soon, the children may begin their own stories or a small group may get together to invent a dramatic story. The teacher can encourage deeper involvement in the story by providing a selection of props and costumes, with opportunities to perform, write (using their emergent literacy skills), or illustrate the stories. With each retelling, vocabulary is enriched and social speech enhanced, and rules of semantics mastered.

For children whose home language is not that of the classroom, the teacher should work to support their first language. It can be a terribly frightening experience for a child to enter a classroom where the teacher speaks in a language she does not understand. The teacher must learn words of greeting and simple phrases in the native language to communicate with the child. Ideally, the teacher should be able to speak the child's first language fluently. As the child socializes with other children in the classroom, words from various languages will be exchanged among the children so that social communication can begin.

Primary Age Language Development

By the time a child enters primary school, her spoken language skills are nearly mastered. She will continue to build vocabulary and learn to express complex ideas verbally. She will get better at explaining cause and effect as her cognitive abilities increase. As her vocabulary and cognitive ability grows, she will be able to describe objects and events more accurately and in greater detail. The child will begin to modify her facial expressions, gestures, and voice inflections to suit the individual with whom she is communicating.

SCENARIO   Jana loudly asks her friend Lucy, "Hey, give me some paper, will you?" When she finds out that Lucy has no paper, Jana quietly approaches her teacher and asks, "Could I have some paper, please?" Jana's goal for communicating with both her

continued

friend and her teacher are the same—to get some paper—but she makes the request to each very differently. She knows that the rules of acceptable communication are different for each person and she can modify her request so that each person is receptive to her.

During the primary years, children develop the ability to think about language. "They can think about and comment on sentence structure, how speech sounds are formed, and the various definitions of words" (Trawick-Smith, 1997). Their increased cognitive abilities, expanded vocabulary, and ability to think about language are most apparent in the popularity of riddles and jokes.

WORDS OF WISDOM Gini relates: "We had six children in our family. When the children got to first grade they began to bring home riddles and jokes. "What has four wheels and flies? A garbage truck!" "Knock, knock. Who's there? Panther. Panther who? Panths or no panths, I'm going swimming!" When the first child began to tell jokes, we were sometimes surprised at the punch line; by the time the sixth one came home with the jokes, we knew all the punch lines. By then, the fun was in knowing that they were at a milestone of some sort that helped them to appreciate the subtleties of language and a good joke."

During their primary years, children begin to build their vocabulary, not only with words learned from teachers, books, and parents, but with words learned from other children. At this age, a child delights in saying or talking about things with words that seem like new discoveries to them or that may be perceived as "forbidden" by adults. Children are in a latency stage for sexual development, so being curious about and discussing topics they may later feel very privately about seems safe at this time. This, coupled with their developing sense of humor and ability to tell jokes, results in an explosion of bathroom humor. Teachers often find themselves laughing silently at the joke while giving the child gentle guidance on appropriate topics for school discussion. Parents may also ask the teacher's advice on how to handle this stage of language development. If expectations at home and school are consistent, this stage may be short-lived.

Primary Age Language Curriculum. The primary classroom curriculum should encourage the verbal exchange of ideas between adults and children, and among children. Because children are building vocabulary and fine–tuning their use of language rules, they need the opportunity to speak, to self–correct their speech, and to pronounce new words. Group projects encourage children to exchange ideas verbally as they search for a solution to a problem. The teacher weaves new vocabulary words emerging from classroom study units into conversations, so that the children hear and begin to use the new words.

Primary age children begin to study language itself. The teacher helps them explore prefixes and suffixes and how they affect the meaning of a word. They may listen to the syllable divisions in words and clap out their rhythm to become aware of the way words are constructed. Much of this language curriculum can be done in the form of games. Small groups of children can try to think of as many words as possible to describe a specific object or concept. They can try to think of all the words that rhyme with a certain word or of opposite-meaning words for a word list. Primary age children can appreciate the beauty and rhythm of language by listening to poetry or prose read out loud. Children enjoy reciting poems such as limericks or poems with repetition, and they enjoy creating original poems that follow those patterns (Figure 7–13).

Children in the primary classroom should be asked to explain their work and their reasoning. The teacher can do this by casually conversing with the children as they work. Asking a child why she chose to do something a certain way or how she came to a conclusion expands her language skills as she defines her thoughts and relays those thoughts to others.

Elementary Age Language Development

During the elementary years, children become very skilled in the use of their primary language. As their cognitive abilities grow and they become more logical thinkers, they use language to persuade others to their point of view, to argue, and to debate. They continue to build vocabulary as they learn and read about new topics in school.

Because peer influences become increasingly strong at this age, the use of slang terms becomes common as a way of identifying with their peers. They may also experiment with swearing as they move into adolescence. Guidance from parents and teachers, paired with positive role modeling, helps to keep elementary age children's language appropriate for the setting. It may be acceptable to use slang terms on the playground during recess to give a friend feedback on a kickball move, but slang terms are not suitable when giving a formal oral report in class. Helping children learn when and where it is permissible to use less formal types of language empowers them to choose to speak appropriately in specific situations.

Elementary children are just beginning to be able to organize their thoughts in notes for giving oral reports. They have the skills to accurately request information and to give information and directions to others. This is a good time to help children feel comfortable speaking in front of groups, before adolescent sensitivity begins to develop.

From eight to eleven, children may be the most proficient at learning a new language (Figure 7–14). "For children who arrive in this country between the ages of eight and eleven they are faster in early acquisition of second language skills, and over several years' time they maintain this advantage over younger arrivals of four to seven years" (Collier, 1987). This parallels Chomsky and Vygotsky's language acquisition theories—that languages are learned easiest at younger ages. Do you wonder why American schools wait until high school to begin the study of languages other than English? Perhaps you will be able to bring about a change in this practice.

Figure 7–13

During the primary years, children increase their vocabulary and begin to study language itself.

Figure 7—14

The elementary years are a good time to have children begin speaking in front of groups.

Elementary Age Language Curriculum. Language curriculum for the elementary child should encourage verbal explanation of their developing logical thinking abilities. Children at this age are beginning to acquire the ability to look at both sides of an issue. They should be encouraged to pay attention to current events and explain several viewpoints. The closer to their lives an issue is, the more they will be able to empathize with it. Examples include such things as examining the pros and cons of having helmet laws for skiers and snowboarders; whether or not there should be school in the summer; whether there should be police in the schools, and whether the price of school lunches should be increased. The issues and topics should come from their own experiences: they should be encouraged to think of both sides of the issue, choose a side, and then explain their choice.

Children should be asked to give oral reports to the class in a manner that does not embarrass or intimidate them. Positive experiences now may help children avoid the fear of public speaking common to many adolescents and adults. The topics chosen should be familiar to the children; they should have some guidelines about formal, appropriate speech (and avoiding the use of slang), and they should be given an opportunity to assess their own presentations. The teacher should publicly thank each child for her presentation and privately offer specific praise for the strong aspects of her presentation while gently suggesting a few specific areas for future growth.

Children in the elementary years can begin to interview other people and create a report based on that interview. The teacher and children can create a list of questions they would like to have answered, identify who the children will interview, and then the chlidren can summarize their findings in a report. Pairing children for the interview works well because they can discuss their findings before creating the report. Interviews give the students opportunities to learn about people from other cultures and other generations, as well as individuals whom they admire and with whom they identify.

Children whose first language is not English, but who have good skills in their first language, can begin to transfer those skills to English. Support for the native language must be provided. It takes four to eight years for a child to master a language to the level of native-speaking children. "At age twelve a non–English speaking student who enters an English-only school environment may lose two to three years of learning in mathematics, science and social studies" (Collier, 1987). Language development issues for children who learn a second language are very complex and are different from the issues for children who are multilingual from birth. The teacher must assess each child's language skills and needs, support their native language, and find ways to challenge and support students in academic subjects as they master their new language.

✳ LANGUAGE DELAYS AND ASSESSMENT OF LANGUAGE

The reasons for language delays in children are numerous. Such delays may be caused by hearing problems, learning disabilities, cognitive function, brain injury, or emotional issues such as extreme shyness. They also may involve problems with the physical structure of the mouth, tongue, lips, or throat, or neurological difficulties that impede the movement of physical structures or hinder cognitive assimilation or expression of language. Communication can also be interrupted by any condition that prevents facial expressions, gestures, or contact.

Common speech delays in children include fluency disorders, of which stuttering is one. A child who stutters hesitates or repeats sounds as she speaks. For some children, such as young children or children learning a new language, stuttering results simply from searching for the correct word. If the teacher is concerned about the child's speech, she should call on a speech and language specialist to make a diagnosis. Delays in articulation of words and word sounds are common in children. The ability to form word sounds correctly, as with any cognitive or physical domain, develops at individual rates. If a child's articulation is so poor that others cannot understand what she is trying to say, or if the child's ability to form words and word sounds is very different from that of other children the same age, a speech and language specialist should be called upon to make an assessment. It is helpful to the specialist if the teacher has observed and documented the child's areas of consistent difficulty. The specialist also should be made aware of whether the child's first language, or home language, is different from the language spoken in the classroom, or if a similar language pattern has been observed in the family or primary caregivers.

Children who have been brain injured may lose their ability to use and understand language. If a child's abilities to use and understand language are deteriorating, this can be a symptom of brain lesions or traumatic brain injury. Therefore, it is very important for the teacher to document the loss of language ability and bring it to the immediate attention of the family, school health personnel, and the speech and language specialist.

Children with hearing loss also have problems with language. If the hearing loss has not been diagnosed or detected beforehand, the teacher should make arrangements with the family and school health staff to have the child's hearing tested and diagnosed. Once a child with hearing loss has been helped to hear at her full potential, the teacher needs to know what the child is capable of hearing and what is the best way to communicate with her. The speech and language specialist is a resource for the teacher to help her understand the most efficient way to communicate with the child. This may include learning and using sign language, wearing a microphone that feeds into a speaker system for the child, using written messages, or making sure the child sees her face when she speaks.

SUMMARY

One of the miracles of child development is language acquisition: the ability of a child to communicate her ideas to others and understand others' communication of ideas to her. By the time children enter kindergarten, they have nearly reached an adult level of language ability in their first language. The preschool teacher has the opportunity to support children as they develop competence in their first language. With a sound foundation in that first language, many children are able to master other languages. Although language acquisition is relatively rapid, it develops in a progressive order in similar ways across cultures.

From birth, children are motivated to communicate with others and attempt to communicate their needs. The response the child receives to her attempts at communication shape the way the child interacts with the environment and other people. Language and communication skills lay the foundation for a child's ability to read and write. Unlike language acquisition, which children are internally motivated to do, children must be externally motivated to learn to read and write.

KEY TERMS

receptive vocabulary	morphemes	semantics
expressive vocabulary	syntax	pragmatics
phoneme		

REVIEW ACTIVITIES

Exercises to Strengthen Learning

1. Observe an infant, a six-month-old, a one-year-old, and an eighteen-month-old child. Observe each child for one hour and document the attempts at communication that you observe. Keep track of gestures, cries, vocal noises, facial expression, and a list of words and phrases the child speaks.

   a. For each age, describe the successful attempts the child made at communication. To whom and what were they communicating? What was the child's reaction to successful communication?

   b. For each age, describe the child's unsuccessful attempts at communication. To whom and what were they trying to communicate? What was the child's reaction to unsuccessful communication?

   c. For each age, describe the child's ability to understand what others tried to communicate to them. Give some examples.

   d. What did you observe in the children's receptive and expressive language abilities? What behaviors of the teachers or other adults facilitated communication and what behaviors impeded communication?

2. Visit a preschool program where there are children who speak more than one language.

   a. What is the primary language of the majority of the children in the classroom?

   b. What other languages do children in the classroom speak with their families or in the classroom?

   c. In what languages are the teachers fluent?

   d. What languages are spoken to children and families by adults in the classroom?

   e. What languages are evident in written materials in the classroom?

   f. What are your observations of the circumstances that influence the language in which a child chooses to speak? (Be attentive to who she is speaking to, what they are speaking about, the child's language ability, the language ability of the person to whom she is trying to speak, the child's comfort level with the individual with whom she is trying to speak, and the authority level of the person with whom she is trying to speak.)

   g. Formulate your conclusions from this experience and from the information in this chapter about preschoolers' experiences in multilingual environments. What was done in the classroom to support a multilingual group of children and what did not support the language development of the children in the classroom?

3. Obtain permission from parents to video- or audio tape a group of three primary age children. Record their responses to the following scenario.

   Mark and Melissa are walking to school. It is a celebration day at school and they are wearing their best shoes and clothes. Mark was responsible for making a sign for the classroom for the celebration and he is carrying it to school. Their walk to school takes them past a large swamp. They are careful to stay away from the edge of the swamp because it is muddy and they do not want to get their good shoes and clothes dirty. Melissa's grandmother told her to be very careful of her good clothes.

   Just as Melissa and Mark are about halfway around the swamp, the wind starts to blow. The sign that Mark made begins to flap in the breeze. Mark holds on tight. Suddenly, a dog runs up and jumps on Melissa with muddy paws. Melissa says, "Oh, no. Go away. You're getting me all dirty." Mark hears Melissa cry out to the dog and turns to shoo the dog away. At that moment, a big gust of wind blows Mark's sign out of his hands into the mud.

   Mark sees how far the sign is away from him and thinks he can step in the mud and reach the sign if he takes one shoe off. Mark steps into the mud with one bare foot and reaches for the sign. His foot sinks into the mud as he reaches farther and farther. Finally, he picks up the sign. As he tries to step out of the mud, he realizes that his foot is stuck in the mud. As Mark stands with his legs stretched out and his sign in his hands, with one foot on the dry ground and one foot in the mud, he says, "What should I do?"

   Ask the children to finish the story. Listen as they discuss the ending as a group and ask them to explain their answers in more detail by asking how and why things happen in their answer. Review the videotape.

   a. Were the children able to explain cause and effect?

   b. How did they use facial expressions, gestures, and voice inflections to communicate?

c. What examples did you observe of children having trouble explaining what they wanted to say?

d. Did the children mispronounce any words; did they make any errors in syntax or semantics?

e. Summarize your observations.

4. Select an issue to discuss with a group of elementary age children. The issue should be one that is current and with which the children are familiar. Issues that children are aware of can be found in a children's newspaper, or on educational television or children's news shows. They may include the environment, laws affecting children, or societal dilemmas. After the children review and consider all viewpoints regarding the topic, ask them to create a news program about the topic.

a. How did the children use language to discuss, debate, and persuade others about the identified issue? How did they use language to decide what should go in the news broadcast?

b. Did the children modify their language from the time they worked in a group together to the language used in the broadcast? How?

c. What were the children's cognitive abilities evidenced by their use of language?

Internet Quest

1. Using the tern *bilingual education,* search for three articles on this topic. Summarize, contrast, and compare the findings in each article.

2. Using the term *infant language,* search for two university laboratories that are doing research on infant language. Summarize the research areas that the labs are investigating.

3. Using the term *language arts curriculum,* find three examples of activities teachers use in their classrooms. Describe the activities and explain why each activity is or is not well designed to strengthen the language abilities of children who are monolingual, multilingual, from various cultures, or have language delays.

Reflective Journal

In this chapter I learned _____ about language and its development.

This will affect what I do as a teacher in the following ways. . .

REFERENCES

Collier, V. (1987). The effect of age on acquisition of a second language for school. *Focus.* Retrieved March 15, 2000, from the World Wide Web: <http://www.nebe.gwu.edu/nebnpubs/focus/02aage.html>.

De Villiers, P., & De Villiers, J. (1979). *Early language.* Cambridge, MA: Harvard University Press.

Gonzalez-Mena, J. (1997). *Multicultural issues in child care.* Palo Alto, CA: Mayfield.

Infant Language Project at the University of Delaware. (1999). Retrieved April 1, 2000, from the World Wide Web: <http://www.udel.edu/ILP/index.html>.

Kratcoski, A., & Katz, K. (1998). Conversing with young language learners in the classroom. *Young Children, 53*(3), 30–33.

LSCP Infant Lab. (1999). The Laboratoire de Sciences Cognitives et Psycholinguistique infant lab. Retrieved May 1, 2000, from the World Wide Web: <http://www.chess.fr/centres/lscp/babylab/newborns.html>.

Machado, J. (1999). *Early childhood experiences in language arts* (6th ed.). Albany, NY: Delmar.

Moore, L. D. (1998, March). Learning language and some initial literacy skills through social interactions. *Young Children, 53*(2), 72–75.

Piper, T. (1993). *Language for all children.* New York: Merrill.

Piper, T. (1998). *Language and learning: The home and school years.* Upper Saddle River, NJ: Merrill.

Saffran, J. (1999). Saffran lab research. Retrieved May 1, 2000, from the World Wide Web: <http://www.psych.wisc.edu/saffran/saffran.research.html>.

Santrock, J. W. (2000). *Children.* (6th ed.). New York: McGraw Hill College Division.

Small, M. (1998). *Our babies, ourselves: How biology and culture shape the way we parent.* New York: Anchor Books.

Trawick-Smith, J. (1997). *Early childhood development: A multicultural perspective.* Upper Saddle River, NJ: Merrill.

For additional learning and teaching resources, visit our Web site at www.EarlyChildEd.delmar.com.

RELATED CAREERS

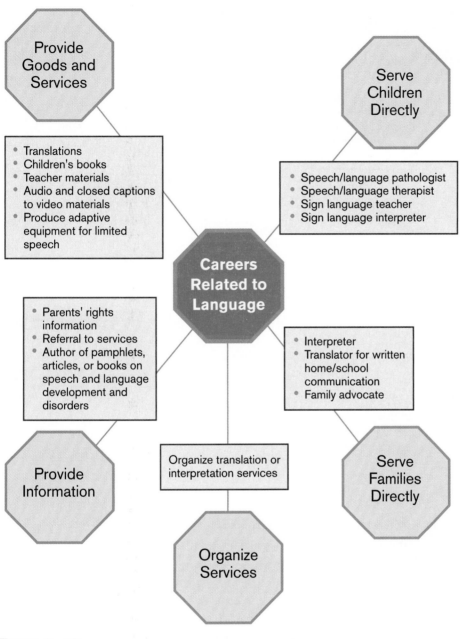

Figure 7–15

Careers related to language.

Learning about and Teaching the Reading and Writing Child

Objectives

After reading this chapter and completing the review activities, the learning teacher should be able to:

1. Explain the conditions that facilitate literacy development.
2. Describe strategies for teachers and families to facilitate children's literacy development.
3. Describe the scope and impact of illiteracy in the United States.
4. Identify conditions that may lead to difficulties in developing reading and writing skills.
5. Discuss the value of multilingual education.

✳ UNDERSTANDING LITERACY

Do you remember the first time you looked at a group of letters and understood that they represented a word? Do you remember the first book you read? Do you remember the first time you wrote your name? Who was with you for these events? How did you learn to read and write (Figure 8–1)?

If you were like most children, these events occurred after the foundation was prepared by a variety of experiences and individuals. It is probably hard to answer these questions because reading has become so natural that you cannot remember *not* reading. Learning to read and write is a developmental process; these events depend, and build on, previous events and accomplishments. Reading and writing do not "just happen." Literacy consists of innumerable cognitive and behavioral threads woven together. Each person's experience is different and so, as a result, are their reading abilities, preferences, and habits. Each also has his own unique writing ability, including the elements of penmanship and style, and how they use that writing.

In *To Kill a Mockingbird* by Harper Lee (1960), the setting is the 1930s and Scout is a girl who enters first grade with the ability to read at a time in history when a teacher was the only adult considered qualified to teach reading in the proper manner. Scout's teacher is critical of her father, Atticus, for teaching his daughter to read. Scout recalls

> "I never deliberately learned to read, but somehow I had been wallowing illicitly in the daily papers. In the long hours of church—was it then I learned? I could not remember not being able to read hymns. Now that I was compelled to think about it, reading was something that just came to me, as learning to fasten the seat of my union suit, or achieving two bows from a snarl of shoelaces. I could not remember when the lines above Atticus's moving finger separated into words, but I had stared at them all the evenings in my memory, listening to the news of the day, Bills To Be

Figure 8–1

Learning to read may seem effortless to some, but it is a developmental process that depends and builds on previous events and accomplishments.

Enacted Into Laws, the diaries of Lorenzo Day—anything Atticus happened to be reading when I crawled into his lap every night." (1960, 1988). HarperCollins Publishers. Used with permission.

Scout does not specifically remember being taught to read, nor does she recall learning to read. For her, the process of learning to read occurred within the nurturing relationship she had with her father and by being exposed regularly to oral reading and the connection between printed text and spoken words. She was immersed in an environment where reading was a useful and necessary way to obtain information or be entertained, and she was raised in a household where reading was valued.

When Scout realizes that she may be prohibited from reading, she says, "Until I feared I would lose it, I never loved to read. One does not love breathing." Reading, for Scout, had been as natural as breathing. In this chapter, we will look at the developmental process of learning to read and write and how that process can be purposefully encouraged for children in their homes and schools so that it seems as natural as breathing and becomes an activity they cherish.

Many believe that learning to read begins at about age four or five when a child first recites his own rendition of the ABCs and begins to copy those big squiggles that people tell him is his name. Actually, learning to read starts long before, when the newborn is first exposed to communication. For the hearing child, reading, writing, speaking, and listening cannot be separated. Hearing the sounds "Ma-ma-ma" or "Da-da-da" and beginning to distinguish between them is the beginning of reading. This is called **phonemic awareness**.

From the very beginning, the child's world is filled with the printed word: the brand name on the car seat, the label on the disposable diaper box, the raised letters on the nursing bottle. This environmental text is an unconscious literacy instruction that contributes to the child's readiness to read and write.

Many factors enter into the learning process as the future reader tries to make sense of the marks on a page, or tries to make such marks himself so others can understand his intended message. Developmental progression and social circumstance affect literacy. In normal circumstances, literacy begins with physical developments: the ability to see and hear and the acquisition of muscle skills (for turning pages or holding a pencil). Social development exacts its influence as the child realizes his place in the family or group, with a resulting desire to participate in pleasurable experiences with other people, and to reach out and be accepted. When reading and writing are natural parts of the lives of people important to the child, literacy comes naturally to the child as well. It is closely aligned with emotional development and feelings of security, self-worth, and competency. When a child has a stable emotional environment, attempting new tasks (such as making marks on a piece of paper or pretending to read) are not risky, but rather are exploratory behaviors that are encouraged and appreciated. Cognitive development plays a significant role in literacy. This accounts for the capacity to make connections between becoming aware of the word "cup," the physical evidence of seeing and feeling the cup and tasting its contents, and then seeing it again the next day and remembering that it is a "cup."

Illiteracy

What would it be like to be unable to read? Look up from reading this page and gaze around the room. Look at all the things you are reading. How many times a day do

---

*phonemic awareness—Hearing and understanding the individual sounds in a language.

you read or write information? How would you function if you could not read? **Functional illiteracy** affects 21 to 23 percent of the adults in America.

These individuals cannot do such things as filling out an employment application, following written instructions, or reading a newspaper (Literacy Volunteers of America, 1999). The ability to read and write has long been considered the measure of a well-educated person. In the past, this ability was restricted to males from privileged families. In colonial times, literacy was pursued to satisfy religious goals and later to foster patriotism and citizenship responsibilities. Still, there was deliberate literacy inequity for certain groups of people: for example, slaves were prohibited from learning to read and write. As our country begins the twenty-first century, the shame of this inequity is perpetuated in individuals with low literacy skills. Reading contributes to societal and individual success, and to the abilities to think, create, critique, and develop intellectually.

SCENARIO   Fred is functionally illiterate and lives in downtown Chicago. His sister, who lives in Harrisburg, Pennsylvania, is sick, but he cannot drive to see her because he has no one who can go with him to read the map or the highway road signs.

Kevin is also functionally illiterate. He pulls his new sweater out of the washer and sees that it is ruined because he could not read the laundry instructions that came with it.

Alice reads at a first-grade level and is married to a man who abuses her. She has considered leaving him, but is unable to become financially independent because she cannot fill out a job application.

What other impact does functionally illiteracy have on people? If we look at specific populations of people, we can see a pattern of problems caused by low literacy skills. There is a heavy concentration of people with low literacy skills among the poor and those who depend on public assistance. About one-half of all adults in federal or state correctional facilities cannot read or write at all. Preschool children with parents who do not read or write are less prepared for school, have poor school achievement, and drop out more frequently than children of parents who read and write (Literacy Volunteers of America, 1999).

The causes of illiteracy are varied. The person may have a learning or physical disability, may have left school early, or may have been prematurely instructed in reading before he was developmentally ready to learn to read. Children who grow up in homes with parents who cannot read and who are not exposed to books, newspapers, or a reading role model may be at a disadvantage in learning to read. Day-to-day concerns about survival and fast-paced lives may limit interactions and intentional experiences that make connections between the spoken and written word. Adult literacy programs attempt to reach those adults who cannot read. However, it is preferable, and easier, to prevent a problem than to try to fix it later.

---

functional illiteracy—The inability to use reading, speaking, writing, or computational skills in everyday situations.

Status of Literacy in United States Children

In 1990, President Bush and the governors of all 50 states established educational goals to be achieved by the year 2000. Two of those goals were ". . . that every adult will be literate and possess the knowledge and skills necessary to compete in a global economy and exercise the rights and responsibilities of citizenship" and " . . . that all children in America will start school ready to learn" (National Education Goals Panel, 1990). The National Assessment of Educational Progress reported that "40 percent of the nation's fourth-graders could not read at the basic level, and a shocking 69 percent of African American and 64 percent of Hispanic fourth graders were not reading at a basic level" (U.S. Department of Education, 1999). From these statistics, we can see that there is much work to be done to improve the literacy levels of children in the United States.

Diversity and Literacy

By the year 2010, no single race or culture in the United States will be in the majority (Washington & Andrews, 1998). Today and in the future, English will not be the first language to which many children are exposed. Many children enter school with basic literacy skills in and speaking languages other than English. The educational system in the United States assumes that English is the language children will be taught to read and write. How does this goal affect literacy for children from backgrounds where languages other than English are spoken? Should children be taught in an English-only environment, or should they be taught English as a second language? Further debate centers around whether the educational system should encourage bilingual or multilingual children who are proficient in more than one language to retain proficiency in all those languages (Figure 8–2).

Figure 8–2

Many children entering school in the United States have basic literacy skills in a language other than English. Helping all students become proficient in more than one language is a goal of most educational systems.

People who support teaching all children only in English argue that English is the official language of the United States. Thus, they reason that children must possess strong literacy skills in English to succeed as adults and participate successfully as citizens. In contrast, those who support children continuing to use their native languages while learning English maintain that cognitive development in areas such as math, logic, and problem-solving skills must move forward and not be slowed down as the child struggles to learn a new language. Providing instruction in their native language, then, allows these children to move forward in those areas of development.

What about encouraging bilingual education so that *all* children are proficient in two languages? "The United States is the only developed country in which a monolingual person is considered educated. American schools tend to have low aspirations regarding language skills for students. All bilingual children experience more by communicating with different people in different ways" (Washington & Andrews, 1998).

SCENARIO Dorthea Jones was born into an English-speaking family. In second grade, she began learning French from her bilingual teacher and found that she liked learning another language. She continued to take French throughout high school, traveled to Paris in her senior year, tutored other French students, and majored in French in college. She is fully literate in both English and French.

Karen Lopez was born into a Spanish-speaking family. Her family moved to the United States when she was five and she began kindergarten. No one in her school spoke Spanish and Karen learned to speak English. Karen continued to speak Spanish at home and English at school and was equally literate in both languages by the end of first grade. When Karen entered seventh grade, she wanted to take Spanish because her goal was to become an interpreter. She was placed in introductory-level Spanish with all the students who spoke only English. Karen quickly became bored with the class and asked to drop it. Her guidance counselor discouraged her from dropping the class because she said Karen would have to learn correct Spanish if she wanted to become an interpreter.

Both Dorthea and Karen were bilingual. Was Dorthea's bilingual ability more valued than Karen's? Why do we encourage and require English-speaking students to study another language in high school and college? Some of the reasons include the belief that studying another language strengthens cognitive abilities and opens doors to understanding the others' cultural values. Would these reasons hold true for both Dorthea and Karen?

As a teacher, what will your values be regarding the multilingual abilities of children in your class? What do you think the policies of your school district or state education department will be in regard to the language or languages curricula that are available for students? "Linguistically and culturally diverse children bring multiple perspectives and impressive skills, from such abilities as code-switching (the ability to go back and forth between two languages to deepen conceptual understanding), to the tasks of learning to speak, read, and write a second language. Those self-motivated, self-initiating, constructive thinking processes should be celebrated and used as rich

Figure 8–3

Pretending to read begins early.

teaching and learning resources of all children" (National Association for the Education of Young Children, 1998).

✳ DEVELOPMENT OF AND CURRICULUM FOR LITERACY

"The term literacy relates to both reading and writing and suggests the simultaneous development and mutually reinforcing effects of these two aspects of communication. **Emergent literacy** originates from children's oral language development and their initial, often unconventional, attempts at reading, usually based on pictures (Figure 8–3). Children's early albeit unconventional attempts at reading and writing are respected as legitimate beginnings of literacy " (Emergent Literacy Project, 1997).

SCENARIO

Emma, eighteen months old, holds a cardboard book upside down, saying "Onna ponna time."

Jake, two years old, holds the book right side up saying, "The hungy caterfiller ate a iceam cone, a pizza, and choco cake and he had a bewwy ache."

Norma, two and one-half, holds the pen in her fist and makes hard scribbles and says, "Dat's a bee and dat's a fower and de bee git de honey from de fower."

continued

emergent literacy—Early attempts at language, reading, and writing that are the foundation for later, more conventional language, reading, and writing skills.

Dushay, five years old, holds the book, turns the pages one by one from the front to the back, and describes the illustrations on each page in detail while running his finger under the words.

Molly, six years old, reads each word, deliberately sounding out the longer words, and then gets a pen and paper and works for half an hour copying down the words from the book.

Coralynn, nine years old, holds a flashlight under her covers at night to get to the next chapter in the Harry Potter book she is reading.

Sheridan, Conway, and Marcus are in fifth grade and are bent over a table closely examining an insect with a magnifying glass. Marcus, who has a clipboard and pencil attached with a string, writes as Sheridan dictates: "It has six legs and two antennae." Conway contradicts and says, "No, look closer, Sher, I thought I saw eight legs, four on a side, and then antennae besides that." Marcus chews on the end of the pencil and says, "How about if we say eight legs and that's it? I can't spell antennae." With his hands on his hips, Conway says, "It's right there in the dictionary in the back of the science book. Look it up."

Lizanne, age twelve, writes in her journal every night before she goes to sleep.

Can you see it? The progression of reading and writing goes from the approximation or imitation phase, into the practice phase, into real reading and writing. This happens over time when other areas of development are in place, as previously mentioned, and it is a wonder to behold. You will be an important part of that process.

In 1998, the International Reading Association and the National Association for the Education of Young Children issued a Continuum of Reading and Writing Development in a joint position statement (NAEYC, 1998):

* Phase 1—Prekindergarten—awareness and exploration—children explore their environment and build foundations for learning to read and write.

* Phase 2—Kindergarten—experimental reading and writing—children develop basic concepts of print and begin to engage in and experiment with reading and writing.

* Phase 3—End of first grade—early reading and writing—children begin to read simple stories and can write about a topic that is meaningful to them.

* Phase 4—Second grade—transitional reading and writing—children begin to read more fluently and write various text forms using simple and more complex sentences.

* Phase 5—Third grade—independent and productive reading and writing—children continue to extend and refine their reading and writing to suit varying purposes and audiences.

✳ Phase 6—Fourth through sixth grade advanced reading and writing—children read and write both to express abstract thoughts and to clarify their thinking.

In Chall's extensive landmark study (1967, revised in 1996) of the best way to teach a young child to read, the results were inconclusive. She investigated and described hundreds of programs and approaches, each of which claimed to be the best method. Many of the methods are products of textbook publishing companies who have hired experts to create reading programs, tested the programs, and then touted the program's positive results. Chall and others since her study have concluded that good teachers use a variety of methods and no one program is the answer for all children. On the other hand, inexperienced or less skillful teachers can be assisted by well-constructed reading programs.

You will notice that there is no one theorist featured in this chapter. There are some basic theoretical approaches that have staunch proponents even today, but we introduce no one major theorist. This is because there are so many slight variations on some major approaches that it is difficult to attribute any one of them to one theorist. Instead, it is important to get acquainted with the approaches. You will be learning more about them throughout your preparation years because the teaching of literacy is the foundation of learning.

✳ Phonics—This method stresses the importance of representing the sounds of language as the first step to reading, with whole words recognized. The phonics method often uses workbooks and large-group instruction to recite sounds and high-frequency words.

✳ Linguistics—Experiences from daily life and words children select themselves are the foundation of this method. It incorporates phonics by teaching the alphabet and the sounds of the letters as a way to form correctly spelled words.

✳ Initial teaching alphabet—This approach emphasizes the importance of learning the alphabet and phonics as the first step of reading and writing.

✳ Individualized reading—This is an approach for beginning readers to self-select what they want to read with the premise that this motivation will promote independent or pupil-teacher work on decoding and reading comprehension.

✳ Language experience—This method emphasizes parallel writing and reading stages, with children writing their own labels for drawings and stories of their experiences using phonetic (invented) spelling, with eventual editing to conventional spelling. This is also called the "whole language" approach.

✳ Basal readers—This is a series of programmed books and exercises designed to build progressively on the previous lesson. Isolated sounds are emphasized in stories and repeated often, with or without pictures. The sentences are constructed for teaching structure and building vocabulary, rather than for meaning. These programs vary from publisher to publisher, but are extensive and extremely prescribed, giving the teacher and children little freedom to pursue their own cultural and other interests.

While methods of teaching reading and writing may differ depending on the approaches espoused by the teacher preparation school you attend, the school district for which you work, and the publishing company that provides the materials, there are some foundational principles. Reading begins best when a child's family helps with language understanding by engaging in discussions and early story reading (Durkin, 1966; Bus, van IJzendorn, & Pellegrini, 1995). Listening to stories repeatedly reinforces the language of text in contrast to spoken language (Pappas, 1991). Naming letters and associated sounds (decoding) by the end of kindergarten is a predictor of successful readers (Riley, 1996; Adams, 1990). When children are able to decode and identify both familiar and unfamiliar words, integrated reading, writing, and spelling instructions are important components of systematic literacy progress. Continued and progressively more complex reading, writing, and vocabulary building should continue through the elementary grades. This is especially important to avoid what Chall, Jacobs, and Baldwin (1990) call *the fourth grade slump*, which is most prominent in children of low-income families.

Literacy development for both reading and writing is best achieved by using a variety of methods. Some are more important early on, such as contact with printed material that supports the child's world, gaining familiarity with alphabet letters and sounds, and recognizing and forming words to receive and express meaning. Other methods are best for later stages when group instruction in reading and writing refinements prevail. At each stage, the task and the method should be matched and, when mastery is achieved, appropriate methods should be selected to help move the child on to the next stage.

Infant Literacy Development

"Emerging literacy begins in infancy as a parent lifts a baby, looks into her eyes and speaks softly to her" (Koralek & Collins, 1997). For children to learn to read, they must first be aware of and understand spoken language (Figure 8–4).

During infancy, children become aware of language; healthy infants are able to hear sounds in the environment and make sounds themselves. They hear the rhythm,

Figure 8–4

"The ground work for early literacy is made by the infant having primary caregivers who speak simply to the child and are nurturing; that is, they respond to the child's cues and language attempts, and make eye contact" (National Association for the Education of Young Children, 1998).

syntax, and word patterns of their native language. They learn to understand and predict what words may be spoken in relation to specific conditions. They know the names of objects and understand much more than they are capable of vocally expressing. "The ground work for early literacy is made by the infant having primary caregivers who speak simply to the child and are nurturing; that is, they respond to the child's cues and language attempts, and make eye contact" (National Association for the Education of Young Children, 1998). By the time a child is one, he has likely spoken a few words, can follow simple directions, has eye coordination, and can use his hands to manipulate objects. These abilities make it possible for an infant to turn the pages in a cardboard or cloth book, listen as a reader labels pictures, and possibly point to pictures of familiar objects when asked to. A one-year-old may also be able to manipulate a crayon or marker to make marks on paper, or on the coffee table (Figure 8–5). Infants whose caretakers read to them enjoy looking at books and the experience and interaction of reading.

What is the role of the infant's teacher in encouraging literacy? It is to provide an environment that is filled with experiences of language and literacy. The infant's teacher should speak to the infant during all routine activities, referring to objects by name and offering reflections on the infant's emotions. The teacher should read to

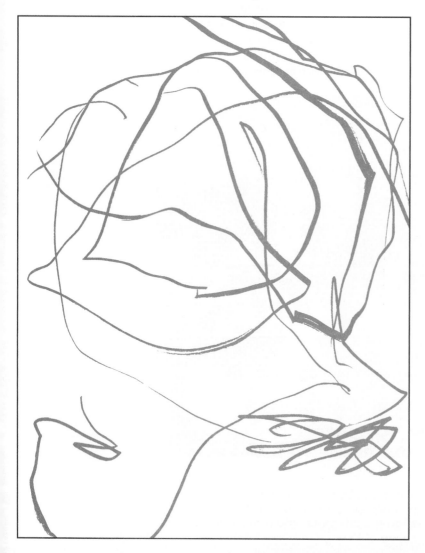

Figure 8–5

A one-year-old may be able to make marks on paper with a crayon or marker.

the infant daily and help him become aware of written language. The teacher should draw attention to daily routines that require writing, such as "I'm going to write your mommy a note to tell her that you ate all your peaches today!" The teacher should then write the note and call attention to it when handing it to the mother. Actions such as this expose the infant to an environment where reading and writing are necessary to function. Does the infant understand every detail of these activities? Of course not; but he will begin to understand that speaking and writing are connected and that marks on paper can convey a message and elicit a reaction in people.

The infant's teacher should work in partnership with the family to demonstrate that reading and writing are a means of communication, by sending notes back and forth and posting notices for parents to read. The teacher should also work in partnership with the family to encourage a literacy-rich environment in the child's home. He can do this in one way by providing labeled pictures of familiar objects for the family to post at home (such as a labeled picture of one of the infant's favorite toys from school). It may be appropriate in some cases for the teacher to supply developmentally appropriate texts or homemade books for the family to look at with and read to their child. The teacher should also be a resource for the parents to locate materials and may guide them to suitable bookstores, public libraries, or sources of free materials.

With all families, the teacher should strive to develop a fruitful relationship so they are receptive to performing literacy activities with their child, such as pointing to and identifying pictures in books. This relationship may lead family members with limited literacy skills themselves to work with a literacy volunteer or enroll in a literacy class. The teacher must be sensitive to family feelings, recognizing what the family is capable of and willing to do in creating a literacy-rich environment for their child. Acknowledging any positive actions taken, no matter how small, is imperative (Figure 8–6).

Figure 8–6

The teacher works with families to encourage a literacy-rich environment.

Carolyn is functionally illiterate. She is the mother of Samuel, who is ten months old. Carolyn likes Samuel's teacher and brings in pictures of him she just had developed. She has double prints of each picture. The pictures include a picture of her, a picture of Samuel's dad, a picture of Samuel with his favorite truck, and a picture of their cat. As Carolyn shows the teacher the pictures, Samuel becomes excited and grabs for them. Carolyn says, "Don't touch!" The teacher asks if Carolyn would like her to laminate a few of the pictures so Samuel can handle them. Carolyn thinks this is a good idea. The teacher mounts four of the pictures on heavy paper, labels them, and laminates them. She has Carolyn help her and reads the labels on the pictures out loud several times. Carolyn takes the pictures and says to Samuel, "Look, here is Daddy! " and points to the picture and word of Daddy. "Where is Mommy? " she says. Samuel points to the picture of Mommy. Carolyn and the teacher laugh and say, "Yes, that's right. That's Mommy!"

During this interaction, the teacher has enhanced her relationship with the parent, provided both the parent and the infant with printed words to connect to the pictures, and has provided a set of objects to enhance the literacy environment in the home.

Infant Literacy Curriculum. The infant's experience with reading prerequisites may occur even before birth when he hears the rhythms of adult voices. In infancy, the sound of the adult's voice, and the interaction and bonding experience, are more important than the reading material's content. Hearing mom, dad, sibling, or caregiver read the Sunday comics, the financial news, or the latest comic book gives the infant the auditory sensations of sustained reading, which is inherently different from conversation. The sound of the human voice comforts infants, as any parent awake at midnight knows; auditory interchange is an important first activity for literacy development in infants.

There are excellent soft plastic books with highly contrasting and patterned color schemes of black, white, and red that can be read to infants starting at a few weeks old, when the infant's eyes begin to focus and adjust. These books are also safe to place within their reach to explore. The older infant should be supplied with cardboard or cloth books that have familiar simple pictures in them, with only one or two words on each page. These books should be available early on for the infant to gaze at while lying down or sitting. Caregivers should also hold young infants and carry on a commentary about what is on the book's pages, because infants understand language before they can speak it. As the infant matures and begins to manipulate objects, these sturdy books should be made available for him to touch and experiment with. When he does this, the infant learns about turning pages and discovers that books are a normal part of the environment. When reading to an infant, as his caregiver talks or asks questions about the objects on the page, the infant is learning that printed symbols can represent objects.

Seven-month-old Zach is being held by his grandmother on her lap. He faces the book and as she turns the pages she

continued

points to the pictures and says, "Dog," "Cow," "Horse," "Bird." Zach is hearing the word, seeing the visual symbol, and forming schemes that connect them together. Eventually, hearing those words will bring the picture to his mind and, later, seeing the words will bring up not only the associated picture but also a categorical assortment of dogs, cows, horses, and birds. The foundation is being laid for reading, understanding, and extrapolation (Figure 8–7).

Toddler Literacy Development

During toddlerhood, the child's command of language grows and enables him to have a conversation with his caregiver about what is on the pages of a book. The toddler is also able to recognize the difference between illustrations and text, and has some understanding that the printed word compels the caregiver to speak. Toddlers can point to pictures when asked and can name some of the pictured objects. They also enjoy having a story be told over and over and begin to be aware that repeated stories follow a pattern, with a beginning, middle, and end. Toddlers enjoy the sound patterns of rhyming words or repeated words. They also discern that there is a "right side up" and an "upside down" to books and begin to turn paper pages in books (not without some tearing, though). Toddlers also begin to make marks on paper with sturdy crayons or pencils and will say the marks represent an object. A toddler who has been exposed to the writing process may explain his written marks as words and may even create rows of marks from left to right (Figure 8–8 on page 282). These activities indicate an awareness of literacy and are the early signs of reading and writing.

Scribbling, or making random marks on a surface with an instrument, is another activity that marks the beginning of the other part of literacy: writing. As children see and then "read" signs like "Stop," "McDonald's," or "Cheerios®," they also want to try writing these words. This conceptualized literacy is an early stage of reading and writing.

Figure 8–7

The love of books begins early.

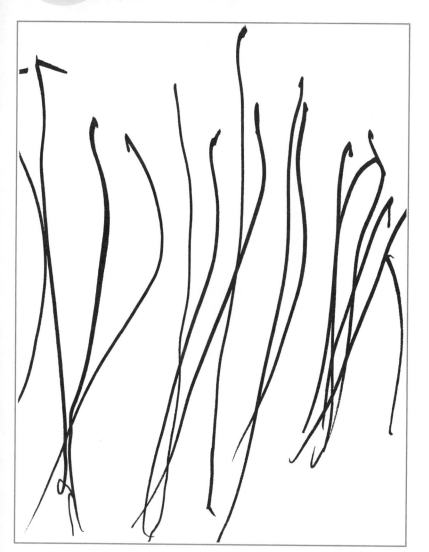

Figure 8–8

Toddlers who have been exposed to the writing process may explain their written marks as words and may even create rows of marks that follow the writing pattern of the culture in which they are being reared.

Their familiarity with, and making connections between the shape and color of, the letters or trademarks sets the course for real reading. Their undeveloped physical skills often keep them from being as successful at writing as they imagine. With time and encouragement, though, the necessary physical skills align with the level of cognitive ability, and more controlled lines like circles and straight lines begin to emerge.

Toddler Literacy Curriculum. The toddler environment for literacy is full of books. They should not just be on a high shelf because they might get torn, chewed, or written on, but instead should be found in different areas of the room, wherever toddlers might go. There should be some books by groupings of soft cushions, some by the potty chair; some near the art materials, and some favorite storybooks by a big chair occupied by an adult who loves to read. Toddlers need readily available books and writing materials that are safe for them to use. Children at this age require sturdy books, nontoxic crayons or markers, and heavy paper or cardboard, and always an adult's close supervision. In a group care setting, children should have a reading area with pillows on the floor or small chairs. "Since toddlers typically do things on the run, toddlers should be free to carry books with them as they go" (Schickendanz, 1999). The books should have pictures of familiar objects or settings and use simple words. A toddler usually has a favorite book that he likes to look at often, and have read to him over and over. He may even begin to talk about the book as he turns the pages, in an imitation of reading. Books made from pictures of familiar people and objects from the child's environment engage him. Toddlers also enjoy looking at catalogs or magazines with an adult, naming familiar objects.

SCENARIO	Mazie has purchased some inexpensive small photo albums for her classroom. She places a photo of each child inside the covers of the albums. She knows that Toolie loves kittens, so she finds pictures of kittens and cats from a magazine and puts them in Toolie's album. Bennett is never far from a toy truck, so she fills his album with all kinds of truck pictures. She allows the children to carry these books around and even take them home if they wish.

Toddlers should have an art area where they can begin to make symbolic representations or drawings of their ideas. They also need adults who will engage in conversations with them about the art activities they are working on. The adult should respond to the toddler's verbalizations by repeating his statement and then waiting for affirmation of understanding, or further explanation, from the toddler. Toddlers' drawing and writing products will be scribbles. Adults should avoid asking, "What's this?" At this stage, children will begin to name their drawings and may even begin to try to print the letters of their names.

All other areas of the classroom should have tools and equipment available for associated reading and writing activities. For example, there should be labeled pictures of bridges and buildings on the wall near the block area and, as a learning complement, hard board books with pictures of bridges and buildings. The kitchen area should have picture cookbooks made from magazine pictures with word labels and laminated pages. Each child's cubby should be labeled with his name and objects in the room should be identified with labels hung at the children's eye level. The teacher may also want to laminate several pages from an old phone book and keeps this child-proof phone book near the toy phone. Photos of the children and their activities should be taken regularly, and labeled, laminated, and hung on the wall at eye level. The teacher must make sure that each child is read to every day. To make this goal a reality, the teacher can enlist the help of classroom aides, parent volunteers, or older children. The teacher should exemplify and model reading books to the children, and help other readers appreciate the value of reading a child's favorite book over and over to him. The teacher should instruct and demonstrate strategies to the readers that will help the child become involved in the reading process. Some approaches may include discussing the illustrations together, trying to predict what will happen next, or allowing the child to "read" to them even if it appears that the child has memorized the book.

Writing implements must be accessible and safe for toddlers. Some writing implements can be secured to various writing stations with string that reaches the writing surface. These should be placed in several areas throughout the room so the toddlers can "make notes" whenever the mood strikes them. There should also be materials such as paint, paint brushes, chalkboards, crayons, paper, and rubber stamps that are readily available for use under adult supervision.

Preschooler Literacy Development

Teachers of young children continue to provide literacy experiences throughout the early childhood years. "These experiences constantly interact with characteristics of individual children to determine the level of literacy skills a child ultimately achieves. Failing to give children literacy experiences until they are school age can severely limit the reading and writing levels they ultimately attain" (National Association for the Education of Young Children, 1998). Children who are three, four, and five years of age take a more active interest in reading when they see immediate benefits. They are in the imitative stage, when everything an older child or adult does will be what they want to do. They will ask for certain books to be read over and over until they can recite them from memory and say proudly, "I can read this book," and they think they really are doing so. They expand their knowledge of familiar words and signs and begin to make the connection between certain alphabet letters and sounds. Printing their name is a big accomplishment for children of this age, usually beginning in all capital letters, often all over the page in random order.

WORDS OF WISDOM

"As a child, my favorite part of a book was the table of contents. I remember curling up beside my grandmother in the big swing on her front porch as she described all the stories found in my favorite Richard Scarry book. After she read the titles and we looked at the pictures, I would try to guess what the story was going to be about—and I loved every minute of it. I always knew that I was having a wonderful time with my grandmother; what I didn't know was that our experiences were laying the groundwork for nearly all the thinking and learning I would ever do" (Arnold, 1997).

Children of this age like to have some independence in their reading activities and will choose familiar books that have predictable outcomes and places to chime in with the reader on key words or phrases. They begin to think of themselves as readers; they start to increase their vocabulary, and are becoming familiar with the structure of a story. Reading a favorite book and hearing familiar intonations and scenarios help them become sensitive to the sound of language. "Phonemes are the smallest units of sound and are coded with alphabet letters. As young children are read to, and hear and become sensitive to rhymes and alliteration, they gain experience in thinking about words in terms of a sequence of sounds. That, along with rich vocabulary and background knowledge seem to enable children to decode print" (Schickendanz, 1999). The role of the family member and teacher is to also point out letters of the alphabet and their sounds. This phonetic recognition is an important foundation for reading.

During their preschool years, children develop the ability to control the marks they make on paper and begin to experiment with drawing and writing by making vertical, horizontal, and circular strokes (Figure 8–9). They now hold the crayon or marker between the first two fingers and thumb (the tripod grasp), not in a fist as earlier, and may begin to show hand dominance (Allen & Marotz, 1999)

Children begin to write by making marks on a page. Over time, as they experiment and practice with vertical and horizontal, circular and straight, dark and light, and lines and dots, they begin to develop direction and mastery over their marks. Additionally, children who have observed others writing and reading written words will attempt to write their own words and stories. The characteristics that distinguish these marks as writing are that they may be made from left to right across the paper, or there may be a series of individual markings to represent letters or words; a few of the marks may look like actual letters (Figure 8–10).

Children will often read back or say what the intended message is. Over time, children learn to make a few letters and begin to make the connection that written letters represent sounds and words.

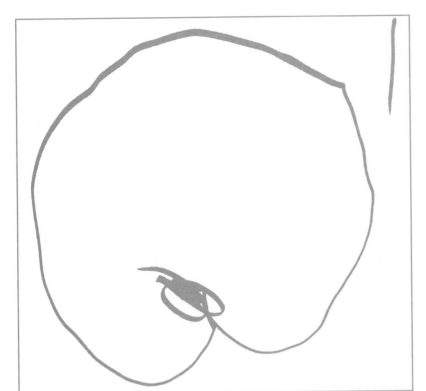

Figure 8—9

During the preschool years, children begin to hold their writing instrument between their first two fingers and thumb (tripod grasp) and begin to experiment with drawing lines and circles.

Figure 8—10

As children experiment and practice with lines and circles, they begin to follow the patterns of written language and may begin to form some recognizable letters.

Children at this age will often write the beginning sound for each word to try to convey meaning by writing. As they sound out words, they spell them as they sound. This phenomenon is called invented spelling and is an expected characteristic of early writing and not a sign of dyslexia or reading problems (Figure 8–11). A later shift to more conventional spelling should take place in the primary classroom, where invented spelling still occurs, however. The teacher's role is to supply children of this age with opportunities to become aware of the written word, and experiment with writing, and support their efforts.

Preschooler Literacy Curriculum. Preschoolers can be aware of the need for, and use and enjoyment of reading and writing. The preschool teacher, along with the child's family, should structure the environment in such a way that reading and writing are an integral part of life. For example, the child learns that lists are made to help remember things, and that checks are written to pay bills. Letters and e-mails are written to communicate with others, addresses are put on mail, and birthday cards carry special messages. Other things preschoolers notice and recognize are logos from favorite fast food restaurants and road signs, and that a heart shape symbolizes love, an "X" a kiss, and an "O" a hug. "As children play in the roles of restaurant workers, chefs, pediatricians, post office workers, grandmothers, grocers, and authors, they experiment with kinds of written language that they expect these individuals to use. As children experiment with written language they find out about its properties and sort out its rules. By engaging in a diversity of play themes children explore diverse aspects of written language" (Owocki, 1999).

The preschool classroom should be arranged so that reading resources and writing tools are available in all areas. For example, the snack area might have menus, order pads, pencils, and a calculator for children to "write" out an individual order and present the customer with a "check" at the end of a meal. Materials for signs are on the shelves along with the blocks, so the label "Emilie's house" can be taped to a

Figure 8–11

Over time, children learn to make a few letters and begin to understand that written letters represent sounds and words.

block construction. Even nonreaders learn quickly that certain signs, such as stop signs, are meant to regulate behavior.

The teacher should arrange the library so it is accessible and contains a variety of books that cater to different literacy abilities, cultural backgrounds, languages, and interests. The book selection can be changed in the library on a regular basis, but favorite books need to remain so children will practice "reading" those familiar books. The teacher should also provide materials, such as heavy paper that has holes on the side so the pages can easily be gathered together, and writing tools to give children the opportunity to make their own books.

Big books are oversized books that enable the teacher to read to a group and have the illustrations and words be visible to all. They inspire great involvement by the children as they explore the pictures on the pages and examine the printed words. The size of the print allows the children to build both their shape awareness and recognition of the printed letters. Additionally children can see the details of the book's illustrations, which leads to close examination and conversations about the illustrations and their relationship to the words printed on the page (Figure 8–12). These big books are sometimes accompanied by the same book in regular size for individual repeated readings later.

Preschoolers must be read to every day, even if it is the same book over and over. With familiar books, the reader should allow children every opportunity to "read" or tell parts of the story himself. This activity of hearing a story over and over and being able to predict what comes next sets the groundwork for higher-level reading skills, making inferences, and drawing conclusions about what has been read. It also enforces the notion that stories have a predictable structure of introduction, climax, and conclusion.

Opportunities to explore the shapes of letters and the differences between letters can come from refrigerator magnet letters, alphabet blocks, sponge letters for

Figure 8–12

Big books allow for group involvement in reading.

sponge painting, and rubber stamp pads and letters. These are not intended for formal lesson use; instead, they provide opportunities to explore. For example, letters made from a variety of textures, colors, and dimensions should be available to touch and attempt to copy with paper, pencils, paintbrushes, and crayons. Labeled items in the room link the object to the written word for it, such as a desk with the letters "d-e-s-k" and a chair with the letters "c-h-a-i-r". Children at this age are beginning to sound out letters and try to make meaning out of them.

> **SCENARIO**   One four-and-a-half-year-old looked at a sign and said, "Where's the ice?" In puzzlement, the teacher asked, "What do you mean? Like ice cubes?" The preschooler pointed to a sign over the door and said, "It says "off ice," so where is the ice?"

At this age, the most important word a child can learn to read is his name. Recognizing comes before re-creating, so the teacher should provide many opportunities for the child to see his name in the classroom throughout the day. The cubby is labeled (along with a photo or recognizable stickers until the children can read), attendance cards are set out for the child to move from "Home" to "School," and lists of jobs and the workers' names are posted. Place cards are handed out at snack and lunch times to designate where each child is to sit. Very quickly, the child of three, four, and five learns to recognize his own name, as well as those of the other children in the class. Cots are labeled so the child can see his name in print, not just to identify space but to have the visual image as he goes to sleep and wakes up. Children's names are used in songs and stories and the teacher call children by the names they and their families prefer. The teacher makes sure to get the pronunciation of foreign names right and to know the proper order of the names. For example, a Chinese child's family name and given name may be in the opposite order of what is standard in the United States. All of these are exercises in literacy, as well as reinforcement of self-esteem by the teacher that let the child experience respect and acknowledgment.

We hope that all children move beyond their preschool years with an enjoyment of literacy. We hope their teachers and families model a love and need for reading and writing. Early reading and writing often occur before children enter school if they have had many varied experiences with books, been provided with writing materials and encouraged to write on their own, and have the requisite developmental skills.

Primary Age Literacy Development

"Because there is little uniformity in the experiences children have during their early years, children enter Kindergarten functioning in literacy at very different levels. They may range in skills typical of a three-year-old to that of an eight-year-old" (National Association for the Education of Young Children, 1998). During the first three years of elementary school, children move from building an awareness and appreciation of the printed word to being able to read from a variety of sources and write for a variety of purposes. What specific skills do children need to master during the primary grades in order to acquire these abilities? Primary age children continue their exploration of phonemic awareness by learning the rules of printed letters associated with spoken words. When children are instructed in phonics, the teacher points out the sounds of letters and words from stories and written tasks that are being used in class. Many English words do not sound like they are spelled and are not spelled like they sound. These words include some of the most commonly used words, such as *the, you, and,* and *was;* they become sight words, or words that are memorized. This is a shift from the invented spelling that takes place in the early primary grades because of the unconventional nature of the English language. Many poor spellers today (are you one?) may have been caught in the difficulties of learning to read and never made the shift from invented spelling to correct spelling.

In the beginning, an inexperienced reader is limited in his ability to store the written word in memory. Reading materials should use short sentences so that slow retrieval and halting reading are not so trying for the student. As skill increases, individual words need to be sounded out less and chunks or sequences of words are read as coherent groups. "The development of language as literacy in the primary classroom is seen as a continuum of earlier experiences. The goal of the language and literacy program in the primary years is for children to continue to develop their ability to communicate orally through reading and writing. Basic tenets of the whole language approach are that spoken and written language interact and influence each other, and that all phases of language development are experience-based" (Gestwicki, 1999). The whole-language approach makes use of big books and the child's own writing about his experiences as the source of the literacy curriculum. The traditional approach to teaching reading and writing is direct instruction through the use of basal readers, work sheets, and handwriting practice, which isolate segments of skills for practice and mastery (Henninger, 1999). Your teacher preparation program's philosophy will influence your pedagogical approach (Figure 8–13).

Before the primary grades, children learn the rules of grammar and syntax by hearing spoken language and having stories read to them. The primary age teacher can now build on this existing audio–based knowledge by drawing examples from materials the children are currently reading or writing about in their lives. The teacher may have a discussion about the use of "him" or "her" and pick examples from a sentence that the student has read. The teacher can also draw on vocabulary, spelling, and

Figure 8–13

The goal of language and literacy programs in the primary years is for children to continue to develop their ability to communicate through reading and writing.

patterns in the student's current reading. "Only when children are taught a combination strategy for quickly and accurately identifying words do they move toward becoming efficient, reflective readers" (Emergent Literacy Project, 1997). Decoding skills, including grammar, meaning, and sounds are required for fluent reading.

> **SCENARIO** Bo is reading the story *Goodnight Moon* by Margaret Wise Brown. This is a story he has heard over and over. He is on the page that says "Good-night, kittens; good-night, mittens." He reads the first line, partly from memory and partly by recognizing the repeated word "good-night." He pauses at the word "mittens." He looks at the picture. He knows there should be a rhyming word; he looks at the letter "m" and remembers how it sounds. With all these clues, he realizes the word is "mitten."

As with reading, the teacher should provide many opportunities for the children to write and to need to write. At this age, children often attempt to write even though they do not know all the rules. They should write frequently and, as they do, they will try to spell the words they want to write (Figure 8–14). Most importantly, the teacher should make reading purposeful and interesting, and model enthusiasm for reading. The teacher should take advantage of every opportunity to help individual children master the skills needed to decode the reading or writing in which they show an interest.

Primary Age Literacy Curriculum. The teacher should arrange the primary classroom in such a way that there is a collection of books suitable for a variety of reading abilities that represent cultural diversity and include a variety of topics

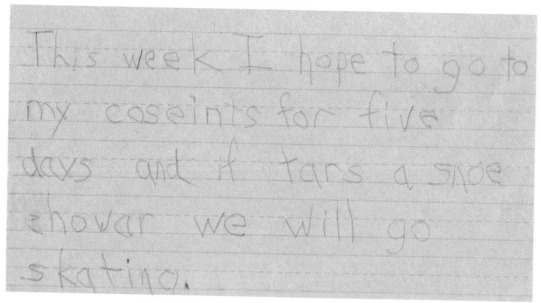

Figure 8–14

During the primary years, children often attempt to write, even though they do not know all the rules.

and forms of literature. To begin a library, the teacher may want to start a collection of the Caldecott, Newberry, and Coretta Scott King award-winning series of books. These books should be made readily available to children for pleasure reading and for integrating with other subject areas, such as social studies, math, science, art, and music. Big books and books with predictable plots and word patterns should also be available in the primary classroom. These are used more for shared reading experiences, where children take more responsibility for reading certain words or supplying predictions or repetitive phrases. As children move through this stage, the complexity of their reading materials increases and they become more independent readers. They can enjoy chapter books that the teacher reads, and eventually their skills will progress enough that they can read them on their own. This is the age when children get hooked on series books and read every one.

Children need to practice the literacy skills of matching upper- and lower-case letters, as well as recognizing words, practicing phonics, and using structural and contextual clues. With these skills, they learn to identify words, analyze punctuation and its usage, and apply grammar rules to word usage by recognizing plurals, contractions, compound words, prefixes, and suffixes. These skills can be isolated on work sheets, included in traditional drills, or incorporated into literature studies or even within the framework of a game as a part of the whole-language approach.

Primary classrooms should also provide a variety of opportunities for children to write. An area of the chalkboard should be set aside for them; easels, markers, paper, and a book-making area should be provided, and activities should be planned that require writing, such as a sign-up sheet to use the computer. More structured activities may include journal writing to capture experiences such as field trips or experiments. Other systematic exercises may include making lists or offering standardized story beginners to be finished creatively. Children may practice specific writing skills by doing author studies, where several books by a single author are read, compared, and analyzed. Disciplined writing skills can be developed with written reports composed using a workshop format.

* Prewrite—Talk about it, brainstorm, think about audience and sequence
* Fastwrite—Jot notes and prepare "first draft"
* Response—Reconsider and share with others for peer feedback
* Revise—Edit and rewrite
* Polish—Proofread and correct into final draft
* Publish—Prepare final copy and share with others
* Evaluate—Assess the product and process (Fields, Spangler, & Lee, 1991)

The teacher should model the necessity of writing by posting attendance and lunch money lists and reminders where the children can see them. The teacher should initially use print, rather than script, so the children can easily decode these writings. Objects in the room should be labeled and signs made to give simple instructions for specific activities. For example, a sign on the bathroom light switch might say, "Turn off the light when you are done." The teacher may also provide mailboxes or e-mail addresses to encourage the children to leave written messages for each other. The teacher also can leave messages for the whole class or a specific child at these addresses.

The teacher's role should encourage the family to read books frequently at home. For children whose families do not speak English, the teacher should support the family's culture and encourage them to read to the child at home in their native language. The classroom library should include books in English, as well as books in the languages the families speak. The teacher should help the families find children's books in their native language through the Internet, by advocating for community libraries to include such books, and by discussing with the families their favorite books that are available in their native language.

The classroom should have computers available for children to use as writing tools. Computers can help children see their words as printed language and can be used to generate a list of spelling words to work on, or allow children to illustrate and print copies of their work. As the children use computers, they can easily correct mistakes they detect, rather than having to erase and write over. Children take special pride in their word processing when it is converted to print (Figure 8–15). The computer is often easier for children with learning disabilities to use to express themselves since writing may be so tedious that they avoid doing it at all. Speech recognition software that converts the spoken word to screen text, which can then be printed, may be used to help young children discover the relationship between language and printed materials, or to help children with learning or physical disabilities write text.

Teachers can help families enrich literacy at home by sending home stories their children have written about pictures they have made or experiences they have had in school. The teacher can also help children make books to take home, and introduce both children and their families to the public library. The teacher may also assist families in obtaining low-cost or free reading materials and writing implements.

The importance of learning to read in the primary years cannot be stressed strongly enough. It is not a case of "now or never," but rather one of "now, or much harder later." School success for the next 10 or more years very much depends on strong literacy skills established in the primary years. Teaching reading will be an important part of your role as a teacher. There is much to learn about reading and many ways to teach it.

My family got a new cat last weekend from Mark and Lissa Sharmeta. It's very fun to play with. It sleeps with me evry night. It can git pretty fisty some times. It is brown and black. It's a very good cat but some times it gits in truble.

By Jimmy

Figure 8–15

Technology can help all children easily express their thoughts in writing.

Elementary Age Literacy Development

SCENARIO

Pat is in the sixth grade. His class is studying a unit on the solar system and space exploration. Pat has been assigned to work on a group report on lunar exploration. He begins his research by reading the 15-page chapter on space exploration in his science textbook. He then goes to the library and looks up several key words in the encyclopedia: "space travel," "moon," and "astronaut." He reads the articles in the encyclopedia and takes notes, and then asks the librarian for help locating newspaper articles from the first lunar landing. On the Internet, he finds a recording of the words spoken by astronaut Neil Armstrong as he took his first steps on the moon. He also finds the construction plans for the lunar lander, and a picture of lunar rocks. His group meets each day to review what each individual has discovered and to plan how their report will fit together. The assignment itself has several parts. Pat has to hand in his note cards, an outline of his report, and a written report; he will participate in a group presentation with one visual aid, and submit a vocabulary list of 20 new words he discovered while doing his research.

Reading and writing skills become more and more crucial as the child moves into the elementary grades. Children not only read and write in language arts classes, but all other subject areas transmit information through higher-level reading. If a child has not mastered reading and writing by the beginning of fourth grade, learning in every other subject area is impaired. By the time children enter the fourth grade, they should be able to:

* read fluently and enjoy reading.
* use a range of strategies when drawing meaning from the text.
* use word identification strategies appropriately and automatically when encountering unknown words.
* recognize and discuss elements of different text structures.
* make critical connections among texts.
* write expressively in many different forms (stories, poems, reports).
* use a rich variety of vocabulary and sentences appropriate to text forms.
* revise and edit their own writing during and after composing.
* spell words correctly in final writing drafts (National Association for the Education of Young Children, 1998).

Elementary age students continue to sharpen the strategies they use to read. They do this by reading and thinking about what they read. Students practice making inferences by predicting outcomes while they read. For example, Jim's fourth-grade teacher is reading *Sarah, Plain and Tall* by Patricia MacLachlan to the class. On October 31, she asks the class to write a short paragraph about what they think Sarah would do for Halloween. Jim's response is, "I think Sarah would have a feast or big dinner. She probably wouldn't go trick-or-treating or anything, but she could invite some people over. I think Sarah would be the same." Jim used his knowledge about

Sarah and her way of life to predict that Sarah would not celebrate Halloween with trick-or-treating or changing into a costume, but would probably celebrate a special occasion with invited company and dinner, as was her custom for other occasions.

During these years, students also continue to build vocabulary, practice spelling, and sharpen grammar skills. As they read and write they are encouraged to generate vocabulary and spelling lists. They must also be able to monitor (to make sure it makes sense) and summarize what they read. These strategies to enhance reading skills occur not only in reading and writing classes, but also while the student reads and writes in all other subject areas.

SCENARIO Josie is reading a math problem that asks her to calculate how much money a vendor earned at a carnival. Josie reads the problem and infers that she will have to add or multiply to reach the answer. She is unsure what a vendor is and looks the word up in the dictionary and adds it to her vocabulary list of new words. When she rereads the problem with this new knowledge, it makes sense to her; she then correctly calculates the answer (Figure 8–16).

Many children in these grades have discovered the pleasure of reading for entertainment. They have favorite authors, share books, discuss what they are reading with each other, and send letters and e-mails to friends to recommend books. If the teacher monitors these activities and is familiar with popular books, he can be included in their discussions and ask questions that encourage them to think more deeply about what they are reading. Just asking, "What do you think will happen?" (about a character in a Goosebumps or Harry Potter book) will lead students to make inferences and summarize what they have read.

Figure 8–16

Reading and writing skills carry over into other areas.

For those students who have difficulty reading at their current grade level, the teacher is the key individual for managing intervention and assessment to determine the areas of difficulty. The teacher will identify resources, communicate with the child's family, and, if appropriate, refer the child to appropriate specialists. The child who has difficulty reading will most likely have trouble with other subject areas, since a child's understanding of a subject largely depends on his reading skills. Such children may need to have the content of other subjects reinforced in ways that do not depend so much on reading. They could listen to textbooks on tape, or learn through discussion or experience. Until their reading skills strengthen, it is important that they not miss out on information in other academic subject areas. For some of these children, reading is a tedious chore. The teacher should look for ways to motivate these children to read and finds ways to make reading purposeful and rewarding for them.

Elementary Age Literacy Curriculum. The older elementary child depends on reading and writing skills to learn and succeed in all subject areas. Teachers in these grades should weave the strengthening of literacy skills and strategies throughout the curriculum. In all areas of the curriculum, the teacher should encourage children to look up words they do not know and draw on current classroom topics for vocabulary and spelling words.

A continued emphasis on the technical skills of reading and writing spans the elementary grades. The teacher can use such strategies as the workshop model, peer tutoring, and interactive instruction through journals. Creative writing of various kinds, such as advertising and first-person adventure narratives, and producing videos based on written scripts can also be used (Schurr, Thomason, & Thompson, 1995).

Listening to good stories never grows old. Dramatic readings of poetry, short stories, and chapter books are still done by teachers in the elementary grades. Ashley Bryant, poet, storyteller, and illustrator, says that poetry, like music, must be heard to get the full effect. He reads with gusto and encourages his audience, whether teachers in a workshop or children in an assembly or classroom, to repeat the lines of Nikki Giovanni's "The Sun Is So Quiet" or Eloise Greenfield's "Honey, I Love." He reminds us that story patterns cross the world with basically the same motifs, which can unite us as human beings.

Storytelling, with its long oral tradition, is a skill that teachers can cultivate to catch the class's attention, and hold onto it through voice inflection, dramatic pauses, and well-timed questions. Using this technique, the teacher can stimulate emotions of empathy, joy, and humor, and even those of sadness or fear. The teacher builds a feeling of community as the students share similar reactions and personal experiences. Using literature, the teacher can lead his students to different kinds of analysis in examining a character's values, actions, and feelings, and the setting in which the story occurs. The students may then make conclusions regarding those factors and their effect on a character's behavior and the plot's outcome. Further extrapolation can lead to discovery of the author's techniques in accomplishing the goals of the book: those of mood or tone, or patterns within the story line, and those of a coherent beginning, middle, and conclusion (Anderson & Lapp, 1988).

Writing in journals is an effective tool for encouraging writing. The teacher may assign a topic on some days, or may have time set aside for free writing and allow a few "pass days" each month. Students and teacher set ground rules for journal entries, such as specifying that they are to be confidential unless an individual reveals that someone is being hurt or may hurt someone else, and that journals are not to be corrected for grammar or spelling. Daily entries are required, but the student usually has a choice of topics to write on.

Everett Lopez, a fifth-grade teacher, generates a list of 25 topics from which to choose for journal entries each month. He offers topics that include subject areas, current events, expression of feelings, and experimentation with different kinds of writing, such as poetry (Figure 8–17).

Another activity that can encourage students to read and write about a variety of topics is a class newsletter. A newsletter allows for all levels of participation and interest: advanced writers can write in-depth, researched articles, while very weak writers can contribute photographs, drawings, or cartoons. Current events, personal interests, or hobbies encourage the student to show his individuality. In such a public forum, students will be inspired to make sure grammar and spelling are correct, and they will naturally be curious about reading each other's contributions. Students may

---

Everett Lopez's Journal Assignment

Journal Choices for January

Happy New Year! Here are 25 topic choices for your January journals. Remember to enter something each day. You will have 20 entries in January. If you choose a pass day, remember to write the date and the word "Pass."

Three goals for the New Year
If I could go on a long winter vacation, I would _____
If I lived in Argentina, I would _____
The funniest thing my family did was _____
My life as an amphibian
The news today made me feel _____
Today's weather
I am really proud of _____
Free writing (your choice of topic)
Free writing (your choice of topic)
Free writing (your choice of topic)
Pass
Pass
Pass
My dream home
No one knew the answer but me about _____
I went to bed and the next thing I knew _____
If I had a dinner party in Peru I would serve _____ and invite _____
My favorite book I read this month was _____
I saw something in the newspaper that _____
I jumped into the pond and _____
My multiplication experience
How I spend my money
Poem of the season
Limerick

Figure 8–17

Journals inspire children to write.

work together to draft the articles. Peer critiques are common practice in collaborative writing projects such as this one.

Students in these grades begin to look outside the required textbook for information. In research activities, they need free access to resource materials. Each classroom must have access to a current encyclopedia, the Internet, a dictionary, atlas, and phone books. The teacher can help students find additional information on academic topics.

Asking children to experiment with various forms of writing increases their writing skills. The teacher may offer several examples of limericks as a model for studying the structure of the limerick, and then ask the class to try limerick writing. Children search for words to fit the pattern. Once they master this structure, they can move on to other poetry forms (Figure 8–18).

Letter writing is another activity in which proficient writing will prove useful to children. The teacher can offer instruction on letter formats and addressing envelopes, and then advance that knowledge by having the students write letters to real individuals. Students can be paired with another classroom to write back and forth, or they can write for free items from manufacturers or to their favorite celebrity. The teacher can also teach students how to communicate through e-mail and follow the conventions of Internet communication.

Motivation seems to be the biggest hurdle the teacher in the upper elementary grades has in developing literacy. Finding materials that address individual skill levels and interests is a challenge. Because reading and writing are the basic skills needed not only for academic success, but also for personal competence and eventual employment, finding and implementing ways of assessing literacy, identifying problem areas, and working on remediation is one of the teacher's most important roles.

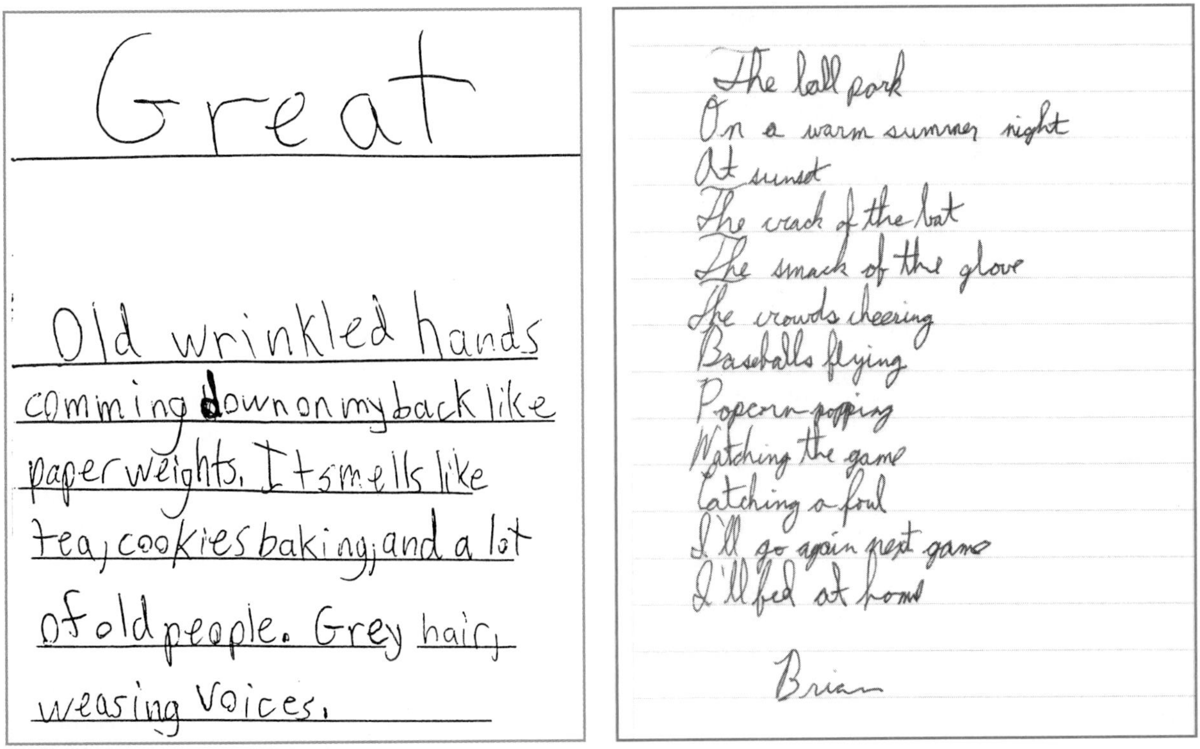
Great

Old wrinkled hands comming down on my back like paper weights. It smells like tea, cookies baking, and a lot of old people. Grey hair, weasing voices.

The ball park
On a warm summer night
At sunset
The crack of the bat
The smack of the glove
The crowds cheering
Baseballs flying
Popcorn popping
Watching the game
Catching a foul
I'll go again next game
I'll fed at home

Brian

Figure 8–18

Experimenting with various forms of writing increases children's writing skills.

✳ ASSESSMENT OF LITERACY

Children's progress in developmental domains, assessment of that progress, and curriculum planning are all closely aligned. When you know about an expected skill or behavior for a certain age, you begin to look for it. You measure what you actually see against what you expect to see, and plan on what to provide to stimulate, reinforce, or expand upon learning. Assessing the early stages of literacy depends on close observation. You need to watch for the infant's ability to grasp the book and bring it to his mouth, or wait for the one-year-old to grab a crayon and make haphazard lines on a piece of paper, or listen to a toddler try to repeat a story he's heard a hundred times. When you see and hear those things happening, you have begun to evaluate the child's progress with reading and writing. As the skills become more defined, you can use more formal measures of assessment to document the milestones as they occur.

Assessment of Literacy Skills

Anecdotal recording, or writing down exactly what you see and hear, is one of the most inclusive methods of assessing literacy skills. Notes are written as the events are taking place, or very shortly thereafter, while the details are fresh in your memory. Dated anecdotal notes, written on a regular basis, that describe the child's reading or writing behavior, are a journal of progress. Comparing these notes to the developmental stages for that age can aid in evaluating whether the child is within the range of expectations.

Checklists and rating scales that contain the linear steps toward reading and writing are helpful. They are easily done, provide criteria to look for, and represent a trustworthy documentation of progress. By seeing what the next step is, the teacher can forge an approach to the kinds of activities to plan for the child within the zone of proximal development (Figure 8–19).

Samples of the child's work, such as the writing samples throughout this chapter, or tape recordings of oral reading, also document the child's progress. Portfolios of child- and teacher-selected work can be used for later assessment. They can contain samples of first and final drafts of the workshop writing process, creative writing pieces, lists of books read, and journals. The portfolio can be the basis for the child self-evaluating his prior work and provide a mechanism for teacher/child conversations that focus on the child's experiences and progress.

The teacher can produce tests to gauge the concepts taught, such as vocabulary tests from stories or other subject areas, spelling tests, timed tests of words recognized by sight, or comprehension tests on selected readings. The presence of written records acknowledges that the teacher knows what experiences and activities the children have had and gives an indication of their levels of mastery of the material.

Standardized tests provide a numerical score or rate the reading level based on performance. In Standards for Assessment (1994) the International Reading Association and the National Council of Teachers of English in a Joint Task Force on Assessment emphasized the importance of multiple perspectives and sources of data that include the teacher as the most important agent. States are using "high-stakes tests" to evaluate teachers, compare one teacher's results against another's, and rate schools against each other. Reading levels are one of the main components of this comparison. This puts pressure on teachers to "teach to the test," adjusting and restricting curriculum to those areas that will be tested. (See Chapter 6 for details on issues related to standardized testing.) As with any outside measurement or one-time assessment, the teacher who knows the child's day-to-day performance is in the position to best judge the authenticity of the test results.

LITERACY RATING SCALE

Child's Name _____

INTEREST IN BOOKS

No interest, avoids	Only if adult initiated	Brings books to adult to read	Looks at books as self-initiated activity

LISTENING TO BOOKS

Wiggly, no attention	Intermittent attention	Listens in one-on-one situation	Listens as part of a group, tuning out distractions

INVOLVEMENT WITH BOOKS BEING READ

Little or no response	Emotional response, laugh, frown	Comments, asks questions	Joins in during reading

HANDLING BOOKS

No voluntary touching	Rough handling	Exploratory manipulation	Books as favorite toys

CONCEPT OF BOOK FORMAT

No idea of front/back, up/down	Holds book right side up but skips pages	Demonstrates front/back concept	Looks at pages left to right

CONCEPT OF STORY BOOK

Labels pictures	Retells story in sequence from pictures	Accurately repeats some story lines	Points to print while accurately retelling from pictures

PRINT IN THE ENVIRONMENT

Notices signs, labels	Asks, "What's that say?"	Reads signs, labels out of context	"Writes" signs to label constructions

(Continued)

Figure 8–19

Literacy rating scale (From Nilsen, B., 2001).

LITERACY RATING SCALE (continued)

BEGINNING READING

Recognizes own name	Recognizes letters in name in other words	Reads simple words	Sounds out letters in unfamiliar words

MANIPULATION OF WRITING TOOLS

Fist hold	High hold on pencil	Adult grip, little control	Adult grip, good control

COMMUNICATION THROUGH WRITING

Communicates ideas through drawing	Dictates on request	Initiates dictation	Draws and writes words

BEGINNING WRITING

Scribbles, no reference to writing	Named scribbles, "Says my name"	Single letters, random	Writes name

WRITING IN PLAY

No reference to writing	Asks for signs, words to be written	Asks for adult to spell words	Sounds out words and writes on own

Figure 8–19 *continued*

Learning Difficulties in Reading and Writing

A print-rich environment and early experiences with print have been emphasized repeatedly in this chapter. Children come to the classroom of any grade with varying degrees of preexisting literacy background upon which the teacher has had little influence. The teacher can work with the family throughout the year, but what has or has not been done in the past is a condition to assess and address in the present. One of the elements of assessment is to determine each child's experience and attitude toward reading and writing, his understanding and competency level, and any limitations that may impede his progress.

Learning disabilities are severe discrepancies between intellect and achievement that interfere with basic reading skills, reading comprehension, and written expression. Two of the most frequent types of learning disabilities that affect reading and writing are dyslexia (a severe difficulty in learning to read, particularly in decoding) and dysgraphia (a severe difficulty in learning to write, including the mechanics of handwriting) (Baroody & Ginsburg, 1991).

Slow or inaccurate decoding skills are the best predictors of difficulties in reading comprehension. Children with learning disabilities can learn strategies for identifying words, decoding more speedily, and reading for better comprehension. Teaching strategies such as presenting information in multiple ways and allowing multiple ways for students to demonstrate learning are accommodations that can help. Spelling instruction can be enhanced by teaching spelling patterns, such as words that end the same but have a different first letter: *bat, cat, fat, hat, mat, pat*. Children with learning disabilities need fewer spelling words, specific feedback for practice, maintenance of previously learned words, dictionary training, and access to computerized spelling checkers.

Children with learning disabilities can be assisted with the content of their writing by structuring the writing experience through planning, composing, and revising. A standardized writing format can help the student organize his thoughts and think about the audience for the writing and the purpose and development of the topic. Handwriting can be a problem for children with learning disabilities. The move from manuscript (printing) to cursive (script) writing occurs in most schools in the third grade. This is also the time when learning disabilities in the area of literacy are becoming most apparent. Dysgraphia slows down the writing process and makes it harder for peer review to take place. Visual acuity and brain dysfunction can cause incorrectly formed letters that interfere with legibility. Using a computer can help the student with writing difficulties and overcome the barrier to producing written work. Speech recognition software can further help a child with writing difficulties to compose. Basic keyboarding will likely become a necessary skill for every child in the future. Accommodations for students with learning disabilities are strategies that all students can benefit from. Diagnosis and formalized Individualized Education Programs guide the teacher in including children with learning disabilities in the class.

Hearing and vision disabilities can also impede reading and writing development. Early identification and intervention is the first step, followed by the provision of adaptive equipment. Depending on the severity, the teacher's modifications may be outlined in an Individualized Education Program.

SUMMARY

For every developmental level, the teacher must supply the students with a safe and engaging literacy environment, a variety of reading and writing materials at the child's developmental level, and planned and spontaneous activities that are challenging without being frustrating. The teacher at all levels must exemplify a love for reading by being seen engaged in recreational reading, showing excitement at looking up and locating information in books, and sharing books with the class. The teacher must demonstrate that reading and writing are useful activities, and find interesting tasks to motivate students to read and write. Lastly, the teacher must be knowledgeable about the skills and strategies that children need to master to become strong readers and writers.

KEY TERMS

phonemic awareness

functional illiteracy

emergent literacy

REVIEW ACTIVITIES

Exercises to Strengthen Learning

1. Collect drawing and/or writing samples from a two-year-old, four-year-old, six-year-old, eight-year-old, and twelve-year-old. To collect the writing samples, supply the children with paper and an appropriate writing implement (keeping safety in mind for the younger children). Try to use a common theme with the children; for example, drawing or writing about their favorite food. Begin with a conversation about the theme to develop a relationship with the child before requesting him to write. Do not give guidance or correct his attempt to write; your task in this exercise is to merely observe.

    a. What was each child's reaction to your request?

    b. How was each child able to respond in writing to your request?

    c. What were some of the writing skills you observed in each child?

    d. What do you think each child's writing abilities reflected about his or her cognitive and physical abilities?

2. Visit a children's library or bookstore. Read two books intended for infants and toddlers, two for preschoolers, two for primary age children, and two for elementary age children. Describe why each book is suited for the particular developmental stage.

3. Interview a reading specialist at an elementary school. What are the most common problems seen and what interventions are taken?

4. Observe a class of an age/grade of your choice. Make a list of all the literacy materials you see in the classroom. Compare your list to a classmate's who visited a different classroom of the same age/grade. What do these lists reveal about the teachers?

5. Interview someone who learned to read as an adult. What was his or her experience in trying to learn to read when he or she was younger? Did he or she have the opportunity to learn to read as a child? What was the experience like as an adult? What does he or she like best about being able to read?

Internet Quest

1. Locate 10 children's books that are about children from at least five different cultures or races. Find two of these books to read and write a book report on each of them. Look at the American Library Association's Web site (http://www.ala.org) for Coretta Scott King, Caldecott, or Newberry Award winners.

2. Scan the International Reading Association's Web site (http://www.reading.org). Summarize your findings. Do they support what you have learned in this chapter about literacy?

Reflective Journal

In this chapter, I learned _____ about children's literacy.

When I am a teacher, I will . . .

REFERENCES

Adams, M. (1990). *Beginning to read.* Cambridge, MA: MIT Press.

Allen, K., & Marotz, L. (1999). *Developmental profiles: Pre-birth through eight* (3rd ed.). Albany, NY: Delmar.

Anderson, P. S., & Lapp, D. (1988). *Language skills in elementary education* (4th ed.). New York: Random House.

Arnold, C. (1997). *Read with me: A guide for student volunteers starting early childhood literacy programs.* Washington, DC: U.S. Department of Education.

Baroody, A., & Ginsburg, H. (1991). A cognitive approach to assessing the mathematical difficulties of children labeled "learning disabled." In H. L. Swanson (Ed.), *Handbook on the assessment of learning disabilities* (pp. 117–228). Austin, TX: Pro-Ed.

Bus, A., van IJzendorn, M., & Pellegrini, A. (1995). Joint book reading makes for success in learning to read: A meta-analysis on intergenerational transmission of literacy. *Review of Educational Research, 65,* 1–21.

Chall, J. S. (1967). *Learning to read: The great debate.* New York: McGraw-Hill.

Chall, J. S. (1996). *Learning to read: The great debate* (3rd ed.). San Francisco, CA: Wadsworth Publishing.

Chall, J. S., Jacobs, V. A., & Baldwin, L. E. (1990). *The reading crisis: Why poor children fall behind.* Cambridge, MA: Harvard University Press.

Durkin, D. (1966). *Children who read early.* New York: Teachers College Press.

Emergent Literacy Project. (1997). Houghton Mifflin. Retrieved March 16, 2001, from the World Wide Web at: <http://www.eduplace.com>.

Fields, M., Spangler, K., & Lee, D. (1991). *Let's begin reading right.* New York: Merrill.

Giovanni, N. (1996). *The sun is so quiet.* New York: Henry Holt and Co.

Gestwicki, C. (1999). *Developmentally appropriate practice: Curriculum and development in early education* (2nd ed.). Albany, NY: Delmar.

Greenfield, E. (1994). *Honey, I love you.* New York: HarperCollins Children's Books.

Henninger, M. L. (1999). *Teaching young children: An introduction.* Upper Saddle River, NJ: Merrill.

International Reading Association and National Council of Teachers of English Joint Task Force on Assessment. (1994). *Standards for assessment.* Newark, DE: International Reading Association and National Council of Teachers of English.

Koralek, D., & Collins, R. (1997). *On the road to reading: A guide for community partners.* Washington, DC: Corporation for National Service.

Lee, H. (1960). *To kill a mockingbird.* Philadelphia, PA: J.B. Lippincott.

Literacy Volunteers of America. (1999). *1999 FACTS on illiteracy in America.* Retrieved March 16, 2001, from the World Wide Web: <http://www.literacyvolunteers.org>.

MacLachlan, P. (1987). *Sarah, plain and tall.* New York: HarperTrophy.

National Association for the Education of Young Children (NAEYC). (1998). Learning to read and write: Developmentally appropriate practice for young children. *Young Children, 53*(4), 30–46.

National Education Goals Panel. (1990). Retrieved March 16, 2001, from the World Wide Web at: <http://www.negp.gov>.

Nilsen, B. (2001). *Week by week: Plans for observing and recording young children,* (2nd ed.). Albany, NY: Delmar.

Owocki, G. (1999). *Literacy through play.* Portsmouth, NH: Heineman.

Pappas, C. (1991). Young children's strategies in learning the "book language" of information books. *Discourse Processes 14,* 203–225.

Riley, J. (1996). *The teaching of reading.* London: Paul Chapman.

Schickendanz, J. A. (1999). *Much more than the ABCs: The early stages of reading and writing.* Washington, DC: National Association for the Education of Young Children.

Schurr, S., Thomason, J., & Thompson, M. (1995). *Teaching at the middle level: A professional's handbook.* Lexington, MA: D. C. Heath.

U.S. Department of Education. 1999. National Center for Education Statistics, *The condition of education 1999.* Washington, DC: U.S. Government Printing Office. 36, 30.

Washington, V., & Andrews, J. D. (1998). *Children of 2010.* Washington, DC: National Association for the Education of Young Children.

Wise Brown, M. (1991). *Goodnight moon.* New York: HarperCollins Juvenile Books.

For additional learning and teaching resources, visit our Web site at www.EarlyChildEd.delmar.com.

RELATED CAREERS

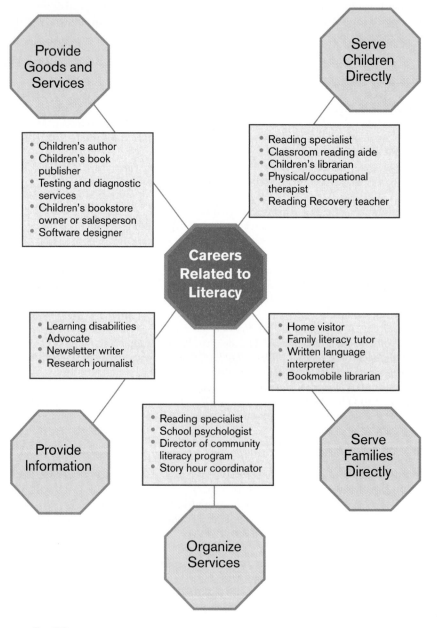

Provide Goods and Services
- Children's author
- Children's book publisher
- Testing and diagnostic services
- Children's bookstore owner or salesperson
- Software designer

Serve Children Directly
- Reading specialist
- Classroom reading aide
- Children's librarian
- Physical/occupational therapist
- Reading Recovery teacher

Careers Related to Literacy

- Learning disabilities
- Advocate
- Newsletter writer
- Research journalist

Provide Information

Serve Families Directly
- Home visitor
- Family literacy tutor
- Written language interpreter
- Bookmobile librarian

Organize Services
- Reading specialist
- School psychologist
- Director of community literacy program
- Story hour coordinator

Figure 8–20

Careers related to literacy.

CHAPTER

9

Learning about and Teaching the Young Mathematician and Scientist

Objectives

After reading this chapter and completing the review activities, the learning teacher should be able to:

1. Identify and describe the mathematics and science concepts children are capable of understanding from birth through sixth grade.

2. Describe teaching strategies the teacher may use to facilitate the understanding of mathematics and science concepts.

3. Explain the national standards for mathematics, science, and technology.

✳ UNDERSTANDING LEARNING AND TEACHING MATHEMATICS, SCIENCE, AND TECHNOLOGY

SCENARIO George Washington Carver (1860–1943) looked at the field of cotton on one side of the lane and noticed that it was much healthier and produced more cotton than the crop on the other side of the lane. He wondered why this was so. What was the difference in growing conditions for the two fields? Both had similar soil, the same seeds were planted in both, and both fields were cultivated in the same manner. He later discovered that, during the previous year, soybeans had been planted in the field where the healthier cotton grew. Carver hypothesized that there might be a link between what was grown on the land previously and the health of subsequent crops. He tested his hypothesis by trying many combinations of crops and was able to conclude that soybeans replenish soil nutrients previously depleted by cotton. Carver was a famous agricultural chemist who discovered many uses for soybeans and peanuts, patented many processes for making paints and cosmetics, and developed crop-rotation methods for farmers to increase their harvest yields (Inventure Place, 2001).

How do we learn about mathematics, science, and technology? Is math just memorizing numbers and how they relate to each other? Is science just a collection of facts related to animals, plants, and the environment? Is technology just mastery of the machines we use every day? It is the exploration of our world, finding that quantity, patterns, and tools exist everywhere. What must happen in our development to prepare the way for these kinds of learning? In this chapter, we will discuss the process and some of the prerequisites for learning about math, science, and technology.

The Scientific Method

SCENARIO Ruana, two and one-half, is playing with four coasters, those small pads that protect tables from sweaty glasses, and is calling them cookies. She says, "Cookies. One for Mama, one for Dada, one for Runa (her name for herself), one for Nana." She looks puzzled as she says, "One for Papa?," because she has no more coasters. She starts over and repeats the doling out of coasters, but ends up without any for Papa again. She starts over and when she gets to the last coaster in her hand she smiles as she places it on the table and says, "And one for Papa and Nana." Ah, she has solved the puzzle. She takes the coasters, puts them in a drawer, and closes it. "Bake 'em in the oven. Ooh, hot! All done!" Then she doles them all out again, doubling up on the last one again.

Ruana is experimenting with physical objects, her social world, symbolism (the round coasters being symbols for round cookies), imaginative play, the concept of numbers, and transformations. She is attempting to figure out what Piaget called "one-to-one" correspondence, knowing that one object when counted or manipulated can only have one corresponding number. While Ruana is not literally counting to five she wants to give five people "cookies" and there are only four coasters. Long before children are counting by reciting numbers or adding and subtracting, they are handling objects and forming ideas or schemes about the quantity of things in their world. Whether it is stones, Matchbox® cars, or cooked macaroni on a high chair tray, quantities of objects form children's mathematical thinking. Ruana apparently has watched raw cookie dough go into the oven in light tan clumps and come out flat, hot, and baked. The cookies were changed, transformed by the heat—a scientific process observed carefully by little eyes and taken into the brain to be played out later with these coasters.

Ruana also made an observation about **correspondence**; she formed a hypothesis about how to solve her problem of not having enough cookies to go around, and tested her hypothesis to see if her solution could be repeated. Both George Washington Carver and Ruana solved problems using the scientific method. Ruana does not know she is doing this, but scientists purposefully use this method to solve problems. The scientific method is the way scientists learn, by asking questions and trying to come up with the answers.

The scientific method involves:

1. making observations about a phenomenon: Crops grow better in some fields than others; there are not enough coasters to go around to everyone.

2. forming an hypothesis to explain the phenomenon: Previous plantings affect the health of subsequent crops; having two people share one coaster will make the coasters come out "even."

3. using the hypothesis to make predictions: If we plant soybeans in the field, then the next cotton crop planted there will be healthier; if I pass the coasters around again and have two people share a coaster, then everyone will have one.

4. testing the hypothesis: Plant soybeans and then cotton in some fields, just keep planting cotton year after year in others, and compare the results; try passing the coasters out again to see if doubling up people will allow the coasters to be passed out evenly.

How do teachers use the scientific method in their practice? No matter what the subject—science, mathematics, art, reading, or just watching children grow—the scientific method is used by observing, wondering, trying something, and watching for the results. It was used unconsciously by Ruana and it is used by all children and adults as they struggle with problems and seek solutions. The teacher, the scientist, and the mathematician use it in a conscious way to seek answers.

SCENARIO

Ms. Kumba is a first-year teacher in a second-grade class. She gets the class list and finds Kara Skellet on it. She is told by the principal that Kara is a child with Down syndrome. She has had experience in her student teaching with other kinds of developmental disabilities, but not this particular one. She and the children begin the first few days of school with activities

continued

correspondence–A clearly defined relationship between two members of a set, or different sets.

designed to learn more about the school in different ways: sketching the outside of the building, measuring the room by counting floor tiles, and taking an inventory of the various materials in the room. They collaborate on a map-making project of the classroom that places it in relation to the rest of the classrooms and to special areas like the gym, library, cafeteria, and emergency exits. She observes all the children as they work on these projects, especially Kara, to confirm her skill levels in counting, reading, writing, and speaking. From her observations she sees that Kara is very sociable and talkative, but has difficulty with reading, writing, and counting. She decides to capitalize on Kara's friendliness and plan appropriate social activities within her range of abilities in which she can take part. Ms. Kumba has used the scientific method to observe Kara and individualize the curriculum for her.

Mathematics, Science, and Technology in Education Today

This is an area where education reform has attempted to make changes. It seems like many people have ideas about what should be taught and how it should be taught, yet when children in the United States take standardized tests, it does not appear that they have learned. In 1997, the United States scored twelfth in fourth grade math assessment behind Singapore, Korea, and Japan in the first three places and other countries such as Czech Republic, Ireland, Hungary, and Australia (National Center for Education Statistics, 2001). This section explores some of the thinking about that.

Who's Afraid of Mathematics, Science, and Technology?

Mathematics, science, and technology are distinct bodies of knowledge, but they are interrelated and thus call for similar roles for the teacher. For this introductory text,

Figure 9–1

Girls are being encouraged to study science.

we will discuss them in parallel where they have corresponding concepts and examine distinctions of each discipline along the way. One of the ways in which they are similar is that some preservice teachers have an anxiety about their own learning and subsequent teaching of these areas, as reported by Unglaub (1997). Perhaps more than 10 percent have this anxiety; perhaps you do. This feeling may influence your preparation and thus propagate anxiety among your students. We encourage you to open your mind to the idea that these subjects are not *hard,* nor impossible for you to learn. Reforms in the last 20 years have resulted in a national emphasis on a more practical, applied, problem-solving approach that can do much to reduce students' anxiety and increase interest, involvement, and competency in mathematics, science, and technology (Figure 9–1). We will review some of these efforts and then look at the teacher's role in facilitating mathematics, science, and technology learning in the developing child.

Calls for Reform. National reports in the last 30 years have criticized education in the United States and called for reforms, especially in the areas of mathematics and science.

Reasons for Educational Reform

* Declining scores on nationwide tests and worldwide comparisons showing mastery levels in mathematics and science declining in the United States.
* Educational research about how children really learn.
* Societal needs for computational skills have decreased because of technology, but the need for problem-solving skills has increased.
* Issues of inequity.

  Research on girls' performance in mathematics and science shows lower interest and scores.

  Conclusive data show that children with special needs have been neglected in mathematics and science learning.

  Learning styles of races and cultures have not been addressed in teaching strategies.

  Research shows that children who have not been successful in mathematics or science in the past are forsaken.

One of the most attention-getting reports was *A Nation at Risk: The Imperatives for Educational Reform* (National Commission on Excellence in Education, 1983), which pointed out changes in the world of work and in society, and called for radical reforms in education to meet these changes. This was followed by the American Association for the Advancement of Science (AAAS) report *Science for All Americans* (1989), which focused on changes in the way science is taught and outlined a plan for the multi-step *Project 2061.* This called for a national consensus on the science content that all children should be learning, with benchmarks to sequence the learning along the way. The National Research Council also presented national curriculum standards in *National Science Education Standards: An Enhanced Sampler* (1993). All of these reports called for teachers to help students actively construct meaning in science through connections between problem solving and the environment.

The National Council of Teachers of Mathematics (NCTM) published corresponding standards and curricula for reform in teaching mathematics, *Principles and Standards for School Mathematics* (2000), which for the first time included preschool.

NCTM emphasized using mathematics for problem solving, communication, reasoning, and making connections to the real world. Technology was incorporated as an important tool for both mathematics and science, as exemplified in an important document by the Committee for Economic Development (1995), *Connecting Students to a Changing World: A Technology Strategy for Improving Mathematics and Science Education*. The unifying theme of these and most other plans for reform is the emphasis on learning activities that begin with concrete experiences before moving on to abstract concepts. Does that ring a bell? Isn't that what Piaget's stages of cognitive development are all about? This is what the constructivist theory of education espouses: "In the hand before it is in the head."

In 1994, Congress passed the Educate America Act (also known as Goals 2000), with goals of improved academic performance in all subjects, including mathematics and science. The specific objectives outlined for mathematics and science learning included teaching the metric system to more closely adhere to global standardization of measurements. Goals 2000 also included increasing the number of teachers with substantive background in mathematics and science by 50 percent, and increasing the number of students, especially women and minorities, who complete undergraduate and graduate degrees in mathematics, science, and engineering (Goals 2000, 1994). Worthy as these and the rest of the goals were, most of them were not achieved for a variety of reasons (see Chapter 3), but progress has been made and a national focus continues. Some researchers explain that "no coherent vision of *how to* educate today's children dominates United States educational practice in either science or mathematics" (emphasis ours) (Schmidt, McNight, & Raizen, 1997).

One strategy that Hurd (1997) says we are overlooking is assisted learning within the family and community (Figure 9–2). Children do not come to school as blank slates. They bring with them various amounts and kinds of knowledge, depending on their home environment. He points out that China and Japan have planned curricula for parents and grandparents to implement starting when the child is

Figure 9–2

Family involvement in homework pays off in higher academic skills.

twenty-eight to thirty months old. Goal 1 of Goals 2000 addresses school readiness, recognizing that the parent is the child's first teacher and that high-quality preschool programs can prepare the child for school. As a new teacher, remember to use the family as a resource and team member in the learning adventure.

Mathematics, Science, and Technology for Every Child

The National Council of Teachers of Mathematics repeats over and over that the goals are for *every child* to have mathematics education; this approach may be generalized not only to mathematics, but also to science or any other academic area.

> The National Council of Teachers of Mathematics states:
>
> "By *every child* we mean specifically
>
> * students who have been denied access in any way to educational opportunities as well as those who have not;
> * students who are African American, Hispanic, American Indian, and other minorities as well as those who are considered to be a part of the majority;
> * students who are female as well as those who are male; and
> * students who have not been successful in school and in mathematics as well as those who have been successful." (NCTM, 1991, pp. 4, 21, 72, 125).

Some children may need accommodations to fully participate in mathematics and science exploration. Children with visual disabilities may need accommodations such as magnifiers, materials written in large print, or alternative ways to communicate processes and findings other than by reading and writing, such as using tape recorders or computerized speech-recognition equipment. Children with hearing disabilities depend even more heavily on multisensory modes of receiving and expressing information and depend more on sight for instruction, directions, communicating their own results, and understanding the results of others. Physical accessibility to materials and equipment should not be a barrier to any child. Children with emotional disturbances may need extra confidence building as they explore mathematics and science concepts and work within a group. Children with exceptional cognitive abilities should be provided with the tools and freedom to extend their activities to a higher level, or perhaps be given responsibility for helping others understand concepts, and regularly allowed to lead explorations, both individually and in groups. Children with limited or no English-speaking skills can fully participate in science and mathematics explorations with graphics and manipulatives to both learn and communicate meaning.

When you begin to look at learning about mathematics, science, and technology not as memorization of facts and symbols, but as active, hands-on construction of knowledge, it becomes apparent that beginning early is more important than ever. The role of the teacher of very young children is to make connections between old and new information, and to help families see opportunities in everyday activities that build on children's curiosity and observation skills. Newsletter articles, take-home activities, and modeling these kinds of interactions are all strategies the teacher can use to encourage family participation in the early learning processes that enhance understanding of mathematics, science, and technology.

✳ THE DEVELOPMENT OF MATHEMATICAL AND SCIENTIFIC THINKING

SCENARIO   Gini learned the multiplication facts by memorizing:

$2 \times 1 = 2, 2 \times 2 = 4, 2 \times 3 = 6.$

Gini's children were presented with the following table and asked to search for patterns, experiment with the table, and draw conclusions. They were encouraged to find the relationship of one multiplication fact to the whole table of facts. Give it a try.

	1	2	3	4	5	6	7	8	9	10
1	1	2	3	4	5	6	7	8	9	10
2	2	4	6	8	10	12	14	16	18	20
3	3	6	9	12	15	18	21	24	27	30
4										
5										
6										
7										
8										
9										
10										

Theories of Learning and Teaching Mathematics and Science

When you examine the various philosophies and conjectures of how people learn, it is apparent that these philosophies have influenced how people teach.

Absorption Theory. Teaching mathematics and science has a behaviorist tradition that Baroody (1987) calls the *absorption theory*. Its psychological view of learning was association through memorization, with repeated reciting of facts. In this way, knowledge is accumulated in sequence, with uniform educational goals for everyone. This is the way Gini learned. This approach was resurrected by the Back to Basics movement of the late 1980s and early 1990s out of great concern for low and declining test scores across the country. This educational design has been opposed by those reformers who espouse the cognitive theory of learning; that is, finding relationships of the parts to the whole, and active construction of knowledge and recognizing the changes in thinking that take place as children develop. This is how Gini's children learned. The philosophical controversy over an "optimum learning process" continues today, with no national curriculum or consensus on what is the best way to teach and learn.

For those visual learners among you, perhaps this diagram will help illustrate the dichotomy between these philosophies (Figure 9–3, adapted from Chaille & Britain, 1997).

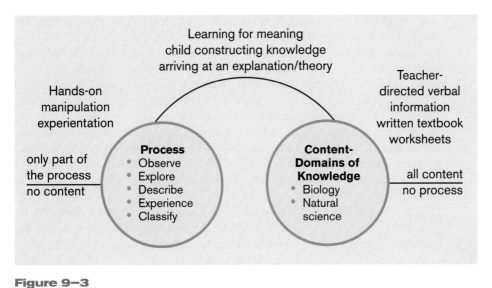

Figure 9–3

Learning for meaning. (Adapted from Chaille & Britain, 1997).

Social Cognition. You will look at the role of mathematics and science teachers together because the basic concepts and approaches to teaching them are very similar. Looking back at what you learned about Piaget's and Vygotsky's theories of cognitive development, mathematics and science knowledge is constructed by the child through experiences with the real world. It begins with sensory explorations of the properties of objects: smooth/rough, warm/cold, round/square, single/many. Through encounters with objects, the child builds knowledge in those three areas Piaget describes as **physical knowledge, logico-mathematical knowledge**, and **social cognition**. With every encounter, the brain either attempts to make a match (association), take in additional information (assimilation), or is in a mental dilemma (**disequilibrium**), when things just do not seem right. These processes, which take place thousands of times a day, collect data and become the basis for additional learning. Kamii (1985), who has studied Piaget's teachings and young children's inventing of arithmetic says, "Number concepts cannot be taught. While this may be bad news for educators, the good news is that number does not have to be taught, as a child constructs it from within, out of his own natural ability to think. Addition does not have to be taught either. The very construction of number involves the repeated addition of '1'" (p. 25). This does not mean that the adult does not have a role, but it does mean that her role is to provide materials and ask questions—not to test knowledge—and to ascertain how the child perceives the objects or problem.

physical knowledge–External, observable features or behaviors of objects, such as color, size, shape, what will happen when the object is dropped.

logico-mathematical knowledge–The internal mental relationships formed about quantity, volume, and relationships such as same/different, more/less.

social cognition–Acceptable social behavior.

disequilibrium–The situation when new information or knowledge is in conflict with present information or knowledge.

Lev Vygotsky

You were also introduced to Vygotsky in Chapter 6 regarding his cognitive development theories and the importance of adult support. In language development and in the formation of mathematical and scientific concepts, Vygotsky's ideas are important ones to understand.

Vygotsky and his adherents remind us of the adult's role in helping the child along by prompting and providing the language for the concepts. Vygotsky recognized the informal knowledge that children gain from hands-on everyday experiences, but he emphasized the importance of adult instruction in procedural knowledge necessary for learning numerical symbols and simple equations. Counting begins as a social interaction between adults and children, supported by adults who model rote counting as a cultural practice. Young children imitate these words without grasping the real meaning they signify. When asked, "How many do you have?" young children do not understand that the answer can be obtained by actually counting objects. They will often give answers like, "All of them," or "Lots." The adult might then continue to scaffold the counting process by pointing to the objects and saying, "One, two, . . . ?" and the child will brighten and say, "Three." Does the child yet have the concept of the quantity of three? Does the child know that if she started counting at the other end of the line, the last number would still be three? Does the child know that if she removed one there would then be only two? It is likely that she does not make the connection.

SCENARIO

Quico's mother is climbing the stairs with him in her arms. She says, "Uno, dos, tres, cuatro, cinco."

Martha's sister says, "Mom, she's got four and I've got three. She's got more than me."

Martha's mother says, "But you have three bigger ones."

Cognitively Guided Instruction. Cognitively Guided Instruction (CGI) (Fennema et al., 1996), is an approach to teaching mathematics developed and researched at the University of Wisconsin. It applies the concepts of problem solving as the primary focus of instruction, with skills based on understanding that the child should develop and explain her own mathematical thinking. It has been effectively implemented and researched on children in kindergarten through third grade. CGI begins with the teacher's knowledge of the child and the ways that children think.

Meaning is constructed by connecting new information with what has already been learned. The greater the variety of connections made, the more opportunities for deeper meaning. Constructing meaning moves from concrete, tangible, sensory experiences to the ability to understand and manipulate symbols mentally. That manipulation of tangibles and abstract concepts needs to be practiced in many contexts to be fully understood. The process is aided by communicating observations to others and receiving feedback about the learning. The learner's own expectations are a significant factor as well. If she expects she cannot learn mathematics or science, then she probably will not, at least not without some major change in attitude. Mathematics, science, and technology literacy requires an acquaintance with the physical world that uses multiple experiences, making connections and having them reinforced by further experiences, as well as feedback from others, and being surrounded with encouragement and the freedom to explore, make mistakes, and try again.

The Problem-Solving Method. The education reform movements all call for the new teacher to have a broader and deeper knowledge of mathematics and science. This does not mean just memorizing facts and formulas, but rather having an understanding of the concepts and the new pedagogy of learning through experiences and problem solving to help your students use strategies of discovery and problem solving. Hiebert et al. (1997) have been studying various ways of teaching mathematics for years; they emphasize problem solving through reflection on experiences, communicating through social interactions, and forming new relationships and connections with prior knowledge (Figure 9–4).

Listen to a statement from *Everybody Counts: A Report to the Nation on the Future of Mathematical Education* (National Research Council, 1989) that encouraged understanding mathematics.

> "Mathematics reveals hidden patterns that help us understand the world around us. . . . Mathematics is a science of pattern and order. . . . Its domain is . . . numbers, chance, form, algorithms, and change. . . . Mathematics relies on logic rather than on observation as its standard of truth; yet employs observation, simulation, and even experimentation as means of discovering truth" (p. 31).

Science depends on mathematics and technology for the tools to analyze data and science provides mathematics with problems to investigate. Chaille and Britain (1997) describe the main themes of inquiry learning in science as: "How can I make it move?" (physics), "How can I make it change?" (chemistry), and "How does it fit or how do I fit?" (biology). Science is an examination of patterns and relationships using logic and creativity. These same characteristics apply to mathematics and technology. Can you see where mathematics and science converge? The student is best served in any subject, including mathematics and science, by learning how to find an answer rather than being required to recite the right answers at the right time. In the fast-changing twenty-first century, teachers who can teach children to follow their own quest for answers through reasoning, problem solving, and finding patterns will indeed be preparing those children

Figure 9–4

Experimentation results in discovering knowledge rather than learning by rote.

for the future. You can begin to see the interconnectedness of what once were known as "subjects" being integrated into learning to listen, observe, reflect, communicate, collaborate, self-correct, and know. Hopefully, these reforms have taken place in your institution of teacher preparation so you will be "taught as you will teach." Research tells us, "Teachers are essentially teaching the same way they were taught in school" (Stigler & Hiebert, 1997), so the way to reform mathematics and science learning is to change the way you learn to be a teacher.

Technology

We have used the word technology several times. As you read it, what visual image did you have? Perhaps it was a computer, and while the computer is probably the most radical technological invention of our time, you need to take a broader view of technology. Technology is the application of knowledge toward useful ends, such as inventing and using tools. The nomad hunters' and gatherers' technologies were spears and sharp stones. The technologies of early agrarian societies were hand-powered farm implements like shovels, hoes, and spades. The technology of the early mathematician was the abacus, and twentieth-century engineers had the slide rule. Scientists have test tubes, Bunsen burners, Petri dishes, and specimen books. But now, from toddlers to mathematicians, scientists, songwriters, and everyone in between, technology is the computer. This contemporary electronic device controls, manipulates, and stores information for a great many scientific and learning tasks. Almost every occupation has such technology, and information technology of all kinds is available to almost every household, from remote controls to computer systems.

Seymour Papert has done some amazing work with children and computers, actually teaching programming language to children. He is a mathematician who studied with Piaget and has contributed to knowledge about artificial intelligence. His thinking has influenced education by exploring how computers can change learning. His book, *Mindstorms: Children, Computers and Powerful Ideas* (1980) was one of the first to consider how children could use computers to learn.

Seymour Papert

(1928–) Papert was born and educated in South Africa, where he was an activist in the anti-apartheid movement. He is a mathematician and one of the early pioneers of artificial intelligence at MIT.

Computers and calculators have changed the way higher-level computational skills are taught. Certainly, we should not give up teaching addition, subtraction, and more advanced skills, but much more complex computations are routinely done with calculators rather than by hand and head. The calculator can be used as a teaching tool as well, helping children to see relationships among numbers, and to better understand place value. Technology has changed what we are able to teach, opening worlds through both sophisticated but inexpensive calculators and computers with Internet access. Learning to use and teach the use of the tools of mathematics and science, and learning to use technologies, including microscopes, telescopes, calculators, and computers, are also part of the teacher's role (Figure 9–5).

Educational reformers also worry that we are not training enough people to understand the basic mathematics and science concepts involved in how our technological devices work, nor how to improve them and create new ones (Committee for Economic Development, 1995). Technology is integrated here in the mathematics and science chapter just as it should be integrated into all curricula, not as a discrete subject but as a tool for learning.

Funding from state budget allocations and private foundation grants for technology (computers, Internet service, printers, and scanners) has made these technological tools available in many schools. Teachers must be knowledgeable in these tools' use and help children to use them wisely.

Figure 9–5

Computers and technology should be tools for learning, not replacements.

WORDS OF WISDOM Debra DeClercq, a kindergarten teacher in Edmonton, Canada, has these words about the use of computers in the classroom.

"I had some teachable moments in my kindergarten classes with the use of technology. A topic of interest would come up in a class discussion and the children and I would check the Internet for answers to our question. The vastness of information and the idea of lifelong curiosity and learning were concepts I wished to share with my students. However, the children would have benefited more from the presence of a classroom aide. When it comes to spending money on education, another adult in the classroom outweighs almost any other resource. This extra adult ensures that more children's needs are met and brings a higher degree of safety into the early childhood classroom."

Learning Mathematics, Science, and Technology—Where and What

Remember Piaget's stages of cognitive development in the context of mathematics and science concepts. Since we are using the developmental or constructivist approach to teaching, the foundation of mathematics and science learning will be formed within the child's developmental stages. What the child is able to do physically, cognitively, socially, and linguistically will enter into the active learning process; therefore, all development affects learning.

The Environment for Exploration. The first role of the teacher is to provide an environment for learning. In the fields of mathematics, science, and technology, this begins with providing psychological safety to try out ideas, collaborate with and challenge others, and make mistakes and explain thinking without the risk of feeling like a failure or being ridiculed. The environment should also include blocks of time for attention, absorbed concentration on a task, reflection, the refinement of ideas and theories, and communication to take place. These intervals represent opportunities for learning; they may be measured in minutes, hours, days, or even weeks (when projects are complex).

The pieces of equipment in the classroom are the tools by which exploration can take place. There should be materials that children can use independently and without hazard, allowing for ways to physically represent the problem or experiment they are working on. "Meaning is developed for tools and meaning is developed with tools and both result from actually using tools" (Hiebert et al., 1997).

Objects, activities, and places in the child's world make the best curriculum for constructing mathematical and scientific principles and applications, and for using existing technology to measure, communicate, and create. All kinds of elaborate pieces of equipment and materials can be purchased, but resourceful teachers find that garage sales, families, and nature can provide what is needed at little or no cost.

SCENARIO   Ms. LaBarre's goal is to teach about condensation and evaporation. She has a photograph of a glass of water with beads of water on the outside. She poses the question, "Where did this water come from? Where will it go over time? What is the temperature difference between the inside of the glass and the outside of the glass?"

Ms. LaBarre is presenting a problem-oriented lesson. Using the constructivist model, can you think of other ways to present this lesson? What equipment would you need? What would you provide so the students could not only test their theories but also explain them to others? Van de Walle (1998) suggests some strategies: Create the environment, pose worthwhile tasks, use cooperative learning groups, use models and provide tools, encourage discussion and writing, require justification of responses, and listen actively (p. 34).

Depending on the children's age, equipment for mathematics and science exploration in a classroom might include:

* Plexiglas®: tubs, small sheets, one large sheet
* tubing, plastic
* containers
* sand/water
* blocks—unit wooden blocks, Unix Blocks®, square wooden blocks (hundreds of them)
* Legos®, Tinkertoys®
* pulleys and hooks
* gears
* balls of varying sizes, densities, and surface materials
* art and writing materials and supplies

✳   magnifying tools

✳   puzzles

✳   games with dice, spinners, matching objects

✳   toys that match numerals, objects, sequence

Adapted from (Chaille & Britain, 1997)

Activities that Construct Knowledge. The mathematics and science curriculum comprises objects on which children can act by producing movement, varying those actions to see the reactions. Learning actually takes place when the change in the object can be observed and measured by the child. The younger the child, the more immediate the reaction or result of an action needs to be. For example, when planting a seed, it takes a *long* time to see a reaction, so such an activity is better suited for older primary and elementary age children.

The following is an example of how mathematics, science, and technology can be integrated into the curriculum with all the other learning areas. This is the *web method* of planning curriculum. In the first step, the teacher asks the children questions to determine what they already know (Figure 9–6 on page 320). This also helps the children focus their thinking on what they know. A plan is then made to address how to learn more through parental involvement, integrating sensory experiences, and using different content areas of language arts, dramatic play, graphic arts, social studies, mathematics, and science (Figure 9–7 on page 321)

An activity appropriate for every age that can be integrated with mathematics and science is reading books. Books for every age level incorporate counting, number, and science concepts, and inspire a sense of wonder. There are also many computer programs for both mathematics and science that can be previewed and incorporated in the curriculum at the proper stage and conceptual level.

Chaille and Britain (1997) pose this question: "Where does the curriculum come from: or, whose question is it?" Some typical activities and opportunities are included in each of these chapters of this book so you can begin to see the kinds of work teachers do. Selecting what, when, and how will be a career-long process.

Using everything around you for observation and problems related to mathematics and science makes the world your laboratory. The classroom can be filled with objects to observe, measure, sort, and classify, and to use as problems and solutions. The students themselves also present opportunities for observation, quantification and experimentation. By observing similarities and differences in objects, by exploring *how* they are different and possible reasons why you can build a curriculum foundation that will fill a whole year or more of learning.

The neighborhood provides opportunities for mathematics in measuring, mapping, and quantifying, as well as a science field site for air, water, animal life, soil samples, growing plants, and businesses that offer opportunities to see raw materials transformed into usable products and services.

✳ DEVELOPMENT AND CURRICULUM IN MATHEMATICS, SCIENCE, AND TECHNOLOGY

Exploring the world around us begins as soon as we are born. As we gaze into the eyes of our adoring family or feel the blanket tightly wrapped around us, as we see the lights moving about the room casting shadows, or hear loud and soft sounds and

Figure 9—6

Curriculum web about dirt.

voices, or the sounds of machinery and rhythms of our own heartbeat, we are integrating experiences and learning concepts. This is the beginning of a lifelong adventure making sense of same and different, and the properties of things and how we can
move them and make them work for us. As we have said before, the concepts of mathematics, science, and technology are not collections of dry facts to memorize, but a
vast world to explore and make sense of. When the teacher approaches these subjects
with wonder, her attitude and expectation influence the students.

Infant Mathematics, Science, and Technology: Development and Curriculum

Even very young children have been found to recognize and pay attention to changes
in quantity.

Curriculum Web to Explore Topics

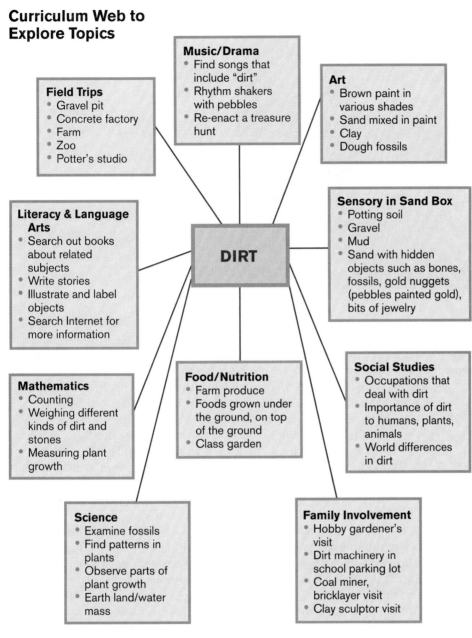

Music/Drama
- Find songs that include "dirt"
- Rhythm shakers with pebbles
- Re-enact a treasure hunt

Field Trips
- Gravel pit
- Concrete factory
- Farm
- Zoo
- Potter's studio

Art
- Brown paint in various shades
- Sand mixed in paint
- Clay
- Dough fossils

Literacy & Language Arts
- Search out books about related subjects
- Write stories
- Illustrate and label objects
- Search Internet for more information

DIRT

Sensory in Sand Box
- Potting soil
- Gravel
- Mud
- Sand with hidden objects such as bones, fossils, gold nuggets (pebbles painted gold), bits of jewelry

Mathematics
- Counting
- Weighing different kinds of dirt and stones
- Measuring plant growth

Food/Nutrition
- Farm produce
- Foods grown under the ground, on top of the ground
- Class garden

Social Studies
- Occupations that deal with dirt
- Importance of dirt to humans, plants, animals
- World differences in dirt

Science
- Examine fossils
- Find patterns in plants
- Observe parts of plant growth
- Earth land/water mass

Family Involvement
- Hobby gardener's visit
- Dirt machinery in school parking lot
- Coal miner, bricklayer visit
- Clay sculptor visit

Figure 9–7

Planning web about dirt.

SCENARIO   Desiree, six months old, and her mother are looking at an animal book. Mother shows her a picture of three rabbits and says, "Three bunnies." Desiree looks with interest. Mother then shows her a picture of three dogs and says, "Three puppies." Desiree looks with interest. Mother then shows her a picture of three kittens and says, "Three kittens." Desiree does not pay attention to the picture. Mother then shows her a picture of four rabbits and says, "Four bunnies." Desiree looks back with interest.

Figure 9–8

Playing with a ball begins a knowledge base about things that are round.

Infant Development in Mathematics, Science, and Technology. In an amazing research project, infants as young as six months old were shown to react to the novel stimulus of pictures of four objects after having been presented with pictures of three similar objects (Starkey & Cooper, 1980). The infants were, of course, not counting, but already displayed a cognitive function that allowed them to differentiate between small sets of objects.

In the sensorimotor stage described by **Piaget** (birth to two years old), the infant moves from reflexive actions to more deliberate ones, using all senses to take in information about all that comes within sight, hearing, or grasp. **Object permanence**, the realization that objects exist even when outside of view, leads the child to the foundation of mathematical and scientific thinking and forming mental symbols. The child thinks, imitates, and begins to use words as symbols for such environmental components as "mama," "dada," "ball," and "dog." Technology skills are developing when an infant uses a spoon to make noise and to feed herself. During this stage, the child is gaining skills in labeling, that part of social/conventional knowledge that is culturally determined, learning the words for objects in her world. The child's logico-mathematical knowledge is beginning to expand with **classification**, making connections between groups of like things.

The child looks at the moon and says, "Ball," looks at an apple and says, "Ball," and looks at her grandpa's head and says, "Ball." The child is using the beginning of the scientific process of observing, comparing, and classifying (Figure 9–8). She is **overgeneralizing**, or placing all objects with a similar attribute in the same class. As she gains the vocabulary for other round objects, her classifications will broaden and differentiate. She will begin rote counting, repeating the numbers she has heard—"One, two, three"—with no concept yet of quantity.

Jean Piaget

You were introduced to Piaget in Chapter 6 on cognitive development. In this chapter, his theories of the development of logico-mathematical concepts are important so we reintroduce you to him here.

object permanence—The cognitive concept that objects have substance external to yourself and that they continue to exist when out of sight.

classification—Arranging similar objects or mentally matching similar ideas into groups.

overgeneralizing—Classifying objects or concepts into a group using only one attribute.

Families and teachers set the stage for experimentation. They provide a safe environment and physical supports for the infant to try things such as batting their hands at a crib toy or trying to crawl. The child learns to attempt new experiences or work toward new outcomes through trial and error. As successes come, the new conclusions are tested to see if they are correct. The scientific method as used in infancy is to observe, wonder, try, and draw conclusions. Future explorers, scientists, mathematicians, and teachers grow out of the freedom to try in an open environment.

> **SCENARIO** Pierra is playing in a tub of water. An adult (family member or teacher) holds the funnel while Pierra pours water in and watches it come out. The adult puts a finger over the hole and Pierra watches the water stop and then watches it come out again when the finger is removed. She plugs the hole with her own finger and watches the water stop and flow again. She is observing, hypothesizing ("If a finger is in the hole the water stops, but it flows out again when the finger is removed"), experimenting, and observing results.

Infant Curriculum for Mathematics, Science, and Technology. The teacher's role is to provide an interactive environment and naturalistic interactions as the child increasingly explores her world. The language of labeling and understanding properties begins with cognitive structures for actual manipulation. "See the red ball. And here's a red car driving up your arm," could be the child's introduction to the concept of the color red. It is connected with objects to feel, body sensations, and a warm exchange with the adult. Once the infant can manipulate objects at will, the teacher should provide various colors, shapes, textures, weights, and kinds of objects for sensory exploration.

"Peek A Boo" is an instinctive game that adults play with infants. What cognitive scheme is this building? You are right: object permanence. While the game is fun for the infant and you, you are building the visual image, hiding it behind the cloth or blanket, and making it appear again. Magic! When the infant grabs for the blanket to pull it away, you know she has a mental image of what is behind it, even when she can't see it. Observation, assessment, interaction, and assessment again; then evaluation and curriculum planning. That's what teachers of infants do. Other activities include providing materials the infant can act upon and move, like balls, vehicles, and toys that reward the action with a noise like a bell ringing or an electronic beep.

Toddler Mathematics, Science, and Technology: Development and Curriculum

No explorer is more inquisitive about the world than the toddler. Newfound freedom, language, and an inner quest to conquer drives the toddler to add to her knowledge about everything in the environment and how those things relate to each other. That's the toddler theme in mathematics, science, and technology.

Toddler Development in Mathematics, Science, and Technology. Now the toddler is entering Piaget's preoperational period and has many more words for round objects. She is differentiating among apples, peaches, oranges, grandpa's head, marshmallows, which are good to eat, and golf balls and snowballs, which are not. This knowledge is acquired in a naturalistic way by the infant using her senses and associating with prior knowledge. Interaction with adults clarifies many of the *mistakes* (not really mistakes but judgments made with limited

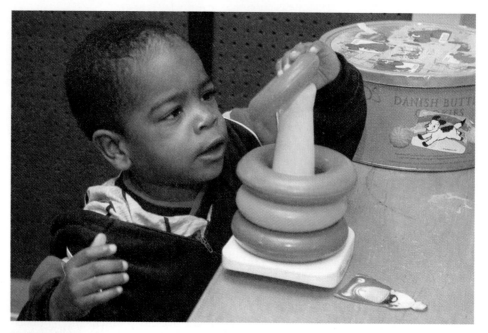

Figure 9—9

Toddlers are making connections between the similarities and differences of objects.

knowledge and experience) toddlers make. Adults say, "Yes, it's round like a ball, but it's an apple. Let's try a piece. Mmm!" or "Yes, this looks like an apple, but it's a pear. It's round like an apple, but it's more pointed on one end. Let's try a piece." "This is white and round like a marshmallow but it's a golf ball. It's hard. We can't eat it." This is the kind of spontaneous teaching that confirms certain classes or concepts of objects the child has associated with prior learning, while at the same time pointing out differences in the properties that differentiate this item from others.

The concepts of big and small take on new meanings, with big cookies being more desirable than small ones, unless there are two small ones or a big one broken up into pieces: they seem like more to the toddler. This judging of quantity or mass is by appearance rather than by counting. The concept of **conservation** has not yet developed.

The toddler may be able to repeat or recite the numbers of counting, "One, two, three, four, five," but may not yet be able to count objects accurately using one-to-one correspondence. Matching and sorting become consuming activities (Figure 9–9). The toddler begins to notice color first by matching and then by separating one color from another, then by responding to "Find the red one," and eventually to accurately naming colors of objects. The same is true for the progression of recognizing shapes and alphabet letters.

Counting is a big task of the toddler years, joining the activities of language development and recitation of a cultural practice. The first step is saying or rehearsing the number words (as mentioned earlier); then when the child has the idea that those words have a relationship to objects, the child will count while simultaneously touching each object. At this stage, they are two separate cognitive activities that may or may not synchronize and yield the "correct" answer. When the child has attained the

conservation—Understanding that the quantity or volume of an object or substance remains the same even though its appearance has been altered in shape or arrangement.

one-to-one correspondence idea, she will touch each object as she says the number, later just pointing to the objects, and eventually just mentally counting the objects. This task is easier when the objects are in a row; it becomes more difficult if they are arranged in a circle or are in a random pattern.

The toddler's world has expanded with her ability to walk and climb, and now her exploration of and experimentation with the world around her has broadened. With language to describe and try to put order to the many new objects in her environment, the toddler begins to form mathematics and science concepts. Inborn curiosity leads the active toddler to explore tangible properties such as size, weight, and shape. The child piles things up and knocks them down, fills and empties, and collects and organizes those actions and reactions.

Toddler Curriculum for Mathematics, Science, and Technology. The toddler is on the move, so the adult should provide objects that can be safely moved, filled, or dumped to provide experience with such concepts as empty and full, heavy and light, always accompanied by a dialogue describing the objects, actions, results, and accomplishments. "You put all the washcloths in the basket, the blue ones and the white ones and the red ones, then you tipped it over and they all fell out! Now you're picking them up and putting them in the basket again. One, two, three . . ."

Meaningful activities involve moving objects such as balls, boxes, and blocks, that include larger and heavier objects, smaller and lighter ones, and things that sink and things that float. Toddlers need containers for sorting, classifying, and dumping things out. They need quantity and variety, and some kind of system to put order to the objects, like shelves, baskets, or containers in which to keep them.

Planned science and mathematics activities are not appropriate for this age, but again that assessment, curriculum, assessment cycle comes into play. The teacher observes what the toddler is able to do and is interested in, provides the materials, equipment, and descriptive language about the objects and actions, and then assesses what actions the child takes. Then the teacher extends the activity by providing a similar but different kind of material or demonstrating another way to use the object. Learning is like a spiral that comes around and around, but rises a little higher each time.

Computer manufacturers are producing child-friendly keyboards and software that appeal to very young children, even toddlers. Even though families are eagerly purchasing them, and urging child care centers to offer computer work as part of the curriculum, child development experts such as Elkind (1998) and Hohman (1998) and computer researcher Haugland (1992) do not recommend computer usage for children under three years of age. Children of this age are still learning through their senses and activity and the computer provides neither.

Preschooler Mathematics, Science, and Technology: Development and Curriculum

Another way mathematics and science are similar is their interdependence on process skills for arithmetic comparing, classifying, and measuring to solve science problems such as observing, communicating, inferring, hypothesizing, and defining variables. The older child now looks at those round objects mentioned earlier and can recognize that they are all round but the pear has a pointed end; and while the apple, pear, and marshmallow are all round and in the food category, the golf ball is not. As the child experiences more of the natural world, she knows that apples and pears grow on trees, while marshmallows come in a package. She may observe the change in the marshmallow over a campfire while the apple or pear, when cooked, may change in a different way. She may then hypothesize why this is and wonder what the marshmallow is made from and how it is made.

Figure 9–10

Preschoolers are beginning to duplicate the patterns they see all around them.

Preschooler Development in Mathematics, Science, and Technology. Without basic knowledge of how the world works, much of science and the patterns of mathematics seem like trickery or magic to the three-, four-, and five-year-old. Moving metal objects with magnets is fun, but the child has no concept of the reason for this power. Preschoolers rub balloons on their hair and stick them on the wall, where they stay, without knowing why this is so. They see water flow from one container to another through a tube, but do not know the pull of gravity is behind it. They see balls of clay made from one big ball, then transformed from several small ones into a big one again, without the concept of volume. They watch the puddle disappear, or the snow melt, or the vacuum cleaner suck up dust without knowing why. It is all *magic* at this age. The role of the teacher is to encourage the magic by planning such experiences and drawing attention to the changes taking place, helping the child be a better observer. The teacher may ask, "Why do you think this is happening?" The teacher should encourage the child to try new and different experiences and help the child accept and organize new information. Those are the kinds of *kid wisdom* that make for wonderful bulletin board postings because the thinking is so fresh, so creative.

Fully into the preoperational stage, three-year-old preschoolers are refining concepts of color, shape, and alphabet letter recognition. They are now sorting objects by their own rules: "These are all yellow," or "These are all round," or "These are light and these are heavy." They are beginning to arrange objects in some kind of order by length, size, or color shade in a process called **seriation** (Figure 9–10). The rules or criteria for arrangement become more complex as their thinking develops.

seriation—Placing objects in order according to some criterion such as size or weight.

Figure 9–11

Montessori materials are designed for learning about specific concepts.

Montessori materials are excellent examples of equipment designed to form cognitive structures. For example, Montessori classrooms have peg sorters with pegs of the same color and diameter but varying heights that are designed to be placed in holes that only allow them to be arranged in height order. This sort of activity helps correlate eye-hand coordination with the concept of sorting by height. These materials are **self correcting** since they are used by the child independently, but will only function when manipulated in the correct sequence or position. The Montessori teacher may initially demonstrate the material. When the child begins to play with the pegs in a random way, initially only trying to insert them into the holes, trial and error leads to closer observation of the importance of color or diameter to the activity's success. This is all without an adult intervening, showing the right way, or giving directions. It is discovery learning, Montessori-style (Figure 9–11).

Counting is refined in the preschool years as the child expands the amount of numbers she can recite. Counting into the teens, 20s, and 30s poses challenges that may take years to perfect. During this time, children are also mastering the concepts of ordinal numbers, which signify position (such as first, last, and middle), and measurement. They do not see the importance of measuring ingredients for a recipe by full measuring cups (just by the number of dips), or starting the measuring tape close to the edge. They also are learning that numbers are sometimes used as identifiers that do not mean quantity, such as house or phone numbers. So much to learn!

Preschoolers begin to understand the concept of time in relation to today, yesterday, and tomorrow. By five years of age, they recognize that the days of the week

self correcting–Educational materials that can only fit together in one way or that give an immediate response as to whether the child is using them in the right or wrong way.

have a pattern and attached meaning like "Saturday is cartoon day" or "Monday we swim at school." However, the concepts of the calendar, maps, globe, solar system, inches, feet, and miles are too abstract for preschoolers. These concepts are representational, and until children move into the next level of cognitive development, most only repeat back numbers, places on a map, days of the week, or names of the planets without true understanding. Teaching for meaning and understanding places the educational value of these activities in question.

Preschooler Curriculum for Mathematics, Science, and Technology.

Naturalistic interactions with the environment are spontaneous for the preschooler. They love to collect, count, sort, arrange, and explore inside and out. The teacher's role is to plan activity centers around materials for play, manipulation, arranging, and rearranging (Figure 9–12). These are called *open-ended materials*. There is no wrong way to play with them (as long as the child does not hurt herself, another child, or the environment). Informal learning experiences come from the child's expressed interest in naturalistic experience. The teacher should observe and use that interest to help the child move to the next level of exploration. This is the zone of proximal development.

Baroody (2000), in his review of preschoolers and mathematics research findings, suggests that early mathematics learning experiences foster mathematical power that has three components. The first is a positive disposition to learn mathematics, that old "can do" attitude where teachers boost confidence with their belief that everyone can understand and use mathematics. The second aspect of mathematical power is showing children that the symbols of mathematics can be used to solve relevant problems like how to divide the snack equally, or provide for five more visitors to the classroom, and to see the why and how of mathematical equations. The third part of mathematical power is the ability to use mathematical inquiry in problem solving and reasoning, and communicating about mathematical principles. Using this approach, the curriculum becomes not just rote learning and memorized feedback of math facts, but posing and solving interesting problems through discussion and coming to an

Figure 9–12

Open ended materials are for arranging and rearranging.

understanding of how the solution is found. This is consistent with the recommendations of the National Council of Teachers of Mathematics (1991, 2000).

Counting, counting, counting is the theme Thompson (1997) recommends: counting in sequence using the word system with all its irregularities, counting for oral and mental calculation; counting for one-to-one correspondence; and counting to measure, indicate position and recognize numbers that are not quantities. Children can be provided with practical addition and subtraction experiences related to supplies, food, and the number of children who can comfortably play in a certain area.

Preschool children begin to play games with each other. Kamii & DeVries (1980) studied these group games in relation to Piaget's theory and saw them as one of the primary ways that preoperational children gain autonomy, define physical skills, and learn to cooperate and be less egocentric. Group games help preschoolers develop socially and morally, and form arithmetical concepts. These group games include racing, chasing, hiding, guessing and games involving verbal commands (p. 35).

SCENARIO	The child turns over a piece of cardboard on the playground and sees all kinds of bugs underneath: "Oh, look at this." The teacher gets a container and helps the child collect several kinds of crawling creatures. They take them inside and she shows the child a reference book with pictures and descriptions of all kinds of insects. "Here, Shanise, see if you can find any that look like those in the jar. Then we will write down the names on this label for the jar." The teacher decides this would be an ideal time to bring out an insect puzzle and some concentration cards with insect pictures to match, and to teach the children a song about insects.

These are structured learning experiences that are also based on the children's interest. Taylor (1993) suggests some general themes for structured activities for young children, such as air, animals, body, clothing, color, community, family, food, health, machines, numbers, plants, senses, shape, size, transportation, water, and weather. By planning curriculum themes based on general concepts, the teacher begins with topics familiar to the children, ones about which they already have first-hand knowledge on which to build.

Computers in preschool classrooms, just as any other equipment, can be used either appropriately or inappropriately based on environmental planning such as where to place the computers and the number of chairs at each one, and the teacher's efforts to introduce, facilitate, monitor, intervene, and extend. Clements (1999) reviews the research to allay early concerns that computers will isolate children. Verbal interaction, social rather than isolated usage, spontaneous peer teaching, software that facilitates collaboration, interactions increased by computers placed side by side, and two seats in front of the computer, all point to positive outcomes. After preparing the environment, selecting the appropriate software is the next important consideration. Haugland and Wright (1997) have developed a scale by which teachers can evaluate software. Haugland's earlier research (1992) indicated that appropriate computer usage in the preschool classroom can result in gains in intelligence, nonverbal and verbal skills, structural knowledge, long-term memory, manual dexterity, and problem-solving, abstraction, and conceptual skills. How computers are used in the classroom is the primary consideration in their effectiveness as a learning tool. Software and Web sites must be carefully selected to meet the children's developmental levels and then integrated into the curriculum.

Primary Age Mathematics, Science, and Technology: Development and Curriculum

Formal schooling should not relegate mathematics, science, and technology to segments in the day and chapters in a book, ending exploration of these areas. While curriculum themes and academic standards may be mandated, delivery of the material is usually at the teacher's discretion. When taking the child's development and natural inquisitiveness into consideration, these subjects can be exciting, rewarding, and yield academic success when woven with high-energy activities.

Primary Age Development in Mathematics, Science, and Technology. There is no magical transformation of thinking once a child enters the primary grades. In the early grades, while still in the preoperational stage, children are concrete learners who need to relate physical properties to concepts. This means that early grades should have mathematics manipulatives in abundance. Pattern blocks, unit blocks, and Cuisenaire® rods (Figure 9–13) are often used as concrete representations of relationships. The relative sizes of the rods and blocks are in even multiples, with the Cuisenaire rods as base 10 and unit blocks as equal multiples of each other. Cuisenaire rods are different colors, in lengths ranging from 1 to 10 inches, and can be combined to make a 10-inch unit.

Children can match 10 ones to make 10, or a two and an eight, or a three and a seven, or a combination of three or more rods to make 10. Informally or with instruction, children can manipulate the rods to see and feel the multiples of one that can make 10.

Unit blocks work in much the same way, but are not colored and are usually wooden, with the basic unit approximately 2″ × 3″ by 6″. They take the shape of equal multiples: a square that is one-half a unit, a double, a quadruple, a triangle, arches, etc. As children build with unit blocks, they are informally constructing knowledge

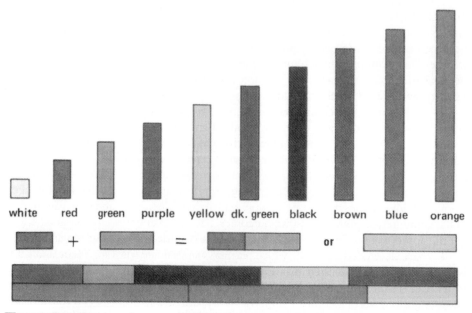

white   red   green   purple   yellow   dk. green   black   brown   blue   orange

Figure 9–13

Cuisenaire® rods. (Printed by permission from ETA/Cuisenaire®, Vernon Hills, IL)

about quantity, space, patterns, and balance, and representing mental images by symbolic objects. They will say, "This is a barn; here's the door and here's the fence" (Figure 9–14). Accessories added to blocks, such as boards for ramps; balls; marbles; play people; paper, markers, and tape for signs; fabrics for textures; and books for ideas about buildings integrate the mathematics, science, social, creative, language, and literacy aspects of block play/work.

	Name	Nursery	Kgn. & Primary
	Square	40	80
	Unit	96	192
	Double Unit	48	96
	Quadruple Unit	16	32
	Pillar	24	48
	Half Pillar	24	48
	Small Triangle	24	48
	Large Triangle	24	48
	Small Column	16	32
	Large Column	8	16
	Ramp	16	32
	Ellipse		8
	Curve	8	16
	1/4 Circle		8
	Large Switch & Gothic Door		4
	Small Switch		4
	Large Buttress		4
	1/2 Arch & Small Buttress		4
	Arch & 1/2 Circle		4
	Roofboard		24
	Number of Shapes	12	23
	Number of Pieces	344	760

Figure 9–14

Unit blocks.

Figure 9–15

Math manipulatives like Unifix® blocks teach concrete concepts.

Unifix® cubes are small plastic blocks of various colors that snap together to lend a physical dimension to counting and comparing quantity and sets. These are an example of a discrete model for counting with each block representing one, as compared to Cuisenaire® rods, which may be in units from one to 10, a continuous model (Figure 9–15).

Older primary age children are entering the stage of understanding sequence and cause and effect. They are beginning to understand the concept of "If I do this, then this will happen," especially when the cause and effect are close together in time and space. First and second graders become adept at telling stories in order of events, "and then . . . , and then . . .". Their attempts at seriation are still by trial and error, with the need to physically manipulate objects to place them in some kind of order.

Primary age children are perfecting and extending their counting skills. Helping this happen smoothly is not easy, when you consider how inconsistent the English language is. First, there is word confusion for numbers above ten: count to 10, listening carefully to the sound of the words. Is there one that sounds different? Now count to 19 and select the number words that are irregular and those that are logical. "Eleven." Where did that come from? Other than the first sounds of the words, 12, 13, and 15 are not as logical as 14, 16, and 19. Then comes 20. All the decade number words add -*ty* but again, some only have the first sounds of the number—20, 30, 50—while 40, 60, 70, 80, and 90 make more sense. Once a child gets over that hurdle, the higher numbers are easy: 101, 1,364, one million, 723,000, 984. These are pointed out by Thompson (1997), along with the explanation that American children's test scores may be unfairly compared to those of Chinese and Japanese children, since they may be affected by these anomalies in the English language counting system. Japanese and Chinese number words are more logical: the word for 11 is 10-one, 12 is 10-two, 21 is two-10-one, and so on.

Some of the standards for grades PreK through two from the National Council of Teachers of Mathematics (2000) include:

* Number and operations—Accuracy in counting, number words and numerals, beginning addition and subtraction, strategies for whole-number computations

* Algebra—Sort, classify, and order objects by size, number, and other properties; sequencing; patterns; representations of symbolic notations; symbols for qualitative and quantitative change

* Geometry—Recognize, name, draw and compare two- and three-dimensional shapes; represent shapes from different perspectives; recognize geometric shapes in the environment

* Measurement—Attributes of length, volume, weight, area, and time and compare objects by these attributes; select appropriate unit and tool for measuring attributes; compare estimates

* Data analysis and probability—Sort and classify objects in sets, represent data using pictures and graphs, discuss experiences as likely or unlikely

* Problem solving—Recognize, analyze, and strategize how to solve problems that occur in experiences that can be solved through mathematical knowledge

* Reasoning and proof—Use pattern recognition and classifying skills to justify answers

* Communication—Use oral and pictorial language to convey mathematical thinking, listen to others and evaluate ideas

* Connections—Use experiences to make linkages between one mathematical concept and another and mathematics and real life

* Representation—Represent understanding through oral and written language, gestures, drawing and symbols

Place yourself in a classroom of a certain age group: toddlers, preschoolers, early elementary, or later elementary age children. Reread the list and think about objects you could bring into the classroom that would help your students establish concepts at their level about each of the above topics. With some thought and creativity, the teacher can provide relevant, hands-on learning experiences that will meet the learning objectives while maintaining the children's interest.

WORDS OF WISDOM Observations and discussions can lead to a scientific investigation. Here is a story from Jennie McDonald, a teacher in Far North Queensland, Australia, about learning through a discovery model.

"We noticed this year that children were bringing a lot of prepackaged food items in their lunch box, which was producing a lot of waste in the rubbish bins at lunch time. Through discussion and reading books, we noted that this was a concern. Our first excursion for the year (to the horror of many of our parents) was to the local dump*!!! We managed to see the dump truck in action and speak with the local "Recycling Man," who shared valuable information about hazardous and useful recyclable materials."

continued

"Lots of discussion about recycling ensued and a "worm farm" to eat all of our food and paper scraps was established as a result. We even decided to have a "nonrecyclable rubbish-free lunch day." Each child could only bring a lunch that consisted of food and packaging that could be recycled. Our Mother's Day presents this year were "mush pots" made from mulched paper and water (dried out) with a seedling planted inside. They were given a head start in their growing life by a dash of our "Worm Wee Fertiliser." The children like to check to see how much "wee" the worms have produced each week and they take it home in turns for their plants."

"Now all our bread scraps go to the birds, food and paper scraps go to the worms, and there are very few nonrecyclable scraps left for our cleaner to put into the industrial bin. This has been a valuable project that has led to a greater understanding of environmental issues."

*"An amusing thing that happened while we were there was that I had told the children that if they wanted to go to the toilet they must go before we leave as there are no toilet facilities at the dump. Lo and behold when we got there, what was sitting in the recycled area—a second-hand porcelain toilet bowl—instantly spotted by the children—and I was left standing corrected!"

Primary age children are very interested in and able to do scientific investigation. They become absorbed in gaining an understanding that the results of similar investigations should be approximately the same. They are beginning to use the technology of thermometers, rulers, scales, and magnifiers to expand their observation and comparing skills. They recognize that patterns and shapes such as circles, squares, and triangles can be found in nature and in the things people build. They are beginning to see that numbers can be used to count anything. In *Doing What Scientists Do: Children Learn to Investigate Their World* (1991), Ellen Doris relates how she holds class meetings to introduce the children to scientific investigation of natural objects in their world. At these meetings, children show their work and ask each other questions. The teacher guides their investigation with work sheets: not the kind where the child circles the correct answer, but the kind that provides places to draw and write about what the "scientist" noticed (Figure 9–16).

Science includes many different fields of study, all of which should be included in the elementary school curriculum.

* Physical science—Properties of objects and materials, position and motion of objects, light and heat, electricity and magnets
* Life science—Characteristics, environments, and life cycles of organisms
* Earth/space science—Earth materials, objects in the sky, changes in the earth and sky
* Science and technology—What technology can do, understanding science and technology, natural versus manufactured objects
* Science and social perspectives—Personal health, characteristics of and changes in populations, changes in environments, science and technology in local challenges
* History—Science as a human endeavor (Rakow and Bell, 1998, pp. 164–167)

The benchmarks of science, mathematics, and technology (AAAS, *Benchmarks for Science Literacy,* 1993) have primary programs helping children use science to investigate and find answers using measuring instruments while working in a team; see patterns, shapes, and motion in the world around them; and perfect counting

Aubrey _____ — *Observation*

Date July 30, 2000 _____

I looked at a flower. _____
_____

A picture of what I saw

Here are some things I noticed: It has Lite steripe
on the backs _____
_____
_____
_____
_____
_____
_____

Scientific field study
includes recording
observations.

skills; learn about tools and their proper uses in carrying out designs to solve problems and produce objects that are useful.

Primary Age Curriculum for Mathematics, Science, and Technology. An integrated curriculum is a way to effectively apply mathematics and science to life situations. When children are creating collages, they are informally studying shape, space, and reactions of glue to paper. Using clay presents opportunities for gaining knowledge about length, width, height, balance, and proportion, and the changes that take place when sculptures are left to dry or baked in a kiln. Music activities can involve the whole body in symbolizing the blowing wind, a growing seed, or a hopping rabbit; the rhythms, melodies, and words repeat patterns that are the foundations of mathematical thinking. Cooking, serving, and eating are favorite activities that involve science and mathematics, as well as physical, social/emotional, reading, speaking, and listening skills.

In *Mathematics Their Way: An Activity-Centered Mathematics Program for Early Childhood Education* (Baratta-Lorton, 1995), all aspects of mathematics foundations are explored with common materials and games for kindergarten through second grade. This resource book provides activities like graphing what kind of sandwiches you like best to counting some new kinds of objects every day. It catches children's imagination and gives tangible experiences on which to build concepts.

Of course, mathematics and science learning is integrated with literacy. Brown (1997) used journals to encourage children to write about how they encountered mathematics and to correlate their experience with a date and activity, using the questions, "What Were You Doing?" and "What Math Did You Do?" as a formula for their writing. Knoll and Halaby (1997) had children pose written mathematics problems for each other in whatever form they needed to communicate: inventive spelling, pictures, numbers, and symbols. These are teaching techniques that involve the learners in both writing and thinking about mathematics in the real world.

> Charlesworth (2000) outlines naturalistic and informal mathematics activities, as well as structured ones like these in the following areas:
> * Operations with whole numbers—Addition, subtraction, multiplication, and division; problems solved with mathematics using concrete materials such as counters, blocks, and chips
> * Patterns—Exploring patterns in nature, using graphs and calculators
> * Fractions—Size comparisons, models of dividing whole into parts
> * Place value—Base 10 blocks and manipulation of decimal points
> * Geometry, data collection, and algebraic thinking—Geoboards, coordinates, experiences with one- and three-dimensional objects, and finding areas
> * Measurement with standard units—Working with rulers, calendars, clocks, thermometers, money

Science activities for primary age children include the following (Seefeldt & Barbour, 1994).

Physical Science.

* Astronomy—Study of heavenly bodies and their motion
* Chemistry—Study of materials found on earth and changes in them
* Meteorology—Study of weather and air
* Physics—Study of matter and energy

Biological Science.

* Plants
* Animals

These science topics can be integrated into all curriculum areas (see Figures 9–6, and 9–7).

Primary age children can now use the computer to expand their literacy and language skills by using it to compose letters to friends and relatives, write stories, or chronicle classroom events. Appropriate computer experiences can improve motor skills, enhance mathematical, critical thinking, and problem-solving skills, and give the child a feeling of power over her environment (Nastasi & Clements, 1994). Children who become proficient with computers have an enhanced self-concept and increased levels of communication, cooperation, and leadership (Clements, 1994; Adams, 1996; Haugland & Wright, 1997; Matthews, 1997).

Four types of Web sites can expand the computer resources in the classroom. Information sites provide reference resources, answer questions, and build knowledge. Communication sites stimulate e-mail interaction between students and people near and far to provide social and informational resources and an expanded view of the world. Children can make friends and have access to famous people through the

Internet. Interaction sites are similar to software programs, with animation, sound, and graphics. These sites can augment curriculum and classroom software. Publication sites can stimulate children's drawing and writing when they realize it will be published where thousands of people can see and read it. Haugland and Gerzog (1998) have also developed a developmental scale tool for evaluating children's Web sites. Given the benefits and opportunities the computer and Internet bring, teachers must be prepared to guide in selecting and using these powerful tools.

Elementary Age Mathematics, Science, and Technology: Development and Curriculum

Mathematics, science, and technology become more separate as subject matter in the upper grades of elementary school, with more teachers having specialized backgrounds, and more male teachers in math and science. This is the age when boys and girls think boys are better at these subjects. It is important for teachers in these grades to dispel the myths by planning ways for girls to find success.

Elementary Age Development in Mathematics, Science, and Technology.
Now in the concrete operations stage, elementary age children continue to expand their logico-mathematical thought. They still need objects to manipulate to work out their theories and ways of addressing problems, but can **centrate** on one attribute to observe and measure, isolated from extraneous information. They can manipulate the symbols of mathematics (numbers) with calculations, both on paper and mentally, and understand concepts of number, weight, and time. Scientific investigations are undertaken with more precision and any variable results can be attributed to variables within the experiment. Communicating about the investigation, whether mathematics or science, is an important part of learning, for the explanation of thinking crystallizes learning, or, at times, reveals and self-corrects flaws in thinking. The student uses technology with greater accuracy to measure and extend her ability to design and implement new or improved technologies (Figure 9–17 on page 338).

Elementary age children can now handle problems with more than one variable, do mental manipulations and reversals, and think through their processes. They can discuss concepts that are more abstract and create and test possible explanations of real problems. Encyclopedias, reference books, and the Internet are sources of new information or confirm previous information. Harlen (1993) suggests that the teacher provide alternative, more scientific ideas only after children have explored their own theories because "it is all too easy to destroy children's confidence in their own thinking and reasoning if their ideas are swept aside by premature presentation of *right* ones" (p. 119).

Elementary Age Curriculum for Mathematics, Science, and Technology.
The elementary grades are important learning years for mathematics concepts, operations, and experimentation. In some states, specialist teachers other than the classroom generalist teach mathematics and science in the later elementary grades (fourth through sixth). You may have a choice depending on

---

centrate—Cognitive ability to take more than one attribute into consideration when making judgments on volume, length, and weight.

Figure 9–17

Children need to use real tools to gain scientific and mathematical information and concepts.

your state certification. However, all teachers need a foundation in mathematics, science, and technology to integrate the subjects for maximized learning.

Some of the standards for grades three through five from the National Council of Teachers of Mathematics (2000) include:

* Number and operations—Place values; fractions; numbers less than zero; fluency in adding, subtracting, multiplying, and dividing whole numbers; strategies for estimation

* Algebra—Generalizations about geometric and numeric patterns, represent unknown quantity with a letter or symbol, express mathematical relationships using equations and how changes in one variable relates to changes in a second variable

* Geometry—Identify, compare, and classify two- and three-dimensional shapes; measure the distance between points on shapes and designs; build and draw geometric objects

* Measurement—Attributes of length, area, weight, volume and size, and measurement strategies; metric conversions; use standard units and tools for measuring

* Data analysis and probability—Collect and represent data using tables and graphs, compare representations of data, predict probability outcomes

* Problem solving—Build new mathematical knowledge through problem solving, apply a variety of strategies to solve problems

* Reasoning and proof—Formulate and assess conjectures, select and use types of reasoning methods for proof
* Communication—Read, write, listen, think, and communicate about problems; learn from the work of others; use the language of mathematics
* Connections—See connections between mathematical ideas, especially equivalence and multiplication; apply mathematical principles outside of mathematics
* Representation—Organize, record, and communicate mathematical ideas through various forms of representations

"The Scientist: Who Is She?" is the title of a section in *Teaching Children Science* (Abruscato, 1999). It is meant to catch your attention. Did it? Did you think the author made a mistake? Mathematics and science carry a male bias, both as school subject areas and as careers. The times are changing, but they are changing slowly. Gender differences in attitude, expectations, and performance in mathematics and science still appear in the upper elementary years. Social pressures, cultural stereotypes, and even adult expectations affect girls' performance. Manning (1998) suggests these strategies: enhance girls' beliefs in their ability, address stereotypic beliefs about girls lacking the ability to learn science and mathematics, plan for collaboration and not competition between boys and girls in all classroom activities, encourage girls to participate in science fairs and mathematics demonstrations, provide hands-on experiences for all. Clara Barton, Marie Curie, Jane Goodall, and Eileen Collins, first woman astronaut, are role models for girls interested in science as a career.

Benchmarks for Science, Mathematics, and Technology. The benchmarks for science, mathematics, and technology for elementary grades are that:

* Scientific investigations can answer physical, biological, and social questions and have a standard format for design, implementation, and reporting, recognizing that variables affect results.
* Mathematics is a study of patterns that can be represented concretely, graphically, and symbolically to describe and predict things about the world around us.
* Technology enables investigators to accurately gather, measure, and communicate results that build on past inventions and lead to new ones, analyzing the benefits and the possible drawbacks (American Association for the Advancement of Science, 1993).

Depending on the school configuration, fourth through sixth grades may be included in the elementary school or fifth and sixth grades may be included in a middle school. The regular classroom teacher may plan mathematics and science activities, or they may be planned by a specialist in those areas or by the teacher/child care provider in an out-of-school enrichment program. The following are included to give you an idea of the kinds of experiences that children can have at this stage.

Van de Walle (1998) presents the following mathematics concepts and activities, the themes of which you will recognize from the NCTM Standards.

* Mental estimation and pencil-and-paper computations with whole numbers—Work with nearest 10 or 100 numbers on paper. "How many ways can you get the answer?"
* Fraction concepts and computations—Begin with squares; follow with rectangles and then circles, dividing them into parts and adding in wholes to get tangible understanding before moving to common denominator concepts

* Decimal and percent concepts and computations—Calculator counting with decimals, real problems such as sales tax computation, batting averages, class voting

* Ratio and proportion—Introduction of geometry concepts such as π (circumference of a circle) and √ (square root), or scale drawing (living space plans)

* Measurement—Standard measures, angles, metric system, volume

* Geometry—Explore one-, two-, and three-dimensional shapes, tanagrams

* Probability and statistics—Coin flips, random numbers

Using the idiom "less is more," teachers are now looking at depth of knowledge rather than just skimming topics. In going beyond superficial knowledge, children learn practical, applicable facts, processes, and procedures that will last a lifetime and is the foundation for later learning. Howe and Jones (1992) recommend a curriculum that includes solar system (systematic observational data, model building, measuring of daylight); earth (water forms and changes, forces of wind, temperature of soil, weather, rocks); physical science (substances and their characteristics and observation of changes under varying conditions); energy, force, and motion (measuring speed, electricity, light, pendulums, machines); life science (cells, organisms, plant and animal behavior); and the ecosystem (hazards to air, water, soil, plants and animals). These topics can be explored using the scientific method of observing, recording, experimenting, observing, and recording.

Parents, administrators, students, and teachers want computers in the classroom, but certain issues need to be addressed. One important issue is that of access. High-income households are more likely to have computers at home, so children from those homes already come to school with familiarity with and sometimes very advanced skills in computer usage. In 1995, only 35 percent of computers in schools were in classrooms (O'Neil, 1995). Computers in labs or libraries are much less used and useful. Papert (1998) stressed the importance of integrating computers into the curriculum. Gender inequity also comes into play, with little difference in computer use by preschool girls and boys, but a significant difference by fourth grade (Haugland, 1992). Teachers can have a strong influence on this by selecting appropriate software, monitoring classroom usage, and encouraging girls to use the computer more often.

✳ ASSESSING MATHEMATICS, SCIENCE, AND TECHNOLOGY LEARNING

Assessment is always placed in this last section in the chapters of this book not because it is last in importance but because of practical considerations. In reality and ideally, assessment should come first. You observe children to find out how much they already know. Children come to school with an amazing, but varied, amount of mathematical and scientific knowledge. Some children have had extensive experience observing nature with families who visit zoos or climb mountains, walk in the woods where they point out flora and fauna, or wade in the ocean. By contrast, some have read books about such experiences. Other children have acquired knowledge from activities where they count stairs or Cheerios® or cans from a kitchen cupboard, and have made connections with the numerical and physical world. And, of course, children moving through the grades in school have accumulated diverse experiences as well. They may have had open classrooms with blocks and microscopes, living things to feed and care for, and quantities of things to sort, classify, and count. They may have had drill and practice in computational skills and "covered" many topics in science. The teacher's first role is to find out each child's developmental level and to then design curriculum to progress from there. Assessment is intertwined with teaching and learning: strands of the same braid, each component depending on the other.

Schools traditionally have used the Iowa Test of Basic Skills to compare students' mathematical knowledge and skills to national averages. Norm-referenced tests have been standardized to a norm group with the assumption that all eight-year-olds or eleven-year-olds will score in a range that accords with the norm group (Figure 9–18). Criterion-reference tests show the achievement in specific areas and are helpful in evaluating complex skills with many components.

In the past, the main mode of assessment was testing, and the purpose was to find out what the child did not know. With the change in how mathematics and science are taught, however, came a change in how learning is evaluated. People have changed their minds both about how to authentically measure what a student knows and can do and about the purposes of this measurement. Alternative assessment measures now include:

* Observations—The teacher sees, hears, and makes note of what a child is doing and infers what the child knows and can do from observational data

* Checklists—Teacher-made itemized lists of process skills or components that can be checked off as each child is observed accomplishing the criteria

* Interviews—The teacher asks the child to explain what process was used or how the answer was obtained

* Journals—Fuqua called them the "Problem-solving Book" with her kindergartners and used them to record problems that occurred in the area of mathematics or science for later reference and investigation (Fuqua, 1997/ 1998)

* Assessment tasks—Working on a project, experiment, or problem as a way of indicating knowledge and skill

Figure 9–18

Schools use tests in a variety of ways.

＊ Portfolios—A collection of the student's work that demonstrates skills and knowledge and which may include work samples, systematic observations, or any of the above tools

＊ Performance assessment—Measurement tools such as checklists or rating scales that look at various factors of performance

An assessment's purpose should be constructive, not punitive. Assessment can monitor the student's learning progress. It can give insight into further teaching strategies that might be successful. Assessment can help teachers make instructional decisions based on observing the process the student is using to achieve the result and analyzing exactly where a problem exists and evaluating the student's achievement level. Assessments used to assist the student and teacher are preferred to those used to measure the teacher or program's effectiveness, for which there are too many variables for the assessment to be valid.

SUMMARY

The natural inquisitiveness of children leads them to explore the world around them. As they do this, they observe, store information, match new information to old, form hypotheses, test them out, and modify theories. They report their findings by telling others what they have observed and learned. This scientific method does not need to be taught, but should be the basis for all learning. In mathematics, children are naturally very interested in quantity, volume, and making sets. The investigation of living things, beginning with themselves and extending to plants and animals, as well as earth and sky, is of great interest as they observe the wonders of nature. Tools and machines used in everyday life form the basis of technological study as children take them apart and eventually mastering their use. The role of the teacher and the curriculum is to build on these natural inclinations to form solid bodies of knowledge and resources to search for answers to questions. The wonder of mathematics, science, and technology brings the world into the classroom and the classroom into the world.

KEY TERMS

correspondence	disequilibrium	conservation
physical knowledge	object permanence	seriation
logico-mathematical knowledge	classification	self correcting
	overgeneralizing	centrate
social cognition		

REVIEW ACTIVITIES

Exercises to Strengthen Learning

1. Spend time with a two-, three-, four-, and five-year-old just counting. Make notes about how the child counts and analyze her "mistakes."

2. Observe two different classrooms of the same grade during a mathematics or science lesson and observe the content, teaching styles, children's involvement, and concepts being taught/learned.

3. Find out about the mathematics and science standards in your state and interview a classroom teacher to find what curriculum changes are taking place to prepare children to meet the standards.

4. Try to find a pre-1960 science and mathematics textbook and compare it to a contemporary version. What differences do you see in content and in teaching approaches?

5. Use mathematics in every day life: find a pizza advertisement with sizes and prices. Using mathematics, find out which is the best buy. Are the price differentials fair?

Internet Quest

1. Find the Web sites for the National Council of Teachers of Mathematics, National Science Teachers Association, and American Association for the Advancement of Science and Research Project 2061, and explore and compare the latest documents and discussion topics there.

2. Using the Dirt Curriculum Webs in Figures 9–6 and 9–7, begin to explore the topic using the Internet.

3. Find and explore Seymour Papert's Web site for families and children.

4. Find three mathematics and three science sites for children of a selected age group and analyze their content according to the standards you found in this chapter.

Reflective Journal

In this chapter, I learned the following about mathematics, science, and technology . . .

Because of this, when I am a teacher I will . . .

REFERENCES

Abruscato, J. (1999). *Teaching children science: A discovery approach* (5th ed.). Needham Heights, MA: Allyn & Bacon.

Adams, P. (1996). Hypermedia in the classroom using earth and science CD-ROMs. *Journal of Computers in Mathematics and Science Teaching, 15*(1/2), 19–34.

American Association for the Advancement of Science (AAAS). (1989). *Science for all Americans.* New York: Oxford University Press.

American Association for the Advancement of Science (AAAS). (1993). *Benchmarks for science literacy.* New York: Oxford University Press.

Baratta-Lorton, M. (1995). *Mathematics their way: An activity-centered mathematics program for early childhood education.* Menlo Park, CA: Addison-Wesley.

Baroody, A. J. (1987). *Children's mathematical thinking: A developmental framework for preschool, primary and special education teachers.* New York: Teachers College.

Baroody, A. J. (2000). Does mathematics instruction for three- to five-year-olds really make sense? *Young Children, 55*(4), 61–67.

Brown, S. (1997). First graders write to discover mathematics relevancy. *Young Children, 52*(4), 51–53.

Chaille, C., & Britain, L. (1997). *The young child as scientist: A constructivist approach to early childhood science education.* New York: Longman.

Charlesworth, R. (2000). *Experiences in math for young children* (4th ed.). Albany, NY: Delmar.

Clements, D. (1994). The uniqueness of the computer as a learning tool: Insights from research. In J. Wright & D. Shade (Eds.), *Young children: Active learners in a technological age.* Washington, DC: National Association for the Education of Young Children.

Clements, D. (1999). Young children and technology. In Clements, D. (Ed.), *Dialogue on early childhood science, mathematics, and technology education.* Washington, DC: American Association for the Advancement of Science.

Committee for Economic Development, Research and Policy Committee. (1995). *Connecting students to a changing world: A technology strategy for improving mathematics and science education.* New York: Author.

Doris, E. (1991). *Doing what scientists do: Children learn to investigate their world.* Portsmouth, NH: Heinemann.

Elkind, D. (1998). Computers for infants and young children. *Child Care Information Exchange, 123,* 44–46.

Fennema, E., Carpenter, T. P., Franke, M. L., Levi, L., Jacobs, V. R., & Empson, S. B. (1996). A longitudinal study of learning to use children's thinking in mathematics instruction. *Journal for Research in Mathematics Education, 17,* 403–434.

Fuqua, B. H. (1997/1998). Exploring math journals. *Childhood Education, 74*(2), 73–77.

Goals 2000. Educate America Act. (1994). PL 103–227 Retrieved March 17, 2001, from the World Wide Web: <http://www.ed.gov/legislation/GOALS2000/TheAct>.

Harlen, W. (1993). *Teaching and learning primary science* (2nd ed.). London: Paul Chapman.

Haugland, S. (1992). Effects of computer software on preschool children's developmental gains. *Journal of Computing in Childhood Education, 2*(2), 3–15.

Haugland, S., & Gerzog, G. (1998). *The developmental software scale for web sites.* Cape Girardeau, MO: K.I.D.S. & Computers.

Haugland, S., & Wright, J. (1997). *Young children and technology: A world of discovery.* New York: Allyn & Bacon.

Hiebert, J., Carpenter, T. P., Fennema, E., Fuson, C. K., Wearne, D., Murray, H., Oliver, A., & Human, P. (1997). *Making sense: Teaching and learning mathematics with understanding.* Portsmouth, NH: Heinemann.

Hohman, C. (1998). Evaluating and selecting software for children. *Child Care Information Exchange, 123,* 60–62.

Howe, A. C., & Jones, L. (1992). *Engaging children in science* (2nd ed.). New York: Merrill.

Hurd, P. D. (1997). *Inventing science education for the new millennium.* New York: Teachers College Press.

Inventure Place: National Inventors Hall of Fame. (2001). *George Washington Carver.* Retrieved March 17, 2001, from the World Wide Web: <http://www.invent.org>.

Kamii, C. (1985). *Young children reinvent arithmetic.* New York: Teachers College Press.

Kamii, C., & DeVries, R. (1980). *Group games in early education: Implications of Piaget's theory.* Washington, DC: National Association for the Education of Young Children.

Knoll, L., & Halaby, M. (1997). Writing to learn mathematics in the primary school. *Young Children, 52*(4), 54–57.

Manning, M. L. (1998). Gender differences in young adolescents' mathematics and science achievement. *Childhood Education, 74*(3), 168–171.

Matthews, K. (1997). A comparison of the influence of interactive CD-ROM storybooks and traditional print storybooks on reading comprehension. *Journal of Computing in Education, 29,* 263–273.

Nastasi, B. K., & Clements, D. H. (1994). Effectance motivation, perceived scholastic competence, and higher-order thinking in two cooperative computer environments. *Journal of Educational Computing Research, 10,* 241–267.

National Center for Education Statistics (2001). *Distributions of fourth grade math scores.* Retrieved March 17, 2001, from the World Wide Web: <http://neces.ed.gov/ssbr/pages/M4Dist.asp>.

National Commission on Excellence in Education. (1983). *A nation at risk: The imperatives for educational reform.* Washington, DC: U.S. Government Printing Office. (ERIC Document Reproduction Service No. ED 279 603)

National Council of Teachers of Mathematics (NCTM). (1991). *Assessment standards for school mathematics.* Reston, VA: Author pp. 4, 21, 72, 125.

National Council of Teachers of Mathematics (NCTM). (2000). *Principles and standards for school mathematics.* Reston, VA: Author.

National Research Council. (1989). *Everybody counts: A report to the nation on the future of mathematical education.* Washington, DC: National Academy Press.

National Research Council. (1993). *National science education standards: An enhanced sampler.* Washington, DC: National Academy Press.

O'Neil, J. (1995). Teachers and technology: Potentials and pitfalls. *Educational Leadership* (Annual), 10–11.

Papert, S. (1980). *Mindstorms: Children, computers and powerful ideas.* New York: Basic Books.

Papert, S. (1998, September 1). *Technology in schools: To support the system or render it obsolete? Milken exchange on education technology.* Retrieved March 17, 2001, from the World Wide Web: <http://www.mff.org/edtech/>.

Rakow, S. J., & Bell, M. J. (1998). Science and young children: The message from the national science education standards. *Childhood Education, 74*(3), 164–168.

Schmidt, W. H., McNight, C. C., & Raizen, S. A. (1997). *A splintered vision: An investigation of United States science and mathematics education.* Boston: Kliewer Academic Publishers.

Seefeldt, C., & Barbour, N. (1994). *Early childhood education: An introduction.* New York: Merrill.

Starkey, D., & Cooper, R. (1980). Perception of numbers by human infants. *Science, 210*(4473), 1033–1035.

Stigler, J. W., & Hiebert, J. (1997). Understanding and improving classroom mathematics instruction: An overview of the TIMSS video study. *Phi Delta Kappan, 79*(1).

Taylor, B. J. (1993). *Science everywhere: Opportunities for very young children.* Fort Worth, TX: Harcourt Brace Jovanovich.

Thompson, I. (1997). Developing young children's counting skills. In I. Thompson (Ed.), *Teaching and learning early number.* Philadelphia, PA: Open University Press.

Van de Walle, J. (1998). *Elementary and middle school mathematics: Teaching developmentally.* New York: Longman.

Unglaub, K. W. (1997). What counts in learning to count. *Young Children, 52*(4), 48.

For additional teaching and learning resources, visit our Web site at www.EarlyChildEd.delmar.com.

RELATED CAREERS

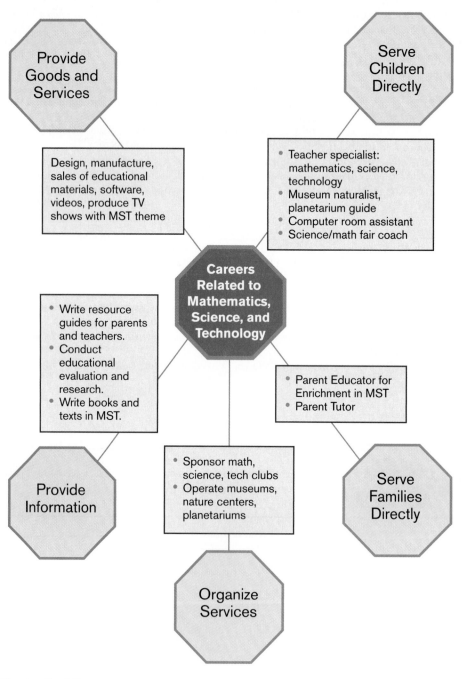

Figure 9–19

Careers related to mathematics and science.

Learning about and Teaching the Creative Child

Objectives

After reading this chapter and completing the review activities, the learning teacher should be able to:

1. Define creativity and explain its sources, inhibitors, and expressions.
2. Describe the development of creativity in children from birth through sixth grade.
3. Explain the teacher's role in nurturing creativity through curricula in visual arts, music, movement, and dramatic arts.

✳ UNDERSTANDING CREATIVITY IN LEARNING AND TEACHING

SCENARIO

✳ Althea hears a song in the wind.

✳ Jasper sees shapes in the clouds.

✳ Kito writes his name in the frost on the windowpane.

✳ Nora organizes her books according to the colors of their covers.

✳ Jason rolls his eyes when asked a question.

✳ Chianna gathers stones to place in a circle and addresses them with an ancient story.

✳ Ezra stops a fight on the playground and gets his friends to talk it out.

Which of these children is using **creativity**? All of them are, of course. None of them has drawn a picture, sculpted clay, written a song, moved to music, or acted in a play, which are the usual understandings or expectations of creativity. Many people deny they are creative because they do not paint, draw, play a musical instrument, or act, yet they are very creative in other ways. Perhaps you are among them. Creativity is an important skill for a teacher and important for a teacher to inspire in children. This is not just because we need art, music, and drama to make the world a more beautiful place. It is not just because we need new products and processes to meet our ever-increasing wants and needs for things. It is not just because we enjoy the novelty of something different. It is all this and more. It is vital because everyday across the world there are problems that need creative solutions and it takes looking at things in different ways to provide possible solutions: not just one right answer, but many choices.

John Goodlad's study of American schools in his book *A Place Called School* (1984) precipitated a movement aimed at nationwide school reform. In his book, he says that many people feel the arts are suitable for preschool and kindergarten, where women teachers dominate, but that these pursuits are put aside for tough subjects like mathematics and science in the subsequent and more masculine world of school in the higher grades. He maintains that the common perception is that the arts are tactile, involving the hands and not the head, in contrast to true intellectualism, as proven through tests of linguistic and quantitative abilities. How does that sound to you? Goodlad disagrees with this attitude and sees the aesthetic education of our children as an undernourished part of the curriculum, thus denying our children the comprehensive general education they need for effective, satisfying living. He further suggests that a beginning point for change would be better teacher education in the arts.

The future of humankind depends on the development of creativity. "There is a widespread belief that the study of math and science seeks right answers, while the study of literature and the humanities accepts creativity. . . . Learning about our world is inherently interdisciplinary. Solving our world's problems requires creative thought"

✳ **creativity**—The ability to originate something new and appropriate by looking beyond common constraints to create something novel and valuable over time.

(Brooks & Brooks, 1993). This chapter explores creativity and its development, and the teacher's role in traditional as well as nontraditional areas of creativity.

✳ THE NATURE OF CREATIVITY

There are many myths about creativity.

- ✳ You are either born with it or you are not.
- ✳ Only geniuses are creative.
- ✳ The majority of creative people are artists, musicians, and inventors.
- ✳ Creative people are a bit (or very) strange.

You already have an idea that the definition of creativity we are proposing here goes beyond the arts. Creativity is an extension of cognition, a way of thinking, or alternate ways of processing information and producing new ideas. Examining various definitions of creativity will broaden your perspective of it. You will look at the origins and stimulation of creativity, barriers or deterrents to it, and the teacher's role in inspiring creativity.

What Is Creativity?

Torrance (1988), who has researched and written much about creativity, relates it to four Ps: person, process, product, and press (referring to kinds of environments). Jackson and Messick (1968) defined four criteria for creativity: thinking of something novel or new, but appropriate; that which makes sense in context; that which uses something familiar in a different way; and that which becomes more valuable and powerful in each new application (Figure 10–1).

Consider the creative idea of generating heat in a wire by connecting a wire to electricity. The wire is imbedded in blankets and in egg incubators, and now even in heaters to warm baby wipes so those little moist sheets are not as cold on the baby's bottom. At one time, heat transference through wire was a new idea; it was used appropriately as a warming mechanism; it found its way into familiar objects; and now it is used in many different ways. The concept originated as a creative idea, became a process, a product, and

Figure 10–1

Children are naturally creative.

Howard Gardner

(1943–) The United States psychologist who developed the theory of multiple intelligences put forward in *Frames of Mind: The Theory of Multiple Intelligences* (1993). He directs Project Zero at Harvard with the mission of applying theory and understanding and enhancing learning, thinking, and creativity in the arts, as well as humanistic and scientific disciplines at the individual and institutional levels.

many more by-products, all as a result of creative people. What began as one idea spurred on others in an evolution and expansion of application.

Creativity is taking a bit of knowledge and changing it, cognitively and practically transforming it into something else. Picasso is said to have formed the sculpture of the head of a bull after looking at a bicycle's handles and seat and Gutenberg combined the winepress and the coin press (which made images on soft metal) into the printing press (von Oech, 1990). "Thinking the impossible" and doing it in a way that is understandable and acceptable to others is the way that Boden (1991) describes creativity. **Howard Gardner** (1993), noted for his theory of multiple intelligences, sees creativity specific to each of them.

Think of how these are used creatively.

* Language
* Math and logic
* Music
* Spatial reasoning
* Movement
* Interpersonal (between individuals)
* Intrapersonal (within oneself)
* Naturalistic

The creative process is a combination of mental processes that lead to the final product, whether it is a new theory, process, invention, or tangible expression of thought. Koster (2001) lists the following as components of that creative process:

* Knowledge—Previous knowledge is the basis for creative thought and action
* Motivation—Inner drive that causes an individual to act
* Skill—Certain skills are needed to create, especially communication skills, whether it is speaking, writing, visual, or auditory productions, manual dexterity and even attention span
* Immersion—Intensely focusing on creating something with the ability to block out distractions
* Incubation—Time to think and process what the person knows and wishes to do
* Production—The tangible expression of the creative process

Creativity's Benefits to the Individual

Contrary to the myth that creative people are eccentric, antisocial, and even emotionally unhealthy, many researchers have found just the opposite. The difference lies in self-actualization versus special talent. Creativity can be the outlet or expression of the emotional/affective domain. Through drawing, painting, music, movement, drama, storytelling, and innovation, a person can express feelings as he can do in no other way. According to Maslow (1970), a self-actualized person lives a flexible life, adjusting and making the most of opportunities and even disruptions, turning them into positives. That is a happy, creative person. The person with a special talent may also be self actualized, but we most often hear of neurotic misfits who have great talent but may waste it or let it become their downfall. The difference is in the personality, or affective traits, that accompany the individual's intelligence, flexibility, and talent.

Creative people can use their creativity in ways that help themselves as well as others. Creativity enhances self-esteem and self-worth. A creative person helps create solutions to problems at home or in the workplace; expresses novel ideas in meetings, gaining peer recognition; or produces new processes and procedures that save time, energy, materials, or frustration. All these applications of creative thinking bring a sense of well-being and accomplishment (Figure 10–2). When a person is creative and can use visualization or mental imagery, performance and health may be positively affected. Being able to separate mind from body can bring release from pain, and Samuels and Rockwood Lane, say, "Creative expression can actually change one's brain wave pattern, and affect a person's autonomic nervous system, hormonal balance and brain neurotransmitters. It can affect every cell in the body, changing the immune system and blood flow to all the organs and creating a healing physiology" (Samuels & Rockwood Lane, 1998).

The creative person can extend these benefits to others by carefully listening and mentally taking the other person's place or point of view. By thinking of a situation from another's perspective, or by feeling his pain or sorrow, the creative person expresses empathy, bringing comfort and support to others. It may not be an invention that changes the world, or a piece of art that hangs in a gallery for all to see, but the personal benefits of creativity to self and others makes the world a better place. Guilford (1981) calls this *personal creativity*, or flexible thinking used in the process of everyday living. This is very necessary in today's world. Another kind of creativity, which results in major discoveries, ideas, inventions, and masterpieces, is what Guilford calls *cultural creativity*. Families, teachers, and the community have the opportunity to inspire both of these kinds of creativity and to ultimately reap the benefits.

Figure 10–2

Creative expression affects the whole body.

Origins of Creativity

So, are individuals born creative? Once again we must look at the interplay of nature and nurture. The three important factors that contribute to creativity tend to be inborn: intelligence, personality, and the capacity to develop. Each can be stimulated or suppressed by outside factors such as relationships and interactions with parents, primary caregivers, teachers, and peers. Emotional or physical trauma can hinder creativity or challenge an individual to find ways to express pain and overcome adversity. Even politics may hinder creativity by setting guidelines that prohibit research or encourage it by funding opportunities for creative endeavors.

Intelligence and Creativity. Development of creativity is intertwined with development in other areas. It is closely connected to **intelligence** and cognitive development; however, as mentioned earlier, IQ and creativity are not necessarily correlated. Creativity is not limited to a few gifted individuals with high intelligence. Wallach and Kogan (1965) found four patterns when they studied intelligence and creativity.

High Intelligence and High Creativity. The individual is flexible, playful, and self-confident; easily adapts to different learning environments; has high attention span and concentration, and questions authority.

Low Intelligence and High Creativity. The individual uses creativity in disruptive ways, lacks motivation in academic endeavors, and has low self-confidence.

Low Intelligence and Low Creativity. The individual lacks the basic level of intelligence to be able to think in creative ways, engages in more physical activity, or passively retreats.

High Intelligence and Low Creativity. The individual achieves in situations where highly structured responses and conforming behavior are rewarded, but has little skill in problem solving or independent actions.

Are all **gifted** individuals creative or are all creative individuals gifted? High creativity (new ideas and problem-solving skills) is only one of the criteria for giftedness. Renzulli and Reis (1997) also include above-average intelligence, high motivation, and the ability to see a project through to completion. Gifted people often demonstrate special aptitudes in art, music, drama, leadership, or interpersonal skills. Computers have unleashed an unprecedented outlet for creativity, from Web site design to entrepreneurial enterprises (Figure 10–3).

Intelligence and knowledge are essential ingredients to creativity because experience must exist as the basis for new ideas; in other words, there have to be some old ideas on which to build. Extremely high intelligence is not a prerequisite. You cannot write a new computer program without knowing how a computer works, design a new electric gadget without knowing about electric current, or create a new recipe without, for example, knowing the effects of baking powder versus baking soda. It is now possible to hum a tune into a computer and have it produced in written musical notation. In this case, you do not need to know how to write musical notes on paper to compose. This was someone's creative technological advance.

intelligence—Ability in a wide range of areas, including vocabulary, numbers, problem solving, and concepts. The ability to learn new information, adjust to new situations, and profit from experiences.

gifted—Normally defined by very high IQ score, but may be defined by remarkable skill in one or more specific areas.

Figure 10-3

Creativity can take many forms, including using the computer to create forms, write newsletters, conduct research, and even compose music.

Convergent and Divergent Thinking.

SCENARIO   The question on the test asked, "What color is a banana?" Bianca quickly wrote "yellow," Armand wrote "white," Ramiro wrote "red," and Lillian wrote "yellow, brown, black, green, and white."

Who is right? What answer was expected? Why did the other children give the *wrong* answers? Test questions usually require one answer that is considered correct. This is **convergent thinking**, or focusing knowledge to converge on one answer. What is required for that right answer? Several knowledge bases converge on the answer. First is the ability to read and process the question to form the response, either by writing or selecting a color swatch or printed word. Experience with a banana by sight or by verbal description is necessary. Knowledge of color names comes into play. Each of these children has further information or thought about the question in a different way. Armand was thinking of the inside of the banana, which is indeed white. Ramiro was thinking of a different kind of banana that he knows best. Lillian has keenly observed bananas and has a repertoire of color words to describe what she has seen. All are essentially correct; it all depends on where they focused their attention and the past experiences they had. Listening to *wrong* answers provides children with insight into their own thinking. Much of the educational system is based on convergent thinking, providing or reciting back what the teacher or lesson has attempted to

---

convergent thinking—The search through present knowledge to converge or match one correct answer.

convey. *Right-answer thinking* is that which von Oech says is attributable to mental locks and barriers to creative thinking (von Oech, 1990).

Divergent thinking is inspired and expanded by the kinds of questions that are asked. The teacher may ask divergent questions as the teacher and students seek solutions together. This is not to try to get the children to come around to the teacher's point of view or answer, but to jointly explore possibilities in questions like:

* What's another way . . . ?
* What might happen if . . . ?
* What are you thinking about . . . ?
* Does that remind you of anything else?
* What are some ways we could find out more?
* Just suppose . . .
* Pretend . . .

Personality and Creativity. Some personality traits that apply to creative people may have positive and negative aspects. Originality may bring impulsivity. Independence is a quality of creativity that may cause problems when it becomes necessary to work collaboratively. The creative person's risk-taking behavior may actually place that person and others in danger. The creative person's sense of humor may not be appreciated by those who do not understand or see the humor. Viewing the world through curious, childlike eyes may cause others to judge the person as naïve, childish, and out of touch with reality. The active, unfocused creative person may have difficulty completing mundane tasks and conforming to society's norms. Do you see how the very characteristics valued in a creative person (child or adult) may cause difficulties in the classroom? We certainly do not want little robots, but be aware that the creative child may not easily conform to classroom expectations. Finding outlets for creativity and common understandings regarding behavior is a learning experience for both the student and the teacher.

✴ THE NURTURE OF CREATIVITY

Certain aspects of creativity are inborn: linked to intelligence, brain physiology, temperament, and personality. These are the raw materials of creativity: nature's contribution, the genetic, the luck of the draw. Now we will look at what can happen to that natural part with help from the family, the environment, and the teacher and how it can be nurtured or, conversely, restricted.

The Family's Role in Creative Development

A family that values creativity by providing interesting conversation, humor, and games, as well as materials, time, and encouragement, can foster creativity in a child. Sosniak (1997) studied the home environment and parental involvement of accomplished artists of all kinds, from sports figures to academicians. In most cases, one or both parents were involved in the child's creative growth. One or both provided the initial training in and supervised practice of the instrument or sport. Tiger Woods, golf master, began at the age of three under the tutelage of his father. Stories of Olympic stars often include the parents' early dedication to the child's sport, often to the point of relocating to be close to expert coaches, or even sending the child to live with the

---

✴ **divergent thinking**—The search for multiple ideas or solutions to a problem.

coach. Another interesting factor in these successful people was that many of them were firstborn or only children, leaving you to wonder if extra attention and autonomy contributed to their creativity. Families of creative people have been found to maintain emotional stability and show a clear understanding and sense of boundaries in relationships, and are usually more complex, varied, and expressive than others (Albert, 1996).

Parents can inhibit creativity by demanding silence, obedience, and orderliness. When a family is governed by rules rather than values, or when emotional closeness and a certain amount of freedom are not present, creativity cannot thrive.

SCENARIO	Hattie was at preschool, where she never played at the sand table or with modeling dough or fingerpaint. She never attempted to play on the climbing apparatus. She seldom approached the easel, with its paints, or the shelves of paper, glue, scissors, and markers. When she was encouraged to do so, she always followed the same pattern of behavior: she would trace her hand. She traced her hand with paint and a small brush; she traced with markers (Figure 10–4). She pressed clay flat and pushed her hand in, but she never freely used materials to mold figures, paint bold strokes or draw circles or lines. Her mother proudly commented that at home all of Hattie's shelves of toys were labeled with pictures and words and the rule was to replace one toy before getting another out to play. Hattie and her mother were models of fashion, impeccably dressed and coiffed.

Do you see the correlation? Hattie will probably do very well in a school where conformity is valued and rewarded. She may select a profession where paying attention to detail and following the rules are necessary. Parents and teachers can socialize a child to value convergent thinking and acting, discount creativity and imagination as less desirable attributes than common sense, follow conventional rules, and be conformist in ideas and actions. Yes, we need people like that in the world, too, but those who have the opportunity to explore and develop creativity are necessary also. Most people need a blend of both convergent and divergent thinking.

Figure 10–4

Sometimes creativity can be repressed.

The Teacher's Role in Creative Development

Creativity, the ability to *think outside the box*, is becoming one of the most valued skills in business, adding to the bottom line. Problems need to be solved effectively and efficiently, and solutions and products need to be developed to meet ever-changing needs. To get the competitive edge, companies must catch the attention of the consumer who can choose among many competing products and services. Companies pay millions of dollars for creative ideas that will translate into billions. It is not just marketing or research and development that value creativity. Any money-saving or money-generating ideas, whether paper reduction, time savers, or new products and services, need someone to come up with them in the first place. Producing ideas is a necessary step in solving problems. Nobel Laureate Linus Pauling says, "The best way to have a good idea is to have lots of ideas" (Crainer, 1998). Where do those ideas come from? Folan (1999) suggests three essential ingredients for fostering creative ideas and problem-solving strategies.

* resources provided by a creative environment that includes multisensory objects
* practice for the mind by exposure to all kinds of new experiences
* time

It takes time in a different environment, and away from pressures, to allow the mind to open and ideas to flow. Does that sound like a classroom? It could be. It should be.

Walberg and Zeiser's (1997) research involving eminent men and women revealed that many creative people experienced stimulating family, educational, and cultural experiences during childhood, and more than half were encouraged to be creative as children by the availability of creative materials in their homes. They worked hard, they were intelligent (but not excessively so), they were creative, and they were thorough. This suggests the role of the teacher as an inspiration for creativity. The classroom should be an environment where there are multisensory objects and new experiences, and the time to explore both (Figure 10–5). It is then that creativity can

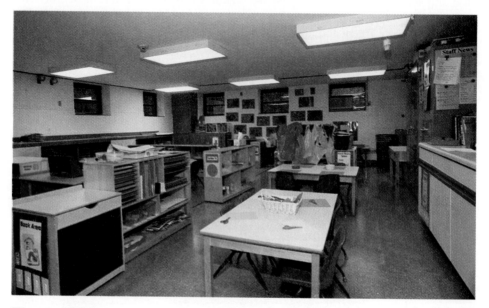

Figure 10–5

An environment full of sensory materials enhances creativity.

result in profits, not of a monetary nature, but of an explosion in learning. Every subject area can enhance, and in turn be enhanced by, creativity: reading, speaking math, science, technology, history, and social studies. The other areas of development—social, emotional, and self-concept—are addressed in the interactions between teacher and child and child and child.

The teacher's role in creativity is to model creativity. Lesson plans are necessary, but the *teachable moment* is an opportunity that cannot be ignored because of a previous plan. The creative teacher considers the opportunity, instantly weighs its potential value against that of the planned activity, and makes a judgment on how to proceed. The creative teacher is resourceful, having an eye for materials or different ways of presenting a concept that will be meaningful to the children. The creative teacher comes to school every day with at least one object to add to the classroom or for the children to explore. The creative and resourceful teacher is always on the alert for industrial surplus, store closeouts, half-price sales, and even recycled materials. Approaching families who have networks and assets to enrich the learning environment is the mark of a resourceful teacher. What better way to learn about anatomy and muscles than to invite a father who is a weight lifter into the classroom to demonstrate the various muscles and how they are strengthened? Or when studying machines, for example, the creative teacher might enlist the support of a family member to bring in a tortilla press, pasta machine, and tomato crusher to make a class dinner. Transforming the ingredients and the mechanics of the tools present lessons that will last longer than reading about these things in a book. You can be creative and inspire creativity in your students. Each day presents opportunities to be creative by setting small challenges for yourself, as in planting your garden rows the opposite of the way you have always done it, driving home on a different route, or listening to a different radio station. Changing routine is creative in itself and opens the door to other creative thoughts and acts.

Creativity relates to every aspect of learning, so the teacher's role is to inspire that creativity. Egan and Nadaner (1988), in the foreword to their book *Imagination and Education*, stated that, "Stimulating the imagination is not an alternative educational activity to be argued for in competition with other claims; it is a prerequisite to making any activity educational" (p. ix). Creative experiences are vehicles for learning in all other disciplines; teachers should integrate creativity into every subject area through open-ended equipment and activities to promote creativity. Look at the list below and sort according to open versus closed materials and activities.

Are the following open (divergent) or closed (convergent) activities?

 ❋ puzzles
 ❋ sand
 ❋ making masks
 ❋ rhythm band
 ❋ collage
 ❋ microphone and tape recorder

This is actually a trick question. You may have marked any one of them open or closed depending on your own experience and the conditions under which the activity was carried out. Puzzles are traditionally considered a closed activity and not a creative one, since there is usually only one way in which a puzzle can be assembled correctly. However, many children take a puzzle and pile up the pieces, or arrange them in some other way than the *correct* way, so puzzles can be creative and open-ended materials, if the teacher allows that to happen. Sand is probably one of the most open-ended activity materials, since there is little explicit direction or right or wrong way to play with sand, except for stringent safety rules about its use. What if a child wants to see what would happen if water were added? What if he wants to use the sand as pretend soup over in the dramatic play area? What if he wants to use the sand to stabilize blocks from tipping over? These are creative uses that may be prohibited in a closed atmosphere. Of course, there are safety considerations and limits to messes that correlate with the teacher's own norms. Making masks could be a very open-ended creative activity, or it could be closed and teacher controlled if the teacher announced, "Today we are going to make cat masks from these paper plates. Here are the strips for the whiskers, a pompom for the nose, and triangles for the ears. I've already traced the eyes so you can cut them out like cat's eyes." The rhythm band is usually an experimentation with instruments that can be struck, rubbed together, or tooted to make a noise as children move around the room, resulting in a cacophony of sound. In that way, it can be an open-ended activity, but you can quickly see how it could become a closed, less creative experience if the teacher insists on directing the beat, the various instruments' timing, and the marching pattern.

Making collages, or collections of objects glued to a foundation, is usually considered an open and creative activity, but it too can be stifled of its creativity when the teacher controls the types of materials and their placement (Figure 10–6). A clown

Figure 10–6

Providing materials with no adult instruction or intervention helps children use their own creativity.

collage planned by the teacher to reinforce shape concepts of circle, triangle, rectangle, and oval is a routine and predictable project that allows little creativity. Beginning teachers might respond, "But they can put them on any way they want." However, the clown, cat, or mask project is already in the mind of the teacher and the children's products will be compared to the outcome he expects in subtle ways. "This looks like a clown's hat to me," the teacher might say as he hands the child the triangle. "Here's a picture of a clown with a round red nose." The child may glue the triangle in the middle of the face because noses remind him of triangles. The child may glue two circles at the base of the triangle because he has closely observed nostrils; the teacher may be puzzled and think this is a strange-looking clown collage. Open-ended activities allow free use of materials, without preconceived notions of the *correct* use, and observing and even asking nonevaluative questions about the child's thoughts as he creates may give the teacher insight into the child's thinking.

Then what about models, coloring books, patterns for projects or technique instructions, such as the *right* way to use the brush, play the song, or follow the script's lines? The teacher who inspires creativity and child-centered teaching does not encourage an environment that is out of control, with no holds barred, no rules, and anything goes. That does not inspire creativity; that inspires chaos. Striving for balance and setting boundaries on creativity are necessary for physical safety. The teacher must also recognize the distinction between creative projects and planned projects that include such things as crafts, training and learning processes, procedures, and basic skills.

The teacher's role as the inspiration for creativity begins with the classroom environment. The physical environment should have materials that can be used in many different ways, at the child's discretion, and with enough time to explore them and finish the creation. Whether it is creating a drawing, painting, or sculpture; listening to, making, or moving to music; or writing a play or acting out an internal scenario, children need blocks of uninterrupted time to sufficiently engage and develop ideas. Of course, every classroom has schedules and time constraints, but a block of time in which the children know there will be no other demands or interference will help him with his creative process. The teacher's other major role is to show respect for the child's work. This is shown not only by providing the uninterrupted time, but also by not interfering or intervening in the child's work. This does not mean that the teacher sets the materials out and goes out for coffee. It means being available and assisting when needed, paying attention to the child's process and progress, and providing a forum for the child to display the work. It means never doing it for the child.

The teacher's comments on creative work are also important to ensure that the child is the one evaluating the work: remember, creativity is an expression from within. Nilsen (2001) suggests these responses to a child's product.

Adult Responses to Children's Products that Do Not Inhibit Creativity

* Not complimenting—Telling a child, "It's beautiful, lovely, very nice," can be an insincere tribute, uttered without even looking, showing nonattention. Instead: "You worked a long time on that."

* Not judgmental—Telling a child, "It's wonderful, it's great," demonstrates that you are not seeing the work from the child's point of view, only your own. Instead: "Would you like to tell me about it?"

* Not valuing—Telling a child, "I love it," takes the focus of satisfaction with the work away from the child and places its value on the viewer's judgment. Instead: "What do you like about it?" *continued*

* Not questioning—Asking the child questions like, "What is it?" and "What is this part?" gives the idea that you expect it to be something or represent an object you can recognize. Instead: "Would you like to tell me anything about it?"

* Not probing—Saying to the child, "Tell me about it," is a command that intimates there is some underlying significance. Instead: "Would you like to tell me about it?" or just a simple, "Hmmmm," shows attention and leaves the door open for the child to make comments without pressure.

* Not correcting—Pointing out things like, "Grass isn't orange; here's a green crayon for grass," indicates there's something wrong with the creation. Instead: do no correct except for such redirection as, "We paint on the paper, not on the wall. Here's a sponge to clean it up."

* Not psychoanalyzing—Inferring psychological significance to work, as in, "He always uses black; I think he's depressed," should be left to the experts. Instead, remember that children are nonrealistic for many years in their color choices and the ability to psychologically analyze drawings takes years of study.

* Not modeling—Do not show what the product should look like, as in, "Today we're going to make a caterpillar from an egg carton like this." Instead: provide a wide variety of materials without having an end product in mind.

* Describing—Give attention to the product or creative behavior and describe it using words for colors, designs, sequence, rhythm, or repeating story lines. In this way, you show respect for and affirm the child's work and provide information. (pp. 231–233)

Not only should children be provided with materials and activities to create musically, visually, or dramatically, they also should have the opportunity to experience the work of others. While the Mozart effect (the premise that playing classical music to infants and toddlers increases their mathematical skills) may have been discredited as a technique for raising IQ, listening to various styles of music can open children's creativity in other ways. They can think about the mood the music inspires, the visual images that appear as they listen, the mathematical pattern of the tempo, the changes in the musical score, and how music is influenced by culture and history. Children should be exposed to all kinds of recorded and live music. The same is true for visual arts. The teacher should include in the classroom prints of famous paintings, as well as examples of art styles from various cultures. The creative efforts of different world civilizations help children develop a broader perspective and acceptance of others. Visiting art galleries and studios, attending musical and dramatic productions, and hosting visiting artists expand the child's world into the arts of the community.

Play's Role in Creative Development

Everyone agrees that play and imagination (or creativity) go together. Play is a natural part of childhood and, if we are honest, a natural part of adulthood as well. Play time is when we do what we want, when we want, the way we want, for uninterrupted long periods. Is it unimportant? Of course not. It is through play that children and adults recreate (analyze that word!) the stories they have seen and heard. It is in play that you can safely stand against an adversary and try different strategies for coping. It is with play that you can say and do things you do not mean and say, "I was only fooling." It is at play that you can experiment with mixing materials, taking things apart, trying different computer keys, or upending a rock to see what is underneath. All of these variations of play help people develop physically, socially, emotionally, and creatively. Singer and Singer (1998), who have studied children's play (and especially how it is affected by television viewing), write that imaginative play helps the child organize and understand the world, experience control over the environment, and express more positive and affective responses.

SCENARIO	Picture a busy day at a bank, with many people queued up in a winding line waiting for the next available teller. An adult is accompanied by a child who is shorter than the rope barrier and promptly ducks underneath. In the space under the counter, the child deals out the stack of deposit slips provided by an adult at the counter. The child piles them on top of each other, then arranges them end to end, then side to side, and then begins to place them on top of each other, crisscrossing them. He then folds some into tiny little tightly packed bundles, wadding some of those up and throwing them toward a wastebasket.

Is the child playing? Is the child creating? Is the child learning? What age, sex, color is the child? What language is the child speaking? Play is the universal world of the child. To be truly effective as learning, play has some needs, foremost of which is a space. It does not need to be large, quiet, or even fully equipped, but it has to be physically and psychologically safe. If children fear being assaulted on a playground, or on a street in their neighborhood, they will have a hard time fully engaging in meaningful play. Another tool for play is an object. It does not have to be the latest educational toy in bright colors, it has to have some way to be acted upon. It is striking how many toys are activated by the push of a button and the power of a battery or computer chip, with the child reduced to standing back and watching the *toy* play. Pieces of paper, sticks, stones, or empty bags or boxes are the kinds of materials that elicit play and imagination. Another play necessity is time. When you are engaging in pleasurable activity, you do not want someone else telling you it is time to stop. You may have just been on the threshold of discovering a new way to arrange those materials or you may be so familiar with them that you begin to transform them mentally into something else. Did the child's trip to the bank fulfill his need for effective play/learning? Did he demonstrate creativity? Bretherton says, "I would like to suggest here that if we must look at the future implications of pretend play in childhood, it may be more profitable to think of it as the hallmark of an emerging artistic and literary ability" (Bretherton, 1998, p. 68). Many see the role of play in childhood as even more important to all cognitive and divergent thinking. Longitudinal studies (Russ, Robins, & Christiano, 1995) indicate fantasy play in first and second graders was predictive of their divergent thinking as sixth and seventh graders. Russ (1996) says, "Developing programs that help children learn to play . . . would be a good investment in the creative futures of our children." As you can see, creative, imaginative play is a valuable part of a child's development.

Inhibitors of Creativity

Did you ever look at some new thing and think, "Why didn't I think of that?" It looks like such a simple idea, now that it is created and manufactured. It seems that some people are more creative than others. Perhaps you are more creative than your friends or siblings, or are you less so? What reduces that curiosity and sense of wonder that is innate in children? We must begin with nature, the genetic controls on behavior and personality. Some people are literal, linear thinkers who are mentally bound by convention and logic, sometimes called *left-brain thinkers*. It appears that cognitive structure may influence creativity either positively or negatively.

The environment may also hinder creativity. This does not mean that an environment devoid of interesting objects, art materials, opportunities for music and dance lessons cannot produce creativity. Rather, an environment that does not allow exploration, manipulation, or trial and error stifles the development of creativity. Such an environment may be found in a very luxurious, affluent home, or it may be at school; the defining circumstance is a setting with few opportunities for creativity where, instead, order, structure, rule-following, convergent thinking, and conformity are valued while nonconformity is not. Surveillance, evaluation, rewards, competition, overcontrol, restricting choice, and pressure are called "creativity killers" in Goleman, Kaufman, and Ray's *The Creative Spirit* (1992). This refers to that restrictive environment where threats or dominance prevent free thought and action. Creativity takes *time*. It cannot be restricted to a 25-minute period between reading and recess. Creativity may even look like inactivity, with the body at rest while the brain is working.

Evaluation, external rewards, and competition are all thought to kill creativity (Amabile, 1989). What does that say about art and music competitions? Creativity is intrinsically motivating. It brings its own pleasure and satisfaction from being able to discover and experiment without too many boundaries. The satisfaction comes from within, not from an adult saying, "That's beautiful." External rewards in the form of adult praise, or money or some other form of materialistic reward have actually been shown to decrease a child's motivation to respond and create (Anderson, Manoogian, & Reznik, 1976).

Stereotypes of all kinds can negatively influence creativity (Figure 10–7). Children learn very early in life what boys and girls are like, and boys trying ballet or girls playing the drums is subtly discouraged. Cultural stereotypes about certain races or cultures being more creative in one specific way may discourage some, while setting false expectations for others. Even political ideologies can hinder creativity. A study in Romania

Figure 10–7

Stereotypical toys can stifle creativity.

showed that an ongoing lack of creativity in a society that traditionally valued conformity also contributes to children feeling disoriented and anonymous (Dinca, 1999).

Another attitude that confines creativity is self-consciousness. When a person is afraid of what others will think of him for having this wacky, far-out idea, or he has little confidence that he has a worthwhile contribution to make, or if he is feeling incompetent, it is difficult to be creative. When you can lose yourself in thought and concentrate on the bigger picture or the big problem, then the creative juices can flow. What this means in a classroom is that the teacher should promote an atmosphere of acceptance and not tolerate put-downs by other children, teasing, or actions that disparage another's ideas, creations, or work. The teacher must be the role model in this. If you could live without self-consciousness, you could be true to yourself, others would see your true self, and you would set yourself free.

If deterrents to creativity are prevented or overcome, creativity may result. So a person can be creative if he has at least a modicum of intelligence, an environment that poses little risk for wrong moves or wrong answers, and lives in a society that values individualism and does not prohibit freedom of expression because of sex, race, or economics. Now maybe you or the children in your class may never discover the cure for cancer, develop the next computer application, or write a hit song like *big C* creators do, according to Gardner (in Goleman, Kaufman, & Ray, 1992). But if you and the children you teach approach learning with open minds and a sense of wonder, looking at the ordinary in extraordinary ways, then your lives will be enriched and you will have earned more than your wages. You and they will have the satisfaction of being creative, making each day a learning adventure.

Creativity and the Arts

We have made the case for the importance of creativity in every aspect of learning. Divergent thinking, problem solving, curiosity, and a quest for different ways of thinking about things transcend all curriculum areas. Creativity is needed for thinking about the principles of mathematics and science, discovering new ways of using machines, speaking and writing, and solving interpersonal problems. Another obvious opportunity for developing creativity is in the arts curriculum, yet we reiterate that this curriculum is not the only place for creativity. The learning teacher should be familiar with the stages of development in the arts and include appropriate activities throughout the day that incorporate the arts with other areas of curriculum. With this concept of creativity and the arts, the curriculum blends the music, visual arts, and drama of different cultures with history and social studies. Focus can be directed to the illustrations in books, as well as the words, analyzing why that particular drawing was chosen and comparing various styles of illustrations. Music can inspire physical movement, touch the emotions, and portray a culture in a way that affects the whole spectrum of the child's development. Role-playing, the first introduction to drama, can help solve classroom problems, or provide the opportunity to act out a historical event, making it real and memorable. In these ways, creativity, the arts, and all areas of development and curriculum are interwoven.

✳ CREATIVE DEVELOPMENT AND THE ARTS CURRICULUM

Children are more imaginative than adults. Creativity seems to decline with age. Why do you think that is? Do you agree or disagree? Think of some of the components of creativity discussed earlier. Everything infants experience is novel and so are their responses.

They are discovering all the objects within their ever-widening reach and acting on those objects with rapidly developing physical skill and strength. They know no constraints, either moral or physical, and so they turn full glasses upside down, put everything that can fit into their mouths, and step off the edges of stairs, tables, or anything else they are standing on. They are trying to make sense of what they see, hear, taste, feel, and smell in light of what they have experienced before, constantly playing a mental matching game. They take those experiences and combine them in new ways. As children grow older and gain wisdom and judgment, the novelty of experience fades somewhat. Some past experiences have been painful or have brought condemnation, as in reaching out to touch a flame or tipping a full glass upside down to see what happens. There is a growing sense of *right* and *wrong*, conventions of society, and the fear of risk. Other forms of play and creativity take place, but none so free as those of the infancy and toddler years (Figure 10–8).

Creativity that finds its outlet in an object requires certain levels of physical development. Eye-hand coordination and fine-muscle control are needed to draw, paint, sculpt, or play a musical instrument. Large-muscle coordination is needed for creative movement. Emotional development, attention span, and the expression of feelings all enter into creativity. Temperament, personality, and emotional state are reflected in the child's creative outlets. Emotions can stimulate poetry, a song, a drawing, or a new way to relate to another person socially. Important people in your life may inspire your creating a drawing, poem, piece of music, or functional object, thus introducing another social aspect of creativity.

Stages of creativity have been observed and formulated by many experts. Lowenfeld and Brittain's (1987) insights into the stages of children's visual art are widely used to demonstrate the progression from scribbling to realism. Several theorists' stages of visual art parallel Piaget's cognitive stages, Erikson's (1950) psychosocial stages, and the development of language and literacy (see Figure 10–9). Gardner (in Healy, 1994) saw three distinct stages corresponding with ages. The visual art of children aged one through eight years expresses itself as spontaneous creativity; for those aged eight through twelve years, it seeks literalism, and for adolescence and beyond, it represents expression and appreciation. Note how the stages of creativity correspond to

Figure 10–8

Children love to play adult roles.

Piaget's Stages of Cognitive Development	Stages of Art Kellogg, Lowenfeld & Brittain, Schirrmacher	Language Development	Writing/ Reading	Erikson's Psychosocial Stages
Sensorimotor (birth to 2 years) • Moving from reflexes to object permanence	**Scribbling and Mark-making** (birth to 2 years) • Random exploration • Nonintentional	**Pre-Language** (birth to 2 years) • Sounds • Telegraphic sentences	**Book-Handling Skills** (birth to 2 years) • Right side up • Front/back • Turn pages	**Basic Trust vs. Mistrust** (birth to 2 years) • Consistent experiences
Preoperational (2–7 years) • Egocentric • Representation of objects and events by appearances	**Personal Symbol and Design** (2–4 years) • Controlled scribbling • Named scribbling	**Beginning Language** (2–4 years) • Acquiring vocabulary, grammar, social speech	**Function of Print** (2–4 years) • Read symbols in context • Reads pictures • Beginning writing	**Autonomy vs. Shame/Doubt** (2–4 years) • Independence • Sensory exploration
	Preschematic (4–7 years) • Generalized symbols recognizable to others • Nonrepresenta-tional	**Language** (4–7 years) • Symbolic language • Humor	**Readers and Writers** (5–8 years) • Decodes print • Invents spelling • Identifies words	**Initiative vs. Guilt** (4–7 years) • Constructive activities • Own decisions
Concrete Operational (7–11 years) • Logical, concrete thinkers • Can conserve, classify, seriate	**Schematic/ Realism** (7–9 years) • Representation of what he knows, not necessarily what he sees			**Industry vs. Inferiority** (7 years to puberty) • Sense of duty • Academic/social competence

Figure 10–9

Stage Comparison of Cognitive and Creative Theorists. (From Nilsen, 2001)

cognitive, emotional, and social stages. According to Amabile's study (1989), the types of creative activities in which children are engaged change over time.

* Toddlers engage in singing, drawing, building, and experimenting with sounds.
* Preschoolers explore painting, word play, dancing, and fantasy dramatic play.
* Early elementary age children experiment with cooking, sculpture, drama, and social relations.
* Upper elementary age children create through storytelling, games, dressing, numbers, and language (pp. 30–31).

As we see from Bergen (1998), kinds of play change with age, with more creative exploration and pretend play declining, and constructive play (play toward an end), games with rules, and symbolic play increasing and stabilizing into adulthood (Figure 10–10).

Just because all children use imagination and creativity, are they all creative? Maslow (1963) theorized that there are two kinds of creativity. *Primary* creativity is what everyone has and uses as they discover the world for themselves and re-create what they experience in words, visuals, or dramatics. *Secondary* creativity is a higher-level function that represents genuine innovation. As you look at the ages and stages more closely, and then look at the teacher's role in inspiring creativity's development, remember that you are usually dealing with primary creativity, but you never know what groundwork and inspiration you are laying for secondary creativity. We would all like to say of our accomplished former students, "I was his teacher." And teachers can take some small credit for their achievements.

Infant Creative Development and Curriculum

"The kernel of creativity . . . is there in the infant: the desire and drive to explore, to find out about things, to try things out. To experiment with different ways of handling things and looking at things" (Amabile in Goleman, Kaufman, & Ray, 1992, p. 57).

Infant Creative Development. Of course, an infant cannot draw, make music, or get involved in dramatics, but in the course of exploring his world, he is banking the sights, sounds, and feelings, storing them for an expressive outlet that will come in the future.

Infants visually track moving objects, and have a preference for patterns of black, white, and red over pastels, and flashing colored lights over white lights. However, the human face is the image they most prefer. They are not yet producing their own work, but are storing mental images for later expression when they have eye-hand

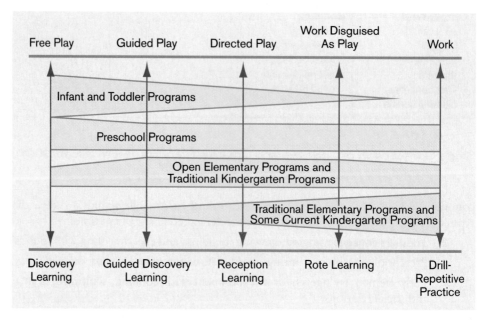

Figure 10–10

The schema of play and learning: four environmental patterns. (From Bergen, 1998. Reprinted by permission of the author and the Association for Childhood Education International)

control and are provided with appropriate materials. The human face, in the form of a rudimentary circle—that first and most important image stored—will likely be the first graphic they produce.

Infants respond to rhythmic sounds in the womb, beginning with the mother's heartbeat. Infants reflexively respond and move in time to music; you can see their activity levels increase with faster beats, slow with the slower tempo of lullabies. Infants also make sounds back when they hear pleasant, soothing intonations. In the second half of the first year, infants bounce and vocalize to music. The infant has enough hand control now to hold an object and bang on things, experimenting with different sounds, whether it's a spoon on the high chair tray or a stick on a rock.

The "Mozart effect" popularized the idea that classical music played to infants raised their IQ. This encouraged many anxious parents to play Mozart and other composers' music to their young children. In the hopes of raising children's academic performance once they entered school, politicians and recording companies distributed classical CDs to new families. Unfortunately, raising IQ is not that easy. The original study (Rauscher, 1994) has been misinterpreted and when it was unable to be replicated, the "Mozart effect" was questioned (Bruer, 1999). However, music's rhythm, its patterned repetition of notes and phrases, has a mathematical connection. Early experiences with music are never without connections to later learning, so providing them for infants is enriching for both their pleasure and their cognitive development.

Infants' reflexes control their movements in the first six months. As they begin to gain control first of head, then of their trunk and arms, and finally their legs in the second six months, they love games like "Peek-a-Boo," pretending to feed a stuffed animal, or imitating Mommy holding the phone or Daddy tying his shoe. Games such as "Peek-a-Boo" and "This Little Piggie" introduce changes in voice when going from talking to storytelling to game playing. These changes in voice inflection are precursors to dramatic play. By the second half of the first year, infants are interested in books with realistic photographs that he can grab, chew, and throw. Repetitive words or rhymes become part of infants' beginning repertoire of words and listening to a story forms the basis of their own attempts at storytelling (which may be unintelligible for a long time). As the child babbles on, listeners comment, "It sounds just like he's telling a story." He is.

Infant Creative Curriculum. A young mother placed her six-month-old in the garden among the pansies. She said in a very soft voice, "This is a beautiful purple pansy. Smell how beautiful its fragrance is. Feel its petals on your cheek. Remember this in your dreams." This is a child on his way to a lovely life (Figure 10–11 on page 368).

The infant's natural environment—first the family bed, crib, or bassinet; then other rooms in his home; the carrier, car seat, blanket, or sling; and eventually wherever the infant goes—is all the equipment he needs. Interacting with the things around him—the sensations of seeing, hearing, touching, tasting, and smelling—begin to build his cognitive structures, stimulating those dendrites to connect brain cells. Planned activities are not necessary, but what is necessary are consistent, loving adults who interact with the infant by first caring for his physical and emotional needs and then initiating interactions and responding to him. Adults who talk, sing, read, and show the infant things in their world are setting the stage for creative development in all areas.

The infant should have a visual environment conducive to exercising focus, including such things as the black, white, and red patterns he will find most interesting in his early months. Colors and patterns to look at can be incorporated in crib sheets, mobiles, and pictures on the wall near the crib or over the changing table. Seeing the colors and patterns sets the stage for later cognitive connections. Since the

Figure 10—11

An infant's interacting with nature adds to his sensory environment.

human face is the earliest vision the child has, pictures of faces and mirrors around the room build the infant's social world. When drawing begins, the face will likely be one of the first objects the child will draw or paint. The infant can experience control of media and produce visual art and even sculpture at an early age. Nontoxic paints, stubby brushes, and safe clay can be provided to the infant as he nears his first birthday. The infant will naturally do this by smearing food on the table, experiencing its texture, and seeing the effects of rubbing, splattering, and scraping it with his fingernails. Infants squeeze foods and form the pieces into balls or feel it squish between their fingers. While some caregivers are not comfortable with encouraging this kind of experimentation, it may help to remember that these are the same kinds of movements and techniques used in painting and sculpting.

SCENARIO At a wedding reception, the dancing began. On the dance floor, several young couples were dancing very close, and holding their babies or toddlers in between them. Older children were making family circles by holding hands and dancing with their parents. The dancers and observers had pleasant memories of that wedding reception.

Providing a blend of music, quiet, rhythms, and melodies gives the infant a foundation on which to later build his own music. Once he is rolling over, creeping, crawling, and eventually walking, the infant needs freedom to explore safely and move in time to music. Playing music during the infant's day can soothe, provide fun, give cues to different kinds of activities, and pave the neural pathways to melodies, rhythms, and words. Moving his arms and legs in time to the music or dancing around the room in his caregiver's arms is enjoyable for the infant and takes no equipment other than a voice, though a radio, tape, or CD may be used to augment that voice.

Listening to music provides warmth and enjoyment, as well as a beginning association of music to emotions that will last a lifetime.

Playing little games with and speaking and reading to the infant with varied facial expressions and voice inflections are the beginnings of the dramatic aspects of the child's development. No planned curriculum is needed; parents and caregivers can do these simple activities that will begin to develop the infant's capacity for creativity. By the end of the first year, the infant is beginning to engage in pretend play by donning Daddy's hat or Mommy's shoes. By providing props for dramatic role-play, the infant is beginning explore stepping into another's role, not as a possible future actor, but as the beginning of empathy, or placing himself in another's situation. This hallmark of cognitive development and emotional maturity has its roots in infancy.

Toddler Creative Development and Curriculum

Now the child is walking and climbing, with creativity motivated by curiosity and sometimes dangerous behavior. There are many ways to get at interesting, but possibly forbidden, objects, like pulling out and climbing up on drawers, or pushing a chair over close by, or even getting a big stick and knocking the object down. The child now has the power to act on his world.

Toddler Creative Development. Toddlers are very observant, taking in the smallest detail of objects and actions around them. This is the beginning of their aesthetic development in differentiating shapes, colors, and textures. Toddlers like to try everything and manipulate writing tools (and such close approximations as lipstick or eyeliner). They use all senses, so all art materials need to be nontoxic, for they will probably be tasted. Toddlers are not yet able to produce drawings or paintings that approximate reality (Figure 10–12). Lowenfeld and Brittain (1987) call this the "Disordered and Random Scribbling Stage."

Figure 10–12

Early experimentation with art materials unleashes creativity.

Toddlers use their whole hand to grip the marking tool, with whole arm movements making haphazard lines on and off the paper. Circles are the first shape they can make, once random scribbles are more controlled. Scribbling is an important developmental phase as toddlers test out the characteristics of media such as crayons, pens, paint, and glue. They see the effect of their actions in a physical representation of their hand's movement. Toddlers often name the scribbles or circles as they draw "Kitty" or "Mommy," showing that they have a mental image, but do not as yet have the physical dexterity to re-create the image on paper.

Most children this age love to sing and dance to music and rhythm of any kind. They sing short phrases from songs and recognize that certain toys like xylophones or drums are connected with music production. They play them with enthusiasm (if not rhythm or melody). During their second and third years, toddlers' muscles are coordinating, so they can move their arms to music, dance simple steps, and jump and twirl. They imitate the dance steps of older children and adults, such as the two-step, hula, or jazz moves. These little dancers delight adults, who shower them with applause and attention. They are beginning to distinguish between songs and have favorites they like to sing over and over, often using them as a way to soothe themselves and prepare for sleep.

This is the true beginning of the theatrical performer. The toddler can mimic the spider creeping up the waterspout, the tired baby, the hungry kitty, and even the angry daddy through body movements, sounds, and words. Realistic props prompt certain behaviors, such as talking on the phone, drinking from a cup, eating with a spoon, or nurturing baby dolls. Toddlers are soon able to transform other objects into the props they need, using them symbolically. A block becomes a car, a stick becomes a fishing pole, and anything becomes a spoon. Toddlers' most recurrent dramatic play themes are the daily routines of eating, preparing for sleep, or taking a bath. Toddlers in households where parents use the telephone a lot will imitate adults on the telephone. In houses where there is a routine of tortilla making, toddlers will imitate the movement of flattening a tortilla. They do these things with extraordinary attention to detail. Toddlers may not as yet be speaking plainly, but their voice inflections and hand and facial gestures mirror what they have seen and heard. Parents in every culture have been startled at the sight of their toddlers re-creating themselves.

Toddler Creative Curriculum. Just as with infants, toddlers' casual, daily living experiences in visual arts, music, movement, and drama are important supporters of creative development. As toddlers look at the pattern the milky spoon makes on the high chair tray, bang out a rhythm with two stones, or use the spoon to pretend to feed the baby, creativity is flourishing. By recognizing these first small actions as steps to creativity, and by encouraging experimentation and providing tactile materials the child can control, the adult is stimulating creativity.

Toddlers are gaining control of their bodies and language, and thus are capable of engaging in experimental activities. Toddlers can be given finger paints (nontoxic of course), or, if the caregiver is comfortable with this, allowed to finger paint with applesauce or pudding. This experimentation with color, texture, and control over the medium is the beginning of creating a masterpiece. Shielding the toddler, walls, and floor with a protective cover is a good precaution; then you can just step back and let him create.

Toddlers also enjoy Play-Doh® and other squishy media to experience the three-dimensional aspect of creations. All visual art projects for toddlers should be for exploration, with no expectations for them making clown faces, bunnies, or caterpillars.

By including interesting visual objects at the toddler's eye level, you encourage his senses to take in color, shape, pattern, and details. Interesting things to look at can be placed on the wall next to the slats in the crib, or next to the changing table, and becoming objects of conversation during quiet moments or routines. Combining things to look at and talk about uses the emotional domain as the link, just as that mother showing her infant the pansy.

Toddlers love music and there are many musicians who have created music that especially appeals to toddlers' interests and need for repetition. Drum-type instruments, bells, and shakers give toddlers the opportunity to experiment with making sounds themselves and compare sounds (Figure 10–13). Listening to different kinds of music—loud and soft, fast and slow—widens toddlers' familiarity with the uses of music. (However, there should also be some quiet time to hear the rhythm of their heartbeats and their own breathing out and breathing in.)

Toddlers are beginning to appreciate silly lyrics. While most cannot yet sing a tune, they can repeat phrases and recognize their favorites as quickly as any "Name That Tune" contestant. Games that incorporate music and body movements are popular at this age, so playing the ever-popular "Ring Around the Rosie," "London Bridge," "Hokey Pokey," and others is only tiresome for the adults, not the toddlers, who love to play them over and over. Singing familiar nursery rhyme songs stretches toddlers' vocabulary and helps them hear rhyming words. Toddlers can often remember the last word of every rhyme or song, such as "Hush Little Baby" when sung over and over at bedtime. These little musical games that come so naturally are important investments in memory expansion as well as creative expression.

Toddlers love dress-up props, such as hats, purses, shoes, and other objects taken from real life, such as plastic dishes, toy fishing poles, and garden tools, in order to act out daily routines. These need not be purchased; they may come from the cupboard or closet, always with a mind for safety, of course. These props set the stage for toddlers to re-create scenarios from everyday life. Adults can join in tea parties, fishing excursions, pretend shopping trips, or bus rides, and in doing so lend authenticity and show approval to the toddler's beginning dramatic performances.

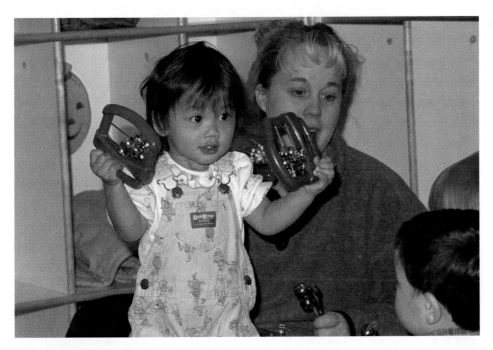

Figure 10–13

Experimenting with sound!

Singer and Singer (1990) advise, "Young children need more structured toys representing commonplace objects in their environment such as home furnishings, dolls, and vehicles in order to engage in pretend play. As children's representational skills become more developed, they are able to use less realistic objects in their play (blocks, clay, pipe cleaners, boxes, cardboard tubs) and can make more transformations. As language increases they are able to communicate more about their pretend acts and dependence on more realistic objects decreases" (p. 85).

Preschooler Creative Development and Curriculum

Preschoolers have language and body control, and have wide knowledge from their experiences that they can use to exercise and express the kind of creative thinking that amazes many adults. One of the most creative areas of this age is language. Preschoolers often create metaphors, giving inanimate objects life and intentions, as in "The star is winking," or "The tree is waving bye-bye."

Preschooler Creative Development. With more developed and sophisticated language, experiences, and developing senses of self in the bigger world, preschoolers seek to re-create thoughts in expressive ways. Preschoolers draw and paint, make up stories and songs, act out carefully observed roles, and combine familiar things in new ways just to see what will happen.

Preschoolers' scribbling becomes more controlled and their creations are even given names. Children at this age hold marking tools with their fingers, and are more intentional about placing marks on the paper. Some geometric shapes and alphabet letters may begin to appear. As children move into the Lowenfeld and Brittain's (1987) Preschematic stage, human figures begin just as a circle, then a circle with lines drawn out from the side and bottom as arms and legs, with more and more detail eventually appearing. This "tadpole man" is not what the child sees, but what he is physically capable of reproducing (Figure 10–14). The human face is first, then arms and legs, and then details like eyes, mouth, hair, ears (and earrings), and, finally, fingers, toes, and knees, usually in that order. Color is used randomly, not realistically; objects float in space, with no relationship between them. Art at this age is personal self-expression and practice with the medium.

This is the beginning stage of learning to draw and drawing to learn. Magaluzzi, founder and philosopher of the Reggio Emilia, Italy, preschools known around the world for their children's creative work, calls children's work "the hundred languages of children, modes of expression, including words, movement, drawing, painting, building, sculpture, shadow play, collage, dramatic play and music" (Edwards, Giandini, & Forman 1995, p. 3) By guiding and closely observing the children and encouraging re-creation of those observations in a variety of art media, the atelierista (art teacher) scaffolds the child's products. This is done by encouraging the children to go beyond their actual capabilities, not by doing it for them, but by supporting, assisting, and providing process skills to accomplish their plans. A preschool in Reggio Emilia contained plastic water tubes and pumps that made a circulatory water sculpture encompassing two classrooms and two floors of the building, inside and outside. The children's ideas were supported by an atelierista whose special talent was water sculpture. In another school, fantastic clay face masks were facilitated by an atelierista who is a sculptor. Children's ideas metamorphosed into reality with materials and processes scaffolded by these teachers.

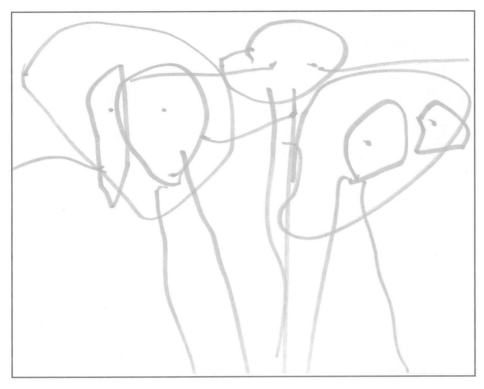

Figure 10–14

Can you see this child between his parents?

Children's drawings in the preschool years are still explorations of the media, but they begin to take on representations of thought, with more and more detail and realism depicted. This movement from nonrepresentational to representational occurs at the end of the preoperational stage, with written language and representation of thought occurring simultaneously. Alphabet letters will often be seen in their artwork as children intertwine the two new skills.

Preschoolers can sing songs, accurately recalling words, music, and movements, and can recognize familiar tunes. Favorites are "Hokey Pokey" and "Head and Shoulders." They are beginning to be able to move to a tempo and tap out simple rhythms on instruments. They often hum or sing during solitary play or when readying themselves for sleep. Songs created by them have little relationship to songs with repeated melodies or choruses, but they love to stand on a stage and belt out original songs for longer than some care to be in the audience. Depending on what they have been exposed to, they may accompany their performances with pretend microphones clutched in the latest singer's style.

Scripts for preschoolers' dramatic play become more elaborate and move toward a more interactive and social realm, away from the monologues of the toddler years (Figure 10–15 on page 374). Preschoolers still have difficulty sustaining roles for a long enough periods of time to really play out their imagined scenes or story lines. Paley's (1990) work in this area demonstrates scaffolding children's ideas of the dramatic episode by having the children dictate the story and the teacher act as director, moving the reenactment along by prompting dialogue and movements. Be sure to read *The Boy Who Would Be a Helicopter* (Paley) to see how she used this technique to help a child with social difficulties be accepted by his classmates.

Figure 10–15

Children replay what they see.

SCENARIO

Wang Lee entered the preschool not knowing any English. She followed the other children around and watched them closely for days, but did not attempt to play. One day, she was opening the cupboards in the play kitchen and found a wok. She put it on the stove, went to the table, and pretended to chop, chop, chop, then scooped her imaginary ingredients into the wok and shook it furiously. With a flourish, she passed the imaginary contents onto a plate and brought it proudly to the teacher. This was the breakthrough. The next day she went to the easel, put on an apron, and painted. She mixed the colors together, pulled the teacher to the easel, and said, "Choc-o-late." She tried the block area, putting together puzzles, and soon was eating at snack time and listening intently at story time. Familiar objects and playing out a familiar role were her bridge into the classroom's world.

WORDS OF WISDOM
Jane Davidson of Delaware has studied children's dramatic play episodes for many years. Here is an episode of dramatic play Jane observed and her interpretation.

"Maddie is crouched in the corner barking, Emily notices and joins her, and soon there is a large collection of dogs barking. The teacher comes over and pets each of the dogs. "Are you a dog family?" she asks. The dogs bark, nodding their heads in agreement. "Who is the mommy dog?" The dogs stop barking for a moment to discuss who they will be in the dog family. Later in the day, the dogs crawl

continued

throughout the classroom barking, generally disrupting other play. The teacher directs them to the blocks to build dog houses, and explains that dogs are not allowed to wander loose without owners. As building progresses, cats also enter the blocks area, and signs are made to distinguish dog houses from cat houses and from integrated dog/cat houses."

Many teachers looking at this play sequence would see the dogs as a disruption to be banned from their classroom. A wise teacher would realize the incredible value of this play. Emily is a shy child who does not often play with others. The dog play not only allowed her to join her peers in play, but also drew her into discussing with others the family structure and type of dog house to build. Making signs showed the children the value and power of writing. Depending on the children's level of writing, they could watch the signs being made and then explain their meanings to other children, or they could participate in the writing themselves. Either way, the children are becoming people for whom writing is a valuable tool. Pretend play is at the heart of a good early childhood classroom. Because pretend play has great meaning to young children, it is a place where much learning can happen. It is important for teachers to gently guide the play to keep it constructive and scaffold it to a higher level, without taking it over or destroying it. In this example, choosing roles, building, and writing were all things that extended the children's play, rather than subverting it.

Playing out roles in the dramatic play area has long been therapeutic for children. They work out sibling rivalry, exercise their will and power, and recite scripts they have heard. Realistic, familiar props help them enter into their roles. When more than one child is playing in that domain, the play takes on a sociodramatic dimension, with negotiation of roles. "You be the little sister and I'm the mother." "No, I'm the mother." "Well, okay, we'll both be mothers." This kind of play incorporates language, physical movement, creativity, cognitive problem solving, and emotional expression, all objectives of preschool programs.

This is the age when children often have imaginary friends. Some may wonder if such children are especially shy, unable to make real friends, or maladjusted in some way. Singer and Singer (1990) have extensively studied children's play and have found that children who have imaginary friends "will be cooperative with friends and adults and may use somewhat more extensive language, while also being somewhat less likely to watch a good deal of television" (p. 104). Davis (1998), in his extensive study of creativity, says that having an imaginary playmate as a child and participating in theater are two dependable predictors of creativity.

Preschooler Creative Curriculum. Experiences children have had as infants and toddlers are now transformed into expressions of their own creativity. They are still experimenting with materials, media, and actions, but are putting them together in new and individualistic ways. Pulaski (1973) found that richer fantasy play was elicited by "minimally structured toys . . . includ[ing] drawing paper, paints, Play-Doh®, wooden blocks, cardboard cartons, pipe cleaners, rag dolls, and costumes." There is more social pretend play with these kinds of materials than there is with puzzles, Legos®, small blocks, or coloring materials. Children's preferences for creating with materials, sound, or dialogue may be seen, although they really are still exploring all these avenues for creativity (Figure 10–16 on page 376).

The environment is part of the child's aesthetic and creative world. Preschoolers often want to take modeling dough, sand, or water to the dramatic play area to have tangible substitute materials to stir and serve. They may want to take markers and

Figure 10—16

Having access to many different art media helps children find success and satisfaction in their own products.

paper into the block area to draw pictures of their buildings, or rhythm instruments into the bathroom to hear the echo. For the sake of orderliness, teachers often discourage such equipment crossover, but this denies children's creative impulses to try out familiar things in different ways. A solution might be to have the children help solve the problems of spills, space, or returning of materials to their storage spaces. The teacher who inspires creativity says "Why not?" more than she says "No."

Art materials should be visible, accessible, and varied. All kinds of drawing implements, such as pencils, crayons, markers, and paints should be available, as well as all kinds of paper and cardboard, including large sheets of drawing and painting paper. Glue, glue sticks, tape, and staplers should be provided so that desired materials can be combined. Materials for collages should be available, including items from nature such as pine cones, straw, twigs, and pebbles, and other items such as cotton swabs and balls, ice cream sticks, stickers, rubber bands, and toothpicks. Children of this age are still nonrepresentational, so there should be no teacher-directed projects or expectation of recognizable products. Such projects and products do not inspire the creative spirit, and may actually diminish the children's confidence in their own creations that come from within.

Blocks are also a part of visual art materials. Children can construct bridges and designs from small plastic or wooden cubes or unit or hollow blocks (wooden frame blocks of multiples of a single unit about 10 inches square). These larger blocks promote dramatic play. Blocks can be laid out flat to become a stage or dancing platform, or stood on end to produce a wall that can be a fortress, platform from which to jump, barrier against the dinosaur or monster, or fence to keep a wild animal contained.

Children's creative work should dominate display areas. Their endeavors, with their permission, may be matted on larger contrasting paper, mounted on bulletin boards, or collected in portfolios. Work that is taken home, which should primarily be of the preschooler's choosing, should be labeled with the child's name by the child, wherever they choose. Showing the children how artists sign their work demonstrates the importance of signing their own work. Of course, the teacher may need to write the child's name on the back of the work if the child's writing is not legible. A date stamp in the art area can be used for fun, as well as to date the backs of works to document the children's progress. The date stamp is a novel way for children to do this, alleviating the teacher of the responsibility (Figure 10–17).

Music and movement can be a big part of the preschooler's day at home and at school. Music can be used as signals for transitions; using certain music just before nap or bedtime is relaxing, predictable, and becomes part of the ritual that many preschoolers find so comforting. Preschoolers can learn the words and melody to songs that especially catch their interest. Hearing their own voice singing is an important goal of the preschool years, so children should have opportunities to sing parts of songs by themselves, without pressure, but in a gamelike way. They learn songs best by singing along with the teacher, joining in on the repetitive parts. Making large song charts with the words in a rebus style, helps with both memorizing the song and prereading overlaying words with recognizable pictures or graphics for words that occur again and again. Before long, the children are pointing to the song charts and learning even long, involved songs. Repetition is the key.

Moving to music, both songs with specific directions to clap or stomp and music that inspires movement with its tempo and melody, should be included in the daily routine. Compositions like "The Flight of the Bumble Bee" or scores from *The Nutcracker* or *The Lion King* defy standing still. Scarves, ribbons, and crepe paper streamers can make the movement more interesting. Preschoolers using rhythm instruments that ring, jangle, or bang are not expected to make music or even a regular rhythm. The activity is intended to give children a sense of control over sound-making instruments. By the end of the preschool years, they may be able to beat out a regular rhythm, but then again they may just be exploring. Take two aspirin and try again tomorrow.

Figure 10—17

Opportunities to use art materials can begin early in life.

Preschoolers can carry out more involved dramatic play situations given the appropriate props. Grocery stores, beauty salons, and restaurants are some of the themes that can be used in a classroom, setting in motion the taking on of familiar roles. Most children have observed behavior in these familiar places and can act out their roles with realism. The traditional housekeeping area of the classroom has taken on a broader definition with these supplementary dramatic settings. The teacher should provide props that reflect the children's culture. The props encourage both boys and girls to take on familiar roles, various occupations, or fantasize with adventure play. Dramatic play elicits language and social interaction while stimulating creativity. Problems that arise afford the opportunity to learn how to solve difficulties without violence through negotiation and compromise.

Creativity and inspiration go beyond these areas into all preschool activities. While the children are looking at gerbils, the teacher can inspire storytelling about what gerbils are thinking or suggest writing a song about the life of a gerbil. Artists' works hung in the classroom can illustrate the use of patterns corresponding to mathematics discussions. Language and literacy are natural vehicles for creativity in storytelling, writing, and reading. The creative teacher inspires creativity in the preschoolers.

Primary Age Creative Development and Curriculum

Erikson (1950) calls the six- to eight-year-old stage one of industry. Children at this age can mass-produce artwork, sing a number of songs from memory, and put on dramatic performances with passionate seriousness. Gardner calls this "the golden age" of creativity, with expression of concerns, as well as hopes, for the world in the children's art, and with their spontaneous enjoyment of music, dance, and poetic language (in Healy, 1994). Primary age children use their creativity to expand activities like writing and illustrating their own books, writing songs and performing them with costumes and choreography, and carrying out elaborate plots in dramatic play. This is the beginning of a peer-comparison stage, so evaluative comments by adults or disparaging comments by peers can have a negative effect on creative efforts.

Primary Age Creative Development. In Lowenfeld and Brittain's (1987) "Schematic" stage, drawings represent thoughts, feelings, and striving for realism. Observers can see this happen over time, as formerly "floating" people and houses now lower toward a baseline. Now there is a sky or ceiling that show the child's spatial awareness and the young artist conquers the dilemma of the horse rider's other leg, or the other eye in a silhouette. Primary age children often portray part of the sun in the upper corner of a picture to represent the whole. Their drawings often take on repeated schemes like flowers, birds, or cars. This newfound realism, however, brings with it a certain loss of spontaneity and creativity, especially as they compare themselves and their work to other children, and emulate some of the themes they see in others' work. Their now-developed small-muscle skills expand their abilities to create in other media, like crafts such as weaving, model making, puppets, and collage.

Primary age children can now make music. They not only can sing, dance, and pound out rhythms, but also can learn to play instruments and read music. Many begin lessons on the recorder, piano, drum, or horn. They also have the large-muscle coordination to follow more intricate dance steps, so they quickly catch on to the latest dance craze. They can accurately sing many of the lyrics of contemporary music (often to the consternation of their parents). Many children at this age participate in dance lessons that may incorporate cultural aspects.

Imitating familiar characters now broadens beyond family roles, expanding to television and movie characters. Primary age children can accurately mimic their favorite singers or adventure heroes. They are still firming up their own identity, so they may at times also imitate each other, taking on mannerisms or speaking styles from their peers. Because they are beyond the egocentric stage, they can use role-play for problem solving. They are also cognitively able to sustain dramatic play, staying with one role and placing themselves in that role physically, emotionally, and linguistically. This makes for extended dramatic play episodes that may range over a few days or even weeks. Because they are most likely selecting same-sex children as playmates, dramatic play at this stage tends to be gender segregated.

Primary Age Creative Curriculum.

As children get older, all their past experiences—those taken in as infants, explored as toddlers, and played at with abandon in preschool—are brought to the stage of industry, when children have an inner drive to create meaningful products that convey their understanding of their world. The products can be seen as windows into the child's mind, as well as opportunities for the child to express feelings and ideas. This also coincides with formal schooling, when preplanned lessons and standards-driven education reduce the time and opportunity for free-flowing creative endeavors. Despite Gardner's labeling this as the "golden age of creativity," conventional behavior; precise, clear thinking; and well-organized learning skills are stressed so vehemently in schools that many researchers call this the "dead period for creativity" (in Albert, 1996). It does not have to be the end of creativity in education, however. The teacher's role is to encourage children's creativity in a quest for knowledge, helping them discover how to learn and learn how to discover.

Now in Lowenfeld and Brittain's (1987) "Representational" stage, children are able to replicate their observations with various types of media. They symbolize mental images on paper, in clay, or with collages, demonstrating their knowledge of the subject. The teacher can use this not only as an expression of creativity, but also as a way to better understand children's thinking. Primary age children convey their knowledge and ideas through visual arts. Teachers can use this ability in subject areas such as science, where the child can document observations by drawing; mathematics, where quantity concepts can be concretely presented; and history and social studies, where projects can re-create neighborhoods, maps, and historical events and figures.

By introducing children to the work of famous artists, the teacher can broaden their world, not just aesthetically, but socially as well. The stories of artists' lives and the cultural and historical events that shaped them bring the children's familiarity with them down to a more personal level.

Children of this age like to play games with rules and musical games that involve jumping or moving to music. These games are important ways to help coordinate muscles and build the social skills of taking turns and cooperating, as well as to develop appreciation for all kinds of music. Music and movement can be integrated into other areas of the curriculum by having the children learn historical dances. Music from various cultures brings another dimension to the global perspective and widens the children's knowledge of sounds, including learning words to songs in other languages. Choreographing movement to words and music helps integrate several mental and physical capacities, while being enjoyable and producing a sense of cohesiveness within a group. This is the age when children really enjoy musical productions. Hearing your own voice singing is an important experience, and the teacher should provide opportunities for the children to do so.

The creative plots of earlier years are now giving way to more realistic enactment of characters, because the children are now reading for themselves and seeking out more realistic literature. They read of real-life adventures and begin to understand the interplay of plot, setting, dialogue, and action/reaction. Choral reading and poetry recitation are favorite activities in which children can give dramatic performances within a structured environment. They enjoy creating puppets and scripts and putting on plays for each other.

Elementary Age Children Creative Development and Curriculum

The decline of the creative spirit as the child matures can be attributed to many factors. The primary reason is one of predictable development. This is the age where industry (Erikson, 1950) is full blown. Children at this age have reached the concrete operations stage in their thinking, logically working out their own theories. Parents are familiar with this as the argumentative stage. Children use their new reasoning ability to argue why they should be allowed to do a certain thing, or they may use creativity to explain why they did a particular deed. They are also keenly aware of their peers and what they think, and the social pressures to conform are often stronger than their creative urges. Conformity is equated with acceptance, and individuality is often rejected as "weird." Singer and Singer (1990), observers of children's play and creativity for more than 25 years, call this pushing creativity underground. "It is clear from observing large numbers of children of diverse backgrounds that pretend play (as well as other kinds of play) goes on well into the early school years and continues either 'underground' in the mind or in more socially sanctioned group forms well into adolescence . . . board games such as Monopoly® often involve additional pretend elements or are the focus of private or shared fantasies well into adult life" (p. 42).

Elementary Age Children Creative Development. Another major factor in the decline of creativity is an educational system that seeks convergent thinking where only the "right" answer is acceptable. This is an emotionally risky environment with heightened anxiety to produce the "right" answer. Gardner, in *The Unschooled Mind* (1991), describes this convergent style of education, where the teacher demonstrates the desired performance or behavior and the student duplicates it as closely as possible. This results in an emphasis on basic skills and memorization without the kind of transformational learning we saw encouraged for math and science teachers in the preceding chapter. The mind only holds so much unrelated information before it casts off what it considers useless; what is relevant and useful becomes a part of the person's real knowledge. Many educators feel it does not have to be one or the other. Teachers can use creativity and transformational methods to help children attain basic skills in mathematics, science, and literacy.

Lowenfeld and Brittain (1987) point out the increasing peer influence, moving out of egocentric thought, and the ability to take on another's perspective. At this age, realism is extremely important, down to the stitching on jeans and the slot holes drawn on the electric plug. Drawings are still one-dimensional but the "X-ray" problem of earlier years has been solved, so that objects that would not appear, such as the horse rider's other leg, are not drawn and the child feels comfortable with that. Girls often draw horses, hearts, rainbows, and fashion models. Boys draw cars, superheroes, and sports figures. There is more of a sense of perspective, with closer objects appearing larger, and often a road or sidewalk converging to the point of a triangle. People in proportionate sizes and visual perspectives in drawing occur at about the same age, both stemming from predictable intellectual development.

Music lessons and participation in chorus and band unite children's interests in music and social activities. Children of this age have a growing awareness of teenage music trends and their yearning to be considered adolescents stimulates that interest.

Figure 10—18

Playing a musical instrument brings many rewards.

The same is true for any dance fad or stylized body movement. Imitation is the byword here and individuality is scorned. Music patterns have mathematical relationships; learning to read music can have a positive effect on mathematical concept learning as well (Figure 10–18).

This is the age for *playing the role*, not in play episodes, but in real life by trying on other persona. Children's search for identity can lead them to adopt the speech, mannerisms, attitudes, and behaviors of others. This can be positive or negative, depending on the role models. The dramatic playgrounds at this age are the mall, the movie theater, and the cafeteria, where clusters of all boys or all girls can be found. Parents and teachers hope the roles the children adopt are ones that will not leave lifelong emotional and physical scars. The latest fads and fashions are indicators of that quest for identity. In their search for individuality, children act out conformity to be accepted. Imitating teenage roles of punk, Goth, gangsta is this age's dramatic play.

Elementary Age Children's Creative Curriculum.

SCENARIO The fifth grader was talking to an adult friend about school. "My art teacher loves us! She lets us use all kinds of neat things and lets us do it our own way."

On the surface, this is a great compliment to the art teacher, interpreting her unconditional acceptance as love. As you think about the sentence, however, there is an additional implication: what about the other teachers? Are they not perceived as loving their students? Why? Could it be that the other teachers rarely let children explore and do it their own way? What implication does that have for discovery learning and creativity?

The best way for teachers to foster creativity is to be creative themselves: to be open to new ideas, to try new things. They should play with the children, not as a playmate, but to present ideas and provide a risk-free environment where all ideas are considered and respected, eliciting responses that draw on creativity. By seeing that every curriculum area can be part of the creative atmosphere, children will become better problem solvers for life; this skill may be more important than any math formula, spelling word, or scientific principle.

Art expression at this stage has moved beyond the symbolism of earlier ages. Elementary age children produce works that range from experimentation with the abstract to intense concentration on details or a single aspect of the work, such as perspective or shadows, while ignoring the whole. Teachers should provide opportunities to practice drawing from still life, and a study of the masters as the children struggle with issues of dimension and content. An even more extensive integration of the arts into science, mathematics, history, and social studies can enrich those studies by helping students see that visual representations are ways of transferring knowledge, as well as expressions of culture and history. Integrating visual arts into content studies gives students expressive outlets and, as Gardner describes, kinesthetic, visual, and spatial awareness.

Children at this age are into the popular music of their time, which often has incomprehensible words and discordant sounds, according to adults. However, popular music is part of the culture and incorporating, rather than ignoring, their musical interests can be a catalyst for some children to find understanding and acceptance. Studying different kinds of music and what makes them different goes beyond learning about music. It involves history, social events that inspire the music, economics, sociology, mathematics, and science. Just the innovations in the music industry, such as technology, cultural reflections, advertising, and changing instruments, can produce issues, topics, and projects that cover many subject areas.

Studying music and movement should include participation. Children of this age are primed for learning to play musical instruments; teachers can introduce and encourage that proclivity by having instruments with which to experiment in the classroom. Singing both traditional and popular music is also an activity this age enjoys. It is not the quality of the student's (or the teacher's) voice that is important here. It is appreciating and being willing to participate in an activity as old as humanity. Making music has always been part of life and it should be included in the present-day classroom.

Elementary age children should be afforded many choices of roles to play. History can come alive when children imagine events as they may have occurred; create scenes, lines, and props; and convey these events to others. Social issues can be discussed in more objective ways if players role-play to work out viable alternatives. Drug use prevention and sexuality discussions often use situational scenarios to practice problem solving. Fun dramatic games such as charades can be used to review literary phrases or scientific principles. Creative teachers make lessons appeal to the children's emotional and creative sides, as well as their cognitive ones.

Some children in this age group become very interested in theatrical productions, which give them the chance to try out different identities in a more structured venue. School and community activities that feature drama are very popular with some children at this age.

✳ ASSESSING CREATIVITY

First, we should discuss the question of why anyone would even want to assess creativity, which is so individual and can take so many forms. Children are characteristically creative, since all things are new to them and they have not yet developed inhibitions or learned social conventions. Children look at and try things in new ways all the time. It is very difficult to assess children's creativity, especially to predict how it will develop into adulthood. Then why attempt to assess creativity? One of the primary reasons is that assessment of creative ability gives a broader insight into cognitive ability. If a school or individual teacher wanted to follow Gardner's (1993) theory of multiple intelligences, then it would be important to know what realm the child's strength lies in and adapt the environment and curriculum to fit that learning style. So here we present some standard creativity measurements.

There are ways to identify children with above-average potential for creativity through both careful observation and formalized tests. Some easy ways to identify creative children include such things as whether they have or had an imaginary playmate, or if their play involves highly creative, involved plots, with props, scripts, and innovative characters. However, you have seen that these are not the only ways of being creative. Both creative behaviors and creative personality traits such as energy, imagination, resourcefulness, and high interest help identify creative or potentially creative children.

Some formal instruments for creative assessment include:

* GIFT (*Group Inventory for Finding [Creative] Talent*) by Rimm and Davis (1980) has inventories with yes-no items for primary, elementary, and upper elementary grades. It has been used with a certain degree of reliability to assess children of white, African American, and Latino heritage; urban, suburban, rural, and immigrant children; and children who are learning disabled or gifted (pp. 80–88).

* *Creative Activities Check List* (Okuda, Runco, & Berger, 1991) for upper elementary students in five domains of art, crafts, literature, mathematics, and public performance. This assessment instrument includes questions such as:"How many times have you . . . ?"

* *Torrance Tests of Creative Thinking* (1966) are the most widely used, with longitudinal validation history, translations in 34 languages, and recent scoring guides and norms (Torrance, 1990a, 1990b). Many subtests and different age-range tests are included in both verbal and visual measurements.

SUMMARY

Creativity is a subject about which there are many misconceptions. Creativity is not just about art, music, or drama, but instead is about thinking and the representation of thought. Teachers have the opportunity and the responsibility to inspire students' creativity, nurture its development, and provide a risk-free environment that allows experimentation. This begins with teachers using creativity to plan learning experiences that allow children to use their curiosity, imagination, and abilities.

KEY TERMS

creativity	gifted	divergent thinking
intelligence	convergent thinking	

REVIEW ACTIVITIES

Exercises to Strengthen Learning

1. Assess your own creativity (Figure 10–19 on page 384).
2. Infants—Observe six- to nine-month-old children, watching to see how they follow their curiosity to explore their world.
3. Toddlers—Play a variety of music for a group of toddlers and observe their various reactions as the tempo and style of music change.
4. Preschoolers—Solicit drawings done by preschoolers of approximately the same age and note the differences in their skill levels, content, and explanations of their drawings.

Creativity Self-Assessment

Rate yourself on a scale of one to five, with five being the highest.

1. **Metaphoric Thinking**
   Do you often use an idea or image from one context to express an idea in another context?

2. **Flexibility in Thinking**
   Do you usually see more than one way to do something or solve a problem?

3. **Independent Judgment**
   Do you regularly take a position that is different from that of your friends and colleagues?

4. **Love of Novelty**
   Do you like to experience unusual ideas, problems, or experiences?

5. **Logical Thinking**
   When giving an opinion, do you usually support your statement with facts?

6. **Visualization**
   Do you often daydream or visualize imaginary events?

7. **Complexity**
   Do you usually prefer perplexing or complex visual images?

Used with permission of Joan Koster, author of Growing Artists

Figure 10–19

Assess your own creativity. (Contributed by permission of Joan Koster)

5. Primary age children—Listen to primary age children as they tell stories of their dreams, dangerous escapades, or visions of the future. Listen for recurrent themes and for how they use language to frame their imagination.

6. Elementary age children—Observe a group of elementary age children as they play on the playground, listening carefully to their play themes, situations, and problem solving. Think about how these reflect their creative development.

Internet Quest

1. Visit Howard Gardner's Web site for Project Zero and explore multiple intelligences and how they can be applied to classroom learning and teaching.

2. Find the Web site that presents the National Arts Education standards and make a science or math lesson plan that incorporates the standards for a selected age group.

3. Find a Web site that is a source of music from many different cultures. Make a tape or CD of music from at least five different cultures to which children could move and dance.

4. Find a Web site that has information about assessing creativity and assess yourself.

Reflective Journal

In this chapter, I learned the following about _____ (age child) creative development . . .

When I am a teacher, I will . . .

REFERENCES

Albert, R. S. (1996, Summer). Some reasons why childhood creativity often fails to make it past puberty into the real world. In M. A. Runco (Ed.), *Creativity from childhood through adulthood: The developmental issues, 72.* San Francisco, CA: Jossey-Bass.

Amabile, T. M. (1989). *Growing up creative: Nurturing a lifetime of creativity.* New York: Crown.

Anderson, N. H., Manoogian, S. T., & Reznik, J. S. (1976). The undermining and enhancing of intrinsic motivation in preschool children. *Journal of Personality and Social Psychology, 34,* 915–922.

Bergen, D. (1998). Stages of play development. In D. Bergen (Ed.), *Play as a medium for learning and development.* Olney, MD: Association for Childhood Education International.

Boden, M. A. (1991). *The creative mind: Myths and mechanisms.* New York: Basic Books.

Bretherton, I. (1998). Reality and fantasy in make-believe play. In D. Bergen (Ed.), *Play as a medium for learning and development.* Olney, MD: Association for Childhood Education International.

Brooks, J. G., & Brooks, M. G. (1993). *In search of understanding: The case for constructivist classrooms.* Alexandria, VA: Association for the Supervision of Curriculum Development.

Bruer, J. (1999). *The myth of the first three years.* New York: Free Press.

Crainer, S. (1998). *Ultimate book of business quotations.* New York: Amacom.

Davis, G. A. (1998). *Creativity is forever* (4th ed.). Dubuque, IA: Kendall/Hunt.

Dinca, M. (1999). Creative children in Romanian society. *Childhood Education, 75*(6), 355–358.

Edwards, C., Gandini, L., & Forman, G. (Eds.). (1995). *The hundred languages of children: The Reggio Emilia approach to early childhood education.* Norwood, NJ: Ablex Publishing.

Egan, K., & Nadaner, D. (Eds.). (1988). *Imagination and education.* New York: Teachers College Press.

Erikson, E. (1950). *Childhood and society.* New York: Norton.

Folan, J. L. (1999). Creativity adds to your bottom line. *Communication World, 167,* 44–45.

Gardner, H. (1991). *The unschooled mind.* New York: Basic Books.

Gardner, H. (1993). *Multiple intelligences; The theory in practice.* New York: Basic Books.

Goleman, D., Kaufman, P., & Ray, M. (1992). *The creative spirit.* New York: Dutton.

Goodlad, J. I. (1984). *A place called school.* New York: McGraw-Hill.

Guilford, J. P. (1981). Developmental characteristics: Factors that aid and hinder creativity. In J. C. Gowan, J. Khatena, & E. P. Torrance (Eds.), *Creativity: Its educational implications* (2nd ed.). Dubuque, IA: Kendall/Hunt.

Healy, J. M. (1994). *Your child's growing mind: A guide to learning and brain development from birth to adolescence.* New York: Doubleday.

Jackson, P. W., & Messick, D. (1968). Creativity. In P. London & D. Rosenhan (Eds.), *Foundations of abnormal psychology.* New York: Holt.

Koster, J. (2001). *Growing artists: Teaching art to young children* (2nd ed.). Albany, NY: Delmar.

Lowenfeld, V., & Brittain, W. L. (1987). *Creative and mental growth.* New York: Macmillan.

Maslow, A. H. (1963). The creative attitude. Modified version of a lecture presented in October 1962 to the Eighth National Assembly of the Canadian Society for Education Through Art held at the University of Saskatchewan in Saskatoon. Greenville, DE: Psychosynthesis Research foundation. In Feinburg, S. G., & M. Mindess (1994). *Eliciting children's full potential: Designing & evaluating developmentally based programs for young children.* Pacific Grove, CA: Brooks/Cole.

Maslow, A. H. (1970). *Motivation and personality.* New York: Harper & Row.

Nilsen, B. (2001). Week by week: Plans for observing and recording young children (2nd ed.). Albany, NY: Delmar.

Okuda, S. M., Runco, M. A., & Berger, D. E. (1991). Creativity and the finding and solving of real-world problems. *Journal of Psychoeducational Assessment, 9,* 45–53.

Paley, V. G. (1990). *The boy who would be a helicopter.* Cambridge, MA: Harvard University Press.

Pulaski, M. A. (1973). Toys and imaginative play. In J. L. Singer (Ed.), *The child's world of make-believe* (pp. 74–103). New York: Academic Press.

Rauscher, F. (1994). *Music and spatial task performance: A causal relationship.* (ERIC Document Reproduction Service No. ED 390 733) Paper presented at the Annual Meeting of the American Psychological Association, 102nd. Los Angeles, August 12–16, 1994.

Renzulli, J. S., & Reis, S. M. (1997). The schoolwide enrichment model: New directions for developing high-end learning. In N. Colangelo & G. A. Davis (Eds.), *Handbook of gifted education* (2nd ed., pp. 136–154). Boston: Allyn & Bacon.

Rimm, S. B., & Davis, G. A. (1980). Five years of international research with GIFFI (Group Inventory for Finding Interests: Grades 6–12): An instrument for the identification of creativity. *Journal of Creative Behavior, 14,* 33335–33346.

Russ, S. (1996, Summer). Development of creative processes in children. In M. A. Runco (Ed.), *Creativity from childhood through adulthood: The developmental issues, 72.* San Francisco, CA: Jossey-Bass.

Russ, S., Robins, D., & Christiano, B. (1995, March). *The affect in play scale: Longitudinal prediction.* Paper presented at the meeting of the Society for Personality Assessment, Atlanta, GA.

Samuels, M., & Rockwood Lane, M. (1998). *Creative healing: How to heal yourself by tapping into your hidden creativity.* San Francisco, CA: HarperCollins.

Singer, D. G., & Singer, J. L. (1990). *The house of make-believe: Children's play and the developing imagination.* Cambridge, MA: Harvard University Press.

Singer, J. L., & Singer, D. G. (1998). Imaginative play and human development: Schemas, scripts, and possibilities. In D. Bergen (Ed.), *Play as a medium for learning and development.* Olney, MD: Association for Childhood Education International.

Sosniak, L. (1997). The tortoise, the hare and the development of talent. In N. Colangelo & G. A. Davis (Eds.), *Handbook of gifted education* (2nd ed.). Boston: Allyn & Bacon.

Torrance, E. P. (1966). *Torrance tests of creative thinking.* Bensenville, IL: Scholastic Testing Service.

Torrance, E. P. (1988). The nature of creativity as manifest in its testing. In R. W. Sternberg (Ed.), *The nature of creativity.* New York: Cambridge University Press.

Torrance, E. P. (1990a). *Torrance test of creative thinking: Manual for scoring and interepreting results. Verbal forms A and B.* Bensenville, IL: Scholastic Testing Service.

Torrance E. P. (1990b). *Torrance tests of creative thinking: Norms-technical manual figural (streamlined) forms A and B.* Bensenville, IL: Scholastic Testing Service.

von Oech, R. (1990). *A whack on the side of the head: How you can be more creative* (Rev. ed.). New York: Warner Books.

Walberg, H. J., & Zeiser, S. (1997). Productivity, accomplishment and eminence. In N. Colangelo & G. A. Davis (Eds.), *Handbook of gifted education* (2nd ed.). Boston: Allyn & Bacon.

Wallach, M. A., & Kogan, N. (1965). *Modes of thinking in young children: A study of creativity-intelligence distinction.* New York: Holt, Rinehart & Winston.

For additional learning and teaching resources, visit our Web site at www.EarlyChildEd.delmar.com.

RELATED CAREERS

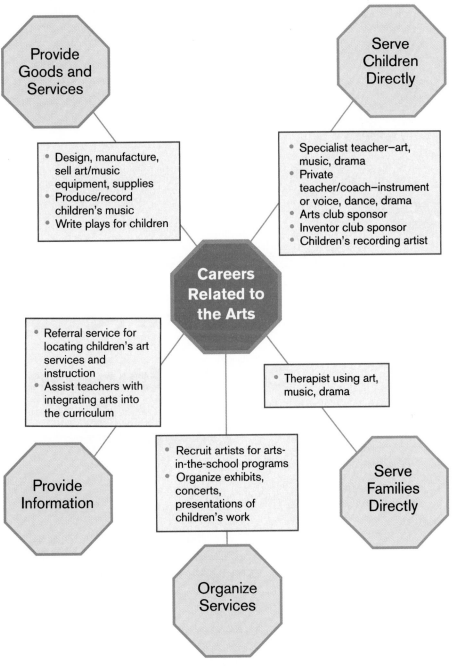

Figure 10–20

Careers related to creative development.

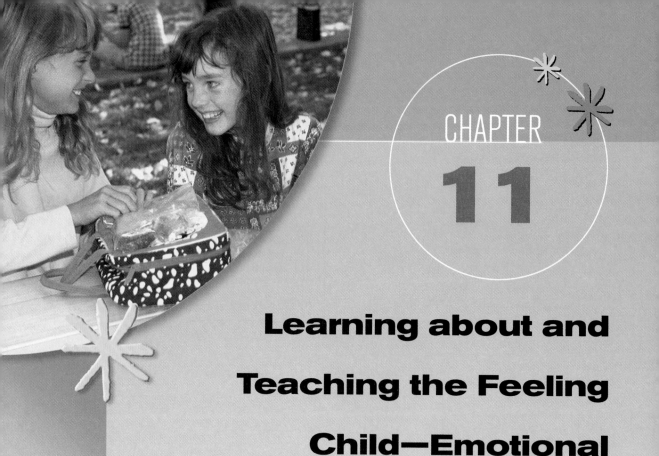

CHAPTER

11

Learning about and Teaching the Feeling Child—Emotional Development

Objectives

After reading this chapter and completing the review activities, the learning teacher should be able to:

1. Explain the impact of emotions on learning.
2. Describe an educational environment that facilitates children's healthy expression of emotions.
3. Predict a range of child behavior based on developmental abilities to process emotions.
4. Describe strategies to reduce stress or the impact of stressful events in the learning environment.

✳ UNDERSTANDING EMOTIONAL DEVELOPMENT IN LEARNING AND TEACHING

SCENARIO Tawani leaves for school with a warm hug from her grandma, who whispers in her ear, "I'll be waiting to see what wonderful things you learn and do at school today."

Alexis passes a big dog on a long chain every day on the way to school. All afternoon, she thinks about what would happen if the chain breaks.

Corey has a sad feeling in his stomach all the time. He misses his dad and his big brother who used to get him ready for school but now they've moved away.

Will any of these children and their learning be affected by the emotions they are feeling? Of course; all of them will. Feelings of security, anxiety, or sadness can permeate the conscious mind, building a positive or negative outlook on learning, socializing with other people, and how you feel about yourself. Teachers must be aware of children's emotions, as well as their physical and cognitive domains.

Emotion, from the Latin *emovere,* which means to move away, disturb, or excite, comes from within the individual, and only in expression, either facial or body movements or sounds or language, can it be communicated. Another word used interchangeably with emotion is **affect,** from which the word "affection" is derived. Affect is the expression of feeling that impresses anyone looking at or listening to a person. **Mood** is another aspect of the emotional being. Davidson (1994) describes mood as "emotional color, affective background," thus distinguishing it from emotion as being more the result of emotions, or of a series of events that cause strong emotions. **Temperament** (which will be discussed in detail later in this chapter) is related to mood and emotion, and is primarily determined by genetics. Temperament is the individual difference that influences how excited you get about events and how you show it. Some people who get good news dance and tell everyone they meet that day. Others are inwardly content without much outward display. Events that influence temperament also influence mood. How much good news does it take for you to dance, sing, and display happiness? Emotions, affect, mood, and temperament are all related, with variations and differences for each individual.

Emotions do not grow; they develop. We are born with the capacity for some basic emotions and spend a lifetime trying to understand, express, and control our feelings and those of others. Built-in reflexes function as emotion, stimulated by some bit of sensory information that causes an immediate reaction (Figure 11–1 on page 390). These reflexes begin even before birth and stay with us throughout life as survival mechanisms. In addition to these instinctive, involuntary, emotional responses,

---

emotion–Strong feelings, positive or negative, accompanied by physiological changes in heartbeat and respiration.
affect–Feelings or emotion expressed or observed; emotional responses.
mood–Prevailing tone or general attitude; frame of mind; disposition.
temperament–The basic style with which an individual responds to the environment; his dominant mood.

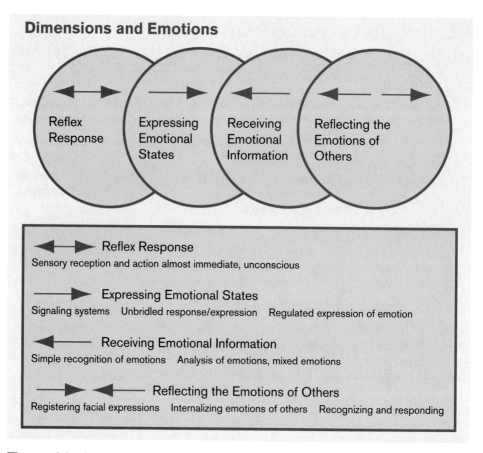

Figure 11−1

Emotional dimensions diagram.

people have more deliberate receptive and expressive sides of emotion. Infants receive sensory information and register one of the core emotions of joy, anger, sadness, or fear. Even very young children know whether the feeling is positive or negative. As cognitive functioning develops, recognizing these emotions becomes more refined into a broader range of joyful feelings from contentment to ecstasy, angry feelings from irritation to rage, and so on. Humans analyze these emotions for causes and connections with past experiences and sometimes even combine them (as mixed emotions) with simultaneously felt related or opposing emotions.

The expressive side of emotion (Figure 11–2) begins with the signaling systems of an infant who snuggles down and goes to sleep peacefully because basic needs have been met, or the outstretched arms of a toddler and the "Uh, uh, uh" that means "I need you to hold me." The expression of emotions progresses to the unbridled tantrums of the two-year-old: "I want my cake now!" It progresses gradually to the more regulated behavior of adults who use words, gestures, and body language to convey inward feelings. "I'd rather have my dessert first, but since everyone else is ordering dinner, I will also." Affect, or outward expression of emotion, differs from culture to culture. Gestures and body language cues are tied very closely to culture, a fact that international businesses have sometimes learned the hard way. Language itself is an important part of emotional expression, with words like love/hate, happy/sad, excited/bored, alert/sleepy, calm/distressed, secure/fearful, and many increments in between used to convey inner feelings. Metaphors are also used to describe emotions such as "head

Figure 11—2

Even before they develop language, children express emotions clearly.

over heels in love," "wired," "dead tired," or "scared stiff." Being able to regulate emotional expression is a developmental process. The infant is unconcerned about how others perceive his crying or the fact that now is not a convenient time for Mommy to begin feeding him. The toddler on the floor of the grocery store screaming for a certain brand of cereal has little control over the tantrum once it is full blown, and needs a patient adult to help her learn how to react appropriately when her desires are not fulfilled. Family patterns and values, interacting with the child's own biological tendencies and the cultural context, affect the child's expression and regulation of emotion (Figure 11–3 on page 392, Dunsmore & Halberstadt, 1997).

The child learns that expressing inner feelings needs to be regulated, either by doing it in a socially acceptable way with appropriate facial expressions, gestures, body or spoken language, or by repressing the feeling. Emotional expression is partly determined by social and cultural expectations demonstrated in such statements as, "Big boys don't cry," or "Say thank you" (even when gratitude is not felt). In Chapter 12, the socially connected emotions of empathy and aggression will be discussed.

Another aspect of emotions involves interpreting the emotions of others. Even newborn infants can sense the emotion in an adult face. Young children use every cue they can to interpret the adult's acceptance or rejection, personalizing those reflected feelings. In other words, if the adult is feeling sad or mad, young children assume they must be the cause. As the child develops socially and cognitively, she is able to more realistically interpret what others are feeling without necessarily internalizing the cause of that expressed emotion. When feelings can be reflected back with empathy to the individual who is having them, full emotional development has occurred.

The teacher's assessment of emotional development is complex and often difficult. Many factors, including the teacher's own perceptions, biases, and emotions, influence her interpretation of a child's emotional state. A child who seems to be developing normally may experience a challenging yet seemingly insignificant incident and revert to emotional coping strategies typical of a younger child. If the teacher is knowledgeable about emotional development, she can help the child handle emotional upheaval and develop future coping strategies. Each developmental stage has its own understanding of emotional feelings, others' emotions, and culturally acceptable regulation of emotional expressions.

The Nature of Emotional Development

Emotions and their expression appear to be distinctive features of the human animal, though there are those who swear their pets express emotions. Exactly which emotions

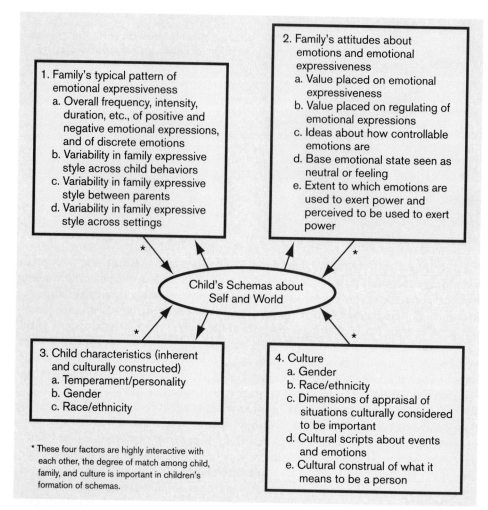

Figure 11–3

How family emotional expressiveness might influence children's formation of schemas. (From Dunsmore, J. C., & Halberstadt, A. G. (1997). *New directions for child development, (77)*, 45–68. Reprinted by permission of Jossey-Bass, Inc., a subsidiary of John Wiley & Sons, Inc.)

and their expressions are universal to all humans is strongly debated. Anthropologist Margaret Mead (Mead, MacGregor, & Bateson, 1951), as well as many recent studies cited by Denham (1998), suggest that the affective (emotional) expression of children depends on that of the parents and culture and thus cannot be interpreted as universal. New brain-imaging technology may soon unlock the mysteries of neural systems, and of universal emotions and their expressions. Until then, we look for clues to indicate what the person is feeling inside by observing and interpreting outward signals.

Core Emotions. Joy, anger, sadness, and fear are the **core emotions** (Campos, Barret, Lamb, Goldsmith, & Stenberg, 1983; Izard et al., 1991). They appear to

core emotions—Inborn emotional responses of joy, anger, sadness, and fear from which all other emotional configurations are derived.

Joy	Anger	Sadness	Fear
Happiness	Frustration	Dejection	Wariness
Delight	Jealousy	Unhappiness	Anxiety
Contentment	Disgust	Distress	Suspicion
Satisfaction	Annoyance	Grief	Dread
Pleasure	Fury	Discourgement	Dismay
Elation	Boredom	Shame	Anguish
Pride	Defiance	Guilt	Panic

Figure 11–4

Core emotions and corresponding emotional clusters. (From Kostelnik, Stein, Whiren, & Soderman, 1998)

be universal, bringing us to the belief that they are inborn and part of the nature of humankind. Researchers like Paul Ekman (Ekman, Davidson, & Birbaumer, 1996) and others have shown photographs of facial expressions to people around the world and have found that people from many different cultures recognize the same expressions for anger, disgust, sadness, fear, or surprise, thereby supporting the theory of inborn emotional patterns. Adult expression of these emotions may differ from one society or culture to another, but even then a basic interpretation of facial expressions seems to be present at a very early age. A research study with Canadian and Chinese infants (Kisilevsky et al., 1998) showed that the infants exhibited similar withdrawal behavior when the mothers' faces were silent and still. They also exhibited similar responses when their mothers smiled, talked, and cooed to them. These universal emotional behaviors indicate that even very young infants from different cultures can interpret adult affect and respond accordingly.

These core emotions serve as later foundations for a wider range of emotions, even for those confusing mixed emotions (Figure 11–4).

Emotional behavior integrates many systems of the sensory, cognitive, social, and physical domains. Internal and external information is gathered by the senses and transmitted to the brain and central nervous system, which then trigger physiological reactions such as breathing and heart rate changes, pupil dilation, sweaty palms, flushing, and nervous bodily activity. Facial expressions, posture, and body movements are all expressions of emotion. The cognitive function of emotion involves analyzing or interpreting these bodily responses and their meaning, which may only take a split second, as in the following examples.

SCENARIO   Craig steps out into the street and immediately jumps back onto the curb, an oncoming car just missing him.

Six-month-old Annetta is fussy and is not comforted by the caregiver's rocking and talking to her. The caregiver goes to the cubby, gets a scarf that Annetta's mother dropped off that morning, and wraps it around the child. Annetta immediately stops fussing, settles down, and falls asleep.

continued

Julian is furiously breast-feeding, making smacking noises. His mother starts to move him to the other breast and he instantly turns red, screams, and flails his arms.

Sensory information processing produces emotional and physical transformations. There are two types of emotional responses: one is the immediate involuntary one of the body mobilizing to deal with an important event, like Craig experienced, or the response elicited when you are sliding toward the guardrails on an icy highway or catch a glimpse of a long-lost friend across a room. Physiological changes are immediate and brief. The sensory signal goes to the *thalamus,* the sensory relay station located deep in the brain, where it is translated into the language of the brain to be processed; a portion of that signal goes directly to the *amygdala,* a structure in the brain where fear and pleasure are registered. The sensory input activates these structures before thinking can and the sensation is analyzed (LeDoux, 1996). The adrenal glands then release *cortisol,* a hormone that triggers physical reactions, including depression of the immune system, tensing of large muscles, blood clotting, and increased blood pressure (Jensen, 1998).

The rational emotional reaction, on the other hand, takes some thinking time that involves an appraisal process for which the brain is prepared at birth. This natural process is altered throughout life as we encounter the actions and reactions of others. It is designed to work like this: an event or circumstance occurs, with information taken in either consciously or unconsciously (or both) and the mind relating the event to memories of past events; an emotional response then occurs, either positive or negative, with their full range of possibilities. The rational mind, the *neocortex,* then decides on the appropriate way to express that emotion (taking into account the setting, culture, and individual style) and responds; this is the regulation phase. The mind considers why this surrounding, event, or person stimulated this particular reaction. Appraisal also occurs after traumatic events, when the mind revisits the event and the emotions it elicited. When Craig thinks about almost getting hit by a car, he can feel it again, but not as intensely, the emotions he felt on that occasion. You may or may not always be able to consciously associate the feeling with a past experience; this is one of the mysteries of emotions. Or reappraising the incident and your emotional response may cause you to form a judgment, "That was silly of me to have that reaction," or "Next time that happens, this is what I'll do." Emotions involve physical sensations, expressive reactions, and cognitive interpretations and reassessments. This is what Goleman (1995) described in his best-selling book *Emotional Intelligence.* He stated that thinking is so closely aligned to emotions that intelligence alone cannot predict a given individual's success. Rather, it is "harmonizing emotion and thought" (p. 27). Goleman pointed out many instances of highly intelligent people whose out-of-control emotions led them to engage in socially unacceptable behaviors. He agrees with Gardner's (1993) theory of the existence and interaction of multiple intelligences, especially interpersonal intelligence.

SCENARIO Here is an example of the interplay of core emotions and learned behavior.

The teacher asks Darren to come to the board to show how he worked out the math problem. Darren hears someone

continued

laugh as he rises from his desk. His palms begin to sweat and his heart rate increases. His face gets flushed. Darren shuffles to the front board and stands with his back to the class, clutching his paper tightly in his hand. He thinks about the day before, when a classmate had trouble reading aloud and someone laughed. He wonders if his classmates are laughing at him now or if they will laugh if he does not solve the problem correctly (Figure 11–5).

Darren is receiving sensory information: hearing the laughter, experiencing physical reactions, thinking about the past experience when a classmate was laughed at, and expressing the emotion of embarrassment and fear of humiliation by turning away and not facing the class. His emotions may even prevent him from clearly reading his paper or thinking about the math problem. If he internalizes his interpretation of ridicule, he may give up, not even attempting to solve the math problem. Or, based on his temperament, his determination to succeed may be heightened. The laughter may have nothing to do with him, but if he thinks it does, it may affect him just as strongly.

The teacher's role in helping children learn depends on her understanding emotions, using aural and visual clues to try to interpret what others are feeling. It is like a dance in which each partner moves in rhythm with each other, reacting to each little step, back and forth. From the moment they are born, infants react: first, with very basic reflexes that help them survive even while totally dependent on adults. They eventually

Figure 11–5

Emotions can have a dramatic effect on learning.

differentiate these reflexes into many deliberate emotional reactions. Emotional development consists of changing responses to surroundings, situations, and people. A very young infant can copy the facial expression of a familiar adult. It even has been found that if the adult is speaking harsh words about another adult or situation, the infant can discern that and not be as upset as if the words were about her (Nelson, 1987). How smart infants are!

Temperament. For infants, children, and adults, the intensity of receptive and expressive emotions is directly related to temperament, the innate tendencies or dispositions that affect interactions with people.

How you react to a situation or event is closely allied to your emotions and personality characteristics. Observing infant behavior presents evidence that babies are different in temperament from the time they are born. Any parent of more than one child is a witness to this as well, marveling at how two children born from the same gene pool could be so different right from the start. Genetic factors contribute to differences in temperament (Bates & Wachs, 1995; Kagan, Arcus, Snidman, Feng, Hendler, & Greene, 1994; Buss & Plomin, 1984). A study of twins, siblings, and adoptees found that identical twins were more alike in temperament than fraternal twins, and biological siblings were more alike in temperament than adopted siblings (Braungart, Plomin, Defries, & Fulker, 1992). This lends further support to the conviction that temperament is biological rather than socialized.

Thomas and Chess (1977) began researching infant temperament in the 1950s, in what became known as the New York Longitudinal Study. They used parent questionnaires to gather information on infant's reactions to their first bath, wet diapers, and first foods, classifying the subjects as having "easy" or "difficult" temperaments. These 140 children were studied into adolescence, when Thomas and Chess (1977) concluded that they could identify nine behavioral traits that describe the child's temperament.

Temperament

Activity level—Typical amount of movement and relative action and inaction

Rhythmicity—Regularity and predictability of bodily functions

Approach-withdrawal—Nature of infant's response to something new

Adaptability—Ease with which initial responses are modified

Threshold of responsiveness—Intensity level required to elicit a response

Intensity of reaction—Energy level of a response

Quality of mood—Amount of pleasant behavior in comparison to unpleasant behavior

Distractibility—Extent to which novel stimuli disrupts ongoing behavior

Attention span/persistence—Extent to which activity, once begun, is maintained

Thomas and Chess found 40 percent were "easy," 15 percent "slow to warm up," 10 percent "difficult," and 35 percent "inconsistent." The stability of these character traits over time into adulthood has been the subject of many studies and differing opinions. Thomas and Chess (1984) agree that the environment's stability has a great influence on whether these characteristics continue or change. Others have confirmed the longevity of certain aspects of temperament (Kagan & Snidman, 1991; Stifter & Fox,

1990; Plomin, Emde, Braungart, & Campos, 1993; Caspi & Silva, 1995), while others cite studies that discount it (Slabach, Morrow, & Wachs, 1991).

| SCENARIO | As a teacher, consider these qualities and see how they might be exhibited in the classroom. |

* Andrea wiggles and is in constant motion, while Camina moves slowly from one area to another.

* Rosa has a bowel movement at about the same time every day, while Sasha could have a bowel movement at any time of the day.

* Maurice notices the new puzzle out on the table, goes right over, and starts putting it together, while Taj watches Maurice and several others before he attempts the puzzle.

* Thanh lines up for the assembly that has been announced over the loudspeaker, while Hillary whines, "But we always have reading time at 10 o'clock. When will we have reading time?"

* Wyatt hears music from the room next door and asks if the class can join in dancing, while Becky continues to work on her map project.

* Dakota raises his hand enthusiastically as soon as the teacher asks, "Who would like to tell about one important finding from the investigation of the slide under the microscope?" while Matthew, who had taken the most notes and made detailed drawings of what he saw, sits silently.

* Brady is described as a friend by everyone in the class; no one lists Jane, who is often moody and argumentative, as their friend.

* Mandze and Troy are working together on a math project. They read the teacher's directions from the poster, assemble the materials needed for the project, and proceed to work on it. Mandze continues to work while Troy goes and gets a drink, stops to talk with another group, comes back and watches Mandze, does a small task, and leaves again.

While there may be other reasons for each of the above behaviors, can you see how basic temperament may influence the children's actions? A teacher who knows the child may need to adjust routines, supervision, and her own actions accordingly.

The Nurture of Emotional Development

According to Thomas and Chess (1977), most infants can be described as one of three types: easy (playful and regular), difficult (irritable, irregular, and responding intensely

Erik Erikson

(1902–1994) German who studied under Sigmund and Anna Freud. He came to Harvard University to study soldiers who had suffered emotional breakdowns, civil rights workers in the South, disturbed and normal children at play, and Native American tribes. He developed the theory of eight stages or conflicts that need to be resolved in order for a person to be independent and functional later in life. His most famous work is *Childhood and Society* (1950, 1963).

and negatively), and slow to warm up (mild, low in activity level, and slow to adapt). Each of these temperaments has an effect on parents' and caregivers' behavior; the cycle repeats and reinforces the temperament. Playful infants get played with; difficult babies may be avoided and not have their needs met; slow-to-warm-up babies may be ignored or not played with as long as the baby needs to respond. The *goodness of fit* (Sprunger, Boyce, & Gaines, 1985), the dynamic relationship between the temperament of the infant and the temperament and parenting style of the parents, is a key factor in attachment, and in whether that attachment is secure or insecure (Figure 11–6). Some easy infants may not get as much attention as the difficult, more demanding ones. However, in a culture that values assertiveness, the difficult behavior is accepted as a positive trait and may result in more attention.

Freedman (1974) found infant temperament differences might also have racial origins, with Chinese American infants more placid than African American and European American ones. This was confirmed 20 years later by the research of Kagan et al. (1994). Stability of temperament throughout stages of development is the important part of this study. How much of the personality and behavior that children exhibit is due to inborn temperamental traits? This brings us back to the old nature/nurture issue.

While one may be born with basic emotions and temperament, there is little disagreement that how the child is nurtured affects her emotional outcome (see Figure 11–6). **Erik Erikson**, a developmental theorist, is best known for his theory about the effect of emotions on development in the human life cycle, with an emotional conflict in each stage that must be resolved. Erikson described eight psychosocial stages of crises, or needs, encountered in the progression from birth to late adulthood (see Figure 11–7). He proposed that if the needs of a given stage are not met, that unresolved issue continues to affect the person

Figure 11–6

Attachment is a key factor in emotional development.

throughout her life. As we look at emotional development later in the chapter, the characteristics of these stages will be examined.

Erikson worked with Freud, but took a more social and cultural view of emotional and social development than Freud did, recognizing that there are many other people in the child's social world who affect her development, while not minimizing the important influence of the parents. Erikson conceptualized stages of developmental conflicts that form later behavior, believing that no deficits were irreversible, but could be overcome more easily than Freud thought.

When thinking about these developmental stages, keep in mind that cultures with different values may also differ in their interpretation and response to their children's development. The autonomy of the self-seeking toddler in some cultures is a mark of animal instinct that must be tamed and subjugated. Strong, harsh discipline may be doled out to reform individual or group behavior. In other cultures, these violent outbursts are ignored and excused as a stage the child will pass through. Free expression of emotion, exercise of independence, and eye contact to indicate attention and close listening may all have very different interpretations in other cultures. Lynch and Hanson in *Developing Cross-Cultural Competence: A Guide for Working with Young Children and Their Families* (1999) suggest some of the following differences.

* Eye contact—Among African Americans, Native Americans, and Latinos it may indicate disrespect; among Asian groups it may be considered shameful.

* Smiling—Among Native Americans and Asians it may not express affection or assent.

* Touching—Patting a child on the head is unacceptable to many Asians and East Indians. Hugging, back-slapping, and vigorous handshaking are not typical behavior among many Chinese and other Asian groups.

* Body posture and positions—Standing with hands on hips, hand gestures, finger pointing, body closeness, and head nodding all have very different interpretations in various cultures.

The teacher should become aware of the cultural values of the children in her class and their families and adapt her behavior accordingly.

Erikson's theory states that how conflicts are resolved throughout development can affect the child's self-concept. Those emotions relate to the stage of cognitive

Infancy (Birth–2½ years)	Trust vs. mistrust Autonomy vs. shame
Early childhood (2½–6 years)	Initiative vs. guilt
Middle childhood (6–12 years)	Industry vs. inferiority
Adolescence	Identity vs. role confusion Intimacy vs. isolation
Adulthood (19–65 years)	Generativity vs. stagnation
Old age (65 years–death)	Ego integrity vs. despair

Figure 11–7

Erikson's stages of socioemotional development.

development, or the extent to which the child is able to think and make sense of the world. The newborn infant has no sense of a separate self separated now from her mother's body; the infant is now one with the crib sheet, the car seat, or the blanket on which she is lying. As the infant develops cognitive structures, she realizes her distinctness from her environment. That feeling of separateness is the beginning of her concept of self.

Self. The emergence of the idea of *self* occurs over time; it is connected with physical, cognitive, emotional, and social experiences and development. Lewis and Michalson (1983) identify five early periods or stages in the development of the early concept of self.

* Birth to three months—Self is undifferentiated from actions and reactions of others, but infant is beginning to interact socially
* Four to eight months—Emerging differentiation, having own intentions
* Nine to twelve months—Differentiation between self and others
* Twelve to eighteen months—Recognizes self in mirrors, photos, movies
* Eighteen months to three years—Articulates self from others

By about eighteen months of age, a child begins to recognize herself as a separate and unique human being. Researchers use a simple test of this perception by placing a dot of lipstick on a child's nose and holding the child up to a mirror. If the child reaches out to touch her reflection, she has not yet met this milestone (Figure 11–8). If the child reaches for her own nose to touch the spot, this indicates the child knows the reflection in the mirror is really her (Lewis & Feinman, 1991). By the end of her second year, the toddler understands that self and others are independent from each other. Now she really can play hide and seek!

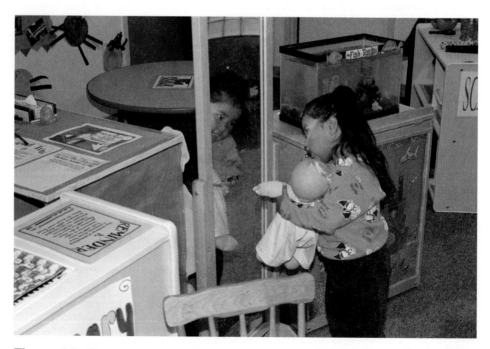

Figure 11–8

Self-identity is discovered when a child recognizes herself in the mirror.

Gaining independence in the second year accompanies this individuation process of the developing self. Erikson's stages point over and over to the developing self-concept of the child attempting to be a separate, competent, independent person. The child who is over-protected and not allowed to try, or the child who is criticized for less than perfect attempts, is receiving negative messages about self-worth.

Self-concept and self-esteem are part of the emotional domain. **Self-concept** is how you evaluate yourself in specific areas, such as appearance, academics, popularity, or athletics. **Self-esteem** is the value, or emotional response, you attach to your self-concept. You look in the mirror and admire your new haircut, arousing good feelings. You pass a person you know on the street and say hello, but get no eye contact or response; your self-esteem may be lowered, if you feel that you must not be memorable or important to that person. The infant who has no knowledge of self and others assumes his primary importance in the world. As a toddler, the child begins to differentiate between herself and others and sees that sometimes other people are the center of attention, like a newborn sibling, or adults talking with each other. Developing the realization that there are other people in the world with their own wants and needs for attention is a difficult task for a young child, and maybe for all of us at one time or another even as adults.

Self-esteem has cultural influences as well. The qualities that one culture values may be the opposite of another's. Through interactions and practice, families convey what is acceptable and desirable as they socialize their children. A culture that values independence and self-reliance will socialize its children toward autonomy, perhaps insisting on separate sleeping rooms from the very beginning. This culture will affirm the child's behavior that indicates individuality and nonconformity and encourages free expression of feelings. Another culture that values allegiance and interdependence does not rush into developing its children's self-help skills, and affirms behavior that imitates and is self-controlled, placing the needs of the group above those of the individual. This shows the child that social connections are more important than self-assertion. Children of either culture will draw self-esteem from meeting the socialized cultural norms.

At a very early age, children are aware of racial differences; many studies have indicated that young nonwhite children express a preference for white dolls or playmates. One of the most influential studies of this type was done by **Kenneth and Mamie Clark** (1939). Many studies since then have either corroborated or disputed the Clarks' study. The implications suggest that teachers must commit to helping all children accept themselves, with race as one factor.

Kenneth and Mamie Clark

The Clarks conducted research on African American children's self-conceptions and identity (1939). Their findings indicated that African American children's racial identity and self-esteem were harmed by segregation. This was used as evidence by the plaintiffs in the *Brown v. Board of Education* (1954) Supreme Court case that found school segregation unconstitutional. In 1971, Kenneth Clark became the first African American president of the American Psychological Association.

SCENARIO   Baby Caroline cries. Mother just sat down at the table to eat. Caroline cries harder.

Three-year-old Anton brings a brightly wrapped present to the birthday party, but throws a temper tantrum when it is time to give it to the birthday child.

continued

---

self-concept—The qualities one attributes to oneself, self-identity.

self-esteem—The valuing of that knowledge based on self and social comparisons.

First graders are lining up to go outside. Half the class is yelling, "Me first! Me first!" and all the class (save one) are disappointed when the lead child is chosen.

Crystal, a fifth grader, is angry when she is denied permission to attend the school dance because her grandparents are visiting from out of town.

The sixth grade voted unanimously to give up their recess time to pack canned goods for flood victims in another state.

Social, emotional, and cognitive development are blended in what Selman (1980) calls **perspective taking,** or the ability to assume another's viewpoint and understand her feelings. Caroline, the infant above, has no empathy for her hungry mother. Caroline only knows she needs something. The preschool child, age three through five, is in the egocentric stage of failing to distinguish between the thoughts and feelings of herself and of others. Anton wants the gift for himself without regard for the birthday child's viewpoint, even when custom dictates that the gift is for the birthday child. Children in the social-informational stage are aware that others have their own perspective, but are still focused on their own. The first graders are in various levels of this stage, some realizing that not everyone can be first, while others are vying to be first even though they know there is a strong possibility it will not be them. Crystal is in the self-reflective stage where she can look at things from another's perspective, knowing her grandparents want to spend time with her, yet respond to a strong self-view of wanting to be with her own friends and attend the dance. The mutual perspective-taking of ten to twelve-year-olds is such that they can see beyond their own need and desire for their recess to defer to the perspective of the needy flood victims. They are willing to suspend their own need for others' needs.

Self-concept and self-esteem influence the movement from being self-centered to empathizing with the perspective of others. When a child has feelings of trust, autonomy, initiative, and industry, she has a self-concept of competency that makes it easier to take the perspective of others. Kurdek and Krile (1982) found these children more popular with peers. If a child has unmet physical or emotional needs, it will be more difficult for her to take another's perspective and give of herself.

Low self-esteem may result in poor academic performance and peer relationships, as well as depression, suicide, anorexia nervosa, or delinquency (Damon & Hart, 1988; Harter & Marold, 1992). Raising self-esteem through emotional support and social approval are not as effective as also helping the child to improve her achievements (Bednar, Wells, & Peterson, 1989) and realistic problem-solving skills (Lazarus, 1991). Competency is the key to self-esteem, making the adult's role one not of offering empty praise but of helping the child achieve success.

Gender and Sexual Development.

SCENARIO   Two-year-old Trina, when asked if she wanted to play with a truck, replied indignantly, "I a goil. I not pway wid twucks."

continued

perspective taking—Empathetic appraisal of another's situation.

Rashid's parents received a note home from the first-grade teacher in which she said she thought he was having a gender identity problem with his long hair. His parents were upset and confused, since it is their religious practice not to cut hair, and Rashid's father has very long hair as well.

How do masculinity and femininity develop? Are they purely physical, determined by nature? Are they learned behaviors, part of cognitive development? Are they emotional, depending on how you feel or how you value certain characteristics and behaviors? As usual, there is no simple answer, but instead an explanation that takes many factors into account. Freud's view was the *identification theory;* that the child between three and five years old develops a sexual attraction for the opposite-sex parent (in males, the Oedipus complex; in females, the Electra complex). When the child finally understands this is fruitless, she transfers allegiance to her mother by the time she is five or six. It is then that the child learns socially acceptable gender behavior. The *social learning theory* emphasizes that gender development occurs by observing and imitating male and female role models such as adults in the home, school, neighborhood, and media.

Gender identity is a biologically based, male-female identification, but also includes such features as appearance, roles, status, and activities that distinguish males from females within a society. We have chosen to include a discussion on gender-role identity in this section about emotions and the developing self. Of course, gender-role identity begins with biological determination of whether the fetus is male or female, which is genetically programmed. A strong influence in socializing to one gender or the other from the moment of birth are words like "strong," "active," and "big" for boys and "pretty," "petite," and "delicate" for girls. Clothes and toy choices, and all interactions and expectations about male and female traits are subtly (and sometimes not so subtly) conveyed as early as the age of two, as Trina told us above.

Children develop their gender identity in stages as they form their image of self. Kostelnik, Stein, Whiren, and Soderman (1998) present five stages.

 * Stage One—General awareness of gender (birth to eighteen months of age). Children are the objects of gender-specific clothing, descriptions, and toys and they begin to form ideas about male, female, and self.

 * Stage Two—Gender identity (eighteen months to three years). Children have learned the labels *boy, girl, he,* and *she* and apply them to others based on hairstyle, clothing, or activities. By two or three years of age, they have learned to label themselves as a girl or a boy, their *gender identity.*

 * Stage Three—Gender stability (four to six years of age). Children at this stage, by the age of six, understand that boys become men and girls become women. However, they still may ask, "When you were little, were you a boy or a girl?"

 * Stage Four—Gender constancy (four to eight years of age). An advanced concept of gender stability, in that gender is constant and permanent. They are still using external cues for gender identification and have inflexible gender-role stereotypes. A four-year-old child insisted, "You can't be a doctor. You have to be a nurse 'cause you're a lady," when his teacher wore a lab coat and stethoscope on Halloween.

gender identity—The child's comprehension that he or she is either a boy or a girl; usually develops by about three years of age.

✳ Stage Five—Gender-role identification (six to eight years of age and older). In this stage, children begin to imitate same-gender adults and describe their own gender in positive terms (pp. 387, 388).

Gender-role stereotypes are beliefs and expectations for male or female behavior. They are labels that may not be accurate for that individual, but even with contradictory evidence are held fast, such as the example of Rashid's hair. Stereotypes of the dominant, independent, aggressive, achievement-oriented male and the nurturing, affiliative, less esteemed and more-helpful-in-times-of-distress female are found in most cultures (Williams & Best, 1982). In a later study by the same researchers (1989), fewer stereotypes were found among people in more highly developed countries. Gender-role stereotyping increases and then peaks in the early elementary years, and then decreases (Bigler, Liben, & Yekel, 1992), probably because of the changes in cognitive and social development during those same years. When stereotypes are reinforced by characters in literature, the media, peers, and role models, sexism (negative treatment of women or men because of their sex) is the result.

Another component of gender identity is sexual orientation. An individual's sexual orientation has to do with the gender to which an individual is sexually attracted. Most people's primary sexual attraction is toward the opposite gender. For some people, however, the primary sexual attraction is toward the same gender. Children develop their gender identity very early, but it is usually during the elementary age years that they become aware of other people's orientations, and how people within their social circles react to the expression of sexual orientation. Most families assume that a child's sexual orientation is toward the opposite gender. It can be very stressful for children to accept that they are attracted to the same gender or to cope with the reactions of others, including family, to their unanticipated sexual orientation. This issue can be so emotionally stressful for young adolescents that behaviors ranging from social withdrawal to suicide may result. Teachers must be aware of their own biases and create an atmosphere of acceptance and support for all children.

While males and females have the capacity for the same emotions, biological factors (such as hormones) and socialization are strong influences over emotional behavior. Another factor in gender identity is ethnicity. Different cultural beliefs and experiences affect female and male attitudes and behaviors. Females who are also members of an ethnic minority experience both racism and sexism. Research shows that the roles of African American and Asian American women and men are slowly moving from patriarchal to more egalitarian, with higher status afforded females than in the past (Kane, 2000; McLoyd, Cauce, Takeuchi, & Wilson, 2000; Lee, 1996). In Mexican American families, the stereotype of the male being a strong provider prevails, but as more women are employed, this, too, is changing (Espin, 1993; Knouse, 1992; Marin, 1994). Women in many Native American tribes are leaders; even in patriarchal tribes, women function as important contributors to the family. Urbanization has caused cultural conflict and modified the values of men and women, and the traditional structure of male and female roles (LaFromboise, Trimble, & Mohatt, 1993; Bennet, 1994). As cultures change, so too will the gender roles and identities of their children and the emotional impact of those roles and identities on their self-esteem.

✳ **gender-role stereotypes**—Rigid notions of male and female behavior.

Stress and Self-Control

| **SCENARIO** | One-year-old Ari screams whenever he sees his mother put on her coat or pick up her purse. |

Rena hears her parents arguing and is sure it is because she has left her room messy on more than one occasion.

Ross has had a stomachache every morning since Kevin's desk was moved next to his and Kevin started whispering threats of beating him up on the playground if Ross does not give him a quarter every day.

Marci just cannot concentrate in school. She hears the teacher's voice and tries hard to listen, but it is just sound. The other children's voices blend together into a blur of noise. She has been working on multiplication in remedial math, but it is so hard to remember on Monday what she worked on last Friday. She knows the teacher is frustrated with her. All she can see and hear clearly are images of what her uncle does to her all weekend when he babysits while her mother is at work.

The news is full of violent incidents in schools, so Darlene has worked out a system of always walking through the halls quickly and facing the door in the classroom in case a stranger enters.

All these children are experiencing **stress**. Can you feel it—the quickening heartbeat and breathing, sweaty palms, knot in your stomach? All of us live in a complex world and the seeming innocence and blissful existence of children are fantasies. Children live under many potential stressors.

Sources of Children's Stress. The child's stress can come from many sources.

Personality. By temperament, some children are more susceptible to changes in their life, no matter how slight, while others seem to be more easygoing and able to cope and adapt to changes.

Fears. Children's fears are age related and also depend on their thinking and reasoning ability, as well as their experiences and socialization (Figure 11–9 on page 406).

Family Stressors. The home, supposedly a haven in a heartless world, is often a place of high stress. Busy schedules can place children under stress, with many worthwhile activities that involve children and adults calling for coordinating the timing of meals, transportation, and supervision. While soccer and music lessons for children and exercise and community clubs for parents may all be worthwhile, they can cause stress. Elkind in *The Hurried Child* (1981) condemns this fast-paced lifestyle as a primary stressor on children who may have many abilities and material resources, but,

stress—Any perceived threat that affects one emotionally and physically.

Age	Source of Fear
0–6 months	Loss of physical support, loud noises, flashes of light, sudden movements
7–12 months	Strangers; heights; sudden, unexpected, and looming objects
1 year	Separation from or loss of parent, toilet, strangers
2 years	Separation from or loss of parent, loud sounds, the dark, large objects or machines, unfamiliar peers, changes in familiar environments
3 years	Separation from or loss of parent, masks, clowns, the dark, animals
4 years	Separation from or loss of parent, animals, the dark, noises (especially noises at night), bad dreams
5 years	Separation from or loss of parent, animals, bodily injury, the dark, "bad" people, bad dreams
6 years	Separation from or loss of parent, the dark, ghosts, witches, bodily injury, thunder and lightning, sleeping or staying alone, bad dreams
7–8 years	Separation from or loss of parent, the dark, ghosts, witches, sleeping or staying alone, life-threatening situations
9–12 years	Separation from or loss of parent, the dark, life-threatening situations, death, thunder and lightning, tests or examinations, school performances (e.g., plays, concerts, sporting events), grades, social humiliation
Adolescence	Appearance, sexuality, social humiliation, violence (at home and in the street), war

Sources: Date from Beardslee, W. R. "Youth and the Threat of Nuclear War." *The Lancet* (September 10, 1988): 618–620; Miller, L. C. "Fears and Anxiety in Children." In *Handbook of Clinical Child Psychology,* edited by C. E. Walker and M. C. Roberts. New York: John Wiley & Sons, 1983; Morris, R., and T. Kratochwill. *Treating Children's Fears and Phobias: A Behavioral Approach.* Elmsford, New York: Pergamon, 1983; Papalia, D. E., and S. W. Olds. *A Child's World: Infancy through Adolescence.* New York: McGraw Hill, 1996.

Figure 11–9

Childhood fears from birth through adolescence. (From Kostelnik, Stein, Whiren, & Soderman, 1998)

because of the demands of that lifestyle, endure the consequences of empty emotional resources. Working families where both parents have the same or opposite work schedules can put stress on the child. Approximately 80 percent of women in the workforce have children. Juggling schedules, physical exhaustion, and divided attentions put stress on the parents and children. Child care arrangements can be stressful, even when the quality of that care is high. Because parents with children are in the workforce, child care is a necessity. In national studies, most child care has been found to be only of moderate quality, however, adding further stress to the child and family.

Separation and divorce which affects more than one million children each year, disrupt many children's emotional stability and is one of the most disturbing events in their lives. Parents separating or divorcing is often accompanied by a change in residence and economic status, and results in emotional trauma no matter how amicable the situation is. Many research studies point to a range of negative effects.

Single-parent families may lack financial and emotional resources. Whether the single parenting is caused by divorce or other circumstances, children raised by only one parent face stresses, including economic ones. Half of the single-parent homes headed by women fall below the poverty line (U.S. Bureau of the Census, 1997, Table 742). Besides the economic stresses, the social isolation and increased responsibility the parent bears alone may compound the situation.

Blended families, where a child is living with one biological parent and the parent's partner can cause adjustment difficulties. Today at least 20 percent of all children are living in a stepfamily. Feelings of insecurity, jealousy, and confusing or opposing value systems add pressure to the children of a blended family.

Child abuse occurs most frequently at home. Children are most vulnerable to being harmed by the people they know best. Family strains, the parent's own abuse as a child, and failure to connect with available resources can result in children becoming the victims of physical, psychological, or sexual abuse. Even though physical scars may heal, such abuse affects the child emotionally for life. Nationally, almost one million children are estimated to be victims of abuse (U.S. Department of Health and Human Services, 2000). This kind of stress affects every other aspect of children's lives.

Out-of-Home Situations. When a child is in a group or classroom with children of another distinctive culture, the continuous, firsthand contact can cause stress. Historic prejudice, hostility, value clashes, customs, and language, may cause **acculturation stress**. From the age of three, children are aware of physical and racial differences. Other differences become apparent as children grow older, and the child who is in the minority group may experience overt or perceived discrimination or diminished self-identity.

School itself is stressful for many children. There is so much publicity today about falling academic achievement that schools, teachers, and children are all under pressure to achieve. Having high academic standards should not be synonymous with stress on children. Qualified, prepared teachers should be able to help children learn in nonstressful ways. With all that is known today about different learning styles, learning disabilities, and the way the brain works, it is inexcusable for children to find school unduly stressful because of academic pressure.

Natural disasters, terrorism, and violence instill fear in children. The Children's Defense Fund (2000) reminds us of the startling fact that every day in America 12 children die from violence (p. 108). While the Columbine High School and other school violence incidents shocked the nation, we must remember that children die every day at the hands of other children and adults, and that other children witness this violence. Television brings immediate images of homes and lives destroyed by natural and human-caused disasters. Children take in these threats as real and personal and can live with the gnawing fear that they may be next.

Children's Reactions to Emotional Distress.
Children react differently to emotional stress, but there are many common reactions.

---

acculturation stress—Emotional disturbance caused by attempts to adapt to a different culture, sometimes called culture shock.

Physical Reactions. Heightened body processes are the physical reactions to stress. Blood pressure, breathing rate, heartbeat, speech problems, frequency of urination, headaches, and stomachaches all may increase. Appetite and sleep patterns may be affected and the child may become more susceptible to colds, flu, and infections.

Psychological Reactions. Inability to focus attention is one of the primary responses to stress. This has important implications for teachers: when a child is suffering from stress of any kind, learning becomes secondary. The child may deny the stress to alleviate the pain. Young children may invent an imaginary friend to share the pain or withdraw physically or mentally from the problem. Long-term use of these strategies may lead to more serious psychological difficulties.

* Regression—A child under stress often reverts to younger behaviors, such as thumb sucking, bed-wetting, whining, and clinginess, as a way of eliciting needed attention.

* Acting out—Impulsive or attention-getting behavior and aggression are often seen in children under stress.

* Coping—Children under stress may have a resiliency that may result from a more easy-going temperament, higher tolerance for pain and frustration, greater intelligence to reason and comprehend, higher confidence and self-esteem, and connections and support outside the family (Monahon, 1993).

Behavioral Reactions. Children from infancy through age seven often choose inappropriate ways to express their emotions (Figure 11–10). Without sophisticated language, an understanding of reality versus fantasy, or knowledge about the difference between perceived and real threats, children react intensely to large and small upsets. Older children are more aware of, but often are less likely to communicate, their emotional upset. They have interpreted social rules about expressing certain feelings and so hide or hold back feelings, which can intensify the emotional disruption. They also take on personal accountability for situations that are not their responsibility, adding to their stress, as in situations involving divorce, child abuse, accidents, or illnesses. Not talking about their feelings of guilt or anger can make the problem worse.

Figure 11–10

Learning to control emotions is often a difficult lesson.

Helping Children Through Stress.

"You don't have to be afraid. There's no such things as monsters."

"Don't feel that way."

"Come on, put on a smile for me. Ah, there it is. Good girl."

"Oh, I know how you feel."

Do any of these statements bother you? All of them should. They all deny and invalidate another's feelings. You can only respond to another's feelings subjectively. There is no way to *really* feel what another is feeling and no way for a person *not* to feel the way they do on demand. What is being encouraged here is to stop expressing the feeling and to repress it. Yet, feelings are a natural part of being human. It is a developmental process to learn to recognize and differentiate among them and to find socially acceptable ways of expressing them. Helping children to do this is one of the teacher's most important roles.

SCENARIO	George falls down while running. He looks up to see his mother. If she looks horrified, he starts to cry. If she smiles and nods, he gets up and continues on his path.

Estelle is bringing her infant to child care for the first time. She watches other parents hand over their infants, kiss them good-bye, and leave.

Carrie is new to preschool. After snack, she jumps up and runs off to play. Another child yells, "She forgot to throw away her stuff." Carrie comes back to the table and watches how another child gathers up his napkin and cup, throws them in the trash, and then pushes in his chair. She does the same.

Lottie and her mother meet some of her mother's coworkers at the grocery store. One woman has on a headdress and another has a dot on her forehead. Lottie sees how her mother smiles and talks with these women.

Jackie is in the grocery checkout line and sees the candy bar display. She reaches for a candy bar and her father says, "No." She wails and flails.

Socialization, learning how to react in social situations, takes place through **social referencing**. When in a doubtful social situation, people look to others for clues about how to act. Sometimes, the referencing may be in conflict with how you really feel, causing you to deny, or refrain from expressing, your real feelings about the experience. George may really be hurt, but he has been socialized to cover his hurt and not cry because it would not be "manly." Estelle may be feeling very guilty about leaving her child and upset at the separation, but not want to make a scene or seem different from other mothers. Carrie learns the expected routines from another child

social referencing—Paying attention to another's expression for cues on how to react.

to find social acceptance. If her mother had avoided these women, Lottie would have formed the beginnings of feelings of bias against people who look different from her and her mother. Because children are learners, they are very open to subtle messages about acceptable and nonacceptable social behavior and expression of feelings. Jackie's father might lose patience with her and say, "Stop that right now," or instead he might say, "I know you want that candy a lot, but that is not the way to let me know it." These cultural scripts help dictate the proper feelings for each situation (Lewis, 1989). When cultural scripts are in conflict with what a person really feels or are in conflict with another culture, uncertainty and emotional turmoil can be the results. The role of the family and the teacher is to find healthy ways for children to learn about feelings and their acceptable expression. Some principles of empathy with other's emotions can help children and adults cope.

Feelings are not to be denied, but need not always be expressed. Jackie is feeling that she is being denied what she wants. Her autonomy is being threatened. Should she be allowed to feel this way? Yes. Should she be allowed to express those feelings the way she did? It depends. How old is Jackie? It is understandable for a two-year-old to exhibit these immature actions. However, by the age of five, a child should know what is considered acceptable behavior and have more control. Certainly by age ten, Jackie should not be acting in such a manner.

Children can be taught the name for what they are feeling without denying the feeling. "I know you are angry because I won't buy the candy, but I want you to have strong teeth so I'm buying yummy apples." Or in the earlier example, Mother could have said, "You were scared when you fell, but it looked like you didn't hurt yourself, so you got up and ran off. If you were really hurt, you could call me for help and I would come." Even as an adult, Estelle might have been giving clues about her uncertainty at leaving her infant at child care that day. The teacher might have said, "I know it is hard to leave your child, but we will take good care of her and she'll be waiting expectantly for you to return at the end of the day." The teacher might say to Carrie, "It looked like you were embarrassed when Tommy yelled at you about the snack clean-up. It's hard to learn all the ways we do things here, but soon you'll be feeling more comfortable with all of it." And Lottie's mother could say to her, "I could see you were curious about my work friends. They have certain beliefs about how to dress that make them look different from us. They are very nice people."

Adults can teach children acceptable ways to express their feelings. Once children have the words to name the feelings and tell how they feel, acceptable ways of expressing them are in order. Gonzalez-Mena (1998) suggests some of the following strategies.

* Usually yelling and screaming are not acceptable, except in times of emergency. "I can't understand you, or I won't be able to listen to you, until you speak in a quieter tone of voice."

* Name calling and obscenities are usually unacceptable ways of expressing feelings. "That's not his name; it's a hurtful word. If you want to refer to him, use his name."

* Negative wishes or threats of violence are unacceptable. "Hurting someone is not the way to let them know that you don't like what they did."

* Encourage the descriptive expression of the feeling, its cause, and its consequences. "You can tell her, 'It hurt my feelings when you told me you didn't want to play with me.'" Or, "You can tell him, 'Ouch! That hurt me!', instead of hurting him back, because then he won't want to play with you again." "You are happy and excited to be chosen for the lead role in the play, but when you talk about it like that, it makes the others feel bad."

Confirm the feeling without agreeing to the cause. "It might feel scary sometimes at night when everything is quiet and dark." "You might feel like doing nothing when you feel so lonely, but sometimes working on a project can help." Adults in the child's life can help the child cope with stress by attempting to alleviate the source of emotional distress. When stress cannot be ignored, active listening can help the child recognize the cues and give names to or identify the feelings: "It looks like you are feeling angry/sad/embarrassed." The adult can help the child find an acceptable way to express the emotion and form a more realistic view of the situation, seeing herself not as the cause but the victim. An important strategy is to discuss possible ways to solve the problem, but not dismiss it as unimportant. Teaching relaxation techniques that ease the physical symptoms of stress and providing positive outlets for the child to find satisfaction and joy in life outside the stressful situation can help when the stressors are unavoidable (Figure 11–11).

One last strategy is very important: paying attention to talk of suicide and referring the child to appropriate personnel (see Figure 4–9 on page 125). Suicide is the fourth leading cause of death among ten- to fourteen-year-olds . Even young children can have self-destructive thoughts and act on them, so it is important to not dismiss hints or subtle symptoms and to get help for the child immediately.

✳ DEVELOPMENT AND CURRICULUM FOR EMOTIONAL HEALTH

Emotions and development are related. Sroufe (1996), in his study of emotions, pointed out that there is order in the development of emotions. Emotions that come later are directly related to those that came before. Emotions are tied to development in other domains, and emotion is both the feeling and the regulation or expression of that feeling. Emotional development unifies all the other domains (pp. 8–9).

Figure 11–11

A listening, caring adult can help the child deal with stress.

Infants and Emotional Health

The core emotions of fear, anger, sadness, and joy first appear as reflexes, such as recoiling at loud noises, wrinkling the brow, or "smiling" from gastric activity. These are not really considered emotions yet, but are the biological framework on which emotional development will be built. They are intrinsic, genetically programmed survival mechanisms that stimulate the parent's instincts to respond.

Emotional Development of Infants.

SCENARIO   Three-month-old Jelani looks up into the eyes of his caregiver, Desi, and quickly looks away when he hears Desi say to her coworker, "I just can't stay an hour later again tonight. This is the third time this week I've been asked to and I don't think it's fair." Jelani begins to cry.

Alexander is working next to Camisha. Camisha begins to adopt some of Alexander's repetitive movements and sounds. The teacher thought Camisha could befriend Alexander and help him with his autistic behavior, but instead it seems to have worked out the other way around.

Attachment, the affectional, emotional bond between living creatures that results in distress when they are separated, has been carefully studied and intensely debated. Ainsworth (1979) and Bowlby (1969) extensively studied attachment in animal and human infants and the negative emotional ramifications when it does not occur. If an emotional bond between an infant and a consistent adult fails to form, lifelong implications result. The great majority of infants are capable of forming close relationships and have the ability to interpret emotional signals. Jelani, above, appears to be able to discern that Desi is talking harshly, but cannot understand that the situation has nothing to do with him, so he becomes upset. You may wonder if Jelani's crying was the result of Desi's words or her tone of voice; or you may think it was an unrelated discomfort, like a hunger pang. Is Camisha's behavior directly related to her emotional response to Alexander's unusual behavior, or is she seeking attention for herself? Is she making an overture to play, or is she exhibiting her own inner disturbance?

An observer of these events interprets the external cues and makes conjectures about their symbiotic relationship with the person's internal states, or emotions. It is difficult, if not impossible, to be sure that one caused the other, because emotions are internal and only their expressions are external, or observable. There may be some other variables as well: inferring that one response elicits the other, or even that they are related, may be misinterpreting the clues. Many researchers believe there is a relationship between the infant's physical and emotional needs being fulfilled, and the later healthy development of social relationships. The importance of attachment has implications for families, caregivers, and teachers who witness the resulting behaviors or misbehaviors.

Attachment is important to emotional development: however, there may not be a critical period immediately after birth, nor do the birth parents necessarily have to be

attachment—The enduring emotional connection between people that produces desire for contact, as well as distress during separation.

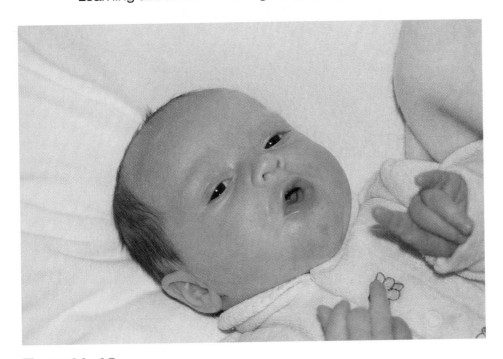

Figure 11—12

The social smile appears at about six weeks of age.

the attached figures. How the need for attachment is fulfilled differs from culture to culture. In some cultures, infants remain in constant contact with their mothers for their first year. In others, the infant has contact with many different people, all of whom are responsible for the infant's care. In some cultures, eye-to-eye contact and conversation are expected, while in others, eye-to-eye contact is avoided and the infant is talked about, but not directly spoken to. In many families and cultures, a grandparent, older sibling, or person who has that responsibility within society is with whom the child associates. All agree, however, that it is desirable for there to be one consistent, responsive adult who provides for the physical and emotional needs of the infant and young child. Some researchers, like Kagan (1987, 1989), believe that the child's genetics, temperament, and resiliency may overcome an attachment deficit, so that an unattached infant is not emotionally crippled for life.

At about two weeks, infants experience joy, expressing contentment or their response to attention with the first semblance of a smile (Figure 11–12). Early smiles are elicited by light touches, blowing on the skin, and light jiggling, with the caregiver's voice as the most effective stimulator. Grins appear between three and four weeks and the actual **social smile**, the intentional response to adult smiles, voices, and touching, appears around six weeks. Not only is the social smile the infant's first intentional communication of her internal state, but it also causes a circular reaction when others smile back. Reinforcing this intentional action encourages it to appear again and again, transforming a very self-centered being into a social being. Visual stimuli captivate the infant between five and eight weeks, with the infant able to fol-

social smile—The infant's earliest smile, usually around six weeks of age, in response to close, positive contact with an adult.

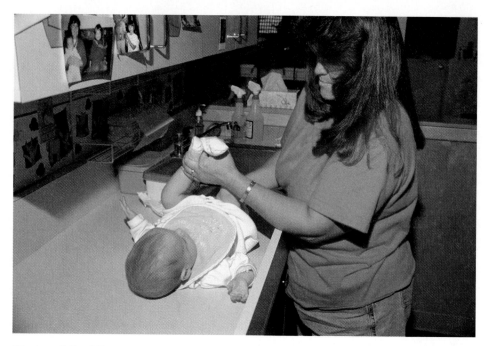

Figure 11–13

A child's emotions are affected by adult interactions during routine care.

low a toy or picture. By four months, the smile is accompanied by laughter, stimulated by such things as rubbing or gently tickling the stomach or neck and "I'm gonna get you" games. By six months, the "Peek a Boo" game brings laughter and by twelve months, smiling is brought about by incongruous movements or actions, like an adult pretending to suck on an infant's bottle or putting the infant's bonnet on her head. By this time, the one-year-old laughs in anticipation of the game or at the approach of the adult playing the game.

Erikson (1950, 1963) calls this stage of psychosocial conflict **trust versus mistrust** that takes place from birth to one year of age. The infant's trust builds as she depends on adults who respond in a reliable, predictable way with nourishment, attention, and warmth. From these interactions, the infant develops trust that the adult will respond, and trust that she herself can communicate her own needs to elicit the desired responses. Infants who do not develop attachments do not develop trust. Later attachments or relationships may be negatively affected by the person's mistrust that others will meet her needs or be responsive. Mistrust may lead to hesitancy in trying new experiences, taking risks, or thinking in new and creative ways.

One issue in emotional development in the first year is the regulation of routines. The infant is building schema, or models and concepts, for coping with her environment and for the regularly appearing adults in her world, and as a result is becoming less concerned that her physical needs will be met. She has built up trust that she does not have to cry for every diaper change or feeding; both she and the caregiver have adapted to each other's schedules, and communication of need is not as important as social communication (Figure 11–13). If attachment has occurred, then

trust versus mistrust—Erikson's first stage of emotional development with the conflict one between confidence in the world and a feeling of uncertainty and hopelessness.

she has the confidence to branch out physically with the caregiver's presence and encouragement providing reassurance.

Curriculum for Infant Emotional Development.

Because we know that attachment is such an important part of emotional development, parents, caregivers, and teachers should do everything possible for infants to be welcomed emotionally. Family support systems and helping professionals can augment the parents' natural instincts to build a relationship with the infant from the moment of birth. While bonding immediately following birth may not be scientifically proven, the infant who is welcomed by gentle handling, smiling faces, and needs that are met has the foundation for a lifetime of successful relationships. The infant is building trust that adults will care for her, confirming and affirming that she is worthy of their love and care. When a parent sneaks off when the child is not aware, that trust is damaged. Caregivers and families should come to an understanding that there will always be a goodbye ritual, so the child knows the family member is leaving. This may incite some momentary distress, but the long-term damage of sneaking away is far more dangerous emotionally.

The physical environment, in addition to the social environment, can help build emotional development. A healthy, safe environment supports the infant's feelings of trust and well-being. Of the hundreds of types of equipment available for infant care, very few are necessities, other than those that ensure safety. What the infant needs most for emotional development are people who respond to her need to be comfortable, well fed, dry and clean, and loved and cared for.

A traditional favorite activity of infants in their first year is "Peek a Boo." The development of object permanence can be observed through the infant's reactions. At the first stage, the infant just accepts the face appearing and then disappearing. Then the infant is surprised when the face reappears, because when it is out of sight, the face ceases to exist in the infant's thinking. When the infant begins to reach up to pull away the hands hiding the face, she has reached the milestone of object permanence, knowing the face exists behind the hands even though she cannot see it (Figure 11–14).

Figure 11–14

The game of "Peek-a-Boo" helps teach the concept of leaving and returning.

In child care settings, maintaining attachment to absent family members is one of the primary ways to enhance emotional development. Photographs, audiotapes, or pieces of fabric or clothing from family members can provide the infant with sensory recall of those closest to her. Attachment to caregivers is important as well, making high staff turnover in child care centers, especially infant rooms, a matter of deep concern. Continuity of caregivers in the infant room builds the trust and attachment the infant needs in her first year of life. She comes to depend on the parent handing her over to another person she knows and trusts. That trust has been won by the caregiver anticipating and responding to the infant's needs. The infant is held for comfort and feeding, gently stroked, patted, rocked, and talked to with a loving voice and affectionate words.

Communication between home and the center is vital to successful infant care. The family member who brings the infant to the center should fill out a form about what kind of night the baby had, and when she was last fed and changed. Throughout the day, the caregivers should make notes on feedings, diaper changes, nap times, and any activities in which the infant was engaged. Any parent or caregiver concerns must be communicated to ensure continuity of care. The infant's moods are cues the adults use in interacting with the child. When the infant is alert, the caregiver offers toys; body games like patty-cake, bicycling with the legs, or gently rolling; storybooks, and playfulness. When the infant is serious and wary, the caregiver comforts and quietly talks and sings to her to give assurances of loving care. When the infant is in active distress, the caregiver promptly gives attention, attempting to find the cause of the infant's distress and then alleviating or soothing it. By being exposed to these responsive caring techniques, the infant builds trust in others and confidence that she is worthy of this love and care.

Toddlers and Emotional Health

SCENARIO   Thirteen-month-old Justin is in the doctor's waiting room. He toddles over to the dollhouse, glancing back at his father several times, and then begins to move the toy furniture from room to room. Another parent and child enter and Justin runs back and hides his face in his father's coat, peeking out at the other child. When the other child stays on her mother's lap, Justin again goes back to the dollhouse and begins to play.

This toddler is beginning the path to independence, but is looking for reassurance that the significant person in his life is still present, if needed. Children will continue to develop more self-assurance and less dependence until that day many years later when she leaves home for college.

Emotional Development of Toddlers.

SCENARIO   Vera's mother arrives at the child care center at the end of a tiring day. She looks forward to reuniting with Vera and anticipates a happy greeting. When Vera looks up from play and sees her mother, she runs to her and punches her in the stomach, yelling "No!"

Vera's mother may feel disappointed, angry, sad, confused, guilty, or embarrassed. What Vera is unable to express other than in this violent, unexpected action is her anger both at

Figure 11–15

Young children have limited ways of expressing their emotions.

her mother for leaving her and because she wants to continue her interrupted play. Woven into those negative emotions is joy at seeing her mother again, but she has no words to express it. Negative feelings overshadow joy and result in this upsetting scene. Vera is now differentiating between self and others and especially those very special people on whom she depends and with whom feels secure. While she may be excited in anticipating the return of her mother, her anger regarding the separation overrides that feeling. Now she may begin to experience distress when her mother begins to prepare to leave the house. She may cling to her mother and cry and act out whenever her mother is out of sight. This **separation anxiety** at around eighteen months marks a milestone in the attachment phase of emotional development. However, it does pass (Figure 11–15).

From one to three years old, toddlers are in a tumultuous emotional stage, seeking to exercise their own will now that they are independently mobile. They are beginning to communicate their wants and needs in words, and investigate everything in their world. The nickname *the terrible twos* describes this period. This new quest for autonomy or self-rule is the stage Erikson (1950, 1963) calls **autonomy versus shame and doubt,** for while the toddler is trying to be self-assertive, her body and thinking processes are still immature, causing some disasters. She thinks she can carry Momma's glass to the kitchen. She tries to get to the top shelf to get the candy she saw big brother hide there. She wants to wear her favorite pajamas, no matter what the destination. When spills and breaks happen, and adult rules prevail, the child feels

separation anxiety—Distress expressed by children between 18 and 24 months old when parent or primary caregiver departs.

autonomy versus shame and doubt—Erikson's second stage of emotional development, this occurs in a child's second year with a conflict between her yearning for independence and her misgivings about self-worth.

failure, both externally, communicated verbally or with body language, and internally. The internalized, "Maybe I'm not as capable as I thought I was," can result in doubt and shame. In situations where the child is not even allowed to try to do things for herself, the doubt and shame are accompanied by the thought, "They won't let me try because they know I can't. They must be right." The emotional task of this period is to experience success in independent activities without too many casualties.

The new freedom afforded by mobility early in the second year still depends on a secure base. Justin returns to his father for reassurance and security, both in glances and then bodily. Mahler, Pine, and Bergman (1975) call this *checking back* behavior, which the toddler indulges in while she practices moving out into the world. Close infantile attachment is difficult to leave behind, as Vera demonstrates. In the second year of life, emotional turmoil overtakes the toddler, as we see in Vera's case. Emotions are widening in range, although the child still has limited understanding of them or language to express them. Simultaneous feelings of joy and anger, frustration and shame, and fear and anger are often so overwhelming that tantrums, biting, hitting, or throwing toys are not uncommon. As intense as the emotions are at this age, they also quickly change from screaming and crying one minute to laughing and hugging the next. What helps the child resolve this crisis is her knowing that the important adult will return and an environment that holds the pleasures of discovery and success. Emde and Buchsbaum (1990) call this autonomy *with* connectedness, or fresh challenges with new ways to maintain connectedness.

The emergence of self in the second year, along with motor development (walking, climbing, fine motor manipulation) and representation (including language), advance the toddler toward autonomy. Joy becomes a feeling of pride when she is praised for successful feats. This independent functioning also begins to change her acceptance of actions by parents or caregivers.

Certain standards for behavior are now being set; there are growing expectations that the toddler will self-regulate. With this new requirement come challenging behaviors of starting and stopping the prohibited action, looking at the caregiver, and then continuing. This indicates the beginning of conscience and developing knowledge of right and wrong, with the accompanying guilt. When the toddler is thwarted from carrying out intended actions, her distress can turn into anger. When she attempts tasks that are beyond her coordination level, she often feels frustrated.

The toddler's new understanding of herself is undifferentiated. If she is scolded or punished for a specific behavior, she extends that displeasure to her whole self: "I am totally bad." And, conversely, when she is praised, the toddler extends it to: "I am totally good." There is no differentiation between an act of behavior and the whole self.

Curriculum for Toddler Emotional Development. Since toddlers are exercising their newfound mobility and increasingly yearn to be independent (but still need to be dependent), this can be an emotionally tumultuous period. Because their expectations of themselves and their abilities are often beyond their physical or cognitive level, they are frequently frustrated and angry. This can erupt into temper tantrums that try adults' patience. To minimize the toddler's frustration, the environment and equipment in it should provide as much opportunity for choice and success as possible. This means that toys should be on shelves that the toddler can reach herself. Toys should be compatible with the child's developmental level, but challenging enough to be stimulating and interesting. Toys should not be too difficult to manage such that they cause frustration leading to anger. If there is more than one child, exact duplicates of toys minimize toddlers grabbing them from others. The atmosphere should be free of stress, with soft areas in the room for quiet times and activities and busy areas separate from sleep areas. A relaxed schedule should include long periods of free play without interruptions. Adults should respond to children's interests by demonstrating toys, extending play, and moving the children on to other activities when they become fussy or disinterested. Lifting and carrying the child should be minimized, saving the adult's back and giving the child independent mobility. Moving the child can be accomplished by holding out your hand or inviting the child to climb or be lifted into your arms. To give comfort and affection, you can sit on the floor and let the child choose to climb in or out of your lap, again giving control to the child, but being available and open to the child's overtures.

Toddlers usually play with objects for a short time before moving on to other objects or areas. One of their favorite things is dumping and filling, with more dumping than filling (Figure 11–16). They have a new *power over objects,* and they will be wielding it. Putting objects *into* a container may need adult assistance; likely no assistance will be needed to get the objects out. Any movable object comes under the toddler's power, so the environment and equipment should be safe. This makes the environment child-centered, with a minimum of "no-no" areas and things that thwart the toddler's will and result in strong emotional outbursts. No matter how well you prepare, however, there will be times when you need to restrict things from the toddler. You can accomplish this with a matter-of-fact statement that gives the reason why she cannot play with the object, even though her reaction may be vocal and violent.

Toddlers achieve feelings of independence when they are involved in activities that require whole body movement, such as games or moving to music, and simple, safe pieces of equipment to climb on, off, into, and out of. With toddlers' increasing ability to control their small muscles, creative art projects and dramatic play also give them a sense of worth. Routines still bring the security they need as a base for their explorations, so new people, equipment, and activities need to be presented slowly, allowing the children time to adjust and make the first move. Fears of strangeness erupt at this age, preparation smoothes the way for all.

Figure 11—16

When toddlers dump things, they are exercising control over objects.

Reading books about emotions with toddlers is an important activity, especially ones with clear art or pictures showing various facial expressions and situations. This helps the toddler learn some of the words for feelings, make associations with facial expressions, and even get cues from the reader's voice. Stories like Eastman's *Are You My Mother?* (1988) include the emotional issues of fear, loss, surprise, humor, comfort, security, and trust. These are all important themes for the toddler.

Allowing the toddler to take an active part in and more control of routines is also a way of establishing her sense of autonomy. While it may be messy, self-feeding is one good way for toddlers to exercise autonomy. They are able to grasp finger foods, begin to drink from cups (usually with spill-proof tops), and use utensils such as toddler-sized spoons and forks. This is the stage when they may give signals for using the potty. Pressure to do this too soon may lengthen the toilet-training process, so adults are wise to let the child take the lead.

Since this is also the beginning of development of a sense of self, successful steps toward autonomy foster a positive self-image. By providing the child with routines and activities in which she can find success, you will be helping her to build the feeling of competency so necessary for shaping confidence and meeting the challenges ahead. You do this not to build the child's vanity or self-centeredness; her pride should be about the struggle and accomplishment ("You tried and tried and you did it!"), about newly acquired skills ("You fed yourself your whole dinner"), or her first expression of caring for others ("That was so nice that you shared your blanket with Grandma. You made her happy. See her smile.").

The toddler's strides in emotional development would seem to point to an increased ability to control emotions, but that may be too much to expect for this developmental age. Because the child cannot regulate and discipline her feelings and responses, adults should try not to place her in situations where she is tempted by things she cannot have or places she cannot go, or places where she must be quiet. This will save both the child and adults a lot of frustration.

Preschoolers and Emotional Health

SCENARIO

※ Kristen says, "I'm mad at you!"

※ Alexia says, "I love you so much, Mommy!"

※ Devonne says, "I don't like it when you do that to me."

Children of this age are often in group settings—preschool, child care, or Head Start—that necessitate sharing and negotiating, and thus more emotional control. Children from three to five are still self-centered, assuming that what they want is what they should have. Piaget and Inhelder (1969) call this *egocentric*. Preschoolers are still learning to control or express their emotions in socially acceptable ways (Figure 11–17), which can make for challenging days for both children and their teacher.

Preschooler Emotional Development. Three- to five-year-olds have usually acquired enough language to begin to express their feelings, especially the core emotions and some of their more defined derivatives. Mixed emotions are still difficult for preschoolers to define and express, but as their vocabulary expands, they connect names for emotions with words. The three-year-old will cry pitifully in embarrassment, but not be able to express in words the shame or guilt she is feeling. The adult's role is to interpret these feelings for the preschooler and give them a

Figure 11–17

Each child sees only one point of view.

name: "You are feeling embarrassed because you wet your pants" or "You are sad that Daddy had to go to work today and angry that he couldn't play with you any longer this morning."

During their fourth and fifth years, children master many self-care tasks, such as dressing, bathing, brushing their own teeth, cutting their own food, and doing small household chores. They can use language not only to communicate needs and wants, but also to express ideas and plans and verbalize their own feelings. Erikson (1950, 1963) calls this stage **initiative versus guilt**, when children can carry out their plans, explore and gain new information, and begin to control their own actions and emotions. When these efforts fall short, self-incrimination, or feedback from adults, may cause them to feel that, because they were *bad*, their plans did not work out or their behavior got out of hand. Adults who shame and belittle preschoolers' independent efforts instill feelings of unworthiness and incompetence. Again, it is important to remember that a child's efforts towards independence, such as toilet training, self-feeding, dressing, and bathing, may occur earlier or later in some cultures than they do in this European American stage.

Preschoolers are expected to assume a much larger role in self-regulating emotions and impulses than toddlers. These children are expected to move beyond toddler temper tantrums and understand certain prohibitions against unrestrained emotional reactions. Preschoolers can delay gratification, defer to others' needs, and accept substitutions for their requests, all without becoming aggressive. They can cope better with high arousal states (Sroufe, 1996). Their independence now allows

initiative versus guilt—Erikson's third stage, in which four- and five-year-olds experience emotional conflict over acceptance or rejection of constructive efforts.

them to operate in the environment without constant supervision and to interact socially with peers, sharing objects and alternating roles. Their emotional development and self-control allow this to occur, if they are children with histories of secure attachments (Sroufe, Schork, Motti, Lawroski, & LaFrenier, 1984). Preschoolers still identify self by physical characteristics: "I'm Clifton. I'm tall and I have brown eyes like my dad."

Saarni (1999) described *socioemotional competence,* advanced social and emotional development, as the skills acquired during the preschool years.

1. awareness of one's emotional state
2. ability to discern other people's emotions
3. ability to talk about emotion in the vocabulary characteristic of one's culture
4. capacity for empathetic involvement in others' emotions
5. realization that an inner emotional state may not correspond to an outward expression
6. awareness of cultural display rules
7. ability to take account of unique personal information about others when inferring their emotional states
8. ability to understand that one's emotional-expressive behavior may affect another person and to take that fact into account in presenting yourself
9. capacity to use self-regulation strategies to modify emotional states

The qualities that deal with emotions are mainly about regulation and expression. In their preschool years, children are learning self-control and acceptable ways to express how they feel because they have a much greater vocabulary and are able to grasp the concepts of hidden inner feelings. They are moving through the egocentric stage, so they are learning that, just because they feel something, other people may not feel or understand it, unless they can make it clear using acceptable words or expressions. Those children who have reached this stage and have the qualities listed previously for socioemotional competence are better liked by peers and teachers (Kurdek & Krile, 1982). Children for whom English is a second language may take more time to develop the expressive skills necessary for negotiation and emotional expression (Eisenberg, Fabes, Bernzweig, Karbon, Poulin, & Hanish, 1993).

Curriculum for Preschooler Emotional Development. The preschool child is building a sense of self-identity. The environment and equipment must support this development, but must also recognize and validate the child's cultural background. Photographs of children in the class or group and their family members; books, pictures, and displays of people who look like them; and familiar music and foods all send a message of recognition and acceptance. Essa and Rogers say, "Keep in mind that self-concept is not something 'taught' during a week's focus on the child as a part of the curriculum. Self-concept is an ongoing concern that should be integral to everything you do in the early childhood program. Certainly activities that enhance children's image of themselves (e.g., songs using children's names, photos of the children in the class) contribute to building self concept. But they are not enough. There must be a constant reminder to the children that they are important and loved and that their world does, indeed, revolve around them in many ways. The way you present curriculum contributes to this feeling" (Essa & Rogers, 1992, p. 17). They recommend a curriculum model that starts with the child and expands into the child's world, while incorporating curriculum activities in eight areas (Figure 11–18).

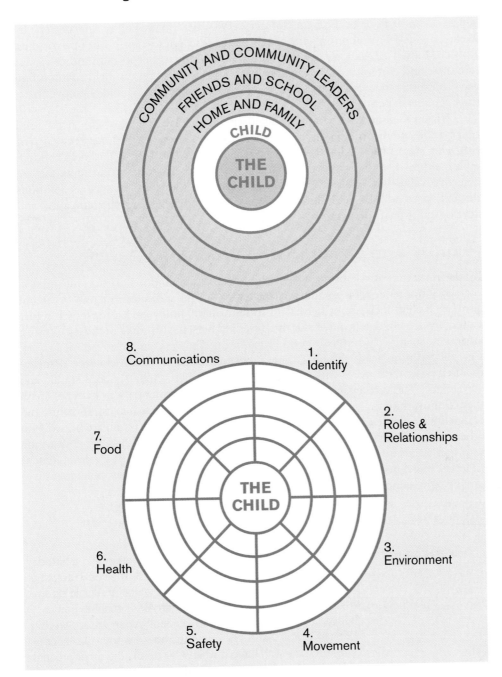

Figure 11—18

Curriculum model that centers around the child and her world. (From Essa & Rogers, 1992)

Using children's natural curiosity as the basis for exploring emotions is another way of helping preschoolers learn about emotions. Feinburg and Mindess (1994) recommend using real events that occur spontaneously, either in the classroom or the community, as vehicles to involve children in exploring their social emotional struggles of sharing and taking turns, as well as more serious issues like wars and violence. They recommend children's literature as a way of bringing out important emotional issues. *Mean Maxine* by Barbara Bottner (1980) deals with bullies. *Tough Boris* by Mem Fox (1994) is about a very tough pirate who cries when his pet parrot dies. Robert Munsch's *Love You Forever* (1986) reinforces the concepts of a mother's long-term love and commitment, no matter what. In this way, you can help children find ways to express their emotions, engage in problem solving, and build cognitive structures for later experiences.

Vivien Gussin Paley combines children's own play scenarios with her careful observation and recording skills in her books (*Wally's Stories* [1981], *Boys and Girls in the Doll Corner* [1984], and *You Can't Say You Can't Play* [1992]), to help children replay and rewrite the scripts of difficult times in the classroom. By gaining a more objective viewpoint of these situations, children are able to try various solutions through pretend play and find comfort, build understanding and empathy, and develop emotional competency.

Primary Age Children and Emotional Health

By the time they reach primary age, children's self-definitions go beyond physical characteristics to encompass inner characteristics. This indicates not only *what* but also *how* a child feels about herself. "I'm tall, smart, funny, and a top-notch figure skater." As the child gets older, she also describes herself with some of the less positive attributes, such as "I'm not so good in math, but I'm very good in reading and art. I'm still trying in math though." **Social comparisons** are when children compare themselves to their peers with respect to abilities, achievements, social status, and appearance. These comparisons also enter their self-assessment: "I'm better at math than Timmy, though." School-related standardized tests, classroom assignments, and competitive activities provide more information the child uses to compare herself with others. Self-worth is increasingly linked with academic performance. When learning tasks and classroom behavioral expectations are not based on children's developmental levels, individual interests, and cultural backgrounds, children may come to premature negative conclusions about their abilities.

Emotional Development of Primary Age Children.

SCENARIO William, age ten, and Cassa, age five, are attending a birthday party for Alex, who is turning six years old. They each select a birthday gift for Alex. William patiently waits for Alex to open his gift and graciously acknowledges Alex's thanks. Cassa keeps saying, "Open mine, open mine." When Alex opens her gift, she grabs it and demonstrates how it works. Cassa continues to play with the gift while Alex opens the other presents and when Cassa gets ready to go home, she cries inconsolably because she cannot take the gift home.

By age five or six, children can recognize some of the mixed emotions they feel, like the happy and excited feeling when going to a birthday party (Wintre & Vallance, 1994). However, mixed feelings of good will, anger, and jealousy about the gifts the birthday child receives are still beyond understanding. The opposing feelings and

---

social comparisons—The stage of emotional development around six or seven years old when the child mentally compares herself to her peers.

their causes will come into consciousness between ages eight and eleven, but children do not yet understand that they can feel them all at the same time.

The primary age child is in the early stages of Erikson's (1950, 1963) fourth stage of psychosocial development. This transitional stage between initiative and industry is a time of rapid change in intellectual, social, and emotional competence. The primary age child moves from self-centered, egocentric thought patterns to much more socially conscious ones, recognizing others' viewpoints and emotions and understanding how they reflect on the child's own image of self. This emotional competence allows the child to expand friendships, feel comfortable in multiple settings, and function in progressively larger groups.

Parental expectations about their child's emotional competence vary across the world. In Warton and Goodnow's study (1991) Japanese mothers, for example, expected emotional maturity, compliance, and ritual politeness earlier than American mothers. All of the mothers from industrialized countries who were studied expected this kind of emotional development by six to ten years old. In less developed countries, children are expected to carry out important tasks that include farming, commerce, and taking care of younger kin; as a result, emotional maturity occurs earlier.

Curriculum for Primary Age Emotional Development. By the time children enter the primary grades, they are able to identify and name their feelings. This ability to identify a greater range of feelings and the intensity of emotions and mixed emotions increase with age. With the development of cognitive, language, and literacy skills, children are increasingly able to express their emotions. The teacher of primary age children should help children learn to clearly express their emotions. This may mean reflecting on a disruptive child's behavior by stating, "You seem angry," or giving children props to identify their emotions. A simple set of circles with faces on them expressing a variety of emotions is one tool a child can use to let others know how she feels.

Children also may use dramatic play to express emotions. Pretending to be an angry parent can help a child deal with a very hurried, tense morning at home. Reenacting significant events such as surgery, funerals, or accidents helps a child to identify and express overwhelming emotions. The teacher should allow and observe dramatic play and join in if this does not erect a barrier to the child's expression of feeling. The only time a teacher should redirect or interfere is if the play may injure that child or another child. Exploring difficult topics of death, illness, and separation can be done safely in dramatic play. As primary children's literacy skills improve, they can begin to express their feelings in writing. They should be given opportunities to label pictures with feeling words or write short paragraphs about how they feel about an event. Children can also read books with characters who discuss feelings related to events, such as Mikey's fear of swimming in *When the Water Closes Over My Head* (Napoli, 1994). In *Yolanda's Genius* (Fenner, 1995), Yolanda's encounter with discrimination, worries over size and appearance, and struggles with life in a single-parent family echo issues that many children of this age face. Finding book characters who have the same feelings they do gives children comfort and confidence.

In the primary grades, children can use artwork to help identify and express emotions. Many children give color or shape to emotions and use these colors or shapes in abstract drawings to help them express feelings. Asking children to draw happy, angry, or proud designs helps make emotions more tangible. Children of this age also enjoy drawing representative pictures of events. They may explain their pictures verbally or label them with feeling words (Figure 11–19 on page 426).

Music is another tool the teacher can use to help manage the emotional climate in the classroom or to help children identify feelings. The teacher can play soothing

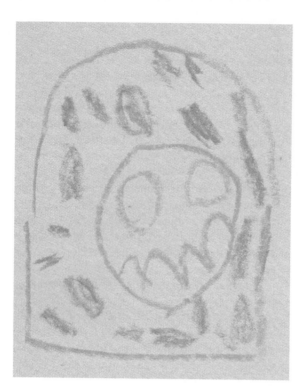

Figure 11-19

Art can help children identify and express their emotions.

background music to reduce stress or have the children listen to a dynamic piece such as "Sorcerer's Apprentice" by Paul Dukas to identify what feelings it sounds like.

Most importantly, the teacher should treat each expression of feeling with respect. Consistency remains important to children at this age and having an even-tempered teacher as a sounding board for discussing feelings helps children mature in their emotional development.

Elementary Age Children and Emotional Health

As children grow increasingly independent, they are expected to have more emotional control and responsibilities. Parental and school standards for behavior are higher, with expectations of less intense expression of emotions than those found in tantrums, whining, yelling, and hitting. Children at this stage are more likely to hold in their emotions, sulk, or demonstrate passive uncooperativeness when angry or upset. In Sroufe's, Carlson's, and Shulman's (1993) research on long-term effects of secure attachment, they found significant differences among children in ego resiliency, self-confidence, self-esteem, and social confidence. Children with secure attachment were better able to form close friendships and more willing to expose their ego to risks by trying adventurous challenges.

Emotional Development of Elementary Age Children.

From eight or nine to twelve years old, children can perform adultlike tasks that Erik-son (1950, 1963) identifies as the upper end of the stage of **industry versus inferi-**

industry versus inferiority—Erikson's fourth stage of emotional development, during the approximate age range of six to twelve years old, in which school age children master adultlike skills that make them feel either competent or inferior.

ority. They can bake cookies, make a bed, build a fort, ride a bike around the block, program a VCR, or design a Web page. They have great energy and are capable of feeling great success. Adult reactions to these efforts affect the child's emotional development. With encouragement and support, children of this age can create and produce sophisticated and remarkable things, enhancing their self-esteem and confidence. Without adult support and recognition of their efforts, children can feel negated and inferior. Erikson recognized that to develop into a fully independent and functional adult, early efforts need to be encouraged and supported; otherwise, emotional disturbances can result that take years to overcome.

By ages ten to twelve, children recognize the possibility of experiencing opposing feelings at the same time. This dilemma causes internal debate and anxiety, and waffling back and forth between the emotions, wondering which one will win out. For children in racial or ethnic groups, this dilemma is especially difficult. By this age, children are acutely aware of how their group is perceived by the white culture (Banks, 1992). Children of non-European background have been found to be "more sensitive to racial cues and develop racial awareness earlier than other children" (Anselmo & Franz, 1995, p. 332).

When considering gender differences in emotions, it is important to begin with the principle that there probably is no biological difference in male and female emotions. Researchers find that both sexes experience love, jealousy, anxiety in new social situations, grief when close relationships end, and embarrassment when they make mistakes in public (Tavris & Wade, 1984). Socialized differences, however, often result in the stereotypes of the female emotional being and the male rational being. There are gender differences in beliefs about emotion and its expression, with females having stronger feelings about relationships and males about being challenged. As children approach puberty, gender identification intensifies and divergence occurs, with attitudes and behaviors becoming more stereotypical, a signal to the outside world of their approaching adult status.

Children with learning disabilities develop increasing awareness and a more realistic view of their abilities as they grow older. They, too, compare themselves to their peers, but if their peer groups include others with learning difficulties, they feel more competent (Renick & Harter, 1989.) Curry and Johnson (1990) suggest that parent and teacher attitudes and labels placed on children with learning disabilities can produce lower self-esteem. Passive rote-learning environments may also reduce these children's motivation to achieve (p. 74). You can see that emotions and attitude influence behavior, and, in turn, behavior influences emotions and attitudes.

Peer acceptance and friendships play an important role in how preadolescent children feel about themselves (Figure 11–20 on page 428). They move from exclusive "best friend" relationships to needing acceptance by a peer group. This transition is sometimes confusing and hurtful, as "best friends" get left behind. The search for peer acceptance may produce feelings of anxiety and fear, or alternate between euphoria and sadness. Physical activity provides a way to overcome negative emotions and give children's minds, bodies, and emotions time to construct more realistic views of themselves and others (Reynolds, 1999).

Curriculum for Elementary Age Emotional Development.
Between the ages of nine and twelve, tremendous changes take place physically and cognitively as children mature into young adolescents. Bodies change, hormones are activated, and children begin to develop the ability to think more logically and systematically. With these changes, come surges of emotions and self-doubt. The teacher should help children continue to learn to identify and express emotions in socially appropriate ways. With their expanded cognitive abilities, children of this age

Figure 11-20

Close friendships are formed at the preadolescent age.

can begin to go beyond simply identifying feelings to being able to analyze the events that led up to those feelings and their resultant behavior. They can begin to see *the other side* of an event, not just their own viewpoint. The teacher should encourage them to develop these abilities by asking them to think about both sides of controversies in the classroom, in world events, and in books or movies.

In the classroom, the teacher should model respect for individual feelings and expects others to do the same. The teacher should find examples in the media of role models for appropriate expression of feelings. Children are sometimes overwhelmed by their negative expressions of emotions, and although they need to examine and process these events, the teacher should also direct their attention to positive events. Children can make a collage of people they admire, saying why they respect those people. Journals are another tool for children this age to express their feelings. This can take the form of guided or free-expression assignments. Drawings or artwork can be used instead of or as an accompaniment to written entries. When the teacher reads these journals, she should not correct grammar or spelling. Her comments should be positive and respectful, such as "I think so too" or "Great thinking!" The teacher must respect the journals' privacy and she should let the children know she feels privileged that they trust her enough to share their thoughts and feelings. When children express their emotions in essays, drawings, poems, or even on work sheets, these products must be treated with respect. They should not be graded or displayed on a bulletin board without the child's permission.

Many commercial workbooks, activity sheets, and curricula are available to help the teacher generate discussions and solidify ideas about emotional expression. However, before using any of them, the teacher should determine their purpose and value. Some curricula overwhelm children with surface exercises, so children begin to respond in the way they perceive is *expected*. It can be much more valuable to initiate an activity in response to an issue or event and allow the children to think deeply about their reactions.

WORDS OF WISDOM Mary Whittaker, a counselor working with troubled families for the last 15 years, recalls a case that caused her to believe in the resiliency of children and to advise teachers to listen and not give up. She met and counseled fourteen-year-old "Sean," the child of an estranged alcoholic father and a financially stressed mother. Left in the care of his seventeen-year-old brother, Sean a year later became heavily involved in substance abuse and was expelled from school. He appeared in a clinic where she was working four years later and she hardly recognized him. "Sean shared that he had once hoped to become an engineer and that his math teacher, who had faith in his potential, had fiercely advocated on his behalf with the school administrators. . . . He felt he had let her down." He entered rehab and returned weeks later looking much better but with very low self-esteem. He joined a group counseling session with younger members who came to look up to him, "awed by the fact that Sean sought treatment on his own, without parental support. . . . Sean readily accepted the leadership role his younger counterparts placed him in and their energy empowered him even further as he enrolled in community college." After two years Sean had completed his degree and received a full scholarship to a prestigious college. He hung onto the belief that math teacher had in him.

Mary reminds teachers: "There is intense pressure on teachers to produce academic success for their students, which requires extreme efforts to also create emotional safety within the classroom. Though Sean was far from an academic success, one caring adult saw his strength and potential, recognizing the difficulties in his life. It was this understanding and support that helped him seek assistance at his lowest point. A teacher's support cannot be fully and immediately recognized, perhaps until years afterward, when the full impact is felt. Sean's story illustrates how influential teachers and other people who work with children can be on the youth in their charge, even if such influence is not readily apparent. In Sean's case, it was years later that he was able to fully appreciate and use this support."

"As families become increasingly pressed for time, money, and support, the classroom may represent the child's only safe haven from a chaotic world that lacks caring and structure. In that context, it is a teacher's challenge to try to create that nurturing environment for learning, knowing that, at any given time, more than half her class may be dealing with issues of parental conflict, divorce, illness, or financial, and emotional stress."

With children this age, more so than with children at younger ages, the teacher must sense when additional help is needed as she supports children in their emotional development. If a child expresses thoughts about depression, suicide, injuring others, or incidences of abuse or neglect, the teacher must tell her that she needs to get more help. The teacher must take control at this point and enlist appropriate assistance from school personnel and the child's family. The child needs to be informed that any confidences regarding the problem may not be kept because helping professionals will need to be told in order to get the child help (Figure 11–21 on page 430). This tightrope of trying to maintain confidentiality while finding the help the child needs is a difficult one that may be seen by the child as betrayal. It is imperative, however, for the teacher to intervene before a tragedy occurs.

✳ ASSESSING EMOTIONAL DEVELOPMENT

Emotional development should be assessed primarily to determine if a child is at risk in order to get her the help she needs. Sometimes, emotions are so masked by behavior that it is very difficult to make a concrete evaluation or diagnosis.

Figure 11–21

The teacher walks a tightrope between trust and confidentiality and the child's safety.

Biological and Emotional Disorders

Two biological disorders that affect emotional competence in varying degrees are autism and Down syndrome. Children with autism often lack awareness of others' feelings, have little or no facial expressiveness, get distressed over trivial changes in the environment, and indulge in abnormal comfort-seeking behaviors when they are upset. While the child with autism does express feelings, they may do so at inappropriate times and with incongruent behavior, such as laughing when another child is crying or crying when she is happy. Children with autism are more likely to show positive feelings when they accomplish something, rather than when they engage in social exchanges. They often avoid eye contact and recoil at physical signs of affection.

Down syndrome affects facial muscles, limiting the range of expressions, and also affects intellectual functioning. While children with Down syndrome tend to be more emotionally placid, with lower arousal points than other children, their abilities to appropriately express or control their emotions are inhibited. Because of the cognitive effects, children with Down syndrome lack understanding of the full range of emotions. For example, they may not be able to differentiate between contentment and ecstasy and they have difficulty connecting the cause with the feeling. Children with various levels of these disorders may be placed in, or *mainstreamed* into, the regular classroom.

There is no clear definition of *normal* emotional health, which encompasses a wide range of behaviors. However, the following may indicate that a further evaluation should be considered.

* Behavior goes to an extreme (not just a little different from usual).
* The problem is long-lasting or chronic.
* The behavior is unacceptable for social or cultural reasons.

∗ The child's inability to learn cannot be explained by intellectual, sensory, or health factors.

∗ The child cannot build or maintain satisfactory relationships.

∗ The child's mood is general unhappy or depressed.

Maltreatment is the most common cause of emotional disorders in children. Children who have an anxious, tenuous attachment or no attachment whatsoever to a parent or primary caregiver, who were neglected, or who were excessively shamed are most likely to have long-term deleterious effects. Children of depressed mothers are also at risk for emotional disorders. They are less likely to receive the emotional nurturing they need; they have a role model who does not display positive affect or emotional competence; and they may not be receiving instruction about appropriate expressive behavior or coping strategies. Children with emotional disturbances or disruptive behavior caused by their inability to control their emotions should be referred for intervention.

Depression is a significant emotional disorder among children; children can become so depressed that they are capable of self-violence. Suicide was the fourth leading cause of death in ten- to fourteen-year-olds from 1993 to 1995 (National Center for Disease Control, 2000). The teacher should be aware of the indicators for depression and suicide. She should seek immediate help from a qualified school professional, such as a social worker, guidance counselor, or psychologist, if a child's behavior indicates that she is depressed or suicidal.

Some warning signs of depression or suicidal tendencies may be:

∗ proneness to accidents.

∗ physical violence toward self, others, or animals.

∗ loss of appetite.

∗ worsening performance at school.

∗ letters, notes, poems, or drawings with suicidal content.

∗ crying spells.

∗ talk of committing suicide.

Adapted from Oregon Health Division, 2000.

A variety of assessment tools are available for evaluating emotional competence and self-esteem. (See the Allen and Marotz [1999] Developmental Profiles in Appendix A.)

SUMMARY

Children's emotions evolve from a few simple reactive emotions at birth to the complex mixed emotions of early adolescence. As other domains develop, children acquire the ability to identify feelings, express emotions in a socially acceptable manner, and perceive the feelings of others. As with all development, emotional maturity depends on the characteristics a child is born with, attainment of early milestones, and having experiences that are not so overwhelming that she cannot cope with them. The teacher should help children move through the stages of emotional development by teaching them to recognize and clarify their feelings, examine and evaluate others' intentions, and discover socially appropriate ways of emotional expression.

KEY TERMS

emotion	gender-role stereotypes	separation anxiety
affect		autonomy versus shame and doubt
mood	stress	
temperament	acculturation stress	
core emotions	social referencing	initiative versus guilt
self-concept	attachment	social comparisons
self-esteem	social smile	industry versus inferiority
perspective taking	trust versus mistrust	
gender identity		

REVIEW ACTIVITIES

Exercises to Strengthen Learning

1. Infants—Visit a hospital nursery and observe the newborns for one hour.
   a. Are any of them relaxed?
   b. Are any of them uncomfortable?
   c. Are they soothed by adult care?
   d. Are they able to soothe themselves?
   e. What are their individual movements like?
   f. How much did they sleep during this hour?
   g. How did adults react to them?
   h. Did you observe possible differences in temperament among the infants?

2. Toddlers—Visit a toddler classroom at a childcare center. Arrive before the families and children. Observe how the toddlers leave their parents.
   a. What did you observe?
   b. What do your observations tell you about individual children's ability to separate and their developmental status?

3. Preschoolers—Observe a preschool classroom during free-play time.
   a. Record all the instances you see of children exhibiting emotional behavior that indicates they are still developing emotional competence.
   b. Describe the behavior, its antecedents, and its results.
   c. Conjecture from what you know about emotional development how the child will react to the same situation two years from now.

4. Primary Age—Observe a group of primary age children during their recess on the school playground. Describe the behaviors that you see that give any indications about social referencing, emotional release resulting from physical activity, or adult intervention in emotional disruptions.

5. Elementary Age—Read the scenario about Darren at the blackboard on page 395 to three teachers of third through sixth graders.
   a. Ask them what they would do in this situation.
   b. Now imagine yourself as the teacher of that class; what would you do?

Internet Quest

1. Search for *emotional disorders in children*. Identify five emotional disorders, the observable behaviors caused by the disorders, and treatment options.

2. Search for *children and stress*. Identify five sources of stress for children and ways a teacher might help reduce it.

3. Search for *sexual orientation*. Summarize two articles about children's sexual orientation from reputable sources. How does environment affect children's emotional development with regard to their sexual orientation? How might this affect learning?

Reflective Journal

What I learned from this chapter about emotional development that was most important to me was _____.

Because of what I learned, when I'm a teacher I will . . .

REFERENCES

Ainsworth, M. (1979). Infant-mother attachment. *American Psychologist, 34,* 932–937.

Allen, K. E., & Marotz, L. R. (1999). *Developmental profiles: Pre-birth through eight* (3rd ed.). Albany, NY: Delmar.

Anselmo, S., & Franz, W. (1995). *Early childhood development: Prenatal through age eight* (2nd ed.). Englewood Cliffs, NJ: Merrill.

Banks, J. (1992, November/December). Reducing prejudice in children: Guidelines from research. *Social Studies and the Young Learner,* 3–5.

Bates, J. E., & Wachs, T. D. (Eds.). (1995). *Temperament: Individual differences at the interface of biology and behavior.* Washington, DC: American Psychological Association.

Beardslee, W. R. (1998, September). Youth and the threat of nuclear war. *The Lancet,* 618–620.

Bednar, R. L., Wells, M. G., & Peterson, S. R. (1989). *Self esteem.* Washington, DC: American Psychological Association.

Bennet, S. K. (1994). The American Indian: A psychological overview. In W. J. Lonner & R. Malpass (Eds.), *Psychology and culture.* Needham Heights, MA: Allyn & Bacon.

Bigler, R. S., Liben, L. S., & Yekel, C. A. (1992, August). *Developmental patterns of gender-related beliefs: Beyond unitary constructs and measures.* Paper presented at the meeting of the American Psychological Association, Washington, DC.

Bottner, B. (1980). *Mean Maxine.* New York: Pantheon Books.

Bowlby, J. (1969). *Attachment and loss* (V. 1). New York: Basic Books.

Braungart, J. M., Plomin, R., DeFries, J. C., & Fulker, D. W. (1992). Genetic influence on tester-rated infant temperament as assessed by Bayley's infant behavior record: Nonadoptive and adoptive siblings and twins. *Developmental Psychology, 18,* 40–47.

Buss, A. H., & Plomin, R. (1984). *Temperament: Early developing personality traits.* Hillsdale, NJ: Erlbaum.

Campos, J. J., Barret, K. C., Lamb, M. E., Goldsmith, H. H., & Stenberg, C. (1983). Socioemotional development. In P. H. Mussen (Ed.), *Handbook of child psychology: Vol. 2. Infancy & developmental psychology.* New York: Wiley.

Caspi, A., & Silva, P. A. (1995). Temperamental qualities at age three predict personality traits in young adulthood: Longitudinal evidence from a birth cohort. *Child Development, 55,* 486–498.

Children's Defense Fund. (2000). *The state of America's children.* Washington, DC: Author.

Clark, K., & Clark, M. (1939). The development of consciousness of self and the emergence of racial identity in Negro pre-school schoolchildren. *Journal of Social Psychology, 10,* 591–599.

Curry, N. E., & Johnson, C. N. (1990). *Beyond self-esteem: Developing a genuine sense of human value.* Washington, DC: National Association for the Education of Young Children.

Damon, W., & Hart, D. (1988). *Self-understanding in childhood and adolescence.* Cambridge, UK: Cambridge University Press.

Davidson, R. J. (1994). How are emotions distinguished from moods and other affective constructs? In P. Ekman & R. J. Davidson (Eds.), *The nature of emotion: Fundamental questions* (pp. 51–55). Cambridge, UK: Cambridge University Press.

Denham, S. A. (1998). *Emotional development in young children.* New York: Guilford.

Dunsmore, J. C., & Halberstadt, A. G. (1997). How does family emotional expressiveness affect children's schemas? *New Directions for Child Development, 77,* 45–68.

Eastman, P. D. (1988). *Are you my mother?* New York: Beginner Books.

Eisenberg, N., Fabes, R. A., Bernzweig, J., Karbon, M., Poulin, R., & Hanish, O. (1993). The relation of emotionality and regulation to preschoolers' social skills and sociometric status. *Child Development, 64,* 1418–1438.

Ekman, P., Davidson, R., & Birbaumer, N. (1996). The nature of emotion: Fundamental questions. *American Journal of Psychology, 190,* 3, 496.

Elkind, D. (1981). *The hurried child.* Reading, MA: Addison-Wesley.

Emde, R., & Buchsbaum, H. (1990). "Didn't you hear my mommy?" Autonomy with connectedness in moral self-emergence. In D. Cicchetti & M. Beeghly (Eds.), *The self in transition* (pp. 35–60). Chicago: University of Chicago Press.

Erikson, E. H. (1950, 1963). *Childhood and society* (2nd ed.). New York: W. W. Norton.

Espin, O. M. (1993). Psychological impact of migration on Latinos. In D. R. Atkinson, G. Morten, & D. W. Sue (Eds.), *Counseling American minorities.* Madison, WI: Brown and Benchmark.

Essa, E. L., & Rogers, P. R. (1992). *An early childhood curriculum: From developmental model to application.* Albany, NY: Delmar.

Feinburg, S. G., & Mindess, M. (1994). *Eliciting children's full potential: Designing and evaluating developmentally based programs for young children.* Pacific Grove, CA: Brooks/Cole.

Fenner, N. C. (1995). *Yolanda's genius.* New York: McElderry.

Fox, M. (1994). *Tough Boris.* New York: Harcourt Brace.

Freedman, D. (1974). *Human infancy: An evolutionary perspective.* Hillsdale, NJ: Erlbaum.

Gardner, H. (1993). *Multiple intelligences: The theory in practice.* New York: Basic Books.

Goleman, D. (1995). *Emotional intelligence.* New York: Bantam Books.

Gonzalez-Mena, J. (1998). *The child in the family and the community* (2nd ed.). Upper Saddle River, NJ: Merrill.

Harter, S., & Marold, D. B. (1992). Psychological risk factors contributing to adolescent suicide ideation. In G. Noam & S. Borst (Eds.), *Child and adolescent suicide.* San Francisco, CA: Jossey Bass.

Izard, C. E., Porges, S. W., Simons, R. F., Haynes, O. M., Hyde, C., Parisi, M., & Cohen, B. (1991). Infant cardiac activity: Developmental changes and relations with attachment. *Developmental Psychology, 27,* 432–437.

Jensen, E. (1998). *Teaching with the brain in mind.* Alexandria, VA: Association for Supervision and Curriculum Development.

Kagan, J. (1987). Perspectives on infancy. In J. D. Osofsky (Ed.), *Handbook on infant development* (2nd ed.). New York: Wiley.

Kagan, J. (1989). *Unstable ideas: Temperament, cognition and self.* Cambridge, MA: Harvard University Press.

Kagan J., & Snidman, N. (1991). Temperamental factors in human development. *American Psychologist, 46,* 856–862.

Kagan, J., Arcus, D., Snidman, N., Feng, W. Y., Hendler, J., & Greene, S. (1994). Reactivity in infants: A cross-national comparison. *Developmental Psychology, 30,* 342–345.

Kane, E. (2000). Racial and ethnic variations in gender-related attitudes. *Annual Review of Sociology, 26,* 419–439.

Kiselevsky, B. S., Hains, S., Lee, K., Muir, D. W., Xu, F., Fu, G., Zhao, Z., & Yang, R. L. (1998). The still-face effect in Chinese and Canadian 3- to 6-month-old infants. *Developmental Psychology, 34,* 629–639.

Knouse, S. B. (1992). Hispanics and work: An overview. In S. B. Knouse, R. Rosenfeld, & A. Culbertson (Eds.), *Hispanics in the workplace.* Newbury Park, CA: Sage.

Kostelnik, M. J., Stein, L. C., Whiren, A. P., & Soderman, A. K. (1998). *Guiding children's social development* (3rd ed.). Albany, NY: Delmar.

Kurdek, L. A., & Krile, D. (1982). A developmental analysis of the relation between peer acceptance and both interpersonal understanding and perceived social self-competence. *Child Development, 53,* 1485–1491.

LaFromboise, T. D., Trimble, J. E., & Mohatt, G. (1993). Counseling intervention and American Indian tradition: An integrative approach. In D. R. Atkinson, G. Morten, & D. W. Sue (Eds.), *Counseling American minorities.* Dubuque, IA: Brown & Benchmark.

Lazarus, R. (1991). Constructs of the mind. In N. Stein, B. L. Leventhal, & T. Trabasso (Eds.), *Psychological and biological approaches to emotion.* Hillsdale, NJ: Erlbaum.

LeDoux, J. (1996). *The emotional brain.* New York: Simon and Schuster.

Lee, E. (1996). Asian American families: An overview. In J. Giordano, M. McGoldrick, & J. Pearce, (Eds.), *Ethnicity and family therapy* (2nd ed.). New York: Guilford Press.

Lewis, M. (1989). Cultural differences in children's knowledge of emotional scripts. In C. Saarni & P. L. Harris (Eds.), *Children's understanding of emotion* (pp. 350–374). Cambridge: Cambridge University Press.

Lewis, M., & Feinman, S. (Eds.). (1991). *Social influences and socialization in infancy.* New York: Plenum.

Lewis, M., & Michalson, L. (1983). *Children's emotions and moods.* New York: Plenum.

Lynch, E. W., & Hanson, M. J. (1999). *Developing cross-cultural competence: A guide for working with young children and their families* (2nd ed). Baltimore, MD: Paul. H. Brookes.

Mahler, M., Pine, F., & Bergman, A. (1975). *The psychological birth of the human infant.* New York: Basic Books.

Marin, G. (1994). The experience of being a Hispanic in the United States. In W. J. Lonner & R. Malpass (Eds.), *Psychology and culture.* Needham Heights, MA: Allyn and Bacon.

McLoyd, V., Cauce, A., Takeuchi, D., & Wilson, L. (2000). Marital processes and parental socialization in families of color: A decade review of research. *Journal of Marriage & the Family, 62*(4), 1070–1124.

Mead, M., MacGregor, F. C., & Bateson, G. (1951). *Growth and culture: A photographic study of Balinese children.* New York: Putnam.

Miller, L. C. (1983). Fears and anxiety in children. In C. E. Walker and M.C. Roberts (Eds.), *Handbook of clinical child psychology.* New York: John Wiley & Sons.

Monahon, C. (1993). *Children in trauma: A guide for parents and professionals.* San Francisco, CA: Jossey-Bass.

Morris, R., & Kratochwill, T. (1983). *Treating children's fears and phobias: A behavioral approach.* Elmsford, NY: Pergamon.

Munsch, R. (1986). *Love you forever.* Scarborough, Ontario, Canada: Firefly Books.

National Center for Disease Control. (2000). Ten leading causes of death, United States 1993–95. Retrieved January 16, 2000, from the World Wide Web: <http://www.cdc.gov/ncipc.osp/leadcaus/ustable.htm>.

Napoli, D. J. (1994). *When the water closes over my head.* New York: Dutton Children's Books.

Nelson, C. A. (1987). The recognition of facial expressions in the first two years of life: Mechanism of development. *Child Development, 58,* 889–909.

Oregon Health Division. (2000). *Warning signs: Possible indicators of increased suicide risk.* Retrieved January 14, 2000, from the World Wide Web: <http://www.ohd.hr.state.or.us/cdpe/chs/suicide/signs.htm>.

Paley, V. G. (1981). *Wally's stories.* Cambridge, MA: Harvard University Press.

Paley, V. G. (1984). *Boys and girls in the doll corner.* Chicago: University of Chicago Press.

Paley, V. G. (1992). *You can't say you can't play.* Cambridge, MA: Harvard University Press.

Papalia, D.E., & Olds, S.W. (1996). *A child's world: Infancy through adolescence.* New York: McGraw Hill

Piaget, J., & Inhelder, B. (1969). *The psychology of the child*. New York: Basic Books.

Plomin, R., Emde, R. N., Braungart, J. M., & Campos, J. (1993). Genetic change and continuity from fourteen to twenty months: The MacArthur longitudinal twin study. *Child Development, 64*, 1354–1376.

Renick, M. J., & Harter, S. (1989). Impact of social comparisons on the developing self-perceptions of learning disabled students. *Journal of Educational Psychology, 81*, 631–638.

Reynolds, K. D. (1999). Schools as a setting for health promotion and disease prevention. In M. M. Racqnyski, & R. J. DiClemente (Eds.), *Handbook of health promotion and disease prevention*. New York: Kluwer Academic/Plenum.

Saarni, C. (1999). *The development of emotional competence*. New York: Guilford Press.

Selman, R. L. (1980). *The growth of interpersonal understanding*. New York: Academic Press.

Slabach, E., Morrow, J., & Wachs, T. D. (1991). Questionnaire measurement of infant and children temperament. In J. S. Trelau & A. Angleitner (Eds.), *Explorations in temperament*. New York: Plenum.

Sprunger, L. W., Boyce, W. T., & Gaines, J. A. (1985). Family-infant congruence: Routines and rhythmicity in family adaptations to a young infant. *Child Development, 56*, 564–572.

Sroufe. L. A. (1996). *Emotional development: The organization of emotional life in the early years*. Cambridge, UK: Cambridge University Press.

Sroufe, L. A., Carlson, E., & Shulman, S. (1993). Individuals in relationships: Development from infancy through adolescence. In D. C. Funder, R. D. Park, C. Tomlinson-Keasey, & K. Widamen (Eds.), *Studying lives through time: Personality and development* (pp. 315–342). Washington, DC: American Psychological Association.

Sroufe, L. A., Schork, E., Motti, F., Lawroski, N., & LaFrenier, P. (1984). The role of affect in social competence. In C. Izard, J. Kagan, & R. Zajonc (Eds.), *Emotions, cognition and behavior* (pp. 289–319). Cambridge, UK: Cambridge University Press.

Stifter, C. A., & Fox, N. A. (1990). Infant reactivity: Physiological correlates of newborn and 5 month temperament. *Developmental Psychology, 26*, 582–599.

Tavris, C., & Wade, C. (1984). *The longest war: Sex differences in perspective* (2nd ed.). San Diego, CA: Harcourt Brace Jovanovich.

Thomas, A., & Chess, S. (1977). *Temperament and development*. New York: Brunner/Mazel.

Thomas, A., & Chess, S. (1984). Genesis and evaluation of behavioral disorders: From infancy to early adult life. *American Journal of Psychiatry, 141*, 1–9.

U.S. Bureau of the Census. (1997). *Statistical abstract of the United States; The national data book*. Washington, DC: U.S. Government Printing Office.

U.S. Department of Health and Human Services. (2000). *HHS reports new child abuse and neglect statistics*. Retrieved March 14, 2001, from the World Wide Web: <http://www.acf.dhhs.gov/news/april00.htm>.

Warton, P. M., & Goodnow, J. J. (1991). The nature of responsibility: Children's understanding of "your job." *Child Development, 62*, 156–165.

Weisner, T. S. (1984). Ecocultural niches of middle childhood. In W. A. Collins (Ed.), *Development during middle childhood: The years from six to twelve*. Washington, DC: National Academy Press.

Williams, J. E., & Best, D. L. (1982). *Measuring sex stereotypes: A thirty nation study*. Newbury Park, CA: Sage.

Williams, J. E., & Best, D. L. (1989). *Sex and psyche: Self concept viewed cross-culturally*. Newbury Park, CA: Sage.

Wintre, M. G., & Vallance, D. D. (1994). A developmental sequence in the comprehension of emotions: Intensity, multiple emotions and valence. *Developmental psychology, 30*(4), 509–514.

For additional learning and teaching resources, visit our Web site at www.EarlyChildEd.delmar.com.

RELATED CAREERS

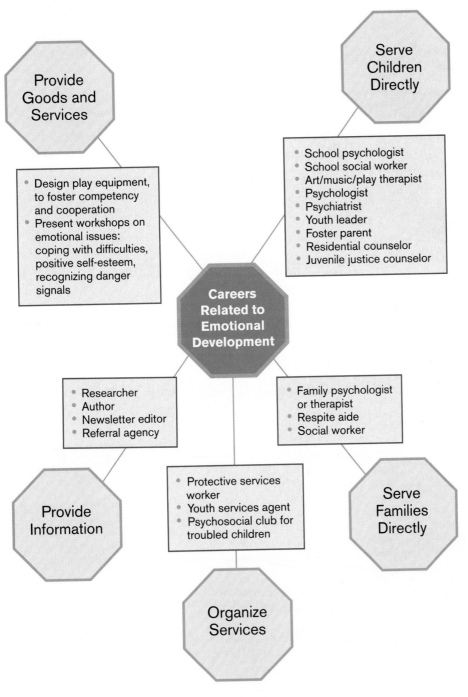

Figure 11—22

Careers related to emotional development.

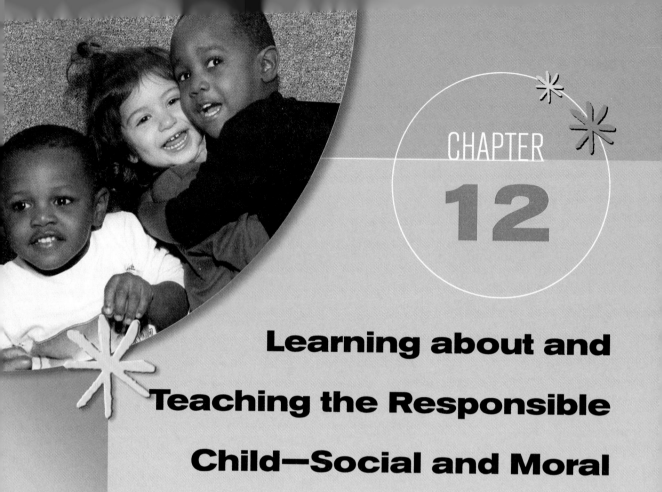

Learning about and Teaching the Responsible Child—Social and Moral Development

Objectives

After reading this chapter and completing the review activities, the learning teacher should be able to:

1. Explain the origins and stages of social and moral development.
2. Identify strategies the teacher can use to promote social competency.
3. Understand how to positively guide children in controlling their own behavior.
4. Reflect on how relationships among home, school, community, and the media can help decrease violence in society.

✳ UNDERSTANDING SOCIAL AND MORAL DEVELOPMENT IN LEARNING AND TEACHING

SCENARIO   Carlos is hours old. His father is holding him aloft and gazing intently into his eyes. Carlos gazes back.

Two-year-old Alonzo is at the beach. He goes over to a child who is playing with a pail and shovel. Alonzo pushes the child aside and takes the pail and shovel back to where he was playing.

Faith, a six-year-old first grader, has just opened her lunch box and sees that her mother has packed applesauce for her dessert. She is carrying her friend Jodi's lunch bag to the cafeteria and sees that Jodi has chocolate cupcakes. She switches her applesauce for the cupcakes and says, "Jodi, here's your lunch."

Krystal is a sixth grader who wants desperately to be part of a group of girls who always eat together in the cafeteria. They giggle and talk excitedly, while Krystal watches with envy, alone and self-conscious about her aloneness.

Learning and teaching are social activities that involve two or more humans interacting in such a way that one or both of them is altered in the way they think and act because of the exchange. The ability to participate in this exchange is paramount to its success. The social nature of human behavior is based upon a set of values infused from infancy forward, during which adults express approval or disapproval of behavior, thus giving the young, inexperienced social being guidance on acceptable ways of speaking and acting toward others. That instruction, both overt and covert, along with the child's emotional nature, discussed in the previous chapter, forms the patterns of socialization.

There are ranges of socialized expectations in each society for sharing, assertiveness, empathy, politeness, repentance, forgiveness of wrongs, aggression, and communication. The learning teacher knows the developmental stages of socialized behavior and its effect on learning within the social atmosphere of the classroom (Figure 12–1 on page 440). As the learning teacher gets acquainted with each child, interpersonal skills will emerge, affecting the whole group in positive or negative ways. The role of the teacher is to instill social characteristics that will primarily ensure physical and psychological safety, and then cooperation and collaboration for the good of the whole group. In this way the classroom is a microcosm of the larger society for which the teacher is preparing the students.

WORDS OF WISDOM Sky Neilson, an early childhood educator in Boston, gives us another way to look at the purpose of school:

"The question 'Why do we send our children to school?' has both personal and general answers. Personally, I would choose to send my child to school in the hopes that she will learn to think critically and equip herself with the necessary tools to succeed in whatever goals she sets for herself. Personally, I believe that the emotional strength she needs to survive in this world, including her time spent in public schools, will come from being raised in a loving family."

"But, as a collective, as a society, this country sends its children to school in an effort to achieve universal basic education as a requisite part of building an egalitarian culture. That is a worthy goal. More recently, people have been fashionably saying that we send children to school 'to socialize them'; I would disagree. The socialization process occurs within the family, with social skills—or lack thereof—being practiced at school. We send the children to public school so that they will have the same opportunity as everyone else. Parental responsibility lies not in making that opportunity work for their children, but in providing the family support to ensure the child can cope with the outside world."

"And when you get right down to it, the answer to our question, 'Why do we send our children to school?' is staring us in the face. And the answer is . . . hope."

"Hope is the thing with feathers,

that perches in the soul.

That sings the tune without the words

And never stops at all."

—Emily Dickinson

Figure 12–1

Children learn social skills from working together.

Do you agree with Sky that socialization is the role of the parent, and not of the teacher? Should the teacher be concerned about **social competence**? Social competence is essential to a safe environment in which learning can take place. Without social competence, chaos would reign, and fear and aggression would preclude learning activity. Building on emotional competence (the ability to control and appropriately express emotions), social competence is its accessory, accompanying behavior that coordinates emotions with actions toward other people. Without emotional control, social interactions may be dangerous. Without social competence, understanding about how emotional expression will be received is absent, making for a lonely, rejected, or misunderstood individual. Goleman (1995) lists the qualities associated with social competence as giving and receiving emotional support; social awareness and processing information accurately; and communicating, problem solving, and self-monitoring. Success in school has been linked with effective social relations (Alexander & Entwisle, 1988). Children become socially competent first through interactions with family members, then with neighborhood friends, participation in school and community activities, and adults other than those in their family.

The teacher's role is to accept developing individual children with their varying degrees of emotional and social competence, as well as to profit from parental guidance. Then, working within the context of the classroom, the teacher can work to ensure that everyone is safe and continuing to develop competent interpersonal skills. These skills will be needed not only in the classroom, but also on the playground, at home, out in the community, and ultimately in the workplace. You probably know people who are brilliant but who cannot sustain a job or preserve a relationship because of poor social skills. Will you be the kind of teacher who concentrates on cognitive development while ignoring the social domain? We hope not; we appeal to you to add social competence to your list of learning and teaching objectives.

Learning about and teaching the social child means more than helping each child develop manners. They also involve social studies, cultural heritage, thinking, decision making, and social science (Welton & Mallan, 1992). By developing these areas, teachers can help children become responsible, caring, and social citizens. The National Council for the Social Studies (NCSS, 1994) has identified 10 thematic or curriculum strands and standards for each grade level.

1. Culture
2. Time, continuity, and change
3. People, places, and environments
4. Individual development and identity
5. Individuals, groups, and institutions
6. Power, authority, and governance
7. Production, distribution, and consumption
8. Science, technology, and society
9. Global connections
10. Civic ideals and practices (p. 15)

These areas are all relevant to the child's world, starting at the place they know best: that of the cultures of their family and the people and groups around them, and

social competence—The ability to act responsibly, independent of supervision or outward control, in interactions with other people; cooperative and self-controlled behavior.

eventually extending that domain to a global perspective. Following established standards helps teachers build a comprehensive, integrated curriculum that begins first with comprehensive knowledge of the learner, including insight into his social world.

How do people become kind, caring, and moral beings like the children in Figure 12–2? Are some people just born benevolent? Are some people just born with an antagonistic and aggressive nature? We explored emotional development and temperament in the last chapter; the realm of social competence and its development is closely aligned with emotional maturation, which demonstrates some of the same inborn characteristics and learned behavior present in social interactions.

The Nature of Social and Moral Development

The infant is born selfish, and is genetically programmed to have personal needs met. It this were not so, the infant would probably not survive. His reflexes are the signals the infant uses to get his survival needs met: turning toward a touch to the cheek or wailing when he is hungry or needs to be held. The infant pays no heed to late night or wee morning hours, how little sleep his parents have had, or if they are doing something else. The infant wants what he wants at the moment the need occurs. How long do these self-serving behaviors last? How does the growing child eventually become considerate of other's needs and feelings? How long does it take until the child gives instead of takes? The answer is different for every human being; for some people (and unfortunately for the rest of us) the answer is *never*.

Birth has been described as the first bio-social-behavioral shift in human development (Cole & Cole, 1996), since prior to birth the infant's development totally depended on the physiological contribution of the mother's body. Biology, or nature, still is a factor in the child's social development. Newborns come equipped with the predisposition to seek and respond to social interactions in such behaviors as attentive looking, smiling, cooing, and soft touches. When the instinctual patterns of sucking

Figure 12–2

Children need to learn to care about each other.

and pausing are interrupted, the parent who expedites its resumption, beginning the entwining of nature and nurture and the beginning of trust in adults.

Many philosophers and theorists have wondered about the origins of how people relate to each other. **Sigmund Freud**, one of the most famous psychiatrists, attributed all social behavior to the biological need for the survival and propagation of the species. He recognized that striving to meet biological and sexual needs throughout their life spans was the underlying motivation for the ways in which people interact with others. He held that gratification of needs during these stages influences adult behavior (1920, 1955). He divided a person's development as follows.

Sigmund Freud

(1856–1939) Trained as a neurologist, Freud developed the psychoanalytic method of treating emotionally disturbed adults by considering the events of their early development as factors in later psychoses. He was one of the first theorists/practitioners to point out the unconscious motives that contribute to behavior.

* Oral stage—In the child's first year, the mouth is the primary source of pleasure, fulfilling the infant's need to suck and get nourishment.

* Anal stage—In the second and third years of life, controlling the urge to defecate brings praise for attaining an important goal.

* Phallic stage—In the fourth year of life, boys become aware of their penis, their sexual feelings toward their mother, and their jealousy of their fathers; girls become aware and resentful of their absence of a penis, blaming their mothers.

* Latency stage—Between ages six or seven and the early teen years, sexual desires are suppressed and energy is channeled into acquiring adult skills.

* Genital stage—From puberty into sexual maturity, sexual urges toward peers of the opposite sex are ultimately for the purpose of reproduction.

Freud (1933, 1964) described the mental structures of personality as consisting of the *id* (present at birth; the unconscious, energetic, and pleasure-seeking element); the *ego* (the gradual realization that self-control and moderation are necessary if you are to operate in the social world in acceptable and satisfactory ways); and the *superego* (society's authority with supersedes individual drives and gratification). See Figure 1–19 on page 135 for a comparison of Freud's stages to those of other developmental theorists. While Freud's theories were framed in the historical perspective of his time, and many dispute them for their unscientific basis, they continue to help us understand the interplay between biology and psychology.

Biology and social development are linked in other important ways other than temperament; a child's inherited intelligence, perception, and ways of thinking also determine, to an extent, human interaction. A certain level of cognitive functioning is necessary to carry out social exchanges. As the child develops cognitively, he better understands other people's motives, desires, and actions, which broaden his choice of reactions or strategies for dealing with other people. The infant only has one mechanism at his disposal to have his needs met: to cry or even scream. If he only has limited brain functioning at his disposal, he has to depend principally, or even wholly, on these primitive methods of expression and communication. As his brain develops its capacity for understanding, he will learn other ways—some very cunning—to communicate with and manipulate the people around him.

The Nurture of Social and Moral Development

". . . No man is an island, entire of itself; every man is a piece of the continent, a part of the main. If a clod be washed away by the sea, Europe is the less, as well as if a promontory were, as well as if a manor of thy friend's or of thine own were. Any man's death diminishes me, because I am involved in mankind; and therefore never send to know for whom the bell tolls; it tolls for thee . . ."

The famous passage from Meditation 17, *Devotions Upon Emergent Occasions,* written by John Donne in 1624 (from Norton, 1962) reminds us that people do not live completely by themselves (Figure 12–3). In all modern societies, children must learn to interact, share, and cooperate by the time they are adults, or they will be unable to function effectively. How do children learn the qualities that enable them to be responsible, nonviolent citizens? This question is discussed daily, sometimes after unthinkable violence has taken place. To be kind, one has to have been treated kindly; to be moral, one has to have seen morality in action. We seek to develop people who can function in society, care about others, and act responsibly. Morality, says Damon (1988, p. 5), is:

* an evaluative orientation toward actions and events that distinguishes them as good or evil and prescribes conduct consistent with good.
* a sense of obligation toward standards shared by the social collective.
* a sense of responsibility for acting on one's concern for others through acts of caring, benevolence, kindness, and mercy.
* concern for the rights of others, justice, and fairness.
* commitment to honesty as the norm in interpersonal dealings.
* awareness that violations may result in emotional responses such as shame, guilt, outrage, fear, and contempt.

Morality is not focused on obedience or the moral rules of others, nor acting in prosocial ways out of politeness or conformity; it is not having a list of positive charac-

Figure 12–3

"No man is an island . . ." (Courtesy of the D.C. Committee to Promote Washington)

ter traits, nor does it necessarily stem from being religious. Instilling morality results from posing moral dilemmas that each person must work out for himself. The socio-moral atmosphere at school has two primary parts: teacher-child and children's peer relations (DeVries & Zan, 1994).

Attachment. You have read about attachment and its importance to emotional development; it is equally important in social development. Secure relationships with important people in his life from infancy onward is the child's foundation for later relationships. One study (Ainsworth, 1979) on infant attachment looked at how responsively mothers fed their infants in the first three months and discovered 10 patterns that correlated to how securely attached the infants were at one year of age. During a child's early years, he and the adults in his life coordinate their behavior, with the adults initially responding to the infant, but very soon the reciprocal dance beginning. Lickona (1991) found that at age three-and-a-half, securely attached children are already more morally mature than those who are insecurely attached. Because the attachment was based on mutual respect, having their own need for love met enabled these children to be more open to the needs of others. He also found that more securely attached children had better peer relations and were better learners. Attachment is, without a doubt, a fundamental foundation for social and moral development (Figure 12–4).

While children with limited mental potential have the ability to become attached, they generally do so at a later age (Cicchetti & Carlson, 1989). Infants who are physically disabled (for example, with sight or hearing difficulties) form attachments, but express those attachments in different ways (Marvin and Pianta, 1992). Infants who are abused even become attached to their abusers (Carlson, Cicchetti, Barnett, & Braunwald, 1989). Infants who are institutionalized where there is no consistent caregiver

Figure 12–4

Children need attachment to an adult for healthy mental, social, and emotional development.

fail to form attachments, to the detriment of their physical, emotional, and social development (Smirnova, 1996; Dubrovina & Ruzska, 1990).

Classic studies of attachment such as Harlow's (1959) with infant monkeys demonstrate that nourishment alone is not enough for healthy emotional and social development. Bowlby's studies (1969) of postwar babies deprived of consistent caregivers, and Ainsworth's studies (1979) of attachment determined that the most securely attached children demonstrate better psychological health later in life. Attachment's importance to later life outcomes relates to the shaping of what Bowlby (1969) calls **internal working models** of the social world, where the person has developed trust in other people's care because of feeling he is worthy of their care. Bretherton (1985) expanded on this principle, proposing that behavior toward others in new social situations depends heavily on that archetype of trust as the model for all other relationships. In other words, when an infant has responsive caregivers, he expects teachers, police, health personnel, store clerks, other adults, and, ultimately, other children to be responsive as well. He has faith and confidence that the model with which he has had prior experience will apply to present circumstances. Such characteristics as curiosity, enthusiasm for solving problems, high self-esteem, and positive relations with teachers and peers all have been found to be strongly linked to the quality of early attachments (Sroufe, 1995).

Moral Development. As people interact, conflicts arise between the needs and wants of one person and those of others. From such conflicts come rules, traditions, and eventually laws that guide individuals, groups, and even countries so that *right* can prevail. That *right* is what is good for society: for example, not speeding so that no one is injured because of the speed of your vehicle, or requiring that goods and services used be paid for, or refraining from physically hurting another person either accidentally or intentionally. There are retributive consequences when a law is transgressed. That is how a moral society works. Laws strive to protect everyone equally and hold each person responsible for his own behavior.

The code of behavior that is broader than law is that of morality. It manifests itself in different ways for different people, depending on some of the same factors discussed earlier. Morality depends on cognitive ability, maturity, and temperament (all biological elements), as well as the influence of family and that of peers, mentors, and teachers. Morality may even depend on the situation, or the individual's perception of that situation. The development of a conscience—that part of us that at some level feels a moral or ethical judgment for a behavior—occurs along a path parallel to that for cognitive functioning. Moral judgments are contingent on reasoning and reflecting to understand the situation and your role in it, as well as expectations that may or may not have been met. Solving the problem or finding an acceptable alternative also relies on your ability to analyze and weigh alternatives and arrive at a logical decision. Toddlers are not yet at the developmental level necessary to make a decision based on knowledge and a set of values or behavioral expectations (Figure 12–5).

We examine moral development along with social development because both progress in discernible stages and are directly relevant to interpersonal relationships. However, we could just as appropriately have included moral development along with cognitive or emotional development because they so closely depend on and parallel each other. Piaget (1932, 1965), the developmental theorist we connect primarily

internal working models—Generalized expectations of responsive or unresponsive caregivers that form in infancy and affect childhood and beyond, representing the self as either worthy or unworthy of care.

Figure 12–5

Children learn to distinguish behavior that is right from behavior that is wrong.

with cognitive development, identified the relationship of moral development with the change in the child's thinking. He felt that children younger than seven are amoral, or lack the ability to reason through a moral course of behavior. The obedient child was the next stage, when the child recognized there was an absolute authority who would punish wrongdoing. Piaget believed that late in childhood or in early adolescence children could see that different situations dictated different behaviors, so absolutes were not always absolute but were instead relative to the situation.

Lawrence Kohlberg was one of the primary moral development theorists. He defined and developed a method of scoring moral development in stages, with accompanying approximate ages (1976).

Lawrence Kohlberg

(1927–1987) Researched moral development and developed a system of moral dilemmas from which levels of moral development could be determined.

* Preconventional—until about the age of nine—Decisions are based on obedience (or rather the avoidance of punishment) or self-gratification.

Stage 0: Egocentric reasoning (preschool years, around age four)

Reason to be good: to get rewards and avoid punishments

Stage 1: Unquestioning obedience (around kindergarten age)

Reason to be good: to stay out of trouble

Stage 2: "What's in it for me" fairness (early elementary grades)

Reason to be good: Self interest

* Conventional—adolescents and most adults—Moral judgments are based on the opinions of others or formal laws, connected with conformity and duty.

Stage 3: Interpersonal conformity (middle to upper elementary grades and early and midteens)

Reason to be good: So others will think well of me (social approval) and I can think well of myself (self-esteem)

Stage 4: Responsibility to "the system" (late teen years)

Reason to be good: To keep the system from falling apart and to maintain self-respect as somebody who meets my own obligations

✳ Postconventional—only a minority of adults—Moral decisions are based on dedication to society and own code, to maintain self-respect and respect of peers.

Stage 5: Principled conscience (minority of adults)

Reason to be good: The obligation of conscience to act in accordance with the principle of respect for all human beings

(Adapted from Lickona, 1991, p. 12.)

According to Kohlberg's stages of moral development, infants are amoral (1976). They have no knowledge of right or wrong; consequently, they have no need of behavioral or ethical guidance. They operate from instinct; their motivation is no more than to satiate their needs. Historically, societies have been ambivalent regarding the relative innocence or evil of infants. At times, sages and intellectuals pointed to children's intrinsic innocence as an attribute to be recaptured, while the general population saw children as miniature adults, financial liabilities, or wild creatures to be tamed and brought under subjugation. Harsh discipline, abandonment, and even infanticide accompanied these attitudes. Reformation philosophers of the sixteenth and seventeenth centuries called on people to consider childhood a sentimental stage of life worthy of protection. In colonial America, however, the Puritans' view of the child as conceived in sin resulted not only in harsh discipline, but also in public education to bring children to God and overcome Satan's influence. The Romantic view of the child came later to America and, to this day, some vestiges of the "sinful child whose will must be broken" still remain. Kohlberg's work sought to enlighten people about the child's moral development being closely entwined with his cognitive and emotional development. The conflict of different philosophies is evident in the various parenting experts who espouse everything from permissiveness to *tough love*.

One of Kohlberg's critics, Gilligan (1982), argues that women tend to respond to moral dilemmas on the basis of caring, personal relationships, and interpersonal obligations. Males, who use abstract concepts of justice and equity, scored higher under Kohlberg's assessment protocol, biasing the scoring against women, who have been taught from childhood to value compassion and social obligations. Others have studied and either supported or disputed Gilligan's claim, but the fact remains that there is need for further study of the gender differences in moral development.

Another criticism of Kohlberg's theory (Snarey, 1985; Edwards, 1982) is that it is specific to middle-class urban societies. It gives lower moral development scores to those raised in collectivist traditional cultures where meeting your obligations to family and community and submitting to elders' authority are the moral principles held in highest esteem. The other criticisms that abound are summarized by Fischer (1983, p. 98) who said that "...it now seems that Kohlberg's first five stages can be accepted as a legitimate description of development of moral judgment in ... white lower- and middle-class males."

There are differing opinions about whether or not schools should teach values. Some would ask, "Whose values? The teacher's? The state's? That of (a) religion?" Because of this disparity, some seek to omit values indoctrination from the curriculum. Others advocate the value of self: "Do what is right for you." However, the apparent moral decline in this country has brought with it a shift in thinking, so that many people believe that helping children grow up to be responsible, caring human beings may be the most important job for parents, teachers, schools, and society. But how is that accomplished? Teaching values and morality is not teaching religion. It is not setting up a strict code of right and wrong to which everyone will adhere. It is instead instilling the universal belief that all people should be treated with respect and

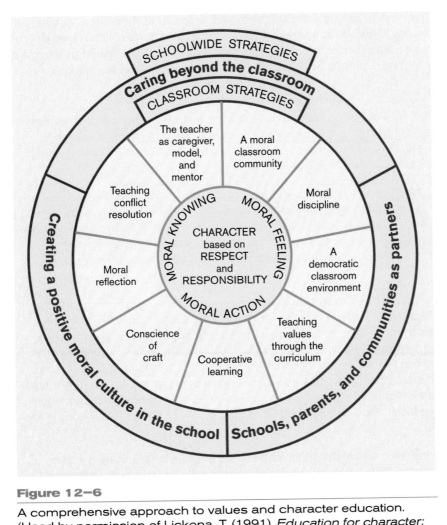

Figure 12-6

A comprehensive approach to values and character education.
(Used by permission of Lickona, T. (1991). *Education for character: How our schools can teach respect and responsibility*. New York: Bantam Books)

equality, and that people must take responsibility for their own actions and the actions of those who cannot be held responsible for their own. Lickona (1991) suggests that teachers can be caregivers, moral models, and ethical mentors if they avoid behavior that undermines a student's dignity and self-esteem, treat their students with respect and love, set a good example along with teaching morals directly, and mentor students one-on-one. He has developed a comprehensive approach to value and character education (Figure 12-6).

Discipline and Guidance. One of the most difficult areas for teachers is classroom control, or how to discipline children who do not abide by the rules. Many years ago, offenses were defined by such behaviors as chewing gum, copying others' work, or not sitting up straight in your chair. Today, the teacher may face defiant, obstinate behavior; threats; physical attacks on other children and even the teacher, as well as an overall atmosphere of disrespect. How can a teacher prepare to deal with these behaviors? The best defense is an offense, as they say in sports, and it is true in this area as well. The adaptive teacher is well prepared in the content of what is to be taught, has a passion for learning and teaching, understands children's developmental levels, and respects children. Such a teacher is much better prepared to set up a classroom and curriculum in which each child feels valued and can find success.

WORDS OF WISDOM

Robert Mills of Indiana has had a long career in child care licensing. In his many visits to child care centers, he has high expectations not only for health and safety standards being upheld, but also for the quality of child/teacher interactions. He writes passionately about those interactions and the need for respect.

"Respect starts with good, sensitive, detailed, regular observations of each child. Respect means accepting and loving each child as he is, and not expecting him to do things before he is ready. When we teach a child anything, we take away his chances of discovering it on his own, forever. And, when a child makes a new discovery, it's like magic. You can see the twinkle in his eye. Instead of trying to teach, we educators need to find ways to create an environment where many, many discoveries are possible."

"Respect means allowing children to be explorers and self-learners and believing in their competence. Respect means giving children *time* to explore, play, solve problems, and learn from their successes and mistakes. Respect means setting up a safe, secure, nurturing, age-appropriate, and challenging environment. Respect means encouraging children to discover available choices and permitting them to make their own, knowing that they will sometimes make bad choices. Teachers must embrace and learn about cultural and physical differences and teach children to respect these differences. We must teach children not to reject each other. Rejection by peers is one of the most painful childhood experiences and is avoidable if we teach 'You Can't Say, You Can't Play,'" as Vivian Paley recommends in her book with that title (1992).

"Respect means setting consistent, reasonable limits for behavior. Respect means trusting in the power of good will and reason to solve problems, maybe not immediately, but eventually, instead of using force or punishment to solve problems."

"Education is not about pumping facts into children; it is about relationships and respect."

Classroom discipline approaches are related to learning theories. Those who espouse the behaviorist philosophy emphasize rewards and punishments as a way of teaching behavior. Strategies such as "counting to three" ("One . . . two . . . three!"), writing the names of "offenders" or the "exemplary" on the chalkboard, or using a system of point accumulation are based on the authoritarian style, which uses praise and threats in an attempt to elicit desired behavior. In contrast, the maturationist philosophy emphasizes the child's understanding unfolding to the point where the child learns self-control of behavior without outside intervention. This perspective is analogous to the permissive discipline style. The constructivist learning theory is based on Piaget's philosophies of learning from experiences, reflecting on those experiences, and forming new patterns of behavior with control from within. As each teacher learns about his own sociological influences and various learning theories, and develops a personal philosophy of teaching, he will develop strategies for classroom discipline that parallel those precepts. Reflect on this as you learn about yourself and the children you will teach.

Violence in the Lives of Children. More attention is given today to social and moral development and mandates for *character education* in the schools because of the increasing numbers of children involved in violence as either victims or perpetrators. (Look back at Chapter 4, where we discussed safe environments. Figure 4–9 on page 125 shows the shocking fact that homicide is the fourth highest cause of death in children from one through nine years of age, rising to third place in the ten through fourteen-year-old bracket, as reported by the National Vital Statistics System data from 1996 (Centers for Disease Control, 2000). "More than half of U.S. public schools reported experiencing at least one crime incident in 1996–97, and one in ten schools reported at least one serious violent crime during that school year" (National Center for Education Statistics, 1998) (see Figure 12–7).

While most of these crimes were in middle and secondary schools, three to ten percent did occur in elementary schools, mainly in the categories of physical attacks, larceny, and vandalism (p. 11). Schools have adopted policies of zero tolerance for violent crimes, suspending students or using some other form of noncorporal punishment. Schools have also adopted safety measures such as *closed campuses* whereby all school visitors must sign in, doors are locked from the outside, and, in a low percentage of schools, students pass through metal detectors as they enter the building.

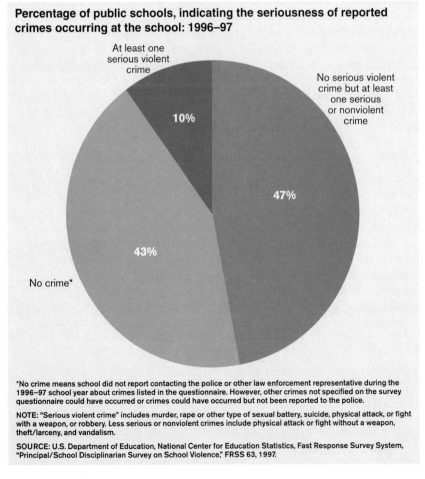

Percentage of public schools, indicating the seriousness of reported crimes occurring at the school: 1996–97

At least one serious violent crime

No serious violent crime but at least one serious or nonviolent crime

10%

47%

43%

No crime*

*No crime means school did not report contacting the police or other law enforcement representative during the 1996–97 school year about crimes listed in the questionnaire. However, other crimes not specified on the survey questionnaire could have occurred or crimes could have occurred but not been reported to the police.

NOTE: "Serious violent crime" includes murder, rape or other type of sexual battery, suicide, physical attack, or fight with a weapon, or robbery. Less serious or nonviolent crimes include physical attack or fight without a weapon, theft/larceny, and vandalism.

SOURCE: U.S. Department of Education, National Center for Education Statistics, Fast Response Survey System, "Principal/School Disciplinarian Survey on School Violence," FRSS 63, 1997.

Figure 12–7

Percentage of public schools reporting crime and violence. (From National Center for Educational Statistics [1998, March]. *Violence and discipline problems in U.S. public schools: 1996–1997* (NCES 98–030). Washington, DC: U.S. Department of Education.)

Following a more proactive model, more than half of all schools have instituted formal school violence prevention or reduction programs that range from social skills training to reviewing and monitoring of schoolwide discipline practices (p. 24).

Some children in America are growing up in *inner city war zones* (Garbarino, Dubrow, Kostelny, & Pardo, 1992). It is not just in urban, but suburban and rural, settings that children witness violence even in schools; it is on television in both fictional programming and factual news. The effects include children displaying symptoms of posttraumatic stress disorder similar to those experienced by Vietnam veterans and children living in war-torn countries. Children are exhibiting sleep disorders such as nightmares, insomnia, and sleepwalking; inability to concentrate; and a general feeling of anxiety and worry. This is not conducive to healthy development or learning. In a later work, Garbarino (1999), while not simplifying the solution, suggests the motive for many teen pregnancies is the search for *someone who loves me* (p. 163). It is the unspoken plea of the fetus, whose development so depends on the mother's health. It is the call to parents to give more attention than money to their child. It likely accounts for the unfulfilled self-love of many children who cannot love themselves because they feel no one else does either. Teachers cannot fix all those things, but they can use some positive strategies to help protect children from being either perpetrators or victims of violence. They can create an environment of acceptance, coupled with a relevant curriculum in which children can feel competent. Teachers can also cultivate conflict resolution from an early age that does not condone any kind of physical action by the adult as punishment or by the child as retribution. Teachers must understand child development and its influence on children's thinking and capacity for self-control. They also must teaching and model prosocial behaviors of caring on a daily basis. In the curriculum areas later in this chapter, some activities and curriculum themes will be suggested to help the learning teacher build resources to prevent violence.

WORDS OF WISDOM Brad Wahl has had a long career in the justice system as a juvenile probation officer. He writes:

"Working with some of the best and extremely dedicated professionals in the nation, we have been able to help salvage the lives of thousands of youth who would have otherwise gone astray. Despite this, I remain haunted by the small percentage of youth we fail to turn around. We constantly ask "Where did we go wrong? What else could we have done?" While we seldom find answers to these questions, and remain confident, in our hearts, that we did everything we could do, we are comforted, for lack of a better word, by a quote from a Supreme Court justice who said, 'How reasonable is it to expect—and over what time and cost—that a 20-year-old rapist can be rehabilitated, when he was not habilitated in the first place?'"

"Teachers, especially those in grades pre-K through six, have a unique opportunity that few, if any others, have. When parents and other family members abdicate their responsibility to properly teach and guide their children in social/moral development, the teacher is often the only significant other left to assume this role. Since this is a moral obligation and not a legal one, teachers have the option to either accept the immense challenge or to turn their heads the other way. This should be an easy choice if you think of it as a life-and-death situation for our young and helpless."

Will you accept Brad's challenge?

✳ SOCIAL AND MORAL DEVELOPMENT AND CURRICULUM

SCENARIO Six-month-old Sara creeps over to Jeffrey and takes the toy he is chewing on. Jeffrey looks at Sara and smiles and gurgles.

Eighteen-month-old Hanna toddles over to Monica and pulls at the toy phone Monica has to her ear. Monica screams and grabs the phone back, hitting Hanna over the head with it.

Four-year-old Teddy watches Gail as she takes off her western boots. As soon as she has them off he grabs them and puts them on. "Hey, I had those," Gail responds. "You had 'em for a long time, now it's my turn." "Okay, but you give them back to me when you're done."

Two second-grade boys are working at one computer station. "How about if I do it for a while and then you do it, okay? But we won't let no girls over here."

The sixth grade is having a bake sale to raise money for their class trip. Andrea was absent for several days during the sale and neither brought baked goods to sell nor worked at the booth. Lois and Kirby are talking when Andrea walks by, "It's just not fair! She hasn't helped at all but she gets to go too. It's just not fair. We just won't talk to her."

Social development involves many other developmental domains, interpersonal relationships, and the child's environment. It becomes more complex as children mature. At early ages, social development consists of overtures and responses to other people as subjects of exploration, and sources of comfort, affection, and fulfillment of needs. Then, as the child's world expands, and interesting objects become desirable even if someone else has them, social development becomes a system of acquiring what you want despite another person's desires. Negotiation and affiliation enter the exchanges as thinking and language skills progress, with social relationships used as a bond and exclusion used as a threat. What is right and fair complicates social relationships, as your own wants and needs conflict with those of others, and you deal with the expectations of significant people like family and teachers. We'll look at how the move from selfish to selfless behavior occurs over time, how play changes from objects to people, and how conscience develops and guides conduct with others.

Infant Social Development and Curriculum

There is no doubt that the infant's brain is ready to be stimulated by social interactions. Early smiles while the infant sleeps are reflexive precursors to ensuing conscious responses, such as smiling in response to adults' cooing and talking. Adults have the responsibility for establishing a social relationship with the newborn infant by getting close, gaze in the infant's eyes, smiling, and saying silly things. Infants need to see, hear, touch, smell, and taste human contact. Attachment is the beginning of social and moral development, with the adult's role being to initiate, reciprocate, interpret, and respond.

Infant Social Development.
When they cry, newborns communicate in what is interpreted as a social overture. They may be crying for a variety of reasons—physical discomforts such as hunger or soiled diapers, a desire for attention, being startled by a loud noise, distress caused by sudden changes, or pain. When adults respond to their cries, infants begin to trust that attention and soothing will come (Erikson, 1963). Newborns have no control of their crying reflex and may continue to cry even after being picked up, held, rocked, changed, or fed. Healthy infants may spend five to 20 percent of their time crying and cannot be trained not to cry (Berg, Adkins, & Strock, 1973; Korner, 1974), but infants whose crying is responded to cry less in the first few months (Bell & Ainsworth, 1972.) This attention is not *spoiling* the infant, but building a supportive, loving relationship that is needed for later social interactions and development in all other domains.

In his first six months of life, the infant has no sense of being different from the surrounding environment. The crib, car seat, and his father's arms all are part of himself, not perceived as separate. While this is hard for us to understand, it probably means that the infant can feel secure and content in those environments as long as other needs are met. Eventually his cognitive structures develop to the point where he associates certain faces, voices, smells, and ways of touching to some special people in his life. The infant comes to depend on these people to be present and responsive. During his first year, the infant's responses are self-focused and programmed; later, he learns to do whatever it takes to have his needs met. By the end of the first year, he is beginning to exert some social control by withdrawing—turning away from the spoon, a plaything, or a smiling auntie—pulling back his social self. The reciprocal dialog between infant and adult frames later exchanges that include words, as well as body language and facial expression.

Social interactions immediately following birth depend on the sex of the child and physical appearance. Female infants are described as "pretty," "beautiful," "petite," or "cute," while male newborns are more likely to be described as "big," "handsome," or "sturdy" (Sweeney & Bradbard, 1988). This is their initiation into the social world and it is perhaps indicative of the way family members hold them for the first time. Female infants are cuddled softly and gently, while male infants are jostled and jiggled. These beginning actions may in part account for female dependence and male independence later in life. The infant's appearance is also a critical factor in social acceptance. Langlois (1986) found that parents interact more frequently and more lovingly with infants they consider attractive than with those they consider homely; this is especially the case for female newborns (Langlois, Ritter, Casey, & Sawin, 1995). Beginning **socialization** instills notions of how you can expect to be treated and how to treat others.

In the second half of their first year, infants are beginning to initiate exchanges by smiling, holding out their arms, creeping and crawling to approach other people, and vocalizing back and forth with people, which precedes child's language development (Figure 12–8). Getting objects from others or keeping objects for yourself is not important at this stage. More important is exploring the other human by touching

socialization—The process of transmitting to children the beliefs, attitudes, and behavioral expectations of a culture.

Figure 12-8

Infants are very interested in each other.

(sometimes squeezing and pinching), pulling hair, and chewing (or biting, if teeth are present). Infants use their same sensory explorations of the environment on people, the family pet, or the grocery cart. This is the stage of object manipulation, taking in information for later use. Infants cry when other infants cry, even as early as two days of age (Martin & Clark, 1987). This display of *emotional contagion* is the first sign of the development of empathy (Eisenberg, 1992).

Infants need no discipline; they are amoral. They are not *good* or *bad*. Their behavior is inspired by their instinct to have their needs met. Their behavior is not intended to *get back* at the adult, or because "He knows I don't like it when he . . ." Infants demonstrate a number of developments, including being able to differentiate themselves from their environment, trusting adults, self-regulating crying, and coordinating muscles to reach out and touch, or move toward or away. All of these actions require the adults in the infant's world to respond and protect, not to discipline.

Infant Curriculum for Social Development. Obviously, if the infant is to learn trust as a basis for future social interactions, family members, caregivers, and teachers must all respond positively to all the infant's social overtures and meet the child's physical and emotional needs. Infants should be held while being fed, so they can look into the eyes of the person feeding them. When they are awake, they should be placed where they can see people and hear voices, and where their vocalizations will receive a complementary response. They should be afforded the opportunity to approach other people by being placed on the floor to roll, crawl, or cruise toward the people with whom they want to be close. They should also have the right to turn away and bury their face in someone's shoulder when the world gets too stimulating. Infants have the right to refuse the overtures of strangers who want to hold them.

Showing the infant his reflection in the mirror is a game that inspires socialization (Figure 12–9 on page 456). At first, the infant does not know the reflection is his own. He will smile, reach out, and coo to that beautiful baby and be happy to see the baby smile back. What a powerful beginning for social interaction!

Traditional games that people have played with babies for many years and in many different cultures have underlying learning concepts.

Peek-a-Boo. Before the infant has attained the concept of object permanence, the face or object disappearing behind the blanket has ceased to exist in the infant's

Figure 12–9

Infants love the baby in the mirror.

memory, so it is magical when it reappears. When the infant reaches for the blanket, thus demonstrating his awareness that the hidden face or object was there all along, he has reached a milestone in cognitive development. The power the infant wields over other people in this game is an important lesson in feeling competent.

Pat-a-Cake. Close physical proximity and gentle movements accompanied by a rhythmic and melodic (or not) adult voice teach the infant acceptance, as well as physical coordination. The various motions and sounds of the rhyme and the excitement at the end with the words "For baby and me!" include the infant in a social group, again a very important lesson.

Bye-Bye. Imitating the motions of others and repeating a simple phrase meet all the criteria for early learning. The game of waving "Bye-Bye" has deeper significance as the infant learns that important people in his life occasionally have to leave him. In the next year, this will become a frightening event, but this game and his immature thinking about absence make this a practice in separation. Physical imitations of another's movement will be practiced over a lifetime, whether waving bye-bye or summoning someone by crooking your index finger.

Roll the Ball. As the ball goes back and forth, the infant learns about more than just the properties of round objects. Taking turns is an important skill in conversation and in almost every aspect of social life. The game can also instill the notion that you must give to get, you must be willing to relinquish possession, and that group activities are more enjoyable when each person in the group performs as expected. All that, in "Roll the Ball!"

Pat the Bunny. Gentle stroking is a skill learned by receiving gentle touches. It can be accompanied by the much-loved tiny storybook *Pat the Bunny* (Kunhardt, 1940), which has a soft piece of fabric to touch and very gentle words to read. Or it can just be gently patting and stroking the infant or holding his hand to reciprocate patting and stroking. This sensory experience lays the foundation for touching other people and animals without being hurtful, which will be needed as the infant turns into a mobile, aggressive, powerful toddler. Hopefully the words "Gently, gently touching" will guide his touches.

Toddler Social and Moral Development and Curriculum

With toddlers' mobility comes the propulsion to move toward (or away from) other people and experiment with the environment. However, they do not yet have the knowledge and self-control to actually participate in social play and refrain from playing with dangerous or precious objects. This makes for tumultuous times in toddler play, with their bodies not yet fully in control, falling over and stepping on each other without meaning to harm anyone. They struggle over toys and have limited speaking abilities to express wants, needs, or apologies. Toddlers are not *terrible* or *bad,* but merely exploring, seeking the autonomy to control their body movements and objects encountered in these forays. Adults must offer opportunities to explore within safety limits; provide permissible places and objects to investigate; and model, guide, and direct the development of acceptable social behavior. The world of "No!" has begun; the toddler is learning moral laws and rules of behavior.

Toddler Social and Moral Development. The stages of play which follow were defined in a study done by Parten (1932) that even today stands as a way of categorizing the increasing complexity of children's play as they learn about their social world. These stages of play occur in sequence as children develop socially and learn to play with each other, as well as materializing all through life when people engage in various levels of social interaction.

* Unoccupied activity—The child is not playing, his eyes are wandering, he shows little interest in or long-term attention to any one activity.

    Example: Anthony is propped up in his infant seat and just looks around the room.

* Onlooker activity—The child watches others play without getting involved. He may get physically close to others' play, and even participate verbally, but he does not actually play.

    Example: Megan stands by the sand box watching other children scooping, sifting, filling, and dumping sand. She does not approach the play area herself.

* Solitary play—The child plays alone, independent of others, using different materials than others are using.

    Example: Salvador stands at the table putting together a puzzle while the others are playing a game of Chutes and Ladders©.

* Parallel play—The child plays independently near other children, using the same or similar kinds of play materials.

    Example: Corrine is in the block area constructing towers with vertical and horizontal blocks, building higher and higher. Darlene is laying blocks end to end around the edge of the carpet. "We're playing blocks together, right?" Darlene asks. Are they?

* Associative play—The children are using the same or similar type of material, talking about what they are doing, exchanging materials, and making their own products.

> Example: Ross and Carmine are on either side of the painting easel. Ross says, "Carmine, I'm painting Jeff Gordon's race car. It's all different colors; that's why he's called the Rainbow Warrior." Carmine says, "Well, I'm painting that other guy's car. My dad says he's faster than Jeff Gordon. I'm gonna make his car red 'cause that's my dad's favorite color."

* Cooperative or organized play—The child is in a group working on a joint project or product. A leader leads the effort and there is a definite "in the group" or "out of the group" identification. (Note: Cooperative does not mean without conflict; it refers to the joint nature of the project.)

> Example: Five children are outside building a snow fort, rolling snowballs into large balls that they place around the perimeter of a space that Frank has marked off with colored yarn. They roll, carry, and place the balls and Frank says, "Yeah, that's it."

Toddlers are most often in the onlooker, solitary, or parallel play stage. They are interested in working with toys and equipment, as well as with people. However, because of their limited language skills and self-centered nature, they cannot yet attain the cooperative play stage (Figure 12–10). Even in parallel play these developmental limitations often lead them into trouble with their peers. They are egocentric and believe that if they want something, they should have it, without considering how other children feel about having toys or possessions taken away from them. Close supervision and many duplicate toys are necessary to keep toddlers from inadvertently hurting each other in their early experiments at social play. This is the age of biting as a way of expressing strong feelings, from affection to frustration, and even though

Figure 12—10

Toddlers are confronting morality.

adults need to keep close watch, biting will still happen. Providing first aid attention to the victim without shaming or placing guilt or blame on the biter is the appropriate action when biting has taken place. Saying, "Ouch, biting hurts" is an appropriate comment the teacher can make to the bitten child, and the biter.

By the end of their second year, children recognize other children and have friendship preferences. They are in the second stage of empathy, when they identify and categorize others' distress signals through facial expressions or crying. Toddlers often offer pacifiers or security blankets as expressions of empathy, even to adults. This giving of comfort as he knows it is a sign of growing awareness of the feelings of others; however, toddlers' social interactions are still at a very rudimentary level. Very young children who have close friendships often have the following characteristics in common (Rubin, 1980): secure relationships with their mothers, relationships with older siblings or children, existing friendships between their mothers, and similar developmental levels, temperaments, and behavioral styles (pp. 26–27).

When their push toward independence and experimentation is in full force, toddlers are forming an understanding of what is acceptable and what is not. Because of their limited knowledge, this does not come naturally, and at times it seems totally inconsistent with their prior experience. For example, how can a toddler understand that having a bowel movement in the toilet brings praise when doing it in a diaper results in disgusted looks and even words of disapproval? Toddlers demonstrate their beginning understanding of what is acceptable by looking at the adult, performing the action, and waiting for a response. They have little moral understanding, but they are forming the rudiments of conscience and making choices. "He's just doing that to get to me!" a frustrated parent may lament. No, he is just doing that to find out what the limits truly are and if this activity is really the activity the parent disapproved of previously. He is seeking to confirm that *this* is the action that is unacceptable. The adult's response should be consistent and impose a logical consequence, such as removing the object or removing the child from the area and redirecting him to another activity. Or, the adult may simply need to just refocus the same action in an acceptable way.

SCENARIO LaMoyne looks at her caregiver as she approaches the wall with a crayon. If uninterrupted, she will scribble with abandon, perhaps looking back at the adult. The ideal teaching response is to catch her before she scribbles and provide a large sheet of newsprint that she can scribble on. If she is not caught in time, the adult should still provide the paper, but also furnish a sponge to help her clean the crayon from the wall. Providing redirection and logical consequences for actions results in an early lesson in self-control, in living a moral life (Figure 12–11 on page 460).

Toddler Curriculum for Social and Moral Development. The curriculum begins with the environment. The toddler classroom environment should contain many duplicates of materials and equipment so there is less likelihood of tugs-of–war over a toy. However, anyone who has been around children knows that the toy the child wants is bound to be the one the other child has, even if an exact duplicate is available. Possession by another makes that object more attractive and desirable.

Adults working with toddlers understand that sharing, taking turns, and playing with others is difficult for them and thus do not insist on these actions. This is not to say that acknowledging such actions is not done, as in, "Oh, Thomas, you shared your blocks with Ashira. She had none and you had many and you gave her some. That is

Figure 12–11

Inappropriate actions, such as writing on the wall, may need to be refocused.

good sharing. Now Ashira will be happy." By pointing out the action's results rather than just saying "Good boy," you reinforce the idea that the way to get along with peers is to share with them. Of course, before long this can backfire when preschoolers threaten, "I won't be your friend if you don't let me play with that." But you have to take on the issues as they come, one step at a time.

Helping toddlers give words to their feelings is a teaching challenge. "Shelby, I know you wanted the truck Kara was playing with. But hitting Kara hurts. You could say, 'Kara, give it to me please.'" Taking it to the next step, give the power to keep possession of it or relinquishing it to the child with the toy by saying, "Kara, listen to Shelby. She says, 'Give it to me, please.' Are you done with it and will you share it with Kara?" In this way, both children learn the give and take of negotiation, even within the confines of their limited language. Since children have a greater ability to understand language than to express it, they know what is being negotiated here, even though they could not manage it on their own. The adult is scaffolding and mediating in the zone of proximal development (Figure 12–12).

The curriculum of caring friendships should be a central aspect of the toddler classroom. Listening to each other, helping each other, serving and cleaning up together, and treating each other with respect are all adult-modeled behaviors and should be topics of conversation throughout the day. Many opportunities should be provided for each child to give someone else a toy, a cup, a blanket, or some other favored or desirable object. When someone is in distress, other children should be invited to help comfort him by giving gentle pats, getting a tissue for his tears, or going to get his favorite blanket. Participating in a caring environment is one of the most important lessons toddlers can learn. They feel competent to be entrusted with the care of another and are building the knowledge that they will be cared for in the same way when they need it.

Safety is the basis for guiding toddler behavior: safety of the child from hazards in the environment, safety of other children and environment from the toddler, and

Figure 12—12

The adult provides the mediation and support to get through tough situations.

psychological and emotional safety for the toddler's growing self-awareness as a competent person. This begins with planning and anticipating what the toddler may try that could lead to danger. Modifying or eliminating questionable things from the environment should happen to prevent accidents or injuries. Respecting and recognizing each child as an individual will lead the teacher to quickly intervene in a positive way: stating the acceptable behavioral expectation, gently moving the child away from the unacceptable activity, and providing a similar but acceptable alternative (remember LaMonte and the crayon earlier?). The teacher should model all behaviors he expects of the child. The teacher should sit on the floor or a chair, for example, and not on the table. The teacher should touch gently. The teacher should ask the child's permission before he picks him up, even if the child does not yet have enough language to give permission. The teacher should control his own anger and use words to express his reasons for that anger. He should also recognize the child's anger and help him find acceptable ways to express it. The word "No!" should be restricted to emergency safety intervention and avoided for all remaining unacceptable behaviors. Intervention, redirection, and logical consequences are strategies the teacher can use to guide toddler behavior. These will lay the foundation for the child's developing self-control and provide knowledge about the ways people treat other people, protect themselves from harm, and care for objects in the environment.

What about *time out*? At times, all people, especially toddlers, lose control of their emotions. The child may get extremely aggressive, repeatedly rejecting redirection, and thus have the potential of harming himself or others. If the child is not able to control his behavior, spending time sitting in a chair does not make sense; the child cannot gain enough control to sit in the chair. What the child needs is help relaxing. A more appropriate strategy would be quiet talking, gentle restraint, and individual attention. This is not the time for a rational explanation of what is acceptable and what is not; understanding is impaired when emotions are heightened. A temper tantrum may be dealt with in the same way, unless the gentle restraint just increases the tantrum. Just staying nearby and waiting it out may be the best strategy, sending a message of empathy and understanding.

Preschooler Social and Moral Development and Curriculum

From three years of age and up, forming friendships is an important part of daily life. These friendships are "mutual preference for interaction, skill at complementary and reciprocal peer play and shared positive affect" (Howes, 1983, p. 1041). Friendships involve playing together and forming emotional bonds. Egocentrism provides the reason for friends at this age, as children are valued for their possessions or willingness to play, but that same egocentrism also interferes with lasting reciprocal friendships at this age. Play is still in the solitary or parallel stages, as children focus on their own actions and are not cognitively or emotionally ready to share ideas or materials, extend play themes, or understand others' viewpoint about play.

Preschooler Social and Moral Development. All developmental domains interact with and contribute to one another. Social and moral development is no exception. The preschool child is developing a strong sense of himself as being different from family and peers, and he is becoming aware of his own unique likes and dislikes, personality characteristics, and appearance. At the same time, the preschooler is forming **social cognition**, an understanding of the social world. He is beginning to be less egocentric, understanding that other people have a perspective that may be different from his own. Preschoolers begin to realize how other people think and feel, what their motives and intentions are, and what they are likely to do (DeHart, Sroufe, & Cooper, 2000). While the preschooler is beginning to understand that other people's perspectives are sometimes different from his own, he is not yet able to actually put himself into their viewpoint. Advancing language development helps preschoolers form social relationships and verbally express empathy by saying "I'm sorry" or "You'll feel better when your mommy comes." They are able to initiate play through invitation ("Wanna play blocks with me?"), requests for toys ("Can I have that?"), and negotiation ("When you get done, can I use it?"). Physically, they are coordinated enough to be able to concentrate more on the people around them doing the same activity, such as riding a tricycle or building with blocks, rather than concentrating completely on accomplishing the physical task.

> **SCENARIO**   Jamie is in the dramatic play area caring for dolls as babies. Alexis comes over and takes a doll from the high chair. Jamie screams, "Get out. You can't play."

Many children have their first school experience as preschoolers, when their families decide they would benefit from having other children to play with for socialization purposes. It is not always easy to adjust from *me* to *we*. Friendships in the preschool years are *momentary* (Kostelnik, Stein, Whiren, & Soderman, 1998), with children engaging in mutual activities because the other child is in the vicinity. Preschoolers may reject other children simply because they do not have the cognitive ability to know how to include them in solitary or parallel play. In a few months, Jamie might welcome Alexis and say, "You wanna be the babysitter? Here's the pizza." Children often have

---

social cognition—Ability to understand the thoughts, intentions, and behaviors of oneself and others.

Figure 12–13

Preschool children are more likely to choose same-sex playmates.

difficulty entering a group that is already playing because they themselves lack the skill of initiating play. A few months from now, Alexis might know enough to precede picking up the doll with, "Oh my, your baby is finished eating. Would you like me to put him to bed so you can take care of your other babies?" Preschoolers are not as gender segregated in their friendships as they will be in their primary years.

Children of this age are likely to choose their friends for nonegalitarian reasons. They most often select friends of the same sex (Figure 12–13). They may chose playmates who have a familiar name (Lansky, 1984), are physically attractive (Bukowski, Newcomb, & Hartup, 1998; Langlois, 1986), are of the same racial group (Shaw, 1973), and are at comparable cognitive and sociability levels (Bukowski, Hoza, & Boivin, 1994). Attracting and maintaining friendships depend on perceived characteristics of sensitivity, kindness, flexibility, and being fun to be with (Hartup, 1970; Shapiro, 1997). However, these characteristics are beyond the capabilities of some preschoolers, so some friendships are based on joint activities, proximity, or momentary need.

The Shy Child.

SCENARIO Three-year-old Alissa clings to her mother's leg and hides her face when anyone else speaks directly to her.

Marcus worries the teacher will ask him a question, so he never raises his hand.

Kara has been in three foster homes in her five years of life. She was placed in foster care after being abandoned by her drug-addicted parents when she was eighteen months old. Kara must be literally peeled from her foster mother when she goes to the Head Start program, crying hysterically. She stops

continued

Figure 12–14

The shy child may be naturally socially withdrawn, going through a stage, or indicating insecure attachment.

crying immediately, but then withdraws to her cubby, where she observes the activities of the day. Despite the teachers' encouragement, she rarely plays, and when she does, it is only in an area where there are no other children playing; then she quickly returns to her cubby.

During their preschool years, some children prefer to be alone in the crowd or feel extremely uncomfortable when given individual attention. Alissa, Marcus, and Kara are displaying **shyness**, responses such as withdrawal from eye contact, physical retreat to a secure base, and an inability or insecurity about speaking in social situations. What should an adult do about the emotional and social development of the shy child? Shyness can be considered from many viewpoints. First of all, the child's nature may make him slow to warm up or less impulsive (Figure 12–14). Infants who exhibit a strong startle reaction are more fearful as toddlers (Calkins, Fox, & Marshall, 1996; Kagan, 1994). Shy biological parents have shy children, even when the child is adopted by outgoing parents (Plomin & McClearn, 1993). Also, identical twin studies show shyness as a strong genetic component (Emde et al., 1992).

On the nurture side, shyness could indicate that the child is securely or insecurely attached (it could be either). The securely attached child uses the parent as a base from which to explore. When the child is in a new situation he finds threatening, for whatever reason, he will seek comfort and safety from trusted adults. The child who is insecurely attached, and does not have this secure base, may not have established trust in infancy or autonomy in the toddler years, and thus is fearful about venturing out physically or socially. Kara obviously has unresolved attachment issues, but with the help of therapists and her foster parents, her scars of abandonment can be healed.

shyness—Behavior in which a person displays an awkward, bashful demeanor, hesitant in social situations, reserved, appearing without self-confidence.

Caspi and Elder (1988) found that shyness (moving away from others) persists over the course of a person's life from very early childhood on. The child's tendency or temperament over the course of his life appears constant. Shyness must also be considered within the cultural context. European American culture, with its assertive, competitive values, considers shyness a negative behavior. However, in cultures where obedience, collective well-being, and submission are valued, inhibited children are considered well behaved and socially competent. Teachers should learn about the cultural meanings of emotional and social behavior for the children in this class.

Morality. Preschoolers learn social, gender, and authority roles. They internalize what behaviors or actions are acceptable or not acceptable, and what is *good* or *bad,* and know that parents and teachers expect obedience and adherence to the rules, whether the adult is present or not, because the adult will be angry if the act is done. Adult response is the measuring stick for right and wrong. Piaget (1932, 1965, p. 335) calls this **heteronomous morality**, the morality of constraint, a system of ethics subject to externally imposed controls. As the child internalizes or accepts behavior standards, the conscience emerges. Conscience formation is very closely tied to culture, for it provides the roles, rules, and activities that are acceptable and unacceptable, and in this way the culture reinforces internalization of the rules. One childhood characteristic is acting on impulse. Self-control develops over time. Self-control, or compliance with rules whether or not an adult is present, requires four kinds of actions (Maccoby, 1980).

* inhibition of movement (stopping an action once it has begun)
* inhibition of emotions (ability to control crying or laughing because of a circumstance)
* inhibition of conclusions (not answering a question or a problem spontaneously without thinking it through)
* inhibition of choice (delayed gratification)

Preschoolers can exhibit some of these some of the time, but it takes a lifetime to display all of them, all of the time.

Guidance. Preschool children are learning roles and rules and at times have limited self-control. Recognizing these developmental characteristics helps the preschool teacher understand the role of planning the environment and setting clear limits, reminding children of the rules in positive terms such as "Walking," rather than "No running," and intervening when preschoolers are out of control emotionally or physically. Cherry (1983) reminds teachers to examine the many possible causes of misbehavior: immaturity, boredom, curiosity, visual or auditory disabilities, family crises, sensitivity to foods or environmental factors, family behavior, physical discomfort or illness, reinforced misbehavior, too many "nos," manipulation, testing limits, personality conflicts, or, in extreme cases, emotional disorders. She suggests a list of alternatives to punitive discipline, including such advice as anticipating trouble, giving gentle reminders, offering choices, giving praise or compliments, deliberately ignoring provocation, providing renewal time, and arranging a discussion among the children (p. 64).

Preschooler Curriculum for Social and Moral Development. Teaching children social and moral skills begins with the adult, as a role model, showing respect and displaying social competence. Displaying qualities such as

heteronomous morality—Morality of constraint; unquestioning obedience to powerful individuals without full understanding of the intent or motives for the rule.

friendliness, helpfulness, concern, and cooperation is the first step in helping children attain these qualities themselves.

The environment as the third teacher (following family as the first, and teacher as the second) should contain a place for each child's belongings so that possessions are kept separate and orderly. The child's name should be on the cubby and used repeatedly throughout the day in a positive, respectful tone of voice. A teacher who complains that the children just call him "Teacher" should be sure that he uses the children's names and help the children remember his name and those of the other adult helpers in the classroom. Name games are enjoyable, help teach names, and raise self-esteem. Preschoolers are not yet generous sharers, but occasional activities where two children share a glue bottle or piece of equipment gives them the opportunity to practice cooperative skills. If the teacher's acknowledges this sharing or taking turns, it is more likely that such behavior will happen spontaneously in the future (Figure 12–15).

Activities can be planned where cooperation (not competition) is emphasized. If one child is finished dressing for outdoors, he can help others get ready. Rather than asking, "Who can be ready first?" which results in children waiting, usually impatiently, for others, turn those who are ready into assistants. Using the word "friend" often throughout the day brings attention and definition to the word. "Mashako, that was a friendly thing to do, helping Carolee open her juice container." Expressing concern for children who are absent encourages caring and empathy: "It's too bad David had to miss school today. We all know how he loves pizza day. His chicken pox won't be gone for a week, so why don't we make him a card? Everyone can draw a picture on it."

Books are great launch pads for discussions and activities that promote friendship. Stories such as the traditional folk tale "Stone Soup" promote the cooperative spirit and show what can be accomplished by working together rather than selfishly hoarding possessions. Activities such as bringing in soup ingredients, working together to make soup or bread, and perhaps serving each other, another class, or families instill pride and help

Figure 12–15

Activities can be planned for cooperation, not competition.

children see service in action. When conflicts arise in the classroom, as they will, the children can be invited to hold a class meeting to discuss the problem. When two people do not get along, they influence the entire classroom atmosphere. Rather than pronouncing the solution as a teacher, convene a class meeting to focus on the problem, and not the people involved. In this process, everyone shares responsibility for the solution. It may not be the solution you would have chosen, but if the children are comfortable with it, it will be upheld.

The following friendship, compassion, cooperation, and kindness activities can be the basis for action and discussion in the preschool classroom.

Activities to Promote Social Development

Friendship:

* Association—Photo flash cards to recognize others in the group
* Conversation—"Little talk area" set up in classroom for cozy chats
* Belonging—Family groups represented in class photo album
* Friendship—Charts of "likes"

Compassion Skills

* Recognition of emotions—Visual and auditory games such as "What's she feeling?"
* Problem solving—Finish the sentence: "When I'm sad I feel . . . ," "It makes me mad when . . . ," "When I am scared I could . . ."
* Expression—Gamecards with descriptions of situations like "When Joey's cat died he felt . . ." or magazine pictures to stimulate speculation, such as "What is she feeling? What could be the reason she feels that way?"

Cooperation Skills

* Cooperation—Establish teams for cleanup
* Consideration of others—Adjustments for others, such as children with disabilities. "What could we do if a classmate couldn't see? . . . hear? . . . run?"
* Negotiation—Scenarios to role-play conflict situations and resolutions

Kindness Skills

* Caretaking—Animal or plant care in classroom
* Gentleness—Share and apply hand cream to each other's hands on a cold wintry day
* Helping—Mini "field trip" to different areas of the room to identify ways to help each other, the environment, and the teacher
* Generosity—Word games with *mine, yours, ours*
* Rescue/Protection—Safety hazard expedition on the playground
* Respect/Encouragement—Tape record compliments, acknowledgments of others' accomplishments, appreciation for beauty, caring, good feelings

Adapted from *The Peaceful Classroom*, Smith, 1993.

As preschool children move from their home arena into a school setting, their world expands. They have contact with people who are different from them and they begin to see how the greater society works. As they solidify their self-identity, they encounter children with different-colored skin and different languages. They meet children who bring curious or unfamiliar foods to school for snack time. They participate in favorite preschool curricular themes about community helpers like firefighters, veterinarians, health professionals, and garbage truck drivers. Through their dramatic play with props from different vocations, they emulate work they see people doing in their neighborhood. This is the beginning of their social studies, understanding the interaction of culture, people, and places. Through activities that graph likenesses and differences, and by participating in decision making, they form the notion that each person has a part to play in society.

A thematic social studies curriculum can be integrated with language, literacy, mathematics, science, art, health, and technology, taking into account children's current levels of large- and small-muscle development. Learning centers can be designed around a theme for children to explore and learn about. The first three strands of the National Council for the Social Studies standards are especially appropriate for preschool children and can be incorporated into the preschool curriculum in the following ways.

* houses and buildings
* community businesses
* playgrounds and parks
* construction sites
* places to eat
* typical food in our community
* languages spoken
* important places in the community
* services and agencies
* local government
* contests and competitions
* community sports
* keeping the community beautiful
* community holidays
* pets living in the community
* community symbols and landmarks
* people in the community

(From de Melendez, Beck, & Fletcher, 2000, p. 84)

The word *community* appears many times in these suggested topics. Begin with the familiar: as the child's experiences broaden, their sense of community expands from the microsystem of family, school, and neighborhood to the macrostystem of national and global community. This is social studies.

When environment, curriculum, schedule, and supervision are all focused on children's developmental levels, and children are surrounded with respect and guidance, discipline problems tend to be minimal and used as opportunities to learn to live together peaceably (Figure 12–16).

Figure 12–16

Caring for other creatures in the environment helps with social and moral development.

Primary Age Social and Moral Development and Curriculum

Once children enter school, the time they spend with their parents and their parents' influence on them diminishes, with time spent with and influence of peers increasing. A child is no longer identified as "Mrs. Smith's son," but instead as "Jacob, that kid in first grade." This shift brings the child greater self-responsibility for behavior, outside the sight and authority of his parents. His new peer group is ruled by power within the group, a power that may be wielded by coercion, charisma, or cooperation. This time of social and moral development will influence the rest of the child's life.

Primary Age Social and Moral Development. Primary age social development centers on children's peer acceptance. In the early school years, same-sex and -race friendships prevail (Schofield & Francis, 1982; Finkelstein & Haskins, 1983; Sagar, Schofield, & Snyder, 1983). In a large study of third and fourth graders, only 14 percent had cross-sex friendships and only three percent has cross-sex primary friendships (Kovacs, Parker, & Hoffman, 1996). Primary age children are better able than preschoolers are to understand not only the behavior of others but also the intent or motive, and can either overlook or react to the behavior based on that motive. They are gaining a better understanding of themselves, so they not only understand others better, but are also measuring themselves against others in terms of skills, appearance, and personality. More realistic self-evaluation in the light of parent, teacher, and peer expectations can bring both pride and guilt or shame (Merrell & Gimpel, 1998). In this shift from parental to peer allegiance, children begin to see discrepancies in adult behaviors and argue vehemently about fairness, consistency, and hypocrisy.

Friendships. Social play for the primary age child is active, including games with rules, rituals, and chants. Piaget (1932, 1965) saw this game-playing as a way to exercise

Figure 12–17

Aggressive behavior happens.

new cognitive structures of conservation, decreasing egocentrism, and balancing one's own desires against society's rules. Game-playing is a training ground for conformist behavior and also for settling disagreements. Primary age children are likely to try to bend the rules so they can win. Hoffman (1980) sees six- to nine-year-olds in the fourth stage of empathy, appreciating other people's feelings, but also becoming concerned about poverty, oppression, illness, and vulnerability. Primary age children are able to empathize with impoverished groups and take an interest in political and social issues. Derman-Sparks and the A.B.C. Task Force (1989) tell of a children's school campaign to designate a handicapped parking space (before the Americans with Disabilities Act was enacted). They discussed why it was needed, where it should be, how it could be marked, and how to deal with people who parked in the spot inappropriately. This is an example of children's natural desires, empowered by the teacher's guidance, to see social justice in action.

Aggression.   Aggression may be considered the opposite of empathy. Antisocial behavior has its beginnings in the preschool years with lack of emotional regulation (Figure 12–17). This is not the rough-and-tumble play mainly engaged in by young boys who are laughing and smiling. Antisocial behavior is accompanied by hurtful words or actions and frowns, furrowed brows, squinting eyes, and clenched teeth and fists. Children's growing aggressiveness is a concern for parents, schools, and society as a whole. Some types of aggression can be part of a natural developmental phase, while others are more serious; all call for intervention and diffusion. The forms of aggression are:

* Accidental—Someone is hurt in the process of play, but no harm is meant.

    Example: running child trips over another child sitting on the floor

* Expressive—Pleasurable sensory experience with no harmful intent

    Example: child is fingering another's long curly hair and pulls hard

* Instrumental—Dispute over objects or rights results in someone getting hurt either defending or trying to get what they want; the intent is not to hurt but to achieve goal

Example: two children are pulling on a toy; one gives a big shove and the other falls over and bumps his head

✳ Hostile—Satisfaction from inflicting physical or psychological pain

Example: child throws chair at another child for no apparent reason

(From Kostelnik, Stein, Whiren, & Soderman, 1998, pp. 327–328)

Children may be aggressive because they have low self-esteem and little self-control. They may have learned that aggression is the way to achieve an end or they may have been instructed to stand up for themselves and fight back. Aggression may have helped them achieve an end in the past, so they repeat it. They have seen countless aggressive actions on television for which they see few negative consequences. Their social inexperience or lack of cognitive development may mean that they do not realize their actions hurt the other person. Preschool and primary age children have difficulty differentiating between accidental and intentional aggression. They feel pain and their natural inclination is to hurt back.

Kostelnik et al. (1998) suggest comparing the following ineffective strategies used by adults to deal with aggression and effective alternatives to those strategies. Ineffective strategies to lower or extinguish aggression either encourage, mirror, or (in non-action) are seen as approval of the undesirable behavior. Giving children punching bags or pillows reinforces the appropriateness of hitting as a way to express emotion. Physical punishment repeats the offense against the child and teaches that, if you are bigger, you can mete out physical pain, exactly the lesson you do not want children to learn. Ignoring aggression sends the message that the adult is condoning it. These strategies do not extinguish the behavior; they increase it. What is effective is a combination of strategies. First, the adult models nonaggression by remaining calm. When children use a strategy other than aggression, the adult can condone that more acceptable choice. Children who feel competent and are given choices are less likely to be aggressive. Direct instruction for nonaggressive behavior may include encouraging cooperation rather than competition, emphasizing helpfulness and prosocial behavior, and giving children ways to feel powerful. Teaching children conflict-resolution techniques can also prevent aggression from escalating to a harmful level. All children in the class can take responsibility for keeping the peace.

Morality. Social, emotional, and cognitive developments contribute to the primary age child's increased awareness of rules that govern behavior. Three categories that emerge are moral rules, such as fairness and prosocial behaviors, and not causing physical or psychological harm; social conventional rules, such as school rules, rules for appropriate appearance, and sex roles and manners; and personal rules, such as personal hygiene and social rules (Turiel, Killen, & Helwig, 1987). The cognitive ability to be able to take another person's viewpoint brings with it a strong sense of reciprocity or fairness. Piaget called this autonomous moral reasoning (Piaget, 1932, 1965). Kohlberg's extension of Piaget's work through the use of moral dilemmas focused on **instrumental morality**, which appears at about age seven or eight. This type of morality is still quite self-centered, with each person looking out for his own needs and interests, which may be different from another person's. Still in what Kohlberg calls the preconventional period, the child follows rules when it is in his own immediate interest (Kolhberg, 1976). Damon (1980) found that a six-year-old's idea of fairness centered on absolute equal distribution, while an older child took other factors

✳ **instrumental morality**—Moral reasoning based on an exchange system of fairness or give and take.

into consideration. He also placed the six- to eight-year-old in the moral stage of recognizing and acquiescing to adult authority, with that recognition as the determining factor of what is right.

Guidance. The early school years may be a major adjustment for children who have never before participated in experiences with formal groups of children. These children must adjust to school rules about lines and waiting; they must adapt to a ratio of a greater number of children to adults; and they also must adjust to, observe, and model themselves after children with varying backgrounds and social behaviors. Misbehavior that Gartrell (1994) calls *mistaken behavior* comes from three sources: experimentation, social influence, and strong needs. When you look beyond the behavior, the motivating factor(s) may vary. The experimenter needs to hear about and see the acceptable behavior for that situation, along with the reasons why such behavior is expected. It is important to determine the source of the mistaken behavior. If it is the family, then the teacher must be careful to maintain respect for the family's influence; the reason may be cultural in nature. Children can learn that what may be right in the family setting is not appropriate in the school setting; a reminder about what is expected may be all that is necessary. If peers or other classmates are the source of the mistaken behavior, it may be necessary to address the entire group. Children with strong needs may display frustration, irritability, hostility, inattentiveness, or isolation from the group, all of which may be attributable to either physical or emotional discomfort. Of course, the school or family health professional should be consulted if that is the case. Emotional discomfort is more difficult to diagnose, making it that much harder for the teacher to determine an appropriate response.

Later in your professional preparation, you will learn more about classroom management techniques (Figure 12–18). In this section and in the next on elementary age children, some discipline approaches will be presented. You can select an approach or combination of approaches that feels right to you and is in accord with

Figure 12–18

Classroom and behavior management is a skill the teacher learns and practices every day.

your own educational philosophy. As you have more experience in the classroom, your approach will continue to develop and evolve.

One of the most appropriate approaches to discipline, especially for younger children, is that of logical consequences. In this approach, the reflecting teacher considers possible environmental causes for the misbehavior, looking to the curriculum and his teaching methods for contributing factors. The teacher then looks at the child's intentions or motivations, which form the basis for the teacher's action. If the child is looking for attention, then the teacher should give him more attention in positive areas. If the child is bored, then the teacher should develop a more stimulating curriculum for him. If the child has little inner impulse control, then moving him closer to the teacher and away from distractions may be the remedy. The misbehavior may result in natural consequences: the child hits others, so he is excluded from play, or neglects to do his homework, so he does not have his contribution for the joint project and is ostracized by the other children. The teacher should impose logical consequences that are connected to the misbehavior. If a child hurts another child, he can help with minor first aid or get a tissue for tears. The child who breaks something must replace it. The child who knocks over a bookcase must stand it up and replace its contents. Logical consequences include reparation for a wrong, repeating the situation with an acceptable outcome, or restricting the child from an activity until he is able to participate in an acceptable way. Logical consequences must be applied consistently, with the child knowing fully the reasoning behind the rule and the possible consequences if the rule is not followed, with uniform enforcement of the consequences. This method emphasizes the preventive approach to discipline and focuses on helping children learn self-control. Sometimes, however, it may be difficult to determine a child's motives, and logical consequences are not always easy to apply in every situation without seeming punitive.

Behavior modification, which is based on the work of B. F. Skinner, explains behavior as pleasure seeking or pain avoiding. In this approach, the teacher gives positive reinforcement for behavior that is deemed acceptable in the form of material rewards, such as stickers, food, or points toward a later event, or less tangible rewards, such as attention, smiles, or overt (expressed) approval. In this approach, negative behavior is met with punishment, such as withdrawal of attention and approval until the behavior is extinguished, time out away from regular activities, or loss of privileges or demerits. In most states, corporal punishment, which involves actually striking a child or hurting them physically, is not allowed. Furthermore, aggression breeds aggression, and physical punishment serves only to set an example for undesirable responses. Behavior modification is probably the most common discipline you have experienced, but it may not be effective in the long run. It can work for the immediate situation, but if the goal is to teach self-control, it is only effective when there is a rewarder or enforcer. The reward portion of behavior modification is denounced by Alfie Kohn in *Punished by Rewards* (1993).

Primary Age Curriculum for Social and Moral Development. One of the best discipline techniques is a well-planned curriculum (Greenberg, 1987). Focusing on prevention, a teacher can help children learn to work together with minimal behavior problems. When the curriculum is relevant, engaging, and meaningful, children do not have the time or inclination to be bored or disinterested. This begins with the classroom environment, as discussed in a previous chapter. Organizational strategies include careful planning for routines, with minimal waiting; smooth transitions from one activity to another through the use of games, music, or fun rituals; and focused group times designed to meet each child's need. The teacher should set a tone of respect, caring for each child, accepting their feelings, expecting them to do the right thing, and helping them when they cannot or will not do so.

At this age, children are interested in playing group games because they have the cognitive ability to understand and follow the rules, the attention span to stay with the game, and the desire to be part of a social group. This brings up the issue of competition in the classroom. If the first six or seven years of a child's life have been spent helping him develop an awareness of others' rights and feelings, he gets a mixed message if all of a sudden he hears, "Who can get dressed for outside the fastest?" with everyone having to wait for the slowest child. How does this coordinate with the objective of creating a caring community? You should rethink ideas about competition in your classroom. What happens when you pit the boys against the girls, or select teams by letting children choose, or reward the winners with a prize? What is the real lesson in these activities? If you think about the long-term implications of the effect your teaching can have on society, stress on being "the best" may be misplaced. You will have to decide for yourself.

Ruth Charney, author of *Teaching Children to Care* (1992), begins the school year with group building: listening, using kind language, enjoying being together, and collectively setting rules for behavior. She works with small groups first and then the children work independently toward a classroom centered on independence and responsibility (Figure 12–19). Her emphasis on cooperation and respect is one model you may wish to consider. Structured discussions of moral dilemmas, following the lead of Kohlberg (1976) and Damon (1988), can heighten children's awareness of them. Real–life ethical quandaries from classroom experiences can also be discussed, with the teacher doing more listening than talking. Many more social and moral development programs have become available recently because of concern over rising violence among young people. Sometimes whole schools adopt a curriculum for peace education, conflict resolution, or character education. Resources such as *Kids Can Cooperate: A Practical Guide to Teaching Problem Solving* (Crary, 1986), *Learn-*

Figure 12–19

Children learn to care and share from working together.

ing to Care: Classroom Activities for Social and Affective Development (Feshback, Feshback, Fauvre, & Ballard-Campbell, 1983), and *The Friendly Classroom for a Small Planet* (Prutzman, Stern, Burger, & Bodenhamer, 1988) provide activities and ideas for teachers who want to incorporate social and moral development into the curriculum.

In the National Council for the Social Studies standards (1994), culture is strand one. Each individual's culture forms his identity, beliefs, and values, as well as his behavior. Culture is unique to that individual, yet recognizing the similarities to and differences among your own culture and the culture of others is the beginning of social studies. This is the theme in the early grades: comparing and contrasting different cultures and their viewpoints on important aspects of life. The teacher should assist this quest by inviting each child to explore his own culture and share his insights with the class. The teacher should also learn all he can about the various cultures represented in his class to be sure the environment has objects, smells, sounds, and pictures that reflect the culture of each child in the class. History, or how people lived in the past, is sometimes a difficult subject to grasp, but inviting children to find out the history of their own families helps them personalize their cultural identity through stories, photo albums, letters, and diaries. Children of this age are beginning to get a sense of the world's immensity and the many differences in climate, geography, and lifestyles of people around the world. Television, the Internet, and other technologies can make faraway places seem very close when studying people, places, and environments. And since children are still self-centered, individual development and identity are also important themes that can be integrated into health education, physical development, family and community, and self-exploration of values and attitudes. Making a book about himself, a favorite activity for a child of primary age, leads him to look at the past, present, and future, with himself as the central figure. Academic subjects can also be integrated into these themes.

Elementary Age Social and Moral Development and Curriculum

This period is one of transition, from the family-oriented child to the independent peer. Friendships are based more on similar attitudes than proximity or parental friendships. Interest in friends of the other gender is beginning, usually earlier for girls than for boys, with crude attempts at being noticed evident in such things as notes, hitting, anonymous phone calling, or telling a third party to bear a message. This is also a transitional time for moral development, with children internalizing the values they admire in others.

Elementary Age Social and Moral Development. As children grow older, they are allowed more independent time, much of which they spend with their peers. The effect of this is that they spend less time with their family, and the family, in turn, has less influence over the child. By the time the child is eleven, he spends more time with peers than he does with his family (Larsen & Richards, 1991). The child is forming his own identity, separate from the one the family has established: the baby, the bright one, or the athlete. The parents' control over the child is now based on reasoning.

Friends are now organized into groups of age-mates, with leaders and followers. Children form loyal friendships with people who help them and share with them in times of need. They may have conflicts, but they recognize that they are still friends (Keller & Edelstein, 1993). These groups share a collective identity (Shulman, Elicker, & Srouve, 1994). Children of this age are particularly concerned about the possibility of being rejected (Parker & Gottman, 1989). Gossip is what Parker and Gottman call "the mortar as well as much of the brick of friendship conversation during middle childhood" (1989, p. 114). Children discuss behavior in light of their cultural norms, testing what friends think so they can to adjust their behavior to be accepted. They compete with each other, and hang out in gender-segregated groups, talking about the other group. Group raids on the other's territory are acceptable exchanges. Girls' friendships are often more intimate than boys', with girls sharing feelings, presents, compliments, likes, dislikes, and embarrassments. Boys are more likely to play physically competitive games with their friends and interact in places that are free from direct adult supervision (Beal, 1994). Beal has witnessed this gender-segregated play throughout the world and theorizes it is biological in nature, to protect the young from premature sexual contact. Boys appear to be socialized to compete with one another in activities bound by rules, while girls are socialized to cooperate and take part in interpersonal activities where the rules are implicit (Cole & Cole, 1996).

Children need to be able to find and keep friends to establish social cognitive skills and social well-being (Figure 12–20). Goodnow and Burns (1985) emphasized the friendship elements of social competence, such as knowing how to make and sustain friendships with likely candidates, ending friendships with friends who are no longer appealing, and achieving resilience in the face of being mistreated or cut off by a friend.

Morality. From age ten through adolescence, children follow their group's rules in Level II, Stage 3, of Kohlberg's stages of moral development, (1976). They see that caring for others and a sense of loyalty are important, especially if this is demonstrated by role models they admire. In a socially diverse society like that in the United States, differences arise between the traditional American mainstream emphasis on individual morality and the collective moral behavior of other cultures or groups. The child encounters a different moral code at school from that at home (de Melendez, Beck, & Fletcher, 2000). Teachers should learn about the cultural groups in the classroom,

Figure 12–20

Organized sports help teach social competence.

highlight their common factors and universal moral values, discuss moral dilemmas and issues, and use the classroom's diversity as an opportunity to learn about a person's right to have a different view (p. 192).

Guidance. A guidance technique used in many schools is reality therapy or control theory, which was first put forward by William Glasser in his book *Reality Therapy: A New Approach to Psychiatry* (1965) and in his later works *Control Theory* (1985), and *The Quality School* (1992). This technique uses psychotherapy practices to help students satisfy their own needs without interfering with others' needs. The elementary age child has the cognitive and emotional maturity to examine a range of choices and consequences, and to accept responsibility for the choices he makes to satisfy his need for love, power, freedom, and fun. "Time out" is used for previously identified misbehavior and is often imposed by the child himself; during time out he may write a plan for how he intends to change his behavior in the future. This method promotes autonomy and responsibility and helps children develop problem-solving techniques for their own behavior and that of others, which is seen as a community effort and shared responsibility. This method requires extensive teacher training and takes time from academic activities, although some would argue that these skills are more important than academics if our students are to be able to function in society in peace.

Elementary Age Curriculum for Social and Moral Development. The National Council for the Social Studies Standard V (Individuals, Groups, and Institutions), is an important one for the elementary age child (1997). At a time when the child's peer group is so important, identifying the characteristics of groups such as families, peers, and clubs, and interactions of people within the group and with other groups, seems like one of those *teachable moments*. Identifying the causes of conflicts between individuals within groups or between groups will help the child understand group dynamics. Standard VI (Power, Authority, and Governance) is also relevant for the child this age, who is struggling with his rights and responsibilities in relationship to the group. This can be integrated with the history of government: distinguishing among local, state, and national governments and outlining government's role in protecting people without threatening democracy. Children of this age are budding consumers, so Standard VII (Production, Distribution, and Consumption) is relevant to their developing awareness of wants and needs, public and private goods and services, and possible career choices. Standard VIII (Science, Technology, and Society) leads them in exploring how lives have changed as a result of science and technology, and Standard IX (Global Connections) expands their concept of what a group is beyond the neighborhood out into the global community. Looking at labels on their clothing and finding on a map where the clothes were made brings a new awareness of the global economy. Standard X (Civic Ideals and Practices) can be implemented in the classroom through democratic principles of individual human dignity, liberty, justice, equality, and the rule of law. Decisions can be made by majority rule, discussions can be held about the "common good," and citizen advocacy efforts can be examined and carried out in relation to current issues. The social studies curriculum comes alive in the classroom when it is connected with the child's everyday life and situations.

Cooperative Learning. Another approach to the curriculum for social and moral development is the cooperative learning method made popular by Johnson, Johnson, and Holubec (1986) and expanded upon by many others. The basic premise is to structure the classroom so students can work collaboratively in small groups, ensuring that all members master assignments, with responsibility for learning not on the teacher or individual student, but rather on the group as a whole. This radical approach has been implemented and researched, and has demonstrated its effectiveness not only in learning outcomes, but also in social and moral development. Slavin (1995) has found that the most effective cooperative learning systems include:

* group goals that reward students for working together.
* individual accountability for mastering the content, with the group responsible for bringing each member to successful assessment.
* equal opportunity for success based on a system of improvement points where the child competes only with himself and his past performance, not with anyone else.

✳ ASSESSING SOCIAL AND MORAL DEVELOPMENT

Assessing social and moral development is done to identify the stage to better understand the child. If a child is having behavioral problems, an evaluation by the school psychologist may be recommended. Assessing social or moral development is done to determine the child's developmental level and evaluate progress when interventions are implemented. Assessing the child's social competence involves observing the child's individual attributes, social skills, and peer relationships. See Katz and McClellan's (1997) list of observation points (Figure 12–21).

For primary and elementary age children, using the research tool *sociometry*, a measurement technique to assess social choice, may be useful. Each child in the class says who his preferred playmates are, with whom he does not play, and states the reasons for both (Asher & Parker, 1989). Diagramming the children's responses reveals the children who have strong social competence and those who are being rejected. An intervention may be planned to help the rejected child learn play-entry strategies and coach him on how to be a friend.

Observing Children's Social Competence

Individual attributes
The child:

* is *usually* in a positive mood.
* does not depend *excessively* on the teacher.
* *usually* comes to the program or setting willingly.
* *usually* copes with rebuffs and reverses adequately.
* shows the capacity to emphathize with others.
* has positive relationships with one or two peers; shows the capacity to really care about them, miss them if they're absent, etc.
* displays a capacity for humor.
* does not seem to be acutely or chronically lonely.

continued

Figure 12–21

Observing children's social competence. (From Katz, L. G., & McClellan, D. E. [1997]. *Fostering children's social competence: The teacher's role.* Washington, DC: National Association for the Education of Young Children. Reprinted with permission)

Social skills
The child usually:

* approaches others positively.
* expresses wishes and preferences clearly and gives reasons for his actions and positions.
* asserts his own rights and needs appropriately.
* is not easily intimidated by bullies.
* expresses frustration and anger effectively and without harming others, himself, or property.
* gains access to ongoing groups at play and at work.
* enters ongoing discussions and makes relevant contributions to ongoing activities.
* takes turns fairly easily.
* shows interest in others; exchanges information with and requests information from others appropriately.
* negotiates and compromises with others appropriately.
* does not draw inappropriate attention to himself or disrupt the play or work of others.
* accepts and enjoys peers and adults of ethnic groups other than his own.
* interacts nonverbally with other children, using smiles, waves, nods, and other appropriate gestures.

Peer relationships
The child is:

* *usually* accepted rather than neglected or rejected by other children.
* *sometimes* invited by other children to join them in play, friendship, and work.

Figure 12–21 *continued*

SUMMARY

Everyone feels better when they have a friend, someone to depend on and test ideas on, someone who will give empathy, advice, and forgiveness. The teacher can support this developing skill by understanding developmental stages, promoting friendships and cooperation in the classroom, serving as a role model by accepting all children, planning a curriculum that promotes positive social interactions, and using a method of discipline that instructs rather than destroys. All of these things need not take place in separate segments of the day, but instead can be part of the entwined strands of academic and affective learning that goes on in the classroom. The teacher's role is to weave these strands together in such a way that no one aspect is overemphasized, but instead interacts with and is an integral part of the support structure. It is imperative that we raise children who have empathy for others, accept social responsibility, and have a well-developed moral code. This is perhaps one of the most important jobs of a teacher or a parent.

KEY TERMS

social competence

social cognition

heteronomous morality

internal working models

shyness

instrumental morality

socialization

REVIEW ACTIVITIES

Exercises to Strengthen Learning

1. Infants—Observe two infants of each of the following ages: a newborn, a two-month-old, a six-month-old, and a one-year-old. Record their individual social interactions with parent or caregiver and compare the social differences between the individual children of the same age and the differences between the older infants and the younger ones.

2. Toddlers—Review the stages of play in the toddler section of this chapter and read more about them in some of the other sources referenced there. Observe a group of toddlers and then a group of preschoolers at play. Make a list of their names and the various stages of play in which you see them engaged. Then obtain a list of their birthdays and check to see if there is any correlation.

3. Preschoolers—Observe a skilled preschool teacher, looking for specific instances where he is providing guidance. Note the strategies the teacher uses to reinforce classroom rules and address misbehavior or acts of aggression. Later, discuss your observations with the teacher to learn about his philosophies and the intent behind his actions.

4. Primary Age—Using the observation points in Figure 12–21, observe three primary age children for at least an hour and assess the social comptence of each.

5. Elementary Age—Read Asher and Parker's (1989) discussion of sociometry and visit an elementary age classroom. Using the sociogram, identify the socially competent children in the classroom. Does this agree with the teacher's assessment? Read one of the latest books on the topic of children and violence and develop ideas about how to recognize, intervene, and thwart violent tendencies in your future classroom.

Internet Quest

1. Investigate one of the following topics: attachment, discipline and guidance, violence in the lives of children, morality, the shy child. Using your findings, write a report to inform the parents of the children in your future classroom about your philosophy regarding this subject.

2. Search for Web sites that feature character education curriculum ideas. Evaluate how effective you think these activities would be.

3. Search for Web sites that provide information on peaceful resolution of classroom conflicts. Evaluate the information and begin to compile resources for your student teaching experience.

Reflective Journal

In this chapter, I learned about social and moral development.
  Because of what I learned, when I am a teacher I will . . .

REFERENCES

Ainsworth, M. D. (1979). Infant-mother attachment. *American Psychologist, 34,* 932–937.

Alexander, K., & Entwisle, D. (1988). *Achievement in the first 2 years of school: patterns and processes.* Chicago: University of Chicago Press.

Asher, S., & Parker, J. (1989). Significance of peer relationship problems in childhood. In B. Schneider, G. Attili, J. Nadel, & R. Weissberg (Eds.), *Social competence in developmental perspective* (pp. 5–23). Dordrecht, Netherlands: Kluwer.

Beal, C. R. (1994). *Boys and girls: The development of gender roles.* New York: McGraw-Hill.

Bell, S. M., & Ainsworth, M. D. (1972). Infant crying and maternal responsiveness. *Child Development, 43,* 1171–1190.

Berg, W. K., Adkins, C. D., & Strock, B. D. (1973). Duration and frequency of periods of alertness in neonates. *Development Psychology, 9,* 434.

Bowlby, J. (1969). *Attachment and loss: Attachment* (Vol. 1). New York: Basic Books.

Bretherton, I. (1985). Attachment theory: Retrospect and prospect. *Monographs of the Society for Research in Child Development, 50*(1–2, Serial No. 209).

Bukowski, W. J. (1990). Age differences in children's memory of information about aggressive, socially withdrawn and prosocial boys and girls. *Child Development, 61,* 1326–1334.

Bukowski, W. M., Hoza, B., & Boivin, M. (1994). Measuring friendship quality during pre- and early adolescence: The development and psychometric properties of the Friendship Qualities Scale. *Journal of Social and Personal Relationships, 11*(3), 471.

Bukowski, W. M., Newcomb, A. F., & Hartup, W. W. (1998). *The company they keep: Friendships in childhood and adolescence.* Cambridge, UK: Cambridge University Press.

Calkins, S. D., Fox, N. A., & Marshall, T. R. (1996). Behavioral and physiological antecedents of inhibited and uninhibited behavior. *Child Development, 67*(2), 523+.

Carlson, V., Cicchetti, D., Barnett, D., & Braunwald, K. (1989). Disorganized/disoriented attachment relationships in maltreated infants. *Child Development, 50,* 716–721.

Caspi, A., & Elder, G. H. (1988). Emergent family patterns: The intergenerational construction of problem behavior and relationships. In R. Hinde & J. Stevenson-Hinde (Eds.), *Relationships within families: Mutual influences* (pp. 218–240). Oxford, UK: Oxford University Press.

Center for Disease Control. (2000). *Ten leading causes of death 1993–1995.* Retrieved January 16, 2000, from the World Wide Web: <http://www.cdc.gov/ncipc/asp/leadcaus/ustable.htm>.

Charney, R. (1992). *Teaching children to care: Management in the responsive classroom.* Greenfield, MA: Northeast Foundation for Children.

Cherry, C. (1983). *Please don't sit on the kids: Alternatives to punitive discipline.* New York: Simon & Schuster.

Cicchetti, D., & Carlson, V. (1989). *Child maltreatment: Theory and research on the causes and consequences of child abuse and neglect.* Cambridge, UK: Cambridge University Press.

Cole, M., & Cole, S. (1996). *The development of children* (3rd ed.). New York: W. H. Freeman.

Coles, R. (1997). *The moral intelligence of children: How to raise a moral child.* New York: Random House.

Crary, E. (1986). *Kids can cooperate: A practical guide to teaching problem solving.* Seattle, WA: Parenting Press.

Damon, W. (1980). Patterns of change in children's social reasoning: A two-year longitudinal study. *Child Development, 51,* 1010–1017.

Damon, W. (1988). *The moral child: Nurturing children's natural moral growth.* New York: The Free Press.

DeHart, G. B., Sroufe, L. A., & Cooper, R. G. (2000). *Child development: Its nature and course* (4th ed.). New York: McGraw-Hill.

de Melendez, W. R., Beck, V., & Fletcher, M. (2000). *Teaching social studies in early education.* Albany, NY: Delmar.

Derman-Sparks, L., & The A.B.C. Task Force. (1989). *Anti-bias curriculum: Tools for empowering young children.* Washington, DC: National Association for the Education of Young Children.

DeVries, R., & Zan, B. (1994). *Moral classrooms, moral children: Creating a constructivist atmosphere in early education.* New York: Teachers College Press.

Donne, J. (1624). Meditation 17, devotions upon emergent occasions. In W. W. Norton (Ed.), *Norton Anthology of English Literature: Vol. 1* (5th ed., p. 1107). New York: Author.

Dubrovina, I., & Ruzska, A. (1990). *The mental development of residents in a children's home.* Moscow: Pedagogics.

Edwards, C. P. (1982). Moral development in comparative cultural perspective. In D. A. Wagner & H. W. Stevenson (Eds.), *Cultural perspectives on child development* (pp. 248–279). San Francisco, CA: Freeman.

Eisenberg, N. (1992). *The caring child.* Cambridge, MA: Harvard University Press.

Emde, R. N., Ploman, R., Robinson, J., Corley, R., DeFries, J., Fulker, D. W., Reznick, J. S., Campos, J., Kangan, J., & Zahn-Waxler, C. (1992). Temperament, emotion and cognition at fourteen months: The MacArthur longitudinal twin study. *Child Development, 63,* 1437–1455.

Erikson, E. H. (1963). *Childhood and society* (Rev. ed.). New York: W.W. Norton.

Feshback, N. D., Feshback, S., Fauvre, M., & Ballard-Campbell, M. (1983). *Learning to care: Classroom activities for social and affective development.* Glenview, IL: Scott, Foresman.

Finkelstein, N. W., & Haskins, R. (1983). Kindergarten children prefer same-color peers. *Child Development, 48,* 806–819.

Fischer, K. W. (1983). Illuminating the processes of moral development. *Monographs of the Society for Research in Child Development, 48*(1–2, Serial No. 200), 97–107.

Freud, S. (1920, 1955). *Beyond the pleasure principle.* J. Strachey (Ed. and Trans.). New York: Norton.

Freud, S. (1933, 1964). New introductory lectures in psychoanalysis. J. Strachey (Ed. & Trans.). *The standard edition of the complete psychological works of Sigmund Freud.* New York: W. W. Norton.

Garbarino, J. (1999). *Lost boys: Why our sons turn violent and how we can save them.* New York: The Free Press.

Garbarino, J., Dubrow, N., Kostelny, K., & Pardo, C. (1992). *Children in danger: Coping with the effects of community violence.* San Francisco: Jossey-Bass.

Gartrell, D. J. (1994). *A guidance approach to discipline.* Albany, NY: Delmar.

Gilligan, C. (1982). *In a different voice: Psychological theory and women's development.* Cambridge, MA: Harvard University Press.

Glasser W. (1965). *Reality therapy: A new approach to psychiatry.* New York: HarperCollins.

Glasser, W. (1985). *Control theory.* New York: HarperCollins.

Glasser, W. (1986). *Control theory in the classroom.* New York: HarperCollins.

Glasser, W. (1992). *The quality school.* New York: HarperCollins.

Goleman, D. (1995). *Emotional intelligence: Why it can matter more than IQ.* New York: Bantam Books.

Goodnow, J. J., & Burns, A. (1985). *Home and school: A child's-eye view.* Sydney: Allen & Unwin.

Greenberg, P. (1987). Ideas that work with young children: Child choice—another way to individualize—another form of preventative discipline. *Young Children, 46*(4), 46–51.

Harlow, H. F. (1959). *Affectional responses in the infant monkey.* Indianapolis, IN: Bobbs-Merrell.

Harlow, H. F., & Harlow, M. K. (1966). Learning to love. *American Scientist, 54,* 244–272.

Hartup, W. (1989). Social relationships and their developmental significance. *American Psychologist, 44,* 120–126.

Hartup, W. (1992). Peer relations in early and middle childhood. In V. B. Vanhasselt and M. Hersen (Eds.), *Handbook of social development: A lifespan perspective* (pp. 345–354). New York: Plenum Press.

Hartup, W. W. (1970). Peer interaction and social organization. In P. H. Mussen (Ed.), *Carmichael's manual of child psychology: Vol. 2.* New York: John Wiley.

Hartup, W. W. (1991). Having friends, making friends and keeping friends: Relationships as educational contexts. *ERIC Digest* (pp. 345–354). Urbana, IL: ERIC Clearinghouse on Elementary and Early Childhood Education.

Hoffman, L. M. (1980). Moral development in adolescence. In J. Adelson (Ed.), *Handbook of adolescent psychology.* New York: Wiley.

Hoffman, L. M. (1991). The influence of the family environment on personality: Accounting for sibling differences. *Psychological Bulletin, 110,* 187–203.

Howes, C. (1983). Patterns of friendship. *Child Development, 54,* 1041–1053.

Johnson, D. W., Johnson, R. T., & Holubec, E. J. (1986). *Circles of learning: Cooperation in the classroom* (Rev. ed.). Edina, MN: Interaction Book.

Kagan, J. (1994). On the nature of emotion. In N. A. Fox (Ed.), The development of emotional regulation: Biological and behavioral considerations. *Monographs of the Society for Research in Child Development, 240*(59), 2–3, 7–24.

Katz, L. G., & McClellan, D. E. (1997). *Fostering children's social competence: The teacher's role.* Washington, DC: National Association for the Education of Young Children.

Keller, M., & Edelstein, W. (1993). The development of the moral self from childhood to adolescence. In G. Noam and T. Wren (Eds.), *The moral self* (pp. 310–336). Cambridge, MA: MIT Press.

Kohlberg, L. (1976). Moral stages and moralization: The cognitive-developmental approach. In T. Lickona (Ed.), *Moral development and behavior.* New York: Holt, Rinehart and Winston.

Kohn, A. (1993). *Punished by rewards: The trouble with gold stars, incentive plans, As, praise and other bribes.* New York: Houghton Mifflin.

Korner, A. F. (1974). The effect of the infant's state, level of arousal, sex and centogenetic stage on the caregiver. In M. Lewis & L. A. Rosenblum (Eds.), *The effects of the infant on its caregiver* (pp. 105–121). New York: John Wiley & Sons.

Kostelnik, M. J., Stein, L. C., Whiren, A. P., & Soderman, A. K. (1998). *Guiding children's social development* (3rd ed.). Albany, NY: Delmar.

Kovacs, D. M., Parker, J. G., & Hoffman, L. W. (1996). Behavioral, affective and social correlates of involvement in cross-sex friendship in elementary school. *Child Development, 67,* 2269–2286.

Kunhardt, D. (1940, 1968). *Pat the bunny.* New York: Western, 1968.

Langlois, J. (1986). From the eye of the beholder to behavioral reality: Development of social behaviors and social relations as a function of physical attractiveness. In C. P. Herman, M. P. Zanna, & E. T. Higgins (Eds.), *Physical appearance, stigma and social behavior: The Ontario symposium: Vol. 3.* Hillsdale, NJ: Erlbaum.

Langlois, J. H., Ritter, J. M., Casey, R. J., & Sawin, D. B. (1995). Infant attractiveness predicts maternal behaviors and attitudes. *Developmental Psychology, 31,* 464–472.

Lansky, B. (1984). *The best baby name book.* Deephaven, MN.: Meadowbrook Press.

Larsen, R., & Richards, M. (1991). Daily companionship in late childhood and early adolescence: Changing developmental contexts. *Child Development, 62,* 284–300.

Lickona, T. (1991). *Educating for character: How our schools can teach respect and responsibility.* New York: Bantam Books.

Maccoby, E. E. (1980). *Social development-psychological growth and the parent-child relationship.* New York: Harcourt Brace Jovanovich.

Martin, G. B., & Clark, R. D. (1987). Distress crying in neonates: Species and peer specificity. *Developmental Psychology, 18,* 3–9.

Marvin, R., & Pianta, R. (1992). Relationship-based approaches to assessment of children with motor impairments. *Infants and Young Children, 4,* 33–45.

Merrell, K. W., & Gimpel, G. A. (1998). *Social skills of children and adolescents: Conceptualization, assessment, treatment.* Mahwah, NJ: Erlbaum.

National Center for Education Statistics. (1998, March). *Violence and discipline problems in U.S. public schools: 1996–1997.* NCES 98–030. Washington, DC: U.S. Department of Education.

National Council for the Social Studies (NCSS). (1997). *Expectations of excellence: Curriculum standards for social studies.* Washington, DC: Author.

Paley, V. G. (1993). *You can't say you can't play.* Cambridge, MA: Harvard University Press.

Parker, J. G., & Gottman, J. M. (1989). Social and emotional development in a relational context: Friendship interactions from early childhood to adolescence. In T. J. Berndt & G. W. Ladd (Eds.), *Peer relationships in child development.* New York: Wiley.

Parten, M. B. (1932). Social participation among preschool children. *Journal of Abnormal Psychology, 27,* 243–269.

Piaget, J. (1932, 1965). *The moral judgment of the child.* New York: Free Press.

Plomin, R., & McClearn, G. E. (Eds.). (1993). *Nature and nurture and psychology.* Washington, DC: American Psychological Society.

Prutzman, P., Stern, L., Burger, M. L., & Bodenhamer, G. (1988). *The friendly classroom for a small planet.* Philadelphia, PA: New Society.

Rubin, Z. (1980). *Children's friendship.* Cambridge, MA: Harvard University Press.

Sagar, H. A., Schofield, J. W., & Snyder, H. N. (1983). Race and gender barriers: Preadolescent peer behavior in academic classrooms. *Child Development, 54,* 1032–1040.

Schofield, J. W., & Francis, W. D. (1982). An observational study of peer interaction in racially mixed "accelerated" classrooms. *Journal of Educational Psychology, 74,* 722–732.

Shapiro, L. (1997). *How to raise a child with a high EQ.* New York: HarperCollins.

Shaw, M. E. (1973). Changes in sociometric choices following forced integration of an elementary school. *Journal of Social Issues, 29,* 143–157.

Shulman, S., Elicker, J., & Srouve, L. A. (1994). Stages of friendship growth in preadolescence as related to attachment history. *Journal of Social and Personal Relationships, 11,* 341–361.

Skinner, B. F. (1938). *The behavior of organisms.* New York: Appleton-Century-Crofts.

Slavin, R. (1995). *Cooperative learning* (2nd ed.). Needham Heights, MA: Allyn & Bacon.

Smirnova, Y. (1996). Personal communication, 1990. In L. A. Sroufe, R. G. Cooper, G. B. DeHart, & M. E. Marshall (Eds.), *Child development: Its nature and course* (3rd ed.). New York: McGraw-Hill.

Smith, C. A. (1993). *The peaceful classroom: 162 easy activities to teach preschoolers compassion and cooperation.* Mt. Rainier, MD: Gryphon House.

Snarey, J. R. (1985). Cross-cultural universite of social-moral development: A critical review of Kohlbergian research. *Psychological Bulletin, 97,* 202–232.

Sroufe, L. A. (1995). Emotional development: The organization of emotional life in the early years. Cambridge, UK: Cambridge University Press.

Sweeney, J., & Bradbard, M. R. (1988). Mothers' and fathers' changing perceptions of their male and female infants over the course of pregnancy. *Journal of Genetic Psychology, 149,* 393–404.

Turiel, E., Killen, M., & Helwig, C. C. (1987). Morality: its structure, functions and vagaries. In J. Kagan & S. Lamb (Eds.), *The emergence of morality.* Chicago: Chicago University Press.

Welton, D. A., & Mallan, J. T. (1992). *Strategies for teaching social studies.* Boston: Houghton Mifflin.

Online Resources

For additional learning and teaching resources, visit our Web site at www.EarlyChildEd.delmar.com.

RELATED CAREERS

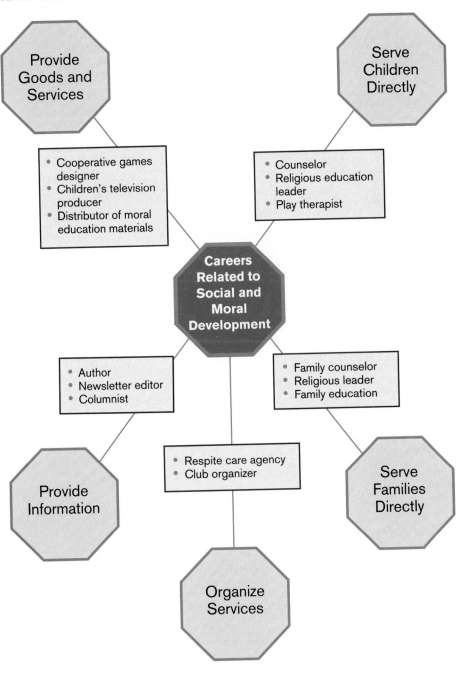

Figure 12—22

Careers related to social/moral development.

CHAPTER

13

Learning and Teaching

as a Professional

Objectives

After reading this chapter and completing the review activities, the learning teacher should be able to:

1. Define "profession" and compare teaching to other professions.
2. Embody, exemplify, and dedicate herself to ethical conduct.
3. Compare professional associations.
4. Describe the teacher's role as an advocate.
5. Identify the teacher's managerial roles.
6. Develop a personalized professional development plan.

✳ LEARNING ABOUT TEACHING AS A PROFESSION

Is teaching a job? Is it a career? We call it a profession, but what does that mean? This chapter will explore this subject to clarify for you what a teacher does besides teach.

✳ WHO IS A PROFESSIONAL?

SCENARIO

✳ Marabella Williams is a brain surgeon, doctor of medicine, and member of the American Medical Association.

✳ Angelo Cruz earned an associate's degree and passed an examination to become a registered nurse.

✳ Jun Tse is an osteopath and a doctor of medicine.

✳ Jane O'Malley is a licensed dog groomer.

✳ Matthew Brown is a kindergarten teacher licensed by the state of Maryland.

✳ Carlos Alvarez is a sixth-grade teacher licensed by the state of California.

✳ Carrie Jump is a Head Start teacher with a CDA, or Child Development Associate, credential.

Which of these people is a **professional**? It depends on the criteria used to define a "profession." Some would say all of these people are professionals, since they belong to groups that establish and enforce standards for professional practice and monitor interactions with the public. Others (Darling-Hammond & Sykes, 1999; Howsam, Corrigan, Denemark, & Nash, 1976; Argyris & Schon, 1974; Schein, 1972; Saracho & Spodek, 1993) would list only Marabella, the brain surgeon; Jun, the osteopath; and Angelo the registered nurse, as professionals. They would list Matthew, the kindergarten teacher, and Carlos, the sixth-grade teacher, as "semiprofessionals" because they have lower occupational status, a shorter training period, and a lower level of societal acceptance. Their communications with their clients are not privileged and have little involvement in matters of life and death. In turn, Jane, the dog groomer, and Carrie, the Head Start teacher, would be classified as "paraprofessionals" (individuals with extensive training who are not licensed or certified). These authorities use the following criteria to define a *profession*.

✳ occupations established and maintained to provide essential services

✳ concerned with a functional need of society

✳ body of knowledge and skills needed for practice not normally possessed by others

---

✳ **professional**—A person with a specialized body of knowledge and skills gained through an extended period of education who meets entrance requirements to the field and who holds high social status.

* members involved in making decisions about standards and practices of the group

* practice and standards are based upon common theories accepted by the group

* organized into autonomous association work that provides guidance and enforces standards of the group

* agreed-upon standards for admission and continuing practice

* protracted period of college preparation

* works to maintain high level of public trust in practitioners

* practitioners have strong service motivation and commitment to competence

* authority to practice derives from client; accountable to group

* accountability to the group eliminates the need for direct on-the-job supervision

Teaching as a Profession

Modern society has myriad divisions of labor (Figure 13–1). These are specializations with specific bodies of knowledge, skill, and expertise in which the public places trust. So is teaching a profession? Let's look at it in light of some of the criteria mentioned previously.

Occupations established and maintained to provide essential services. The public education system is an institution, with nearly 3.2 million people bearing the title *teacher* who provide essential services to individuals and society. When your title describes your occupation, everyone has an idea of what you do on the job. No one would argue that teaching is not an essential service performed to educate children and prepare them for the future.

Concerned with functional need of society. Is it a public function and need of society that its citizens be educated? Is society so complex that teachers are necessary for cross-generational learning? In the United States, people must be able to read and write to fully participate in public life by informed voting

Figure 13–1

What is a professional? A professional is a lifelong learner.

for local, state, and national political candidates. The private function of education is to prepare people to contribute to their own and their family's well-being by earning a living. The teacher's function is to enhance the child's opportunity to learn.

Body of knowledge and skills needed for practice not normally possessed by others. Whether or not teachers must possess an exclusive body of knowledge is one of the main areas of dispute. Teachers should be knowledgeable in content area, pedagogical skills, and child development. Some people do not value teachers' knowledge and some teachers do not have enough depth of knowledge to warrant respect. This is an area national reform movements are addressing in calling for higher standards, greater accountability of teacher preparation institutions, and more uniform assessments to regulate entrance into the field. Many states are now requiring teachers to pass a standardized test, such as the National Teacher Examination (NTE), which consists of Core Battery Tests, Specialty Area Tests, and Professional Skills Tests. The Educational Testing Service introduced Praxis in 1993 (ETS, 1999), a rigorous series of tests that many states are adopting.

Members involved in making decisions about standards and practices of the group. Teaching has not had the decision-making power of other fields. Laws at the federal, state, and local levels often define the teacher's role, sometimes without input from practitioners. School administrators often manage in a top-down, bureaucratic style. More and more school districts are moving to site-based management and team decision making, but an individual classroom teacher does not have the authority or autonomy to define their practice the way a doctor or lawyer does.

Another way to look at this is that teaching is a continuous decision-making process. There is no professional *cookbook* or manual containing instructions that, when followed, turn out the same product each time. Teaching human beings is an individualized interaction between people who each have unique thinking and behavior. When an action is taken by either the teacher or the student one, the other interprets it within a unique framework; her response is generated almost instantaneously, based on past education and experience. A teacher sees that a child is out of her seat. The teacher must interpret if the child is neglecting her assigned task, coming to the teacher for help, or going to the bathroom. Each of those interpretations call for the teacher to react in a different way, and different teachers also react in different ways depending on their education, experience, and personal teaching philosophy. There are just too many possibilities for a uniform response. Yes, teachers are involved in day-to-day, moment-by-moment decisions, but they are not as actively involved in institutional decisions.

Practice and standards are based upon common theories accepted by the group. There is no one, single accepted theory of teaching. There is an assortment of philosophies and practices that have been studied in every conceivable way, but since teaching and learning are art more than they are science, and reflect an ever-changing culture and society, one theory does not serve all purposes. Many attempts have been made to develop position statements and definitions of bodies of knowledge in each content field, such as mathematics, science, reading, social studies, and the arts. Pedagogy research and models abound, and teacher educators try to instill in their students the viewpoint the teacher educator believes in. Thus, teaching outcomes vary from institution to institution and even from professor to professor. Therefore, the field of teaching's more independent approach is based on the teacher's judgment, which is formed in her preparation years and modified by experience.

Organized into an autonomous association that promotes guidance and enforces standards of the group. Teaching professionals usually belong to professional organizations, but there usually is no requirement that they do so. These associations may be unions that represent the members in bargaining situations and provide professional development opportunities. Teachers' unions advocate primarily for benefits, working conditions, and teacher involvement in decision making, but draw the line at any kind of self-regulation of their members. Professional associations may also specialize in a content area or theory, or focus on a particular age range of students, bringing members together for conferences, and publishing journals to keep members informed. Membership in these organizations is voluntary and they have no authority over the profession. This is different from the medicine and law, whose organizations control entrance and exit from the profession by setting standards and censuring those who violate their ethical codes.

Agreed-upon standards for admission and continuing practice. Individual state laws determine how teachers enter and continue in the field. While these laws are similar, they are not uniform nationally. Because the demand for teachers in certain geographical locations and specialized fields periodically exceeds the supply, entrance requirements are at times relaxed or ignored. The shocking fact is that more than 12 percent of new teachers enter the classroom without any formal training at all, and 40 states allow districts to hire teachers who have not met the basic requirements for emergency or standard licensing (Darling-Hammond, 1996). While this laxity brings criticism to the field, it is a matter of practicality. If there were a dire need for physicians or lawyers, would hospitals or law firms accept unlicensed people? Probably not.

Protracted period of college preparation. Public school teacher requirements in all states call for a minimum of a bachelor's degree. In spite of this, nearly one-fourth to one-half of secondary teachers did not major or minor in the subjects they are teaching, especially mathematics and science. The nation's poorest school districts are the most likely places for teacher qualification standards to be relaxed or ignored (Ingersoll, 1995; Oakes, 1990). As educational requirements for other occupations rise, the bachelor's degree will no longer be sufficient for teachers. Masters degrees and extended postgraduate professional development are necessary for a society where rapidly changing and growing knowledge are required to prepare the workforce (Figure 13–2).

Works to maintain high level of public trust in practitioners. In a recent Phi Delta Kappa/Gallup Poll (Rose & Gallup, 1998) of attitudes toward public schools, only about half of the respondents gave their community schools a grade of A or B, and less than half felt that children were getting a better education than they had. Media reports about state and national student test scores and individual instances of teacher incompetence have eroded some of the trust that society had in teachers and schools. The increase in home-schooling, private school enrollment, and voucher movements are indicators of this lost trust.

Practitioners have strong service motivation and commitment to competence. Most people who enter the field of teaching do so because they are strongly motivated to educate children. Sometimes these high ideals are tarnished by day-to-day lack of support for teachers or by teachers feeling unprepared to meet the needs of the students they serve. This may result in teachers ques-

Figure 13–2

Professionals have a high level of education.

tioning their career choices, frustrated, jaded, and lacking the idealism they brought to the profession.

WORDS OF WISDOM Listen to Patrick Patterson's excitement and hopes two weeks before his first second-grade teaching assignment.

"I'm curious about what the students and faculty are going to think of me. Right now, I feel overwhelmed and scared because I've never done this before. However, I'm also excited and amazed that I have such a wonderful opportunity in my life, and I am not going to waste it. I feel very fortunate that, despite my inexperience, the district that hired me trusts me. There's a lot of support in the school, but I'm really nervous about meeting the students. I've set up an open house for parents and students for the week before school starts, just for my classroom."

"I'm very excited. I can't explain how excited I am! I'm responsible for 21 students. It feels like I'm going to have an impact on their lives and I'm honored to have the chance. I hope all new teachers realize what an opportunity they've been given. That's why I'll do the best job I can."

Teacher's motivation to serve is sometimes questioned by the public when teachers' unions advocate for higher wages and benefits, and when teachers' salaries are higher than the average in the communities where they work. A teacher's commitment to competence may be difficult, because teacher competencies are not clearly defined. It sometimes takes years to see the results of competent or ineffective teaching.

Authority to practice derives from client; accountable to the group. Clients (or students) do not have the freedom to select their teacher as they can select their doctor, lawyer, or hairstylist. The school is a coercive institution that is sanctioned by law. Students must attend. This may not always prove pleasant for the student or the teacher, but neither has much choice in the matter. In our inequitable society, choices are more available to people in the higher-income tax brackets, who can send their children to private schools.

The teacher is hired by the school district, not the individual student or parent, so the authority to assign a child to a particular teacher is the prerogative of the district. This is unlike other professions, except for public defenders and public health clinics. Freedom of choice in these cases is limited by your ability to pay for alternative services.

Accountability to the group eliminates the need for direct on-the-job supervision. Teachers often work without direct supervision in their day-to-day teaching. As mentioned previously, professional associations do not censure individual teachers or hold them accountable for their professional actions or practices; that is the responsibility of the school or administration.

The majority of teachers are women, while the majority of administrators are men. In this gender-segregated organizational structure, supervision and decision making reflect the traditional male-dominant culture. Medicine and law are also predominantly male. Teaching will be considered more "professional" when men do not dominate society and when more men become teachers.

Recommendations for Professionalizing Teaching

For teaching to be more professionalized, the National Commission on Teaching and America's Future, in *What Matters Most: Teaching for America's Future* (1996), makes the following recommendations.

* Get serious about standards for both students and teachers by:
— establishing professional standards boards in every state to oversee teacher licensing based on performance, knowledge, and skill.
— insisting on accreditation for all schools of education and closing inadequate schools.
* Reinvent teacher preparation and professional development by:
— developing extended, graduate-level teacher preparation programs and internships.
— creating and funding mentoring programs for beginning teachers and evaluate their teaching skills.
— creating high-quality sources of professional development.
* Meet the increasing demand for teachers by:
— developing multiple pathways for recruitment.
— providing incentives for teachers in shortage areas and financial assistance to help low-wealth districts hire qualified teachers.
— streamlining hiring processes and eliminating barriers to mobility.
* Encourage and reward teacher knowledge and skill by:
— developing a career continuum that links assessments to compensation.
— removing incompetent teachers.
— setting goals and incentives for national board certification in every state.
* Create schools organized for student and teacher success by:
— investing more in teachers and technology than in administration.
— providing capital for school improvements.
— selecting administrators who understand teaching and learning and can lead high-performing schools.

Professionalizing teachers began with the development of normal schools into the early days of the National Education Association (NEA). NEA contends that there needs to be a more uniform entrance standard, a code of ethical conduct and practice, and a way for the profession to hold individual teachers to the standard (1975). One organization working toward this end is the National Council for Accreditation of Teacher Education (NCATE), which develops standards and accredits teacher-preparation institutions. NCATE's motto is, "A competent teacher for every child." Hopefully, you will receive preparation in an institution that upholds the NCATE Standards. Ethical conduct, of course, is another matter, and is up to you.

Professionals Act Ethically

"Child Care Teacher Accused of Murder"

"Teacher Convicted of Child Sexual Abuse"

"Teacher Charged with Pornographic Internet Business"

Headlines like these can be seen almost daily in newspapers and lead off many local television newscasts. People are shocked and disturbed when those who have been entrusted with their children misuse that trust, and acted illegally or immorally with respect to the children. In these circumstances, the children's protectors have become molesters and agents of harm. As mentioned earlier, professions have established codes of ethics about how members should act toward their clients. Teaching has no unified code. While various professional associations have such codes, the organizations do not have the authority to revoke a teacher's license to practice.

Of course, harmful behaviors such as those mentioned previously are also illegal and should be addressed by the criminal justice system. However, there are many other instances where an action is not illegal or immoral, but requires the teacher to use her judgment so that no psychological harm comes to the client, in this case, the student. These ethical dilemmas have no clear right or wrong answers or solutions, but call for the individual to exercise her discretion based on her values and principles. Professional ethics go beyond personal morals and values by affirming the profession's moral commitments. A code of ethics provides a profession with "a vision of what the professional should be like and how they should behave, . . . guidance in making choices that best serve the interests of their clients, a tool to help members of the profession articulate their core values . . . a justification for a difficult decision" (Feeney & Freeman, 1999, p. 10).

What would you do in the following situations?

SCENARIO A new child enters your classroom midway through the year. She barely speaks to you or the other children. A more experienced teacher suggests that you have her read out loud in front of the class every day so she becomes accustomed to speaking in public. The other teacher is coming to your classroom this afternoon to show you how to carry out this initiative.

The parent of a child in your class has confided to you she has extra food stamps she would like to donate so you can purchase an afternoon snack for the class on her child's birthday.

continued

A colleague from down the hall leaves her class every afternoon to have a smoke. While she is gone, she calls in a parent volunteer who is also a friend of hers to supervise her class. This is against school policy.

These situations place the teacher in the position of making hard decisions. Often you are torn between two sides, neither of which feels right. That is an ethical dilemma. Professional teachers associations have codes of ethics that help their members make decisions based on principles of responsibility and equity.

NEA's Code of Ethics for the Education Profession states that the educator should accept responsibility not to harm, intentionally embarrass, or discourage a student from learning, nor deny a student's rights on the basis of any form of discrimination, and that she will act fairly and responsibly toward the student, keeping personal and academic student information confidential. Members should not misrepresent their competency or qualifications or assist others in doing so, nor disclose private information about a colleague, make false statements, or accept gifts that may influence their professional decisions (NEA, 1975).

The American Federation of Teachers' (AFT) Code of Ethics, adopted in 1976, calls on members to commit themselves to developing each student's potential, working objectively to advance students' knowledge, and providing educational opportunities for all students. It also publicly commits teachers to be dedicated to a democratic heritage, take responsibility for political awareness and citizenship, and enhance the public image of education. Members also dedicate themselves to quality education, raising professional standards, and attracting worthy persons to the profession, as well as supporting the organization. Members commit to doing an honest job for their school districts and keeping the Code.

The National Association for the Education of Young Children's (NAEYC) Code of Ethical Conduct (1998) is similar to the AFT and NEA Codes. It also emphasizes ethical responsibilities to families, such as not denying access to their child's classroom, informing and involving them in policies, advising them about decisions that directly affect their child, and keeping personal and academic information confidential. The Code stresses communicating openly with the family and working together for the good of the child. The Code also mentions the responsibility of showing mutual respect, trust, and cooperation to colleagues.

These codes of ethics come from three large membership organizations. While there are many areas of similarity among them, there is no single unified code of ethics to guide teachers. Nor is there a uniform code of ethical standards tied to licensing.

The Professional as a Member of an Association

There seems to be a club for everyone and everything. There are organizations for knitters, dog breeders, race car fans, and people named Bill Smith. Any group with something in common may form an association and recruit more members. When people of like interests band together, they do so for recognition, support, and advancement of their commonality. They form a network in which to trade information, skills, products, or experiences. The same thing is true for the teaching profession. There are two major kinds of organizations: unions and associations. Unions may or may not be voluntary, depending on the school district in which you live. Associations, however, are voluntary. Either may charge dues to join, which are usually deductible from your taxable income.

Teachers' Unions. The two major teachers' unions were mentioned earlier. NEA is strong in suburban areas, while AFT is stronger in urban school districts.

NEA (known then as the National Teachers Association) was founded in Philadelphia in 1857 for the purpose of promoting teaching as a profession and the cause of public education. It claims to be the oldest and largest organization committed to advancing public education, with 2.3 million members and affiliates in every state. Its membership includes teachers from preschools, public schools, and universities. In the past, NEA focused more on educational issues and reform, but in the 1960s it became more of an advocate for economic benefits for its members, not avoiding such things as collective bargaining, striking, mediation, and other labor tactics as it had in the past. In 1966, it merged with the American Teachers Association (ATA), an African American association that brought with it advocacy for civil and human rights of all educators and children. Administrators also belong to NEA, which causes some controversy and is seen by some as a conflict of interest. NEA acts as a labor union, but also sees itself as a professional association.

AFT is the only teacher organization affiliated with the American Federation of Labor-Congress of Industrial Organizations (AFL-CIO). AFT's roots are in the early 1900s, when it was formed to organize those working in public education, especially in large cities. Its more militant stance has been criticized as unbecoming of a professional organization, but its effectiveness as an advocate for its members forced NEA to change to a more proactive stance or risk losing members to AFT. AFT is dedicated to teachers in public education and excludes membership by administrators and nonpublic schoolteachers. Its late president, Albert Shanker, was a respected spokesperson during his long career as AFT's leader. Although it is considerably smaller than NEA, at about 900,000 members, AFT's affiliation with AFL-CIO heightens its influence.

Teacher's unions such as NEA and AFT work just as any labor union does: to collectively bargain on behalf of their members for better wages, benefits, and working conditions. They promote public education on a national, state, and local level, especially by enhancing educational opportunities for all social classes, races, and minorities. If you work for a district whose teachers are represented by a union, you usually must become a member. Union dues, which can amount to several hundred dollars a year, are automatically deducted from your salary. If you refuse to join, the dues are still deducted, since you will benefit from any contractual negotiations the union provides. As a member, you will receive a variety of publications with articles related to education. Both unions provide extensive professional development offerings for their members, especially in the summer. They fund research on curricula and many other educational issues. They provide legal assistance to protect members against claims of malpractice or other charges. Insurance and savings plans are available at group rates.

NEA and AFT have engaged in serious merger negotiations over the past few years. If the two unions did merge, they would provide a powerful unified voice for their members. However, AFT's ties with AFL-CIO present a problem. If AFL-CIO went on strike, it might expect AFT to do so as well, and NEA is reluctant to have that expectation extended to its members. NEA members also have strong feelings about uniting with the 72 other unions in AFL-CIO, which represent 13 million blue-collar workers and other professionals, including child care workers who belong to unions such as the Communications Workers of America, the International Brotherhood of Teamsters, the Screen Actors Guild, and the American Federation of State, County, and Municipal Employees. AFT, however, sees its relationship with AFL-CIO as augmenting its power in promoting legislation and pressuring for reform.

Whether or not you join a teachers' union will depend on the type of school you work in—private or public—and if the teachers in that school are represented by NEA or AFT. Beyond your union membership, you may also choose to join another kind of professional organization.

Professional Associations. One effective way to continue learning and work for changes within your profession is to join a professional association. Professional associations formulate standards for teaching and for learning-specific content areas, share teaching strategies, and address issues affecting different-age learners, different abilities of learners, and specific philosophies of education. As a member, you usually receive a journal and other publications that advise you of the latest information related to that group's interest. There may be local or state chapters as part of the national organization. These associations often sponsor conferences and workshops, which provide a forum for you to present your research findings, as well as hear those of others. The Web sites, listserves, and chat rooms of these special interest groups keep you up-to-date without you having to leave home and link you to colleagues around the world. The list that follows contains some of the many professional associations of special interest to educators. You will recognize some of them from previous chapters.

* American Association for the Advancement of Science (AAAS) <http://www.aaas.org>
* American Council on Teaching of Foreign Languages (ACTFL) <http://www.actfl.org>
* Association for Supervision and Curriculum Development (ASCD) <http://www.ascd.org>
* Association of Childhood Education International (ACEI) <http://www.asaenet.org>
* Council for Exceptional Children (CEC) <http://www.cec.sped.org>
* International Reading Association (IRA) <http://www.reading.org>
* Music Teachers National Association (MTNA) <http://www.mtna.org>
* National Association for the Education of Young Children (NAEYC) <http://www.naeyc.org>
* National Association for Gifted Children <http://www.teachermagazine.org>
* National Council for the Social Studies (NCSS) <http://www.ncss.org>
* National Council of Teachers of English (NCTE) <http://www.ncte.org>
* National Council of Teachers of Mathematics (NCTM) <http://www.nctm.org>
* National Science Teachers Association (NSTA) <http://www.nsta.org>

The Professional as an Advocate

The professional teacher has the responsibility to act as an **advocate** as part of carrying out her duties. There will be many instances in your career when you will witness injustice, want to make a policy change, or need to take a position on an issue about which you feel strongly. A professional advocates based on her knowledge and the ethical code of her profession, so her advocacy is not self-serving but truly for the ben-

---

advocate—One who pleads the cause of another.

efit of another. This altruistic action is not done for praise or reward, but to actively express a belief. The following sections list some instances where your advocacy may be needed.

Advocate for the Child and Family. We cannot even begin to guess what teaching will be like by the time you complete your preparation and enter the field, but it appears that, unfortunately, certain challenges facing families in the United States will as yet be unsolved. You will be teaching children and becoming involved with their families in ways you never imagined. The teacher's role is becoming more like that of a professional in the field of human services. You cannot address a child's learning without taking into consideration the family situation from which the child emerges each day. If that situation is one that lacks the basic necessities of life, then it may fall upon you to help match the family's needs with available services. Previously, we discussed the fact that a hungry, anxious, or hurting child is not able to learn. We remind you again of that. With your responsibilities as a professional and your knowledge of community resources, you may be the link to help families receive the services vital to the academic success of their children. You may have to *go to bat* for a family to help them to receive those services. This is not to suggest that you act as a bountiful benefactor, but rather as an advocate. You can empower the family by helping them define their strengths and needs and find the services they need, acting as a go-between, another voice, or a conduit for information. You do not do it for them; you do it with them (Figure 13–3).

Another family advocacy role you may play is to prevent or overcome inequities. If any place should be a level playing field, it should be school, but unhappily that is not always the case. Even though civil rights legislation was passed two generations ago, racism and bigotry have not been eradicated and are powerful forces against which we all must fight. Whether it is in person-to-person interactions, equitable testing, or showing respect for other cultures and beliefs, a teacher is a role model of acceptance and tolerance. Stand up for equal treatment and advocate against injustices wherever they are

Figure 13–3

The professional teacher is an advocate for families.

found: on the playground, in school policies, or in the teacher's lounge. Not only is this right; it is also the law.

You can advocate for respecting diversity in your classroom and your school by planning curricula and using teaching strategies that meet the learning needs of students from diverse cultural, ethnic, and linguistic backgrounds. This is also true for differing developmental levels, abilities, and disabilities. Your attitude of acceptance is the positive behavior that the Brophy and Good (1974) study did not see: waiting for answers, equal interactions, frequent positive feedback, seeking their equal participation in activities, making eye contact, and holding high expectations. Teachers are advocates for *all* students: by listening, challenging, appreciating, and encouraging.

Of course, the teacher's first responsibility is the child's well-being. Increasing numbers of children need either special services or evaluations to determine what they need. Schools are overwhelmed with the number of children with special needs and the costs, and sometimes the individual child's needs are lost in the bureaucratic process. As a child advocate, you can and should push for action that needs to be taken on behalf of the child. Maybe the child needs a hearing or speech evaluation. Maybe the evaluation has been done, but nothing is happening as a result. You have to take a stand and move the process along.

Another way you may have to be an advocate for the child and her family is in reporting suspected child abuse. This was discussed previously, but is repeated here. You may think it strange to discuss this under advocacy, but if you look back at the definition, you will see that the child cannot or will not plead for help. The family may not plead for help by actually asking for it, but the plea consists of a family member neglecting or abusing a child for whatever reason. You can defend the child and be instrumental in getting assistance for the family so they can stop the cycle of abuse. You are advocating for both the child and her family when you report an honest suspicion of abuse or neglect. The case of Kitty Genovese, a woman who was beaten to death in New York City more than 20 years ago, is a reminder of what happens when people do nothing. Many people witnessed the beating, but all were reluctant to intervene, with the inevitable tragic result. Hopefully, you will never have to take such a serious life-or-death advocacy position, but if you can make the way smoother for a child and her family, this will have lifelong positive effects. Take a stand.

Advocate for the Community. Schools are financed with national, state, and local funding. Schools with the lowest tax base commonly have the greatest need for monies to repair buildings, purchase supplies and equipment, and pay teacher salaries. You may need to be an advocate in the community to help with its quality of life. Is there a youth center that needs a few volunteer hours? Does the neighborhood need to organize a community watch so people feel safe? Does the area need a grocery store, or streetlights replaced, or a library branch? Whatever needs to be done in the community to make it a safer, nicer place to live is an area where you can get actively involved and make a difference. Perhaps community members just need to know how to get organized. Maybe they need someone to help them start a letter-writing campaign.

Community-based partnerships are another way that schools and teachers can address issues that place students at risk, such as poverty, substance abuse, violence, crime, teen pregnancy, HIV/AIDS, and suicide. Community schools can become the hub of services, from Head Start to adult education, by providing before- and after-school programs, including meals offered for the full year and during school vacations. Schools can host health clinics; social service offices; music, dance, and drama lessons; Saturday classes for enrichment, or computer studies for children and adults. Teachers can be the impetus for such programs that make the school the center of the community.

These partnerships can work in other ways as well: the community can become a resource for the school. Volunteer organizations can provide mentors for children who need a consistent and concerned adult friend. Businesses can adopt a classroom and provide extra materials and books that can make a difference in student learning outcomes. Organizations can band together to provide scholarships and incentives for perfect attendance or academic improvement, not just excellence. Small businesses can involve students in job-shadowing and apprenticelike programs that give students a clearer and more realistic image of real-life employment. All these programs need an organizer and that can be you, the teacher, who knows what these things can mean for children, families, the school, and the community.

There are any number of projects that have had amazing results because a few people cared enough to get them started. That is a way you can advocate for the community and ultimately affect the lives of the children you teach.

Advocate for the Profession. You are a representative of your profession. Whenever you make a purchase at a neighborhood store, park your car and put money in the meter, or write a note home to the family of a child in your class, you are representing the whole profession. If you are not courteous to the clerk, if you skip the meter or park in a spot reserved for people with disabilities if you are not entitled to do so, or if you spell words incorrectly or write a sarcastic note, you are misrepresenting the teaching profession. Some people may judge all teachers by the way you present yourself. What kind of a teacher do you want your students to remember you as? You are an ambassador of the system of education. If you misuse the trust placed in you, all teachers are indicted by your actions. This is a big responsibility, certainly, but on the other hand, if you inspire, encourage, and light the spark of curiosity and quest for knowledge in your students, your impact will be mighty indeed.

The Professional Teacher as a Manager

A manager is one who oversees, supervises, and takes charge. The teacher has many areas to manage in taking responsibility for the classroom environment, the curriculum, student behavior, record keeping, and, most of all, herself. Maintaining a competency level in all of these areas requires planning, self-control, and sometimes knowing when to seek help. Three categories of management responsibility follow.

A Time Manager. One of the skills you will need to develop is managing your time, both in and out of the classroom. In the classroom, your day is segmented, perhaps not by your choice, but by forces beyond your control. You will have mandates for what curriculum areas must be covered in a year's time, so you will have to break down those expectations into units of smaller and smaller segments, until you can see manageable components that can be covered in a day or a week. This is lesson planning. Future courses will help you develop this skill. It is a fact of life that the clock governs your day. The children must be finished with a certain task by the time lunch begins. You must budget time to include cleanup, or you will be left with it at the end of the day, and the children will have no closure to the lesson or activity on which they were working (Figure 13–4 on page 500).

A related skill is the record keeping that accompanies lesson plans. It is not enough to plan and do; children's individual progress must be documented. Determining their progress and achievement is based on the hard evidence of your record keeping, whether you do it with portfolio entries, anecdotal records, or scores in a grade book. Assessing learning outcomes in a useful format is a necessary part of the teacher's job.

Figure 13—4

The professional teacher is a time manager.

A Resource Manager. Every school or program has a limited budget for equipment and supplies. The teacher is responsible for wisely managing those resources. If the children use up all of the paint in the first half of the year, what will you do for the remainder of the year? If the paper supply runs out in March, then what? Knowing what you have available and how to budget your resources are valuable and necessary skills. This will come with experience, but, unfortunately, it is the lesson is usually learned from a bad experience, when you run out of something and have to forego an activity because you lack the necessary resources.

These situations call for the teacher to be resourceful. Imagination, inventiveness, initiative, and networking can produce amazing results. Families can often provide interesting and abundant materials that the children can use to turn trash into treasures. Sometimes, you may even have to plan fundraisers for materials or special projects. These can be learning experiences for the students if they are involved in setting up a cookie factory and store, or buying in bulk, repackaging, and reselling. They learn mathematics as they figure cost and profit. They combine artistic and language skills to make posters and write advertising copy. They experience satisfaction when they see what they have accomplished.

A People Manager. This phrase is not meant to connote manipulation, but instead is used here to remind you that as a teacher you work with people: students, parents, coworkers, maintenance and office staff, and other school professionals such as nurses and social workers. Teaching is a social activity. When I meet teacher candidates who never smile, who can hardly speak because they are so shy, or who have no friends among their fellow learning teachers, I wonder how they can overcome their lack of social skills so they can relate to all the people mentioned above? Maturity helps. At 40, I was much more comfortable with all ages and kinds of people than I was at 20, but do you have to wait 20 years, through 20 classes of students, for these social skills to develop? It probably takes more than maturity. Is it self-confidence?

Will therapy help? What will make the difference? Can these social skills be developed or are they either present or absent? This is something to consider when you select teaching as a career. You will be interacting with many other people in addition to the children in your class. If you think this will be too stressful, you may want to look at the related-career charts included at the end of each chapter. They include some related careers that do not involve as much social interaction. It is up to you to assess your own sociability and decide what is right for you (Figure 13–5).

Working with people, both children and adults, requires many skills. Can you think of some? Patience is usually at the top of the list. Not everyone will be kind, gentle, and easy to get along with. Repaying those difficult people in kind only multiplies anxiety and hard feelings. Being patient about trying to understand the other person's position goes a long way toward helping your day, and hers, run smoother. Listening skills are also necessary: not only listening to the words, but also watching for body language cues and undertones that may convey a different message. The professional teacher learns to use listening more than talking to learn about another person. This practice also gives you time to frame your thoughts before you speak, something everyone could benefit from. Extending courtesy to all, not just those in positions above you, is something to practice as well. Learn from each person who comes along, for everyone has something valuable they have learned in life; if you are patient and open to suggestion, you will recognize this gift. In teaching—as in life—you will meet many people who are very different from you. Use these opportunities to learn about and appreciate the differences.

✳ THE PROFESSIONAL AS A LIFELONG LEARNER

Because you have chosen the field of education, you know that learning is the foundation of your profession. You have begun your education and have a tentative plan,

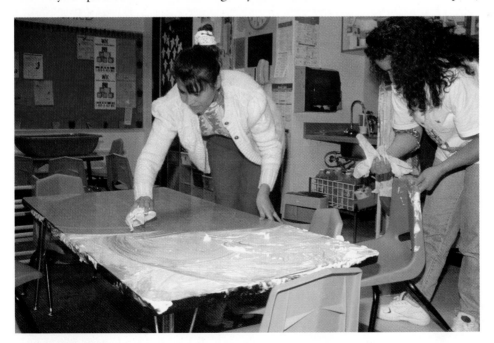

Figure 13–5

The professional teacher is a collaborator.

perhaps laid out by the college you attend and regulated by the state in which you live. To achieve any goal, you must have a plan, although you may veer from the pathway when existing plans are modified into new plans. Begin now to think about that plan in three phases: your preparation, as you fulfill the learning requirements for your chosen profession, your induction, as you launch yourself into the profession after fulfilling the basic requirements, and your continuing education, as you strive to keep current in your field.

The Preparation Plan

We began this textbook with the question, "Why do you want to become a teacher?" Hopefully, the discussions in this book have helped you consider, reconsider, and commit yourself to a career goal based on accurately evaluating your interests, talents, and resources. Figure 13–6 should help you review what has brought you to the point of deciding to pursue a career in teaching. Assess your strengths in the areas of knowledge, skills, and dispositions and determine what you need to develop in each of these areas. They will all be needed to succeed in college coursework and field practice.

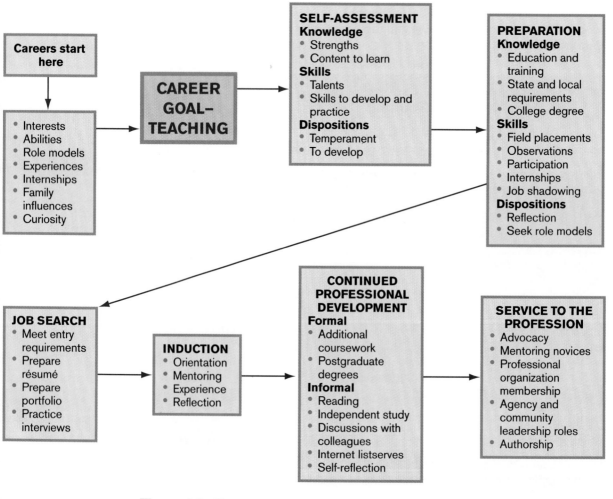

Figure 13–6

Pathway to a career in teaching.

The college you are attending has already decided on the courses they believe will best prepare you for your career goal, which you must clarify for yourself and communicate to your college advisors. Sometimes, differences in terminology or assumptions on both sides make for misunderstandings and a detour from your intention.

WORDS OF WISDOM   Here's a story from Barbara.

"One of my sons transferred to another college in his sophomore year of college after he changed his career goal from communications to secondary math teacher. He attended that college for three more years and when he was in his last year I asked him, 'When are you going to take any education courses?' He had not gone to any advisement sessions; he had just chosen math courses and others he thought he needed and was in his final year as a mathematics major, but not a mathematics *education* major. His goal was thwarted and discouragement set in because, due to his own misunderstanding, he had inadvertently detoured from his original career plan. He's made the most of his college degree, but he's not a teacher—maybe someday."

Seek advice, ask questions, be an advocate for yourself. Be sure you know the state requirements for your intended career goal and check with your college advisor to ensure that the courses you are taking will prepare you for that goal. If you are undecided as to what you want to do, take the most versatile courses you can to keep your options open as long as possible.

During your college preparation, you will have to take required courses in which you will wonder why you are sitting there. It is up to you to make every course relevant to your intended goal. If assignments seem difficult, get help. If they seem vague, get clarification. If they seem boring, find a way to apply them to subjects in which you are interested. If you are writing a research paper, tie it to a previous research subject that interested you. Challenge yourself to make all of your education relevant. You never know when a bit of knowledge that you accumulated in a course you thought was a waste of time will be called for and you will lament, "I wish I had paid more attention!" In other words, make the most of your preparation coursework, for it is the base on which you will build—and you know what happens to buildings on shaky foundations!

Entry Requirements

Your career choice and state requirements will determine the college preparation, degree, and type of practice you will need. Good outcomes for children depend on well-qualified teachers, so if you are really serious about working with children to help them develop, do the best you can in this preparation period.

Depending on your career choice and where you live, you may be facing a state or national teacher examination. Prepare for that examination by learning the content as you go along, rather than depending on cramming before the test (a strategy that may have worked in the past). These tests cover a very large body of knowledge that it is almost impossible to learn in a short time. Learning is a cumulative process. If you can, review samples of the test so you will know what to expect in terms of question formats and content areas. You may also have to be observed in your teaching or produce a video of your teaching. Many avenues of help are available to help you find success in these projects. Find out the requirements for teacher licensure in your state and start early to plan for them. The next section will assist you in your postgraduation phase, which may seem like a long way off, but which you should start planning for now.

The Induction Plan

You should begin to prepare for that first interview for your first teaching position now. Even though that interview and teaching position may be years away, there are some things you can do now to prepare.

Résumé and Cover Letter. First of all, you will need a résumé that presents your academic achievements and work experience. List the institutions of higher education you have attended and the courses you took or degrees you obtained, highlighting your GPA (grade point average) if it is 3.0 or better. In another section, list your employment experience, which may not be related to your career goals, but indicates your dependability and responsibility. Related experience, either in employment or field experiences, practicums, or volunteer work, should be documented, informing potential employers of the practical experience you have had. You can list the types of duties you performed and add letters of reference or evaluations from these experiences as addenda to your résumé. Participation in campus or community activities, such as attending conferences, volunteering at children's events, or mentoring fellow students, can give your résumé an edge. You can use reference books, Web sites, and your college career planning office to help you develop your résumé.

The résumé cover letter is as important as the résumé itself, for it portrays your written communication skills, attention to detail (it should be perfect, as should the résumé), and, most of all, your enthusiasm and interest in the particular position you are applying for.

Professional Portfolio. Start an organizational system for storing and *retrieving* important samples of your work, articles you have written, course notes, and resources. As you get ready for your first interview you will select some pieces from this file to include in your **professional portfolio**. You should carefully select the best work you have done, pieces that best represent the progress you have made and the kind of teacher you are. Wolf (1996) suggests that the portfolio *not* be a scrapbook of eye-catching and heartwarming mementos, nor a bulging steamer trunk of assorted papers and projects. It should be a carefully selected collection of your work samples, along with narrative, reflective essays that convey the essence of your teaching philosophy and practice.

The types of information you may want to include are:

* Facts—Background and experience, including your professional résumé (with identifying information, education, work experience, special skills, and community service), copies of your degrees and credentials.

* Recognitions—Awards; honorary society memberships; letters of commendation from students or parents (from your student teaching placement), professors, and employers; newspaper articles about you.

* Products—Examples of your work, such as lesson plans and student projects, photographs of your student teaching activities, video/audiotape of a lesson (Johnson, Dupuis, Musial, Hall, & Gollnick, 1999).

* Reflections—One of the most important parts of the professional portfolio is your educational philosophy. This is a concise but well-thought out statement of your vision for your classroom environment, your approach to curriculum,

---

professional portfolio—A collection of your work that demonstrates your competencies and accomplishments.

your beliefs about the teacher's role in the lives of children and their families, and the special interests, skills, and strengths that you bring to teaching.

One important activity you can begin now (but that will be an ongoing process throughout your professional preparation) is developing your educational philosophy. Throughout this book, you have been presented with information about child development, stages of learning, and how to effectively teach within those parameters. Different philosophies or approaches have been mentioned. Suggestions have been made for learning and teaching in the various developmental domains. You have researched subjects of interest to you on the Internet, seeking answers to your own questions. You have reflected on this knowledge, measured it against and correlated it with your own opinions and experiences, and thought about how your own teaching will be affected by what you have read and discussed in class. You are forming an educational philosophy, a set of values and beliefs that will frame the kind of teacher you will become. Over the years, you will probably change your approach. You will perfect some things and totally reject others that you find impractical or uncomfortable. Begin to think about your educational philosophy in light of these categories.

Classroom Organization. What kind of a person are you? That will guide how you organize your room. Will it be highly organized with labeled shelves and items grouped together by use and type, or will items appear and move to various parts of the room as they are used and modified? Will you arrange the furnishings in groupings, rows, or right angles to each other? Will you have personal items from your own collections and interests around the room or will the room contain items carefully chosen to correlate with the lesson? Will you develop a daily schedule that you will follow fairly consistently or will you extend some activities and eliminate others as student interest increases or decreases? Will you inform students of your room organization plan or will you plan the environment with the students?

Teacher's Role. How do you see your role in the classroom? Are you the conveyor of important information the students must absorb, and do you measure your success by their ability to repeat concepts in a variety of ways, including on tests? Will you be doing most of the talking, with the children listening, or will the children be talking and moving about the room at will? Will you be giving directions, with the students listening and then acting? Do you see yourself as a facilitator, providing learning experiences and leading the children to actively explore materials, but perhaps not necessarily meeting the lesson's objective? Do you see yourself as an evaluator or as an encourager of self-evaluation? Will you make decisions about the classroom or will you involve the students in decision making (Figure 13–7 on page 506)?

Motivation and Discipline. How will you get children to do what you want them to do? Will you set up a system of rewards? Will you set up a system of punishments or demerits? Will you emphasize them attaining grades or achievements that will make you happy or will you encourage self-motivation, without external reinforcement? Will you stress the necessity of preparing for the next grade, the test, and the future, or will you allow them to choose between working and not working, whatever the natural consequences may be?

Think about these areas as you continue to learn and develop as a teacher. When you are student teaching, you will have the opportunity to try various strategies and see which ones are most comfortable for you. Your educational philosophy will be as personal and individual as your portfolio, but you may want to begin with your own school experiences and how they influenced the kind of teacher you want to be. You may want to include your goal for each student, whether it is learning, getting along with others, or finding acceptance and self-confidence. Along with that, you may want to explain what values you want to instill in your students along with content learning.

Figure 13-7

The professional teacher has many decisions to make.

In the area of curriculum, you could describe your strongest areas and how your interests and strengths will influence your teaching. You should also include a statement about including every child and family and recognizing each child's uniqueness as an asset to be prized.

You can see from these suggestions that much thinking needs to go into this essay. It need not be extremely long or complicated, but as with any document that represents you, it should be articulate, grammatically correct, neatly presented, and defensible. This may provide the basis for the interview questions you will be asked, so be sure it is in your own words so you can explain your positions. Producing this document should encompass all you know and feel about teaching.

You can use your professional portfolio during interviews to enhance your presentation of yourself and your qualifications. You can also use it to anticipate questions about your teaching philosophy and experience and expand upon your answers. The portfolio should give you confidence, for by getting it ready you have already thought out your beliefs and practices.

The portfolio is useful for more than job searches. Many school districts use the professional portfolio as a way to authentically assess a teacher's effectiveness (Doolittle, 1994). The portfolio, constructed with the advice of colleagues, can show a teacher's development and improvement over time. You will use the skills you gain in portfolio preparation again and again.

Orientation and Mentorship. Once they are hired, new teachers like Patrick Peterson, whom we heard from previously, need some help getting started. Patrick had to prepare the classroom and make decisions about what he would need that had been left by the previous teacher, who accumulated teaching materials for 30 years. He sought assistance from a fellow teacher with a few years experience to help him make better decisions about the materials' usefulness. He already sounds like he feels he will be supported in his school. It is important to seek out an experienced and trusted teacher to serve as a **mentor**, someone to whom you can go with large and small questions and for advice and commiseration. While this person does not function as your supervisor, she can be helpful in many matters.

Continuing the Learning Process

You probably have thought to yourself and perhaps even yelled out loud, "I can't wait until I've graduated and I'm done with school!" The pressures of assignments and budgeting time, money, and energy along with schoolwork can be extremely stressful. Learning is hard work. But remember: you are preparing not for a job, nor even a career, but a *profession*. A professional makes a lifelong commitment to her field. You may move from grade to grade, school to school, or even from being a teacher to being an administrator, to being a college professor, but you are embarking on teaching as a profession. A teacher who is not continually learning is not a role model of students' learning. If the teacher is not learning, why should the student?

One of the characteristics of a profession is that it is dynamic. It never stays the same. New theories, technologies, and strategies come along to expand the knowledge base and change professional practice. As new medicines and surgical procedures are perfected, you expect your physician to keep up on them and use them to your benefit. As new laws are passed and precedents set, you expect your attorney to be aware of how they might advance your case. Even as new dry-cleaning procedures, computer programs, or technological advances come along, you expect your service provider to access those things and so you can benefit from their use. The same is true of the teaching profession. You will need to find ways (which may be presented as a mandate) of continuing to learn. The professional associations discussed previously provide one way to keep abreast of issues and new approaches. Most of these associations publish journals, as well as books, that offer the very latest information in the field.

Informal Professional Development. You can learn independently through reading and your own research. As you teach, you will find that there are certain areas or subjects about which you need to know more. Reading other teachers' experiences can give you insight or comfort. Professional journals and books, as well as the Internet, can provide you with resources. As you discuss your teaching with colleagues in the lunch room, at the bus stop, or in the parking lot, learning opportunities abound. Just relating an incident to another teacher can give you new ideas about how to interpret or approach it differently next time. On-line discussions through listserves can expand your ideas and serve as a forum for your questions and ideas. Writing in a diary or journal can be an emotional outlet for your own feelings of anxiety, anger, frustration, and, hopefully, happiness with victories. These reflections are milestones as you look back at them over the years and see how far you have come.

Formal Professional Development. Advancing in a profession usually means pursuing further degrees or at least continuing with formalized learning such as college courses, extended workshop sessions, or focused professional conferences.

mentor—An experienced and trusted fellow teacher who assists a new teacher with advice.

Public school districts offer in-service training on subjects pertinent to the teachers of that district. Other community offerings include workshops or speakers sponsored by the the local chapters of professional organizations (Figure 13–8). The Internet offers a range of new possibilities for learning. On-line courses can link you to the leading authorities of the day and colleagues around the world in a community of learning that is not bound by time and place. Distance education offers the possibility of lifelong learning.

Service to the Profession. Teaching others is another way to learn. Throughout this book, we have presented the idea that learning and teaching go hand in hand. You may be asked to present a workshop or make a conference presentation on a specific topic. When you prepare a presentation, you investigate, plan, research, agonize over presentation style and order, prepare meaningful handouts, and think about how to actively engage the audience. The process of getting ready to make a presentation teaches you about the subject and about yourself. The more you offer to teach your peers, the more you will learn yourself. One day, you may write articles and books and teach college courses yourself. No one ever learns the lesson as well as the teacher. Another role you may take on later in your career is that of mentor. If you had the good fortune to have a mentor yourself, you have a role model and proof of the important role a mentor can play in a new teacher's career.

Membership in local professional organizations can also provide you with learning opportunities when the organization offers professional development opportunities for its members. Newsletters and journals published by professional organizations keep you current on issues and trends in the field. Participating as a leader in professional organizations is another way to develop professionally. You can learn parliamentary procedure by participating in board meetings, network with other leaders in the community, and learn new skills. Public speaking, that dreaded activity, can be cultivated in the relative

Figure 13–8

The professional teacher shares knowledge and experiences with colleagues.

safety of a small group of colleagues in a professional organization. These are important ways to serve the profession while learning and developing yourself.

SUMMARY

We have been on a journey with you, introducing you to famous contributors to the field of education, as well as teachers, parents, and children who had words of advice or stories for you. We have given you glimpses into knowledge areas you will examine much more closely in the next few years of preparation. We have suggested exercises to strengthen your learning and guided searches of the Web, as well as exploration of your own perceptions and thinking. All through the journey, we have emphasized learning before teaching, so let us remind you one more time to *learn* about your students before you begin teaching them. If you do that, they will learn what you teach.

We hope that someday you receive a tribute like the one this first grader wrote as he nominated his kindergarten teacher for " a teacher of the month" award (Figure 13–9).

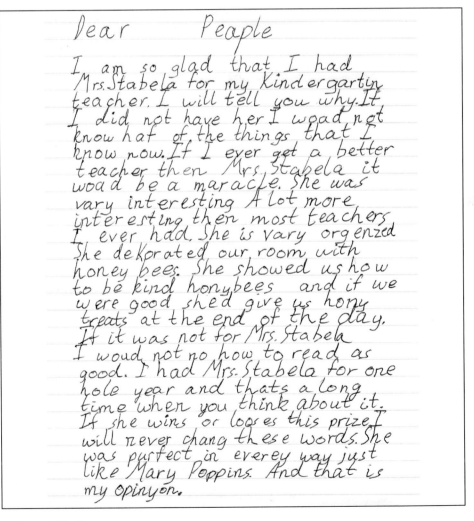

Dear Peaple

I am so glad that I had Mrs. Stabela for my Kindergartin teacher. I will tell you why. It I did not have her I woad not know haf of the things that I know now. If I ever get a better teacher then Mrs. Stabela it woad be a maracle. She was vary interesting A lot more interesting then most teachers I ever had. She is vary orgenzed She dekprated our room with honey bees. She showed us how to be kind honybees and if we were good shed give us hony treats at the end of the day. If it was not for Mrs. Stabela I woud not no how to read as good. I had Mrs. Stabela for one hole year and thats a long time when you think about it. If she wins or looses this prize I will never chang these words. She was purfect in everey way just like Mary Poppins. And that is my opinyon.

Figure 13–9

A student's tribute to his teacher.

KEY TERMS

professional

advocate

professional portfolio

mentor

REVIEW ACTIVITIES

Exercises to Strengthen Learning

1. Infants—Child care teachers are becoming more professionalized. Investigate what the qualifications are in your state for the teachers/caregivers of our very youngest children. Because they do not have to have advanced degrees, these teachers are considered paraprofessionals. Interview three teachers of infants and ask them what they think about professionalizing the field of child care and the advantages of and barriers to that change. How is their job the same or different from the fifth-grade teacher, other than the ages of the children they teach?

2. Toddlers—Many early childhood teachers belong to professional associations. Gather information on three associations to determine what they offer their members, how much the membership costs, and what the association offers in the way of professional development.

3. Preschoolers—Head Start has a strong advocacy role for teachers and family workers. Find out in what way Head Start is involved in advocacy.

4. Primary age—Primary age children often need help getting organized and taking care of things like lunch money, library books, and so on. Observe two classrooms to see what systems the teachers use to help the children learn these organizational and management skills, and then watch to see those skills modeled by the teacher.

5. Elementary age—Teachers who have been in the profession for many years have a wealth of good advice. Seek out some veteran teachers and ask how their teaching has changed over the years. What advice would they give you as you seek your first teaching position? What should you look for in a school that would make it a good place to work?

Internet Quest

1. This chapter contains many Web site addresses for professional associations. Select three that interest you and find out more about them.

2. Search for information on how many teachers your state is expected to need in the next five years.

3. Search for information on issues that advocacy groups are involved in to influence policy. Where do you stand on these issues?

Reflective Journal

In this chapter, I learned the following about the profession of teaching . . .

Use your prior Reflective Journal entries to begin writing your educational philosophy for your professional portfolio.

REFERENCES

American Federation of Teachers (AFT). (1976). *Code of ethics, American Federation of Teachers, AFL-CIO.* Washington, DC: Author.

Argyris, C., & Schon, D. A. (1974). *Theory in practice.* San Francisco, CA: Jossey-Bass.

Brophy, J. E., & Good, T. L. (1974). *Teacher-student relationships: Causes and consequences.* New York: Holt, Rinehart & Winston.

Darling-Hammond, L. (1996, November). What matters most: A competent teacher for every child. *Phi Delta Kappan,* 193–200.

Darling-Hammond, L., & Sykes, G. (Eds.). (1999). *Teaching as the learning profession: Handbook of policy and practice.* San Francisco, CA: Jossey-Bass.

Doolittle, P. (1994). Teacher portfolio assessment. *ERIC/AE Digest.* (ERIC Document Reproduction Service No. ED 385 608)

Educational Testing Service. (1999). *The Praxis Series.* Retrieved March 16, 2001, from the World Wide Web: <http://www.ets.org>.

Feeney, S., & Freeman, N. K. (1999). *Ethics and the early childhood educator: Using the NAEYC code.* Washington, DC: National Association for the Education of Young Children.

Howsam, R. B., Corrigan, D. C., Denemark, G. W., & Nash, R. J. (1976). *Educating a profession.* Washington, DC: American Association of Colleges for Teacher Education.

Ingersoll, R. M. (1995). *Schools and staffing survey: Teacher supply, teacher qualifications and teacher turnover, 1990–1991* (p. 28). Washington, DC: National Center for Educational Statistics.

Johnson, J. A., Dupuis, V. L., Musial, D., Hall, G. E., & Gollnick, D. M. (1999). *Introduction to the foundations of American education.* Boston: Allyn and Bacon.

National Association for the Education of Young Children (NAEYC). (1998). *The National Association for the Education of Young Children code of ethical conduct.* Washington, DC: Author.

National Commission on Teaching and America's Future. (1996). *What matters most: Teaching for America's future.* New York: Author.

National Education Association (NEA). (1975). *Code of ethics, National Education Association.* Washington, DC: Author.

Oakes, J. (1990). *Multiplying inequalities; The effects of race, social class, and tracking on opportunities to learn mathematics and science.* Santa Monica, CA: RAND Corporation.

Rose, L. C., & Gallup, A. M. (1998, September). The 30th annual Phi Delta Kappa/Gallup poll of the public's attitudes toward the public schools. *Phi Delta Kappan, 80,* 41–44.

Saracho, O. N., & Spodek, B. (1993). Professionalism and the preparation of early childhood education practitioners. *Early Child Development and Care, 89,* 1–17.

Schein, E. H. (1972). *Professional education.* New York: McGraw-Hill.

Wolf, K. (1996). Developing an effective teaching portfolio. *Education Leadership, 53*(6), 34–37.

For additional learning and teaching resources, visit our Web site at www.EarlyChildEd.delmar.com.

RELATED CAREERS

Figure 13–10

Related careers.

Appendix A

Developmental Profiles

Child's Name _____ Age _____

Observer _____ Date _____

DEVELOPMENTAL CHECKLIST

BY 12 MONTHS, does the child:	Yes	No	Sometimes
Walk with assistance?			
Roll ball in imitation of adult?			
Pick up objects with thumb and forefinger?			
Transfer objects from one hand to other?			
Pick up dropped toys?			
Look directly at adult's face?			
Imitate gestures: peek-a-boo, bye-bye, pat-a-cake?			
Find object hidden under cup?			
Feed self crackers (munching, not sucking, on them)?			
Hold cup with two hands and drink with assistance?			
Smile spontaneously?			
Pay attention to own name?			
Respond to "no"?			
Respond differently to strangers and familiar persons?			
Respond differently to sounds: vacuum, phone, door?			
Look at person who speaks to him or her?			
Respond to simple directions accompanied by gestures?			
Make several consonant-vowel combination sounds?			
Vocalize back to person talking to him or her?			
Use intonation patterns that sound like scolding, asking, exclaiming?			
Say "da-da" or "ma-ma"?			

(From Allen, K. E., & Marotz, L. R. [1999]. *Developmental profiles: Pre-birth through eight* [3rd ed.]. Albany, NY: Delmar.)

Child's Name _____ Age _____

Observer _____ Date _____

DEVELOPMENTAL CHECKLIST

BY TWO YEARS, does the child:	Yes	No	Sometimes
Walk alone?			
Bend over and pick up toy without falling over?			
Seat self in child-size chair?			
Walk up and down stairs with assistance?			
Place several rings on stick?			
Place five pegs in pegboard?			
Turn pages two or three at time?			
Scribble?			
Follow one-step direction involving something familiar: "Give me ___." "Show me ___." "Get a ___?"			
Match familiar objects?			
Use spoon with some spilling?			
Drink from cup holding it with one hand, unassisted?			
Chew food?			
Take off coat, shoe, sock?			
Zip and unzip large zipper?			
Recognize self in mirror or picture?			
Refer to self by name?			
Imitate adult behaviors in play—for example, feed "baby"?			
Help put things away?			
Respond to specific words by showing what was named: toy, pet, family member?			
Ask for desired items by name: (cookie)?			
Answer with name of object when asked "What's that"?			
Make some two-word statements: "Daddy bye-bye"?			

(From Allen & Marotz, 1999)

Child's Name _____ Age _____

Observer _____ Date _____

DEVELOPMENTAL CHECKLIST

BY THREE YEARS, does the child:	Yes	No	Sometimes
Run well in forward direction?			
Jump in place, two feet together?			
Walk on tiptoe?			
Throw ball (but without direction or aim)?			
Kick ball forward?			
String four large beads?			
Turn pages in book singly?			
Hold crayon: imitate circular, vertical, horizontal strokes?			
Match shapes?			
Demonstrate number concepts of one and two? (Can select one or two; can tell if one or two objects.)			
Use spoon without spilling?			
Drink from straw?			
Put on and take off coat?			
Wash and dry hands with some assistance?			
Watch other children; play near them; sometimes join in their play?			
Defend own possessions?			
Use symbols in play—for example, tin pan on head becomes helmet and crate becomes space ship?			
Respond to "Put ___ in the box," "Take the ___ out of the box"?			
Select correct item on request: big vs. little; one vs. two?			
Identify objects by their use: show own shoe when asked, "What do you wear on your feet?"			
Ask questions?			
Talk about something with functional phrases that carry meaning: "Daddy go airplane," "Me hungry now"?			

(From Allen & Marotz, 1999)

Child's Name _____ Age _____

Observer _____ Date _____

DEVELOPMENTAL CHECKLIST

BY FOUR YEARS, does the child:	Yes	No	Sometimes
Walk on line?			
Balance on one foot briefly?			
Hop on one foot?			
Jump over object six inches high and land on both feet together?			
Throw ball with direction?			
Copy circles and crosses?			
Match six colors?			
Count to five?			
Pour well from pitcher?			
Spread butter, jam with knife?			
Button, unbutton large buttons?			
Know own sex, age, last name?			
Use toilet independently and reliably?			
Wash and dry hands unassisted?			
Listen to stories for at least five minutes?			
Draw head of person and at least one other body part?			
Play with other children?			
Share, take turns (with some assistance)?			
Engage in dramatic and pretend play?			
Respond appropriately to "Put it beside ___," "Put it under ___"?			
Respond to two-step directions: "Give me the sweater and put the shoe on the floor"?			
Respond by selecting correct object—for example, hard vs. soft object?			
Answer "if," "what," and "when" questions?			
Answer questions about function: "What are books for"?			

(From Allen & Marotz, 1999)

Child's Name _____ Age _____

Observer _____ Date _____

DEVELOPMENTAL CHECKLIST

BY FIVE YEARS, does the child:	Yes	No	Sometimes
Walk backward, heel to toe?			
Walk up and down stairs, alternating feet?			
Cut on line?			
Print some letters?			
Point to and name three shapes?			
Group common related objects: shoe, sock, and foot: apple, orange, and plum?			
Demonstrate number concepts to four or five?			
Cut food with knife: celery, sandwich?			
Lace shoes?			
Read from story picture book–in other words, tell story by looking at pictures?			
Draw person with three to six body parts?			
Play and interact with other children; engage in dramatic play that is close to reality?			
Build complex structures with blocks or other building materials?			
Respond to simple three-step directions: "Give me pencil, put book on table, and hold comb in your hand"?			
Respond correctly when asked to show penny, nickel, and dime?			
Ask "How" questions?			
Respond verbally to "Hi" and "How are you"?			
Tell about event using past and future tenses?			
Use conjunctions to string words and phrases together– for example, "I saw a bear and a zebra and a giraffe at the zoo"?			

(From Allen & Marotz, 1999)

Child's Name _____ Age _____

Observer _____ Date _____

DEVELOPMENTAL CHECKLIST

BY SIX YEARS, does the child:	Yes	No	Sometimes
Walk across balance beam?			
Skip with alternating feet?			
Hop for several seconds on one foot?			
Cut out simple shapes?			
Copy own first name?			
Show well-established handedness; demonstrate consistent right or left handedness?			
Sort objects on one or more dimensions: color, shape, or function?			
Name most letters and numerals?			
Count by rote to 10; know what number comes next?			
Dress self completely; tie bows?			
Brush teeth unassisted?			
Have some concept of clock time in relation to daily schedule?			
Cross street safely?			
Draw person with head, trunk, legs, arms, and features; often add clothing details?			
Play simple board games?			
Engage in cooperative play with other children involving group decisions, role assignments, rule observance?			
Use construction toys, such as Legos®, blocks, to make recognizable structures?			
Do 15-piece puzzles?			
Use grammatical structures: pronouns, plurals, verb tenses, conjunctions?			
Use complex sentences; carry on conversations?			

(From Allen & Marotz, 1999)

Child's Name _____ Age _____

Observer _____ Date _____

DEVELOPMENTAL CHECKLIST

BY SEVEN YEARS, does the child:	Yes	No	Sometimes
Concentrate on completing puzzles and board games?			
Ask many questions?			
Use correct verb tenses, word order, and sentence structure in conversation?			
Correctly identify right and left hands?			
Make friends easily?			
Show some control of anger, using words instead of physical aggression?			
Participate in play that requires teamwork and rule observance?			
Seek adult approval for efforts?			
Enjoy reading and being read to?			
Use pencil to write words and numbers?			
Sleep undisturbed through night?			
Catch tennis ball, walk across balance beam, hit ball with bat?			
Plan and carry out simple projects with minimal adult help?			
Tie own shoes?			
Draw pictures with greater detail and sense of proportion?			
Care for own personal needs with some adult supervision? Wash hands? Brush teeth? Use toilet? Dress self?			
Show some understanding of cause-and-effect concepts?			

(From Allen & Marotz, 1999)

Child's Name _____ Age _____

Observer _____ Date _____

DEVELOPMENTAL CHECKLIST

BY EIGHT AND NINE YEARS, does the child:	Yes	No	Sometimes
Have energy to play, continuing growth, few illnesses?			
Use pencil in deliberate and controlled manner?			
Express relatively complex thoughts in clear and logical fashion?			
Carry out multiple (four to five)-step instructions?			
Become less easily frustrated with own performance?			
Interact and play cooperatively with other children?			
Show interest in creative expression—telling stories, jokes, writing, drawing, singing?			
Use eating utensils with ease?			
Have good appetite? Show interest in trying new foods?			
Know how to tell time?			
Have control of bowel and bladder functions?			
Participate in some group activities—games, sports, plays?			
Want to go to school? Seem disappointed if must miss day?			
Demonstrate beginning skills in reading, writing, and math?			
Accept responsibility and complete work independently?			
Handle stressful situations without becoming overly upset?			

(From Allen & Marotz, 1999)

GROWTH AND DEVELOPMENT DURING SCHOOL-AGE YEARS (SIX TO TWELVE YEARS)

Gross Motor

Increasing motor skills for participation in games and working with others
* can use rollerblades or ice skates
* able to ride two-wheeler
* play games such as baseball

Fine Motor

Increasing fine motor skills
* can put models together
* likes crafts
* able to play musical instrument

Cognitive

Increasing cognitive skills for participation in games and working with others
* master concepts of time, conservation, and reversibility
* enjoys board games and plays cards

Language

Mastering oral and written communication skills
* vocabulary increases
* language abilities continue to develop

Sensory

Able to concentrate for long periods of time

Socioemotional

Learning rules and norms of a widening social, religious, and cultural environment
* become more active, cooperative, and responsible family member
* win approval from peers and adults
* obtain place in peer group
* build sense of industry, accomplishment, self-assurance, and self-esteem.
* develop positive self concept
* exchange affection with family and friends without seeking an immediate feedback
* adapt moral standards for behavior

(Adapted from Estes, M. E. Z. [1998]. *Health and physical examination.* Albany, NY: Delmar.)

Appendix B

Evaluation of Infant/ Toddler Environment

How can you tell if your baby's home base is a place where infants or toddlers learn what they need to learn?

Here's what infants or toddlers might ask if they could choose their own setting for maximum learning:

Will I be held when I want or need to be held?

How many places are there where I can:
pull myself up? ___   reach? ___   kick? ___   jump? ___
climb up? ___   climb in? ___   climb over? ___   climb on? ___
go through? ___   go under? ___   go in and out? ___   see myself? ___

How many different places are there for me "to be" and explore—places that feel different because of light, texture, sound, smell, enclosure, and sight lines?

When you put me in an infant swing or bounce chair, am I only there for a short time?

Can I get out when I want to get out?

How often do I go out of the room?

How often do I go outside?

How often do I go for stroller or cart rides?

How often can I get out of the stroller/cart and walk/crawl around?

How often do I get to play with messy things such as water, sand, dough, paint?

Are there duplicates and a variety of toys?

Are there duplicates and a variety of "stuff," and real-life objects I can reach?

What is there to: transport? _____   push/pull? _____

collect/dump? _____   throw? _____

Do I get to feed myself as soon as I can hold a spoon, bottle, or cup?

Do I have to wait to be changed or use the toilet?

When I talk my talk, will someone listen and talk back?

When you talk to me, will you look at me and use words I am learning to understand?

Will someone read to me, a lot?

Will you make me feel special and appreciate me for who I am, the way I am today?

(Reproduced by permission. *Prime Times: A Handbook for Excellence in Infant and Toddler Care* © 1996. Redleaf Press. St. Paul, Minnesota.)

Appendix C

Playground Rating System
(Ages Three–Eight)

Instructions:

Rate each item on a scale from 0–5. High scores possible are: Section I—100 points, Section II—50 points, and Section III—50 points, for a possible grand total of 200 points. Divide the grand total score by two to obtain a final rating.

Section I. What does the playground contain?

Rate each item for degree of existence and function on a scale of 0–5. 0 = not existent; 1 = some elements exist but not functional; 2 = poor; 3 = average; 4 = good; 5 = all elements exist and function.

___ 1. A hard-surfaced area with space for games and a network of paths for wheeled toys.

___ 2. Sand and sand play equipment.

___ 3. Dramatic play structures (playhouse, car, or boat with complementary equipment, such as adjacent sand, water, or housekeeping equipment).

___ 4. A superstructure with room for many children at a time and with a variety of challenges and exercise options (entries, exits, and levels).

___ 5. Mound(s) of earth for climbing and digging.

___ 6. Trees and natural areas for shade, nature study, and play.

___ 7. Zoning to provide continuous challenge; linkage of areas, functional physical boundaries, vertical and horizontal treatment (hills and valleys).

___ 8. Water play areas, with fountains, pools, and sprinklers.

___ 9. Construction area with junk materials such as tires, crates, planks, boards, bricks, and nails; tools should be provided and demolition and construction allowed.

___ 10. An old (or built) vehicle, airplane, boat, car that has been made safe, but not stripped of its play value (should be changed or relocated after a period of time to renew interest).

___ 11. Equipment for active play: a slide with a large platform at the top (slide may be built into side of hill); swings that can be used safely in a variety of ways (soft material for seats); climbing trees (horizontally positioned mature dead trees); climbing nets.

___ 12. A large soft area (grass, bark mulch, etc.) for organized games.

___ 13. Small semiprivate spaces at the child's own scale: tunnels, niches, playhouses, hiding places.

___ 14. Fences, gates, walls, and windows that provide security for young children and are adaptable for learning/play.

___ 15. A garden and flowers located so they are protected from play, but with easy access for children to tend them. Gardening tools available.

___ 16. Provisions for the housing of pets. Pets and supplies available.

___ 17. A transitional space from outdoors to indoors. This could be a covered play area immediately adjoining the playroom that protects children from the sun and rain and extends indoor activities to the outside.

___ 18. Adequate protected storage for outdoor play equipment, tools for construction and garden areas, and maintenance tools. Storage can be separate: wheeled toys stored near the wheeled vehicle track; sand equipment near

(From Frost, J. [1990]. *Play and playscapes*. Albany, NY: Delmar.)

the sand enclosure; tools near the construction area. Storage can be in separate structures next to the building or fence. Storage should help children pick up and put equipment away at the end of each play period.

____ 19. Easy access from outdoor play areas to coats, toilets, and drinking fountains. Shaded areas and benches for adults and children to sit on within the outdoor play area.

____ 20. Tables and support materials for group activities (art, reading, etc.).

Section II. Is the playground in good repair and relatively safe?

Rate each item for condition and safety on a scale of 0–5. 0 = not existent; 1 = exists but extremely hazardous; 2 = poor; 3 = fair; 4 = good; 5 = excellent condition and relatively safe, yet presents challenge.

____ 1. A protective fence (with lockable gates) next to hazardous areas (streets, deep ditches, water, etc.).

____ 2. Eight to 10 inches of noncompacted sand, wood mulch (or equivalent) under all climbing and moving equipment, extending through fall zones and secured by retaining wall.

____ 3. Size of equipment appropriate to age group served. Climbing heights limited to six to seven feet.

____ 4. Area free of litter (e.g., broken glass, rocks), electrical hazards, high-voltage power lines, sanitary hazards.

____ 5. Moving parts free of defects (e.g., no pinch and crush points, bearings not excessively worn).

____ 6. Equipment free of sharp edges, protruding elements, broken parts, toxic substances, bare metal exposed to sun.

____ 7. Swing seats constructed of soft or lightweight material (e.g., rubber, canvas).

____ 8. All safety equipment in good repair (e.g., guardrails, signs, padded areas, protective covers).

____ 9. No openings that can entrap a child's head (approximately 3½–9 inches). Adequate space between equipment.

____ 10. Equipment structurally sound. No bending, warping, breaking, sinking, etc. Heavy fixed and moving equipment secured in ground and concrete footings recessed in ground. Check for underground rotting, rusting, termites in support members.

Section III. What should the playground do?

Rate each item for degree and quality on a scale of 0–5. 0 = nonexistent; 1 = some evidence but virtually nonexistent; 2 = poor; 3 = fair; 4 = good; 5 = excellent. Use the space provided for comments.

____ 1. Encourages Play:

Inviting, easy access

Open, flowing, and relaxed space

Clear movement from indoors to outdoors

Appropriate equipment for the age group(s)

(From Frost, 1990)

   ___   **2.** Stimulates the Child's Senses:

Changes and contrasts in scale, light, texture, and color

Flexible equipment

Diverse experiences

   ___   **3.** Nurtures the Child's Curiosity

Equipment that the child can change

Materials for experiments and construction

Plants and animals

   ___   **4.** Supports the Child's Basic Social and Physical Needs:

Comfortable for the child

Scaled to the child

Physically challenging

   ___   **5.** Allows Interaction Between the Child and the Resources:

Systematic storage that defines routines

Semi-enclosed spaces to read, work a puzzle, or be alone

   ___   **6.** Allows Interaction Between the Child and Other Children:

Variety of spaces

Adequate space to avoid conflicts

Equipment that invites socialization

   ___   **7.** Allows Interaction Between the Child and Adults:

Easy maintenance

Adequate and convenient storage

Organization of spaces to allow general supervision

Rest areas for adults and children

   ___   **8.** Complements the Cognitive Forms of Play Engaged in by the Child:

Functional, exercise, gross-motor, active

Constructive, building, creating

Dramatic, pretend, make-believe

Organized games, games with rules

   ___   **9.** Complements the Social Forms of Play Engaged in by the Child:

Solitary, private, meditative

Parallel, side-by-side

Cooperative interrelationships

   ___   **10.** Promotes Social and Intellectual Development:

Provides graduated challenge

Integrates indoor/outdoor activities

Involves adults in children's play

Regular adult-child planning

The play environment is dynamic—continuously changing

(From Frost, 1990)

Appendix D

Early Childhood Environment Rating Scale

The following two excerpts from the Early Childhood Environment Rating Scale (ECERS) (used with permission) show rating scales that measure the environment of the early childhood classroom for infants/toddlers and for preschoolers. You will note the range from an unacceptable to a fully met criterion. The full ECERS measure other aspects such as: space and furnishings, personal care routines, language-reasoning, activities, interaction, program structure, and parents and staff. The ECERS scoring system can be used confirm areas that are excellent and to indicate areas that need improvement.

Inadequate		Minimal		Good		Excellent
1	2	3	4	5	6	7

4. Room arrangement for play

Inadequate	Minimal	Good	Excellent
1.1 No interest centers* defined	3.1 At least two interest centers defined.	5.1 At least three interest centers defined and conveniently equipped (Ex.: water provided near art area; shelving adequate for blocks and manipulatives).	7.1 At least five different interest centers provide a variety of learning experiences.
1.2 Visual supervision of play area is difficult.	3.2 Visual supervision of play area is not difficult.	5.2 Quiet and active centers placed so as not to interfere with each other (Ex.: reading or listening area separated from blocks or housekeeping).	7.2 Centers are organized for independent use by children (Ex.: labeled open shelves; labeled containers for toys; open shelves are not over-crowded; play space near toy storage).
	3.3 Sufficient space for several activities to go on at once (Ex.: floor space for blocks, table space for manipulatives, easel for art).	5.3 Space is arranged so most activities are not interrupted (Ex.: shelves placed so children walk around, not through, activities; furniture placement discourages rough play or running).	7.3 Additional materials available to add to or change centers.
	3.4 Most spaces for play are accessible for children with disabilities who are enrolled in the group. *NA permitted.*		

Note for clarification

*An interest center is an area where materials, organized by type, are stored so they are accessible to children and appropriate furnished play space is provided for children to participate in a particular kind of play. Examples of interest centers include art, blocks, dramatic play, reading, nature/science, and manipulatives/fine motor.

Question

(7.3) Are there any additional materials available to add to the interest centers?

Inadequate		Minimal		Good		Excellent
1	2	3	4	5	6	7

4. Room arrangement

—Inadequate* space used for either routines or play. —Arrangement of room makes it impossible to see all children at all times (Ex.: children hidden from caregiver by high furnishings; diapering table placed so caregiver unable to see other children while changing diapers).		—Routine furnishings placed to provide space for play. —Open area used for crawling, walking, and play. —Arrangement of room makes it possible for caregiver to see all children at a glance. —Sufficient space used for play so children are not crowded.		—Routine care areas conveniently arranged (Ex.: cribs placed for easy access, diapering supplies at hand, hot running water available where needed, feeding tables on easy-to-clean floor). —Areas for quiet and active play separated (Ex.: by low shelves). —Young infants given space and materials to explore while protected from more mobile children.		—Variety of learning experiences available in both routine and play areas (Ex.: mobiles over diapering table changed often, many age-appropriate toys in play areas). —Materials with similar use are placed together to make interest areas with suitable play space (Ex.: infants: rattle or soft toy area; toddlers: books, music, push toys, manipulative toys, gross motor area). —Traffic patterns do not interfere with activities.

5. Display for children

—No pictures or other materials displayed.		—Some colorful pictures or other materials displayed (Ex.: mobiles, photos). —Content of display is not frightening to young children (Ex.: no witches, animals with frightening faces).		—Many colorful, simple photographs or pictures displayed where children can easily see them, some within easy reach (Ex.: in feeding area, near cribs, on floor, or low in crawling areas). —Mobiles or other colorful hanging objects for children to look at. —Caregiver talks to children about displayed materials (Ex.: responds to child's interest in picture; points out displayed items).		—Scribble pictures done by toddlers displayed in toddler rooms. —Photographs of children in group, their families, pets, or other familiar faces displayed on child's-eye level. —Pictures protected from being torn (Ex.: clear plastic over pictures). —Pictures and mobiles changed periodically.

(Reprinted by permission of the publisher from Harms, Thelma, *Early Childhood Environment Rating Scale.* (New York: Teachers College Press. © 1990 by Teachers College, Columbia University. All rights reserved, p. 12.)

Appendix E

Frost-Wortham Developmental Checklist

MOTOR DEVELOPMENT: PRESCHOOL (FINE MOVEMENT)

Level III (approx. age three)	Introduced	Progress	Mastery
1. Places small pegs in pegboards	___	___	___
2. Holds a paintbrush or pencil with the whole hand	___	___	___
3. Eats with a spoon	___	___	___
4. Buttons large buttons on his or her own clothes	___	___	___
5. Puts on coat unassisted	___	___	___
6. Strings bead with ease	___	___	___
7. Hammers a pound toy with accuracy	___	___	___
8. Works a three- or four-piece puzzle	___	___	___

Level IV (approx. age four)	Introduced	Progress	Mastery
1. Pounds and rolls clay	___	___	___
2. Puts together a five-piece puzzle	___	___	___
3. Forms a pegboard design	___	___	___
4. Cuts with scissors haltingly and pastes	___	___	___
5. Eats with a fork correctly	___	___	___
6. Holds a cup with one hand	___	___	___
7. Puts a coat on a hanger or hook	___	___	___
8. Manipulates large crayons and brushes	___	___	___
9. Buttons buttons and zips zippers haltingly			

Level V (approx. age five)	Introduced	Progress	Mastery
1. Cuts and pastes creative designs	___	___	___
2. Forms a variety of pegboard designs	___	___	___
3. Buttons buttons, zips zippers, and ties shoes	___	___	___
4. Creates recognizable objects with clay	___	___	___
5. Uses the toilet independently	___	___	___
6. Eats independently with a knife and fork	___	___	___
7. Dresses and undresses independently	___	___	___
8. Holds and manipulates pencils, crayons, and brushes of various sizes	___	___	___
9. Combs and brushes hair	___	___	___
10. Works a 12-piece puzzle	___	___	___

(From Frost, J. [1990]. *Play and playscapes.* Albany, NY: Delmar.)

SOCIAL PLAY AND SOCIALIZING: PRESCHOOL

	Introduced	Progress	Mastery
Level III (approx. age three)			
1. Engages in independent play	———	———	———
2. Engages in parallel play	———	———	———
3. Plays briefly with peers	———	———	———
4. Recognizes the needs of others	———	———	———
5. Shows sympathy for othres	———	———	———
6. Attends to an activity for 10 to 15 minutes	———	———	———
7. Sings simple songs	———	———	———
Level IV (approx. age four)			
1. Leaves mother readily	———	———	———
2. Converses with other children	———	———	———
3. Converses with adults	———	———	———
4. Plays with peers	———	———	———
5. Cooperates in classroom routines	———	———	———
6. Takes turns and shares	———	———	———
7. Replaces materials after use	———	———	———
8. Takes care of personal belongings	———	———	———
9. Respects the property of others	———	———	———
10. Attends to an activity for 15 to 20 minutes	———	———	———
11. Engages in group activities	———	———	———
12. Sings with a group	———	———	———
13. Is sensitive to praise and criticism	———	———	———
Level V (approx. age five)			
1. Completes most self-initiated projects	———	———	———
2. Works and plays with limited supervision	———	———	———
3. Engages in cooperative play	———	———	———
4. Listens while peers speak	———	———	———
5. Follows multiple and delayed directions	———	———	———
6. Carries out special responsibilities (for example, feeding animals)	———	———	———
7. Listens and follows the suggestions of adults	———	———	———
8. Enjoys talking with adults	———	———	———
9. Can sustain an attention span for a variety of duties	———	———	———
10. Evaluates his or her work and suggests improvements	———	———	———

(From Frost, 1990)

Glossary

accommodation—Modification of prior information forming a changed schema (Ch. 6).

acculturation stress—Emotional disturbance caused by attempts to adapt to a different culture, sometimes called culture shock (Ch. 11).

advocate—One who pleads the cause of another (Ch. 13).

affect—Feelings or emotions expressed or observed; emotional responses (Ch. 11).

assimilation—Absorption of new information, forming expanded schema (Ch. 6).

association—Matching new information with what is already known (Ch. 6).

asthma—Condition that causes breathing difficulty because of obstructions in airways of the lungs. The U.S. Department of Education recognizes asthma as a disability when it affects a child's education (Ch. 5).

attachment—Enduring emotional connection between people that produces desire for contact, as well as distress during separation (Ch. 11).

autonomy versus shame and doubt—Erikson's second stage of emotional development, which generally takes place in a child's second year with the conflict between independence and misgivings about self-worth (Ch. 11).

axon—Long process of a neuron that transmits impulses away from the cell body to other neurons. Usually one axon per neuron; can subdivide to connect with many dendrites (Ch. 6).

behaviorism—The theory that views learning as the most important aspect of development and states that behavior can be objectively measured through stimulus-response relationships (Ch. 1).

bell curve—A common type of bell-shaped graph that displays the normal distribution of statistical frequencies of items, features, or attributes with the average, and usually majority, feature falling most frequently in the median, and with lesser/greater values/frequencies displayed either side of normal (Ch. 1).

bias—Actions of discrimination against a person or group based on prejudice (Ch. 1).

centrate—Cognitive ability to take more than one attribute into consideration when making judgments on volume, length, and weight (Ch. 9).

cephalocaudal—Progression of muscle control from head to feet (Ch. 5).

classification—Mentally arranging or matching similar objects or ideas into groups (Ch. 9).

conservation—Understanding that the quantity or volume of an object or substance remains the same even though its appearance has been altered in shape or arrangement (Ch. 9).

constructivism—Interplay between biological development and experiences in which a person constructs knowledge unique to that individual (Ch. 6).

convergent thinking—Search through present knowledge to converge or match one correct answer (Ch. 10).

core emotions—Inborn emotional responses of joy, anger, sadness, and fear from which all other emotional configurations are derived (Ch. 11).

correspondence—Clearly defined relationship between two members of a set or different sets (Ch. 9).

creativity—Ability to originate something new and appropriate by looking beyond common constraints to create something novel and valuable over time (Ch. 10).

cross-generational learning—Knowledge that is transferred form the older generation to a younger one (Ch. 3).

cultural competence—Working knowledge of the values, beliefs, customs, food, and language of various cultures (Ch. 1).

culture—Patterns, beliefs, thoughts, manners, tastes that are common to a group of people and passed on from generation to generation (Ch. 2).

curriculum—Planned activities for learning a skill or concept (Preface).

deductive reasoning—Coming to a conclusion by applying a general principle to a specific fact. For example: Sugar tastes good. Cake has a lot of sugar in it. Cake will taste good (Ch. 3).

dendrites—Strand-like fibers emanating from the neuron, the receptor sites for axons (Ch. 6).

development—Qualitative changes in physical, cognitive, social, emotional, creative, and language domains that proceed from simple to complex according to a universal systematic progression (Ch. 5).

development—Progressive physical, psychological, and social changes in human beings (Preface, Ch. 5).

disequillibrium—When new information or knowledge is in conflict with present information or knowledge (Ch. 9).

divergent thinking—Search for multiple ideas or solutions to a problem (Ch. 10).

ecology—Biological term referring to the mutual relations between organisms and their environment (Ch. 1).

egocentrism—Interpretation from an individual's own point of view; the inability to mentally place oneself in another's position physically or emotionally (Ch. 6).

emergent literacy—Early attempts at language, reading, and writing that are the foundation for later more conventional language, reading, and writing skills (Ch. 8).

emotion—Strong feelings, positive or negative, accompanied by physiological changes in heartbeat and respiration (Ch. 11).

equilibrium—Process of new information finding order and structure with prior information. When new information is not linked to prior information, the individual is in a state of disequilibrium (Ch. 6).

Eurocentrism—Focus of beliefs and concerns relevant to Western societies (Ch. 1).

exosystems—Those spheres of influence that indirectly affect individuals over which they have little or no control (Ch. 1).

failure to thrive—Undernutrition that seriously affects physical growth and development, as well as emotional and cognitive development (Ch. 5).

functional illiteracy—Inability to use reading, speaking, writing, and computational skills in everyday life situations (Ch. 8).

gender identity—Understanding by a person that he or she is either a boy or a girl; usually develops by about three years of age (Ch. 11).

gender-role stereotypes—Rigid notions of male and female behavior (Ch. 11).

gifted—Normally defined in very high IQ scores, but may be defined by remarkable skill in one or more specific areas (Ch. 10).

growth—Physical changes throughout the lifespan that can be measured quantitatively (Ch. 5).

heteronomous morality—Morality of constraint; unquestioning obedience to powerful individuals without full understanding of rule's intent or motives (Ch. 12).

inclusion—Students with disabilities are educated in primary settings with some age or ability peers, with supports and services provided as needed (Ch. 1).

Individualized Education Program—Education plan developed by a committee comprising parents, school administrators, and sometimes the affected student, that describes the special education and services designed to meet the needs of a student with a disability (Ch. 2).

inductive reasoning—Coming to a conclusion based on the examination of individual facts. For example: The cake tastes good, the candy tastes good, and the pie tastes good. All have sugar; therefore, sugar must be the common ingredient that makes them taste good (Ch. 3).

industry versus inferiority—Erikson's fourth stage of emotional development, which falls in the approximate range of six to twelve years old, in which school age children master adultlike skills that make them feel either competent or inferior (Ch. 11).

initiative versus guilt—Erikson's third stage in which four- and five-year-olds experience an emotional conflict over acceptance or rejection of constructive efforts (Ch. 11).

institutional bias—Unequal access to the benefits produced by a system which is supported and integrated throughout the system (Ch. 3).

instrumental morality—Moral reasoning based on an exchange system of fairness or give and get back (Ch. 12).

intelligence—Strong abilities on a wide range of tasks, including vocabulary, numbers, problem solving, and concepts. The ability to learn new information, adjust to new situations, and profit from experiences (Ch. 10).

internal working models—Generalized expectations of responsive or unresponsive caregivers that form in infancy and affect childhood and beyond, representing the self as either worthy or unworthy of care (Ch. 12).

learning disability—"Disorder in one or more of the basic psychological processes involved in understanding or using spoken or written language, which may manifest itself in an imperfect ability to listen, speak, read, write, spell, or to do mathematical calculations" (PL 101–476) (Ch. 6).

least restrictive environment—Instructional setting most like that of nonaffected peers that also meets the needs of a student with a disability (Ch. 1).

logico-mathematical knowledge—Internal relationships formed about quantity, volume, and relationships such as same/different, more/less (Ch. 9).

macrosystems—Systems that exercise power over vast resources or numbers of people based on values, traditions, and beliefs over which individuals have no control (Ch. 1).

maturation—Genetically determined patterns of changes in development that occur over time (Ch. 5).

maturationist—One who espouses the theory that the child will learn and develop according to a genetically determined pattern from conception through adulthood, with the role of the adult to support and follow the child's lead (Ch. 1).

mentor—Experienced and trusted fellow teacher who assist a new teacher with advice (Ch. 13).

metacognition—Ability to reflect on one's own thinking process; thinking about thinking (Ch. 1).

microsystems—Interpersonal relationships experienced in face-to-face settings, including family, school, youth groups, and religious organizations (Ch. 1).

milestones—Markers of significant developmental behavior attained in an orderly progression, but at individual rates (Ch. 1).

mood—Prevailing tone or general attitude; frame of mind; disposition (Ch. 11).

morpheme—Units of meaning of language, root words, prefixes, and suffixes (Ch. 7).

nature—Inborn genetically coded capacities and limitations of an individual (Preface).

neuron—Nerve cell (Ch. 6).

nurture—Environmental and experiential influences on development that occur through social interactions (Preface).

object permanence—Cognitive concept that objects have substance, external to oneself, and continue to exist when out of sight (Ch. 9).

overgeneralizing—Classifying objects or concepts into a group using only one attribute (Ch. 9).

partnership—Two or more individuals or organizations working together toward mutually beneficial goals (Ch. 2).

pedagogy—Art or practice of teaching according to a particular philosophy or method (Preface).

perspective taking—Empathetic appraisal of another's situation (Ch. 11).

phoneme—Each separate individual sound in a language (Ch. 7).

phonemic awareness—Hearing and understanding the individual sounds in a language (Ch. 8).

physical knowledge—External, observable features or behaviors of objects, such as color, size, shape; what will happen when object is dropped (Ch. 9).

prejudice—Attitude of prejudging, usually in a negative way; a rigid and irrational generalization about an entire category of people (Ch. 1).

primary caregiver—Individual who provides the majority of physical, social, emotional, and economic support to a child (Ch. 2).

professional—Person who has a specialized body of knowledge and skills attained through an extended period of education, who meets entrance requirements for the field, and who holds high social status (Ch. 13).

professional portfolio—Collection of work produced by a teacher that demonstrates competencies and accomplishments (Ch. 13).

proximodistal—Progression of the control of muscles from the body's center out to the fingers (Ch. 5).

receptive vocabulary—Words an individual understands and can act upon (Ch. 7).

scaffolding—Adult providing direction and support to help a child accomplish what would normally be beyond the child's abilities (Ch. 6).

schemes (schema)—Piaget's term for a mental structure that provides a model for action in similar circumstances; organized patterns of individual knowledge of objects and their relationships (Ch. 6).

self-concept—Qualities one attributes to oneself; self-identity (Ch. 11).

self-correcting—Educational materials that can only fit together in one way or that give immediate response as to right or wrong (Ch. 9).

self-esteem—Valuing of qualities one attributes to oneself based on self- and social comparisons (Ch. 11).

semantics—Meaning of words and sentences (Ch. 7).

separation anxiety—Distress expressed between eighteen and twenty-four months when parent or primary caregiver departs (Ch. 11).

seriation—Placing objects in order according to some criterion such as size or weight (Ch. 9).

shy—Behavior of withdrawal from social contact, exhibiting an inability to speak or insecurity in social situations (Ch. 12).

social cognition—Child's understanding of the social world, which leads to socially acceptable behavior (Chs. 9, 12).

social comparisons—Stage of emotional development around six or seven years old when the child mentally makes comparisons to peers, affecting the child's own self-worth (Ch. 11).

social competence—Ability to act responsibly, independent of supervision or outward control, in interactions with other people; cooperative and self-controlled behavior (Ch. 12).

social referencing—Attention to another's expression for cues as to how to react to an unusual event (Ch. 11).

socialization—Process of transmitting the beliefs, attitudes, and behavioral expectations of a culture to its children (Ch. 12).

standardized tests—Tests designed to be taken by a large number of classrooms and schools and administered, scored, and interpreted in the same way, no matter where they are administered (Ch. 6).

stereotype—Assumptions of what people are like based on previous associations with them or with people who have similar characteristics, or based on information received from others, including the media, whether true or false (Ch. 1).

synapse—Small gap between interconnecting neurons (Ch. 6).

system—Organization of individual units that functions as a whole (Ch. 3).

temperament—Theory of human development that emphasizes the enduring aspects of personality considered to be inborn (Ch. 11).

theory—Framework of ideas or principles that guides the interpretation of facts and acts as a basis for action (Ch. 1).

trust versus mistrust—Erikson's first stage of emotional development with a conflict between confidence in the world and feeling uncertainty and hopelessness (Ch. 11).

zone of proximal development—Support provided by adults that helps children to accomplish actions they will later be able to accomplish themselves (Ch. 6).

Index